Mastering Communication in Contemporary America

Theory, Research, and Practice

Mastering Communication in Contemporary America

Theory, Research, and Practice

Melvin L. DeFleur
Syracuse University

Patricia Kearney
California State University,
Long Beach

Timothy G. Plax
California State University,
Long Beach

Mayfield Publishing Company
Mountain View, California
London • Toronto

Library of Congress Cataloging-in-Publication Data

DeFleur, Melvin L. (Melvin Lawrence)

   Mastering communication in contemporary America : theory, research, and practice / Melvin L. DeFleur, Patricia Kearney, Timothy G. Plax.
        p.   cm.
     Includes bibliographical references and index.
     ISBN 1-55934-097-5
     1. Communication.   I. Kearney, Patricia   II. Plax, Timothy G.   III. Title.
P90.D442   1992   92-4797
302.2—dc20   CIP

Manufactured in the United States of America
10 9 8 7 6 5 4 3 2 1

Mayfield Publishing Company
1240 Villa Street
Mountain View, CA 94041

Sponsoring editor, C. Lansing Hays; managing editor, Linda Toy; production editor, April Wells-Hayes; copyeditor, Margaret Moore; art director, Jeanne M. Schreiber; cover and text designer, Janet Bollow; illustrators, Pat Maloney and Susan Carolla Iannone; manufacturing manager, Martha Branch. Cover image: Pat Maloney. The text was set in 10/12 Bembo and printed on 45# Mead Pub Matte by R. R. Donnelley.

Acknowledgments and copyrights continue at the back of the book on page 453, which constitutes an extension of the copyright page.

Preface

The two goals of *Mastering Communication in Contemporary America* are straightforward: The first objective is to present a text that explains in readable terms the nature and applications of principles of human communication derived from a growing body of classical and contemporary theory and research. The second is to present the discussion in ways that are sensitive to the needs and interests of all kinds of students and users, whatever their background or origins. Each of these goals needs further explanation.

To try to achieve the first objective, the book explains the process of communication within the framework of both linear and transactional models that have been specially developed for the text. These general models provide an organizing framework used throughout for presentation of concepts, principles, theories, and research findings relevant to understanding the complexities of human communication. To this end, the authors have brought together a rich body of knowledge from a number of disciplines that provide insights into how this can be accomplished. That body of research, theory and applications is discussed in ways that bridge the intellectual moats that traditionally separate scholars in various fields.

The first eight chapters discuss the basics of verbal and nonverbal interaction, their personal and social implications, and how they take place in contexts that include interpersonal, small group, organizational, and mediated communication. In this way, the student is provided with a strong *foundation* of concepts, principles, and research-supported theories that clarify the nature and consequences of human communication. The second half of the book uses this foundation to focus on practical *applications*—improving the reader's ability to communicate more effectively in a wide variety of applied situations and settings. These include effective self-presentation, influencing others, resolving conflicts, and overcoming shyness and apprehension—plus an extended section of three chapters focused specifically on public speaking.

The insights into communication theories and their practical applications presented in *Mastering Communica-tion in Contemporary America* are not unique to people of a particular racial, ethnic, or gender identity. These are fundamentals that *everyone* who wants to improve his or her mastery of communication needs to understand. However, the second goal of the present text can be seen in the decision to include in its title the phrase *"in Contemporary America"*. That phrase calls attention to the fact that the authors present their material in ways that are responsive to the concerns and sensitivities of students from the various racial, ethnic, and gender categories that bring such fascinating diversity to the American population.

While attention to diversity has recently become popular in academic circles, the development of *Mastering Communication in Contemporary America* preceded that trend. The book took more than eight years to complete. Its multicultural orientation is based on long-term commitments and extensive professional experiences of each of the authors relevant to understanding the needs of under-represented people. The professional activities in which the three authors have engaged include the following: design and implementation of graduate programs for African-American students, basic research on the social and psychological foundations of prejudice and discrimination toward African-Americans, studies of the adaptation of immigrant Asian-Americans to new ways of life in the United States, receipt of a teaching award from an Asian-American student association, developing a federally-funded doctoral program aimed specifically at recruiting and training Hispanic and Native American women, teaching university-level classes for Native Americans at remote sites on reservations, and providing leadership in furthering the prospects for equality of women in the academic profession.

These professional activities provided the authors with deep concern for the special problems posed by minority status in coping with the mainstream American society. More to the point, they helped the authors in identifying ways in which to prepare *Mastering Communication in Contemporary America* so that it could focus on the fundamentals of communication while being deeply aware of the needs and feelings of students from a variety of backgrounds.

Overall, then, this book is intended first and foremost as a text presenting basic theoretical and practical analyses of the human communication process. At the same time, it makes abundant use of examples, concepts and research that help clarify multicultural issues that are a part of that process. Those seeking a powerful political statement or an ideology-based advocacy position will not find it in *Mastering Communication in Contemporary America.* It is a book about communication first and foremost. Discussions of minorities or others with cultural uniqueness are brought in where they are relevant to the objective understanding of the nature of communication in our society. They have been included because they are a realistic part of contemporary America and the communication processes that must be understood within it.

Our book is specifically dedicated to the late Gordon T. Anderson, who brought the team together in 1983. His plan was to develop an innovative book that would draw freely from all of the social sciences to integrate explanations, insights, and guidelines concerning human communication in critical areas of human interaction. It was his belief that it was appropriate in an introductory text to include innovative chapters with completely new formulations that had not been presented by previous authors.

But what are those innovative approaches that make this book different from its competitors? The first example, in the beginning chapter, is an integration of the linear and transactional approaches to understanding both simple and complex forms of communication. Theoretical explanations and principles are provided that apply in every subsequent chapter as the discussion moves from simple messages between two people to more complex situations, such as organizational communication and public speaking. A second example, in Chapter 2, is a comparison of the critical similarities and differences between human and animal communication that will help the student understand what makes human communication unique. A third, in Chapter 5, is an examination of interpersonal communication from a developmental point of view. It discusses how people initiate interpersonal relationships, maintain them, or disengage from each other by exchanging particular kinds of messages. In the area of small groups, we use a theoretical perspective that expands on more traditional approaches to contexts by showing the influence of norms, roles, ranks, and controls as rules for specifying who can say what to

whom for what purposes. In the early chapters, we develop a theory of the nature of group cohesion by showing that it can be based on sentiment, personal reward considerations, work assignments, or mutual role dependency. There are a number of additional innovations in theoretical perspectives throughout.

The book also presents chapters not found in other texts. For example, an entire chapter (Chapter 9) deals with the presentation of self. While this concept is mentioned in many books, this text develops it very fully, focusing on the uses and control of messages in impression-formation, attribution, affinity-seeking, and changing unwanted impressions. Another unique chapter discusses communication with media—not mass media but traditional forms, such as letters, memoranda, and more contemporary media based on new technologies. These are the media students will have to use in the workplace: computer networks, fax, voice mail, and telecommunication conferencing.

Our reasons for presenting new theories, perspectives, and chapters, as well as the more traditional material of the introductory communication text, is to help students develop conceptual strategies for thinking about and engaging in communication as they cope with problems on a daily basis. Thus, it is not our purpose to have students leave the course merely with a list of memorized concepts and definitions. We are trying to provide them with a working command of effective tools of communication and insights into understanding how these work so that they can manage everyday situations competently long after they have graduated.

The authors want to give formal recognition to Margaret H. DeFleur, who prepared the original draft of Chapter 7, "Communicating Within Organizations." In addition, we are indebted to many others who made important contributions to this book, and to the following people for their insightful comments: Jack M. Bain, Michigan State University; Michael J. Beatty, Cleveland State University; Julie A. Burke, Bowling Green State University; Ann L. Darling, University of Utah; Lawrence W. Hugenberg, Youngstown State University; Robert Kastenbaum, Arizona State University; Richard A. Katula, Northeastern University; Raymie E. McKerrow, University of Maine; John L. Williams, California State University—Sacramento; and Donald D. Yoder, University of Dayton.

Brief Contents

Part One   Basics of Communication   2

Chapter 1   The Communication Process: An Overview   4

Chapter 2   Verbal Communication   32

Chapter 3   Nonverbal Communication   66

Chapter 4   Listening as Communication   98

Part Two   Communicating in Distinctive Contexts   124

Chapter 5   Communicating Interpersonally   126

Chapter 6   Communicating in Small Groups   156

Chapter 7   Communicating Within Organizations   188

Chapter 8   Communicating with Media   220

Part Three   Managing Personal Communication Processes   248

Chapter 9   Presenting Oneself Effectively   250

Chapter 10   Influencing Others   282

Chapter 11   Coping with Conflicts   312

Chapter 12   Overcoming Shyness and Apprehension   336

Part Four   Communicating in Public Settings   362

Chapter 13   Preparing the Content   364

Chapter 14   Speaking Before a Group   396

Chapter 15   Public Speaking: Polishing and Fine-Tuning   422

Contents

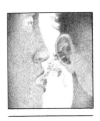

**Part One
Basics of
Communication   2**

Chapter 1
The Communication Process:
An Overview   4

The Significance of Communication in Human Life   6
   Communication Skills in Contemporary Society   7
   *Speech and Language as the Foundation for Thought
     and Society*   7
   COMMUNICATION COMPETENCE SCALE (CCS)   8
Defining Communication   9
Communication as Process: A Linear Model   12
   Stage 1: Deciding on the Message   14
   Stage 2: Encoding the Intended Meanings   14
   Stage 3: Transmitting the Message   18
   Stage 4: Receiving the Message   19
   Stage 5: Decoding or Interpreting the Message   19
Interactive Communication: A Simultaneous
     Transactions Model   21
   Simultaneous Encoding and Decoding   22
   Simultaneous Role-Taking and Feedback   23
   Simultaneous Influences of Prior Communication   23
   Simultaneous Influences of Physical Surroundings   23
   Simultaneous Influences of Sociocultural Situations   23
   Simultaneous Influences of Social Relationships   24
Achieving Accurate Communication   25
   Factors Creating Distortion   25
   An Index of Fidelity   27
   Living with Limited Accuracy   27
Chapter Review   28
Key Terms   29
Notes   30
Additional Readings   31

Chapter 2
Verbal Communication   32

Communication without Language   35
   Communicating with Inherited Behavior Systems   37
   Communicating with Learned Signs and Signals   39
The Controversy over Whether Animals Can
     Use Language   41
   Intelligent Creatures in the Sea   41
   Trying to Teach Apes To Talk   43
   Implications of the Animal Studies   46
   Human Beings Without Language   47
The Semantics of Human Communication
     with Language   49
   The World Outside and the Meanings in Our Heads   49
   Troublesome Concepts in a Multicultural Society   51
   Symbols and Their Referents   53
   VERBAL IMMEDIACY SCALE   54
   Structural Features of Language   59
Chapter Review   60
Key Terms   61
Notes   62
Additional Readings   63

Chapter 3
Nonverbal Communication   66

The Relationship Between Verbal and Nonverbal
     Communication   69
   Complementing Our Verbal Meanings   70
   Regulating Verbal Interaction   71
   Substituting Actions for Words   72
   Contradicting Our Verbal Meanings   72
   Interpreting Nonverbal Communication   73
The Use of "Things" in Nonverbal
     Communication   74
   The Body as Message   74
   Arousing Meanings with Artifacts   75
   Sending Messages with Clothing   76
   Sexual Communication in the Workplace   79
"Actions" That Communicate   81
   Body Movements and Gestures   81
   Nonverbal Uses of the Voice   82
   Eye Contact as Communication   83
   Meanings Associated with Space and Distance   84
   Communicating with Touch   87
   TOUCH APPREHENSION MEASURE (TAM)   88
   Meanings Associated with Time   89
Communication as an Integrated Process   90
   The Importance of Nonverbal Immediacy   90

Applying the Immediacy Principle   92
Chapter Review   92
Key Terms   93
Notes   94
Additional Readings   96

Chapter 4
Listening as Communication   98

The Listening Process   101
Listening as Behavior   102
What We Gain from Effective Listening   102
Actions Required of an Effective Listener   105
The Listening Encounter   107
Sender/Receiver Reciprocity   108
Sender/Receiver Similarity   111
Barriers and Misconceptions That Impair
     Listening   112
Inaccurate Assumptions About Listening   112
Five Barriers to Effective Listening   113
RECEIVER APPREHENSION TEST (RAT)   114
Planning for Effective Listening   117
The Importance of Planning   117
Features of a Sound Plan   117
Chapter Review   120
Key Terms   120
Notes   121
Additional Readings   122

Part Two
Communicating in
Distinctive Contexts   124

Chapter 5
Communicating Interpersonally   126

Basic Features of a Communication Context   130
Physical Settings: Places Influence Communication   130
*Sociocultural Situations: Goals Influence
     Communication*   130
*Social Relationships: Rules of Interaction Influence
     Communication*   130
Communication in an Interpersonal Context   132

Characteristics of Interpersonal Communication   133
Reasons for Initiating and Maintaining Relationships   135
Engagement: The Decision to Encounter   138
The Critical First Moments   139
Small Talk as Big Talk   139
The Skills of Small Talk   141
SMALL TALK SCALE   142
Management: The Decision to Linger   144
Assessing the Rewards and Costs   144
Revealing Core Information About Self   145
Communicating with an Intimate Other   147
Disengagement: The Decision to Leave   147
Causes of Relationship Disengagement   148
Saying Goodbye   149
"Fifty Ways to Leave Your Lover"   150
Chapter Review   152
Key Terms   152
Notes   154
Additional Readings   155

Chapter 6
Communicating in Small Groups   156

The Nature of Small Groups   159
Basic Features of a Group   160
The Influence of Group Size   160
Types of Small Groups   161
Sociocultural Situations: Why People Communicate
     in Small Groups   162
Communication Goals in Intimate Groups   162
Communication Goals in Task-Oriented Groups   166
Social Relationships: Rules for Communicating   171
Stages in Group Development   171
*Informal Rules for Communicating in
     Intimate Groups*   172
Rules for Communicating in Task-Oriented Groups   176
SARGENT AND MILLER LEADERSHIP SCALE   178
*Communication Codes in Formal Decision-Making
     Groups*   179
Group Cohesion and Disorganization   181
Distinct Bases of Cohesion   181
*Communication Breakdown and Group
     Disorganization*   182
Chapter Review   183
Key Terms   184
Notes   186
Additional Readings   187

Chapter 7
Communicating Within
Organizations   188

Sociocultural Situations: Why People Communicate
      in Organizations   192
   Society's Need for Organizations   192
   Bureaucracy as a Prerequisite   193
The Classical Theory of Bureaucracy   193
   The Emergence of the Rational Society   194
   Weber's Principles   194
Management-Oriented Approaches to Organizational
      Communication   195
   Human Use Perspectives   196
   BEHAVIOR ALTERATION TECHNIQUES (BATS) AND
      MESSAGES (BAMS)   198
   Human Relations Perspectives   200
   Human Resources Perspectives   205
The Flow of Messages Within Large
      Organizations   206
   Formal Communication Through Official Channels   207
   Informal Communication in Organizational Settings   210
   Distortion of Messages in the Grapevine   211
   Consequences of Organizational Communication   213
Chapter Review   215
Key Terms   216
Notes   217
Additional Readings   219

Chapter 8
Communicating with Media   220

Face-to-Face Versus Mediated Communication   223
   Why Media Matter   224
   The Personal and Social Influences of New Media   225
Traditional Written Media   227
   Letters   227
   COMMUNICATION TECHNOLOGY AVOIDANCE
      SCALE   228
   Memoranda   231
Telephones and Related Media   232
   Using the Phone   232
   Using Fax   234
Computer Networks   236
   Types of Networks   236
   Electronic Mail   239
Teleconferencing   241
   Computer Conferencing   242

   Audio Conferencing   243
   Video Conferencing   243
Chapter Review   244
Key Terms   245
Notes   246
Additional Readings   246

Part Three
Managing Personal
Communication
Processes   248

Chapter 9
Presenting Oneself Effectively   250

The Impressions We Make in Initial Encounters   254
   What Research Tells Us About Initial Impressions   254
   Problems in Initial Encounters   258
Presenting Yourself in Encounters That Really
      Matter   261
   Goals in First Meetings   262
   Preselecting Your Impressions   263
   Sizing Up People   265
   Getting People to Like You   267
Deciding What to Say   269
   Self-Disclosure in Initial Encounters   270
   Talking with New People   270
   GENERAL DISCLOSIVENESS SCALE   272
Changing Old Impressions   275
   The Inflexible Nature of Preexisting Impressions   275
   Resistance to Change   276
   Constructing New Realities   277
Chapter Review   277
Key Terms   278
Notes   279
Additional Readings   280

Chapter 10
Influencing Others   282

The Importance of Persuasion in Everyday Life   286
Formulating a Definition   286
   Linear Versus Transactional Views of Persuasion   288
   A Formal Definition   289

The Dynamics of Influence   289
  Using Coercion to Gain Compliance   290
  Persuading People to Conform to Social Expectations   290
  Cognitive Reorganization to Achieve Behavior
     Change   292
Understanding Resistance and Yielding   299
  Resistance as Reaction to Persuasion Attempts   299
  STUDENT RESISTANCE SCALE   300
  Types of Resistance   302
  Types of Yielding   303
Communication Strategies for Influencing
     People   304
  Recognizing Receiver Characteristics   305
  Features of Effective Messages   305
  Credibility of the Source   306
Chapter Review   307
Key Terms   308
Notes   309
Additional Readings   310

Chapter 11
Coping with Conflicts   312

The Nature of Conflict   315
  Formulating a Definition   317
  Consequences of Conflicts   318
Personal Styles of Coping with Conflict   321
  ARGUMENTATIVENESS SCALE (ARG)   322
  The Competitive Style   323
  The Collaborative Style   324
  The Compromising Style   324
  The Avoidance Style   324
  The Accommodation Style   324
Common Causes of Conflict   325
  Meanings as Primary Cause   325
  Contextual Factors That Can Generate Conflict   326
Successful Conflict Negotiation   328
  Defining Negotiation   328
  Guidelines for Negotiation   329
Chapter Review   332
Key Terms   333
Notes   333
Additional Readings   334

Chapter 12
Overcoming Shyness
and Apprehension   336

Communication Apprehension as a Common
     Reaction   340

  Apprehension as a Personality Trait   340
  The Influence of Apprehensive Experiences   342
Causes of Communication Apprehension   342
  Common Contextual Sources of Anxiety   342
  How We Learn to Be Characteristically
     Apprehensive   345
Consequences of High and Low Communication
     Apprehension   349
  PERSONAL REPORT OF COMMUNICATION
     APPREHENSION-24 (CA)   350
  Evaluations in the Classroom   351
  Assessments in Interpersonal Encounters   352
  The Reactions of People at Work   352
  Influences on Careers   353
Dealing with Stage Fright   354
  The Contributions of the Context   354
  What the Speaker Brings to the Problem   354
Reducing Communication Apprehension   355
  Systematic Desensitization   355
  Cognitive Restructuring   356
  Skills Training   358
Chapter Review   358
Key Terms   359
Notes   360
Additional Readings   361

Part Four
Communicating in
Public Settings   362

Chapter 13
Preparing the Content   364

Three Steps for Getting Started   367
  Choose the Topic   367
  Determine the Purpose   369
  Analyze the Audience   371
  AUDIENCE ANALYSIS SURVEY   372
How to Research the Topic to Find Supporting
     Materials   374
  Rely on Personal Knowledge and Experience   374
  Make Use of What Others Know   375
  Criteria for Selecting Evidence   376
Organizing a Speech to Inform   377

A Basic Format for Informing 377
Outlining the Informative Speech 380
Six Rules for Increasing Effectiveness 382
Organizing a Speech to Persuade 384
*A Basic Persuasion Format: Monroe's Motivated
    Sequence* 384
Outlining the Persuasive Speech 387
Seven Strategies for Persuading 390
Chapter Review 392
Key Terms 393
Notes 393
Additional Readings 394

Chapter 14
Speaking Before a Group   396

Public Speaking as Extended Conversation 399
"Planned" Spontaneity 400
Recognizing and Responding to Audience Feedback 400
*Adapting to the Audience Through Collective
    Role-taking* 401
Selecting a Mode of Delivery 402
Reading from a Manuscript 402
Delivering a Memorized Speech 403
Impromptu Delivery 404
Extemporaneous Speaking 404
Five Ways to Establish Credibility 405
Demonstrating Competence 405
Generating Trust 407
Exhibiting Composure 409
Communicating Sociability 410
Displaying Extroversion 410
Performing the Speech: Beginnings, Middles, and
    Endings 411
Act I: Managing Initial Impressions 412
Act II: Strategies to Keep the Plot from "Sagging" 413
Act III: The Famous Final Scene 416
Enhancing Immediacy 417
NONVERBAL IMMEDIACY BEHAVIORS (IMM) 418
Chapter Review 419
Key Terms 420
Notes 420
Additional Readings 421

Chapter 15
Public Speaking:
Polishing and
Fine-Tuning   422

Five Strategies for Making Your Language More
    Interesting 428
Use Imagery Imaginatively 428
Strive for Simplicity 429
*Employ Intense, Animated Language to Add
    Excitement* 430
Maintain Rhythm for Emphasis 432
Orchestrating Applause 433
Developing and Using Sound Bites 433
Managing Applause 434
Developing Your Own Rhetorical Style 435
Dramatic Style 435
Animated Style 436
Humorous Style 436
HUMOR ORIENTATION (HO) SCALE 438
Chapter Review 439
Key Terms 440
Notes 440
Additional Readings 441
Glossary 443
Acknowledgments 453
Index 455

Mastering Communication in Contemporary America

Theory, Research, and Practice

Part One

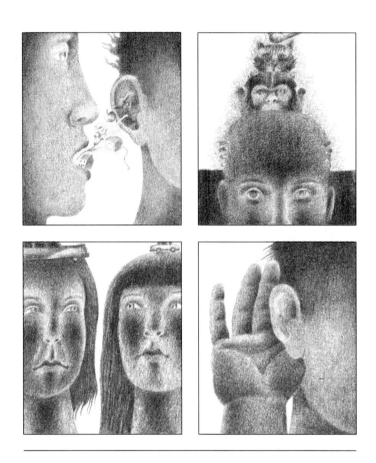

Basics of Communication

The first four chapters of this book focus on the basics of communication faced by people regardless of their backgrounds or origins. They develop a theoretical framework that guides discussions of various applied aspects of the communication process thoughout the remaining chapters. This conceptual framework integrates what communication theorists refer to as a "linear" view of communication with what we refer to as a "simultaneous transactions" model. It shows that communication can be analyzed as a step-by-step process moving from a sender to a receiver. At the same time, communication must be seen as a complex set of simultaneous exchanges between interacting senders and receivers of messages where both act as "communicators." This book shows that these are not competing perspectives.

In Chapter 2, human and animal communication are contrasted in a comparative perspective, not so much to learn about ways in which animals communicate, but to gain essential insights into the distinctive basis of the process among human beings of different backgrounds and origins. Thus, the chapter clarifies the nature of language and shows in detail how people uniquely use symbolic processes to arouse and share parallel meanings.

The third chapter in this part shows how human beings communicate without words, sometimes with patterns that differ among various racial and ethnic groups. Chapter 3 shows how nonverbal communication is as much a part of human exchanges as is the use of speech and language. By using their bodies, actions, and objects, people use gestures, signs, and signals to enrich and extend their meanings. Understanding the basics of human communication, then, requires a full understanding of both the verbal and nonverbal dimensions of the process.

Finally, Chapter 4 analyzes listening as a basic part of the human communication process. Through an analysis of the listening encounter, and the nature of sender/receiver reciprocity, it points out common misconceptions about listening as well as the characteristics of the effective listener. In particular it reviews misconceptions and barriers that can reduce the accuracy and effectiveness of communication in a diverse society.

Chapter 1

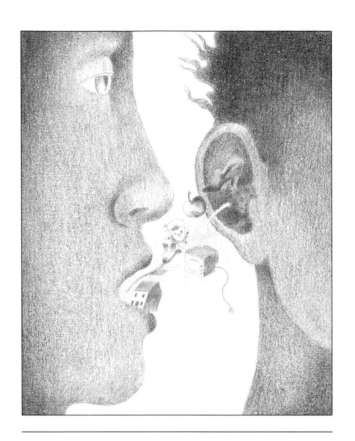

The Communication Process: An Overview

Contents

The Significance of Communication in Human Life
Speech and Language as the Foundation for Thought
  and Society
Communication Skills in Contemporary Society

Defining Communication

Communication as Process: A Linear Model
Stage 1: Deciding on the Message
Stage 2: Encoding the Intended Meanings
  The meaning of meaning
  Symbols and meanings in memory
  Role taking to assess probable interpretations
  Encoding as automated behavior
Stage 3: Transmitting the Message
Stage 4: Receiving the Message
Stage 5: Decoding or Interpreting the Message

Interactive Communication: A Simultaneous Transactions Model
Simultaneous Encoding and Decoding
Simultaneous Role-Taking and Feedback
Simultaneous Influences of Prior Communication
Simultaneous Influences of Physical Surroundings
Simultaneous Influences of Sociocultural Situations
Simultaneous Influences of Social Relationships

Achieving Accurate Communication
Factors Creating Distortion
An Index of Fidelity
Living with Limited Accuracy

Chapter Review

Key Terms

Additional Readings

Key Questions

- In modern society we communicate in many ways, by talking, making speeches, telephoning, sending messages via fax or computer, and using our mass media. Is human communication a different process in each of these settings? Or is it the same basic process wherever it occurs?

- Why are effective communication skills more important today than at any previous time in history? In other words, why does one have to acquire such skills to be able to get along with others, get ahead, and achieve other objectives in contemporary society?

- How can the complex activity of human communication be studied systematically in such a way that understanding how it works can lead to a greater command of important skills required for relating to other people?

But the most noble and profitable invention of all other, was that of Speech, . . . whereby men register their Thoughts; recall them when they are past; and also declare them to one another.

Thomas Hobbes
Leviathan, 1651

Human communication is a truly remarkable process. Clearly the most complex form of behavior in which we engage, it sharply separates us from other members of the animal kingdom. Through the use of words and other signs and symbols for which we share meanings, we perceive, evaluate, and respond to the physical and social world around us. Communication is not only the basis of human thought, it is the means by which each of us develops an individual pattern of beliefs, attitudes, and values—the personal attributes that bring us to understand, misunderstand, accept, or reject others who are like or unlike ourselves. In that sense, communication is the foundation of an effective democratic and multicultural society.

Communicating well or poorly can spell the difference between success and failure in human relationships of almost every kind. Most of us already have deeply established communication habits that serve us well or poorly and may be difficult to change. But whatever skill we may possess, we can always improve. Gaining in the ability to communicate with and influence others brings significant rewards.

Improving the ability to communicate is precisely what this book is all about. This first chapter examines in overview the fundamental nature of human communication. Chapters that follow will look at the process in more detail. Without the understanding these chapters provide, improving basic communication skills would not be possible. Subsequent chapters explain how communication takes place effectively—or ineffectively—in various settings and situations with which we all must cope. Later chapters also discuss understanding others who are different, making good impressions on new acquaintances, maintaining valued relationships over a long period, communicating effectively in large and small groups, and speaking in public.

As will be clear, this text is not just a "how to do it" manual or handbook. Acquiring effective communication skills requires detailed insights concerning every feature of the process. It rests on an understanding of the nature of speech and language, of verbal and nonverbal communication, and of how to listen effectively. In other words, practical skills are built on an understanding of concepts, principles, and theories that explain the human communication process as it takes place in a variety of contexts for many purposes. That knowledge has emerged from decades of systematic study and research on how communication takes place, how it can go wrong, and what the consequences are likely to be. This text presents principles and generalizations based on communication research and shows how they can be usefully applied.

The number of settings in which people communicate is almost unlimited: intimate conversations between two people, discussions in small groups, transmission of messages within large organizations, and public speeches where one person talks to an audience, to name a few. People also communicate using various media such as the telephone, fax machine, and computer network, as well as mass media such as newspapers, the movies, and television, whereby messages may go out to millions of people. A question that comes to mind immediately is whether human communication is a different process in each of these settings or follows the same principles wherever it occurs. As we will see, both answers are true. That is, unique factors characterize communication in each context, but the process by which people construct meanings and transmit them to others, who then interpret and respond, is essentially similar in all contexts, large or small, formal or intimate. Thus, in spite of the elaborate technology used in some communication settings, a solid case can be made that *verbal* communication, using speech and language along with some *nonverbal* actions such as gestures and facial expressions, is the fundamental form by which we arouse meanings in each other.

The Significance of Communication in Human Life

No field of study has more important implications for our lives in contemporary society than that which looks systematically at the process of human communication. Everything we do, from making friends to governing a nation, would be impossible if human beings were unable to communicate with speech and language. It is no exaggeration to say that communication *is at the heart of human existence*. Indeed, all of the great advances in civilization that have occurred since prehistoric times—in government, law, science, education, religion, the arts, and many others—depended on improved systems of communication. About 40,000 years ago our direct forebears, the Cro-Magnon, developed the ability to speak. Earlier hominids, such as the Neanderthal, were unable to do so because of the physiological structure of their tongue, facial muscles, and voice box.[1] Developing speech and language separated the Cro-Magnon from other hominids and from related animal species.[2] With the ability to think, reason and communicate in complex ways, the human species went on to invent writing, then printing, and in modern times to develop our sophisticated electronic media. It was those long and often difficult changes—constantly extending our ability to communicate more swiftly, widely, and accurately—that enabled us to advance far beyond the level of our primitive forebears.

Speech and Language as the Foundation for Thought and Society

The insight that speech and language provide the foundation of human thought and the basis of societal life is a very old one.[3] As early as the 17th century it had become clear that the ability to use words to convey ideas from one person to another was what separated human beings most sharply from animals. In 1690 the English philosopher John Locke published an analysis of these relationships in his famous *Essay Concerning Human Understanding*. Although his style of writing now seems old-fashioned and sexist by contemporary standards, what he said remains true:

> God having designed Man for a sociable Creature made him not only with an inclination, and under a necessity to have fellowship with those of his own kind; but furnished him with language, which was to become the great Instrument, and common Tye of Society. Man therefore had by Nature his Organs so fashioned, as to be fit to frame articulate sounds, which we shall call Words. But this was not enough to produce language; for Parrots, and several other Birds, will be taught to make articulate

Sounds distinct enough, which yet, by no means are capable of Language.[4]

In other words, Locke saw that human beings are social by nature and use language as a basis of their group life. In addition, while the sounds people use in communicating can sometimes be imitated, animals cannot use them to communicate in the way human beings do.

Locke went on to point out that the process of *thinking* also depends on the use of words because they "stand as Signs of Internal Conceptions," that is, as "Marks for the Ideas within his own Mind."[5] Thus, Locke concluded that the use of speech and language is a necessary condition for organizing human society on the one hand, and for engaging in imagination and individual thought on the other. These remarkably accurate insights remain consistent with our knowledge today.

Communication Skills in Contemporary Society

In today's society a command of effective communication is far more critical than at any previous time in history. Skills in communicating with others and managing human relationships have become more important than those related to working with one's hands. In fact, shortly after the mid 20th century, we emerged into what scholars call the "information society." That is, we now collectively spend more time and energy manipulating "symbols"—words and numbers—that we do manufacturing "things."[6]

As we move into the future, goods will increasingly be produced by computerized machines rather than human beings. Even now our economy is more devoted to "services" than to production of hard goods. These trends have only begun and will certainly continue. In such an information society the ability to communicate effectively will truly be at a premium. Thus, relating to others, gaining their approval for our ideas, and eliciting positive evaluations of us are the kinds of skills that will increasingly count in achieving success.

Also ahead is a requirement of increasing sensitivity to the nature of the distinctive ethnic, religious, racial, and regional cultures that make up our collective way of life. The ability to use appropriate words to guide the way we think about and act toward each other is as much a critical communication skill as is using proper grammar and syntax.

As later chapters will show, critical communication skills include more than the ability to formulate and

Communication Competence Scale (CCS)

Instructions   The following are statements about how people generally communicate with others. Answer each item as it relates to your *general* style of communicating in *most* social situations. Complete the questionnaire by indicating the extent to which you agree or disagree with each statement—by noting whether you:

5 strongly agree   2 disagree
4 agree   1 strongly disagree
3 neutral/undecided

_____ 1. I find it easy to get along with others.

_____ 2. I adapt to changing situations.

_____ 3. I treat people as individuals.

_____ 4. I interrupt others too much.

_____ 5. Others find it "rewarding" to talk with me.

_____ 6. I deal with others effectively.

_____ 7. I am a good listener.

_____ 8. My personal relationships are cold and distant.

_____ 9. I am easy to talk to.

_____ 10. I won't argue with someone just to prove I am right.

_____ 11. My conversation behavior is not "smooth."

_____ 12. I ignore other people's feelings.

_____ 13. I generally know how others feel.

_____ 14. I let others know I understand what they mean.

_____ 15. I understand other people.

_____ 16. I am relaxed and comfortable when speaking.

_____ 17. I listen to what people say to me.

_____ 18. I like to be close and personal with people.

_____ 19. I generally know what type of behavior is appropriate in any given situation.

_____ 20. I usually do not make unusual demands on my friends.

_____ 21. I am an effective conversationalist.

_____ 22. I am supportive of others.

_____ 23. I do not mind meeting strangers.

_____ 24. I can easily put myself in another person's shoes.

_____ 25. I pay attention to the conversation.

_____ 26. I am generally relaxed when conversing with a new acquaintance.

_____ 27. I am interested in what others have to say.

_____ 28. I don't follow the conversation very well.

_____ 29. I enjoy social gatherings where I meet new people.

_____ 30. I am a likable person.

_____ 31. I am flexible.

_____ 32. I am not afraid to speak with people in authority.

_____ 33. People can come to me with their problems.

_____ 34. I generally say the right thing at the right time.

_____ 35. I like to use my voice and body expressively to communicate.

_____ 36. I am sensitive to others' needs of the moment.

Calculating Your Score

1. Add together your responses to items 4, 8, 11, 12, and 28 = _____ .

2. Add together your responses to all the other items.

3. Then, complete the following formula:

   CCS = 30 − Total from step 1 = _____ .

   Then, + Total from step 2.
   YOUR TOTAL CCS SCORE = _____ .

Interpreting Your Score

Possible range of scores: 36–180. (If your own final CCS score does not fall within that range, you made a computational error.) The absolute mean = 108.

Individuals high in CCS (above 108) are generally more sensitive, flexible, and assertive communicators than those lower in CCS. Of course, the higher your score, the more competent the communicator you perceive yourself to be. Importantly, this score reflects only how YOU perceive yourself as a communicator. You might want to let a partner, parent, brother/sister, or co-worker complete the scale on you as well. Then compare their total scored responses with your own!

Reference

Weimann, J. M. A model of communicative competence. *Human Communication Research, 3,* 297–333.

Philosophers and other scholars started analyzing the nature of human communication and its influences on individuals and society many centuries ago. By the 18th century, relationships between words, thought, and action were relatively well understood. British philosopher John Locke set forth insightful analyses of these relationships that remain valid today.

transmit appropriate messages. The act of human communication includes *receiving* messages as well as sending them. Effective listening, then, is as important in communication exchanges as is effective talking. For that reason we devote an entire chapter to the listening process. Moreover, communication does not take place in a vacuum, but always occurs in some kind of surroundings—that is, some type of social and cultural setting, or **context.** No matter what our way of life, type of work, or daily activities, we relate to each other in contexts ranging from small, intimate groups to large, impersonal organizations. In addition, we are often called on to present ideas systematically to others in various group situations. An important part of acquiring proficiency in relating to and influencing other people, then, is gaining skills in public speaking.

The down side is that the skills needed to communicate effectively to different kinds of people in various contexts are not easy to acquire or improve. One's communication style, habits, and abilities are built up over an entire lifetime. They cannot be set aside easily and new ones substituted, like changing one's clothes. Nevertheless, with determination, understanding of principles, and frequent practice, it is possible to learn to communicate more effectively.

Defining Communication

Against the background we just sketched, we need to focus specifically on the details of what constitutes communication. It is not a simple task. In fact, the nature of

In today's society, the ability to communicate effectively has become more important to most people than manual skills required to produce things. Fewer and fewer people in our society work with their hands. In the modern workplace, people manipulate information and perform services requiring a high level of skill in relating to others. The ability to communicate accurately and sensitively can make the difference between success and failure.

communication has been debated since history began. Ancient proverbs from the Masai, the writings of Confucius, and early European scholars such as Plato and Aristotle, to mention only a few, reveal a deep interest in such issues as how personal meanings for the world outside our minds are acquired through the use of speech and language, how they represent reality, and how people are influenced through both public speaking and teaching as forms of human communication.[7] Since writing began, a long list of philosophers, scholars, and teachers have tried to understand the essential features of human communication. They have left a legacy of important treatises on such topics as oratory, rhetoric, dialogue, persuasion, elocution, and grammar that deepen our contemporary understanding of human communication.[8]

In recent times, social scientists throughout the world have tried to identify the nature of communication by trying to understand communication as it takes place among both animals and human beings. This approach provides a *comparative* perspective, which means studying

the ways in which communication occurs among all animal forms, from simple to complex, and then sorting out what is common to all. This strategy is best seen in the work of psychologists who have defined communication among all living forms in the following way: *Communication occurs when one organism (the source) encodes information into a signal which passes to another organism (the receiver) which decodes the signal and is capable of responding appropriately.*[9]

This general or "comparative" strategy is so broad that it reveals only a partial understanding of human communication. However, it provides a useful beginning point. For example, it shows that one "organism" (animal) initiates the process; some sort of encoding occurs; information moves across space; decoding is accomplished by a receiver; and then a response is made. Those are indeed important features of communication, but there is a lot more to human communication than that. People communicate in ways that never occur among animals. Therefore, at some point we need to *contrast* animal and human communication so as to understand what makes human communication unique and different. We will return to this issue in the next chapter by comparing animal with human verbal communication in order to understand better the fundamental nature of language and how it sets us apart from other creatures in the animal kingdom.

But what are the essential features of the human communication process? We can formulate a definition, but it has to include *all* forms of human communication— not only people communicating in face-to-face private or public settings, but with media, such as letters, telephone, print, film, broadcasting, and so on. Finally, such a definition must take into account the fact that people communicate with themselves. That is, they use language in the process of generating meanings for themselves, just as they do in arousing them in others.

With these conditions in mind, we begin with the following foundation definition: **Human communication** *is a process during which source individuals initiate messages using conventionalized symbols, nonverbal signs, and contextual cues to express meanings by transmitting information in such a way that similar or parallel understandings are constructed by the receiving party or parties toward whom the messages are directed.*[10]

At first glance, this definition looks hopelessly long and complicated. But on closer inspection it is little more than a *list* of important factors that are involved when people communicate with each other. As we will see, cer-

tain aspects of communication are not included; these will be added later. In addition, while the definition includes elements that human beings share with animals, it does set forth ways in which human communication is different. Therefore, it provides a good foundation for understanding what concepts and principles are needed for our analysis.

But what is in the list? The definition begins by stating that communication is a *process*. To explain, any process is a series of stages in which something undergoes transformation at each step. In communication, human beings serving as sources formulate meanings that will make up messages. It is these meanings that are transformed during the process. Stated simply, the source's thoughts and ideas (meanings) are formulated into messages by selecting appropriate symbols (sometimes referred to as "encoding"). These messages are then transformed into verbal sounds and/or visible nonverbal signals that can move across space. Receiving individuals then see or hear them and transform them back to their own symbolic understandings of thoughts and ideas. Presumably, the meanings constructed by both sender and receiver are similar. (All of these features are different from their counterparts among animals.)

Included in the definition is the idea that a message consists not only of conventionalized *symbols* (words, grammatical rules, and syntax structures that are part of

Human communication takes place when a sender decides on and initiates a message by coding it into language symbols and nonverbal signs. Those who receive the message reconstruct its meanings from their own understandings of those symbols and signs. Many additional factors, such as the context in which communication takes place, play a part in determining its nature, accuracy, and consequences.

language), but of standardized *nonverbal* cues plus *contextual* signals and factors that imply meanings. Thus, a source person normally expresses intended meanings with words, gestures, and actions, but often the setting within which the communication takes place adds additional meanings. For this reason all three of these concepts—symbols, nonverbal signs, and context—are included. (These issues will be discussed in detail in subsequent chapters).

Note also that the definition highlights the idea of similar or parallel *meanings* in the communicating parties. As we will see more fully later in this chapter, meaning is a form of internal or subjective behavior that occurs as responses to words or other standardized signs and signals. To the degree that the subjective meanings aroused in each party are similar, they are *parallel*. If that is the case, the communication between the parties is complete or *accurate*. If the meanings are different, the communication process has suffered some kind of *distortion* and the result is limited accuracy.

While the word **communicator** commonly designates the person who initiates a message, in the present analysis both the source and the receiver are "communicators." Therefore, the terms **source** and **sender** will be used throughout this book to identify an individual who formulates and transmits a message, while the term **receiver** will identify the communicator to whom that message is directed, and who constructs his or her own version of what it means.

The foundation definition conceptualizes communication as a *linear* process. Although this is not the final way we will define and discuss human communication, it does provide a good point of departure. The linear view implies that communication occurs when one person begins the action and another completes it. That is, a person serving as a source begins by formulating the message and transmitting it to another person, who then receives and interprets it. Later, as will be made clear, we will go beyond this linear process in order to show that ongoing communication between interacting parties is a series of transactions that are far more complex. However, we need to understand communication as a linear process in order to identify a number of vital aspects of message formation and interpretation.

While we will look closely at *both* of these views in order to understand the basic nature of human communication, the linear analysis must be considered first. The reason is that linear processes are *embedded* within the ongoing interactive communication activities that occur when people converse or even make speeches. What this embedding idea refers to is that when communicating people are engaged in a complex and ongoing exchange, they repeatedly go through linear stages as they communicate back and forth, taking turns as source and receiver. That is, when one person is acting as a sender, she or he formulates a message and transmits it to the other, who receives and interprets it. Then the receiver serves as a source, sending back a response.

Usually, people quickly take turns in such transmission and reception activities. In fact, they may even perform them simultaneously, providing subtle messages to each other before, during, and after their turns. However, even subtle messages are formulated, transmitted, and received. The point is that ongoing and even simultaneous message transmission and reception are made up of patterns of linear exchanges that are embedded in a complex process of communicative interaction.

To simplify the communication process, and as an aid in identifying every aspect of it, we can analyze the process, or break it down into each of its component parts. In this case these are the stages that are mentioned in our earlier definition—including various activities occurring at each.

Inevitably, such a step-by-step analysis of communication is somewhat artificial, as it would be to analyze breathing or walking in this manner. Everyone communicates so automatically that it scarcely seems necessary to look at it one stage at a time. In everyday life we communicate almost continuously, but we seldom try to break down our communication into stages. However, in order to gain skills in communicating it is essential to understand every step in the process thoroughly so that we can identify potential problem areas and formulate strategies to minimize the effects of various pitfalls.

Communication as Process: A Linear Model

The stages or steps involved in the human communication process can be simply illustrated by considering an elementary communicative act, involving only two people. The source or sender will initiate the exchange with a sentence consisting of only three words, and the receiver will respond with a single gesture. Using that example, we will set forth formally a very basic *linear model* of the communication process. The term **linear** indicates that the process moves like a straight line, from a beginning to an end through specific stages.[11] A model is simply a careful and succinct description that summarizes

A Linear Model

Basic Stages in the Human Communication Process

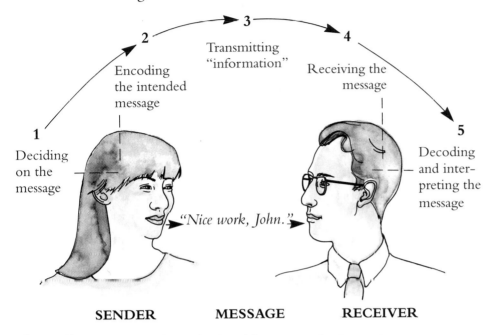

An act of human communication can be viewed for purposes of analysis within a basic linear perspective so as to understand what is happening at each stage. Within this perspective, a message is decided on and formulated by a sender. It is transmitted after conversion into information that can move from sender to receiver. It is decoded and interpreted by a receiver, who makes use of meanings stored in memory.

what takes place. Some models are verbal—set forth in ordinary words and descriptive sentences—and are the easiest to understand. Others are graphic and depict the situation in drawings; still others use mathematical symbols and equations to portray what they represent.

A limitation of the linear model is that in reality an act of communication does not simply start, like turning on a tape-recorded message, and go through stages to a point where it stops and the switch is turned off. The linear view describes communication in that oversimplified way. Nevertheless, if the stages of the basic linear model can be made clear, even in an artificially simple example, then complex interactive communication, which we will examine in a later section, can be more easily understood because it incorporates *exactly the same set of basic principles* (plus a number of others).

Our basic strategy of analysis, then, will be to stop an ongoing conversation between two people at a point where one person decides to transmit a message to the other. We will enter the ongoing process and artificially slow it down so as to look at it stage by stage—like looking at a film projected slowly, one frame at a time. In this sense, we will examine everything that happens from the time one human being initiates a meaningful message and transmits it to another. We will also include what takes place when the receiver, in turn, understands the message and transmits an acknowledgment back to the initiator.

In our example, one individual says to another, "Nice work, John," and the other smiles in return. Despite its simplicity, this exchange, using only three words and a nonverbal gesture, provides a basis for understanding the steps involved in the linear view of human communication. Essentially, the process involves five distinct stages, summarized as follows:

1. *Deciding on the message.* A person serving as a source decides on a message to be sent to a receiver (or sometimes more than one) so as to achieve a desired goal.

2. *Encoding the intended meanings.* The source searches his or her memory for specific words and gestures and their associated meanings that can be put together in a pattern which will describe the desired facts, ideas, and images.

3. *Transmitting the message.* The message is transformed by voice (or other means) into physical information (like sound waves) so that it can overcome distance, and the message moves in this form from sender to receiver.

4. *Receiving the message.* The receiver attends to the physical information as it arrives and identifies the symbols into which it has been coded.

5. *Decoding or interpreting the message.* The receiver searches and compares the incoming symbols with meanings stored in her or his memory and selects those that seem best for interpreting the message.

As the following sections will show, each stage in this basic linear model includes important ideas and concepts that help us understand the basic nature of communication within this linear framework.

Stage 1: Deciding on the Message

We assume that any person initiating an act of communication has some *intention* in mind. Of the many goals that people attempt to achieve through communication, most are simple and obvious, but others are complex and difficult to ascertain. In our example, where the three-word message is "Nice work, John," the source or sender's purpose is simple—to express a sentiment that will reinforce a meaningful social relationship. A key principle here is that communication begins when the sending person constructs a message that he or she feels can be interpreted by the receiver so as to accomplish the goal.

An important consideration in deciding on the goal to be achieved by a message is that once it is understood by the receiver, it is irreversible, that is, *irrevocable.* In other words, it is difficult or even impossible to retract, or remove from the mind of a receiver, a thoughtless message or one transmitted in haste or anger. In courtroom communication, the judge sometimes rules that "the jury will disregard that last answer of the witness." But it does not

work that way. People are not like tape recorders where messages can be conveniently erased.

Stage 2: Encoding the Intended Meanings

After the goals are clear, the source person must construct the message by selecting from memory a pattern of words to represent her or his intended meanings. This is what is meant by the term **encoding.** Often, our messages will include not only words but also gestures or other cues associated with particular meanings. The term **symbol** will be used here to refer to the various words, gestures, signs, signals, or other cues (verbal or nonverbal) whose conventional meanings people usually understand. Thus, to construct and encode a message, we select some pattern of symbols to represent our intended meanings.

Although our example is elementary, involving only the symbols, "nice," "work," and "John," selecting just the right symbols so that they are closely associated with our desired meanings, and so that we believe they will be understood by the receiver, is a remarkably sophisticated task. To gain a perspective on this part of the process, we first need to understand the nature of "meaning" itself. Then we can look at ways in which senders try to determine whether their receiver will understand their encoded message.

The meaning of meaning.   Essential to the encoding process is the concept of meaning. The nature of meaning, and the part it plays in thinking and communicating, has been debated for thousands of years. Despite this continuing attention, it remains one of the most perplexing aspects of human behavior. Meaning is difficult to define, study, and analyze. Nevertheless, we need to understand the nature of meaning as completely as we can because it lies at the heart of the encoding process, which is fundamental to both thinking and human communication.

The central reason why the nature of meaning is such a problem is that it is *subjective* behavior. That is, meanings occur "in our heads," where no one but ourselves can experience them, and so we have no way of directly observing another person's meanings. That simple fact poses an insurmountable barrier for those who want to study meaning scientifically through a process of detached observation. Science is supposed to deal only with what can be directly observed. Yet, we can make some *assumptions* about meaning that will make it less mysterious.

One way of understanding human communication is to view it as a linear process that takes place in stages. It begins with the sender, who seeks to accomplish specific goals. To do this, the sender formulates a message by selecting verbal symbols and nonverbal signs he or she believes will be interpreted by the receivers in desired ways as it is transmitted. The receivers then decode and interpret the message. If the process has worked accurately, the meanings intended by the sender will parallel those reconstructed by the receivers.

First, meanings are neither ethereal nor ghostlike. We assume they are a form of *behavior*—that is, responses we make, within ourselves, to objects, events, and situations we encounter in the world around us. Those responses are the different kinds of images, understandings, feelings, and factual beliefs that are aroused within us when we encounter some part of reality (a dog, a house, our mother, etc.). It is easy to see that we "encounter" such things through our *senses*, by seeing, feeling, hearing, smelling, or tasting them. It is also easy to see that after many such encounters, we *learn* a specific pattern of internal subjective experiences—a set of habitual meaning responses that we make to each kind of object, event, and situation.

But what about meanings for words? We learn to make responses to words, or other symbols, that are the same as (or very similar to) the way we experience meaning for things in our world. Therefore, the term *meaning* has a double implication: Not only does it imply subjective

responses to aspects of *reality*, but it also implies the same kinds of responses to the *labels* we impose on that reality (in the form of words and other symbols). We learn such symbols because we are reared and live in a language community, where we have been taught since infancy to associate specific patterns of inner experiences with each symbol in the vocabulary we share with others. As a result of these learning experiences since infancy, each member of a particular language community winds up with (1) a set of remembered subjective experiences associated with various things, conditions, and situations in reality, and (2) an extensive remembered repertoire of symbols (a vocabulary) and a huge set of corresponding subjective responses associated with those symbols.

This implies that one's inner meaning experiences can be aroused in either of two ways: (1) One can experience (respond to) the reality first-hand through the senses, or (2) one can have similar experiences indirectly as a response to the symbol which labels that aspect of reality.

It is this uniquely human ability to use learned symbols to arouse meanings that makes it possible to communicate with other people and to communicate with ourselves (to *think*) by using language to arouse internal meanings. Meaning, then, is the key to understanding human beings as thinking and communicating creatures. For our purposes, **meaning** can be defined as *subjective responses that individuals learn to make, either to objects, events, or situations in reality that they experience through their senses, or to socially shared symbols used to label those aspects of reality.*

We normally assume that the meanings one person experiences for a particular aspect of reality are basically the same as those of another. Therefore, we assume that an object like a rose looks the same to all of us—that it arouses the same experience of "red" (except for the colorblind) and that it has the same perfumed smell, feel, and presumably taste (if one is so inclined). The symbol "rose," used to label those realities, is also supposed to arouse pretty much the same experiences in each of us. Unfortunately, as we will see in some detail, a sender's meanings may not be the same as his or her receiver's, which can result in distortion and misinterpretation of the message.

Symbols and meanings in memory The way symbols and meanings are stored in memory is an important consideration for understanding the encoding stage. Social scientists in recent years have developed elaborate theories of memory in which such meanings are stored.[12] In some ways, our memory structure is like those of modern computers (but infinitely more intricate). The key concepts are *traces* and *schemata*. **Traces** are imprinted records of experience registered in the brain by electrochemical activities of its nerve cells. They record the images, recollections, and other elements of experience that we associate with every word or other symbol in our repertoire.

Traces are organized into *schemata* (singular: *schema*) representing concepts with which we are familiar, rather than in just a random jumble. A **schema** is a pattern or *configuration* of traces of meaning that have been organized and recorded in a person's memory.[13] Such configurations are made up of all the stored memory traces of understanding, feeling, imagery, or other interpretations that a person associates with some specific aspect of reality or with the word, phrase, or idea labeling that aspect of reality. Some schemata are simple, like "chair," "fork," or "shoe." Others are more elaborate. For example, when we recall the Fourth of July, we might experience a pattern of meanings that include fireworks, patriotism, flags,

parades, and perhaps other ideas and images. Thus, the Fourth of July schema brings together a number of meanings into an organized configuration. Another example might be an idea, such as "democracy," or a particular ceremony, such as "Ben's bar mitzvah." Thus, rather than storing our remembered meanings in a random jumble, we organize them into schematic patterns of varying complexity that aid in the recall of "clusters" of related traces of experience.

The schema idea is helpful in describing the structure of a particular message that is selected and encoded for transmission to one or more others. We can think of a message as a number of such organized schemata, developed initially from the meanings associated with each word and combined according to our shared rules of grammar and syntax. Referring again to our simple example, we construct an organized message from the schemata for "nice," "work," and "John." In so doing, these individual schemata are put together in a sequence that meets the requirements of syntax and grammar in our language community. For example, we would not formulate a message of "work John nice"—that would violate such well-understood rules. Instead, we place them in a sequence following rules of ordering such words that we all understand and share. Thus, our combination brings together all the meanings of "nice work, John" into one overall configuration of meaning.

Looking at the message again, and focusing *only* on those verbal and nonverbal meanings the sender wants to arouse, we assume it is an organization of schemata that include all the implications, ideas, and aspects of interpretation the sender intended when formulating the message. These include both important and unimportant elements, as well as all the sender's objective and subtle meanings. That pattern is the overall intended meaning of the entire message.

Stated concisely, at the encoding stage the sender has to *sort* among his or her traces and schemata and *decide* which symbols match the meanings he or she intends. The individual then *selects* those symbols, plus the appropriate rules for their combination, that can form a message which is both appropriate to the occasion and consistent with the goal. Then, she or he *constructs* the message pattern to be used. Even when this has been done, however, the encoding process is not complete.

Role-taking to assess probable interpretations Another major problem at the encoding stage is predicting whether the receiver will understand the message as composed and how he or she will respond. Even with

A Schema as an Organization
of Meanings in Memory

A schema is a set of traces of meaning that have been organized in a particular configuration in a person's memory. Many schematic structures include abstract ideas, such as "animals" and "people" in this diagram, and increasingly concrete levels of organization of memory under each. Some are not organized in a hierarchical manner but are simply sets of linked recollections, such as one's recall of the images and plot of a movie, recollections of a graduation ceremony, or a great shopping trip.

a simple message, such as "Nice work, John," is it possible that the receiver will not understand the intended meaning? Of course it is. The receiver may interpret the message as consistent with the goal of expressing an honest sentiment—or may see the message as one calculated to manipulate him. Furthermore, senders often choose words that receivers cannot easily understand, perhaps because the receivers lack memory structure for particular words, as in the use of unfamiliar slang or jargon, or they have a limited vocabulary. This problem of matching the symbols used to encode a message with the probable capacity of the receiver to interpret intentions and

Meanings for the words, nonverbal cues, and features of contexts that we use in human communication are stored in human memory. Those meanings are organized into schemata, which are configurations of traces registered in the brain by electrochemical activities of nerve cells. Schemata provide the basis for the concepts that we use in relating to the world we perceive and in communicating about that world with each other. Without an unimpaired and adequately functioning brain, therefore, a person could not participate effectively in the human communication process.

meaning accurately and appropriately is a critical aspect of communication.

How can a person initiating a message assess the *probable* interpretation the receiver will make? Actually, we make this assessment all the time and we do it very quickly, if not always accurately. Technically, it is called "role-taking."[14] This refers to the source mentally placing himself or herself in the shoes of the other party so as to try to understand the best way to encode the intended meanings so that the receiver can interpret them.

Role-taking, then, is an important part of the encoding stage and can be defined as *an activity of a sender by which the likelihood is assessed that a receiver will be able to interpret the intentions and meanings of a particular form of a message.*

If role-taking suggests the receiver is not likely to understand the message if formulated (encoded) in a certain way, the sender quickly makes revisions before transmission. This may sound complicated, but we all do this every time we communicate, and in different ways depending on the nature of the receiver. For example, we engage in role-taking when we communicate with a child—encoding the message in simplified symbols and using appropriate meanings. We also do it with many other categories of people so as to help them understand, or to refrain from arousing feelings we wish to avoid.

The assessment of probable interpretations by role-taking, then, is a significant part of the message-encoding process.

Encoding as automated behavior   As suggested, the encoding process is unbelievably fast—so fast that it rivals the speed of even the most sophisticated computer. In an instant we can formulate a message, engage in role-taking, and revise what we want to say—even when using long strings and patterns of symbols with associated meanings. This speed implies that encoding behavior is "automated," so that we are not even aware of the steps we follow while doing it.[15] Examples of automated behavior include typing on a keyboard, playing a piano, and driving a car. When we do those things, we do not consciously plan, select, and then execute each finger movement or other action; instead, our selections, and executions take place at a very high rate of speed, automatically, without conscious awareness. Encoding messages that incorporate the meanings we intend is done even faster.

Stage 3: Transmitting the Message

The third stage in the communication process requires that the message span the distance between the parties (unless it is communication with oneself). In the example, "Nice work, John," the message is transformed into patterned *physical* events—agitations of air molecules that we know as sound. (In a print version these would be patterns of light waves by which gestures or actions are made visible.) This is accomplished by the various parts of the body the sender uses to produce the information relevant to the phrase "Nice work, John."

These physical events are called **information.**[16] It is this information that moves across space in patterns representing words and related aspects of the message. This information serves as *stimuli* (a term from psychology) that the receiver's sensory organs can detect. If the message had been transmitted in written form, it would have had to conquer distance as visible patterned marks against a contrasting background. Here the information stimuli would be visual. If a medium, such as a telephone or computer network, had been involved, the device obviously would have played a part in transmitting the information from one party to the other.

Although the term *information* has many common meanings, the way we are using it here, to identify physical events in transmission, is convenient in discussing the movement of messages across space. One reason is that

An important skill in communicating effectively is role-taking. This requires sensitive insight into ways in which different kinds of receivers are likely to interpret words, nonverbal cues and other features of a message. In a society made up of people who come from very different backgrounds, role-taking skills are critically important.

it helps clarify the nature of "meaning." What we are saying is that meaning does *not* move across space. Remember that meanings are subjective experiences of both the sender and the receiver, who depend on the functioning of their central nervous systems and memories. Meanings, then, lie at the beginning and end of the communication process within the memory of each party involved.

Stage 4: Receiving the Message

In the fourth stage of our linear model the person to whom the message was directed becomes the principal actor. Briefly stated, the receiver first *perceives* the incoming information and transforms it into symbols. Patterns of information transmitted by the message initiator are picked up as stimuli by the receiver's sensory organs. These are then identified as specific words, in a recognizable pattern, along with any nonverbal or other observable cues. Only then will the assignment of meanings (decoding) begin.

The term *perception* has both common and technical meanings. Many people use it loosely as a synonym for "belief" when they say something like, "It is my per-

ception that our candidate will win the election." A more precise meaning is that used in technical discussions by psychologists and other social scientists. When they use the term, **perception** means *seeing, hearing, or feeling something (with the senses) and then identifying what it is within the interpretations learned from one's language and culture.*

Thus, perceiving refers to identifying and classifying a physical object within a system of meanings—like recognizing a small red spherical object as an "apple." Or, it can refer to hearing a pattern of sounds, such as the spoken word "apple" and identifying its meaning as the spherical object. Perception is important in human communication in that receivers have to identify the words making up a message before they can arouse within themselves the appropriate meanings they have stored for those words.

Stage 5: Decoding or Interpreting the Message

After the words and other symbols of the message have been perceived and identified, the process of **decoding** can take place. In fact, it occurs in an automated way at a very rapid rate. That is, we are able to receive and re-

A remarkable feature of human communication is how rapidly people can encode, transmit, receive, and decode messages with complex meanings. The selection of symbols by a sender, and their arrangement into appropriate grammatical form in the right sequences, takes place swiftly. The same is true of the instantaneous reconstruction of their meanings by receiver. These aspects of communication are at an automated level, like the movements of a skilled juggler who can keep several objects in the air at the same time.

spond to long clusters of words and patterns of symbols almost instantaneously. Stored in the receiver's memory are thousands of schemata, organized structures of verbal symbols, grammatical patterns, and nonverbal signs that have recognizable meanings. The incoming symbols are first distinguished from others similar to them and specifically identified. A quick search is then made for possible interpretations. In the case of our simple three-word example, the receiver almost instantly perceives it as "Nice work, John"—and then sorts out the associated meanings stored in his or her memory. When this happens, the linear process is complete.

It is important to realize that even within this linear view of the communication process, the receiver is actively involved in constructing meanings for the incoming information. In so doing, she or he draws on enormous personal resources of learned meaning responses, based on traces organized into schemata, plus habits, opinions, beliefs, attitudes, values, and factual information stored in memory. That is, the receiver's interpretations are certainly related to the intentions of meaning built into the message by the sender. However, they are not just passive arousals of the sender's meanings. They are *active reconstructions of meaning* derived from the traces, schemata, and images stored in the receiver's memory.

Our linear model can be easily transformed into an *interactive version* by adding a stage in which the receiver becomes a sender and transmits a **feedback** message as a response.[17] In our example, we indicated at the beginning that after the sender said, "Nice work, John," the receiver would respond with a smile. A smile under such circumstances is a nonverbal gesture used as a feedback message. It is a conventionalized signal that functions like a word in that it has a fairly standardized meaning in our society. In this case it means something like "I like what you said."

Such an interactive version is just an extension of the linear model in that returning messages follow exactly the same steps outlined earlier. To understand this feedback, no new concepts or stages are required. The activity begins as a goal (to supply the sender with an acknowledgment); a message is selected so as to hopefully arouse an intended meaning; it is delivered or presented (in the nonverbal form of a smile in this case); and it is received by acts of perception and interpretation. Thus, feedback of this type is the same step-by-step linear process between the two parties as discussed earlier. It may be with the use of simple gestures; it may be based on complex verbal messages as in ordinary conversation; or the message may take some other form like clapping, booing, or yawning.

Needless to say, face-to-face communication is seldom as simple (and never as slow!) as in our example. And, as mentioned, it is much more than the start-stop linear process we have outlined. Communication flows back and forth between people, and as they engage in role-taking and feedback, what they have said or done earlier shapes what they say next. However, by scrutinizing what takes place within a series of linear stages, we were able to sort out aspects of the process that will help in understanding later chapters. Various concepts, such as meaning, symbol, verbal, nonverbal, context,

Role-Taking and Feedback

Role-Taking

He will like this

"Nice work, John."

I like what you said

**SENDER
AND
RECEIVER**

Feedback

**RECEIVER
AND
SENDER**

Adding the process of feedback modifies the basic linear model. However, the process it depicts is still linear. That is, the feedback message moves from the receiver (who now acts as a sender) back to the sender (who now acts as a receiver) through the same five stages as in the basic model. Adding role-taking modifies the model even further to make it more interactive. Even with these additions, however, the linear model is useful mainly for analyzing each stage of human communication separately, and not as an accurate depiction of the process in its full complexity.

memory, perception, role-taking, and feedback, provide keys to developing a deeper understanding of the nature of this basic and essential form of human behavior.

Interactive Communication: A Simultaneous Transactions Model

Looking beyond the linear process just described, we can now put together a broader and more inclusive view of communication that describes how it usually takes place in more realistic terms. We do this by developing a *simultaneous transactions model* of human communication as it takes place between people who engage in conversations or other interactive message exchanges.

Although the phrase "simultaneous transactions" may sound like technical jargon, neither term implies any specialized meaning beyond its dictionary definition. When used to describe the communication process, simultaneous implies that both parties involved are

undergoing the same kind of experience at the time. A **transaction** is simply any kind of exchange—that is, an activity that occurs between, and mutually influences, all parties acting together in some way. As explained earlier, a model is a kind of summary of the essential features of something, such as a process.

As will be seen, the simultaneous transactions model does not challenge the validity of the linear view of the communication process discussed previously. On the contrary, it subsumes or incorporates it. To explain, we set forth the linear model in order to *analyze* the act of communication—that is, to break it down into its constituent parts and stages. Our task now is to *synthesize* that linear process with other aspects of the communication process by pulling together not only the stages already discussed but also a number of other critical features of the process into a broader, more realistic description of what happens when people communicate interactively.

We can sum up the essential ideas of a simultaneous

Receiving a message requires that the individual first perceive the symbols and nonverbal cues transmitted by the sender. Once they have been identified, the receiver can decode the meanings they have for him or her by reference to schemata stored in memory and interpret the sender's intentions.

transactions model of the human communication process in six basic propositions. That is, communicating parties simultaneously:

1. *encode and decode messages.* All parties involved act as senders and receivers at the same time.

2. *engage in role-taking and feedback.* These processes take place as each party decodes messages and encodes replies.

3. *are influenced by their prior communicative interactions.* What people say and the way they respond during a given transaction depend greatly on what has been said previously.

4. *are influenced by the physical surroundings within which the transaction takes place.* People communicate differently in various places.

5. *are influenced by the sociocultural situation within which their communication takes place.* What people say is almost always a part of an ongoing situation that has sociocultural definitions, such as a date, family dinner, or work activity.

6. *are influenced by the social relationship that exists between them.* Any ongoing relationship between communi-

cators, or the fact that they are strangers, will have a significant influence on their transactions.

Taken together, these six propositions form a realistic description of the nature of face-to-face communication—a model of how it occurs under a wide variety of circumstances, ranging from a conversation between intimate friends to a speaker's public address to a live audience of strangers.[18] The model is less applicable to mediated communication, such as when communicators use computer networks, and it is not relevant to the case of mass media, where professional writers or broadcasters transmit messages to audiences whom they never see.

Simultaneous Encoding and Decoding

The first proposition in the model indicates that while encoding messages, people also receive and decode incoming verbal or nonverbal messages from others. Thus, even as one person is speaking, the other may be encoding a reply. This is not inconsistent with the linear model described earlier. What this proposition of the transactions model implies is that those processes occur simultaneously as each party formulates and interprets messages continuously, speaking and responding, listening and replying.

An important feature of interactive (as opposed to simple linear) communication is feedback. The sender is alert to verbal and nonverbal indicators as to how receivers are responding as the message is being transmitted. If the receivers provide positive indicators, the message is being well received. If the feedback seems negative, there may be a need for revision of the message or a change in communicative strategy.

Simultaneous Role-Taking and Feedback

The second proposition in the model is actually an extension of the first: The messages of each party, and the interpretations constructed by each, are simultaneously influenced by the role-taking assessments and the feedback they mutually provide. Thus, even as a person speaks, he or she is simultaneously assessing the listener's response on the basis of feedback and is modifying the formulation of further parts of the message as that feedback is being transmitted.

Simultaneous Influences of Prior Communication

The third statement is obvious: What people have already said or heard determines what will follow. Thus, the coding, decoding, and interpretation of messages by communicating parties usually builds on or is an extension of prior message content. All parties simultaneously take this prior message content into account as the exchange continues.

Simultaneous Influences of Physical Surroundings

The influence of physical surroundings on communication is not always clear, but in many cases the place where it takes place has a strong influence on both what and how messages are exchanged. Obvious examples of the influence of physical context are the ways communication is different in a discussion among close friends at a favorite watering hole, at a funeral home where a memorial service is being held for a loved one, or at a rowdy New Year's Eve party in a friend's home. Thus, the influence of physical context must be a part of our model.

Simultaneous Influences of Sociocultural Situations

People do not just get together in random groupings and begin communicating. They do so because communication is part of social situations that have meanings within their culture. These can be one-time get-togethers such as weddings, parties, or religious ceremonies, or ongoing situations such as people encounter at work. What

A Simultaneous Transactions Model

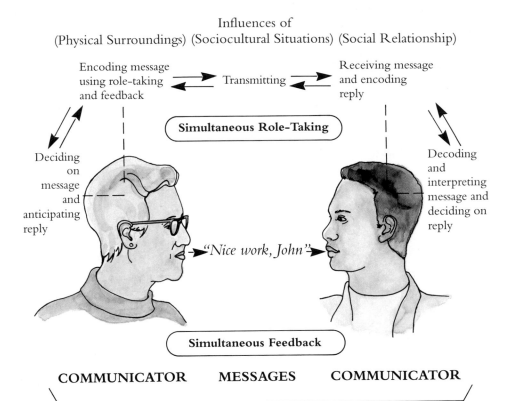

Influences of
(Physical Surroundings) (Sociocultural Situations) (Social Relationship)

Encoding message
using role-taking → Transmitting →
and feedback

Receiving message
and encoding
reply

Simultaneous Role-Taking

Deciding
on
message
and
anticipating
reply

Decoding
and
interpreting
message and
deciding on
reply

"Nice work, John"

Simultaneous Feedback

COMMUNICATOR   MESSAGES   COMMUNICATOR

Influences of Prior Communication

The simultaneous transactions model is complex because it depicts the process of face-to-face human communication as a set of reciprocal activities in which each party engages at the same time. They simultaneously encode and decode messages, transmit them to each other, engage in role-taking and feedback, and formulate replies even as the other person is transmitting. Moreover, significant influences on the process arise from what they have said before, the physical setting they are in, the sociocultural nature of their ongoing activity, and the kind of relationship existing between them.

is said, to whom, and in what way is heavily influenced by the situation. At a party where people have only recently met, for example, the conversations that take place among people getting to know each other will very likely focus on "small talk," as people size each other up without revealing much about themselves. When it's a fishing vacation among close friends, however, conversation topics are quite different as a great deal of self-disclosure takes place. The situation that brings people together, then, is an important part of a transactions model.

Simultaneous Influences of Social Relationships

Finally, the sixth proposition states that communicators are simultaneously influenced by any social relationships already existing between them. That is, relationships such as those between spouses, friends, acquaintances, or supervisors and subordinates at work can strongly influence both the content of messages and the way in which they are transmitted and received. Even if the communicators have never met before, that absence of a relationship heavily influences what they communicate to each other. Thus, the social expectations and rules of relationships shape the way messages are encoded or decoded, the effectiveness of role-taking assessment, the amount and kind of feedback, and even the amount of self-disclosure each party provides for the other.

The simultaneous transactions model, then, is a general view that applies to a broad spectrum of situations, relationships, and contexts within which people communicate. It brings together all the elements and stages discussed in the linear analysis, and adds the influences of a number of factors that impinge on the human communication process as it takes place in various settings for many purposes. We will use this model extensively in the chapters that follow as we explore ways in which people communicate for different purposes in interpersonal and group contexts.

Achieving Accurate Communication

Whether we consider it within a linear perspective or as a more complex set of transactions, communication is seldom if ever perfect. It is either incomplete or distorted in various ways in that the meanings of the message as interpreted by the receiver always differ to some degree from those intended by the source. A number of factors and conditions lead to this lack of congruence.[19] To understand the limitations on completeness and accuracy within which people communicate, we need to look first at what *totally accurate communication* really means. Although such a level is rarely achieved, regardless of the parties or the circumstances, a theoretical model of what complete accuracy would be like will offer a useful basis of comparison with what actually happens when people communicate.

But what *is* accurate communication? Put simply, accurate communication means that all of the sender's intended meanings are reconstructed by the receiver (in the stage of decoding and interpretation) so that they match. This seldom happens because accuracy can be eroded in two basic ways. One is because understanding is *incomplete*: The receiver simply fails to reconstruct at least some of the subjective meanings from the incoming message that were intended by the sender. The other is through **distortion**, which occurs when the source's intended meanings become compounded with, or displaced by,

unintended implications as the receiver reconstructs the meanings of the message.

If communication is to be regarded as totally accurate, then, the sender and the receiver must have closely similar internal subjective meaning experiences as a result of the formulation, transmission, reception, and interpretation of the message. If understanding is incomplete, or if the receiver constructs alternative or additional meanings, communication accuracy is eroded.

Clearly, these definitions of accurate, incomplete, and distorted communication tie the concepts of meaning and interpretation directly to the intentions of the sender. The sender's intended meanings become the standard or criterion by which the accuracy of the transaction is judged.

Factors Creating Distortion

How does such distortion take place? That is, how do unintended meanings displace or become compounded with those that the sender wanted to arouse in the receiver? There are an almost unlimited number of ways, and one of the goals in various chapters of this text is to show many common factors that introduce distortion in what receivers interpret from the messages transmitted to them.

In large part, distortion arises because communication is much more than just using words and other symbols to express ideas to others. We have indicated that three broad categories of techniques are used, either deliberately or unwittingly, to arouse meanings in others. Each offers abundant opportunities for distortion.

First are the *verbal*—the spoken, written, or printed—symbols and patterns (grammar and syntax) of language itself. These are usually selected deliberately, but poor choices can be made that distort meanings constructed by the receiver. For example, the use of the term "man" to refer to all human beings implies a lesser status for women, and the use of racial labels such as "Negro" rather than "African-American" carries distorting connotations not acceptable to people of such ancestry.

A second opportunity for distortion is provided by those things and actions that we use in *nonverbal* communication. These can be very complex and confusing. For example, winking while scolding a child in front of others can be intended to negate the meanings included in the verbal scolding, but children may not understand. Whether nonverbal cues are used deliberately or unin-

Total Accuracy in Communication

$\mathbf{M_s}$
Meanings Intended
by Sender

$\mathbf{M_r}$
Meanings Interpreted
by Receiver

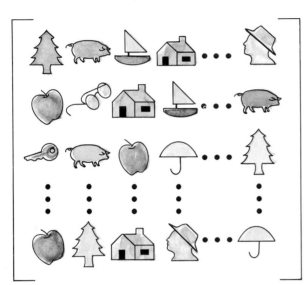

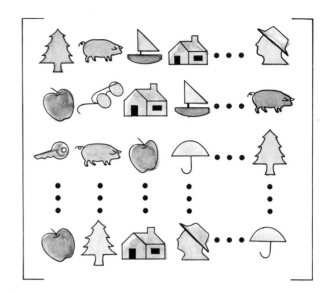

Where $\mathbf{M_s} = \mathbf{M_r}$, then $\mathbf{I_F} = 100\%$

The degree of accuracy of communication between a sender and a receiver can be conceptualized theoretically by an *index of fidelity*. That index would be 100% if every element and nuance of both denotative and connotative meaning in the message encoded by the sender were decoded and interpreted by the receiver in precisely the ways that the sender intended. It would be zero if there were no similarities of meaning between the two. Realistically speaking, total accuracy probably is impossible between two human beings, except for very trivial messages. However, such an index provides a useful conceptual model.

tentionally, they can cause others to construct distorted meanings.

Third, features of the setting or *context* within which the communication takes place may offer opportunities for distortion. A message such as "I love you" said sincerely after a romantic candlelight dinner may be interpreted differently from the same words uttered to a person met an hour earlier in a singles bar. Later chapters will discuss the influences of contexts at length, but for now what we can say is that the sociocultural and physical settings within which communication takes place can introduce subtle or obvious cues into the process. These often influence the meanings intended by the sender and those constructed by the receiver without either party realizing the cues are there.

Again, we note that receivers are always active parties in the communication process. That is, they bring to the act of interpreting the message their own individual repertoires of remembered understandings, which include many private and subjective shadings of meaning for words, things, actions, and settings that may not be universally shared in the general language community and the specialized cultures of the communicating parties. Nevertheless, those unshared "connotative" shadings may be used to construct a receiver's meanings of a message. Because they are private, personal, and unshared, rather than standardized and shared, they create distortion in communication.

These discussions of verbal symbols, nonverbal cues, and connotative meanings imply that the schematic structure of the memory of one person is unlikely to be the same as someone else's. Thus, distortion in communication depends on the *degree to which the sender's and receiver's combinations of memory traces and schemata for encoding and decoding are identical.* If all elements of meaning, imagery, implications, and connotative and denotative interpretations intended by the sender are *exactly the same* as those aroused in the experience of a receiver, the communication would be perfect!

Thus, we can define complete and accurate communication much more specifically than we did earlier. *Complete and accurate communication occurs only if the total combination of traits and schematic configurations of meaning intended and developed by a source is identical to those constructed and experienced by a receiver.* If, on the other hand, the degree of matching is less than 100%, communication has been either incomplete or distorted.

Obviously, complete and accurate communication in the sense defined above is very unlikely in the real world. But as a theoretical idea, it is useful for thinking about what actually does take place when people communicate. The real question is how close do people come to this theoretically perfect situation when they transmit and receive messages? What we need is a measure of such congruence.

An Index of Fidelity

Given our refined definition of complete and accurate communication, we can describe (at least theoretically) an **index of fidelity** for any act of human communication. Such an index will describe a way in which a message transmitted by a sender can be assessed for accuracy against that received and interpreted by another party. To do so we must imagine a long list of all the details and elements of meaning that a source intended to represent in her or his message. Then we imagine a similar list of the details and elements of meaning as these are reconstructed by a receiver of that message. By comparing the two lists, element by element, we could calculate a percentage, based on the proportions of the lists that match perfectly.

Viewed in this way, fidelity could range from 0%, where there is no match of the elements of meaning in the respective lists of sender and receiver, to 100%, where the match is perfect. However, it would be difficult to make such a calculation without exhausting interviews of each party. Still, an index of fidelity is useful as a *conceptual model*, providing an elementary theory and a pre-

cise definition for understanding the concept of error-free communication.

As we have stressed, an almost unlimited number of factors operate to reduce the index of fidelity of any communicative exchange. In later chapters, many of these factors will be discussed at length. They include such problems as choosing the wrong words, misreading the context, sending misleading nonverbal signals, failing to listen, not assessing the nature of feedback from the audience, ignorance about the receiver's cultural background, and dozens more. Thus, even in the case of a simple message of only a few words it is possible for the fidelity index to be low. When messages are long and complex, the prospects for inaccurate communication are very great indeed.

Living with Limited Accuracy

Our discussion of incompleteness and distortion may make it seem that we can *never* communicate with other human beings at a high level of accuracy. Actually, we may not need to do so! Other features of the human communication process permit people to get along pretty well without totally complete and accurate paralleling of meanings between themselves. In other words, in most of our communicative exchanges we do not require an index of fidelity of 100%. In fact, we can get by with accuracy levels well below that level. To illustrate, let us assume that your boss comes by and says:

> "I wonder if you would mind going down to the legal department and talk with Mr. Murakita. He has a mortgage contract that was signed a couple of days ago, and we may need it for the three o'clock meeting this afternoon. You might want to go over it with him so that you will understand the terms."

Suppose now that another person comes up a few moments later and asks, "Exactly what did the boss say?" Your response might be:

> "Well, she told me to go see Mr. Murakita to get a contract that was just signed. Then she said she wanted me to read it in time for the meeting this afternoon."

Essentially, your version may sound pretty close, but it is not totally accurate. In fact, the index of fidelity is rather low. For example, the boss asked you "if you would mind." Furthermore, she did not say that she wanted you to read the document, she merely said that "you might want to go over it." Looking closely, a number of such differences exist between the version encoded and transmitted by the boss and that decoded and interpreted by you.

At the same time, the basic elements of meaning are close enough so that you can do what the boss expects. The sender's and receiver's combinations of meaning elements and schemata contain enough similarity *for practical purposes*: (1) You understand that there is a document; (2) you know that you are to get it; and (3) you realize that you are supposed to read it and be ready for the meeting. Those elements are about all you need to comply rather closely with the boss's wishes.

The point is that in any message there is both a **surface meaning,** such as the whole range of intended elements the boss formulated into the message, exactly as she worded it, and a **deep meaning**—the basic ideas that can be understood well enough for practical purposes. Thus, although the index of fidelity between the message transmitted by the boss and the version understood by you is rather low, the deep meaning of essential ideas is sufficiently similar for coordinated action.

Despite this flexibility, even deep meanings are often interpreted incorrectly. What we noted earlier about the many ways in which communication distortion can take place applies to deep meanings as well as to surface meanings. No one expects a fidelity level of 100% in human communication. If a reasonable amount of fidelity can be attained at the deep meaning level, the transaction can serve well enough. Unfortunately, as will become increasingly clear, high levels of fidelity are not easy to attain at *any* level of meaning.

The important lesson of this review of accuracy is that reasonably complete communication at a sufficiently high level of fidelity doesn't just happen, but must be carefully planned and managed at every stage. Adequate fidelity in communication occurs only when the sender understands both the goals he or she wants to achieve and the characteristics of the receiver that make accurate communication likely. Fidelity is enhanced when the message is selected and constructed verbally and nonverbally in such a way that barriers to communication will be minimized.

Chapter Review

- While almost all animals communicate, speech and language are unique and critical to human beings. They provide the basis for their ability both to engage in thinking and to relate to each other in complex group and societal patterns. In today's society, understanding the process of communication and acquiring effective communication skills is essential for everyone who has to cope with a complex social environment. We have moved from a society based on the production of things to one in which communication and the exchange of symbols is our central activity. That change is likely to accelerate, leaving behind those who are not able to communicate effectively.

- While one-sentence definitions have many limitations, they can highlight the major concepts that need to be understood. For that reason, communication was defined as a process in which an individual initiates messages using verbal and nonverbal signs and symbols to express meanings in such a way that similar or parallel understandings are aroused in all of the communicating parties. Thus, concepts such as process, symbol, and meaning are significant for understanding communication.

- A linear model analyzes the communication process as a series of stages. When people communicate, these stages take place so automatically and rapidly that they seldom even think about them as separate steps. However, by analyzing an act of communication, using only a three-word message and looking at it step by step, the critical features of the behavior can be brought out.

- Essentially, communication takes place when a person identifies a goal or purpose, constructs a message from her or his repertoire of symbols and their meanings, and then transmits or delivers that message using various parts of the body and brain. The term *meaning* is at the heart of communication. Essentially it is the internal or subjective responses we make, either to aspects of the reality around us or to the labels we impose on that reality. The sender's message in physical form transcends distance and is detected as stimuli by the receiver's sensory organs. Once those stimuli are perceived and identified as particular language symbols, decoding and interpretation take place and the receiver's meanings are constructed. Often, the receiver formulates a return message, following the same steps, to provide feedback to the original sender.

- A broader synthesis of the communication process is provided by the simultaneous transactions model of the influences and actions of communicating parties. The six propositions of this model state that while communicating, the parties simultaneously encode and decode messages and engage in role-taking and feedback. They are influenced by their prior communicative interactions, the physical setting, the social situation, and their social relationships.

■ Whether considered as linear or as transactions, complete and totally accurate communication between sender and receiver is unlikely because a variety of factors create distortion. An index of fidelity is at 100% if all elements of meaning intended by the sender are exactly the same as those in the meanings constructed by the receiver. The index is at 0% when these meaning structures do not match at all.

■ Total accuracy is not necessary in most communication situations. This is because most message transactions result in arousal of deep meanings that serve the practical needs of the communicators. Even so, it is likely that inaccuracies will occur in communication, even at a deep meaning level.

Key Terms

Communication, human   A process during which source individuals initiate messages using conventionalized symbols, nonverbal signs, and contextual cues to express meanings by transmitting information in such a way that similar or parallel understandings are constructed by the receiving party or parties toward whom the messages are directed.

Communicator   A person who either sends or receives a message during the communication process.

Context   A physical setting and/or a sociocultural situation in which communication takes place. Examples are a church or an office (physical setting) and a wedding or a sales meeting (sociocultural situation).

Decoding   The assignment of meaning to symbols perceived by a receiver in the communication process.

Distortion   An outcome of communication in which the source's intended meanings become compounded with, or displaced by, unintended implications as the receiver reconstructs the meanings of the message.

Encoding   The assignment of symbols to meanings that a source or sender intends to transmit to a receiver.

Feedback   Messages provided in an ongoing manner by a receiver in response to a message being transmitted by a source or sender. Such messages may be verbal or nonverbal.

Fidelity, index of   A (theoretical) way in which a message transmitted by a sender can be assessed for accuracy against that received and interpreted by another party.

Information   Physical events, such as agitations of air molecules that enable a receiver to hear the voice of a sender, or in the case of written messages, the light waves that make written symbols visible. Such information makes it possible to transcend space or time in the communication process.

Linear   A process that moves like a straight line, from a beginning to an end through specific stages.

Meaning   Subjective responses that individuals learn to make, either to objects, events, or situations in reality that they experience through their senses, or to socially shared symbols used to label those aspects of reality.

Meaning (deep)   The basic ideas implied by a message that can be understood well enough for practical purposes.

Meaning (surface)   The entire set of meanings encoded into source's message, whether they are essential to understanding its basic ideas or not.

Perception   The psychological process of seeing, hearing, or feeling something (with the senses) and then identifying what it is within the interpretations learned from one's language and culture.

Receiver   A person who attends to, perceives, and interprets (decodes) the message information transmitted by a source.

Role-taking   An activity of a source or sender by which the likelihood is assessed that a receiver will be able to interpret the intentions and meanings of a particular form of a message.

Schema   A pattern or configuration of traces of meaning that have been organized and recorded in a person's memory.

Signs   Stimuli in our environment to which we have learned to make a patterned response.

Source or sender   A person who formulates, encodes, and transmits a message to one or more receivers. In some cases, groups or agencies can serve as sources. (In discussing public speaking, the term *speaker* is often used to designate sources or senders who are presenting a talk.)

Symbols   Words, numbers and other marks, objects, or signs to which we have learned to associate patterned meanings that by established conventions are shared by other members of our language community.

Trace   Imprinted records of experience registered in the brain by electrochemical activities of its nerve cells.

Transaction   Any kind of exchange—that is, an activity that occurs between, and mutually influences, all parties acting together in some way.

Notes

1. Howells, W. W., Neanderthal man: Facts and figures. In *Proceedings of the ninth international congress of anthropological and ethnographic sciences.* Chicago, 1968; also: Trinkhaus, E., & Howells, W. W., (1979). The neanderthals. *Scientific American 241,* 118–133.

2. The family Hominidae (humanlike creatures) began to develop as a variation of the order Primata several million years ago. As evolution proceeded, such creatures grew larger and their brain-to-body-mass ratio increased; by about 1.8 million years ago they were walking upright. After the genus *Homo* emerged, our ancestors began making tools and using fire. However, cultural development remained at a stone-tool level throughout the Pleistocene period. Modern *Homo sapiens sapiens,* in the form of Cro-Magnon, can be traced back no farther than around 90,000 years. They were the first human beings physiologically capable of using speech and language, which may have been fully developed only as recently as about 35,000 or perhaps 45,000 years ago. It was this communication ability, enabling Cro-Magnon to engage in reasoning, organized recall, and the transmission of solutions to complex problems to new generations, that provided the foundation for a rather sudden and increasing elaboration of human culture. By 15,000 years before the present, *Homo sapiens sapiens* was widely dispersed in Europe, Asia, and Africa, and about 10,000 years ago the great Neolithic era of agriculture and village life began. For a detailed discussion of the fossil record and its implications, see: Lieberman, P. (1984). *The biology and evolution of language.* Cambridge, MA: Harvard University Press.

3. The relationship between language, thought, and social life has been well established by research in such fields as anthropology, linguistics, philosophy, and sociology. See, for example: Whorf, B. J. (1956). In J. B. Carol (Ed.), *Language, thought and reality.* Cambridge, MA: MIT Press; Mead, G. H. (1934). *Mind, self and society: From the standpoint of a social behaviorist.* Chicago: University of Chicago Press; and Bronowski, J. (1978). *The origins of knowledge and imagination.* New Haven, Conn.: Yale University Press.

4. Locke, J. (1975). In Peter Niditch (Ed.), *An essay concerning human understanding* (p. 402). Oxford: Clarendon Press. (First published 1690.)

5. *Ibid., p. 402.*

6. See: Bell, D. (1973). *The coming of post-industrial society: A venture in social forecasting.* New York: Basic Books.

7. See: Becker, H., & Barnes, H. E., (1961). *Social thought from lore to science* (3rd ed.) (pp. 3–131). New York: Dover Publications. Also: Cornford, F. M. (Trans.) (1941). *The Republic of Plato.* London: Oxford University Press, 1941. See especially Part III, Books XXIV–XXVIII, pp. 221–264.

8. See: Harper, N. (1979) *Communication theory: The history of a paradigm* Rochelle Park, NJ: Hayden Book Company; Trenholm, S. (1991). *Human communication theory* (2nd ed.). Englewood Cliffs, NJ: Prentice-Hall.

9. Ellis, A., & Beattie, G. (1986). *The psychology of language and communication* (p. 3). New York: Guilford Press.

10. Additional support for this definition is provided by W. Barnett Pearce and Vernon Cronen's "coordinated management of meaning theory." These communication scholars argue that as people try to make sense of their world, they act on the basis of the meanings they ascribe to an event. They further argue that failures in communication represent the ability of individuals to coordinate their different interpretations of events. For a full statement of this theory see: Pearce, W. B., & Cronen, V. (1980). *Communication, action, and meaning: The creation of social realities.* New York: Praeger.

11. Studying the act of human communication within the framework of a linear model began with the work of Claude E. Shannon and Warren Weaver in their *Mathematical Theory of Communication* (Urbana, Il: University of Illinois Press, 1949). A model of communication was presented based on the components of Source → (encoding) → Message → Channel → (decoding) → Receiver. Their model included the concept "noise," which is any factor that reduces fidelity (accuracy).

12. Detailed reviews of this rapidly developing field are found in the following sources: Cermak, L. S., & Craik, F. I. M. (Eds.). (1979). *Levels of processing in human memory.* Hillsdale, NJ: Lawrence Erlbaum; and Bower, G. (Ed.). (1977). *Human memory: Basic processes.* New York: Academic Press; Green, J. (1984). A cognitive approach to human communication: An action assembly theory. *Communication Monographs 51,* 289–306; Green, J. (1989). Action assembly theory: Metatheoretical commitments, theoretical propositions, and empirical allocations. In B. Dervin, L. Grossberg, B. J. O'Keefe, & E. Wartella (Eds.), *Rethinking Communication* (Vol. 2, pp. 117–128). Newbury Park, CA: Sage.

13. The schema concept was first used by Frederick C. Bartlett in his classic work *Remembering* (London: Cambridge University Press, 1932). For an explanation of contemporary thinking about the nature of schemata and how they influence the communication process, see: Crockett, W. H. (1988). Schemas, affect, and communication. In L. Donohew, H. E. Sypher, & E. T. Higgins (Eds.), *Communication, social cognition, and affect* (pp. 33–51). Hillsdale, NJ: Lawrence Erlbaum; Trenholm, S. (1991). *Human communication theory* (2nd ed.) (pp. 65–68). Englewood Cliffs, NJ: Prentice-Hall.

14. The activity of role-taking, sometimes called "taking the role of the other," comes originally from the writings of George Herbert Mead, a philosopher and sociologist of the early 20th century. He developed a general theory called symbolic interactionism, which maintains that human communication, using symbols with conventional rules of meaning, is the basis of the thinking abilities of human beings and of the social rules they share for behaving predictably in society. See: Mead, G. H. (1934). *Mind, self and society: From the standpoint of a social behaviorist.* Chicago: University of Chicago Press. For excellent discussions of role-taking and of symbolic interactionism more generally, see: Littlejohn, S. W. (1977). Symbolic interactionism as an approach to the study of human communication. *Quarterly Journal of Speech 63,* 84–91; and Delia, J. G., & Grossberg, L. (1977). Interpretation and evidence. *Western Journal of Speech Communication 41,* 32–42.

15. For a readable account of the implications of automaticity, see: Bargh, J. A. (1988). Automatic information processing: Implications for communication and affect. In L. Donohew, H. Sypher, & E. T. Higgins (Eds.), *Communication, social cognition, and affect* (pp. 9–32). *Hillsdale, NJ: Lawrence Erlbaum.*

16. A long tradition in the study of communication is based on information theory, which was originally derived from thermodynamics. Basically it is a major concept in the study of signal transmission, including noise, entropy, and redundancy. Our usage here to refer to the physical means by which messages move across space (i.e.,

transmission) is consistent with that background. See: Shannon, C., & Weaver, W. (1949). *The mathematical theory of communication.* Urbana: University of Illinois Press.

17. The term *feedback* comes from a field called cybernetics, which is the study of the automatic control systems formed by the nervous system and the brain that stabilize functions of the human body. It came into the study of communication through the work of Norbert Wiener in his seminal book, *The Human Use of Human Beings: Cybernetics and Society* (Boston: Houghton Mifflin, 1954).

18. This view of human communication parallels in part what has been described as the "rules perspective." Communication scholars arguing this perspective indicate that people learn the rules for communication within differing situations and that the use of these rules is highly contextualized. For complete discussions of the rules perspective, see: Shimanoff, S. B. (1980). *Communication rules: Theory and research.* (Beverly Hills, CA: Sage; and Sigman, S. J. (1980). On communication rules from a social perspective. *Human Communication Research, 7,* 31–51.

19. The term noise is often used to lump together and label various kinds of physical and other influences that reduce the accuracy of communication. It comes originally from the classic formulation of Shannon and Weaver, op. cit. For a complete elaboration of Shannon and Weaver's formulation see: Broadhurst, A. R., & Darnell, D. K. (1965). An introduction to cybernetics and information theory. *Quarterly Journal of Speech, 51,* 442–435; Krippendorf, K. (1975). Information theory. In G. Hanneman & W. McEwen (Eds.), *Communication and behavior* (pp. 351–389). (Reading, MA: Addison-Wesley, and Littlejohn, S. W. (1989). *Theories of human communication* (3rd Ed.) (pp. 42–64). Belmont, CA: Wadsworth.

Additional Readings

Dahnke, G. L., & Clatterbuck, G. W., (1990). *Human communication: Theory and reseach.* Belmont, CA: Wadsworth.

This is an excellent edited book of essays written by well-known scholars in the field of communication. The topics covered represent the areas of research that have been the primary points of inquiry over the past two decades. Each essay is clearly written and accessible to beginning communication students.

Fisher, B. A. (1978). *Perspectives on human communication.* New York: Macmillan.

One of the older survey-type overviews of communication theory, this book explains in simpler terms what were in their original form highly complex perspectives on human communication. This book provides the reader with a good idea of where the field of communication was two decades ago and thus provides a good comparative base for more contemporary books.

Littlejohn, S. W. (1991). *Theories of human communication* (3rd ed.). Belmont, CA: Wadsworth.

Now in its third edition, this upper-level text surveys both social and psychological theories of human communication. It effectively incorporates a discussion of contemporary research into explanations of classic and contemporary theories while presenting complex material in a readable style.

Stacks, D., Hiskson, M., III, & Hill, S. R., Jr. (1991) *Introduction to communication theory.* Fort Worth, TX: Holt, Rinehart, and Winston.

This text is different than most of the others on the market. It provides an overview of both empirical and rhetorical theories of human communication in an effort to blend perspectives. It is difficult to read in spots, but overall it provides a good survey of the field of communication.

Trenholm, S. (1991). *Human communication theory* (2nd ed.). Englewood Cliffs, NJ: Prentice-Hall.

This text presents a good survey of the history, the nature, and the status of human communication theory. Theories are described in terms of their emphasis on particular communication problems and the specific context of communication. This is a good intermediate-level book that can be suitably used by the introductory student.

Chapter 2

Verbal Communication

Contents

Communicating Without Language
Communicating with Inherited Behavior Systems
  Use of the senses
  Genetically determined abilities
Communicating with Learned Signs and Signals
  Learning to signal
  Acquiring meanings for natural signs

The Controversy over Whether Animals Can Use Language
Intelligent Creatures in the Sea
  Communication among whales
  Dolphins as communicators
Trying to Teach Apes to Talk
  Assessing ape intelligence
  The early language experiments
  Ameslan and Yerkish
Implications of the Animal Studies
Human Beings without Language
  The case of "Anna"
  The case of "Isabelle"

The Semantics of Human Communication with Language
The World Outside and the Meanings in Our Heads

How meanings are acquired
Concepts as configurations of meaning
Concepts as the basis of perception
Troublesome Concepts in a Multicultural Society
Symbols and Their Referents
  Symbols as labels for meanings
  The principle of arbitrary selection
  The principle of conventions
Specialized cultures: Implications for communication
  The meaning triangle
  Denotations versus connotations
Structural Features of Language
  Vocabulary: The building blocks of language
  Grammar: Rules for constructing conventional patterns
  Syntax: The architecture of language
  Redundancy

Chapter Review

Key Terms

Notes

Additional Readings

Key Questions

- Will we ever be able to talk to animals? That is, if we learn their languages one day, will we be able to converse with whales, dolphins, chimpanzees, or other creatures?

- Many attempts have been made to teach animals to use human languages—often by using manual signs, computer-controlled symbols, or other means. What have we learned about both animal and human communication from these efforts?

- When I see an object, such as a *rose* or a *rhinoceros,* are my inner meaning experiences the same as yours? No one really knows. But if that is true, how can we ever be sure we are talking about the same thing when we use such words to refer to those particular objects?

- We know that people who speak different languages use entirely different words to label the same thing, such as *avion, flugzug,* and *plane* as symbols that mean "aircraft" (as in Spanish, German, and English). How do entirely different labels come to be used to indicate exactly the same object?

A word is a vehicle, a boat from the past, laden with the thought of men we never saw; and in coming to understand it we enter not only into the minds of our contemporaries, but into the general mind of humanity continuous through time.

Charles Horton Cooley
Social Organization, 1909

In 1900 a retired Berlin schoolteacher, Wilhelm von Osten, bought a horse. He called him Hans and began to train him in a most unusual way. With the aid of a blackboard and other devices, Herr von Osten taught Hans to recognize numbers and count out their value by tapping his forefoot on a small wooden platform. The schoolteacher was very patient with his new pupil and aided him in getting it right. At first, he took the horse's hoof in his hands and showed him just how to tap, over and over until he could do it by himself. He then taught him the right answers to all kinds of problems. When asked for a number, such as 10, Hans would obediently tap 10 times. The teacher was pleased with his pet and decided to go on to more advanced problems. To his delight Hans caught on very quickly, and soon the horse could answer amazingly complex questions put to him by his trainer. He seemed to be able to add and subtract and even multiply and divide, always signaling the correct answers to his trainer by taps of his hoof on the little platform. Herr von Osten was not a showman or a professional animal trainer, and he was certainly not trying to deceive anyone by displaying the abilities of his horse. He was as much surprised as anyone at how clever Hans turned out to be.

The horse's reputation grew rapidly, and after several years Hans was attracting widespread attention. The idea that an animal could communicate with human beings was very exciting. Furthermore, the level of intelligence required to perform the tasks accomplished by Hans was far beyond what anyone had attributed to a horse before. Finally, experts were coming from all over Europe, and even other parts of the world, to see "Clever Hans" (as he became known). Some were convinced that it was all a fake, and they tried to expose Herr von Osten as a fraud. But no one was able to detect any deception, and many came to believe that Clever Hans might provide the key to a whole new understanding of animals.

Many authorities felt that the discovery of the horse's amazing capacity was an important breakthrough. It seemed clear that the animal—and perhaps all animals—had a level of intelligence very close to that of human beings. In particular, it appeared that Hans was understanding and using *language.* Although he lacked a voice, his hoof-tapping seemed like an effective alternative, just as hearing-impaired people were able to substitute hand signs for the sounds of words and use language in that form.

In 1904 a German psychologist, Professor Oskar Pfungst, decided to make a thorough study of Clever Hans and determine once and for all if the animal was actually able to understand and use human language.[1] With the owner's permission, the psychologist conducted all kinds of tests to determine the animal's true abilities. What he discovered was that Hans was a very clever horse indeed—but not in the way people thought. Actually, Hans was receiving unintentional "cues" from his owner that enabled him to start and stop tapping in just the right way! The bond between the animal and his owner was so strong that Hans could detect the most subtle movements and facial expressions of the schoolteacher when he was waiting for Hans to tap out answers. What Herr von Osten was doing without realizing it was nodding his head in an almost undetectable manner as he silently counted to see if Hans would reach the correct number of taps. Such unintended movements (some as small as a fraction of a millimeter) were cues to Hans to keep tapping. When the owner stopped moving his head, changed expression, moved back, or smiled as the correct number was reached, Hans simply stopped tapping.

What confused many observers for a long time was the fact that Hans was able to tap out the right number to answer problems posed by a stranger even if his master was not present. That certainly ruled out deliberate deception with secret signals. But eventually, Professor Pfungst found out that Hans could not correctly solve a problem if the answer was not known to the questioner or if Hans could not see or hear his audience.

The conclusion finally reached was that Clever Hans had no grasp of human language whatever. The answer was much simpler. The horse had learned to read a great

In recent times the case of "Clever Hans" has re-entered the debate among scholars as to whether or not animals can understand and use language using the principles involved in human communication. It was concluded in 1904 that Hans was not really able to do arithmetic but was actually responding to subtle and unwitting cues provided by human beings. Today, there is a question as to whether animals studied in communication experiments can actually use language or whether they are really demonstrating the "Clever Hans effect."

variety of subtle cues as to when he should start tapping and indicators of when to stop when enough taps were reached. In fact, he learned to read amazingly subtle cues from strangers as well as his master. When other people came to watch Hans perform he was able to read their expressions of anticipation, encouragement, and satisfaction, just as well as those of his master. When such cues were absent, Hans was just another nice horse.

What is important about the story of Clever Hans is that it helps us understand the nature of language by showing the sharp *contrast* between human and animal communication. In this chapter we will use what psychologists call a **comparative perspective** that will provide a better understanding of the unique features of animal communication based on inherited and learned signs versus human verbal communication based on culturally shared meanings for symbols. This perspective will extend both the linear and the simultaneous transactions models by looking closely at the use of language, a cat-

egory of behavior occurring only among human beings.

It is easy to assume mistakenly that a clever animal, like Hans, can learn to use language. If we make this incorrect assumption, it blurs the distinction between human capacities and those of other species. At present, the case of Clever Hans has come once again to the forefront of knowledge as social scientists try to understand the many kinds of communication systems used by various species. Particularly important are distinctions between three types of behavior systems: those based solely on *inherited* functions, those based on *learned* signs and signals, and those depending on *language,* which requires individual learning of meanings that are conventional, that is, standardized within a shared culture.

Communication without Language

Virtually every creature in the world—including many microscopic forms—uses some set of techniques to communicate.[2] As we will see, there are essentially two major ways in which they do this. Some animals *inherit* their communication abilities, whereas others *learn* to influence other members of their species. There are many gradations of complexity within these two broad categories, but each serves the creatures well who use them.

It has been apparent since the earliest times that animals communicate with each other. They bark, sing, click, howl, croak, shriek, and use distinctive patterns of action to generate numerous signals, not only to members of their own species but to others as well. Long before science was invented, people understood that such signaling was related to coping with significant aspects of the animal's environment, such as locating food, finding a mate, establishing territory, and warning of danger. Human beings have been closely involved with animals since prehistoric times. They have feared them as predators, depended on them for food, domesticated them as beasts of burden, and tamed them as companions. Many societies even elevated animals to the status of gods. Thus, it is not by chance that we are fascinated with the question of their ability to communicate.

But the issue that has been of greatest interest to nonspecialists and researchers alike is whether there can be interspecies communication between animals and human beings. The belief that human beings and animals might be able to talk to each other through language has deep cultural roots. Some of our most ancient legends tell of conversations between animals and people. In the sixth century B.C., Aesop's fable of the fox and the grapes portrayed the animal communicating in human terms. The fox could speak and think just like a human being. Among many Native American groups, legends of animals communicating with people were very important and were used to teach concepts and principles to children.

Today, the idea that animals can use language, and that human beings can exchange ideas with them, is very much alive. Parents read bedtime stories to young children in which they describe animal-human conversations. Some of the most delightful experiences of childhood were our introductions to Goldilocks and the three bears, Little Red Riding Hood and the wolf, and Uncle Remus and his animal companions. Many such stories were originally from Africa, Asia, or elsewhere, and they enriched our childhood experience. Only later, as we grew older, did we somewhat reluctantly realize that it was only make-believe. Even so, we continue such fantasies into adulthood as we read the daily funny papers, where such animals as cats, dogs, penguins, opossums, birds, alligators, and even ants carry on sophisticated conversations using an extensive human vocabulary.

Those who study animal communication scientifically must set aside the fantasies and fables of childhood. The object of scientific studies of animals and their behavior is to determine objectively how animals communicate and the consequences of such activities. As we will note later in this section, the first scientific studies of animal communication were undertaken long ago, but the majority of such research has been done in modern times.

More than anything else, it was the perspective offered by Charles Darwin in the 1850s that provided an organizing theme for scientists who became interested in studies of animal communication, especially as it compared with that of human beings. Darwin's theories offered the vision of evolutionary development, beginning with simple forms and eventually resulting in complex creatures, including human beings. That idea fired the imagination of scientists of all disciplines. By 1866 the concept of a **phylogenetic continuum** had been developed. That is, animal species could be arranged along a kind of scale, according to such criteria as their learning capacities and abilities to communicate in complex ways. The simplest animals were on one end of the scale and the most complex on the other.

When the field of psychology developed later in the 19th century, the question of how human beings were to be classified or positioned on this phylogenetic continuum came under great debate. To provide answers, psychologists undertook intensive studies of all kinds of animals in order to assess the different capacities and behavioral characteristics of various species. We noted earlier that this strategy is referred to as a comparative perspective. Today, psychologists are joined in this task by zoologists (those who study animals), entomologists (specialists in the study of insects), and communication specialists who study human beings.

Because of their great neural complexity, learning capacity, and elaborate cultures, human beings are now seen as at the upper end of the phylogenetic continuum. Apes, whales, dolphins, and so on, are ranked somewhere below them in behavioral complexity and learning capacity. Obviously somewhere below those are other kinds of animals—various mammals, birds, fish, insects, and so on, down to the simplest creatures.

The fascination with comparative studies (see Table 2.1) is that some rather romantic enthusiasts think they might unlock the secrets of how animals communicate with each other in "languages" that are not yet understood (and that human beings might learn). What a world it would be if human beings could command those codes (if indeed they exist)! The ancient dream of talking with

The cultures of virtually every society have included the idea that human beings can use language to talk with animals and that they can talk to each other. Reinforcing this belief were our childhood experiences with Walt Disney's creations or more sophisticated communicators such as the White Rabbit from *Through the Looking Glass.* Such beliefs have been with us from the time of Aesop to television's Mr. Ed. Talking with animals remains a romantic hope, even though modern research raises serious doubts that it will ever be possible.

animals might at last be realized. As this kind of research began, no one knew what might be found and it was one of the most exciting challenges of science.

In the sections that follow, we will review what we now know about the capacities of various animals to communicate and their techniques of communication. As indicated earlier, our goal is not to learn about animals as such, but about ourselves. In other words, a look at animal communication at various points along the phylogenetic continuum will provide an important comparison and contrast with the nature of human communication processes.

Communicating with Inherited Behavior Systems

Animal communication based on inherited biological systems (and not dependent on learning) is far more common than any other form. It is very effective for survival, but at the same time, it has severe limitations, as we shall see in this section. Inherited communication techniques are widely found among insects. A brief look at the ways in which they solve their problems of communication will show the sharpest possible contrast with ways used by human beings.

Insects are the most numerous animals on earth. Although no one is certain how many separate species exist (it increases from time to time as new forms are discovered), there are many hundreds of thousands and insects are the most successful of earth's creatures. Various kinds of ants were foraging among forests of conifers and cycads more than 100 million years ago. Most of the common insects we know, such as the lowly cockroach, have not changed much in millions of years. Many scientists are convinced that if this planet suffers a major catastrophe in which all human life is destroyed, insects will thrive on what is left. One reason insects have been around so long is that they handle very effectively all activities which are important for their survival: Regardless of whether they are solitary or live in complex social systems, all insects engage in communication needed to find *food,* protect themselves from *danger,* and to provide for *reproduction.*

Use of the senses   Insects, like human beings, depend on their senses in order to communicate. They receive sounds, see light, feel objects in the physical world, and detect various kinds of odors. Some insects use all four of these sensory modalities in their communication; others use only three or fewer. Usually, one sense predominates, while the others are secondary. The most important sense among the majority of the world's insects is smell. The importance of scent in insect communication was first discovered just after the beginning of this century.[3] We know now that many kinds of chemical secretions are used by insects and other animals. Collectively called **pheromones** (pronounced "ferro-moans"), they are released in the air or are deliberately used to mark trails, territory, or readiness for mating. Insects can detect these chemical signals in incredibly minute concentrations and adjust their behavior according to their implications.

Table 2.1

Animals Whose Communication Patterns Have Been Investigated in Scientific Studies

TYPE OF ANIMAL	NUMBER OF STUDIES REPORTED	TYPE OF ANIMAL	NUMBER OF STUDIES REPORTED
Alligator	1	Lemming	1
Anuran	1	Lemurped	4
Ape and gorilla	16	Lizard	4
Baboon	4	Lobster	1
Beaver	2	Marmoset	5
Bird (all species)	183	Monkey (all species)	75
Bushbaby	1	Mouse	21
Cat	7	Muntjac	1
Cattle	7	Mussel	1
Chamois	1	Otter	1
Chimpanzee	21	Periplaneta	1
Chinchilla	1	Pig	1
Chipmunk	1	Pika	1
Coyote	1	Pinneped	1
Crab	14	Prairie dog	2
Crayfish	3	Protozoa	1
Deer	3	Rabbit	3
Degu	1	Raccoon	1
Dog (tame and wild)	5	Rat	18
Dolphin and porpoise	6	Reindeer	2
Eland	3	Salamander	1
Elephant	1	Seal	2
Elk	2	Sea lion	2
Fish (all species)	32	Shrew	2
Fox	2	Shrimp	3
Frog (all species)	14	Skunk	1
Genet	2	Snake	3
Gerbil	8	Squirrel	11
Gibbon	3	Tadpole	1
Guinea pig	4	Tasmanian devil	1
Hamster	10	Tiger	1
Horse and pony	4	Toad	4
Insect (all species)	97	Whale	6
Jacana	1	Wolf	5
Lamb	3	Zebra	2

Source: Compiled from the titles of 1,027 citations obtained through a computer search of *Psychological Abstracts,* 1966 to 1986, using the descripters "Animal" and "Communication." The table underestimates the number of studies of some animals due to limited information in some titles about specific species under investigation. The table also excludes numerous books, monographs, and technical reports not cited in the data base searched.

Some insects depend heavily on sight. Bees are a good example. Professor von Frisch and his associates studied bees from various parts of the world for decades, and a very intricate system of communication was slowly revealed. All bees, everywhere, perform a kind of "dance" to indicate distance and direction to food sources. They all do it in much the same manner with only minor variations between species and locales. Generally, the bees do a "round" type of dance to indicate food sources between 25 and 100 meters away, and a quite different "sickle" dance to indicate more extensive distances. Painstaking experiments showed that there are a number of additional patterned dances for various purposes. In addition, bees use sound, smell, and touch to provide other signals. Finally, more recent studies indicate that bees can orient themselves to the sun and its daily angles to judge direction and distance, even on cloudy days.[4]

In comparison, the senses of human beings are not as keen as those of many insects. Our most acute sense is sight, and we use it to detect nonverbal cues. However,

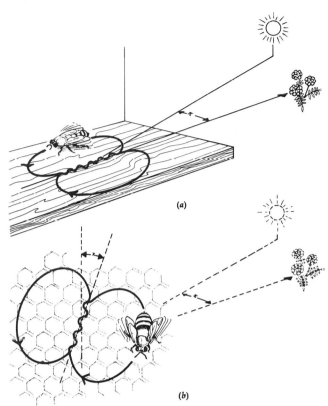

(a)

(b)

Insects communicate in complex ways by using behavior systems that are inherited. Honeybees, for example, locate sources of food, return to the hive, and perform characteristic patterns of movements (sickle or round "dances"). From these movements, other bees obtain indicators of direction and distance to a food source. They are able to use the sun for directional orientation. Most insect communication is based on the senses of smell, sight, and sound, and usually concerns basics, such as food, danger, or readiness to reproduce.

our verbal communication is based primarily on the production and detection of sound. In basic oral communication, then, the voice is obviously our principal tool, and effective listening is a critical part of the process. At the same time, seeing, touching, and even smelling the individual with whom we are communicating can sometimes be important. In this way, human and insect communication are similar.

Genetically determined abilities   While the tools of communication used by insects can be impressive, they are rather rigidly fixed and limited by their genetic endowment. In this sense, insects are very different from human beings. That is, insects *inherit* the ability to use whatever sensory receptors or other parts of their bodies are needed to form and receive signals. For example, bees

do not teach their offspring to perform their complex dance movements; they inherit the ability to perform the dance.

Adaptive behavior patterns that are inherited, unlearned, and universal in a species are often called **instincts.** Their nearly total dependence on instinctual forms of communication makes insects unlike animals higher on the phylogenetic continuum. While higher animals may display instinctual patterns in many aspects of their behavior, they are much more dependent on learning in order to adapt to their environment. That generalization applies to their patterns of communication as well as to other forms of behavior.

In overview, human beings and insects have at least *some* common features in their systems of communication. Both depend on the use of sight, hearing, smell, and touch to originate signals and to detect signals from their fellow creatures. Human beings are confined to hearing and listening in most of their communication, although sight and even touch can be part of the process. Dependence on sight may have been much more important to human beings earlier, before speech became possible.

With these conclusions in mind, we turn to an examination of communication in which instincts fixed by genetic determination are less important. Much of the signaling behavior widely found among animals higher on the phylogenetic continuum is based on the use of **signs**—events in the environment that they associate with and use to anticipate subsequent events. Signs are acquired by learning, although they may be shaped or limited by inheritance. A major purpose of this part of our analysis will be to show that communication among such animals is based mainly on learned responses to forms of behavior occurring *naturally* in the animal's repertoire.

Communicating with Learned Signs and Signals

Anyone who has lived with a much-loved pet understands that communication between a human being and an animal can be both subtle and extensive. Like Clever Hans, dogs, cats, parrots, and other typical animal companions are much more intelligent than most people realize. It doesn't take them long to figure out how to master their environment, whether it is a back yard or an urban apartment. They develop ways to let the people know that they want to be fed, that they want out (or in), that strangers are present, and so forth. They have little trouble in initiating signals to beg tidbits or treats, to indicate that they want to go along in the car or on a walk, or that they want to play. Again, like Clever Hans, our pets quickly learn to pick up subtle cues related to human habits and family routines. Anyone who has seen pets suddenly make themselves scarce at bath time will realize the subtlety of the cues they can read. No wonder owners sometimes conclude that their pets really can understand human language.

Learning to signal   Like human beings, animals mainly depend on sound to signal to each other. The calls made by birds and other creatures are easily interpreted by others of their species as signs that stand for such interpretations as warnings of danger, the need to flee, and readiness to mate. Some signs are directed toward and interpreted by other species. Warnings to predators are unmistakable as animals seek to protect their young.

While it was once thought that instincts played a dominant role in almost all animal communication, experiments with birds have forced scientists to revise their views. Recordings have been used to study the songs of various species of birds. First, it was discovered that chaffinches (small sparrowlike birds) raised in isolation (in soundproof boxes) couldn't sing like normal members of their species. At the age of 9 months all they could do was make rather raucous noises. However, if they could listen to tape recordings of the normal chaffinch song when they were young, they learned to sing normally as early as ten days after hatching.[5] Thus, learning was a critical factor in their communication.

Birds also communicate with patterned movements. Watching young birds still in the nest shows that when the adults approach the babies use various parts of their bodies, such as wide-open beaks and wing flutters, to indicate they want to be fed. Adult birds use various mating "dances" and aggressive postures when danger threatens. All of these movements, postures, and sounds can be regarded as signs, whose meaning is understood by the initiator—and presumably by other similar birds, or in some cases, even by other species.

There is no doubt that inheritance places important limitations on the signs used in the communication systems of birds as well as other animals. Because of its inherited biological structure, a sparrow will not learn to sing like a nightingale. The best it can do is to learn to chirp like other sparrows. While some birds have a capacity to imitate sounds, in the wild they communicate according to the patterns characteristic of their species. Thus, their signs are based on actions within their natural repertoire, and they do not invent new bird calls or agree among themselves to signal each other in novel ways.

The important lesson provided by studies of the use of natural signs among birds is that learning plays an important role in all aspects of their behavior. Instincts are still very important and govern such matters as migrations, nesting, selections of foods, procreation, and rearing of the young. Their communication, while far more complex than that of lower creatures, is still limited to signs based on patterned movements and sounds that may be acquired in part by learning but which are sharply limited by inheritance.

Acquiring meanings for natural signs   Among mammals (whose position on the phylogenetic scale is nearer the top) the ability to acquire meanings for complex signs is considerable. We noted at the beginning of the chapter the unsuspected abilities of Clever Hans to detect extremely subtle facial expressions, postures, and bodily movements among those watching him perform. Those human cues served as natural signs for Hans. Without instruction, he acquired the "meaning" that they were signals to begin or stop tapping his foot. The signs the horse learned can be regarded as "natural" because they were not prearranged by Hans, a human being, or any other agency. They simply occurred in the horse's environment, and he learned to associate them with behavior that led to reward.

Animals in the wild detect a large number of complex natural signs to which they learn appropriate responses. They use these to anticipate and adjust to the problems they encounter in their environment, including coexistence with other creatures. Thus, such mammals as wolves, deer, elk, panthers, and other large animals communicate important messages to each other that help in their survival. Depending on their species they may also communicate social signals indicating dominance, submission, and leadership, along with the usual messages concerning danger, protection of young, presence of food, and so on.

At the same time, we must not confuse natural signs with language. The natural signs used by animals, including those they learn to use as well as those they inherit, are *very different* from the words, rules, and patterns (syntax and grammar) used by human beings. Thus, the communication patterns among species relatively high on the phylogenetic continuum are limited by inherited capacities and techniques and are based mainly on learning to respond to complex natural signs. The signs that animals use are neither *arbitrarily selected* by the creatures that use them nor are their meanings *shared by conventions* among themselves. As we will show, these are two of the major features of human languages.

Communication between human beings and animals can be sensitive, but it is based on the animal's considerable capacity to learn meanings for natural signs. For example, the gestures and actions of the pet owner come to have predictable consequences for such animals, enabling them to respond in complex ways. But this is not the same as using language symbols or nonverbal actions with meanings based on shared cultural conventions among human beings.

What all of this means is that human language has technical features that set it apart from the communication systems used by even the highest animals. Left on their own, animals have never developed language. They communicate, often very effectively, by other means—pheromones, inherited behavior patterns, learned natural signs, or combinations of all three.

Two questions obviously follow from these conclusions: First, isn't it possible that some species actually are using language and we have not yet figured out their codes? Second, isn't it possible that some of the more intelligent animals would be *capable* of learning to use language if human beings took the trouble to teach them? These two questions have been vigorously studied in recent years, and a considerable controversy has raged around the conclusions reached.

The Controversy over Whether Animals Can Use Language

Learning a language is difficult, even for human beings. Are any animals capable of such a feat, even at a very elementary level? Can any creature other than a human

being be taught to speak? Or, if other communication tools, like hand signs, have to be used, can any animal acquire an understanding of rules for arranging signs in patterns to produce meaning? These are critical questions whose answers will show whether human beings are close to, or far apart from, other animals in their ability to communicate.

The capacity to learn is at a maximum among animals near the top of the phylogenetic scale. These include such creatures as dolphins and whales, both of which are mammals that have complex brains. Another important category is made up of chimpanzees, gorillas, and other large primates. All of these remarkable animals have fascinated human beings for centuries. In recent decades, a number of interesting experiments have been conducted to try to understand their learning capacity and whether they can be taught to communicate with language.

Intelligent Creatures in the Sea

One fascinating category of mammals are the *cetaceans,* which include the large and small whales, porpoises, and dolphins. In recent decades, human beings have taken a special interest in whales. Their complex communication signals, in particular, can be hauntingly beautiful. Such "songs" have been recorded and studied for many years. Some whale fans have gone so far as to set them to music—writing background symphonies that bring out their patterns. True devotees maintain that these complex noises are, in fact, a language whose secrets are as yet known only to the underwater giants. At least some enthusiasts assume that we will eventually be able to talk to these great creatures of the ocean depths. Dolphins are also held in particularly high regard by human beings. They are sleek and beautiful, and they seem both intelligent and friendly. There is a large lore concerning their affinity to people, and various marine exhibits and TV shows in which the animals perform complex tricks, have led the public to believe they have near-human qualities.

Communication among whales   The plight of whales has become a topic of special sensitivity among those who are concerned about problems in our environment. Concern about these great animals has led at least a few people to take sometimes drastic measures to stop the practice of whaling. Motivated by the prospect that whales may face extinction, and assumptions that the creatures have extraordinary intelligence, individuals have risked their lives in various kinds of confrontations with whaling

vessels and their crews. Given such commitment, it is little wonder beliefs persist that whales have their own language and that human beings may someday be able to converse with them. Adding to the mystique is the fact that whales seem quite gentle. Indeed, most appear to be friendly to divers and even sightseers in boats as long as they do not bother their young.

There is no doubt that whales make elaborate noises. Their "songs" consist of patterned sounds that carry for miles through water. One reason is that the frequency range they use is quite low. Such sounds travel better under water than those of high pitch. Recordings show that whale songs not only have complex variations of pitch and intensity but also can go on for many minutes or even hours. In addition, among some species they seem to change from year to year and in exactly the same way all over the world. No one knows quite what to make of this. What it does indicate is that learning plays a significant role in their production and that the songs are not simply determined by inflexible inheritance.

Because some whales are more than 80 feet long—too big to study in a laboratory—little has been done in placing them in experiments that might reveal more details about the nature of their communication systems. For decades, however, extensive observations have been made of their migrations, mating, care of the young, be-

Few creatures have stirred our imagination and sympathy more than whales. Even though they are huge, these mammals do not appear to be aggressive or dangerous. Extensive observations indicate that they are both intelligent and tolerant of human beings. While some people maintain that their "songs" are a kind of whale "language," many experts remain skeptical and believe that their complex sounds serve the same functions that sound signals serve for other animals—mainly as indicators of food, danger, or readiness to mate.

havior toward each other, and so on. Still, while we know a great deal about whales, we have not made much real progress in understanding their communication capacities and limits.

One thing that excites many fans is that the brains of whales are very large—which they take as indication of high intelligence. In addition, they are not aggressive, as is the case with many other large mammals. They are often observed to be concerned about each other, and in fact, instances have been reported of whales being protective toward injured human beings swimming or diving among them. Such reports have resulted in generally favorable attitudes toward whales. All of this has led some advocates to propose that the giant creatures are even *more* intelligent than human beings and that it is essential we learn their language so as to have their guidance!

Those who have observed whales systematically for many years hold other views. Most knowledgeable people agree that whales are marvelous animals and clearly need protection for their survival. However, there are few scientific grounds for assuming they are anywhere near the equal of human beings in intelligence. Their brains are not particularly large in comparison to their huge body mass. Furthermore, their elaborate "songs" are probably no different in function than the songs of birds or even frogs. Animal researcher Roger Payne suggests that their songs are related to such typical animal problems as survival, leadership, mating, territorial claims, and the like.[6] At this point it seems unlikely that some mysterious "whale language" will eventually be decoded.

Dolphins as communicators   Porpoises and dolphins are small enough to keep in tanks and observe in a systematic way. In fact, since the 1950s there have been many successful efforts to do so. In particular, bottlenose dolphins have been extensively studied. They are the familiar and lovable creatures of Sea World animal acts and television shows about "Flipper" (who was actually several different dolphins).

One young woman lived for several weeks with a dolphin—in a shallow tank where suitable sleeping and eating arrangements were available for both creatures. Although dolphins are large and powerful, with strong jaws and teeth, the animal never harmed the woman. In fact, the dolphin was intensely interested in his companion and stayed with her constantly.[7] Like other dolphins, it was able to mimic human vocal sounds and easily learn to associate patterned sounds of words with ideas. Altogether, it was a fascinating experience, but not much was learned about dolphins' ability to communicate.

In recent times, experiments with dolphins and similar cetaceans have become much more sophisticated. For example, in 1984 zoologists Louis Herman and associates reported an experiment in which they taught two dolphins a system they likened to human language. The animals were taught to associate particular behavior with such objects as a ball, a frisbee, and a hoop. They also learned signals for actions, such as spit (out), touch, and fetch. Finally, they were trained in such ideas as "bottom" and "surface" (of the water). These signals were put together into combinations so that the animals could respond to "fetch the hoop from the bottom," and so on. The dolphins had no problems in learning to respond to such patterns.[8]

What do these observations of the cetaceans tell us about communication among whales and dolphins? Certainly they provide fewer answers than we would like. However, some things seem clear. These animals are very intelligent by comparison with other members of the animal kingdom. On the other hand, we cannot assume they approach human beings in that respect. They obviously can learn to respond to signs in complex ways—perhaps even more readily than many other animals—but it would be unrealistic to conclude at this point that they use a language we do not yet understand.

Trying to Teach Apes to Talk

Most Americans easily recognize chimpanzees. These animals seem cute and intelligent, and in a grotesque way apes look rather like human beings. Because of this, some people think they ought to be able to behave like people—especially when it comes to the use of language. In fact, a number of attempts have been made to teach chimpanzees to speak and to instruct gorillas or other primates to use sign language, special symbols, computers, and the like. In many ways, the results of these attempts are surprising. They are also very controversial.

Assessing ape intelligence   The classic study of the intelligence of larger primates is that of Wolfgang Köhler, the German psychologist who performed ingenious experiments to understand the problem-solving abilities of chimpanzees.[9] When World War I broke out in 1914, he was stuck on the remote island of Tenerife in the South Atlantic (where a German anthropoid station was maintained). Professor Köhler used the time to devise a series of puzzles for his chimps to solve so that he could determine the upper level of their abilities. He found that the apes were smart but that they had clear limitations on intelligence. The animals were able to stack boxes to reach otherwise unreachable food, to break off and use a tree branch to rake a banana into a cage, and to solve a number of similar spatial and tool-using problems. Köhler concluded that while apes behave intelligently, they remain far behind human beings. We still believe that today.

It is a giant step from figuring out how to use a stick to rake a banana into a cage to learning to speak a language. Furthermore, how does one go about trying to teach an ape to speak? Should the animal be raised in a laboratory setting where systematic lessons can be provided under controlled conditions? Or should the animal be reared in a human home, surrounded by language to imitate plus loving encouragement to do so?

The early language experiments   In the first of the classic efforts to answer these questions, psychologists Winthrop and Louise Kellogg decided in 1931 to see if a chimpanzee could learn to speak.[10] At the time, they believed that one reason apes did not do so was because they were not raised in a language environment. Human infants, on the other hand, are in constant contact with language-using adults who offer reward and encouragement for attempts to learn to talk. As it happened, the Kelloggs were expecting a baby. They decided to acquire an infant chimpanzee and raise it in an identical manner with their own child. Their infant son, Donald, and the chimp, Gua, were bathed, fed, diapered, and treated affectionately in exactly the same manner. Both were equally encouraged to use words and were coached extensively.

It didn't work. The chimp and the baby got along very well, but at the end of 3 years, Donald was growing up to be a normal boy while Gua was developing into a normal chimp. Donald learned speech in the manner typical of his age, putting together words into simple sentences. Gua was never able to speak a word. On the other hand, Gua was a bright animal and quickly learned to respond to a number of simple verbal commands. Furthermore, the chimp far outstripped Donald in manual dexterity and within a year could swing about in vigorous chimplike fashion while the boy could only toddle awkwardly.

In 1947 a somewhat similar project was undertaken. There was no human baby present, but Keith and Catherine Hayes raised a chimp, Vicki, in their home.[11] They coached her constantly in the use of specific words, helping to form sounds by manipulating Vicki's lips. After 6 years, however, the chimp had learned to vocalize only three approximations of English words—"mama," "papa," and "cup" (and perhaps "up"). She did so only in a hoarse whisper with great difficulty, and there was no firm indication that these "words" had the same meanings they have for people.

The home-rearing experiments with Gua and Vicki were generally failures in terms of their original goals. Yet, in one way they were great successes. They forced a clear recognition that the animals had difficulty because their *vocal physiology was not able to form speech sounds*. We know now that the vocal tract, larynx, and other soft tissue structures that human beings use to generate and control complex sounds are quite different among other primates.

Furthermore, an elaborate brain is required for speech. The chimpanzee does not appear to have clear counterparts of those areas in the human brain that are essential to human speech (Broca's and Wernicke's areas).[12] What all of this means is that apes are not going to learn to talk. Their bodies are not designed for it, and it would be rather pointless to make further attempts along these lines.

Ameslan and Yerkish   On the other hand, young apes are far better at manual dexterity than are young human beings. They spontaneously make many expressive gestures and finger movements. This led comparative psychologists to conclude that they should try to take advantage of this natural endowment, by using a means of communication not requiring the apes to speak. If this could be done, then perhaps apes could be taught to "talk" with human beings without the use of the voice.

One solution to the problem occurred to psychologists Beatrice and Allan Gardner. Why not try sign language, such as the finger positions and movements used by hearing-impaired people? In 1966 they acquired a chimp they named Washoe (after the Nevada county where they lived) and began to teach her the American Sign Language—sometimes called Ameslan—that is used by the hearing impaired.[13] They chose the version with single signs for whole words, rather than the kind requiring the user to spell out letters. Here, no vocalization was involved, and the chimp could take advantage of her natural manual dexterity.

Teaching Washoe the signs wasn't easy. The chimp was housed in a special trailer surrounded by a big yard with a high fence—a rich environment resembling a human home. Both the Gardners and other teachers spent long periods with Washoe every day, conditioning her to make the right signs for various objects and actions. At the end of the 4-year experiment, the experimenters believed she was able to use or respond to some 160 signs. What seemed even more exciting to them was that the chimp sometimes spontaneously put two, or even three, signs together. At least some of these combinations appeared to "make sense." The chimp used signs such as "gimme tickle," "go sweet" (which the experimenters interpreted as a request to be taken to raspberry bushes to eat berries), and even "Roger Washoe tickle" (seen as a request to play with her trainer).

While the results seemed gratifying, there were serious limitations in what Washoe could do. On no occasion did she put together anything abstract, novel, or inventive, although she lived in an environment where there were numerous possibilities to make such combinations. Her signing behavior was restricted to the here and now, never referring to the past or future. Virtually all of her spontaneous signing related to food, treats, or other personal needs of the moment. Most important,

there was no evidence that she developed an understanding of *syntax,* that is, rules for putting signs together in consistent patterns that themselves provide meaning. In short, the effort was inconclusive.

Perhaps the most dramatic of the sign language experiments was the effort by psychologist Francene Patterson to teach Koko, an African gorilla, to communicate with Ameslan. She acquired the animal as an infant and established it in special quarters. Gorillas are large and powerful, with a reputation as being bad-tempered and ferocious. Working with several assistants, Patterson patiently taught the animal to make signs and associate them with specific meanings (such as "food," "drink," and "more"). Later, this was extended to include many more signs and their associated meanings. No dangerous behavior was encountered, and the animal developed an extended repertoire of the signs, which were used in many sequences. Some of them seemed to Patterson to be appropriate to communicate simple requests and responses

The gorilla "Koko," shown here with her trainer Francine Patterson, was taught to respond in a variety of ways to commands and signals using American Sign Language. The gentle creature seemed to some observers to be able to signal back to human beings with combinations of signs as though the animal could use language. However, statistical analysis of the patterns used by Koko caused some experts to doubt that they were anything other than occasional chance configurations of the learned hand signs one would expect in any random distribution of such actions.

to queries from the trainers. Generally, Koko seemed to be the equal or superior of Washoe in the use of signs.[14]

Other attempts to surmount the lack of vocal physiology have been made by teaching apes to use "artificial languages." For example, a chimp called Sarah was taught by David Premack to manipulate pieces of plastic of various colors and random shapes.[15] Through conditioning, the ape was taught to associate various objects and actions with these plastic "words." Then, to try to develop primitive rules of syntax, various combinations were given meanings. Sarah did learn to use sequences of her pieces of plastic. In fact, after extensive training it seemed to the experimenters that she had mastered simple abstractions and conceptual relationships, such as identifying things by color and indicating whether an object was "over," "under," or "beside" another. Perhaps the most significant finding from the work with Sarah was that she could learn and use simple rules for associating meaning with combinations of her plastic pieces. On the other hand, she was limited by the characteristics of all apes: She had a very short memory span and her use of the synthetic "language" was restricted completely to the here and now.

Finally, the computer age extended our ability to study possible language use among animals. Early in the 1970s, psychologist Duane Rumbaugh developed a system for teaching a chimp called Lana. Initially, the animal was placed in an environment that did not require the presence of a human handler.[16] It was a laboratory-like room that contained a kind of keyboard. Each key corresponded to a "word" in an artificial language called "Yerkish" (after Robert Yerkes, a famous comparative psychologist). Pressing the key, on which was displayed a special symbol, caused a visual display with the same symbol to light up. It was possible to press several keys and get a string of symbols lit up on the special display. Outside the room, the experimenter had a similar keyboard. Because it was also wired to the visual display, two-way signaling with the ape was possible. A computer interfaced the two devices and kept track of the results.

Training began with the use of a single key (which Lana could press to get rewards) and was soon extended to combinations of the symbols the chimp had to master. If Lana used the symbols in the proper sequence to request rewards, she got what she asked for: various foods, drinks, tickling, a trip outside, and even a movie to watch. As in the case of Sarah, in the Premack experiment, Lana was able to master a number of such behaviors.

In spite of the elaborate controls and the computerized

apparatus, the Yerkish experiment did not reveal much that was new. An extended analysis of "conversations" with Lana in the computer-assisted experiment brings into sharp focus the essential limitations that have been found to characterize the abilities of apes in all of the animal studies:

> Lana has been prone to converse whenever she must do so in order to receive something exceptional or whenever something not in accordance with the routine delivery of foods and drinks has occurred—in short when some practical problem arises for her. She has never in conversation commented extensively on this or that as children and adults are inclined when their attention or motivation shifts unpredictably. For Lana, language is an adaptive behavior of considerable instrumental value for achieving specific goals not readily achieved otherwise."[17]

In general, then, it seems to make little difference whether an animal is raised in a warm human environment or in a sterile laboratory. They still remain locked into an animal world that is very different from that of human beings.

Implications of the Animal Studies

What are the overall implications of these studies and experiments with animals? Are we as human beings located on the phylogenetic continuum in terms of communication ability at a position only *somewhat* above that of the apes? Or do we have unique capacities and abilities that so *far exceed* those of even the brightest animals that a tremendous gap exists between us?

Many critical psychologists have rejected the conclusion that these animal experiments show *any* language usage or capacity at all. They base their rejection on two grounds. First, careful studies of films and videotapes taken to record the training of many of the chimps, and the gorilla Koko, seem to show the **Clever Hans effect.** That is, there was evidence that these intelligent animals could detect what their trainers wanted them to sign, and they obligingly complied to get approval or rewards. This interpretation has raised serious doubts about whether the animals involved had any real conceptual ability or had mastered even the crudest idea of syntax. On the other hand, the Clever Hans effect was ruled out of the Rumbaugh experiments with Lana, the chimp in the computer-controlled environment. The trainer was not even in the room until after she had mastered the signals.

The most damaging criticism comes from the statistical evidence. The number of times the animals used various signs and signals both singly and in various combinations was carefully tallied. Out of the thousands of such usages, a certain number of combinations would be expected if only *chance* were at work. That is, even in the most random set of events, at least some combinations will be found that "look" meaningful. In fact, the analyses showed that the combinations occurred almost exactly in proportion to what one would expect if indeed only chance were at work. Thus, enthusiastic experimenters may have focused on those few chance occurrences and unrealistically concluded that they represent language usages, while ignoring the huge numbers of meaningless combinations far more typical of animal behavior.

Human Beings Without Language

But what if human beings were the subjects rather than apes? And what if the object were not to get them to speak but to deny them access to language? What would be the consequences? Would people invent and use language anyway? If so, what kind? It goes without saying that any deliberate use of human beings in such experiments is morally unthinkable. However, a number of events in history have placed human infants in just such circumstances, and accounts of the results have survived. For example, the Greek historian Herodotus reported that Psammetichus, King of Egypt, had several children raised by nurses who were forbidden to speak to them in order to find out if the children would first utter the Egyptian tongue or some other. Reportedly, when the children tired of the goat's milk they were being fed, they asked for bread in the Phrygian tongue! Centuries later, when Emperor Frederick II of Austria attempted to repeat the experiment, the children died. This confirmed the existing belief that children raised without speech would have no souls and, therefore, lacked vitality.

During the 18th century, King James IV of Scotland arranged for two children to be placed on the island of Inchkeith in the care of a woman who could not speak. He was seeking proof for the widely held belief that children raised under these circumstances would speak Hebrew, the tongue of Adam. According to reports sent to the King, when the children began speaking, "they spak guid Hebrew."[18] (It is wonderful what experimental results one can obtain if one is king!)

Contemporary observations do not support the idea that children come into the world naturally predisposed to speak one language or another, or indeed any language

at all. We do know, however that the *absence* of a language environment in early life appears to have drastic consequences for a developing infant. While no one in recent times has deliberately performed experiments on this issue for obvious reasons, some reliable information on the effects of isolation from language in early age is available. Careful *case studies* have been made during the last several decades of children who were raised under conditions where they had no contact with human speech. These can be regarded as "natural experiments," and they illustrate what happens when human beings are denied normal participation in the language learning process. Two specific cases can be summarized where extended observations were made on such children after they were placed in more normal environments following their discovery.[19]

The case of "Anna" Anna (name fictionalized) was the second illegitimate child of a sturdy young woman who lived on and operated her grandfather's farm in a northeastern state during the late 1940s. The grandfather was a man of stern morals and strongly disapproved of this new evidence of his granddaughter's indiscretions. The newborn child was given up for adoption, but this did not work out for various reasons. Within weeks, the mother had to take the infant back to the farm in spite of the grandfather's wrath. To avoid trouble, the baby was confined in a small attic room on the second floor, out of the grandfather's sight.

> Anna was left almost without attention. Ordinarily, it seems, Anna received only enough care to keep her barely alive. She appears to have been seldom moved from one position to another. Her clothing and bedding were filthy. She apparently had no instruction, no friendly attention. It is little wonder that, when finally found and removed from the room in the grandfather's house at the age of nearly six years, the child could not talk, walk, or do anything that showed intelligence. She was in an extremely emaciated and undernourished condition, with skeleton-like legs and a bloated abdomen. She had been fed on virtually nothing except cow's milk during the years under her mother's care.[20]

After she was discovered, Anna spent about a year and a half in a county home. She learned to walk, feed herself, understand simple commands, to be more or less neat, to remember people, and the like. She made little progress toward speech. It began to be clear that her inherited intelligence level was very low. At this time she was moved to a home for retarded children, where with systematic training she made greater progress. After 4 years she could dress herself, bounce a ball, eat fairly normally, and conform to normal toilet habits. More important, she had begun to speak. At age 9 she was at about the level of a 2-year-old, with a number of words in her vocabulary and several simple sentences to express her wants.

Unfortunately, Anna died when she was 10. She had made additional progress and could brush her teeth, string beads, play lovingly with a doll, and help other children. Anna's early experience had obviously had a devastating effect on her and may have been the cause of some mental retardation. In addition, there were some grounds for believing that her mother was at the low end of the normal intelligence scale. But, considering that when she was found she was a pathetic and animal-like creature, her psychological development at the time of her death provides a striking contrast. In particular, Anna had made considerable progress in learning language. Even with her limitations, she was far above the level of the chimpanzees or other primates in mental ability and communication skills. However, while in the earlier solitary environment, she had remained at a level little different than that of an ape.

The case of "Isabelle"   Only 9 months after the plight of Anna came to light, another American child of almost identical age was discovered living under isolated circumstances. This case cleared up many of the questions caused by Anna's low mental ability: Isabelle (name changed) was the illegitimate offspring of a deaf-mute mother, who had been confined with her. The mother was of normal intelligence, but she had suffered an injury that left her blind in one eye and without the ability to hear, speak, read, or write.

At the age of 22 this unfortunate young woman became pregnant. Her family was deeply ashamed and locked her up in a darkened room during her pregnancy. After the birth of the baby, both mother and child were confined in the same room for a period of 6½ years. Finally, the mother escaped, carrying Isabelle in her arms, and was immediately brought to the attention of the authorities. They placed both her and Isabelle in a hospital.

Since the mother was unable to communicate with the child, Isabelle's environment during her confinement was one entirely without speech. In her new environment she could at first make only strange croaking sounds. She was as terrified of strangers as a wild animal after capture. She was, from the standpoint of language development, every bit as bad off as Anna. Moreover, her health had suffered during her isolation. She was wan and thin, and her legs were badly bowed from rickets caused by im-

proper nourishment and lack of sunshine. (In fact, the soles of her feet came nearly flat together so that she could not walk.) This was later corrected by surgery. With proper diet and care, her health became generally good.

When Isabelle was first brought to the hospital, the authorities thought she was feebleminded. She was completely unable to respond to human speech. When it was finally established that she was neither deaf nor feebleminded, a university professor who specialized in speech therapy undertook to give her language training. Isabelle's progress under this tutelage was truly remarkable. Within 2 weeks she was making her first attempts to identify toys by name when they were presented to her (ball, car, etc.). Within 2 months the child knew dozens of words and could volunteer simple sentences. After a year of training, Isabelle could write, count up to 20, and give a simple summary of a story that had been read to her. After a year and a half, she had a vocabulary of between 1,500 and 2,000 words and could respond to complex questions in a manner very close to that of any child of her age.[21]

Within a short time Isabelle was placed in a regular school. She did very well, experiencing neither learning difficulties nor problems in social adaptation. She had passed through all of the usual childhood stages in learning to read and write, but at an accelerated pace. As she continued in school her earlier experiences became less and less an influence. Later, Isabelle went on to marry and lead a normal life. Her identity, of course, remains a secret.

The conclusions from these two cases are similar to those reached by investigators who have studied others like them. These children, while in environments without speech, developed much like animals. But when removed from isolation and placed in a language community, they began to acquire human characteristics. That transition was slower in the case of Anna, probably because of her limited mental ability. It was very rapid in the case of Isabelle, who was in every respect of normal intelligence.

There are two important lessons to be derived from these two cases. First, human beings, like other animals, are limited in their development of communication skills by their inherited capacities. Anna appears to have been unable to progress rapidly due to a low level of learning ability passed on from one or both parents. Isabelle, on the other hand, inherited a more normal capacity and progressed far more rapidly. Second, high learning capacity is not enough. The ability to use speech develops only in the social environment of a language community. Even an intelligent human being raised in isolation will be unable to communicate beyond an animal level if he or she is denied access to a language culture. That culture includes shared meanings for words and conventional understandings about the rules for their use.[22]

Keeping in mind the perspective derived from animal studies and human beings without language, we turn now to an analysis of language itself, with two purposes in mind. The first is to show in detail how human beings use language to accomplish those processes of communication discussed briefly in Chapter 1. Our second purpose is to gain sufficient insight into the nature of language that it will no longer be a mystery as to why we are unable to use it to communicate with animals, or they with each other.

The Semantics of Human Communication with Language

Speculation about how human beings use language to communicate probably began over council fires in caves when prehistoric people were first learning to speak. By the time written records of the ideas of great thinkers started to accumulate, much was already known about language and how it is used to create internal understandings of external reality. In this section we will take advantage of not only the insights of early philosophers but also a host of scholars and scientists who have added to our knowledge during the succeeding centuries. Today, the study of relationships between the objects, events, and situations of reality, the words we use to label them, and the meanings we construct for both, is called **semantics.** The relationships it studies lie at the heart of verbal communication with language.

The World Outside and the Meanings in Our Heads

One of the problems of great concern to philosophers in ancient Greece, India, China, and the Arabic world was the question of *how we know reality*. That question has continued to hold the attention of many kinds of scholars right up to the present day,[23] because it is a logical beginning point in discussing the nature and functions of language. Answers to the question provide the key to understanding how human beings *perceive* their physical and social environment, *think* about the world around

them, and *communicate* their thoughts to others and themselves. Thus, the issue of how we know reality must be answered before insight can be gained into communication transactions as well as into such critical "mental" activities as perceiving, remembering, and reasoning. As we have noted, it is these activities that enable human beings to lead elaborate social lives and to develop and pass on complex cultures.[24]

By "knowing reality" we mean acquiring internal images or understandings—*personal meanings*—that are our subjective responses to objects, events, and situations existing outside our heads, but which we contact with our senses. (We discussed this idea briefly in Chapter 1, pp. 14–16.) If those personal meanings are shared by everyone within a particular human group—if they have similar or *parallel* meanings for the same aspects of reality—it provides a necessary basis for language-based communication.

But communication is based on more than consensus about parallel meanings. An additional requirement, of course, is some system of *labels* for those meanings—verbal or nonverbal cues such as words or gestures that can be initiated by a sending individual. These enable a receiving person to construct his or her internal meanings for whatever aspect of reality has been labeled.[25] In Chapter 1 we discussed how thousands of years ago human beings began to develop languages for precisely this purpose. The patterned sounds of words, used in accordance with rules for their sequences and forms, have been the basis of speech and language ever since.

How meanings are acquired   To understand the critical importance of language for human thought and behavior, we need to discuss in greater detail than we did earlier how individuals *acquire* meanings through a process of experience and learning. The goal here is to explain the nature of "concepts."

We have repeatedly pointed to the importance of *learning* in language acquisition and use. The internal images and other experiences we have for aspects of reality are acquired by both systematic and random *experience*.[26] For example, most of us learned about the quality of being "hot" through some probably rather painful experience when we were children. As we were growing up, hundreds of similar experiences provided us with well-remembered lessons about a long list of qualities, attributes, and characteristics of the objects and events we encountered. That process of learning took place as a result of either *direct* experience or, in some cases, *indirect* or

As children experience the world around them, they learn from others that specific words stand for distinct categories of objects or situations in reality. They learn to connect specific organizations of their own internal experiences (meanings) either to the words or to perceived aspects of reality that are labeled. Thus, for each word a relationship is learned connecting a feature of reality, a symbol, and shared meanings associated with both. Such meaning triangles, along with rules of syntax and grammar, make human communication possible.

vicarious contact, as when someone vividly described something to us.

In Chapter 1 we explained that those aspects, or *attributes,* of objects, actions, and situations we experience in reality, are recorded and stored ("imprinted") in memory by biochemical processes controlled by the brain. We referred to these as *traces*—stored recollections of experiences we have had with the external world around us. Meanings, then, are made up of remembered impressions of things, events, or situations that exist outside our-

selves but which we have experienced directly with our senses, or indirectly via descriptions provided by others.

Concepts as configurations of meaning   A special problem arises when we have repeated experiences with some "set" or class of similar objects, events, or situations and we need to recognize individual instances of that set over and over. In this situation we develop ways of quickly recognizing individual members of the set on a routine basis. It would be cumbersome and inefficient, to say the least, to have to search laboriously through complexes of imprinted traces and put together a fresh pattern of meaning for every single object, action, or situation we encounter as we move through our day. Each would have to be dealt with as though we had never encountered anything similar before. To cope efficiently and routinely with the world around us, then, we need easy mental techniques for recognizing, classifying, and responding to repetitive experiences of our environment.

To deal effectively with that problem, we organize into patterns the traces of meaning in our memory for various *categories* of objects, events, and situations we repeatedly encounter. That is, we develop a general schema (Chapter 1, pp. 16–17) that more or less fits all objects, events, or situations appearing to be in the same class. This makes for great efficiency because the schema as a whole can quickly be recalled and used to recognize and classify any particular representative of a category on the basis of what we think all its members have in common. This makes it unnecessary to examine and consider a host of unique characteristics of a particular member. In other words, such a schema becomes for each of us our organized configuration of meaning for *all* members of that category, regardless of any variations among individual members of that class.

If this process sounds abstract, consider a simple example. Children in today's world acquire traces of meaning for the family's "television set" at a very early age. In their home they can easily distinguish the family receiver from the stove, table, bed, or any other object in a room. What has taken place is that after repeatedly experiencing the television's shape, colors, and sounds through their senses, a set of traces are stored in their memory concerning its characteristics. These traces permit them to recall the attributes of their particular television set. These set it apart from dissimilar objects, enabling them to recognize it whenever they confront it. That schema, or configuration of attributes in memory, is the meaning of "television set" for that individual.

However, an additional step is needed before "television set" can become a workable part of the shared vocabulary the children will use for recognizing, dealing with, and talking about such objects with other people in their language community. It needs to be transformed from a unique schema applying only to the set they have at home to a *more general construction of meaning*—a "concept"—that identifies all such sets, wherever they are encountered. That, of course, requires additional learning and a process of *abstraction*. When a child begins to learn that a particular configuration of attributes applies not just to the television set at home but to a whole *class* of such things, wherever they are, the process of forming a concept of "television set" has begun.[27]

Generally, then, to learn a concept the individual must understand that certain basic attributes present in a particular object, action, or situation are also present in an entire category of such phenomena. This brings us to the following definition: A **concept** is a labeled set or configuration of attributes by which any particular instance of a whole class of similar objects, events, or situations can be recognized.

Concepts, then, are more than just labels for private or personal schemata of meanings. Because we form concepts by abstracting a common set of attributes, those schemata can be "shared." That is, people of a particular language community, who learn and use words in the same way, develop parallel—that is, very similar—inner experiences of essential attributes when they hear or see a particular label for a class of similar objects. If they encounter a single representative of that class, they are able to use the shared label and experiences of its basic attributes to classify and interpret it as a member of a category. Thus, those who speak English share the abstracted commonly held meanings assigned by conventions to such labels as "touchdown," "ticket," and "team." Because we share those labels and their meanings, we can identify and classify a particular set of actions as a "touchdown" or a specific group of people as a "team." In short, virtually every word in our language is a concept in that it is a label for a widely shared schema—a cluster of meaning attributes of some class or category of objects or events.

We can note in passing that concepts and their meaning need not be confined to "real" things that have physical existence, like stones and trees. People long ago formed concepts for abstract shapes, such as "triangle" and "circle," that had no physical counterparts. Indeed, human beings have words that label concepts for thousands of ideas that have no physical counterparts. Labels for states of existence, such as "beauty," "love," and "justice," provide obvious examples. Others are those for patterns, like "orbits," "cycles," and "trends." Some concepts even refer to things that we know full well do not exist, such as "Santa's reindeer," "Klingons," and "goblins."

Concepts as the basis of perception The process of perception is based squarely on the use of concepts to interpret and classify sense impressions. In Chapter 1 we noted that the term *perception* has a relatively precise technical meaning (pp. 19–20): the act of perception refers to "making sense," that is, attaching meaning to some aspect of reality apprehended by the senses. In terms of the present discussion, perception takes place when an individual sees, hears, touches, tastes, smells, or otherwise experiences something, and interprets and understands it as an instance of some familiar class or category. For example, the child who sees a new television set in the store window, rather than the one at home, has to "make sense" out of it (assign meaning to it) by recognizing it as an instance of the concept "television set."

The remarkable thing about human beings is that those same meanings can be aroused within us by merely detecting the *name* of a concept as well as by experiencing the real thing. Our habits of perception and assignment of meaning are so well developed that we can experience the essential attributes of a television set not only by seeing the physical object but merely by hearing someone say it, by reading the words, or even by just thinking of them.

Troublesome Concepts in a Multicultural Society

While labels, meanings, and concepts are at the heart of human thought, perception, and communication, they are also at the heart of a number of significant problems existing in our contemporary society. People not only learn to label television sets and recognize they make up a class of objects with a set of relevant attributes, they do the same with *categories of people* as well.

Unfortunately, some of the labels applied to certain categories of people are linked to negative meanings that have come to be shared in our society. This has not been by chance. Distinctive labels with associated pejorative meanings have been used by dominant groups in every known society to identify various categories of people

"Concept"
Human Being

A concept is a general construction of meaning for some set of objects, situations, actions, or states of existence that has been labeled with a shared convention in our language community. That construction of meaning is based on a process of abstraction in which the attributes common to the entire class or category are understood. Concepts enable us to perceive, recognize, and respond to the many features of reality with which we must cope.

whom they want to discredit or prevent from attaining full dignity as human beings. Even among preliterate people, the name they apply to themselves often means something like "the people," whereas their names for those outside their group imply a lower order of life.

The traditional pattern of racial and ethnic relations in the United States, say before World War II, provided an instructive example. During those times, every racial and

ethnic group had a slang name capable of arousing schemata of meaning experiences of a negative nature. Those labels are so offensive today that it is difficult to list them even in a historical context in a book like this without risking criticism that harm is intended. It is not, however, and the lessons these historical examples provide can help in understanding similar problems that remain with us today.

In an earlier America, power was maintained by the dominant group, which was mainly white Anglo-Saxon Protestants, by labeling various ethnic, religious, or racial minorities in such a way as to maintain their position as "second-class citizens." Various categories of people were referred to as *niggers, wops, kikes, mackerel-snappers, spics, krauts, gooks, micks, slopes, polacks, and hunkies,* to mention only a few. Indeed, everyone who was not in the dominant class had an ugly label (although they were widely used by almost everyone). The important point is this: *All were concepts that aroused specific configurations of negative meaning about those so labeled.* As far back as 1922, Walter Lippmann gave the name *stereotypes* to such configurations of negative meanings.[28]

Maintaining these labels and stereotyped meanings as part of the general culture, through repeated use, jokes, and even portrayals of minority people in the mass media, served to down-grade everyone who was a member of one of the labeled categories. This effectively shaped the routine perceptions of the dominant group regarding the others. It made it psychologically easy and efficient to interpret members of these categories as of lesser worth. That, in turn, made it seem natural to segregate, discriminate against, and deny equal status to members of the labeled minorities. It was not necessary to examine the unique characteristics of each member of such a category; each was assumed to possess uniformly the set of negative characteristics of the stereotype defining the entire group. Thus, our earlier abstract discussion of labels and concepts, and their influence on perception and action, has profound implications when we move from television sets and Santa's reindeer to categories of human beings who are labeled and perceived within a uniform set of pejorative meanings.

Is that all in the past? Have we effectively stopped using pejorative labels for people and interpreting individuals within a perspective of negative concepts that presumably apply to all members of a category? The answer is obviously no. Many people who are members of minority or disadvantaged classes are still fighting that same battle. Continuing attempts are being made to get the majority to abandon pejorative labels in favor of different ones that arouse either neutral or favorable images. Thus, "old people" are thought to prefer being called "senior citizens." Those who were once called "cripples" vastly prefer to be labeled "physically challenged." Kids who were once called "retards" are now referred to and thought of as those in need of "special education."

To some, such efforts may seem extreme. However, it must be remembered that the labels used for categories of people, and the schemata of meanings shared for those labels, strongly influence the way they are perceived, understood, accepted, or rejected by other human beings. Thus, in a society increasingly sensitive to the needs of all its citizens, learning and using different labels that avoid stereotypes seems a small price to pay.

Symbols and Their Referents

Human beings use many different kinds of cues, signs, and labels to refer to the various types of organized and shared meanings we have discussed. We noted in Chapter 1 that one convenient way of referring to all of those many kinds is simply to call them "symbols." This term has come into wide use for that purpose.

Symbols as labels for meanings   Most of the symbols we use in communication are ordinary words. Many other symbols are not actually words but are nonverbal cues or signs used in much the same way. Here we can include special clothing (e.g., a police officer's or airline pilot's uniform that implies a specific set of meanings), religious shapes and forms (crosses, crescents, and stars used to communicate particular ideas), and so on through military insignia, tattoos, and a host of gestures, postures, and actions.

The most significant point that can be made about this broad category of symbols is that they all serve as *labels* in some way for organized sets of meanings. That is, they provide cues to which people respond by experiencing internal images, feelings, and understandings. In terms of the explanations developed in previous sections, we can put all the ideas together in the following definition: **Symbols** *are socially agreed-upon labels that we use to arouse conventionalized meanings stored in schemata within our memory system.*[29]

This formulation provides an extension of the definition of communication that we formulated in Chapter 1 (p. 11). It does so by specifying more precisely the nature of symbols—including nonverbal symbols and signs, such as actions or objects that arouse conventionalized meanings in ourselves and others.

The principle of arbitrary selection   Where do symbols come from? That is, how does a given language community originally select a particular word or other symbol for its members to use as a label for a given concept? There are no clear rules; in fact, the selection process is **arbitrary**—rather random and sometimes even capri-

Verbal Immediacy

Instructions   Please respond to each of the statements in terms of the way you perceive yourself communicating generally with acquaintances, colleagues, or friends. For each item, indicate how often you find yourself responding in your normal conversations with others. Use the following options:

0 never   **3** often
1 rarely   **4** very often
2 occasionally

____   **1.** I use personal examples or talk about my experiences with others.

____   **2.** I ask questions and encourage others to talk.

____   **3.** I get into discussions based on something someone else brings up even when this doesn't seem to be part of what I wanted to talk about.

____   **4.** I use humor in my conversations with others.

____   **5.** I address others by name.

____   **6.** I can easily recall others' names.

____   **7.** People like to talk to me.

____   **8.** I initiate conversations with others.

____   **9.** I include others in conversations by referring to what "we" are doing or what "our" plans are.

____   **10.** In conversations with others, I give specific feedback to them by commenting directly on what they are saying.

____   **11.** I sensitively handle issues I know others don't want to talk about.

____   **12.** I ask how individuals feel about an issue, task, or relationship.

____   **13.** I encourage people to stop by or telephone whenever they want to talk.

____   **14.** I ask questions to solicit others' viewpoints or opinions.

____   **15.** I praise or compliment people's work, actions, or comments.

____   **16.** I can talk about anything with just about anybody.

____   **17.** People usually address me by my first name.

Calculating Your Score

Simply add together each of your responses to all 17 items.

YOUR VERBAL IMMEDIACY SCORE = ____.

Interpreting Your Score

Response options should range from 0 to 68. (If your own score does not fall within that range, you made a computational error.) Often, the words or symbols we choose to use in our everyday conversations arouse predictable meanings in others. One such predictable association includes certain word choices and language strategies that appear to reduce physical or psychological distance between people. We call these behaviors "immediacy behaviors." Normally, we think of immediacy as nonverbal behaviors, such as standing physically close to someone or maintaining prolonged eye contact. (See Chapter 3 for an extended discussion of nonverbal immediacy.)

However, immediacy can also include the use of specific labels (e.g., using first names rather than formal titles) and communication strategies (e.g., using humor, complimenting others, encouraging people to talk). When individuals select specific verbal immediacy behaviors to interact with others, they simultaneously trigger feelings of positive affect or liking. They might also stimulate meanings or feelings of intimacy or closeness.

The research on immediacy is unequivocal: The higher your verbal immediacy score (above 45 or so), the more people will find you an attractive communicator. Other research indicates that immediacy is a good way to get others to like you. People generally feel more motivated around immediate others and work hard to please them. In short, people perceive immediate others to be warm and friendly; they find them easy to talk to, and they prefer spending time interacting with them. Clearly then, we know that the verbal symbols we select have important implications on how others perceive us.

References

The original version of this scale was designed to assess teachers' verbal immediacy in the classroom. For purposes of this book, however, we thought it would be more interesting to tap your own level of immediacy while conversing with others. Consequently, this survey is a revised version of the original.

Gorham, J. (1988). The relationship between verbal teacher immediacy behaviors and student learning. *Communication Education, 37,* 40–53.

Gorham, J., & Zakahi, W. R. (1990). A comparison of teacher and student perceptions of immediacy and learning: Monitoring process and product. *Communication Education, 39,* 354–368.

cious.[30] For example, in English we say *horse,* in Spanish *caballo,* and in German *pferd.* No one can say exactly how these labels came to be associated with that particular kind of animal. Most words are like that—their original selection was arbitrary. If we all agreed, we could use the sound "clop" to refer to a horse, but earlier people who developed English arbitrarily chose what we now use.

For some words we can uncover origins. Many contemporary words in English, which is a composite of a number of ancient and relatively modern languages, can be traced back to historical or even prehistoric sources. For example, the term *father* is an obvious derivation of the Latin *pater.* That, in turn, is identical to the same but much older Greek *pater.* An even earlier term found in ancient Sanskrit is the word *pitar.* There are indications that it originated as part of the very earliest languages used by human beings. In fact, a number of words that appear in many modern languages can be traced back to an ancient common source—a "mother tongue" that was spoken in northern and eastern Europe and parts of Asia somewhere between 6,000 and 8,000 years ago.[31]

Aside from this heritage, the process of selecting words to signify and arouse particular meanings is capricious. Whoever those ancient people were who began using *pitar* to signify male parenthood could just as easily have chosen something quite different. In fact, in other parts of the world totally different sound patterns came into use to signify that particular human relationship. The principle of arbitrary selection, then, indicates that when new concepts are formed, the process of labeling them does not follow some rigid or systematic rule. For that reason, Americans use *gasoline* in their cars, the British use *petrol,* and the Argentines use *nafta,* even though they are all chemically the same.

The principle of conventions   While the original assignment of a symbol as a label for a concept can be arbitrary, once the assignment has been made the situation changes sharply. To be used as a tool for communication, the link between a symbol and its **referent** —the object, situation, or event to which it refers—has to be predictable, stable, and relatively unchanging. Otherwise, its use in communication would be impossible. This stability is achieved by the use of *conventions* of definition and usage.

A **convention** is a rule that people of a given language community agree to follow. Such conventions state that whenever a person initiates a particular sound pattern (as in a given word) or a specific action (used as a nonverbal symbol), the meanings to be aroused in both sender and receiver are those set forth in the rule and none other. (The same conventions apply to written symbols, of course.)

It is a simple idea, really, and one that virtually everyone understands. To do otherwise, and let people use whatever meanings they wished for a particular word or nonverbal symbol, would result in an Alice in Wonderland world of chaos and would make communication impossible. To stabilize such conventions and preserve them over time, dictionaries are used to provide relatively fixed meanings, at least for verbal symbols.

Specialized Cultures: Implications for communication   In a complex multicultural society, both the original selection of symbols and the establishment of conventions of meaning associated with them can present a number of distinctive problems. This is because there is not only a *general* culture in which conventional meanings for words are widely shared, but there exist within the society a great variety of groups who also have *specialized* cultures. Within such cultures, specialized words and unique meanings can be different from those existing in the general culture. This means that such activities as encoding, role-taking, and feedback must be conducted with great sensitivity.

But what are "cultures," and why is it important that they be understood by people who want to improve their ability to communicate? Anthropologists generally define culture as the *way of life* shared among a given people who make up a particular society. That way of life is made up largely of solutions to problems of living that the group has accumulated as a heritage from the past. Each generation adds more solutions, and the accumulated culture is passed on from one generation to the next. Those solutions include not only the physical artifacts (tools, machines, art objects, etc.) routinely used by the group, but also its language, customs, and all shared beliefs, attitudes, values, and patterns of behavior. That definition describes very well a *general,* or "mainstream," culture within a society.

But one size (or culture) does not fit all in a complex society, as there are many kinds of Americans whose way of life is somewhat different from that of the majority. It is these distinctive, more localized patterns of culture that make the American people so interesting and rich in diversity. For example, among Native Americans in the United States, more than 100 different cultures exist that set each tribal group off, not only from the larger society as a whole but from each other as well. They maintain specialized ways of life that are rich with their own traditions, language, and shared orientations. The people

involved value these distinctive patterns of culture and often go to considerable lengths to maintain them because they believe they are of significant value.

In much the same way, the entire American population is a complex mosaic of various racial, ethnic, religious, and national-origin groups. Some people were brought to the United States forcibly from Africa. Others flowed through Ellis Island by the millions during the great immigrations of the 1800's and the early half of this century. Still others came more recently from Asia, Mexico, and Latin America. Thus, we have a long list of specialized cultures maintained and valued by people from virtually every part of the globe. All of us are tied together as citizens by the general American culture, but we are also distinct in ways we feel are important.

In an earlier America, national policy tried to force these diverse people into a "melting pot" system, insisting that everyone assimilate as soon as possible so as to become similar in language, customs, beliefs, and so on. It didn't work—or, perhaps more realistically, it worked only to a limited degree. People retained many of their unique cultural distinctions despite strong pressure. Today, cultural pluralism more closely represents our national policy. This policy dictates that peoples' differences must be respected and that all specialized cultures be equally valued.[32]

The implications for communication are that each of these distinctive cultures is to a greater or lesser degree a separate **language** community. Within each, specialized words, gestures, and other symbols are often shared—signs and symbols whose subtle meanings may not be easily understood by outsiders. These can reduce accuracy when communication takes place between people from very different cultures. On the other hand, our mutual participation in the general culture, along with its corresponding more-or-less standardized language community, is usually sufficient to permit reasonably accurate communication to take place between diverse people.

The meaning triangle   We can now bring together the ideas and principles we have discussed concerning symbols, the meaning of concepts, and how they represent "the world outside". The relationships between all three can be represented by the simple diagram on page 57. This diagram is an elaboration of one that was first proposed in 1946 by Ogden and Richards, who aptly called it the "meaning triangle."[33] The **meaning triangle** shows that meaning, symbol, and referent constitute a kind of system. Within a culture, each element is linked by a convention. The *referent* is whatever object, situation, thing,

The Meaning Triangle

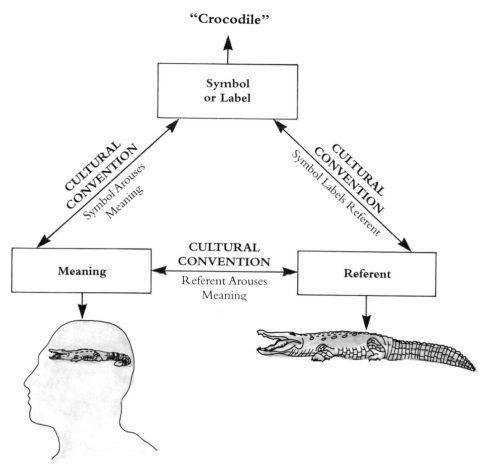

Every symbol (word or standardized nonverbal gesture) in our vocabulary can be thought of in terms of a *meaning triangle*. The triangle depicts the relationship between the symbol, what it labels in reality, and the meaning experience we have for both. Cultural conventions provide rules for linking the symbol, referent, and meaning among those who share the same language. Because we share thousands of such meaning triangles, we can use language to communicate with others and with ourselves.

or even make-believe concept, to which we have assigned some meaning. The *meaning* is the internal configuration or schema of memory traces subjectively aroused in us either by apprehending the referent itself with our senses or by receiving a cue from another person. The *symbol,* of course, is the word, gesture, object, or behavior we use as a cue to arouse the meaning in another (or even in ourselves).

The conventions are the rules of our particular language community that stabilize the meaning triangle. The first, C_1, links the *referent* and the *meaning* with a rule that a specific pattern of internal experiences is the expected way of perceiving and understanding that aspect of real-ity. A second, C_2, links the *symbol* and the *meaning* with an agreement that perception of the symbol will arouse the same meanings (in us or in another person) as does the referent itself, even though the latter may not be present. Still another, C_3, completes the system with a shared agreement that the particular *symbol* will stand for, and be the label of, the *referent*. The arrows in the meaning triangle show these relationships.

Conceptualizing language symbols in terms of configurations of schemata and meaning triangles probably will not, just by themselves, be of immediate practical utility in communicating more effectively with one's boss, roommate, or special friend. Nevertheless, such

Table 2.2

The Fine Art of Euphemization

PREFERRED CONTEMPORARY EXPRESSION	MORE TRADITIONAL TERM
revenue enhancement	taxes
preowned automobile	used car
home equity loan	mortgage
signed authorization	signature
visually impaired	blind
hearing impaired	deaf
speech disabled	dumb
significant mobility limitation	crippled
developmentally disabled	retarded
nondisabled	normal
sanitation technician	janitor
solid waste	garbage
solid-waste disposal facility	dump
experience positive gratification	enjoy
low socioeconomic status	poor
underclass	poor people
economic deprivation	no money
placed on furlough status	laid off
separated	fired
dentures	false teeth
halitosis	bad breath
feminine hygiene product	douche
recycled apparel	used clothes
initial investment	down payment
collateral damage	civilian deaths
revisited	bombed again

Source: Assembled from various newspaper stories, government reports, magazine articles, advertisements, and brochures.

theoretical models do identify the nature and definitions of basic features of the communication process that may otherwise be difficult to understand—and they do so far better than vague descriptions. For that reason, models are an important part of the foundation on which effective communication skills are acquired.

Denotations versus connotations   One potential source of confusion in communication not shown in the meaning triangle is the problem of unique personal meanings versus shared or standardized meanings. We discussed this in the previous chapter in terms of reducing the fidelity of communication. If the conventions of the meaning triangle are followed strictly, the use of a symbol in a message transmitted to a receiver will evoke only its **denotative** meaning within the relevant culture.[34] If that is the case, accuracy will be high. The meanings aroused in each will be restricted to those governed by established conventions. However, there is always the problem of **connotative** meanings.[35] These may be part of the personal meanings that an individual uniquely as-

sociates with a referent because of past experience or as a result of membership in a specific culture. If that is the case, use of the symbol in a message will arouse those private and unshared meanings and reduce the accuracy of the communication.

Personal connotative meanings can be illustrated easily. For example, suppose that you ask me if I have a pet and I say, "Yes, I have a dog." It may appear that communication has been complete and accurate. However, you may have connotative meanings for the concept "dog" that bring to mind the attributes of a large, brown, friendly, and gentle dog that wags its tail when petted. My dog, however, has different attributes. It is a mean, little, white mutt that barks nastily and nips at strangers. Our mutual connotative meanings have limited the degree to which our communication can be accurate, and they have reduced the index of fidelity.

Many people in such fields as advertising, politics, and social service are deeply aware of the problems that can be caused by negative connotations which become part of a concept's shared meaning. One of the clearest examples of unacceptable connotations in the use of a word in American society is that of "man." Until recent decades, the term was commonly used by virtually everyone as a symbol referring to "mankind," "humanity," or "human beings in general." With the rise of the feminist movement, and the development of its sensitive culture, however, that convention became unacceptable to many women and men because the connotation of the word *man* is that humanity is masculine, with an implied meaning that women are of a lesser status. For that reason, today most college textbooks, do not use the generic term *man.* Instead, they use *humankind,* or a similar inclusionary term, to refer to people in general, regardless of their gender.

Although connotations often bring about inaccuracy, they are not always undesirable. They can be a source of delight in certain kinds of messages. Poets, novelists, and even spellbinding orators often try to arouse a flow of colorful subjective meanings within their audiences by a rich attachment of connotative meanings to the symbols they select.

Structural Features of Language

The meaning triangle on page 57 aids in understanding important aspects of the ancient problem of how we know reality and how we communicate about it. However, merely showing the system for a single referent, its symbol, and its meaning is scarcely enough to represent an entire language. For that reason additional structural aspects of language must be added. These include *vocabularies, syntax, grammar,* and *redundancy,* all of which are necessary conditions for verbal communication with language.

Vocabulary: The building blocks of language Every known language has an extensive vocabulary—a long list of symbol-referent conventions for communicating about various aspects of the physical and social world. These are the building blocks out of which messages are constructed. The authoritative *Oxford English Dictionary* lists about 500,000 words. To this could be added about another half million terms used in specialized technical and scientific fields by English speakers.[36] In contrast, German has about 185,000 words. French has fewer than 100,000. Chinese has at most about 50,000 characters, each standing for a word. However, each of these languages provides for the same level of richness of expression as words can be combined to indicate virtually any intended meaning.

To represent the entire English vocabulary, including all technical words, in the form of meaning triangles we would need up to 1 million diagrams (there would have to be a separate diagram for every word). It is a staggering thought to say the least. However, none of us carry around anything even close to a million meaning triangles in our head. In order to conduct our daily routine, most of us can get by nicely with about 5,000 words. On average, an educated person will have a vocabulary of about 15,000 words. Truly able communicators will have many more. For example, William Shakespeare, who had one of the largest vocabularies of any English writer, used an estimated 30,000 different words to write his plays and sonnets.[37]

Grammar: Rules for constructing conventional patterns To the requirement of vocabulary we can add the necessity of grammar, which is a critical aspect of any language. Grammatical structures themselves imply meanings. That is, different variants of symbols (tenses, verb forms, and so on) arranged into grammatically conventionalized sequences, indicate meanings that are not implied in the specific words in a message. The same words in different grammatical patterns form distinct messages.[38]

The grammatical conventions of some languages are far more complex than those of others, and many languages use forms that have no counterparts in English. For example, English speakers do not assign a masculine or feminine status to nouns, as some languages require. In Spanish, any house *(casa)* is feminine and takes an "a" ending, whereas any "building" *(edificio)* is masculine and takes an "o" ending. For every noun one must remember whether it is masculine or feminine and pronounce it accordingly. Native English speakers learning Spanish often find this difficult.

By comparison with the grammars of some languages, English grammar is simple. We use nouns to indicate objects and verbs for action. Our system of nouns is neuter in terms of the masculine-feminine distinctions noted above. We do make an important distinction between actions that occurred in the past, are occurring in the present, and will occur in the future, and we conjugate our verbs differently in each of these tenses. Furthermore, we use separate sets of adjectives and adverbs to modify the meanings of nouns and verbs.

Some languages do all of this very differently. For example, the Navajo language uses only two major categories of verbs—neuter and active—for which English has no counterparts. However, in each category, the Navajo have from five to seven different ways of conjugating their verbs that imply important distinctions. In addition, the implications of nouns, verbs, adjectives, and adverbs can be compounded into a single term. In the Navajo language it is possible to indicate with only one word the meaning that "the round solid object that was formerly in motion is now at rest."[39]

Syntax: The architecture of language   Syntax refers to rules for ordering words in a sentence or any expression in such a way that their meaning is clear. In some languages, word order does not matter very much. For example, Russian speakers can say "The dog looks at the cat" in fifteen different ways (all the possible combinations of the six words). That is, the sender can arrange the words in any order she or he likes and the receiver will understand very well. In other languages, such as English, the rules of syntax are far more rigid, and odd arrangements of words can produce bizarre implications and interpretations.

Redundancy   One of the features of English, and many other languages as well, is **redundancy**—that is, a message formulated in English usually contains a lot of words that are not actually needed. For example, take the sentence "The English language is actually a very redundant form of speech." The essential message contained in that sentence could be reduced to the simple statement "English is redundant." Why the extra baggage? There is no certain answer, but one can speculate that on occasions when it is difficult to hear, or transmission is incomplete, enough of the meaning remains when some words are lost for the deep meaning to be interpreted well enough for practical purposes.

What all of these considerations of vocabulary, grammar, syntax and redundancy imply is that the use of language for even basic communication is an extraordinarily sophisticated activity. In Chapter 1 we oversimplified the process of human communication with the use of a sentence of only three words ("Nice work, John"). In terms of the issues discussed in this chapter, that would require only three meaning triangles of the type shown in Figure 2.1 plus a few simple rules of grammar and syntax. In reality, after people decide what they want to say and why, they have to consider thousands of meaning triangles and rules to encode their messages into appropriate symbols that are likely to be understood by their intended receiver. After transmission has taken place, the receiver also has to use thousands of similar triangles in order to perceive, recognize, and decode the meaning of the incoming symbols.

In short, even in our most mundane interactions we make use of a communication system of incredible complexity, subtlety, and richness. There is nothing like it in the animal world, and it is unlikely there ever will be. Accurate human communication depends on an elaborate vocabulary of linked symbols and referents in the memory of both sender and receiver. From these sets of labels and schemata, the sender will formulate and transmit the intended message and the receiver will reconstruct its meanings. Such a transaction depends on well-honed abilities to put symbols together into grammatically correct sequences following rules of accepted syntax and to interpret the additional meanings these conventions imply.

Chapter Review

■ Early in the century a great controversy began over whether or not animals could communicate with language. The value of this controversy was that it brought about enthusiastic efforts to clarify the nature of language and the question of whether only human beings use it. After decades of animal studies, it appears there is a huge gap between the abilities of human beings to communicate and the communication abilities of animals nearest to us on the phylogenetic continuum.

■ Not all animals communicate in the same way. Insects rely on inherited communication systems that depend on the senses. They make and detect sounds, produce chemical substances called pheromones, and use sight to orient themselves to food, danger, and reproductive activities. At positions farther up the phylogenetic scale, learning becomes increasingly important and the role of inheritance is mainly one of limitation.

■ Attempts to teach animals such as chimpanzees to talk have not been successful because they cannot generate the complex sounds required. Numerous attempts have been made to communicate with primates. Such efforts have based communication on movements or actions animals can make, such as signing in the manner of the hearing-impaired, and using plastic symbols or even computerized systems to probe the potentials of primate ability to communicate with something like language. All such attempts are mired in deep controversy. Statistical analysis of patterns of "words" put together by chimps in experiments shows random distributions. At present it seems there is no convincing evidence for language ability among animals. While animals do communicate extensively, and often very effectively for the purposes they need in life, they do so in ways that do not parallel those used by people.

- Human beings require language in order to develop normally. If they are denied such an environment, thought, perception, and social relationships are impaired. They remain at an animal-like level.

- A semantic analysis of verbal communication recognizes that each of us has to acquire an enormous set of labels for internal and subjective images, interpretations, and experiences that are associated with specific aspects of the world outside our heads. We learn inner meanings not only for concrete objects that make up the physical world, but also for situations, relationships, activities, and conditions that make up our complex social life. In addition, we learn meanings for ideas that have no physical counterparts and even for things we know do not exist.

- Concepts are clusters or configurations of attributes that are jointly agreed upon as shared meanings for the aspects of reality or fantasy about which we communicate. Concepts are critical to perception, interpretation, thinking, and remembering. They enable each person to "know reality" by classifying sense experiences into meaningful categories. However, some concepts that include numerous negative attributes are used by groups to dominate others. Such concepts are commonly called stereotypes, and they pose deeply troubling problems in a democratic society.

- By using symbols, human beings attach labels to concepts. Then, by establishing conventions of usage, those same symbols refer to both the object and the meaning. The three ideas—meaning, symbol, and referent—form a triangular system, with each pair stabilized by a convention. The initial choice of a symbol to label a referent and its meaning may be arbitrary, but once consensus is reached regarding the convention, meanings are stabilized.

- American society is a complex mosaic of specialized cultures whose origins lie in the pre-European experience of indigenous people or are a consequence of patterns of forced or voluntary immigrations of the past. Each specialized culture represents variations of the principle of arbitrary selection and conventional meanings for at least some words, gestures, and actions used in communication.

- Language is composed of thousands of such systems, plus elaborate rules for putting symbols together, as in sentences composed of words. The subtlety and complexity of human communication can be appreciated by realizing that just to get by at a simple level requires knowledge of about 5,000 words and their meanings, and an educated person will, on the average, command about 15,000 such meaning systems. Truly able communicators may be able to use up to 30,000. Important structural aspects of language include connotative meanings, grammar, and syntax. These can introduce meanings that are not contained in the conventional usage or that go beyond the meanings of the separate words used in a message.

- Finally, the conditions necessary for communicating with language are many. They include a relatively large and complex brain, a memory system capable of storing vast numbers of meaning triangles, numerous conventions of grammar, a full grasp of syntax, a recognition of problems of connotative meanings, and a speech community in which parallel systems exist in the memories of other participants. No other creatures in the animal kingdom possess these conditions necessary for communicating with language. It is little wonder, then, that we cannot talk with whales, dolphins, or apes. The remarkable thing is that we can communicate with each other within a sufficient level of accuracy to go about our daily routines.

Key Terms

Arbitrary (selection) The sounds and/or letters used to form words that refer to particular meanings within a given language are not initially selected by clear rules, but in rather random or even capricious ways. Once selected and established in use, however, the relationship between the word and whatever it refers to becomes fixed.

Clever Hans effect The mistaken belief that an animal can use language as do human beings because it makes complex responses or initiates behavior using combinations of signs and signals. Such combinations can be a result of the animal responding to subtle cues unintentionally provided by an experimenter, or they may simply represent chance occurrence among a large number of unpatterned behaviors.

Comparative perspective   The study of animals (including human beings) that is based on a strategy of looking for general laws of behavior common to many species.

Concept   A set of labeled objects, situations, or events that can logically be grouped together and thought about as making up a class or category because they share similar properties or attributes.

Connotative (meanings)   Personal or unshared meanings that an individual uniquely associates with a referent because of past experience.

Convention   A rule adopted within a particular cultural group (or language community) that specifies what patterns of meaning are to be labeled with what particular word or nonverbal sign.

Denotative (meanings)   Meanings that by established convention are to be aroused and experienced by a particular symbol.

Instincts   Adaptive behavior patterns that are inherited, unlearned, and universal in a species. Many animals have instincts concerning such behavior as migration, reproduction, and communication. Human beings do not have such inherited patterns.

Language   A complex of shared words, nonverbal signs, and rules for their use and interpretation according to agreed-upon rules within a particular human group or society.

Meaning triangle   A diagram showing that meaning, symbol, and referent constitute a kind of system, with each element linked by a convention.

Pheromones   Chemical secretions used by insects and other animals in communication processes. They are released in the air or are deliberately used to mark trails, territory, or readiness for mating.

Phylogenetic continuum   The idea from evolutionary theory that animals can be arranged along a kind of scale in terms of the complexity of their bodily structures and organization.

Redundancy (in language)   Including more words in a message than are actually needed to express deep meanings.

Referent   The object, situation, or event to which a symbol refers.

Semantics   The study of relationships between words and their meanings, and (sometimes) of rules that can add meaning when human beings use language for verbal communication.

Sign   An event in the environment that animals (and human beings) learn to associate with and use to anticipate subsequent events. Examples: clouds are followed by rain, the sight of the dish (for dogs) is followed by the availability of food, (for human beings) a red light indicates that one must stop.

Signal   Noises or patterned movements that animals can make to which others of their species can respond. Examples: cries or postures that typically imply such matters as danger, the presence of food, or readiness to mate. Human beings also use many kinds of signals (whistles, bells, waving flags, etc.).

Symbol   A label used by participants within a language community to arouse standardized meanings for aspects of reality. The initial selection of a label for that to which it refers is initially made in an arbitrary manner. However, before the label can be a part of the vocabulary of a language the connection between label and labeled must be maintained consistently by an established convention.

Syntax   Rules for ordering words in a sentence or any expression in such a way that their meaning is clear.

Notes

1. Pfungst, O. (1907). *Das pferd des Herr von Osten: der Kluge Hans.* [Clever Hans: The Horse of Mr. von Osten]. Leipzig: Joh. Ambrosius Barth.

2. Sebeok, T. A. (1977). *How animals communicate.* Bloomington: Indiana University Press.

3. Sladen, F. W. (1902). "A scent-producing organ in the abdomen of the worker Apis mellifera" [a species of bee]. *Entomology Monthly Magazine, 38,* 208–211.

4. Dyer, F. C., & Gould, J. C. (1981). Honey bee orientation: A back-up system for cloudy days. *Science, 214,* 1041–1042.

5. Bright, M. (1984). *Animal language* (p. 88). Ithaca, NY: Cornell University Press.

6. Crail, T. (1981). *Apetalk and whalespeak: The quest for interspecies communication* (p. 222). (Boston: Houghton Mifflin).

7. Ibid., pp. 34–37.

8. Herman, L., Richards, D. G., & Wolz, J. P. (1984). Comprehension of sentences by bottlenosed dolphins. *Cognition, 16,* 129–219.

9. Kohler, W. (1925). *The mentality of apes* (E. Winter, Trans.). London: Routledge and Kegan Paul.

10. Kellogg, Withrop N. & Kellogg, L. A. (1967). *The ape and the child: A study of environmental influence upon early behavior.* New York: Hafner. (First published by Whittlesey House in 1933).

11. Hayes, C. H. (1951). *The ape in our house.* New York: Harper.

12. Geshwind, N. (1970). The organization of language and the brain. *Science, 170,* 940–944.

13. Gardner, T., & Gardner, R. A. (1969). Teaching sign language to a chimpanzee, *Science, 165,* 664–672.

14. Patterson F., & Linden, E. (1981). *The education of Koko.* New York: Holt, Rinehart, and Winston.

15. Premack, A. J. & Premack, D. (1972). Teaching language to an ape. *Scientific American, 227,* 92–99.

16. Rumbaugh, D. M. et al. (1975). Conversations with a chimpanzee in a computer-controlled environment. *Biological Psychiatry, 10,* 627–641.

17. Rumbaugh, D. M. Gill, T., von Glasersfeld, E., Warner, H., & Pisani, P. (1977). Language behavior of apes. In T. A. Sebeok &

J. Umiker-Sebeok (Eds.), *How animals communicate* (p. 250). Bloomington: Indiana University Press.

18. Briffault, R. (1927). *The mothers: A study of the origins of sentiments and institutions* (pp. 23–24). London: George Allen and Unwin.

19. In an earlier era, much was made of so-called feral children who were supposedly raised by animals. These reports meet no scientific standards as research evidence and remain little more than unfounded claims. For that reason they will not be cited here.

20. Davis, K. (1947). Final note on a case of extreme isolation. *American Journal of Sociology, 52,* 433.

21. Mason, M. K. (1942). Learning to speak after six and one half years of silence. *Journal of Speech Disorders, 7,* 303.

22. Berger, C. R., & Bradae, J. A. (1982). *Language and social knowledge: The social psychology of language.* London: Edward Arnold.

23. Cherwit, R. A. & Hikins, J. W. (1986). *Communication and knowledge: An investigation in rhetorical espistemology.* Columbia: University of South Carolina.

24. Gregg, R. B. (1985). *Symbolic inducement and knowing: A study in the foundations of rhetoric.* (Columbia: University of South Carolina Press.

25. Adler, R. B., Rosenfeld, L. B., & Towne, N. (1986). *Interplay: The process of interpersonal communication.* New York: Holt, Rinehart, and Winston.

26. This is the position of the "empiricists" in philosophy, who rejected earlier positions that we came to know through a process of reasoning and the use of logic. The empiricist position provided an important foundation for the development of science as based on observation, which requires empirical observation.

27. Jacobs, S. Language. In M. L. Knapp & G. R. Miller (Eds.), *Handbook of interpersonal communication* (pp. 313–343). (Beverly Hills, CA: Sage.

28. Lippmann, W. (1922). *Public opinion* (pp. 1–19). New York: Macmillan.

29. Hickson, M. L., & Stacks, D. W. (1985). *Nonverbal communication.* Dubuque, IA: William C. Brown.

30. Goss, B. & O'Hair, D. (1988). *Communicating in interpersonal relationships.* New York: Macmillan.

31. McCrum, R., Cran, W., & MacNeil, R. (1986). *The story of English* (pp. 51–53). New York: Elisabeth Sifton Books, Viking.

32. For an extended discussion of the background and consequences of the multicultural aspects of American society, see: "Race and ethnicity," and "Sex and age inequalities." In M. L. DeFleur, W. V. D'Antonio, & L. DeFleur, *Sociology: human society* (4th ed.) (pp. 294–374). New York: Random House, 1984.

33. Ogden, C. K. & Richards, I. K. *The meaning of meaning.* New York: Harcourt Brace. And: Adler, R. B., Rosenfeld, L. B., & Towne, N. *Interplay: The process of interpersonal communication.* New York: Holt, Rinehart, and Winston.

34. Bettinghaus, I., & Cody, M. *Persuasive communication.* New York: Holt, Rinehart and Winston.

35. Ibid.

36. McCrum, Cran, & MacNeil, op. cit., p. 19

37. Ibid., pp. 102–103.

38. Schegloff, E. A. (1972). Notes on a conversational practice: Formulating place. In D. N. Sudnow (Ed.), *Studies in social interaction* (pp. 75–119). New York: Fress Press.

39. Hoijer, H. (1964). Cultural implications of some Navajo linguistic categories. In D. Hymes (Ed.), *Language and culture in society: A reader in linguistics and anthropology* (pp. 142–153). New York: Harper and Row.

Additional Readings

Adler, R. B. & Rodman, G. (1991). *Understanding human communication* (4th ed.) (Ch. 3, pp. 59–87). (Fort Worth, TX: Holt, Rinehart, and Winston).

> Chapter 3 effectively discusses the nature of language and the misunderstandings that incur when we communicate. These authors consider such important topics as how language shapes our perceptions and the relationship between language use and gender. This chapter can serve as a good reference for undergraduates trying to understand this important area.

Davis, F. (1978). *Eloquent animals: A study in animal communication.* New York: Coward, McCann & Geoghegan.

> This interesting book about the study of animal communication reviews the most important research that has been conducted in this area. Questions are set forth and answered about the communication patterns of apes, fish, ants, bees, crickets, frogs, birds, whales, dogs, and chimps. The results of technical reports are explained in lay terms. This book can be recommended for undergraduate audiences.

Ellis, A. & Beattie, G. (1986). *The psychology of language and communication.* New York: Guilford Press.

> This book presents a psychological perspective on human communication. Its early chapters review a number of studies of communication among animals to show how they communicate both with inherited processes and through learned signs. Remaining chapters discuss ways in which human beings use symbols and language.

Jacobs, S. Language. (1985). In M. L. Knapp and G. R. Miller (Eds.), *Handbook of interpersonal communication* (pp. 313–344). Beverly Hills, CA: Sage.

> This is an excellent advanced essay most suitable for students with some background in language and discourse analysis. It covers the central problems and basic properties of language. Its careful review of the research on language and linguistics contributes to the reader's understanding of this area.

Lieberman, P. (1991). *Uniquely human: The evolution of speech, thought, and selfless behavior.* Cambridge, MA: Harvard University Press.

This easy-to-read book brings together findings from cognitive science, anthropology, and linguistics to answer important questions about ways in which human beings are different in their communication behavior from every other species. It shows how language developed among human beings in relatively recent times, and how this enabled human beings to think and act in complex ways. That, in turn, enabled *Homo sapiens sapiens* to develop the complex cultures that so sharply separate human beings from other animal forms.

McCrum, R., Cran, W., & MacNeil, R. (1986). *The story of English.* New York: Elisabeth Sifton Books, Viking.

This source is highly recommended for understanding the origins of our language and how it has spread to become the most widely used in the world. It discusses not only the historical sources of English but also the variations used by people in different social backgrounds in many societies. It offers important insights into ways in which languages evolve and change due to the contacts people have with each other and the evolution of societies over long periods of time.

Chapter 3

Nonverbal Communication

Contents

The Relationship Between Verbal and Nonverbal Communication
Complementing Our Verbal Meanings
Regulating Verbal Interaction
Substituting Actions for Words
Contradicting Our Verbal Meanings
Interpreting Nonverbal Communication

The Use of "Things" in Nonverbal Communication
The Body as Message
Arousing Meanings with Artifacts
Sending Messages with Clothing
    Communicating status and power
    Dressing to fit in
    Communicating inner feelings
Sexual Communication in the Workplace

"Actions" That Communicate
Body Movements and Gestures
Nonverbal Uses of the Voice
Eye Contact as Communication
Meanings Associated with Space and Distance
Communicating with Touch
Meanings Associated with Time

Communication as an Integrated Process
The Importance of Nonverbal Immediacy
Applying the Immediacy Principle

Chapter Review

Key Terms

Notes

Additional Readings

Key Questions

- Does our "body language"—our gestures and postures—reveal far more of what we are thinking and feeling when we communicate than do our verbal messages? If so, is this a kind of separate language we can master so that we can read people's private thoughts and emotions?

- What can we tell about people's positions in society and their personalities by looking at what they are wearing? That is, does the way a person is dressed provide clues as to her or his social and psychological characteristics?

- What does it mean when a person wears expensive-looking jewelry or uses such objects as gold fountain pens, designer eyeglasses, and a fancy briefcase or handbag? Do these "things" provide clear messages about who the person is and how he or she thinks?

- How do such behaviors as the use of space or time, and such factors as body postures, voice tones, eye movements, and touch, provide meanings that go beyond those implied by what people say verbally when they communicate?

I loved the old man. He had never wronged me. He had never given me insults. For his gold I had no desire. I think it was his eye! Yes, it was this! He had the eye of a vulture—a pale blue eye, with a film over it. Whenever it fell upon me, my blood ran cold; and so by degrees—very gradually—I made up my mind to take the life of the old man, and thus rid myself of the eye for ever.

Edgar Allen Poe
"The Tell-Tale Heart"

Jerome knew that he was late for the interview, and he suspected that Mr. Kim, the personnel director, would be annoyed to be kept waiting. However, Mr. Kim didn't say anything about it, and, after shaking hands and introducing himself, he smiled and said warmly how nice it was to meet Jerome. He invited him to have a seat. Jerome really wanted the job, and he knew that he could do the work. After all, he did have a degree in public relations, and he had gotten good grades in all his courses. All he had to do was explain to this guy how well qualified he was, and he would be in.

They sat facing each other in comfortable leather chairs in Mr. Kim's attractive office. Jerome noticed right away that Mr. Kim was both slim and a neat dresser. His conservative blue suit and tasteful maroon tie seemed somehow to suggest both competence and dignity. Even his shoes looked expensive, and Jerome noticed that his stockings were much longer than his own, covering Mr. Kim's entire lower legs. He suddenly felt awkward because his own short socks left a lot of hairy leg showing. He squirmed to get his cuffs down.

I probably should have bought a new suit, Jerome thought. He had gained a lot of weight last year, and his coat and trousers were stretched and wrinkled from being too tight. He hoped that Mr. Kim wouldn't notice the small spots on the lapel. In the back of his mind, he observed that Mr. Kim's hair was neatly trimmed. Darn, thought Jerome, I should have gotten a haircut too. He suddenly realized that he looked pretty shaggy and that he really ought to do something about his dandruff.

To get started, Mr. Kim reached into an expensive-looking leather case and took out a pad and a beautiful gold pen. Then he glanced at an elegant watch, and said, "Well, Jerome, let's begin." As Jerome looked at the pen, he realized that Mr. Kim's fingernails were neatly trimmed and immaculate. Suddenly, he felt like sitting on his hands to hide the grime under his own ragged nails.

By this time, Jerome was getting nervous and felt that somehow he wasn't making the right impression. He cleared his throat several times and squeezed his hands together. Finding it hard to look Mr. Kim directly in the eye, he shifted his gaze from the floor to the ceiling and then glanced quickly at the different objects in the room.

As the personnel director asked various questions, Jerome felt less and less confident. He realized that the interview was not going as well as he had hoped. Even though he explained about his grades, and about how much he liked to work with people, Mr. Kim did not seem enthusiastic. However, he remained polite. Jerome hoped for the best.

Finally it was over. As they were walking toward the door, Mr. Kim explained rather briskly how pleased they were that Jerome had applied. He told him that there were a number of candidates, but that if they decided he was the one they would be in touch right away.

———————

Needless to say, Jerome did not get the job. Obviously, there were a number of things that sent the wrong messages to the personnel director. It wasn't so much what Jerome said in verbal terms that posed a problem, it was the accompanying *nonverbal* meanings interpreted by Mr. Kim that did him in. Jerome's use of such factors as time, gestures, clothing, and bodily appearance were not helpful. Mr. Kim's dress, office, and "artifacts" (pen, leather case, and watch) sent other kinds of messages. Thus, the interview illustrates ways in which human communication includes exchanges of nonverbal messages as well as the verbal variety discussed in the previous chapter.

In this chapter we discuss how nonverbal signs and signals function in the simultaneous transactions model of human communication. As we will see, they are far more than mere additions to or extensions of what we say. Our nonverbal activities are an inseparable part of the human communication process.

The Relationship Between Verbal and Nonverbal Communication

Many people are convinced that meanings associated with our actions, postures, facial expressions, and similar activities are even more important than what is said.[1] Indeed, some scholars maintain that nonverbally transmitted meanings contribute as much as 90% to our interpretation of other people's behavior.[2] That is a considerable exaggeration. In this text we will show that neither the verbal nor the nonverbal dimensions of communication should be interpreted without considering the other.

While there is no question that the signs and signals we send through nonverbal communication provide meanings that can alter, amplify, or limit people's understandings of the words we use, nonverbal factors are, like our words, a part of the overall human communication process—one that cannot be separated from our use of spoken language. Thus, an effective command of communication skills is not possible without understanding fully how meanings encoded and transmitted nonverbally are part of the process.

Generally, communicating with the voice (or by print) in words and sentences constitutes verbal communication. Nonverbal communication, which uses the same principles outlined in Chapter 1, obviously does not use words and sentences. **Nonverbal communication** can be defined as *the deliberate or unintentional use of objects, actions, sounds, time, and space so as to arouse meanings in others.* This essentially linear view is useful for purposes of analysis. However, as already explained, our more comprehensive simultaneous transactions model synthesizes both linear verbal and nonverbal exchanges, plus contextual factors, into an overall view of communication as an ongoing interactive process.

It is difficult to distinguish neatly between verbal and nonverbal processes. As the simultaneous transactions model indicates, people do not communicate just in one mode or the other, or even rapidly shift back and forth. Their ongoing communication uses both systems at the same time. That is, while speaking words and sentences, all parties in the transaction simultaneously supplement or even modify their meanings with the use of a host of gestures, actions, and other nonverbal cues.

A simple illustration of the use of nonverbal cues to include different meanings of our verbal message is the emphasis provided by the sounds we make when speaking. For example, the sentence "I hate chocolate ice cream" can be pronounced a number of different ways with the stress and emphases supplied by various tones. And, if accompanied by specific actions or gestures (e.g., crossed fingers or a wink to another person), the message can take on still other meanings, even though the words remain the same.

There are enormous numbers of ways in which a sender can include subtle implications and nuances of meaning in a message without using words. Posture, movement, time sequence, space, eye contact, clothing, bodily ornaments, gestures, facial expressions, tone of voice, and even odors can all stimulate meaning in a receiver. This chapter reviews how all parties in communication transactions use such nonverbal means to modify meanings in messages conveyed by words.

There is a considerable mystique surrounding the idea of nonverbal communication. Called **body language** by some people, it has been popularly touted as a means by which the "true" feelings and intentions of people can be read and understood by a shrewd observer armed with a knowledge of what nonverbal signs "really mean."[3] The implication is that the words of a speaker do not openly convey his or her actual meanings and feelings and that the true intentions must be read in the nonverbal cues accompanying the verbal message. Nothing could be further from the truth, and this implication is *not* intended in this book. One writer has recently pointed out some of the mistaken ideas associated with this aspect of human communication:

A phrase that comes readily to mind is "body language," and there has been a book from the popular press with that phrase as its title. The topic has everything: the hope of reading the romantic intentions of one's girl- or boyfriend, the adventure of outsmarting a shrewd salesman, the sure thing of predicting the next move of a poker-faced gambler, the surprise of "reading through" the white lies of one's friends, the advantage of knowing what a prospective employer wants to hear.[4]

In contrast, our position is that nonverbal cues are an important part of the behaviors that human beings use to arouse meanings in others, but they are not some sort of separate code that has a life of its own. Indeed, they can often be misread to a point where serious consequences follow.

People's gestures, actions, and postures provide dimensions of meaning that can modify in various ways what they say with words. Nonverbal communication makes use of objects, actions, vocal sounds, the eyes, space, time, and touch. It is not a separate language in itself, but an inseparable part of the human communication process.

There are four fundamental ways in which we use nonverbal cues to extend, enrich, or modify our verbal messages to others. Most commonly, we use them to *complement* or *reinforce* the meanings we intend in our verbal messages. Equally important is the fact that we rely extensively on nonverbal behaviors to *regulate* the flow of our ongoing communication transactions with others. However, nonverbal cues on some occasions can serve as *substitutes* for words. Or, more rarely, they may actually *contradict* what we say (but not in the sense of the popular beliefs noted earlier). We now look briefly at each of these uses.

Complementing Our Verbal Meanings

The most frequently found relationship between verbal and nonverbal communication is that where the two *complement* each other. Almost everything we say verbally is accompanied by nonverbal actions, expressions, and other behaviors that supplement or reinforce the meanings contained in our talk. One common form is the case where nonverbal communication serves to **frame** our

verbalizations. That is, as we talk to another person, we may jab the air with our finger for emphasis, extend our palms upward, roll our eyes, tick off points by touching the tips of the fingers one after the other, shrug our shoulders, and so on. Such actions are intended to convey subtle meanings that emphasize, complement, and reinforce what we are saying.

Usually, such actions are subtle or even barely noticeable. At times, however, such "framing" is done with great enthusiasm. People jump up and down, clapping their hands while saying such things as "I got an A in chemistry!" Or, if the individual who crumples up his or her grade report throws it on the floor and says "damn!" through clenched teeth, such nonverbal cues clearly indicate less enthusiasm. Whatever their form, such actions are important in that they assist others in understanding the emotional meanings we attach to the message we are transmitting. An important part of learning to communicate and understand the meaning of others is a full understanding of the implications of such framing cues.[5]

This need to complement and frame our meanings with nonverbal signs and signals runs very deep. It is even done when people can't actually see each other, such as when they talk on the phone. They nod, smile, shrug,

One of the most common forms of nonverbal communication is the use of gestures to complement what we are saying. We unwittingly frame our verbal messages with actions and expressions that convey elements of meaning which reinforce and enrich our verbal messages. In many cases, these can make our intended meanings better understood.

and point to supplement what they are saying. Some even make elaborate pointing and body movements to accompany such verbal meanings as "make a right turn," "go to the second light," and so on.

Regulating Verbal Interaction

While supplementing the meanings of our verbal messages may be the most obvious use of nonverbal behavior, one of the most subtle is in **regulating** our conversations.[6] Here, the nonverbal cues are not used as part of an encoded message, but as signs and signals making up informal "rules of order." Employing nonverbal actions and gestures to regulate the flow of talk among people is almost always done with little awareness on the part of the participants. Even for observers it can be difficult to detect such efforts unless one knows exactly what to look for.

For example, in ordinary conversation we usually take turns talking. Normally, we wait until the current speaker stops before responding. Then, when we have the floor, others listen until we signal that it is appropriate for someone else to talk. These rules of order are intricate,

but they are really quite powerful in regulating the flow of conversation. Now try to imagine a conversation between several people where there were no such rules. It would be chaos! No one would know whose turn it was to talk, when to start or when to stop. Individual speakers would be constantly struggling to hold the floor, and everyone would be chattering at once.[7]

But what are these "turn-yielding" cues that we send to each other to regulate the flow of talk? Careful study of people conversing shows that *eye contact* is certainly one.[8] Looking away from a person talking to you and focusing on another individual, for example, tells the speaker, "OK, I listened to you, but now it is the next person's turn." Or, if we are talking, we may "sign off" with a shrug, a hand gesture, or simply a change in vocal tone as we "wind down." On the other hand, if we want to continue and another speaker tries to take over, we send the signal "but, but, but," in a kind of motor-boat stutter, that says, "Hey, I am not through, and I want to say more." Similarly, to head off a competitor, we may increase volume and continue, or nod our head to say, "Sure, I know you want to say something, but wait a minute." Other cues include catches of breath, voice inflections, eye movements, and gestures. A command of

Common Emblems Used in the United States

Recall that emblems have direct verbal equivalents established by conventions. Can you "translate" verbally what each of the following emblems supposedly means to Americans? How many of these do you suppose are interpreted similarly in other societies?

Placing an imaginary halo above your head

Poking your index finger into your cheek and twisting it back and forth

Making lips with rapid hand and thumb movements

Licking forefinger and marking the air

Blowing on your fingertips and then rubbing your nails on your shirt

Pretending to pull up each trouser leg to the knees

Making a telephone or beer mug with thumb and little finger alongside your cheek

Licking your lips back and forth

Pulling on your nose over and over again

Rubbing your thumb across your fingertips over and over again

Pretending to play an imaginary violin

Holding two fingers in the air in the shape of a "V"

Twirling your index finger in the air to make horizontal circles

Nodding your head up and down or side to side

Cupping your ear and leaning forward

such nonverbal cues is an important part of learning to be a good conversationalist.

Substituting Actions for Words

Even though nonverbal communication generally parallels, extends, and supports our verbal messages, occasionally we *substitute* actions for words. For example, people commonly use nonverbal gestures or facial expressions rather than words when trying to communicate such emotions as dismay, disgust, frustration, hostility, or love. The patterns of behavior that people use

in doing this vary from one culture to the next. In the American society, many nonverbal gestures have relatively straightforward meanings that can be translated into direct verbal terms.[9] There are a number of conventional gestures that most people understand, including the hitchhiker's raised thumb, rotating the first finger around one's ear, sticking out the tongue, and blowing a kiss. Communication specialists have chosen the term **emblems** as a name for this category of nonverbal gestures that have direct verbal translations which are widely understood.[10] The box at the left lists some common emblems that are widely used in the United States.

While the meanings of standardized gestures or emblems are reasonably clear, other nonverbal substitutes for words may be vague and difficult to read as we relate to others. For example, if after a minor argument one person says, "OK, let's forget it," and the other shrugs, one interpretation might be a good-natured "shrugging it off." Another might be "It is useless to argue with you." The point is, interpreting nonverbal behavior that does not have clear conventional meanings can be risky. Indeed, the very impreciseness in the link between nonverbal messages and their intended meanings can be a source of serious errors in a receiver's meaning constructions that lowers the index of fidelity for the communication.

Contradicting Our Verbal Meanings

While it is not common, nonverbal actions or expressions sometimes openly *contradict* what we are transmitting in verbal terms. For example, when the husband shouts angrily, "Look! I said I was sorry!" the wife is likely to interpret the nonverbal message to say, "I'm not sorry at all!" But rather than being accidental, this form of nonverbal communication is usually deliberate. That is, people are usually quite aware when they are transmitting or receiving contradictory nonverbal cues. For example, as children we all at one time or another received a stern reprimand or warning communicated in front of others by an authority figure, such as an aunt or a grandparent. But a single wink accompanying such a message could simply turn the entire meaning around: "What I am saying in words is for *public* consumption in this situation, but you and I understand *privately* that my real message is quite different."

Some people believe that our nonverbal messages are both unwitting and unintentional. This leads them to the conclusion that the "true" meanings of our verbal messages are revealed by nonverbal cues. It would be an interesting world if we could somehow discover a person's true intentions or real message just by careful attention to their nonverbal cues. Poker buffs are particularly fond of this idea. They scrutinize every twitch and eye movement of their competitors in a game to try to divine whether she or he is holding a powerful hand or is merely bluffing. At the same time, the ability to offer a "poker face" (a total absence of nonverbal cues) is considered essential to the accomplished player. However, as many an impoverished but wiser player has discovered, making decisions on the basis of such cues can be an uncertain business at best. The really successful poker player telegraphs disinformation with the subtle use of nonverbal cues intended to deceive the others.

The detection of lying is another area that focuses on nonverbal cues that somehow "leak" the truth. Some people maintain that it is possible to identify nonverbal gestures, expressions, and postures that indicate when an individual is lying or arguing a position counter to her or his beliefs.[11] The best-known form of such detection is the use of a *polygraph* (commonly called a "lie detector") to identify activity in the autonomic nervous system occurring when people are not telling the truth. The assumption is that individuals have little or no control over such indicators as changes in heart rate, increased electrical conductivity of the skin, and other physiological phenomena triggered by internal mental conflicts accompanying lying. The major problem with such an assumption is that it does not hold for many people. Some subjects who are telling the absolute truth blow the needles off the graph, whereas others who are "lying in their teeth" can control their inner activities. For that reason, lie detector findings have not been admitted as evidence in courts and have recently been banned from use by employers.

The belief that true meanings are revealed by nonverbal cues may have merit when messages are inconsistent or in conflict. For example, the individual who tells another "I love you," but who at the same time is rummaging through the refrigerator, seems to be saying, "You're OK, but at the moment a sandwich is more important to me." This apparent inconsistency is unlikely to inspire confidence in the verbal message. At the same time, it would not seem wise to conclude that the speaker is lying with words and really does not love the person. It is possible that she or he is just hungry.

One of the most interesting ways in which verbal and nonverbal messages can convey different meanings is with the use of *sarcasm*. Adults understand this mode of communication very well and usually have little trouble sorting out the true meaning of a verbal message delivered sarcastically. They recognize that the nonverbal message implied by the sarcastic tones of voice and facial expressions represents the real meaning.

Children and adolescents, on the other hand, are often relatively unskilled in identifying true meanings when sarcastic cues are used in communication. Generally, they are more literal: In a contradictory message where the words say one thing and the sarcastic manner says something else, the meaning to which they respond is that contained in the words.[12]

Generally, then, the relationship between verbal and nonverbal communication is primarily one of *symbiosis*, or mutual dependence. Human communication in its richest sense relies heavily on both. What we have tried to show is that while we sometimes substitute nonverbal cues for words or even contradict our verbal messages with gestures, facial expressions, and actions, most of the time the two systems complement each other.

Interpreting Nonverbal Communication

While we have stressed the subtle quality of much of our nonverbal communication, there are occasions when it is loud and clear. For example, students who get restless near the end of a lengthy lecture period are experts at sending blatant nonverbal signals. They send unmistakable "leave-taking" cues—shuffle books, put pencils away, yawn, look not-so-furtively at the clock, cough, gape at the door, slide forward on their seats, stretch, whisper to their friends, and transmit other conspicuous signals that carry the meaning "Professor, it is time to stop talking and let me escape."

Communication difficulties arising from inadequate understanding of the importance of nonverbal communication are commonplace. Unless the process of nonverbal communication is well understood—and used effectively—it is inevitable that we will confuse others and become confused ourselves. For example, most of us have been in situations where we have been very tired and have either yawned or momentarily dozed off while someone was presenting a message that he or she judged to be very important. While we might understand completely that the act was involuntary and that our behavior was due solely to great fatigue, the other person will surely read "I am bored by you" and will be very likely to feel resentment.

One reason that speaking (as a mode of communication) is often more effective than writing is that we can include nonverbal cues to enrich and emphasize our meanings. That is, when written communication is used, the *absence* of nonverbal cues can pose problems. For example, a manager who relies solely on written memos will be unable to transmit nonverbal messages that might express the urgency of what is being communicated. Consequently, employees receiving the message may glance at it and then toss the memo into a pile of other papers "for future examination." Days or weeks later, that manager probably will be irate at the lack of employee responsiveness. When a fuss is made, the employees will no doubt express surprise at management's spontaneous outburst. Thus, the absence of nonverbal cues on even the most basic level of interaction can leave us insecure, with incomplete understandings of the intended meaning of a verbal message.

The Use of "Things" in Nonverbal Communication

Having stressed the symbiotic nature of verbal and nonverbal communication, we turn to a more detailed study of nonverbal transactions. For purposes of analysis, we will use an analytic approach and look separately at a number of specific nonverbal communication strategies and activities. By this means we will identify and discuss a number of distinctive ways in which people arouse meanings in others without using words.

In this section we discuss three major nonverbal strategies that we use to indicate to others information about ourselves or about some other topic that we want them to interpret and believe. Each of these strategies depends on the use of "things." These include the *body* itself, which sends numerous messages, the various possessions or *artifacts* with which people transmit ideas about themselves to others, and the special category of *clothing* by which individuals communicate many "layers" of meaning.

The Body as Message

To a greater or lesser degree, the things used in nonverbal communication are under the sender's control and can be manipulated, modified, selected, or excluded to incorporate intended meanings in messages transmitted to others. The possible exception is the use of the body itself. Some body-related messages can be controlled through various means. However, some (e.g., those related to age, height, skin color, general body configu-

ration, and perhaps in some cases, weight) are not subject to voluntary change.

Being tall or short is a matter of genetics rather than choice. Nevertheless, even such a simple fact as one's height can carry a nonverbal message. Many short men feel at a disadvantage among their taller peers. In our culture, commanding height among males implies greater authority, leadership qualities, and power. Being short suggests the opposite. For that reason, short men sometimes buy special shoes that add to their stature. A woman can be tall and be thought of as glamorous—up to a point, after which people may regard her as ungainly. Short women complain that they suffer a special disadvantage in competitive arenas, such as the business world, where everyone else is taken more seriously because they seem more physically impressive.

Skin color is so obviously related to social meanings in our society that it scarcely needs to be reviewed. Among African-Americans, particularly prior to recent decades, a rule of long standing was that a lighter-skinned individual had social advantages over one of similar appearance but darker skin. But among those of any race, skin *condition* can also carry powerful nonverbal messages. For women and for men as well, appearance of the skin—especially on the face—has powerful emotional connotations. Wrinkles, oil, hair, dryness, blemishes, sagging, and scars are widely regarded as signaling undesirable meanings. The preferred conditions are those that communicate youth, sexual desirability, and robust health. An enormous skin-products industry thrives on attempts to control such messages.

While it may be tempting to dismiss such efforts at beautification as mere vanity, an abundance of research on the experiences of attractive versus unattractive people shows that being handsome or pretty can bring definite advantages.[13] In the simplest terms, the majority of Americans fully believe in one way or another that "beautiful is good." The opposite of that proposition is all too obvious.

Along those lines, one bodily condition that conveys troublesome meanings in contemporary society is being fat. Because of the message that excessive weight sends to self and others, a large proportion of the American population is dieting, or thinking about dieting, or feeling bad that they can't lose weight. For those who are obese, our language contains a long list of epithets (negative terms) that convey the unpleasant evaluations accompanying the condition. These messages are so powerful that a significant number of people regularly prod themselves into jogging, dancing to jazz music, and going

Among the "things" we use in nonverbal communication, perhaps no other can arouse more complex meanings than our body. People read nonverbal meanings into our messages based on our height, weight, skin color and condition, and overall body configuration. A body that deviates significantly from the norm may transmit nonverbal messages of many kinds.

to gymnasiums or exercise spas to punish off excess pounds. In more extreme cases, being fat is so feared that individuals undergo surgery or deny themselves food to a point of virtual starvation.

Modifying the body to make it seem more attractive to self and others has been a feature of human existence since prehistoric times. Tattoos, filing the teeth, extending the lips or ears, and binding the feet to prevent normal growth, are all ways that have been used to communicate beauty or some special status. Americans today are no exception; in addition to dieting and exercising, some rather drastic approaches to body modification are in use. Some women have silicone devices inserted to make their breasts larger and firmer. A growing number of young males take steroid compounds and pump iron to make their muscles bigger. An increasing number of males and females of all ages troop to plastic surgeons to get big noses made smaller, faces tightened, and excess fatty deposits removed by liposuction. The message resulting from these transformations: "Look at me, I'm young, slim, attractive, and sexy."

Even those of us who do not care for such draconian measures do not hesitate to use more widely accepted means to make us look better. We have our hair curled, dyed, razor-cut, streaked, or at least "styled," in order to achieve that "natural" look. If we can afford it, we get manicures and pedicures, facial massages, body wraps, wax applications, tanning treatments; we apply layers of cosmetics, insert artificial lenses into our eyes, and generally suffer whatever it takes to modify our body so that it will encode and send messages to others so as to arouse the meanings we desire.

The point is that our body is available to us as a communication device. While we can scarcely make ourselves taller or shorter, or change our skin color, it is subject to considerable manipulation and change depending on how far we want to go and what we want to communicate.

Arousing Meanings with Artifacts

Our simultaneous transactions model of communication (Chapter 1, pp. 21–25) indicates that the physical surroundings in which communication takes place add their own dimensions of meaning as messages are exchanged between participants. Those surroundings include not only places but the use of **artifacts** (physical objects that we possess) to communicate meanings to others about our personal and social attributes. Many people, perhaps most, seem to have a profound need to have others believe that they are physically attractive and have other qualities which others admire. For example, they want others to believe that they enjoy a social rank of significant status and prestige and that they are accepted by groups they feel are important. Those needs may be based on the proposition that if others respond to them favorably, then they too can legitimately hold comforting beliefs about themselves.[14]

Artifacts are used by individuals in our impersonal society to signal their *position in the social order*. This translates for the most part into messages about wealth, status, and power. One of the most obvious ways in which we communicate to others our location in the social structure is through the display of "things," both large and small, that have become meaningful symbols of rank. These include artifacts as obvious and expensive as homes, furniture, and automobiles, and as seemingly insignificant as eyeglasses, earrings, purses, and briefcases. These possessions communicate to others a great deal about us as individuals—where we belong in the social class system, the financial resources we command, and our tastes, hobbies, and interests.

In the American society, perhaps no single possession communicates more than one's dwelling, including its location and contents. Even the address of one's home or apartment can speak volumes. People form impressions based simply on whether the dwelling is large or small, well or poorly furnished, in a nice neighborhood or on the "wrong side of the tracks." For example, on many applications for credit individuals are asked whether they are homeowners (presumably implying stability and financial responsibility) or renters (presumably suggesting instability and risk).

At work, an office can become a stage where one's power and status are communicated. One kind of message is transmitted by the large and elegant office with a nice view, a rug on the floor, paintings and sculptures on display, and handsome wood furniture. Add an outer office with a secretary and the rank goes up even further. In contrast, a small windowless room with metal furniture and linoleum on the floor, or even worse, a cubicle with walls that do not reach the ceiling, places one much farther down in the "pecking order."

Among possessions that signal position in the social structure, few match the communicative ability of the automobile. Different messages are transmitted by the limousine, the sports convertible, the sensible four-door sedan, the pickup truck (with gun rack), the station wagon, and the heavily reworked older vehicle with a homemade air scoop on the hood. These are more than mere indicators of preferences in types of vehicles. They

are artifacts that signal "locations" in our complex society in terms of the resources, tastes, and values of their owners.

Even small artifacts, such as rings, wristwatches, eyeglasses, and briefcases, send messages about our personal qualities. For example, the seemingly insignificant plastic device that some males place in their shirt pocket (where they insert an array of different pens and pencils) sends a message. These have become popularly known as "nerd packs" on the presumption (right or wrong) that those who use them are serious but socially inept types, like engineers or computer experts.

Other artifacts that send messages are the gold fountain pen favored by affluent lawyers (versus the drugstore felt-tip model that most of us carry). The Crucifix or Star of David on a slender gold chain sends a message. Other artifacts that send nonverbal signals are wedding and engagement rings, an alligator handbag (versus the plastic copy), a leather briefcase (versus vinyl models), designer sunglasses, Rolex watches (versus Timex models), and heavy gold chains worn by men with shirt unbuttoned to the waist.

In short, the world of "things" provides us with almost unlimited choices for transmitting messages about meanings we value to other people. That is not to say the meanings they construct will be the ones we have in mind. In fact, the index of fidelity may be low indeed in such nonverbal encounters. The reason is that the rules of communicating nonverbally with artifacts are not uniformly established in our culture. Indeed, the very artifacts we regard as signaling high status and good taste may be seen by others as tacky signs of low class and poor judgment. For that reason, the use of artifacts in communicating significant information about ourselves must be approached with care and sensitivity in order to avoid potential "boomerang" effects.

Sending Messages with Clothing

The use of clothing to signify one's place in society is an ancient form of nonverbal communication. The technology of weaving to make cloth, replacing animal skins for clothing, goes back to the Neolithic era. By biblical times, clothing had become deeply established as one of the ways in which a person's social level could instantly be identified. The poor wore shapeless garments, woven of coarse gray wool (or other fiber in warmer areas) that was left natural (i.e., not colored with dyes). Those of higher rank had much finer clothing made of fabrics decorations were appropriate at each level and severely limiting what those of lower ranks could wear.

As Western societies moved into modern times, particularly during the late 19th century, ready-made clothing was developed. Early in the 20th century, volume production, low cost, and wide distribution made it available to virtually everyone. This brought great change: As the use of such garments spread, status and power could no longer be determined readily on the basis

A number of features of the human body are subject to alteration. Various parts can be stretched, filed, tattooed, or otherwise modified. People in some societies choose deliberately to change their bodies in order to communicate various kinds of conventionalized nonverbal messages. In other societies such modifications do not imply specific and culturally shared meanings, and they are not as easily interpreted.

woven with delicate skills and often colored with bright dyes. Furthermore, fashions for the elite changed quickly, making garments obsolete even when they had been only slightly used. Only the wealthy could afford such change for the sake of change.

Communicating status and power During the 15th and 16th centuries, as the rigid structure of medieval society began to erode somewhat, those in power were concerned about preserving their social ranks. Specifying by law who could dress in what manner was one means that the status quo was preserved. Both the nobility and the Church backed laws that prescribed elaborate codes of dress, setting forth what colors, types of cloth, and

During the 15th and 16th centuries, people in positions of power used elaborate clothing as nonverbal messages testifying to their high social rank. Fine cloth and elaborate designs were very expensive. The more cloth used in a garment, and the more intricate its fashion design, the higher the rank and greater the power that it signified.

of what people were wearing in public. The shop girl and the heiress, or the banker and the clerk, began to dress in rather similar ways. Thus, both appearance and styles in clothing became less obvious as overt signs of rank. That became increasingly true when the designs of the great fashion houses came to be quickly copied, mass-produced, and marketed through nationwide retail chains.

What has happened in recent times is that very *subtle* codes of dress have come into use for both men and women. These provide nonverbal cues that enable those "in the know" to recognize those of "gentility" (presumably of higher social status). Thus, clothing continues to distinguish those who believe themselves to have more refined tastes from those who do not understand or choose to ignore the rules of "proper" dress.

Many of these codes identify appropriate attire for individuals in positions of power and status in the business and professional world. Among women in such settings, a relatively clear set of rules prevails as to appropriate garments to be worn at work. A dark business suit, conservative blouse, and plain pumps with high heels are said to command respect. Gaudy, informal, or casual clothes are likely to signal weakness. For example, a professional woman who came to the office in a lace suit or pink ensemble with sequined shoes would cause raised eyebrows. Blue jeans at work for such a female executive would not even be imaginable.

Men in the business world have parallel codes that are said to communicate status, financial means, and recognition of good taste (read "high rank"). For example, males who adhere to such rules would never even think of wearing a striped seersucker suit to a board meeting. Similarly, if one wears a patterned tie, then neither the coat nor the shirt should have a pattern. Either a subdued club tie or one with quiet slanted stripes would be appropriate for the office, but bright ties with conspicuous designs would be regarded as sartorial atrocities. Suits with a flashy European cut would be perceived as inappropriate for most conservative, traditional business situations.

Moreover, in the overall ensemble, one must always be conscious of color. For women, black suits and dresses are thought to connote strength and potency. For men, any color is fine as long as it is either somber gray or dark blue. Patterns, other than a faint pin stripe or perhaps a subdued chalk stripe, are regarded as gauche. Brown shoes worn with a gray or blue suit are a disaster. Hosiery is a must for women. For males, stockings should always cover the lower leg to just below the knee. A clear view of a naked stretch of hairy male leg between stocking and trousers is perceived as gross and disgusting.

But how much attention should be paid to such rules? Whether you personally think such elaborate codes are important, trivial, or even silly, a significant number of people in our society continue to make judgments about the social nature and inner characteristics of individuals on the basis of what they wear. Furthermore, the men and women who do feel such dress codes are important are likely to be the ones who are "in charge"—often they are the bosses who have the power to hire, fire, promote, and give raises. They reach yes/no decisions on such matters, depending on their judgment about individuals who report to them. Do the dress requirements they regard as important play *some* part in forming and maintaining their judgments? There is every reason to believe they do. Thus, the ideas of traditional power-holders about what clothing is appropriate may be worth looking at closely.

Finally, because the way we dress signals rank and power, it can have an influence on the way we are treated even in the most casual and impersonal encounters (in stores, banks, car dealerships, etc.). In contemporary society we must deal every day with strangers in a host of such circumstances, and perceptions of our probable purchasing power made on the basis of how we are dressed are a key to how we will be treated.

Dressing to fit in   But there is far more to clothing as nonverbal communication than just the dress-code idea we have inherited from ancient sources.[15] For one thing, we dress so as to be socially acceptable—to "fit in" with different kinds of groups. An obvious case is the uniforms characteristic of some occupational categories, such as nurses, police officers, and airline pilots. However, prevailing dress codes among other categories are rather like uniforms, identifying who is "in" and "out."

Appropriate dress can be important for all kinds of group identifications. There are even codes governing recreation. Those who play tennis dress differently from those who go jogging. Such recreations as skiing, sailing, hiking, fly-fishing, riding, and hunting all require different "costumes." While people widely believe that clothes make a difference in social acceptability and popularity, is it really true? Researchers Madelyn Williams and Joanne Eicher found that it is.[16] Their research showed that both popularity and liking are related to the clothes people wear.

Even ordinary social events are governed by clothing rules. It is not uncommon to be asked to an informal gathering, such as an outdoor pool party, and be told to

Different types and styles of clothing are commonly used in modern society as nonverbal indicators of where the individual fits into the complex occupational structure. There are both clear and subtle codes of dress, not only for different types of work, but also for different social occasions and even different types of recreation.

"dress casually." On the other hand, sometimes it is difficult to forecast just what that means. A woman, taking the hostess at her word, may arrive at the party dressed in white cotton slacks and a new T-shirt. To her mortification, she may discover that all the other guests interpreted "casual" to mean silk sport jackets rolled up at the sleeves!

Communicating inner feelings Clothing is often used to communicate how we feel—or at least what we want others to *think* we feel. For example, people traditionally wear dark colors at a funeral to communicate that they feel grief and respect for the deceased, whether they do or not. They generally dress in restrained colors to go to church so as to signal their religiosity and concern for the dignity of the service. To demonstrate that they too are just plain folks, politicians campaigning in rural areas commonly wear an open-collared shirt with their sleeves rolled up, or a farm jacket and feed-company cap.

Generally, then, clothing is far more than something we wear for modesty or to keep from getting cold. It is also an extraordinarily complex system of nonverbal communication that can be used to signal what we are as persons and where we are (or would like to be) in the social structure.

Sexual Communication in the Workplace

One of the areas of communication in contemporary life that has become increasingly difficult for both men and women is that of gender relationships on the job. Differing conceptions by men and women of the rules of interpretation of nonverbal behavior—related to the body and to various artifacts and clothing in the context of the workplace—may contribute to significant sexual misunderstandings.

To understand how this has come about, we need to begin by noting that since World War II more and more women have moved into the labor force. A consequence is that contacts between males and females in the workplace have risen sharply. That increase was accompanied by a growing number of verbal and nonverbal communication problems that have now placed sexual harassment high on the agenda of public discussion.

Many women today are deeply troubled by nonverbal (or verbal) messages of a sexual nature that make them uncomfortable, afraid, or even unable to continue their employment. These women often maintain that men "just don't get it"—that even after repeated protests men fail to understand that gestures, actions, and verbal messages with sexual meanings are unwelcome and can cause female workers great distress.

Did he or didn't he? As a result of the Senate confirmation hearings on President Bush's nomination of Clarence Thomas for a position as a Justice of the Supreme Court, the issue of sexual harassment has been high on the public agenda. Anita Hill, a former subordinate of Thomas when he was director of a major federal agency, claimed in a confidential FBI interview that he had initiated numerous messages to her concerning sexual matters. She interpreted them as messages of sexual harassment by her (then) boss. Her secret report was "leaked" to the media, and she was asked to testify publicly during the televised hearings. The confrontation created great controversy when he vehemently denied all charges and she steadfastly insisted that they were true.

On the other hand, when women who feel victimized define those messages as "sexual harassment," the males involved are often astonished that what they said or did was interpreted as offensive. We are not referring here to gross and outright disgusting behavior, such as misuses of power for sexual advantage, coarse propositions, obscene language, or actual physical abuse. No one can fail to misunderstand that kind of sexual harassment. We are referring instead to nonverbal behavior such as staring, whistling, facial expressions and gestures used in flirting—or verbal messages that a woman "looks sexy," telling off-color stories, or even making mild sexual innuendos). Many men indeed "just don't get it" with respect to such communications—they can't understand why women object to such messages, which they see as "just joking around" like "men always have" in ways that "mean no harm."

How can such misunderstandings occur? Has there been a moral collapse on the part of males in the workplace, to a point where they insist on harassing women who detest it? Or is the explanation that such women are being unrealistically oversensitive when they define traditional forms of male behavior as unwelcome and unacceptable? An alternative explanation is that neither of these is true. What may be happening is that meanings associated with the body, and with various artifacts and types of clothing, became quite different for men and women as the workplace gender balance changed over the past several decades. For example, for working women, remaining slim, using modest amounts of makeup and perhaps a bit of scent, wearing a nice suit, stockings, high heels, matching accessories, and adopting a flattering hair style may be seen as merely following the norms of appropriate dress in the contemporary business world. For men, those same features of the body, artifacts, and clothing may send messages of "sexiness" or even "enticement." This is because, in part, meanings used by men to interpret women's nonverbal behavior continue to be based on traditional peer-validated interpretations developed, shared, and retained *before* the massive entry of females into the workplace.

But how could such traditional meanings survive that long, after half a century? For one thing, a virtual sea of mass media content stresses the theme that *women seek and welcome the attentions of men.* The media pose such behavior models daily for all of us as they construct and strongly reinforce social interpretations of reality for both males and females. For example, the movies began their emphasis on the role of "sexual enticer" for females during the silent-picture era, when they posed the model of the seductive "vamp." The same industry emphasized the enticing "sex goddess" during the decades just before and following World War II. The sexy-female-interested-in-men is still emphasized in virtually all of our media. For example, television places heavy emphasis on the female as "erotic" in sitcoms, soap operas, evening drama, and even in popular game shows, such as "Wheel of Fortune." In addition, a great deal of media content is advertising. Huge industries focus on selling a long list of products with open sexual appeals. Women are portrayed as preoccupied with being seductive and attractive to men. Thus, sexual enticement remains a deeply established, heavily reinforced, and culturally legitimized activity emphasized by our mass media for females in our society.

After seeing such advertising and media content day after day, men tend to believe that women deliberately engage in sexual enticement and value male sexual attention. Furthermore, it has always been the accepted role of men, stemming from training since childhood and frequently reinforced by communication among peers, to take the lead in male-female relationships. Thus, taking the sexual initiative seems "natural" for many men, in or out of the workplace.

In contrast, the women's movement that arose after World War II began to pose entirely new role models for females that rejected the concept of sexual enticer and promoted conceptions of gender equality, especially in the workplace. Changes in official policies opened opportunities for women in virtually every sphere of employment. These new role models and shared conceptions have reinforced an expectation of equality on the part of females. Many women feel that the role of sexual enticer has *absolutely no place on the job,* and they insist on a gender-neutral work environment. However, this is not fully understood by many of their male coworkers.

Our simultaneous transactions model, which makes the context of communication a significant feature of the process, helps in understanding these meaning conflicts. Because of the traditional male definitions of women outlined earlier—heavily reinforced outside the workplace by our media—nonverbal and verbal sexual messages to females seem appropriate to many men. These men continue to believe that it is up to them to make advances and that females will welcome them *in any context.* What they "just don't get" is that females with more contemporary orientations define these as completely inappropriate, and even disgusting, in the physical setting, sociocultural situation, and social relationships of work. Until traditional males are able to engage in more sensitive role-taking, sexual communication in the workplace will remain a problem and confusion over what constitutes sexual harassment will continue.

"Actions" That Communicate

A number of actions, postures, and activities are part of the nonverbal dimensions of human communication. Among them are facial expressions and gestures, variations in the use of the voice, and messages transmitted by the eyes. The use of space, touch, and time can also introduce special meanings into ongoing transactions. In this section we will touch briefly on all of these as part of the human communication process.

Body Movements and Gestures

The study of body movements—including gestures, postures, and facial expression—is important in understanding nonverbal communication.[17] As a specialty, that study is called **kinesics**.[18] A person's overall body orientation or posture typically communicates his or her level of interest, liking, and openness. For example, simply by watching a couple engage in conversation from afar one can sometimes guess rather accurately whether or not they are psychologically close and interested in one another. Some of the indicators are displaying direct, frontal body orientation (or close side-by-side seating), open arm gestures (as opposed to folded arms across the chest), and forward-leaning. If such postures and movements are evident—along with head-nodding, smiling, and giving eye contact—it is a good guess that the couple is enjoying each other's company a great deal.

Nonverbal gestures are even easier to decipher. Earlier, we discussed emblems, noting that they are gestures which have specific conventions of meaning in our culture.[19] Because this is the case, emblems are often used as effective substitutions for talk. A good example is simply putting your index finger to your lips, which everyone sharing our culture understands to mean "shhh" or "be quiet."

Another category of gestures is *illustrators*—hand and arm movements that demonstrate and reinforce meanings intended by verbal messages.[20] For example, pointing to your sweater on the chair while explaining that "it's lying over there," is an illustrator. Others include stretching your arms over your head to emphasize your level of fatigue, slapping your hand against your head in an effort to recall a thought, punching the air with your fist to accentuate a word or phrase, and using your hands to show length when describing the fish you caught (or the one that got away).

Another category of gestures is *adapters*—unintentional hand, arm, leg, or other bodily movements used to reduce stress or relieve boredom.[21] For example, waiting endlessly for your turn at the doctor's office may elicit such actions as pencil-tapping, nail-biting, or chewing on eyeglass frames. Excessive use of such adapters is often a result of fears and anxieties, such as concern about making a presentation or delivering a speech. Such actions are common among students giving their first talk in front of a class. Many try to calm themselves by pacing or dancing across the room, twisting their hair or moustache, rocking back and forth on the heels, pulling on their ears or nose, and shuffling notecards.

While these kinds of bodily activities are common, most of us are unaware that we use such adapters. However, observers are quick to interpret nonverbal adapters as indicators of nervousness, insecurity, or anxiety. In this sense they can be a problem if not controlled. It goes without saying that the last thing we want is for others to perceive us as lacking confidence during such communication situations as a job interview, a public presentation, or asking someone for a date.

Nonverbal Uses of the Voice

Our vocal tones often indicate to others that we are happy, sad, confident, nervous, culturally refined, boorish, and so on. The study of such nonverbal uses of the voice is called **vocalics,** and it is an important category of communication behavior. The basic idea is that we surround the words we use with many kinds of voice-quality cues that contribute significantly to people's judgments about us, and directly or indirectly, to the meanings of our messages. Put simply, *how* you say something can at times be as important as *what* you say.

Nonverbal vocal cues can take many forms—pitch, tone, rate, volume, and accent patterns in speech all make big differences in how verbal messages are interpreted. For example, if a woman greets a man by saying "hello," what are the implications when her voice quality is flat and matter-of-fact? Now suppose the reply is "breathy" and a bit drawn out. Does the subtle meaning change? For both males and females, voice quality is often associated with suggestions of size, intelligence, and sexuality.

Accents are another category of vocalics. These can cause endless problems in misjudging the intelligence, emotions, and personalities of people who speak in ways that seem different and strange to us. For example, people from the Midwest seem to talk through their nose, and such a nasal voice quality may be perceived negatively by listeners from other geographic areas. The same can be true of the Texas drawl and the speech patterns heard in the Deep South. Such speakers are often assigned characteristics of laziness and ignorance. A Kentucky hill-country accent can result in a mental subtraction of about 10 IQ points when the listener is from another part of the country.

Speech patterns used by many poor urban African-Americans may be judged very negatively by well-educated whites. Pronunciations characteristic of people raised in some parts of New York City (especially in Brooklyn) do not inspire confidence among westerners. Regional, racial, and ethnic accents, then, bring with them a curious baggage of positive and negative attributions about the speaker's personality.[22] However, there is absolutely no relationship between any such accent and level of intelligence. It is a serious mistake to assume that since a person pronounces words in an unfamiliar way, his or her intelligence is low (or high) or that the individual has any other personality trait.

Not only do we assign personal and social qualities to those who talk differently than we do, but we also make judgments about people's current emotions based on vocalics.[23] Tone of voice is particularly important in this process. Hearing two people in the next room or upstairs speaking loudly brings an assumption that they are arguing and are angry with each other. One may not be able to understand the words, but the level of hostility often seems unmistakable because of the vocalics.

As a matter of fact, research suggests that negative emotions are much more likely to be identified accurately from vocalic cues alone than are positive ones.[24] It appears to be easier to tell if someone is sad, disappointed, or angry from voice tone, level, and pitch than if the person is happy, relieved, or thrilled. Some individuals appear to be more skilled than others in deciphering vocalics to determine how someone feels.[25] But neither the personal and social attributions most listeners make nor their judgments about emotions are always accurate.

While the rules for interpreting the meanings of vocalics are not standardized, one reason that nonverbal aspects of the voice are so commonly used to make judgments about people is that they are very visible. That is, the nature of one's voice and speaking style is one of the first things we notice about another person. When we are in a communication situation with someone we have just met, or about whom we know very little, we have to try to understand what that person is like in order to deal with the situation. Vocalics may be one of only a few discernible guidelines we have available.

Eye Contact as Communication

Novelists, poets, and songwriters have always been fascinated by eyes. Their works lyrically describe the character traits that different types of eyes reveal and the subtle messages that eyes can transmit. There is a great deal of lore about eyes that are "shifty," "steely," "beady," "innocent," or "jaded." The idea that we communicate with our eyes, then, is deeply rooted in our popular culture.

A less romantic view of the role of eyes in nonverbal communication is called **oculesics,** which refers to the study of eye contact and pupil dilation in nonverbal communication. People use their eyes to indicate their degree of interest, openness, and even arousal as they commu-

nicate. Even simple eye contact with another has meaning on some occasions. For example, one of the rules of public address is that speakers are supposed to maintain eye contact with people in their audience.

What assumption do we make when receivers of our message look down or away? It is clearly a negative signal, and most of us readily conclude they're not interested in what we have to say. Similarly, teachers, politicians, clergy, or anyone else making a public presentation can become threatened and concerned when the audience fails to meet their gaze. A parent will scold a child for not "looking at me when I'm talking to you!" (the kinesics here is usually a finger vigorously shaken at the hapless child). Another example is loss of eye contact when you happen to be browsing through a magazine during an exchange with a friend. He or she is likely to ask, "Am I boring you?"

Research on eye contact supports our popular beliefs only up to a point.[26] Even though eye contact generally communicates positive feelings toward another, staring can be interpreted as a sign of hostility and aggression. Keep in mind that eye contact communicates the degree of interest or arousal between persons. Whenever we feel extreme sentiment, whether that sentiment is in the form of anger or of love, a degree of interest or arousal is triggered. Thus, we are likely to express *both* emotional extremes through eye gaze, and we have to look to other communicative behaviors to determine the particular emotion revealed.

Popular lore further has it that the lack of eye contact is a certain clue that someone is *lying.* So firmly established is this so-called fact that people who suspect another person is lying demand that he or she "look me in the eye when you say that" in an effort to solicit the truth. (Their own oculesics will include a glaring stare at this point). The problem with this "fact" is that a considerable number of studies of the detection of deception have failed to confirm its validity.[27] In fact, most people learn very early to lie quite successfully while steadily holding eye contact with an accuser. As children most of us were able to fool our parents in this way.

On the other hand, for the most part, we do gaze at others less when we feel embarrassment, guilt, or sadness. If we feel such emotions, our most common response is to avoid interacting with others. For example, at a dinner party, the last thing we want our host to do is provide undue attention to the fact that we spilled red sauce all over the white linen tablecloth. If we contribute to our embarrassment further by spilling the wine as we try to wipe up the mess with our napkin, we do not appreciate eyes on us at such a time. Similarly, when we experience either guilt or sorrow, we would rather hide than face the open confrontation implied by eye contact.

Many conventions are used in connection with oculesics in nonverbal communication. For example, the rules of eye contact between professor and student in the college classroom are well understood. When the instructor poses a question, students quickly learn to escape from having to provide an answer by avoiding the professor's gaze. They examine their fingernails, glare at their books, study the floor, or gape at the ceiling—anything to avoid being called on. The rules of flirting with the eyes are also well defined. Gazing or even repeatedly glancing at someone "across a crowded room" is likely to result in some kind of response, at best a smile, at worst bored indifference.

Meanings Associated with Space and Distance

Some of the most subtle aspects of nonverbal communication are associated with the use of both space and distance as these influence meanings we arouse in others. Such considerations are something that most people seldom think about, but they have important implications for communication. The study of the meanings communicated by the use of space and distance is called **proxemics.** Two uses of space are important in understanding human communication behavior. The first is *territoriality.*[28] The second, a quite different concept, is *personal space.*[29] Each provides special insights into the shaping of meanings for others in the communication process.

The term **territoriality** refers to a common tendency characteristic of both animals and human beings. That is, many species define some fixed or semifixed space to claim or stake out as their own. When we as individuals engage in this behavior, we feel that some territory belongs to us exclusively, but we willingly share other territory with family or friends. Still other territory involves only temporary ownership.

Regardless of the level of exclusivity, we respond to territorial "invasion" as if we have a right to that space. For instance, the most primary form of territory may include your office, your room, your side of the bed, or even your chair. Should others attempt to encroach on your rightful domain, you may feel frustrated, angry, or downright hostile. More public, and thus less exclusive, are forms of territory that provide only temporary "ownership," such as a parking spot, a table reserved at a restaurant, or a seat or desk in a particular class. Even though technically we have no rightful claim to such public territories, we may respond as if we actually own that parking spot, table, or seat.

The second proxemic concept is **personal space**—the immediate zone we carry around with us during our daily interactions with others. It is like a "bubble" that moves with us. That bubble of personal space often contracts and expands, depending on where we are, what we are doing, and who we are with. In other words, the degree of personal space one allows with others is determined by the nature of the relationship, the topic under discussion, gender, age, and cultural background.[30]

Anthropologist Edward T. Hall has identified distinctive extensions of personal space in various cultures in terms of *zones* of distance related to our various interpersonal activities and transactions.[31] Briefly, Hall's zones can be categorized as follows: The first is a distance of zero (touching) to a distance of 18 inches, which defines the *intimate* zone; a second ranges from 18 inches to 4 feet to encompass the *casual-personal* zone; then, 4 to 8 feet for the *socio-consultative* zone; and finally, beyond 8 feet for the *public* zone. Each of these zones tells us something about the nature of the relationship the conversants share. Obviously, for lovers and close friends or family members, the distance between them during intimate interaction is likely to be limited. When a teacher lectures to a large class, the interaction probably will require space boundaries more typical of the public zone.

Hall's zones have important implications for the study of nonverbal communication. It's very difficult, if not impossible, to talk about intimate topics from a distance of 5 feet or more. Instead, we "move in" to each other when we wish to discuss a secret, share an embarrassing experience, or make very personal comments. Thus, as we move in closer and closer, we imply a change in the meaning and content of our messages.

Gender and age are also factors in determining the size of one's personal space. Females tend to interact at closer distances with other females than do males with each other. Not surprisingly, mixed sex dyads (male-female couples) interact at closer distances than do either female-female or male-male pairs. Furthermore, children and adults use space differently. Since rules concerning appropriate distances to maintain in communicating are learned, it is not surprising that young children comprise the greatest percentage of "space invaders." They overrun each other's territories and blithely penetrate the distance zones of adults. As they get older, they learn to follow the rules.

Great variability exists from one cultural group to the next as to the rules governing proxemics. For example, compared to those of other societies, people in the United States seem almost paranoid about space. We are a *noncontact-oriented* people. That is, we avoid spatially close (intimate zone) interactions except with members of our immediate family or our close friends. Asians, Indians, Pakistanis, and northern Europeans (except Germans) are also noncontact people. In contrast, Arabs, Latin Americans, and southern Europeans (particularly male Italians) are identified as more *contact oriented.*[32] In fact, for many Americans, attempting to maintain space with Latin or Arabic friends or business acquaintances, sometimes seems similar to a fencing match. As they move forward, the Americans keep moving back.

Differences also exist among African-Americans, whites, and Hispanics. African-Americans maintain the closest interaction space and Hispanics the greatest. Research suggests that those variations are more a function of socioeconomic status than of racial or ethnic identification. Shawn Scherer found that such differences were not present when the people interacting were all from the middle class or all from lower strata in the social system.[33]

Some of the more interesting research on territoriality and personal space involves *encroachment,* or space invasion. Experiments on encroachment require a confederate (who is aware of the purpose of the study) to violate subjects' territories or personal space. The subjects, of course, remain unaware of the experiment or what is to happen. An observer then records each subject's response to the encroachment.

One of the best-known experimental designs of this nature was pioneered by Robert Sommer.[34] He had confederates approach tables in a library occupied by a single other person. Each confederate would sit at the table directly across from the occupant, or right next to him or her, or a few seats away. Observers sitting at nearby tables reported that subjects' reactions to this space invasion were fairly consistent. In almost all cases, victims of the invasion experienced anxiety and then attempted to reduce it by increasing the distance between themselves and the encroacher. Some set up barriers by redistributing their books, book bags, and other materials around them. Others shifted themselves away from the intruder. Only a few defied the invader by glaring. Others gave up and took flight by switching tables or leaving altogether.

Subsequent studies confirm these findings. Almost always, people respond to space invasion in one of two ways—*fight* or *flight.* The most common response to en-

There are many cultural variations in *proxemics,* meanings associated with space and distance. In some societies, shared cultural rules for the use of space call for people to stand very close to each other when they communicate in person. In others, the rules are that a greater distance be maintained.

croachment on public or more temporary territory is flight.[35] Evidently, people recognize that no one really "owns" such space. For example, if someone stands too close to you in an elevator where you are the only other occupant, you are more likely to move over and construct barriers (pointing your books in the direction next to the encroacher) than you are to complain or to shove the person aside. Nevertheless, you may know of some individuals who become agitated and engage in fight responses to territorial violations. More than once, you've probably seen an angry driver yell or even get out of his car when someone took the only parking space available.

Fight responses are more common when invasions occur within primary or exclusive territory. The legal

Preventing Territorial Invasion

Dogs, cats, and other animals are pretty good at staking out their territory by "spraying" the boundaries with their urine. If you've ever moved your dog or cat to a new house or apartment, you've probably had a lot of cleaning up to do initially. This is especially true of those environments that were inhabited previously by another animal.

In many ways, human beings are little different from animals. While we seldom stake out our territory with urine, we do construct elaborate fences or walls around our property, post "keep out" signs on our doors or gates, and sign legal documents of ownership. These are all ways we ward off potential encroachers. Researchers categorize our stakeouts in four ways:[1]

1. *Markers.* We strategically place objects to "mark" out our spot. Examples are leaving a sweater on the table to let others in the cafeteria know that the table "belongs" to you. Book bags, a partially filled glass or cup, and caps or hats all make excellent markers. Such markers allow us to leave the territory temporarily without worrying that someone else will take over. Curiously, feminine markers (a girl's jacket or a woman's purse) are less likely to ward off invaders than are male markers. Given the research on fight versus flight responses to invasion, why do you suppose feminine markers are less discouraging to encroachers?

2. *Labels.* Labels are markers with your name or some other symbol on them. Mothers are known to label their kids' clothes before they leave for college. Checks and credit cards are labeled with your legal name. Signs marked "reserved" communicate to others that the table (or chair, room) is being held for someone else. T-shirts, baseball caps, license plates, and brass door plates use a variety of labels, not only to communicate a slogan but also to identify the owner.

3. *Offensive displays.* Clenching your fists, leaning forward, glaring, and just looking "mean" are examples of offensive displays. Such displays are very effective at preventing invasion. After all, who would want to mess with Dirty Harry when that vein in his temple starts to pulse and his arms move toward his side?

4. *Tenure.* By being there first and staying the longest, we can prevent others from taking over the space. One of the authors comes from a family of seven kids and happens to be one of the younger family members. Like all families, they had so-called assigned seats around the kitchen table. But now that they are all older and living elsewhere, you might expect the seating at homecoming dinners to change. Even with a different table these days, the older siblings still dominate the "best seating," making it necessary for others to pull up a folding chair! You may have always "slept on that side of the bed," "sat in this chair in the den," or "had the desk closest to the window." As a result, your tenure acts to prevent others from encroachment.

1. Knapp, M. L. (1978). *Nonverbal communication in human interaction* (2nd ed.) (pp. 116–120). New York: Holt, Rinehart, and Winston.

system, police force, and insurance carriers provide services, penalties, and financial restitution to victims of territorial invasion. By such formal means, homeowners are supposed to be protected from thieves, men and women from rapists, authors from plagiarists, and rock bands from overly zealous groupies. Across all of these instances, a fight response is expected and typically condoned by our society. Note, however, that fight need not necessarily involve hitting someone or other types of physical force. Fight reactions can range from polite forms of requests ("Would you please move your books to the other end of the table so that I can have the room I need to study?") to enraged commands ("Just what do you think you're doing? Get away from me, you creep!"). Whether your response to space invasion is fight or flight, it's apparent that personal space, distance, zones, and territory are very important to all of us. (For further information on this topic, see the box above.)

Communicating with Touch

Closely related to the use of space in communicating is *touching* to transmit nonverbal messages. The study of touch as a means of nonverbal communication is called **haptics** and is in many ways a logical extension of proxemics. That is, in order to touch someone to convey meaning it is necessary to be very close to them (that is, space is at a minimum). As we will see, touching is a far more flexible and meaningful form of nonverbal communication than most people realize.

The importance of touching begins early in life. One body of evidence for the importance of touch to infants comes from classic research on animals. Psychologist Harry F. Harlow studied newborn monkeys that had been separated from their mothers and were kept in isolation. He discovered that they would cling for hours to a wire mesh surrogate (substitute) mother wrapped in soft cloth. However, infant monkeys caged with other infant monkeys survived as well as those that were exposed to the cloth surrogates. Still others, without either a cloth surrogate or other infant monkeys to touch, had clear problems. They developed socially maladaptive behaviors and became violent when caged later with the other monkeys.[36]

It is not clear that Harlow's findings apply to human beings, and infant human beings cannot be subjected to such experiments. However, there is evidence that touch does play a vital role in early childhood development.[37] During infancy, touching and stroking seem to satisfy important emotional requirements. In fact, without being touched at all, human babies may not even survive. A number of specialists who study early childhood have concluded that there is a relationship between extreme touch deprivation and mortality.[38] Evidence for this can also be derived from observations made at an earlier time of infants in orphanages. Some writers argue that the mortality rate of almost 100% of infants left in orphanages during the 19th century, and even the early 20th century, was due primarily to the lack of touch. In those institutions, infants were not picked up, talked to, or cradled; they were just cleaned, fed, and left by themselves. As a result, many died. Those who survived typically became maladjusted or retarded.[39]

Infants who develop under normal family circumstances are touched very often until they are about 2 years old. Then, the frequency of touch begins to decrease. Thereafter, people are touched at a decreasing rate throughout life. In fact, senior citizens may be touched very little, or not at all.[40] Despite this withdrawal from

One of the most important areas in the study of nonverbal communication is "haptics"—the use of touch. The importance of touch begins early in life when it plays a vital role in the well-being of the very young. It continues throughout life, and studies indicate that among older people who are deprived of being touched, health problems can arise.

touch, most people of all ages continue to enjoy being touched and touching others.

But just what are the benefits of touch for adults? Perhaps some answers to that question can be seen if we ask, "What happens when we *fail* to get our needed quota of touch?" A number of correlational studies suggest that health problems often arise. For example, a variety of allergies and certain skin diseases are common among those who are deprived of touch.[41] Other research shows that normal speech development may be affected as well.[42] Most important, without the comfort of touch, all of us are likely to succumb more easily to stress in our daily lives.[43] We feel greatly comforted and reassured during crises when someone offers both verbal and nonverbal reassurance through touch.

Comfort and reassurance are not the only significant meanings communicated by touch. Depending on the kind of touch employed, such actions can communicate dislike or aggression. Poking someone on the chest while making a strong point can arouse hostility. More often

Touch Apprehension Measure (TAM)

Instructions This instrument is composed of 14 statements concerning feelings about touching other people and being touched. Please indicate the degree to which each statement applies to you by marking in the blank beside the item:

5 strongly agree   **2** disagree
4 agree   **1** strongly disagree
3 are undecided or neutral

While some of these statements may seem repetitious, take your time and try to be as honest as possible.

____ **1.** I don't mind if I am hugged as a sign of friendship.

____ **2.** I enjoy touching others.

____ **3.** I often put my arms around others.

____ **4.** When I see people hugging, it bothers me.

____ **5.** People shouldn't be uncomfortable about being touched.

____ **6.** I really like being touched by others.

____ **7.** I do not show my emotions by touching others.

____ **8.** I do not like touching other people.

____ **9.** I find it enjoyable to be touched by others.

____ **10.** I do not like being touched by others.

____ **11.** I dislike having to hug others.

____ **12.** Hugging and touching should be outlawed.

____ **13.** Touching others is a very important part of my personality.

____ **14.** Being touched by others makes me uncomfortable.

Calculating Your Score

1. Add together your responses to items 1, 2, 3, 5, 6, 9, and 13 = ____ .

2. Add together your responses to items 4, 7, 8, 10, 11, 12, and 14 = ____ .

3. Complete the following formula:

TAM = 42 − Total from step 1 = ____ .

Then, + Total from step 2. YOUR TOTAL TAM SCORE = ____ .

Interpreting Your Score

Possible range of scores: 14–70. (If your own final TAM score does not fall within that range, you made a computational error.)

The midpoint on the TAM is 42. If your score falls well above that midpoint, you can be classified as a "touch approacher"; below the midpoint, a "touch avoider." Touch approachers like to touch others and, in return, to be touched. These high touchers are apparently unaware of the norms for touching and often touch even when others find it annoying. Research indicates that with the same sex, males are typically more avoidant than females; but with the opposite sex, females are more avoidant. Protestants are more touch avoidant than non-Protestants; older, married persons are more touch avoidant of opposite-sex friends.

References

Andersen, P. A., & Leibowitz, K. (1978). The development and nature of the construct touch avoidance. *Environmental Psychology and Nonverbal Behavior, 3,* 89–106.

Richmond, V. P., McCroskey, J. C., & Payne, S. K. (1987). *Nonverbal behavior and communication: A workbook and study guide* (2nd ed.). Edina, MN: Bellwether Press/Burgess.

than not, however, we consider touch to be positive because it usually communicates attraction. We touch those we like and avoid touching or being touched by those we don't.

Touching, then, can transmit messages intended to arouse meanings ranging from the most tender and significant to those that are offensive or even repulsive. Some people are "touch avoiders" who would never touch a stranger and who feel very uncomfortable with gratuitous pokes, pats, hugs, or kisses. Others are "touch approachers" who just can't seem to wait to get their hands on people.[44] In any case, understanding the rules of touching is critical in relating to others.

Meanings Associated with Time

Have you ever noticed that some people are always late no matter how hard they try to be on time? By the same token, you may know others who are so punctual that they can be downright annoying. The study of the way in which people use time to transmit nonverbal messages is called **chronemics.** Like other forms of nonverbal communication, it can be far more complex and subtle than people generally realize.

Populations in modern urban industrial societies are preoccupied with clocks, watches, and time. In simpler societies, the position of the sun was the rough regulator of daily routines, life proceeded at a slower pace, and schedules were far less compelling. In societies such as ours, almost all activities are regulated by the clock and people have to be far more conscious of closely measured time. To appreciate our society's concern with time, count the number of clocks in your home or office and consider the number of watches you own (or would like to own!). Or imagine how many times a day you glance at a timepiece or ask someone else the time. One of the first things we teach young children is what it means when the "big hand" is in one position and the "little hand" is in another.

There are remarkable individual differences in people's tolerances for early or late time schedules. These seem related to one's biological clock, as is the case with jet lag, but on a more permanent basis. For example, those who are "owls" work best at night and drag around lethargically in the morning. They have difficulty relating to the "sparrows" who wake up early, usually without an alarm, singing the equivalent of "Zippity Doo Dah."[45] Such early birds literally chirp their way through breakfast and chatter cheerfully to teachers and friends as they arrive for an early morning class. Parking is rarely a problem for them; they are the first into the lot.

Conversely, owls sleep late in the morning if they possibly can. Or, if they absolutely must get up, they require both a snooze alarm and a wakeup call. Breakfast is out of the question—they just sit glumly with a cup of coffee, trying slowly to get their act together. (Owls never cite breakfast as their favorite meal.) However, owls become more and more functional as the day wears on. About the time the sparrows are at a low, say mid-afternoon, owls are starting to peak.

Chronemics encompasses not only our rules, ethical beliefs, and individual personality differences related to time but also the study of how people actually schedule their actions within a temporal framework. In particular, the focus is on what this means to others. For example, what does the host actually mean when she or he indicates that the party will begin at 7:00 P.M.? Most people understand a 7:00 P.M. party to mean that it will begin some time between 7:30 and 8:00—a half-hour to an hour later. Their behavior reflects their understanding of that meaning, and they arrive within that time frame. The host or hostess is not offended that they did not arrive promptly at 7:00 P.M.

What would be the implications if a guest used the rules of the work ethic and arrived at the party at 6:30 P.M.? Or what is the meaning if a guest arrives at 9:45 and then leaves at 10:00? Most people also understand that this informal time frame does not apply to a job interview scheduled precisely for 9:30 A.M. If the interviewee arrives late, what meaning does that communicate?

We also share a set of meaning conventions related to time *intervals.* When friends call and claim they'll be along "in a minute," how long is that? How long is "a while," "a day or so," or "sometime soon"? Such informally specified intervals permit a wide range of actual behaviors—but there are limits. If "in a minute" stretches to several hours, it sends a message that may not be intended and is very unlikely to be appreciated.

Misunderstandings over time intervals are commonplace because of these imprecise meanings and because of individual variations in actual behavior associated with them. Some folks are punctual and take time literally. When they say a "minute" or an "hour," that's exactly what they mean. Others flexibly use time by expanding a second, minute, or hour well beyond limits of courtesy. Regardless of individual differences, however, we tend to judge others' punctuality by our own conception of and value for time. If we are punctual ourselves, we are likely to become angry or concerned when others fail to adhere to our expectations. If fuzzy definitions of time are more to our liking, we can be taken aback when someone arrives on time or early.

More closely related to problems of communication are psychological time orientations that are reflected across cultures and societies. For instance, some societies, like those of the Chinese and Native Americans, place great emphasis on the *past*. Such societies rely heavily on tradition and respect the advice and wisdom advanced by their elderly. *Present*-oriented societies, like those found in the Philippines and many Latin American countries, choose to live for today. In contrast to these past and present preoccupations, Anglo-Americans reflect more of a *future*-oriented society.[46] Consequently, we share beliefs that tomorrow will bring us greater health, wealth, and happiness. In the meantime, we collectively subscribe to the idea of working hard today while saving up for later. These general time-related orientations help shape our own actions and our interactions with and expectations of others. Because of our familiarity with this future orientation, we often find it difficult to understand how others fail to plan for their future in terms of their careers, family, education, and eventual retirement.

Communication as an Integrated Process

In previous sections our approach to discussing nonverbal communication has been analytical—that is, we have picked the process apart, element by element, showing how each complements or modifies our verbal messages. Using this kind of analysis we have discussed separately how meanings are aroused through the *things* we use (artifacts, clothing, and features of our bodies) or our *actions* (movements and gestures, voice, eyes, touch, and managing space or time).

At this point we need two notes of caution. The first is that the tendencies and generalizations we have pointed out are just that. They are probabilities greater than chance that people will act in particular ways; they are not iron-bound or universal laws of behavior. That is, even though some forms of nonverbal behavior seem supported by research and it makes intuitive sense to us, that does not mean everyone always behaves that way. Because that is the case, a particular generalization may fail to match up with our own personal observations or experiences.

The second note of caution is that all the nonverbal uses we have discussed need to be considered as a system of factors acting in a simultaneous transaction with one another. That is, all must be considered as a part of the simultaneous transactions model we set forth in Chapter 1. Thus, their influence on meanings of both sender and receiver is not element by element, but is a kind of integrated package. When people communicate they do so *as whole persons in a particular context.* In a simultaneous way, then, as they transmit verbal messages to each other, they frame their messages by using artifacts, movements, gestures, their voices, and their eyes. While doing those things they are also managing space and time. Thus, as we see the simultaneous transactions model developed more fully, it is clear that it is both the verbal and the nonverbal systems which do the communicating, rather than either of these elements alone. Finally, as we will see in chapters that follow, the influence of the context will have to be added as an additional part of this holistic view so as to understand the entire process.

The Importance of Nonverbal Immediacy

Viewing human communication as a holistic or integrated process provides insight into ways in which we use nonverbal communication to get others to like us— to establish friendships or develop closer relationships with others. Verbal communication is clearly a very important part of that process. At the same time, however, we can achieve and manage our relationships by simultaneously using a number of nonverbal behaviors as part of our overall communication strategy.

Because we use nonverbal behaviors to get others to like us does not mean that we do so in a deliberate, calculated, or even conscious way. Using nonverbal strategies to influence others to perceive us positively can be as unwitting and spontaneous as distancing ourselves from those we find unattractive or disgusting. Recognizing what we do to achieve those relational outcomes is an important part of developing an effective communication strategy. Once we know how to initiate or promote positive outcomes, we are in a better position to exert at least some degree of control over our own behaviors and, eventually, how others respond to us.

The use of nonverbal signals and actions that promote physical and psychological closeness with others is called *nonverbal immediacy* behaviors.[47] Immediacy is a product of a number of related behaviors contributing to perceptions of closeness, liking, or affect. According to Albert Mehrabian and others, the nonverbal immediacy behaviors which, when used together, result in those perceptions include smiling, head-nodding, forward-leaning, eye contact, touch, open gestures, and standing close to someone.[48]

In developing and maintaining close personal relationships, nonverbal immediacy is important. Verbal messages are supplemented with various actions and postures that contribute to perceptions of closeness, liking, and positive feelings. These include smiling, head-nodding, forward-leaning, touching, and eye contact.

Establishing a sense of physical closeness with some-one relies on what we have called proxemic, kinesic, and haptic nonverbal behaviors. That is, by moving closer, leaning forward, and increasing our use of touch we are effectively decreasing the physical distance between our-selves and another person. However, psychological closeness is more difficult to describe. Most of us have experienced that state when we locked eyes with that "special someone" across a crowded room. In other words, we need not be physically close to be psycholog-ically close with another. Instead, we might smile, nod our heads affirmatively, and maintain eye contact. Taken together, these particular nonverbal immediacy behav-iors all contribute to perceptions of psychological and/or physical closeness.

In order to understand the importance of immediacy behaviors, we need to consider a modern version of phi-losopher Jeremy Bentham's (1789) "principle of utility," which Mehrabian has applied to his **immediacy prin-ciple.**[49] Specifically, it maintains that people approach things and others they like or prefer and avoid those they don't like or don't prefer. According to the principle, ap-proach/avoidance implies physical as well as psycholog-ical and social distance. However, if we find ourselves together with someone we dislike, we're not always able to put distance between ourselves and the offensive in-dividual. In fact, we may find ourselves in the unenviable position of having to spend an entire evening sitting next to someone we loathe. Unable to rearrange the seating, or otherwise move elsewhere, we are forced to rely on nonverbal behavior to increase distance. We can do this by looking away, frowning, turning our body to the side, or leaning in the opposite direction. By such actions we are able psychologically to reduce or even avoid contact.

In more positive circumstances we may find ourselves near, but unable to talk in meaningful ways with, some-one we regard as special. The house may be full of guests or the folks may be staying up late watching TV. In that case, we are likely to initiate or simulate psychological closeness by gazing longingly, sharing smiles, and "ac-cidentally" touching one another.

One of the more fascinating results of the research on nonverbal immediacy behaviors is that immediacy often begets immediacy. That is, when we engage in nonverbal immediacy behaviors with someone, the probability is high that our target will respond in kind. For example, some individuals laugh in such a contagious way that an entire room can become hysterical. There are some professors who smile, joke, and give eye contact to reduce distance. Usually, the class reciprocates in like manner.

We know that using nonverbal immediacy behaviors is an effective communication strategy in efforts to develop positive relationships with others. Basically, this strategy works because when someone engages in immediacy behaviors with us, we often assume that they do so because they like us. And, when we see that the person apparently likes us, approves of us, and enjoys being with us, we feel like returning those feelings. Clearly, nonverbal immediacy behaviors are hard to resist. For example, even if you have had an argument with your best friend, it's extremely difficult to stay angry or aloof when she hugs you and tries to make you laugh.

Applying the Immediacy Principle

We suggested earlier that people usually do not deliberately try to develop nonverbal immediacy in a conscious way. However, there is no reason why that cannot be done. Should you discover that your supervisor or someone else who has control over your behavior is an ogre and picks on you, you might apply the immediacy principle. The next time you see him or her, go right up and shake hands. Initiate a conversation; smile a lot; give a lot of strokes, like head-nodding or laughing at jokes; and maintain eye contact. It probably will not have an effect right away. But keep it up and changes probably will occur. If all goes according to plan, you may find the individual responding to you in a much friendlier way. If you're still not satisfied with the results, try it again and again. It is very likely that sooner or later the person will come around.

One of the more interesting side effects of this planned use of the immediacy principle may reside with you. Over and over, students who have deliberately used the strategy report confusion in their own feelings toward the targeted other. They begin to reassess their own original assessment of the person and tentatively conclude that maybe, just maybe, he or she isn't all that bad.

Before you conclude that using the immediacy principle is the panacea for mending all bad relationships or for inducing everyone to like you, the drawbacks of using immediacy behaviors need to be understood.[50] All too often, people misunderstand nonverbal attempts aimed at eliciting psychological closeness. Some may misperceive our efforts as flirting, or even a blatant sexual "come on." Liking is one thing; total intimacy obviously is quite another. As we saw earlier, if a sexual invitation or an advance is not welcome (as in the workplace), the consequences can be devastating to all parties concerned. Thus, under certain circumstances, attempts at too much immediacy may not be a good idea after all.

Another potential problem is that immediacy often results in more, not less, communication with others. If that's what you want, fine. However, once you have initiated immediacy behaviors with someone, you may find it extremely difficult to limit or control the interaction. It is especially difficult if there is a need to terminate it gracefully. For example, it may be essential to initiate immediacy with a client in order to get a sale or close a deal. When the transaction is concluded, however, it's time to move on to other customers. However, the client may be unwilling to disengage from an interaction that was positive and reinforcing.

Generally, then, the principle of immediacy and the nonverbal behaviors comprising immediacy are among the most important strategies we can use to maximize our effectiveness as communicators. No other single aspect of nonverbal communication has been found to be more closely related to perceptions of liking and approval. When people engage in the immediacy behaviors of approach that we have just discussed, they are perceived by others to be more popular, well liked, responsive, and sensitive. Those who behave in opposite ways are likely to be labeled as aloof, unresponsive, tense, awkward, and insensitive. At the same time, as we have suggested, the principle of nonverbal immediacy has to be applied with careful anticipation of consequences.

Overall, this chapter has shown that nonverbal communication is an extraordinarily complex process. It is not a separate language by which we can read the secret thoughts and intentions of people, but a part of the transaction processes by which people simultaneously arouse meanings in others. As part of those processes, nonverbal communication includes the use of a great variety of things and many categories of actions. If techniques of nonverbal communication are well understood, however, we can use them to increase greatly our effectiveness as communicators.

Chapter Review

■ Nonverbal communication refers to the deliberate or unintentional use of objects, actions, sounds, time, and space to arouse meanings in others. Such cues do not constitute a separate code that is independent of our

Chapter 3   Nonverbal Communication   93

verbal communication. They are a vital part of the simultaneous transactions involved in ongoing communicative interaction.

- Although there is a mystique that would have us believe nonverbal behaviors reveal our true feelings and intentions while our words tend to hide truth, this idea is not supported in fact. Verbal and nonverbal transmissions rely on an interrelated system of symbols, signs, and signals with which people communicate their meanings to others.

- Nonverbal communication takes many forms. These include complementing our verbal meanings, regulating verbal interaction, such as in turn-taking, and substituting actions for words, particularly when we express strong emotions. At times our nonverbal cues can even contradict our spoken message. Overall, nonverbal communication can make our verbal message more easily understand; at other times, it can result in confusion.

- We use a great many "things" in our nonverbal communication. These include the body, which is capable of sending many kinds of messages. The broad category of "artifacts" identifies many other kinds of objects that we use in nonverbal communication. These include our dwelling and its contents, our car, and even the small objects—such as eyeglasses, jewelry, purses, and briefcases—that we carry or attach to our body.

- Clothing is one of the most meaningful of the artifacts we use to communicate nonverbally. Since the dawn of history, people have defined their rank, power, resources, personal tastes, and group memberships with the clothing they wear. Today, we dress to communicate such meanings as status and power, social acceptability, occupational role, sexual attractiveness, and inner feelings.

- Sexual communication in the workplace has become a widely discussed problem in American society. Some

behavior by males is grossly offensive by anyone's interpretations. However, many common forms of nonverbal, or even verbal, communication may be defined as joking and harmless by men while they are interpreted as disgusting and sexually threatening by women. Male and female meanings for such messages may be related to a traditional male culture reinforced by the mass media, significant changes in the status of women in society, and failures in role-taking on the part of many men.

- There are many kinds of actions that communicate meanings to others. Body movements and gestures (kinesics) are one example. The nonverbal use of the voice (vocalics) is another form of action providing meaning to those who listen to us. Using the eyes (oculesics) has long been considered an important means of communicating. Space and distance carry their own meanings. The study of touching as communication (haptics) shows that this form of nonverbal communication can transmit very important messages, especially to those for whom we have special feelings. Finally, time (chronemics) is associated with many kinds of actions that imply meanings.

- Taken together, many of the actions that we use in nonverbal communication—especially proxemic, kinesic, haptic, and oculesic behaviors—aid in establishing and maintaining closeness with others. These immediacy behaviors include eye contact, touch, forward-leaning, head-nodding, smiling, and others. In combination, these nonverbal behaviors of approach signal to others, "I like you and I care about you."

- Finally, even though this chapter analyzes nonverbal communication in an analytic manner, we need to keep in mind that we actually communicate as whole persons in ongoing situations.

Key Terms

Artifacts   Physical objects that we possess, such as jewelry, handbags, pens, and briefcases (or even homes, cars, and offices) that provide meanings to others about our personal and social attributes.

Body language   The idea believed by some that bodily actions, gestures, and other nonverbal behavior reveal more of our "true" thoughts and feelings than does our verbal behavior.

Chronemics   The study of the way in which people use time to transmit nonverbal messages.

Emblems   A category of nonverbal gestures that have established conventions of meaning providing direct verbal translations.

Frame   The use of nonverbal gestures or other actions while talking so as to emphasize, complement, and reinforce what we are saying.

Haptics   The study of touch as a means of nonverbal communication.

Immediacy principle   The generalization that people tend to approach things and others they like or prefer and avoid those that they don't like or don't prefer.

Kinesics   The study of body movements—including gestures, posture, and facial expression—that are used for nonverbal communication.

Nonverbal communication   The deliberate or unintentional use of objects, actions, sounds, time, and space so as to arouse meanings in others.

Nonverbal immediacy   Physical and psychological closeness to others, a condition that can be established through the deliberate use of nonverbal signals and actions.

Oculesics   The study of eye contact and pupil dilation in nonverbal communication as people use their eyes to indicate their degree of interest, openness, and even arousal.

Personal space   The immediate zone we carry around with us during our daily interactions with others.

Proxemics   The study of the meanings communicated by the use of space and distance.

Regulating   Using nonverbal signs and signals as informal "rules of order" to regulate the flow of talk among people who are communicating verbally.

Territoriality   A common tendency characteristic of both animals and human beings in which they define some fixed or semifixed space to claim or stake out as their own.

Vocalics   The study of the way in which vocal tones indicate meanings to others, such as that we are happy, sad, confident, nervous, culturally refined, boorish, and so on.

Notes

1. Fast, J. (1970). *Body language.* New York: Evans; Birdwhistell, R. (1955). Background to kinesics. *Etc., 13,* 1955, 10–18; Burgoon, J. K., & Walther, J. B. (1990). Nonverbal expectancies and the evaluative consequences of violations. *Human Communication Research, 17,* 232–265.

2. Mehrabian, A. & Farris, S. R. (1967). Influence of attitudes from nonverbal communication in two channels. *Journal of Consulting Psychology, 31,* 248–252.

3. Argyle, M., Alkema, F., & Gilmour, R. (1971). The communication of friendly and hostile attitudes by verbal and nonverbal signals. *European Journal of Social Psychology, 1,* 385–402; Argyle, M., Sater, V., Nicholson, H., Williams, M. & Burgess, P. (1970). The communication of inferior and superior attitudes by verbal and nonverbal signals. *British Journal of Social and Clinical Psychology, 9,* 221–231; Mehrabian, A., & Wiener, M. (1967). Decoding of inconsistent communications. *Journal of Personality and Social Psychology, 6,* 108–114; Burgoon, J. K., Manusov, V., Mineo, P., & Hale, J. L. (1985). Effects of gaze on hiring, credibility, attraction, and relational message interpretation. *Journal of Nonverbal Behavior, 9,* 133–146.

4. Dittman, A. T. (1987). The role of body movement in communication. In A. W. Siegman & S. Feldstein (Eds.), *Nonverbal communication and communication* (2nd ed.) (p. 37). Hillsdale, NJ: Lawrence Erlbaum.

5. Not all complementary framing is done with overt actions and gestures. Sometimes "nonverbal" cues are included in written or printed verbal messages. This is done not only by using phrasing that permits "reading between the lines" but also by including gesturelike cues. For example, we have all written and received letters where "Ha Ha" or "Just kidding" has been inserted into the text.

6. Regulators are acts that maintain and regulate the back and forth nature of speaking and listening between two or more people communicating. Ekman, P., & Friesen, W. V. (1969). The repertoire of nonverbal behavior: Categories, origins, usage and coding. *Semiotica, 1,* 49–98.

7. Duncan, S. D., Jr. (1972). Some signals and rules for taking speaking turns in conversations. *Journal of Personality and Social Psychology, 23,* 283–292; Duncan, S. D., Jr. (1974). On the structure of speaker-auditor interaction during speaking turns. *Language in Society, 2,* 161–180; Weiman, J. M., & Knapp, M. L. (1975). Turn-taking in conversations. *Journal of Communication, 25,* 75–92.

8. Collier, G. (1985). *Emotional expresssion.* Hillsdale, NJ: Lawrence Erlbaum. P. 95; Kendon, A. (1967). Some functions of gaze-direction in social interaction. *Acta Psychologia, 26,* 22–63; Exline, R. V. (1971). Visual interaction: The glance of power and preference. *Nebraska Symposium on Motivation.* Lincoln: University of Nebraska Press, 163–206; Burkhart, J. C., Weider-Hatfield, D., & Hocking, J. E. (1985). Eye contact contrast effects in the employment interview. *Communication Research Reports, 2,* 5–10.

9. Ekman, P., Friesen, W. V., & Bear, J. (1984). The international language of gestures. *Psychology Today, 18,* 64–69.

10. The use of the term *emblem* to describe nonverbal acts that have a direct verbal translation was introduced by: Efron, D. (1941). *Gesture and environment.* New York: King's Crown Press. See also: Ekman, P., & Friesen, W. V. (1969). The repertoire of nonverbal behavior: Categories, origins, usage, and coding. *Semiotica, 1,* 49–98.

11. Riccillo, S. C. Physiological measurement. In Philip Emmert & L. L. Barker (Eds.), *Measurement of communication* (pp. 267–295). New York: Longman.

12. Knapp, M. L. (1978). *Nonverbal communication in human interaction* (2nd ed.) New York: Holt. Pp. 21–22.

13. Berscheid, E., & Walster, E. (1972). Beauty and the best. *Psychology Today, 5,* 42–46; Algozzine, R. (1976). What teachers perceive—children receive. *Communication Quarterly, 24,* 41–47; Dion, K., Berscheid, E., & Walster, E. (1972). What is beautiful is good. *Journal of Personality and Social Psychology, 24,* 285–290.

14. Social psychologists in the sociological tradition refer to this generalization as the basis of the "looking-glass self," whereby people develop beliefs about themselves on the basis of the reactions others make to them. It is a concept developed by Charles Horton Cooley early in this century. See: Cooley, C. H. (1964). *Human nature*

and the social order (p. 185). New York: Schocken Books. (First published 1909)

15. Sybers, R., & Roach, M. E. (1962). Clothing and human behavior. *Journal of Home Economics, 54,* 184–187; Rosenfeld, L. B., & Plax, T. G. (1977). Clothing as communication. *Journal of Communication, 27,* 24–31; Taylor, L. C. & Compton, N. H. (1968). Personality correlates of dress conformity. *Journal of Home Economics, 60,* 653–656; and Molloy, J. T. (1975). *Dress for success.* New York: Warner Books.

16. Williams, M. C., & Eicher, J. B. (1966). Teen-agers' appearance and social acceptance. *Journal of Home Economics, 58,* 457–461.

17. The study of the expression of emotion with the use of the face and other parts of the body is an ancient one. It goes back to the 1600s when artists were concerned with ways to capture human emotion on canvas. A classic work is: Darwin, C. (1965). *The expression of emotions in man and animals.* Chicago: University of Chicago Press. (First published in London 1872)

18. Birdwhistell, R. L. (1970). *Kinesics and context: Essays in body-motion communication.* Harmondsworth: Penguin.

19. Ekman, P., & Friesen, W. V. (1948). The repertoire of nonverbal behavior: Categories, origins, usage, and coding. *Semiotica, 1,* 49–98.

20. Ibid.

21. Ibid.

22. Addington, D. W. (1968). The relationship of selected vocal characteristics to personality perception. *Speech Monographs, 35,* 492–503; Addington, D. W. The effects of vocal variations on ratings of source credibility. (1971). *Speech Monographs, 37,* 242–247.

23. Soskin, W. F. (1963). Some aspects of communication and interpretation in psychotherapy. Paper presented at the meetings of the American Psychological Association, Cleveland, 1963. Cited in Kramer, E. (1963). Judgments of personal characteristics and emotions from nonverbal properties of speech. *Psychological Bulletin, 60,* 408–420.

24. Scherer, K. R., & Oshinsky, J. S. (1977). Cue utilization in emotion attribution from auditory stimuli. *Motivation and Emotion, 1,* 331–346; Wiggers, M. (1982). Judgments of facial expressions of emotions predicted from facial behavior. *Journal of Nonverbal Behavior, 7,* 101–116; Manusov, V. (1990). An application of attribution principles of nonverbal behavior in romantic dyads. *Communication Monographs, 57,* 104–118.

25. Snyder, M. (1974). Self-monitoring of expressive behavior. *Journal of Personality and Social Psychology, 30,* 526–537.

26. Von Cranach, M. (1971). The role of orienting behavior in human interactions. In A. H. Esser (Ed.), *Behavior and environment: The use of space by animals and men* (pp. 217–237). New York: Plenum. Mazur, A., Rosa, E., Faupel, M., Heller, J., Leen, R., & Thurman, B. (1980). Physiological aspects of communication via mutual gaze. *American Journal of Sociology, 86,* 50–74.

27. Ekman, P., & Friesen, W. V. (1948). The repertoire of nonverbal behavior: Categories, origins, usage, and coding. *Semiotica, 1,* 118; Hocking, J. E., Bauchner, J., Kaminski, E. P., & Miller, G. R. (1979). Detecting deceptive communication from verbal, visual, and paralinguistic cues. *Human Communication Research, 6,* 36–46.

28. For a detailed discussion of this concept, see: Altman, I., (1975). *The environment and social behavior.* Monterey, CA: Brooks/Cole

29. The classic discussion of this idea is that of: Hall, E. T. *The hidden dimension.* Garden City, NJ: Doubleday.

30. Richmond, V. P., McCroskey, J. C., & Payne, S. K. (1987). *Nonverbal behavior in interpersonal relations* (pp. 118–128). Englewood Cliffs, NJ: Prentice-Hall.

31. Hall, E. T. *The silent language.* (1959). New York: Doubleday.

32. Watson, O. M. (1970). *Proxemic behavior: A cross-cultural study.* The Hague: Mouton.

33. Scherer, S. E. (1974). Proxemic behavior of primary school children as a function of their socioeconomic class and subculture. *Journal of Personality and Social Psychology, 29,* 800–805.

34. Sommer, R. (1969). *Personal space: The behavioral basis of design.* Englewood Cliffs, NJ: Prentice-Hall.

35. Ibid., p. 291.

36. Harlow, H. F. (1959). Love in monkeys. *Scientific American, 200,* 68–74.

37. Nguyen, T., Hesin, R., & Nguyen, M. (1975). The meanings of touch: Sex differences. *Journal of Communication, 3,* 92–103; Montagu, A., *Touching: The human significance of skin.* New York: Harper and Row; Heslin, R., & Alper, T. (1983). Touch: A bonding gesture. In J. M. Wiemann & R. Harrison (Eds.), *Nonverbal interaction* (pp. 47–75). Beverly Hills, CA: Sage. Thayer, S. (1986). History and strategies of research on social touch. *Journal of Nonverbal Behavior, 10,* 12–28; and Thayer, S. (1988). Close encounters. *Psychology Today, 22,* 30–36.

38. Montagu, op. cit., p. 75.

39. Adler, R., & Towne, N. (1990). *Looking out/looking in.* Forth Worth, TX: Holt, Rinehart, and Winston. Burgoon, J. K. & Saine T. (1978). *The unspoken dialogue: An introduction to nonverbal communication.* Boston: Houghton Mifflin.

40. Richmond, McCroskey, & Payne, op. cit., p. 138. See also: Watson, W. H. (1975). The meanings of touch: Geriatric nursing. *Journal of Communication, 25,* 104–112.

41. Montagu, A. (1978). *Touching: The human significance of the skin* (2nd ed.). New York: Harper and Row. Fisher, J. D., Rytting, M., & Heslin, R. (1976). Hands touching hands: Affective and evaluative effects of an interpersonal touch. *Sociometry, 39,* 416–421.

42. Despert, J. L. (1941). Emotional aspects of speech and language development. *International Journal of Psychiatry and Neurology, 105,* 193–222; Hill, S. D., & Smith, J. M. (1984). Neonatal responsiveness as a function of maternal contact and obstetrical drugs. *Perceptual and Motor Skills, 58,* 859–866.

43. Richmond, McCroskey, & Payne, op. cit., 1987, p. 141. See also: Montagu, A. (1971). *Touching: The human significance of the skin.* New York: Columbia University Press.

44. Andersen, P., & Liebowitz, K. (1978). The development and nature of the construct touch avoidance. *Environmental Psychology and Nonverbal Behavior, 3,* 89–106.

45. Richmond, McCroskey, & Payne, op. cit., pp. 177–179.

46. Malendro, L. A., Barker, L., & Barker, D. A. (1989). *Nonverbal communication* (2nd ed.) New York: Random House.

47. Mehrabian, A. (1971). *Silent messages.* Belmont, CA: Wadsworth; Mehrabian, A. (1981). *Silent messages: Implicit communication of emotion and attitudes* (2nd ed.). Belmont, CA: Wadsworth.

48. *Ibid.,* see also: Andersen, J. F. (1979). The relationship between teacher immediacy and teaching effectiveness. In D. Nimmo (Ed.), *Communication yearbook 3* (pp. 543–560). New Brunswick, NJ: Transaction Books; Andersen, P., & Andersen, J. (1982). Nonverbal immediacy in instruction. In L. L. Barker, (Ed.), *Communication in the classroom: Original essays* (pp. 98–102). Englewood Cliffs, NJ: Prentice-Hall.

49. Mehrabian, op. cit., p. 1. See Bentham, J. (1823). *An introduction to the principles of morals and legislation* (Rev. ed.). London: W. Pickering. (First published 1789)

50. Richmond, McCroskey, & Payne, op. cit., pp. 203–204.

Additional Readings

Burgoon, J. K., Buller, D. B., & Woodall, W. Gill (1989). *Nonverbal communication: The unspoken dialogue.* New York: Harper and Row.

> This is a relatively advanced textbook about nonverbal communication. It is well written and comprehensive in reviewing the relevant research literature. Innovative thinking is particularly apparent in the discussions about the relationship between the verbal and the nonverbal aspects of communication. Also important, the authors of the text are well known for their research in this area.

Burgoon, J. K., & Saine, T. (1978). *The unspoken dialogue: An introduction to nonverbal communication.* Boston, MA: Houghton Mifflin.

> This introduction to the study of nonverbal communication is suitable for the beginning student. Material is presented in simple terms in order to guide readers who are not familiar with this area. The book also provides undergraduate students with guidelines for communicating nonverbally. A great deal of emphasis is placed on the functions of nonverbal communication.

Knapp, M. L. (1978). *Nonverbal communication in human interaction* (2nd ed.). New York: Holt, Rinehart, and Winston.

> This is a revision of the first complete undergraduate textbook on nonverbal communication within the field. The chapters are well written and easy to read. Research from all of the social sciences is presented. Its numerous examples guide the reader through some relatively complex research findings.

Malandro, L. A., Barker, L., & Barker, D. A. (1989). *Nonverbal communication* (2nd ed.). New York: Random House.

> This undergraduate textbook provides an excellent overview of selected topics in nonverbal communication. Emphasis is placed on the body, clothing, movements and gestures, face, touch, voice, the senses, and culture. The book is clearly written and interesting. Numerous cases are included.

Richmond, V. P., McCroskey, J. C. & Payne, S. K. (1991). *Nonverbal behavior in interpersonal relations* (2nd ed.). Englewood Cliffs, NJ: Prentice-Hall.

> This text presents a consolidated overview of the field of nonverbal communication. Each chapter is short and clearly written, making it appropriate for the undergraduate. Notable extras in this book (as compared to others) are chapters on teacher–student and intercultural relationships. This book is suitable for both lower- and upper-division undergraduates.

Chapter 4

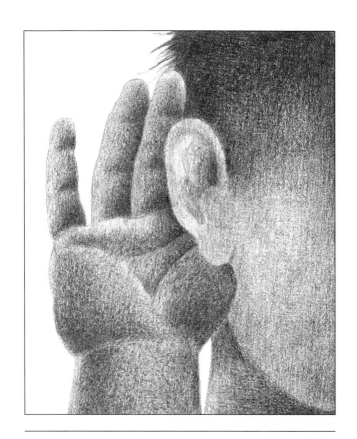

Listening as Communication

Contents

The Listening Process

Listening as Behavior
What We Gain from Effective Listening
  Acquiring needed information
  Evaluating and screening messages
  Listening as recreation
  Listening as a requirement for social efficacy
Actions Required of an Effective Listener
  Active versus passive reception
  Listening as observable action

The Listening Encounter

Sender/Receiver Reciprocity
  Responsibilities of senders
  Responsibilities of receivers
Sender/Receiver Similarity

Barriers and Misconceptions That Impair Listening

Inaccurate Assumptions About Listening
  "Listening is easy"
  "It's just a matter of intelligence"
  "Listening requires no planning"
  "Read better, listen better"

Five Barriers to Effective Listening
  Physical conditions
  Personal problems
  Cultural differences
  Prejudices
  Connotative meanings

Planning for Effective Listening

The Importance of Planning
Features of a Sound Plan
  Understanding our current listening skills
  Preparing ourselves to listen
  Controlling concentration
  Showing alertness and interest
  Searching actively for meaning
  Keeping active while listening
  Suspending judgment about message and source

Chapter Review

Key Terms

Notes

Suggested Readings

Key Questions

■ How is "listening" a critical feature of the communication process, and what does it mean to be an effective listener? In other words, does it really make any difference how hard one tries to listen to what other people are saying?

■ Do we really have to try to listen intently to everything that people say all of the time? That seems very difficult—and rather boring. How do we sort out what is important to listen to and what we can safely ignore?

■ How is effective listening related to the social skills that are important in modern society? In other words, how does listening play a part in developing abilities to meet people, get along with them, and effectively manage important social relationships?

■ What are the concrete steps we can take in order to improve our ability to hear what others are saying? Moreover, how do we do that when we don't particularly like those we are listening to or don't want to hear what they are saying?

"Weren't you listening?" [she asked]. "I guess not,"
[he replied]. He tried to pay attention now; he had to
force himself to concentrate. . . . He didn't intention-
ally "not listen," he just simply didn't hear all the
time, too easily absorbed in his thoughts.

Ridley Pearson
Under Currents, 1988

Mike glared at everyone in the executive conference room. He had just severely and publicly repri-manded one of his immediate subordinates. The rebuke was highlighted by the fact that it was Paul—Mike's right-hand executive director, who was being admon-ished for "not bothering to *listen* to what Mike was saying."

All of the other directors were stunned. They had always felt that Paul was Mike's favorite. None would have ever expected such open hostility during a staff meeting. Even more surprising was the fact that it was Paul's "lack of attention" which had aroused Mike's anger.

Although now calmer, Mike continued his point. His message was now more broadly targeted:

"Every one of us at this table," Mike said pointedly, "is paid one hell of a lot of money to do an effective job of managing the operations of this corporation. Whether any of you like it or not, *I* am the vice-president here. That means that I'm your *boss* and that I'm *in charge.* It is my butt that ends up in a sling when any one of you screws up! So, when I'm talking I expect every one of you to listen *very carefully* to *each and every word!* That also means that I better be able to *tell* that you are listening to me when I look at you! Do you all understand me?"

All heads nodded vigorously. Mike again focused his attention and concentrated his comments on Paul:

"I don't know how many times I have had to tell you, Paul, that most of your mistakes around here follow directly from your not listening to what I am telling you. Now 'read my lips.' You are officially on notice. If I sense again that you're not listening, I am going to put a letter of reprimand in your personnel file. And any subsequent failure to listen to me will bring even more severe disci-plinary actions! Do you understand me, Paul?"

Paul was sweating, and his back was pressed tight against his chair. The lines of tension on his face revealed the stress of the situation:

"Yah Mike," Paul said shakily, "I understand—and I am truly sorry. It won't happen again. I promise that I will always listen when you are talking and I'll *look* like it as well."

At this point, the time for Mike's next meeting had arrived and the weekly staff meeting was over. Mike pulled himself up out of his chair and indicated that he would "see you guys later."

When the staff meeting was over, and Mike had departed, Paul looked around and said apologetically:

"Well guys, I feel pretty stupid. Mike was really mad, huh? I had no idea that it looked like I wasn't listening. The fact is, I wasn't, and I didn't realize it. I guess my mind just wanders sometimes. I'm really sorry to have put the rest of you in such a difficult situation. I guess I did screw up, and I need to concentrate on what people say to me. I just had no idea that it was such a problem."[1]

———————————

Paul's tendency not to listen to his boss is by no means unusual.[2] We saw in the previous chapter that many men fail to listen to women in the workplace when the women object to the men's sexual messages. But listening failures are by no means restricted to the work environment. In fact, from time to time, all of us fail to take note of what people are saying, even if they are giving us vital infor-mation. Some of us may be like Paul, a chronically poor listener, and not be aware of it. The fact is, however, few people are truly competent listeners who are able to wring all of the meanings intended by the source out of every message they receive. At the same time, listening and making interpretations of meanings intended by senders is an integral part of communication process as we have discussed it in both our linear model and the more comprehensive simultaneous transactions model.

In this chapter we focus on the receiver and look closely at this essential part of the human communication process. We show that effective listening is not only im-portant as a part of developing a theoretical understand-ing of the basic nature of human communication, but it is also one of the most important communication skills.[3]

Why don't we listen to people at a high level of effectiveness? At least part of the reason is that we take listening for granted. We assume that we already understand what listening is all about, and therefore, there is no need to learn anything more. We also assume it is easy to be a good listener. In fact, like Paul, many of us probably assume we already have effective listening skills, even when we do not. Both of these assumptions are unwarranted. We cannot assume that our listening skills are already at a maximum, and we certainly cannot assume that effective listening is simple or easy.[4]

However, there is hope! Listening is a *skill* that is a result of *learning*. It is not "inborn"—we do not become competent as a listener because we inherit the capacity from our parents. We learn to attend to, analyze, and comprehend messages directed toward us, just as we learn other skills. What this means is that even someone like Paul can become an effective listener. Further, if the foundations of listening skills are understood, anyone can improve their ability to sort out more fully the meanings of what people are saying to them.

As with many aspects of human communication that we have already covered, listening is a complex process. But, like the other parts of the linear and transactions models we have discussed, listening is a process that can be analyzed in order to be better understood. Briefly

stated, becoming a more effective listener requires an understanding of our limitations, strategic planning for improvement, and systematic practice. If this sounds like hard work, you have just listened effectively!

This chapter will begin, then, with an analysis and description of the listening process so as to portray what each of us needs to know about its basic nature. Next, it will examine the process from one point of view of good and bad listening.[5] Finally, in a step-by-step fashion, it will discuss just how each of us can plan so as to improve our listening skills.

The Listening Process

Systematic efforts to unravel the behaviors involved in listening can be traced to social science research done as early as the 1920s.[6] Since that time, a considerable body of evidence has accumulated showing the important aspects of the process. We need, therefore, to define listening in a way consistent with that body of evidence. Unfortunately, over the past half century, hundreds of investigators have proposed different definitions of listening. In fact, to list and discuss even the more popular among them would require at least an entire textbook. Nevertheless, a basic definition is needed to identify the factors that warrant discussion.

Listening is an essential and active part of the communication process. While listening, a receiver attends to and perceives patterns of physical information transmitted by a sender, and transforms them back into the symbols and nonverbal cues into which the message was originally encoded. The listener then interprets their denotative and connotative meanings using his or her own schemata and other stored experiences in memory.

Listening as Behavior

For our purposes, we will define listening in a nontechnical way. It can be viewed as a form of behavior that is a part of the communication process—an active effort of attention and perception on the part of a person toward whom a message has been directed. In other words, it is part of the transaction that takes place between people as they communicate. More formally, **listening** is *an active form of behavior in which individuals attempt to maximize their attention to, and comprehension of, what is being communicated to them through the use of words, actions, and things by one or more people in their immediate environment.*

Most people think of listening mainly in terms of using the ears, attending closely to verbal messages. In our analysis, listening also refers to monitoring the nonverbal and contextual aspects of messages. We showed in the previous chapter the variety and subtlety of the meanings that can be included in messages by nonverbal means. Thus, in the simultaneous transactions view of human communication that we are developing, listening includes attending to and interpreting all of the ways in which people use words, actions, and things intended to arouse meanings in their receivers. Thus, it is more than just hearing spoken words.

Note also that included in the definition is the concept of "immediate environment." This refers to meanings that are included in the source's message due to the *context* in which the transmission takes place. Effective listening requires attention to those aspects of a message as well, because they can be both complex and diverse as influences on interpretation.[7] For example, what we interpret can be very different as we listen to people in familiar and unfamiliar places, to people we know very well versus individuals we have just met, in group situations versus one-on-one. Another kind of context is provided by different media that may be a part of the communication process—telephone, radio, TV, and so on. Each of these sets of conditions constitutes a different context, a different "environment," that has its own influences on the listening experience.[8]

We also emphasized in previous chapters that what something "means" to us is based on the accumulation of both indirect and direct experiences we have had during our lifetime.[9] This provides for a set of personal internal meaning responses for each of the huge number of symbols, gestures, rules, and so on that make up our language and nonverbal signs. Only when the sender's and the receiver's bases of experience are sufficiently *similar* can meanings of the parties involved be parallel, permitting individuals to share the same interpretations. Comprehension, therefore, depends immediately and directly on the existence of parallel meaning experiences, which can accurately be produced only by effective listening.

The preceding discussion implies that effective listening is no accident—that it is not an "automatic" form of behavior. While it is true that some aspects of listening are habitual or reflexive, others are certainly not.[10] Therefore, we cannot simply stand around talking to people and expect that high-quality listening is just going to "happen." To provide for accurate communication, both parties in the transaction need to be actively and consciously involved in attending to and comprehending what is being transmitted by the other by all of the means we have discussed.

To be done well, listening is something that we must deliberately and consciously *manage.* In other words, successfully attending to and comprehending what is communicated to us will be achieved only if it is deliberately set as a key objective—an objective we can achieve if we work hard and systematically. Furthermore, it is not a part-time pursuit. We must set this objective whenever we communicate with other people.

At the same time, it is possible to listen too intently! It would be impulsive, unreasonable, and even impossible to give our total attention to what is being communicated to us at all times, in all situations, and via all media. That would be a tidal wave of information with which no normal person could cope. Furthermore, much of it would be either a ghastly bore or a total waste of time. We can all think of any number of circumstances where we wouldn't want to involve ourselves intensely in the task of attending to and comprehending whatever information was sent our way. Stated more simply, an important prerequisite to effective listening is the acquisition of skills in discriminating between what we should pay attention to and what we can safely ignore.[11] The importance of being able to listen selectively but well is closely linked to the essential objectives or goals of the process.

What We Gain from Effective Listening

Listening serves at least three primary purposes in our lives.[12] There is some disagreement about their order of importance, but there is solid consensus that all three are part of this form of human behavior. One reason we listen is to *acquire information.* Another is for the purpose of *evaluating and screening* information as it is being presented to us. Finally, we often listen just for *recreation.*

Acquiring needed information   Obviously, some information is important and central to our well-being, whereas other kinds may be trivial. For example, when a person goes to the doctor to learn the results of a recent test for cancer, or AIDS, or another serious illness, that individual is in a situation where the information is extremely important. Even our friend Paul would become a very effective listener in such a situation. On being presented with the information that the neighbor's cousin planned to visit, however, most of us might be more like Paul at his worst.

Most information that we seek fits somewhere between these extremes. Much of it has some importance to us. Every student knows, for example, that on those days when, for any number of reasons, it is necessary to miss a class, the information presented will be essential to an upcoming test. It is one of the basic laws of higher education! When this situation occurs, most people seek out someone they know in the class to tell them what was said. Here, they will be at the mercy of their informant's ability to listen and comprehend the information that was discussed. In turn, their own ability to listen will govern how well they acquire the needed information from their secondary source. (This could be a kind of double jeopardy unless both parties are gifted listeners.)

At a low level of importance are all those daily messages that make up minor news and gossip about people, situations, conditions, or events of only limited significance to us. The key here is not to attend with bug-eyed intensity to all such information, but to develop the ability to monitor the ongoing information flow to which we are exposed. In that way, we can *sort out* that which has true significance in our lives. For that category, we can raise our attention to a high level of intensity and listen very closely indeed. To a large extent, then, our ability to discriminate *as* or even *before* we listen will determine the degree to which we can successfully screen important from trivial information and successfully attend to and comprehend the latter.

Evaluating and screening messages   We noted earlier that the second reason people listen is to *evaluate* information. This purpose is inseparably linked to that of information-seeking. We seldom just listen aimlessly or randomly, with the same level of attention to whatever is coming our way. Rather, as previously noted, we are usually on the lookout for specific forms of information that are important to us, at least to some degree. However, most of us are exposed to so many people, and to

We live in a daily tidal wave of messages. Only through selective listening can we acquire information that we vitally need. From the host of sources that transmit an abundance of messages to us daily, we learn to evaluate and screen out those that have little significance. We listen with care to those that have relevance to our needs, interests, or well-being.

such large numbers of messages, every day, that the overload is too much to handle.[13] We must be able to sort through and evaluate quickly both the *relevance* and the *accuracy* of the information we receive when interacting with others. As indicated earlier, we must be able to discriminate efficiently among the flood of information we receive, and select for more intense listening that which is both trustworthy and important to us.

In order to select information effectively, we need a set of **criteria** according to which appropriate judgments can be made. These will permit us to evaluate the *source* of incoming information and the *characteristics* of what is being said against whatever we have selected as standards for judgment. Such criteria are quite personal, but they are based on common sense and past experience and are not difficult to formulate. Such criteria would normally include ways of deciding whether a source is *credible,* whether what the person is saying is *believable,* and whether the message is *important* to us in any way.

Such criteria for selective listening provide grounds for judging the degree to which what is being heard is accurate or inaccurate, reliable or unreliable, and even honest or dishonest. For example, when a used-car salesperson solemnly tells you that "this car has only been driven to church on Sundays by a little old lady," is he or she credible? Are his or her claims likely to be true? If you detect a faint, painted-out sign on the door that looks

like "taxi," common sense suggests we should exercise caution. On the other hand, when the professor says, "We will have a test on Friday, and it will cover Chapters 6 through 10, plus the material covered in the lectures," common sense tells you to listen closely to this credible source, that the message is important and that it can be believed.

Effective listening for acquiring and evaluating information, then, does not occur in a passive manner. It takes place as we actively receive, interpret, and evaluate both the source and the message against those criteria that we believe to be adequate guides for accepting or rejecting what is said.

Listening as recreation   Of the three main reasons people listen, *recreation* is the easiest to discuss. A great deal of our listening comes under the heading of amusement, fun, or diversion. We engage in this form of listening when we socialize with relatives or friends, attend concerts, turn on our stereo, or view television. In fact, we listen recreationally in most interpersonal situations that are not defined specifically by our need to acquire accurate information. Recreational listening allows us to interact with people we like for the sole purpose of enjoying each other's company.

At the same time, all recreational listening may not be fun and games (so to speak). It all depends on how we

In selective listening, we learn to use a variety of criteria for judging the characteristics of the source and the trustworthiness of their messages. Invoking these criteria enables us to determine whether the source is credible and what he or she is saying is believable. In that way we can decide on appropriate actions, such as purchasing a used car that a salesperson claims has only been driven to church by a little old lady.

define what we are doing. The way we classify a particular listening experience can have a significant influence on what we perceive and how we interpret the incoming information. It may be perfectly harmless just to enjoy much of the listening that we do. However, when we define certain types of listening as "simply recreation," it changes our conception of the importance and quality of the information we are receiving.

In fact, classifying certain kinds of listening as recreational can be damaging. That is, when we use the term *recreation* we normally think of synonyms like amusement, diversion, entertainment, leisure, and relaxation. If we are listening in this mode, it is unlikely that we will be alert to certain kinds of information that might have real importance to us. For example, if a professor regularly provides a lot of entertaining jokes and interesting illustrations during his or her lecture, the important points of the presentation probably will be lost on students who have defined it as recreation. They will be able to remember the jokes and the amusing examples, but not the essential principles and concepts that were being illustrated. In fact, a great deal of poor listening that goes on in the world results from the tendency to think of the process as recreational. Consequently, students flunk tests and can't figure out why. After all, they came to every class and "listened carefully."

Listening as a requirement for social efficacy The term **social efficacy** means being competent as a social person—being able to form, manage, and maintain all kinds of social relationships in a positive manner. As we have indicated, success or failure in the vast majority of such human encounters will depend on how well we are able to listen to what people are communicating by verbal, nonverbal, and contextual means.

Learning to listen skillfully, then, is no trivial matter. It can spell the difference between a successful experience in the workplace, with promotions and rewards for effective performance, and stagnation in a dead-end job. Good listening skills are practical tools for developing smooth and comfortable social relationships on which professional success depends.[14] In fact, an important aspect of any form of work is just "getting along with the people you work around."[15]

Outside the workplace, effective listening contributes to successfully meeting people, enjoying the company of friends, maintaining family ties, initiating and maintaining a love relationship, and many other similar experiences. All of these activities depend largely on our ability to hear what people are telling us, to sort out the true

meanings of their messages, and to respond in ways that meet their needs.

Actions Required of an Effective Listener

We deliberately included the word *active* in our definition of listening, because the degree to which we actively listen to someone directly influences our effectiveness.[16]

Active versus passive reception Passive listening, that is, the passive reception of messages, occurs when little or no *effort* is exerted by a receiver. The kind of effort we are concerned with is that which contributes to our close attention to and careful comprehension of what is being communicated. Depending on the circumstances, there are a number of reasons people are passive listeners. Obviously, the causes of passiveness can include complex problems associated with mental and physical illness, but these need not concern us here. Usually, passiveness stems from conditions as basic as boredom, hunger, disinterest, and apathy. Of the four, the simple lack of interest is probably the most frequent.

Some people take great pride in their ability to avoid making an effort to listen. Some of these individuals can avoid listening, while successfully remaining unnoticed for their lack of effort. This is not to say that it is always bad to act like we are listening when we are not. In fact, we sometimes need to appear as if we are not listening when we really are, or vice versa.

Ironically, most people to whose messages we are exposed are absolutely sure that what they have to say is both profound and critical to our survival. They expect and even demand that we appear highly attentive. Typically, we give them what they want—we look and act like we are listening, even though we are not. We look observant, and perhaps nod wisely from time to time, but our mind is miles away. In some cases, this listening mode is totally justified. The problem is that it can become habitual. If it is used when information important to us is being transmitted, such passive message reception can result in a singularly unsuccessful listening experience.

Active listening, or the active reception of messages, occurs when the receiver makes a substantial effort to maximize attention to, and comprehension of, what is being communicated. As mentioned earlier, when the receiver exercises such effort, the likely result is not only greater attention and comprehension on the part of the receiver, but greater enthusiasm and appreciation on the part of the source. There simply is no better prerequisite to high-quality communication than the active reception of messages. It is almost impossible to listen closely without being actively involved in what is being communicated. That kind of feedback motivates the speaker and can make the entire transaction a far better experience than occurs when listeners are in a passive mode.

Our "activity imperative" applies even when a particular encounter ends in disagreement. Whatever the situation, if individuals listen actively, there is a very good chance they will have listened far more carefully to what the other has to say. Once understood, it may be that the differences between points of view are not as great as initially perceived. Effective listening, then, can be a beginning point for conflict resolution.

It is common sense that the degree to which we find a person interesting will dictate how much effort we exert to listen to what that person has to say. We have a tendency to disregard individuals who, at first glance, appear to be dull or uninteresting. A major problem is that truly interesting people are in dreadfully short supply. Fortunately, however, almost every person is interesting in *some* way. One key to becoming an effective listener is to try to look for and isolate at least one interesting thing about each individual with whom we interact. In this way, individuals who initially appear terminally boring or totally uninteresting can be redefined as worth listening to.

Listening as observable action   Effort and activity when listening, as we have discussed them so far, are internal or motivational characteristics. That is, they are factors that operate "in our head" to influence us as good listeners. Such internal factors are not observable by others. However, the characteristics of an effective listener can also be discussed as *observable actions* that make us "look the part." For example, what are the external and recognizable actions, expressions, and other behavioral signs that enable someone to identify and classify a person as a "good listener"? This is a very important consideration for understanding the relationship between a sender and a receiver.[17]

People easily recognize those who are actively listening to them in contrast to those who are "tuning them out." They do this by noticing a variety of signs or cues. It is not easy to describe what it is they look for or see, but the factors are real enough. If you stop and think about what we are saying, you can almost close your eyes and see someone you know who is a good listener. He or she has a certain way of reacting as you talk.

It is not enough to say that good listeners "look and act like good listeners."[18] Yet, as vague as this may sound, they do stand out from poor listeners. For one thing, good listeners focus their full concentration on individuals to whom they are attending, and their bodies communicate receptivity to what is being said. This is a very subtle nonverbal skill, but people who are concentrating on another's message tend to lean forward slightly, with eyes fixed on the speaker, and perhaps almost imperceptibly, they nod in agreement from time to time. The opposite is to stare off in the distance, with eyelids partially closed, perhaps arms crossed, leaning backward, and with a bored look or a slight frown.

Even a cursory examination of the face of a person engaged in active listening illustrates a variety of distinctive cues. Observable eye contact, an alert and amiable expression, and an obvious focus on the source person are all typical of the "look" of a good listener. In this way, then, a necessary (but not sufficient) condition for effective listening is being *perceived* and *classified* by others as a good listener on the basis of observable signs and behaviors.[19]

Looking like a good listener contributes to effective listening in at least two important ways: First, when someone is perceived to be a good listener, the person doing the communicating is likely to feel sympathetic toward that individual. Accordingly, the sender makes more of an effort to ensure that her or his message will be understood clearly. This is not easy. Making an effort to maximize understanding for the listener involves a great deal of what we called role-taking in Chapter 1. Role-taking is accomplished by means of *adaptation* on the part of the sender.

Adaptation is a central feature of our explanation of listening. As we are using the term here, **adaptation** refers to various ways in which both senders and receivers independently modify how they think and behave toward each other. The results of this modification or adaptation include a type of joint posturing that contributes to the sharing of meaning.[20] This idea of adaptation will become more relevant in subsequent sections of this chapter. For now it is enough to say that a good listener can influence significantly the amount of effort exerted by persons sending messages simply by "looking like" a good listener.

The second way that looking the part influences effectiveness occurs when a listener initiates a characteristic pattern of responses that others can identify. That is, conducting oneself in ways necessary to be perceived by others as a good listener requires that certain *standards* of good

To be an active participant in a communication process, and to make a positive impression on a sender, receivers have to "look like" they are listening. People talking always assume that what they are saying is important and that their listeners will be absorbed in the messages directed to them. Looking bored or otherwise inattentive is a very negative form of feedback and is sure to result in an unpleasant experience for the person speaking.

listening conduct are met. To be perceived as a good listener, a person must exhibit a combination of activities that taken together, are easily identified and associated with high effort and motivation. What is interesting about doing so is that performing these actions can actually change the person's habitual behavior.[21]

Let's take the case of a below-average listener like Paul, whom we described at the beginning of the chapter. Such an individual would find it very difficult to behave so as to be regarded by others as a good listener. In effect, it would involve changing deep-seated or habitual behavior patterns that have minimized this person's listening effectiveness. However, such deliberate attempts are important keys to improvement. If a poor listener takes the appropriate kinds of actions, a real transformation can take place. New listening behaviors can displace the habitual ones.

The underlying principle is that over a short time, people who work hard to try to create an impression of self tend to become what others perceive them to be. This means that if Paul, the ineffective listener, successfully exhibits the required "look," two conditions will likely result: First, he not only will *appear* to be a good listener in his work situation but also will *be* one. Second, if Paul's efforts toward change continue successfully in situations outside of work, the result will be a true transformation. Paul, "the problem case," will in fact become Paul, "the

good listener," not only to his boss but to everyone else as well.

The Listening Encounter

Our discussion of listening has included descriptions of the behaviors of both senders and receivers. We made it clear in earlier chapters that the actions of both are important and that communication is a transactional process where all parties are active. However, it is the receiver of messages who carries most of the burden in accomplishing the actual level of listening effectiveness. Nevertheless, if accuracy of communication is to be high, *both* (or *all*) of the individuals participating in an encounter must adapt to each other. To explain what we mean, we will continue our earlier discussion of adaptation between sources and receivers.

Active attempts to adapt can produce a number of positive outcomes for a listener. For example, adaptation helps to promote and maintain *attention,* which in turn can improve message *comprehension.* When this happens, communication *accuracy* improves, and the meanings intended by the source are more likely to be interpreted accurately—that is, in a parallel reconstruction of meaning by the receiver.

Sender/Receiver Reciprocity

We indicated that senders and receivers adapt to each other in order to minimize the influence of factors that can obstruct understanding of their messages. There are a host of such factors, including language limitations, personality differences, and membership in various social categories (defined by age, gender, race, education, and so on). Mutual adaptation is a means of getting around these potential barriers to accurate and easy communication. However, if this kind of adaptation is to occur, certain *responsibilities* must be met by both parties. By meeting these obligations, each will be able to communicate more accurately with the other. Thus, the responsibilities of being an adequate sender merge with those of performing as an effective listener. Only when these obligations are jointly met can communication accuracy be improved.

Successful adaptation to each other in a communication encounter, then, is a condition of *sender/receiver reciprocity*. This is a contemporary term that communication scholars use for what George Herbert Mead called "in-terpersonal adjustment" early in this century.[22] It is a process based on both role-taking and feedback, which are basic to both the linear and the transactions models discussed in Chapter 1. Feedback, as you recall, provides messages from a receiver back to a source revealing how the receiver is interpreting and responding to the message being transmitted. When each of the parties engages in both role-taking and feedback simultaneously, adapting their behavior to each other, they are engaging in **source/receiver reciprocity.**

Simple illustrations of such reciprocity are the following: If I begin to talk, you start to listen . . . which makes me more systematic in my presentation. If you cup your hand behind your ear, I talk louder . . . which causes you to lower your hand . . . leading me to speak more softly. If I make a joke, you grin . . . which makes me smile back. If I say something you like, you nod in agreement . . . which motivates me to provide more positive comments . . . which makes you blush. Or, at a somewhat more complex level, seeing that I am a woman, you avoid using certain four-letter words . . . which makes me feel that you are not being natural. Or, noting that you are a

Effective role-taking and active feedback are the bases for sender/receiver reciprocity. In this interactive process, both the verbal and nonverbal messages each communicator sends to the other result in a high level of understanding on the part of each as to how well messages are being understood and what reactions they are provoking.

male, I refrain from comments that might suggest any form of sexual interest . . . which leads you to conclude that I am "cold." At a very sophisticated level, you may mentally formulate a rebuttal to my argument even as I am presenting it . . . which leads me to anticipate just such a rebuttal, and therefore, I systematically incorporate counterarguments into my message.

Such sender/receiver reciprocity can be analyzed by looking at the role-taking activities and feedback signals and the consequent personal "adaptations" of each party, separately or jointly, as "reciprocity." Reciprocity, in other words, is the combined influences of such behaviors on *both* parties as they adjust to each other.[23] Thus, adaptation and reciprocity are similar, but not the same.

Understanding the need for reciprocity helps in understanding the responsibilities of both the source and the receiver. In the present analysis, because we are concentrating more on listening than on transmission, we will necessarily give more attention to the responsibilities of receivers. At the same time, the behavior of listening is so closely linked to that of the sender (because of the need for reciprocity) that it is difficult to isolate the responsibilities of one party from the other. However, using an analytic strategy, we can include a separate discussion of the obligations of each.

Responsibilities of senders Those responsibilities that are unique to the sources of messages include the following: a consideration of *what* is to be communicated, the *way* in which it is to be phrased, *where* it will be transmitted, *who* is to receive the message, and the *consequences* of what will be said. Taking each in turn:

1. Senders have a responsibility to understand *what content is to be communicated* before it is actually stated (see goal-setting as explained in Chapter 1, p. 14). Common observation indicates that much of the content that people communicate is not well thought out. In fact, poorly structured messages are common. This type of message confuses further the already difficult listening process. That is, how can receivers ever be expected to listen effectively if senders are lax in the formulation and preparation of the meanings they try to transmit?

2. Senders should consider carefully *the way a message is to be communicated* because this has a substantial effect on the way it is received. Should it be a formal statement, transmitted solemnly; or should it be said in an informal manner, with kidding and joking as a part of the transmission? Deciding how a message will be communicated

is part of planning how it is to be received. Obviously, then, how a message is sent will influence a receiver's ability to listen to it. There is no single or universal way to transmit messages effectively. It is the source's responsibility to select the way of sending a message that is most appropriate to his or her intended meanings and which will assist the receiver in listening to the full implications and nuances of what is being said.

3. In deciding how a message can be most effectively articulated, senders should consider carefully the importance of context—meanings added because of contextual factors. The context can control both how a message is interpreted and whether listening occurs successfully. As discussed in Chapter 1, there are many kinds of contextual factors. However, the real issue when engaging in role-taking concerning the setting is to make absolutely sure that the context is appropriate for the message to be communicated.

4. Individuals sending messages to others should be certain that the nature of the receiver, that is, *who* is to receive the message, is considered in the design of the message. This responsibility may seem too obvious to mention, but experience has shown that senders often ignore role-taking and are totally insensitive to their audience. They use words that their receivers cannot understand, phrasings that are inappropriate, and even words that can arouse hostilities on the part of their audience. As we have explained in earlier chapters, many kinds of people, such as women, minorities, the elderly, or people of specific national origin, can be sensitive to phrasings or words that imply a lack of awareness of their particular sensitivities. When such errors occur, listening effectiveness can be significantly reduced.[24]

5. Senders must consider the *consequences* of a message prior to its transmission. An old saying is that you "can't unring the bell." Back in Chapter 1 we noted the issue of *irrevocability* in communication—that you can't take back what has already been said. At one time or another, many of us regret having said the wrong thing to someone. It doesn't even have to be something that is obviously inappropriate. In fact, most of us avoid saying things to people that we feel will trouble them. Such communication seriously limits a receiver's ability to listen.

Generally, then, senders have a responsibility to phrase their messages in responsible ways, to deliver them in appropriate contexts, to understand the sensitivities of

One of the significant features of a message transmitted by a sender is that, once said, it cannot be taken back and its influence on the receiver conveniently erased. Individuals sending messages have a responsibility to understand the sensitivities of the people who will receive them and the feelings that they may invoke. This is especially important in a society made up of many kinds of people with different sensitivities.

their audiences, and to avoid clouding the task of listening by offering inappropriate content. If these responsibilities are abrogated, listening will be impaired.

Responsibilities of receivers   Just as senders have clear responsibilities, there are a number of obligations unique to receivers. These include being discriminating in the amount of *effort* devoted to a particular message, assessing the *intent* of the source, appreciating the implications of the *context,* understanding the *nature of the sender,* and avoiding *overreacting* to what is being said. We can look at each of these ideas more closely:

1. Receivers should determine the amount of *effort* necessary for both maximum understanding and comprehension of what is communicated. Effort is important to being an effective listener. However, not all messages are worth listening to, so receivers should be discriminating in their efforts to listen. The idea that all receivers are going to exert 100% of their energies whenever they listen is unrealistic! Most of us would wear out quickly if we listened intently in every encounter. But we should be able to determine from what is initially communicated

how important it is for us to make the considerable effort required for effective listening. This type of decision involves discriminating carefully among the goals we discussed earlier—information seeking, evaluation, and recreational listening.

2. Receivers should be able to understand the reason(s) *why* a particular message is being communicated. In some respects this responsibility is an extension of number one above. That is, receivers need to be able to distinguish between important and unimportant information. They also need to be able to identify information that is either relevant or irrelevant to them personally. The person who calls on the phone, unsolicited, with a sales pitch about why we should buy insurance against falling meteors, may not have our best interests at heart. Good listeners ask themselves such questions as: Why is this individual sending this message to me? Is what is being said important? Is what this person is saying worth what it will cost me to listen? The simple act of asking these kinds of questions can alter significantly the way a message is received.

3. Receivers should always consider *where* they are when interpreting a given message. There are a number of obvious reasons why where a message is transmitted can shape the way it is received. The social and physical contexts within which messages are transmitted and received can alter the way receivers listen. For example, two individuals at a job site discussing the solution to a work problem probably will be more attentive listeners than if they were to discuss the same problem in a bar after work. Declarations of undying friendship after the consumption of large amounts of alcohol may not have the same level of validity as those made under more sober conditions. As with the other receiver responsibilities we have discussed, the issue of discrimination is important. In order to be effective listeners, we need to be able to discriminate competently among various communication contexts.[25]

4. Receivers should take into consideration *who* is communicating the message when interpreting it. There are a number of ways to explain this particular receiver responsibility. One is in terms of source "credibility," or believability. Messages sent by trustworthy transmitters are almost universally listened to by receivers. Unfortunately, many of the people we come into contact with are not highly credible. How believable we perceive a sending person to be can vary substantially. Moreover, in certain situations, even if we don't perceive an individual to be particularly trustworthy, what he or she has to say may have the ring of absolute truth. In other words, who is speaking, as well as what that person says, can have an effect on the effort we are ready to expend to listen.

5. Receivers should make every attempt not to *overreact* to either what is being said or how something is being communicated. Often, receivers forget that an important and primary objective of all communication encounters is to come as close as possible to sharing meaning experiences. Failure to recognize this objective can arouse a variety of ill-advised responses to incoming messages. Inappropriate responses can decrease overall listening effectiveness. For example, if an individual compliments us on our appearance one day, it may be tempting to conclude that she or he is doing so because of a romantic interest. This may be far from the truth. Or, if on another occasion, an individual disagrees with our point of view, we might conclude that he or she "has it in for us" and is an enemy. Again, we may be way off target.

Sender/Receiver Similarity

We showed in Chapter 2 that the use of language in communication is possible only because human beings have an enormous *memory* capacity. Each of us learns and stores personal meanings and shared symbol-referent conventions in elaborate "schemata." Thus, we are able to communicate as we do because we have such a high capacity for learning and remembering.

Effective listening, of course, depends partly on that same ability to recall previous experience. That is, our ability to listen is based on the experiences we have had that parallel those of the source of the message. Listening cannot be effective unless we can experience some degree of *shared* meaning with the individual transmitting a message. This is what is meant by **sender/receiver similarity.** When we attend to and make an effort to comprehend what such an individual is saying, we will succeed or fail, depending on whether we can construct meanings that are the same or very similar to those intended by the source. Efforts to increase fidelity in communication are widely used in business and industry where the "bottom

Receivers have a special responsibility not to overreact to a message. Often, a person transmitting a message does not intend to arouse hostility or some other strong response, but it happens because of inappropriate reaction on the part of receivers. If that takes place, the prospects for further effective communication between the parties are drastically reduced.

line" is cost-effectiveness in the workplace. One corporation, a manufacturer of space satellites and vehicles, cuts the costs of hiring new people by creating new work teams out of previously unacquainted employees.[26] Whenever a new item is being considered for inclusion into the company's line of products, a group of current employees who have not previously worked together are assigned to work on the feasibility of the idea. This can raise the level of accuracy in their communications about the new product, which increases their efficiency and productivity.

Essentially, this is a problem in effective listening. We noted above that *shared experience* is one important key to competency in this task. Effective listening skills are an important component of the factors that enable people to work together efficiently and harmoniously as a team. Therefore, in forming such teams it is important to improve listening skills by providing opportunities for team members to share certain kinds of experiences. In particular, they need to get to know each other as individuals so that, in a team situation, they will be able to understand and anticipate how each of the others will assign meaning to the messages they send and receive.

Several approaches to getting employees acquainted very quickly have been tested. One particular procedure has proven to be quite effective. After the teams are created, provision is made for members to spend the time necessary to get to know each other well enough to be able to work together. This is done by providing for one-on-one interactions between all possible pairs in the team. After spending sufficient time in one encounter, individuals switch and pair up with another member of the team. This activity continues until each member of the work team has had a chance to get acquainted with every other member. Employees communicate with and listen to each other during all of these encounters. Because these are people who have already worked with the company a while and are familiar with the general type of work they will be doing, each has had experiences that can contribute to their understanding what other members will say to them. They are all members of the local community; they tend to be similar in terms of education; they have a similar income level; they tend to share a common life style; and they have many other characteristics and experiences in common. In short, because of these similar stored experiences they quickly become able to listen effectively to each other.

How does this example increase our understanding of listening skills in general? The important principle is that listening effectively is easy or difficult depending on the degree to which the sender and receiver are similar. For example, college students can communicate and listen to each other in such a way that accuracy is relatively high. They can do so even if they are from different schools because they share many common experiences. However, a college student and a person of similar age who went directly from high school to work in a factory will have a much more difficult time listening to each other effectively. The point is that similarities or differences in the ability of people sending messages to recall similar experiences for the construction of meaning (while listening) will help or hamper understanding. There really is no magic solution to the problems that dissimilar people have in listening to each other. This principle of the influence of differences must be kept in mind when attempting to listen to someone from a very different background. Additional listening effort probably will have to be made to try to grasp fully what that person is saying.

Barriers and Misconceptions That Impair Listening

In addition to those we have already discussed, a number of other factors can reduce our listening effectiveness, and, subsequently, the fidelity of our communication. These include several inaccurate *assumptions* that many people make about the process. They also include a variety of physical, cultural, and psychological *barriers* that need to be understood and taken into account.

Inaccurate Assumptions About Listening

Ineffective listening may result from inaccurate assumptions.[27] There are at least four common misconceptions made by poor listeners. These include the idea that listening is *easy*, that it is just a matter of *intelligence*, that it requires *no planning*, and that improving *reading skills* will improve listening.

"Listening is easy"   In our discussion about recreational listening, we indicated that thinking about listening as "fun" or "relaxation" changes the way we attend to and understand what is being communicated. A common misconception related to this idea is that "all listening is easy." Certainly, some of the listening we do is easy, but most of it definitely is not. As we have emphasized, effective listening is a complex activity that requires effort. Moreover, good listeners are not "born"; they are *made*—through hard work. Approaching listening with the assumption that it is effortless, amusement, play, or in any other way just "easy" is certain to lead to difficulties in interactions with others.

"It's just a matter of intelligence"   A second common misconception about listening is that all smart people listen well. The conclusion that seems to follow from such an assumption is that "I am smart, therefore I am already a good listener." Unfortunately, this is a *non sequitur* (not a logical conclusion). Recall our example of Paul. He is no dummy, but he is not a good listener. We are certainly not suggesting that dumb people make good listeners. What we are saying is that smart people, dumb people, or those in between can be either good or bad listeners.

"Listening requires no planning"   A popular belief is that because we engage in a great deal of listening every day, we need not plan in order to do it more effectively. That is, the large amount of listening we do routinely automatically makes us good listeners. This is a totally inaccurate assumption. It is true that all of us engage in a multitude of communication interactions every day, and that whenever we assume the role of a receiver in an interaction we do something that *resembles* listening. Unfortunately, most of us neither practice good listening skills nor have the ability to assess the effectiveness of our own listening behavior.

What do we actually learn, then, from most of the listening we routinely do on a day-to-day basis? We learn almost nothing. Effective listening follows from having planned carefully, not just from sheer frequency of doing it. (We will return to the topic of planning for listening later in this chapter.)

"Read better, listen better"   A rather curious but misguided assumption is that by improving our reading ability, we will also improve our ability to listen. This idea is founded on the belief that there is a transfer of what is acquired in learning one skill to another, even though what is learned is different. This is an interesting idea, but no educational research has shown that this transfer actually occurs. There are certain skills that can generalize across a variety of activities, such as being able to run fast, which probably would help in making a touchdown at a football game. But listening and reading are not based on enough common skills to allow for the same kind of transfer.

Five Barriers to Effective Listening

In addition to the incorrect assumptions just discussed, a number of additional barriers to effective listening need to be considered.[28] What we mean by a "barrier" is any condition, either in the context or one that is personal to the listener, which functions to reduce accuracy in communication. Most of these barriers to effective listening can be grouped into five broad categories: *physical conditions* that hamper the process; *cultural differences* between communicators that pose barriers to understanding; interference caused by *personal problems;* attitudinal *prejudices;* and the ever-present problem of *connotative meanings.*

Physical conditions   Although this may be obvious, it is surprising how often sheer physical noise can interfere with effective listening. Not so obvious is the fact that many people tend to ignore such obstacles and assume that they make no impact on their communication. Nothing could be further from the truth.

Noise interference can come from any number of causes external to listeners, and often these are beyond their control. They include sounds caused by printers, typewriters, lawn mowers, dishes, aircraft, or any other source that physically interferes with our ability to hear. Other types of external barriers are loud voices in the background that either distract us or limit our ability to receive messages. If a speaker cannot be asked to move to a quieter location, listening effort and concentration must be especially high.

Personal problems   The most obvious personal conditions that can pose barriers to good listening are those that affect us physically. Sickness, exhaustion, and discomfort caused by illness, all influence our ability to listen effectively. Overindulgence in alcohol, or even food, can leave an individual with a reduced listening capacity. Another set of conditions that can reduce personal well-being includes things we have on our mind that distract us—financial problems, a sick child, a stressful relationship with a loved one, or a preoccupation with a future event. We can also be so overextended at work or study that we are unable to concentrate effectively on other matters.

Cultural differences   Many of the problems of ineffective listening are brought about by cultural differences between the communicating parties. We saw in the previous chapter that women in the workplace often find that men "just don't get it" when they repeatedly tell

Receiver Apprehension Test (RAT)

Instructions   The following statements apply to how various people feel about receiving communication or listening to others. Indicate if these statements apply to how you generally feel by noting whether you:

5 strongly agree   2 disagree
4 agree   1 Strongly disagree
3 neutral/undecided

_____ 1. For the most part, I feel comfortable when listening to others on the phone.

_____ 2. It is often difficult for me to concentrate on what others are saying.

_____ 3. When listening to members of the opposite sex, I find it easy to concentrate on what is being said.

_____ 4. I have no fear of being a listener as a member of an audience.

_____ 5. I feel relaxed when listening to new ideas.

_____ 6. I would rather not have to listen to other people at all.

_____ 7. I am generally overexcited and rattled when others are speaking to me.

_____ 8. I often feel uncomfortable when listening to others.

_____ 9. My thoughts become confused and jumbled when reading important information.

_____ 10. I often have difficulty concentrating on what others are saying.

_____ 11. Receiving new information makes me feel restless.

_____ 12. Watching television makes me nervous.

_____ 13. When on a date I find myself tense and self-conscious when listening to my date.

_____ 14. I enjoy being a good listener.

_____ 15. I generally find it easy to concentrate on what is being said.

_____ 16. I seek out the opportunity to listen to new ideas.

_____ 17. I have difficulty concentrating on instructions others give me.

_____ 18. It is hard to listen or concentrate on what other people are saying unless I know them well.

_____ 19. I feel tense when listening as a member of a social gathering.

_____ 20. Television programs that attempt to change my mind about something make me nervous.

Calculating Your Score

1. Add together your responses to items 1, 3, 4, 5, 14, 15, and 16 = _____.

2. Add your responses to items 2, 6, 7, 8, 9, 10, 11, 12, 13, 17, 18, 19, and 20 = _____.

3. Complete the following formula:

   RAT = 42 − Total from step 1 = _____.

   Then, + Total from step 2. YOUR TOTAL RAT SCORE = _____.

References

The original RAT was developed by Buddy Wheeless and can be found in:

Wheeless, L. R. (1975). An investigation of receiver apprehension and social context dimensions of communication apprehension. _Speech Teacher, 24,_ 261–268.

For research supporting the validity of this scale, see:

Beatty, M. J. (1981). Receiver apprehension as a function of cognitive backlog. _Western Journal of Speech Communication, 45,_ 277–281.

Beatty, M. J., Behnke, R. R., & Henderson, L. S. (1980). An empirical validation of the Receiver Apprehension Test as a measure of trait listening anxiety. _Western Journal of Speech Communication, 44,_ 132–136.

Interpreting Your Score

Possible range of scores for the RAT: 20–100. (If your own final RAT score does not fall within that range, you made a computational error.)

The average or median score for the Receiver Apprehension Test (RAT) is 60. Higher scores reflect greater receiver apprehension. If you scored above 70 (or even above the median of 60), you are considered high in receiver apprehension. Because your level of RAT is dispositional or traitlike in nature, we know that, as a rule, high RATs have trouble processing information from others. That is, high RATs tend to miss out on crucial information while listening to others, and they often misinterpret the information they do receive. Research indicates that individuals high in receiver apprehension experience more anxiety while listening to difficult or provocative material. Moreover, high RATs are negatively associated with the amount of information they assimilate on a variety of topics. In other words, high RATs experience more anxiety while listening, and that anxiety interferes with their ability to concentrate or process information.

If you scored low in RAT (below 50 or the median of 60), you aren't as likely to experience the same kinds of listening problems that high RATs do. Low RATs are able to adjust to others and focus actively and attentively on what others are saying. Without the anxieties that high RATs experience, low RATs are able to comfortably process large amounts of information, and what they do process is likely to be more accurately interpreted or perceived.

Many of us are more moderate in our receiver apprehension (between 50 and 70). Consequently, we are more situational in how we listen to or process information. Sometimes we may have more difficulty listening than at other times; moreoever, it may be easier to listen to particular individuals more than others. The truth is, we may occasionally *need* some level of arousal when listening to others—to prevent us from becoming too comfortable and falling asleep on the speaker.

them that sexual advances are inappropriate in that setting. This is a classic case of a cultural barrier to effective listening. We saw that in part this communication failure is brought about because of major differences in the cultural worlds of traditional males versus contemporary working women. Many men do not feel they have to listen because they already "know" how women feel and what they want, namely, the very attentions women find objectionable.

Differences in cultural beliefs of this kind occur widely. Individuals from low-income backgrounds can have difficulty in listening to the affluent; management may not listen carefully to the complaints of labor; those from dominant groups in society do not always hear what minority people are saying. In all of these situations, pre-existing systems of beliefs are shared within a particular group. Those beliefs define various features of reality and make it difficult to hear what is being said by persons who have different interpretations of those same features.

Prejudices A fourth set of barriers to effective listening, personal **prejudices,** come from certain cultural differences found among various kinds of people in society. Thus, individuals may share with others like themselves negative attitudes based on unrealistic beliefs regarding a particular category of people (e.g., see "stereotypes," pp. 51–53). Common examples are anti-Semitism, shared biases among whites concerning African-Americans, and so on. The personal behavior resulting from such shared beliefs is a tendency to "prejudge" *any* member of the negatively defined category, regardless of that person's individual merits.

Such prejudices can pose significant barriers to effective listening. They prevent us from perceiving and understanding the actual characteristics, abilities, or intentions of an individual simply because he or she is a member of the negatively defined category. Thus, it doesn't matter what that individual is actually saying, the message is perceived within the framework of the stereotypes and other negative beliefs that are the basis of the shared prejudice.

Prejudices can truly mislead us because, like the traditional males in our discussion of sexual harassment, we may not even know we hold a particular bias. Thus, such an unwitting predisposition can influence how we listen, or fail to listen, without our actually realizing it. We are not referring here just to well-documented prejudices, such as those focusing on race or ethnicity. They are obviously important. Beyond those, we may have a difficult time listening objectively to someone of virtually *any*

Barriers to Effective Listening

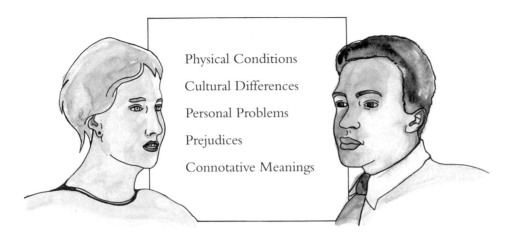

Physical Conditions

Cultural Differences

Personal Problems

Prejudices

Connotative Meanings

kind of category if we are convinced that such people usually lack judgment or cannot perform effectively in some areas. For example, we may "tune out" individuals who do not have a college education, who have limited income, who are older, or younger, assuming that they could not possibly appreciate the concerns and viewpoints of someone like ourselves. Particularly subtle are prejudices concerning physical attractiveness. We noted in Chapter 3 that many people tend to overrate the competence and capacities of males or females who are unusually handsome or beautiful, while seriously underestimating the abilities of those who are unattractive or disabled.

Generally, then, prejudice against categories of people is an especially difficult problem in listening. We noted in Chapter 2 that in all acts of perception we use labeled categories as "concepts" to "make sense" out of the world around us. We have to do that to achieve efficiency in coping with aspects of reality we encounter repetitively. However, if we have prejudices toward a labeled category of people, listening to what one of them is actually saying is influenced by the schemata of beliefs we have constructed for that entire category. Like the mirrors in amusement parks that distort images, such prejudicial schemata cause misleading interpretations that contort the meanings we construct as we process their messages. That is, our beliefs about the entire category in which that person can be classified become part of her or his incoming message. In this way, we construct meanings and interpretations that were never intended by the source of the message, and the index of fidelity is reduced as accuracy is eroded.

Connotative meanings   A final category of barriers to effective listening is represented by the *connotative* meanings we read into messages. As we explained in Chapter 2, connotative meanings are those personal, subjective, and unshared interpretations we have for verbal and nonverbal symbols and signs. Obviously, these are not part of the meanings intended by the source, and when we build them into our interpretations of an incoming message, listening is impaired and accuracy in the communication is reduced.

The influence of connotative meanings on accuracy is a vexing one. It stems from the fact that both senders *and* receivers have connotative meanings associated with the symbols used in a message. The former unwittingly use them in encoding messages; the latter in decoding and interpretation. It is a vexing problem because it is hard to detect. We have all come away from encounters feeling that we completely understood and totally agreed with someone. Later we discover that the other person recalls a completely different version of what took place and what we thought the agreements were! Often, we conclude that the person either has a faulty memory or is deliberately misrepresenting what was said. What we may be experiencing in this situation is an erosion of accuracy in communication due to the very different connotative meanings in the encoding/decoding processes of sender and receiver.

What can be done about this influence on listening? Very little. Usually, neither party realizes they are failing to separate connotative and denotative meanings. However, as listeners, we can be aware of the problem. If we find ourselves in that stressful situation of recalling a communication differently than the other person, we can then search for sources of connotative confusion brought into the transaction by each individual.

Planning for Effective Listening

We have emphasized repeatedly that effective listening is a critical communication skill; that it can be learned; and that it requires both effort and planning. This chapter has provided an analysis of the overall listening process, the characteristics of good and bad listening, and the sources of various barriers to effective listening. All of this is intended to provide a solid foundation for thoughtful planning so as to be able to perform this vital task better.

The Importance of Planning

In this chapter, we have presented in a systematic manner the principal factors that can provide the basis of an effective plan for improving personal listening skills. Clearly, the details of such a plan will depend greatly on the personal characteristics and circumstances of individuals, the kinds of communication situations they frequently encounter, the degree of their determination to learn and improve, and their current level of skills.

However, before discussing the general features of such a plan, it seems fair to ask: Is it *really necessary*, or even realistic, to work out a systematic personal plan for effective listening? Or is this just some kind of odd "academic exercise"? The answer is that it is entirely up to each individual. The decision will depend on some combination of one's goals and aspirations, plus one's motivations and self-discipline. However, one thing is certain—ineffective listeners with low motivation are *not* likely to formulate such a plan, and they are *most* likely to be unable to improve their skills. If that is the case, as we have shown, the consequences will be bleak.

Those who really want to improve their listening skills need to recognize at the outset that it will have costs. No one claims that it is easy, or that it is even enjoyable, and it may seem like more trouble than it is worth. However, in deciding whether to use the guidelines provided by this chapter to develop a systematic plan to improve listening skills, the following points are worth considering: As we have forcefully emphasized, in today's complex world, *social* skills are far more important than manual or even technical ones. It is those individuals with high competency in relating to and influencing people of all kinds of backgrounds and cultural origins who become executives, administrators, successful professionals, and (generally) leaders in their fields. Those social skills depend heavily on being able to communicate effectively, which as our simultaneous transactions model shows, includes being a first-rate receiver and listener.

Features of a Sound Plan

Developing a strategy for effective listening involves incorporating all of the factors we have discussed in this chapter. Such a plan can be viewed as a series of steps we can take to make use of those features that will improve both our listening skills and our ability to interpret messages more accurately. Listed below are seven specific activities that provide the broad outlines for improving competence in listening.

Understanding our current listening skills The first step in assembling our listening plan is to make sure we clearly understand our present level of skills as listeners. Because each person is a unique personality, and because there are important individual differences (in attitudes, intelligence, interests, and many other factors) between people, each of us performs the role of listener in a somewhat unique way. Communication scholars designate these individual characteristics that have an influence on our own communication accuracy as **receiver eccentricities.** Simply put, they are those personal attributes and individual personality differences that help or hinder our capacity to receive and interpret messages accurately.

Logically enough, before we can begin to refine our listening skills, we need to identify our current strengths and weaknesses as listeners—our receiver eccentricities. These will be the foundation on which to develop a plan as we attempt to improve as listeners. Remember, our overall objective is to sharpen our skills while minimizing our weaknesses. Part of minimizing weaknesses involves the "unlearning" of poor listening habits and replacing them with good ones.

To illustrate, are there any personal problems, illnesses, or stressful conditions in our lives that will reduce our listening effectiveness? Can we understand people whose cultural characteristics are different from our own? Do we understand our personal prejudices well enough so that we can listen closely to what people of all kinds are really saying? Are we making inaccurate assumptions about the listening process of the kind we discussed earlier? Perhaps all of those problems, if they are present,

Features of a Sound Listening Plan

Understanding your current listening skills

Each of us is a unique individual who performs the task of listening in characteristic ways. The individual attributes that influence how well you listen are called your *receiver eccentricities.* You need to understand your own eccentricities as a beginning point for an effective listening plan.

Preparing yourself for listening

Begin to prepare yourself by understanding the concept of *sender/receiver reciprocity.* This requires that you be open and sensitive to all kinds of source persons and to the content of what they are saying.

Control your concentration

This requires learning to concentrate actively on what a person is saying. Such concentration rests on the distinction between *active* and *passive* listening. Such concentration must be selective, of course, with the greatest effort directed toward important messages and irrelevant ones screened out.

Show alertness and interest

It is important to *appear* to be listening, even if your attention sometimes wanders from what a speaker is saying. The act of trying to show interest actually does result in more effective attention to and understanding of a sender's message.

Search actively for meaning

Search actively for the *essential meanings* in messages being sent by a source, and summarize them on an ongoing basis in your own terms. Seek every clue to take into account how the sender's special background may influence what is being said.

Keep active while listening

This can be difficult, but it pays off. Avoid slipping into a passive manner of receiving, with accompanying daydreaming and distraction. Keeping active may require *changes in behavior,* such as adjusting posture, more active breathing, or other shifts away from a relaxed mode.

Suspend judgment about message and source

Premature judgments about a person's intentions, qualifications, or actual positions can interfere with what is being said. It is essential, therefore, to *withhold early closure* about the real meanings being transmitted, and wait until after the entire message has been heard.

cannot magically be set aside. But bringing them to a level of awareness is the first step toward minimizing their negative impact on our listening skills.

Preparing ourselves to listen   In the second step of the planning process we begin to prepare ourselves to listen. As we have discussed previously, effective listening is largely a product of the attained degree of what we discussed as adaptation and reciprocity between senders and receivers. Preparing ourselves for listening, then, requires that we be sensitive in relating to others. We must be open to all kinds of source persons and receptive to what they are saying.

One way of preparing ourselves for this type of receptivity is to guard as much as possible against any hidden barriers to listening effectiveness. Part of this activity requires that we be ready to make an effort to fulfill those receiver responsibilities considered earlier. A useful analogy is that we have to be like a runner who is warming up and getting ready for the upcoming race. This means preparing ourselves to adapt to the speaker and achieve the required level of sender/receiver reciprocity. It also means anticipating the need to expend effort, to assess the intent of the person transmitting the message, to understand the implications of the context, and recognizing the danger of overreacting.

Controlling concentration   The third step of planning places an intense emphasis on controlling our level of concentration. Here we begin to expend the effort needed to be a good listener. This step addresses the question: How actively do we concentrate on what others say to us? What we are considering here is related to our earlier discussion of active versus passive listening. Remember, our approach is based on the idea that effective listening is no accident. It requires that we deliberately and consciously attend to and try to comprehend what is being communicated to us. At the same time, a good listening plan will allow us to maintain a reasonable amount of control over our concentration. As we noted earlier, some messages need not be given the same level of attention as others. When they seem important, however, the time has come to *really* concentrate.

Showing alertness and interest   The fourth step in a good plan is to decide how effectively we show or demonstrate alertness and interest to a sender when we listen. Recall Paul, who was reprimanded by his boss so harshly for not *appearing* to be listening. In earlier sections we discussed what good listeners "look like"—that is, how they engage in specific kinds of overt behaviors which lead senders to believe they are listening intently to what is being said. No suggestion was made that this should be "faked." Looking the part does, in fact, improve communication accuracy. Often, senders will try to communicate more effectively when they have a good listener.

Searching actively for meaning   The fifth step in a listening plan is to provide for deliberate concentration on the intended meaning of messages. That is, in this step we need to develop ways to construct for ourselves the meaning the source intends. This requires that we understand any significant cultural differences between ourselves and the source as well as grasp how our personal prejudices may distort meanings of messages from people who are different from us. We can engage in reverse role-taking by trying to understand the purposes of the source's choice of symbols, nonverbal cues, and rules of syntax and grammar. This brings us back to our earlier notion of sender/receiver reciprocity. Our point here is that if we are to comprehend messages accurately, we need to look for *every clue* as to what the person is trying to say. Here we take into account the person's characteristics, possible connotative meanings, and implications of the setting or context. If in doubt we can ask questions, provide feedback, and follow up with requests for further details. Only if all of these strategies are used effectively in our constructions of intended meanings will communication be accurate.

Keeping active while listening   A sixth part of a good plan is to consider ways that will help us maintain a high level of activity during listening. Many people would like to be effective listeners but simply refuse to be active during the process. Some can't seem to exert any effort at all. Other individuals truly intend to listen actively, and they expend the necessary effort in the initial stages of an encounter. But for one reason or another, as communication proceeds their level of activity declines. Motivation subsides; the degree of effort decreases; and they misinterpret the message. In all probability, most of us have experienced such decreases in activity for one reason or another. Consequently, this is a critical step in the formulation of a good listening plan.

Maintaining our determination to listen is a little like "psyching ourselves up" to run a race. Numerous competitors have lost a race because they failed to develop the right mental outlook. Also, a runner must actually cross the finish line first in order to be the winner, not just lead most of the way. In the context of listening, our efforts to attend to and comprehend messages need to last the duration of the entire encounter. If listening deteriorates before our interaction is finished, we will likely miss something critical. Unfortunately, there are no "magic keys"—no universally effective approaches—to maintaining a high level of listening activity. The only suggestion we can offer is that each of us needs to use whatever personal resources and determinations that are within us to continue listening until the sender has completed transmitting his or her message. Only one thing is certain: It is not an easy task.

Suspending judgment about message and source   The final aspect of a good listening plan is to recognize the need to minimize any tendency we might have to make premature judgments about either the source person or the message. Recall our discussion of barriers to listening. We emphasized the problem of both cultural differences and personal prejudices. We noted that both serve as the basis of selective perception and that they shape many of our judgments. How we feel about a sender influences what we construct from the messages we receive from that individual.

It is not easy to separate one's feelings about the person, and the labeled categories he or she represents, from the meanings of a message that the individual is sending. However, if we can recognize our idiosyncratic biases, we should take them into account in our listening plan. This kind of deliberate assessment of our own predispositions flags problem areas for us. Having an awareness of these limitations on objectivity provides us with an important insight we need to limit their influences on us.

In overview, the preceding seven-part plan is complex. It may not be possible to start doing all of the activities at the same time, but even if you can be successful at one or two as a start, your listening skills will have improved. Later, additional parts can be incorporated.

Chapter Review

- Effective listening is one of the most important of all communication skills. Fortunately, it is one that we acquire as a a result of learning. This means that it can be analyzed, understood, and improved.

- Listening can be defined as a process in which individuals make the effort necessary to maximize their attention to, and comprehension of, what is being communicated to them by one or more people in their immediate environment. In short, it means playing an active part as a receiver in the transactions that make up accurate human communication.

- People listen to acquire information they need, to evaluate incoming messages, and for recreation. However, defining most listening as recreational can be problematic, leading us to ignore or treat lightly information that may be critical to our goals.

- Learning to listen well is an important part of getting along with others, influencing people, and getting them to think of us in positive terms, and this skill helps us to understand the requirements of a wide variety of social situations. These are the activities that can spell the difference between success and failure in many kinds of social circumstances and relationships.

- While passive listening is perfectly all right for some activities, a far more active effort is often required. Looking the part is an important strategy. Overt actions, expressions, bodily postures, eye contact, or other signs that one is concentrating on a speaker provide incentives for that individual to try to communicate clearly.

- During the listening encounter, a condition of reciprocity develops between source and listener if the communication is successful. This reciprocity depends in part on the degree to which sender and receiver have fulfilled their mutual responsibilities toward each other. Each makes adjustments to the needs and requirements of the other.

- Senders' responsibilities include formulating messages clearly, using an appropriate style of transmission, being aware of the influence of context, understanding the unique characteristics of the receiver, and assessing ahead of time the possible consequences of the content. Receivers' responsibilities include being discriminating in the amount of effort devoted to listening to a particular message, assessing the intent as well as the nature of the sender, appreciating the implications of the context, and avoiding overreacting to what is being said.

- Listening effectiveness is reduced to the extent that people assume listening is easy; that it is just a matter of intelligence; that it requires no planning; or that because they read well, they listen well. It can also be hampered by physical conditions, personal problems, prejudices, and connotative meanings.

- Barriers to effective listening arise from five major sources: physical conditions, personal problems that are distracting, cultural differences that exist between sender and receiver, personal prejudices that lead to distorted perceptions of senders, and connotative meanings that make it difficult to reconstruct what another person is trying to say.

- A systematic plan to improve listening skills includes understanding our current skills, preparing to listen, controlling levels of concentration, showing alertness and interest, searching for the full meaning of a message, maintaining a high level of effort, and suspending judgments that can be influenced by biases and prejudices.

Key Terms

Adaptation   Various ways in which both message senders and receivers independently modify how they think and behave toward each other during the transmitting and receiving processes.

Criteria (in listening)   Standards by which we decide whether a source or sender is credible, whether what the person is saying is believable, and whether the message is important to us in any way.

Listening   An active form of behavior in which individuals attempt to maximize their attention to, and comprehension of, what is being communicated to them through the use of words, actions, and things by one or more people in their immediate environment.

Prejudice   A configuration of emotionally held beliefs that results in a person making judgments about another individual before he or she even begins to communicate or interact.

Receiver eccentricities   Personal attributes and individual differences that help or hinder our capacity to receive and interpret messages accurately.

Sender/receiver reciprocity   Successful adaptation to each other in a communication encounter by engaging in both role-taking and feedback simultaneously.

Sender/receiver similarity   A condition in which both the message sender and the receiver have had sufficiently similar learning experiences in their language community so as to have acquired parallel meanings for verbal and nonverbal signs and symbols.

Social efficacy   Being competent as a social person—that is, being able to form, manage, and maintain all kinds of social relationships in an effective manner.

Notes

1. This account is based on an actual incident that occurred when one of the authors was serving in an executive role in a major corporation.

2. Listening problems are endemic in industry. In a recent survey of training directors in Fortune 500 industrial and Fortune 500 service corporations, 59% of those studied reported that they had formal training programs for employees to improve their listening skills. See: Wolvin, A. W., & Coakley, C. G. (1991). A survey of the status of listening training in some Fortune 500 corporations. *Communication Education, 40,* 152–164.

3. Bostrom, R. N., & Waldhart, E. S. (1988). Memory models and the measurement of listening. *Communication Education, 37,* p. 1.

4. Kelly, C. (1967). Listening: Complex activities and a unitary skill. *Speech Monographs, 34,* 455–466.

5. Watson, K., & Barker, L. (1985). Listening behavior: Definition and measurement. In R. Bostrom (Ed.), *Communication yearbook 8* (pp. 178–197). Beverly Hills, CA: Sage.

6. Rankin, P. T. (1926). *The measurement of the ability to understand spoken language.* Unpublished doctoral dissertation, University of Michigan. University Microfilm Publication No. 4352, 1952.

7. Nichols, R. G. (1948). Factors in listening comprehension. *Communication Monographs, 15,* 154–163; and Nichols, R. G., & Stevens, L. A. (1957). *Are you listening?* New York: McGraw-Hill.

8. DiGaetani, J. L. (1980). The business of listening. *Business Horizons, 57,* 40–46.

9. For complete discussions of the accumulation of experiences see: Baddeley, A. D. (1976). *The psychology of memory.* New York: Basic Books; and DeFleur, M. L., & Plax, T. G. *Human communication as a biosocial process.* Paper presented at the International Communication Association, Acapulco, Mexico, 1980.

10. Goss, B. (1982). Listening as information processing. *Communication Quarterly, 30,* 304–307.

11. Barker, L. L. (1971). *Listening behavior* (Englewood Cliffs, NJ: Prentice-Hall; Meyer, J. L. & Williams, F. (1965). Teaching listening at the secondary level: Some evaluations. *Speech Teacher, 15,* 299–304.

12. Brooks, W. D. & Heath, R. W. (1985). *Speech Communication* (5th ed.) (pp. 89–90). Dubuque, IA: Wm. C. Brown; Weaver, C. H. (1972). *Human listening: Processes and behavior.* Indianapolis, IN: Bobbs-Merrill.

13. Hamilton, C. & Parker, C. *Communicating for results* (2nd ed.) (p. 20). Belmont, CA: Wadsworth.

14. Sarbin, T. R., & Allen, V. L. (1968). Role theory. In G. Lindzey & E. Aronson, (Eds.), *The handbook of social psychology* (pp. 488–567). Reading, MA: Addison-Wesley.

15. Taylor, A., Rosegrant, T., Meyer, A., & Samples, B. T., (1986). *Communication* (4th ed.) (pp. 143–145). Englewood Cliffs, NJ: Prentice-Hall.

16. Pearson, J. C., & Nelson, P. E. (1985). *Understanding and sharing* (3rd ed.) (pp. 57–61). Dubuque, IA: Wm. C. Brown.

17. Howell, W. S., (1982). *The empathic communicator.* Belmont, CA: Wadsworth.

18. Mehrabian, A. (1967). Orientation behaviors and nonverbal attitude communication. *Journal of Communication, 16,* pp. 324–332.

19. Samovar, L. A., & Mills, J. (1986). *Oral communication: Messages and responses* (6th ed.) (pp. 84–85). Dubuque, IA: Wm. C. Brown.

20. DeFleur & Plax, op. cit.

21. Bandura, A. (1977). *Social learning theory.* Englewood Cliffs, NJ: Prentice-Hall

22. Mead, G. H. (1934). *Mind, self and society: From the standpoint of a behaviorist* (Charles W. Morris, Ed.). Chicago: University of Chicago Press. See the discussion of interpersonal "adjustment," bottom of p. 44.

23. This idea resembles what has been shown in research on how individuals vary in the degree to which they attend to others. This attentiveness has been studied as an aspect of "involvement," "perceptiveness," and "other-oriented perceptiveness." See: Cegala, D. (1981). Interaction involvement: A cognitive dimension of communicative competence. *Communication Education, 30,* 109–121; Cegala, D., Savage, B., Brunner, C., & Conrad, A., (1982). "An elaboration of the meaning of interaction involvement: Toward the development of a theoretical concept. *Communication Monographs, 49,* 229–248.

24. For a discussion of which receiver characteristics can affect listening see: Plax, T. G., & Rosenfeld, L. B., (1979). Receiver differences and the comprehension of spoken messages. *Journal of Experimental Education, 48,* 23–28.

25. For a discussion of environmental characteristics that are thought to affect listening see: Watson, K., & Barker, L. (1985). Listening behavior: Definition and measurement. In R. Bostrom (Ed.), *Communication yearbook 8* (p. 185). Beverly Hills, CA: Sage.

26. This example is drawn from the experience of one of the authors who served as an executive in such a corporation for several years.

27. Brooks, W. D. (1974). *Speech communication* (2nd ed.) (pp. 80–84). Dubuque, IA: Wm. C. Brown.

28. Hansford, B. (1988). *Teachers and classroom communication* (pp. 43–46). Orlando, FL: Harcourt, Brace, Jovanovich. Watson & Barker, op. cit., pp. 183–185.

Additional Readings

Barker, L. *Listening behavior.* (1971). Englewood Cliffs, NJ: Prentice-Hall.

> Though an older text, this is still an excellent statement of the field of listening. Barker effectively overviews the basic principles and perspectives, and provides students with guidelines for improving their listening behavior. This book was written with the undergraduate in mind and is well suited for the introductory student.

Beatty, M. J., & Payne, S. (1984). Listening comprehension as a function of cognitive complexity. *Communication Monographs, 51,* 85–89.

> This now-classic study investigates the relationship between an individual's level of listening comprehension and his or her degree of cognitive complexity. The results suggest that people who process information in complex ways tend to comprehend more information than those who do it more simply. The study provides several insights into the development of listening skills.

Watson, K., & Barker, L. (1985). Listening behavior: Definition and measurement. In R. Bostrom (Ed.), *Communication yearbook 8* (pp. 178–197). Beverly Hills, CA: Sage.

> This chapter reviews and analyzes most published research literature on listening behavior. The authors do an effective job of discussing the various definitions of listening and the variables that affect listener comprehension. They also carefully outline the pros and cons of various listening tests that have been published over the past several decades.

Weaver, C. H. *Human listening.* (1972). Indianapolis, IN: Bobbs-Merrill.

> This introductory book is a solid entry-level statement about the field of listening. Materials are presented in a simplified fashion, and the reader is provided with meaningful examples throughout. This text is consistently cited in published research on listening, and it is a good compliment to beginning communication courses.

Wolvin, A. D., & Coakley, C. G. (1991). A survey of the status of listening training in some Fortune 500 corporations. *Communication Education, 40,* 152–164.

> This recent study reports the results of a survey of training directors of Fortune 500 corporations. The study suggests that the training of premanagers and managers in the skills of effective listening continues to be perceived as an important part of industrial training programs.

Part Two

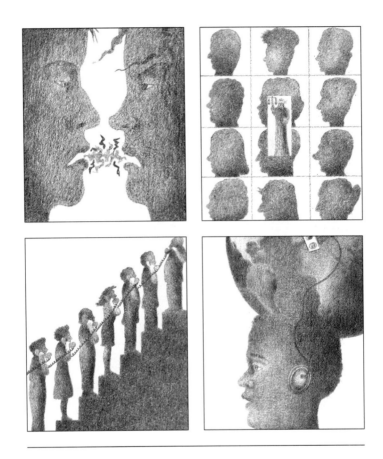

Communicating in Distinctive Contexts

Part 2 of this book looks at communicative exchanges as they take place in a number of different contexts. Such contexts are characterized by distinctive physical settings and sociocultural situations in which communication is governed by rules that define social relationships between participants. In Chapter 5 we look at how people who communicate in dyads, or interpersonal pairs, develop close and intimate relationships through the exchange of messages. We also see how such relationships are maintained over time and how people communicate in special ways to terminate those that are no longer rewarding.

The focus then shifts to communication in small groups. Chapter 6 shows that there are a remarkable number of different types of small groups in modern society. They range from the intimate relationships of the family to the more formal exchanges of the committee. Each of these groups serves different and important functions for their participants, and each constitutes a distinctive communication context.

Contemporary life is deeply dependent on large and complex organizations. Chapter 7, dealing with communication within organizations, shows how all of the communication concepts and processes the book has already addressed aid in understanding the communication patterns in such groups. It also shows that there are many kinds of communication unique to this context. Anyone participating in the labor force in today's multicultural society needs to understand the nature of these formal and informal processes.

In today's technological society, communicating with media is commonplace. Chapter 8 shows that each medium—letters, memos, the phone, fax, computerized electronic mail and various forms of telecommunication conferencing—has its own advantages. At the same time, each places its own limitations on the communication process. In addition, each of the media that has been introduced into society has created its own special effects on the social order.

Chapter 5

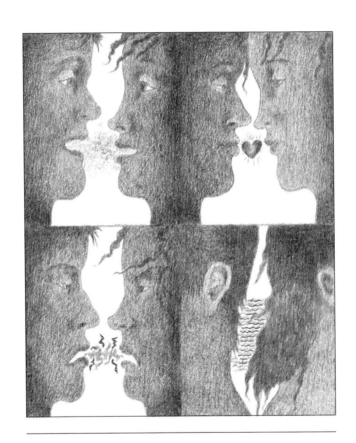

Communicating Interpersonally

Contents

Basic Features of a Communication Context
Physical Settings: Places Influence Communication
Sociocultural Situations: Goals Influence
    Communication
Social Relationships: Rules of Interaction Influence
    Communication

Communication in an Interpersonal Context
Characteristics of Interpersonal Communication
    Interpersonal communication begins with the "self"
    Interpersonal communication is fully transactional
    Interpersonal communicators share physical
        proximity
    Interpersonal communication is shaped by social roles
    Interpersonal communication is uniquely irreversible
    Interpersonal communication is unrepeatable
Reasons for Initiating and Maintaining Relationships
    Constructing and maintaining a positive self-image
    Coping with daily problems
    Maximizing rewards and minimizing punishments

Engagement: The Decision to Encounter
The Critical First Moments
Small Talk as Big Talk
    Auditioning for friendship
    Controlling self-disclosure
    Painless interaction
The Skills of Small Talk
    The importance of eye contact
    Providing nonverbal immediacy

The importance of names
Drawing out the other person
Keeping it light
Accentuate the positive

Management: The Decision to Linger
Assessing the Rewards and Costs
Revealing Core Information About Self
    Testing the water
    Labeling the relationship
    Achieving full disclosure
Communicating with an Intimate Other

Disengagement: The Decision to Leave
Causes of Relationship Disengagement
    The pressure for an explanation
    Acceptable assignments of blame
Saying Goodbye
    Establishing distance
    Disassociation
"Fifty Ways to Leave Your Lover!"
    Withdrawal/avoidance
    Ending on a positive tone
    Machiavellianism
    Open confrontation

Chapter Review

Key Terms

Notes

Suggested Readings

Key Questions

■ Each of us constructs a set of beliefs about who we are, where we fit in the social order, and how other people evaluate us. That self-concept is the foundation on which we develop relationships with other people. How do we go about building this self-image, and why is it that most of us construct one that is quite positive and flattering?

■ What is "small talk"? Is it as trivial and meaningless as some people say? If so, why is it that people who have just met almost always engage in a great deal of small talk before they reveal their deeper thoughts and ideas to another? Is it possible that such seemingly inconsequential communication serves a critical function in establishing social relationships and getting to know someone well?

- What communication strategies do people use when they want a relationship with another person to develop into an intimate one? How can they tell when the other person is trying to move in the same direction? What mistakes can be made along the way that will lead to a termination of the relationship?

- What do you do when you want to end a relationship? How can it be done peacefully and in stages so that it does not end in an open confrontation and emotionally draining fight? Can certain communication strategies be used to achieve disengagement that leaves the parties without hard feelings?

Some authors feel that all rational analysis, not just the scientific methodology, does a disservice to the mystical elements that are central to the experience of love. . . . The proper "knowing about love" is crucial to enable us to fulfill the promise of the experience.

Willard Gaylin
1987

Looking back, Cecelia found it difficult to understand how she had first been attracted to George. Maybe it was because she had never been quite sure of who she was or what she really wanted out of life. But one thing was clear to her now. She never *ever* wanted another George!

It had started out almost by chance when she met George at a Magarita's Halloween party. She had been intrigued when he seemed so well informed about the things she liked. They had spent almost an hour in small talk, and when he asked if he could call her, she agreed and gave him her number.

The first time they went out should have alerted her, but she missed all of the subtle cues. George talked a lot about difficulties with his parents and the problems he was having in the department where he worked. She talked about her interests in art and music, but did not actually tell him a lot about herself.

After that they went to movies and concerts, becoming more and more intimate. Within a couple of weeks George was coming to her apartment for meals. Then he began staying over. Finally, he moved in and it seemed as if it was going to be a stable and fulfilling relationship. In fact, for several months they were very happy.

But by Christmas, Cecelia clearly saw a side of George that she had not understood before. It wasn't so much that he did anything really bad. It was more his attitude toward her and their relationship. George stayed in bed in the morning until Cecelia had breakfast ready. He never volunteered to do any of the cooking or even take out the garbage. He expected her to do the laundry, go to the store, and keep the apartment clean. But, to be fair, he was generous when it came to sharing costs and that wasn't a problem.

Cecelia remembered very clearly the event that marked the beginning of the end. She had been asked to stay late at the office by her boss, Mr. Lipman. She didn't mind because they had been working on an important contract, and Mr. Lipman was always very thoughtful and helpful. But when she got back to the apartment at around 8:00, George was furious. He demanded to know where she had been and why she had not been there to prepare dinner. She got mad and they had a terrible fight. It was after midnight before they both calmed down.

Even though they had made up, it was never quite the same. Each of them made an effort to be polite and concerned about the other, but the relationship was clearly going downhill. Cecelia began to see George as both selfish and self-centered. He accused her of being bitchy and punishing. In retrospect, she guessed that he probably was right.

By Easter it was clear that they were finished. Cecelia asked George to sleep on the couch, and she stopped fixing his meals. She deliberately stayed out after work, and George was usually absent when she finally did get home. Finally, he moved out while she was away visiting her mother, and they have not even talked on the phone since.

The changing relationship between Cecelia and George illustrates *interpersonal* communication, which is the focus of this chapter. The study of interpersonal communication looks at the kinds of messages people use in the three stages Cecelia and George passed through. At first, they developed close ties to each other. Then they tried to keep a troubled relationship going. Finally, they disengaged themselves from emotional attachments that were no longer rewarding.

Interpersonal communication is the first of several "contexts" or settings that will be discussed in the next several chapters. Therefore, our first task in the present chapter will be to clarify the nature of a "context" and discuss how it can influence meanings intended by senders and interpreted by receivers.

But why is it important to analyze communication within particular kinds of contexts? The reason is that the different kinds of physical and social settings in which communication takes place have strong influences on what is said, by whom and with what effect, regardless of who is communicating and about what. Therefore, we need to identify the major features that make up any type of context and see how these influence the communication process. In the next four chapters we will look closely at several different contexts: *interpersonal, small groups, organizations,* and *media*.

Basic Features of a Communication Context

In the formal description of the simultaneous transactions model that we set forth in Chapter 1 (pp. 21–25), we indicated six essential propositions regarding ways in which people communicate. The last three of these (numbers 4, 5, and 6) indicated that communicating parties are simultaneously influenced by their *physical surroundings,* the *sociocultural situation* in which their transactions take place, and the *social relationships* that shape the interactions between them. It is precisely these three features of the transactions model that identify what is meant by the *context* in the study of communication.

Physical Settings: Places Influence Communication

In his *Merchant of Venice,* William Shakespeare included the oft-quoted line "All the World's a stage, And all the men and women merely players." That metaphor identifies quite well what we have in mind by the physical setting or place as an aspect of context. People do act out their parts in physical surroundings that serve as a kind of "stage" in which human dramas take place as people speak their lines. That physical stage includes not only buildings, such as a school, concert hall, or restaurant, but places, like a beach, parking lot, or park. The physical context shapes communication insofar as it either inhibits or encourages certain kinds of messages. For example, one would be unlikely to discuss deeply romantic issues while waiting for a subway in a crowded station. One might well be prompted to do so in a romantic restaurant where soft music is playing and the lights are dim.

Like stages, physical settings also have "props." We discussed in Chapter 3 how nonverbal "things" are used

in communication. These become part of a context because they are often an integral part of either the place or the sociocultural situation within which the communication takes place.

Sociocultural Situations: Goals Influence Communication

People do not come together randomly and engage in recurrent communication for unknown purposes. They get together with other individuals so that they can accomplish *goals* in sociocultural "situations" that they could not achieve by individual action alone. Cecelia and George, in our opening example, were seeking satisfactions by establishing a live-in situation that neither could have achieved alone. Sociocultural situations include those typically found among people in socially organized interaction, such as on a date, relaxing with the family at home, working, playing, worshiping, studying, getting medical treatment, or undergoing some significant ceremony, like a wedding, funeral, or final exam.

Such sociocultural situations are organized around *goals* that people pursue through communicating with each other in such settings. These are not only "social" because people interact in a patterned manner, but they are also "cultural" insofar as the ways of life that different kinds of people follow define the goals they set. Those goals shape the general content of their messages. For example, the messages transmitted and received by a group of people participating in a bar mitzvah are not the same as those exchanged by the same individuals in a pick-up basketball game or even while eating lunch after the contest. These are distinctive sociocultural situations.

The sociocultural situation, then, is a significant feature of a context because it focuses participants on goals they are jointly pursuing. Those goals define the drama that is played out between communicating parties. Each different situation places its own limits on what is likely to be communicated, and it encourages who is likely to say what to whom for what purpose and with what effect.

Social Relationships: Rules of Interaction Influence Communication

Within a particular sociocultural situation, people seldom just communicate at will with anyone whom they choose whenever they feel like it. Virtually every context in-

An important feature of any context in which communication takes place are the physical surroundings in which messages are transmitted and received. Because of cultural definitions of what is appropriate and inappropriate in particular places, each type of surrounding promotes or inhibits certain types of verbal and nonverbal message content.

cludes elaborate rules that dictate who can communicate what messages to whom. Those rules provide a clear pattern of social organization to many communication contexts. For example, the general **norms** (social rules) of a courtroom situation dictate that people talk about crimes, torts, and evidence—not about baseball games, pie recipes, or modern art. Other general norms require that the group meet at a particular time, that onlookers remain quiet, that participants dress appropriately and conduct themselves in an orderly, dignified manner, and so on.

There are also rules that specify a pattern of **roles,** definitions of appropriate behavior for particular participants, who perform specialized parts in a clear "division of labor." The distinctive roles of attorneys, judges, witnesses, and jurors shape the messages each transmits to the others in a pattern of social relationships. Furthermore, clear rules define the *rank* each participant enjoys in the situation. **Ranks** are communicated via various kinds of permissible verbal and nonverbal messages that provide meanings of authority, power, and prestige. The black robe of the judge, plus the impressive judicial bench, even the courtroom as a whole, speaks to his or her high rank. In fact, in one way or another each participant in the situation transmits verbal and nonverbal messages that identify where he or she fits in the various social ranking levels in the situation.

Finally, all of these norms, roles, and ranking considerations are enforced by messages designed to **control** those who would deviate, disobey, or otherwise disrupt these social relationships. For example, when the judge bangs her or his gavel and demands "order in the court," few fail to understand that this is a message transmitted for purposes of social control. Even in more casual settings, rules of interaction dictate who says what to whom about what. In our opening example, Cecelia and George followed our society's general norms, roles, ranking, and controls in each of their situations. When they began dating, the general norms and roles prevailed concerning who should ask for the phone number, who should invite whom to what social function, and probably who should pay for the dinner or movie. When they became a couple, there was supposed to be a division of labor (about cooking, cleaning, taking out garbage, etc.). Later, when the relationship deteriorated, various attempts were made to control the other through different kinds of verbal and nonverbal messages.

The rules governing communication in a given context of social relationships, then, are the general *norms* that all parties are expected to follow, the specialized *roles* they play in the division of labor, the ways in which *ranks* de-

People do not come together to communicate in random ways. They do so in contexts that are defined in part by the goals sought in particular kinds of sociocultural situations. These can range from serious meetings held for religious purposes to recreational situations in which people's main purpose is to have fun. In each case, the overall goals of the sociocultural situation provide definitions of who says what to whom in what manner.

fine each participant's authority, power, and prestige, and the *social controls* exercised by both verbal and nonverbal communication. As we look at different types of contexts—interpersonal, small group, and organizational—these will be key factors in describing and understanding how and why communication follows distinct patterns in different social situations.

Generally, then, the transactions model specifies that senders and receivers are simultaneously influenced by their *physical surroundings,* the goals defined by *sociocultural situations* in which they communicate, and the *social relationships* that influence the kinds of messages they send and receive. It is precisely these three concepts (and the ideas included in each) that define the meaning of context.

Communication in an Interpersonal Context

Interpersonal communication is a process of using language and nonverbal cues to send and receive messages (between individuals) that are intended to arouse particular kinds of meanings. In that sense, it is no different from any other form of human communication. What does set it apart is that it is focused specifically on interactions between two people.

We have already indicated that interpersonal com-

munication is a general communication context. However, the contextual features outlined earlier may change from time to time as the parties move from one physical setting and sociocultural situation to another, or as their relationship changes over time. Thus, in the systematic study of interpersonal communication, researchers recognize that interpersonal affiliations are not static; they are constantly being modified. As in the case of Cecelia and George, they often move back and forth from lesser to greater levels of intimacy.

After specifying more precisely what we mean by interpersonal communication, we will review it within a framework of: (1) **engagement**—the process by which people try to move their relationships from an impersonal to a personal basis, (2) **management**—the communication strategies people use to maintain valued interpersonal ties, and (3) **disengagement**—communication strategies people use when they are attempting to withdraw gracefully (or not so gracefully) from a close association with another.

It will become very clear that interpersonal communication incorporates all of the verbal and nonverbal concepts and principles of listening discussed in previous chapters. Above all, this chapter will show that interpersonal relationships, good or bad, do not just "happen." They are outcomes of communication exchanges that are thoughtfully managed or awkwardly bungled.

Characteristics of Interpersonal Communication

Some theorists argue that interpersonal communication is really a matter of degree and is not restricted by the number of people involved in the exchange.[1] In this book, however, the process of interpersonal communication is discussed within the context of two major background features: The first is that interpersonal communication takes place in the **dyad**, which is a technical term for two people in a relatively enduring social relationship.[2] The second major feature of interpersonal communication, as we are analyzing it, is that as the individuals involved come to know one another better, their relationship tends to move from impersonal to personal; that is, they become increasingly close and intimate. With these two features in mind, we can identify six key characteristics of interpersonal communication:[3]

Interpersonal communication begins with the "self"   The term *self* is central to the process of communication and will be referred to in a number of chapters in this book.[4] **Self** can be defined as *that pattern of beliefs, meanings, and understandings each individual develops concerning her or his own personal characteristics, capacities, limitations, and worth as a human being.* In other words, the self (sometimes called the "self-image" or "self-concept") consists of our personal conceptions of *who* we are, *what* we are, and *where* we are in the social order. Our position in the social order is determined by how we are classified into the categories and criteria judged as important in our society. The self, then, is our personal and subjective configuration of beliefs about how we are classified and evaluated (by ourselves and others) in terms of socially important standards.

The significance of the self-image or self-concept for present purposes is that who, what, and where we think we are dictates to a large extent how we relate to and communicate with others. Considering our biological, psychological, and social makeup, and their evaluation by society, we bring to our relationships with other persons rather complex conceptions of ourselves as human beings. Furthermore, when we communicate with another person, we quickly form a set of beliefs (right or wrong) about who, what, and where *they* are in the social order. By the same token, those with whom we communicate bring to the process complex conceptions of who, what, and where *they* are in terms of important categories and criteria. In addition, they quickly form an

Our beliefs about who we are, what we are, and where we are located in the social order are derived from the evaluative responses we think others make to us. In turn, these beliefs about ourselves dictate to a considerable extent ways in which we relate to and communicate with other people. In other words, our strategies and modes of interpersonal communication are heavily influenced by our concept of "self."

image about us. In a very real sense, then, we can recognize at least four "images" at work in the process of interpersonal communication—my self-image, my image of the other, the other's self-image, and the other's image of me.[5]

These four patterns of belief about self and others truly can influence interpersonal relationships. For example, a young university professor may believe that she is attractive, hard-working, liberal, intelligent, independent, and a feminist. Another person, a young blue-collar worker who is a high school dropout, may have the self-image that he is clever, a bit reckless, hard-working, a born gambler, irresistibly attractive, muscular, and committed to the notions of male dominance and superiority.

Suppose now that by some strange set of circumstances these two individuals were brought together on a blind date. While Hollywood might design a scenario whereby the pair overcome their differences and wind up romantically in each other's arms, in the real world these two would have a great deal of difficulty communicating in a way that would bring them closer together.

We have seen in previous chapters that people who are very different may or may not have the same set of beliefs about each other that they entertain personally about themselves. These differences can serve as serious barriers to effective interpersonal communication. For example, the young woman in our imaginary blind date would be likely to form an image of the young man as a "dull, macho boor." He, in turn, would be likely to put together an image of her as "stuck-up, pushy, and hostile."

The selves or images that we construct of others, and that we project upon them as we engage in interpersonal communication, are what in ancient times were called *personae*—the central and unique characteristics of an individual that set her or him off from others.[6] At the turn of the century, Charles Horton Cooley called them **personal ideas.** He described them as the set of beliefs and evaluations (ideas) that we devise about specific other persons as a result of our interactions with them.[7] Today we would be more likely to call them our beliefs (schemata of meanings) about the *personalities* of the other individuals (derived from the same root word). A modern term for personal idea is "implicit personality."

While you may never have realized that there can be as many as four distinct personal ideas or images present in a conversation between two people, the situation is actually even more complex. After all, when you talk to someone, you cannot help but imagine what that person is thinking about you. Does he or she see you as gauche or sophisticated, attractive or plain? Do you seem interesting or dull? Is what you are saying clear or confusing? And, in much the same way, through sensitive role-taking the other individual is doing exactly the same thing, putting together an image of what you are thinking about him or her. Thus, there are two additional images present during any interpersonal conversation—what you think your image is in the mind of the other person, and what that person feels is the image you have constructed about her or him.[8]

By now it may seem that there is an army of images produced by mutual role-taking that are present and playing a part in what initially seemed like a simple two-person exchange. Nevertheless, it is true that all six personae are involved, and that these images of self and other help shape what is said and what is understood. Fortunately, the process of interpersonal communication takes place so rapidly that most of us ignore these complexities and simply carry on our conversations. At the same time, if one wants to gain skill in interpersonal communication, these self and other images offer possible points of attention around which to analyze present limitations and develop more effective strategies.

Interpersonal communication is fully transactional   More than in any other context, interpersonal communication is based on our simultaneous transactions model.[9] As communicators, each party uses verbal and nonverbal symbols and signs to construct messages around his or her intended meanings. At the same time, the receiver brings similar, or possibly different, meanings to the task of receiving and interpreting that message. Information is sent back in the form of feedback, and each communicator adjusts by role-taking for the next phase of the process. Thus, each party simultaneously influences the other's behavior while being affected in return.

Interpersonal communicators share physical proximity   Simply put, people have to be near each other in space to engage in interpersonal communication. To be sure, they might talk on the telephone or exchange letters, but that is mediated communication and it lacks important elements of the interpersonal process we are discussing. Interpersonal communication takes place with two individuals engaging in face-to-face interaction. This rules out all forms of impersonal exchanges or those in which interaction is carried on over longer distances. For example, we cannot have an interpersonal relationship with a rock star, movie actor, sports figure, or television personality who has no knowledge of our existence as a member of the audience.

By being in close physical proximity, communicators are able to increase their chances for understanding each other accurately and efficiently. This result is accomplished more easily with the accessibility of feedback. When we communicate one-on-one in close physical proximity, we are able to recognize even the most subtle verbal and nonverbal cues that tell us whether or not we're being understood as intended. We can instantly detect the eyebrows that suddenly go up, the hint of a frown, eyes that "glaze over," tears beginning to form, a jaw that tightens or relaxes, a nose that "turns up," a meaningful shift in body position, and other nonverbal cues that provide important feedback.

In interpersonal communication such subtle and obvious reactions are immediate and frequent, but in other communication contexts they may not be readily observed. As a result, in the face-to-face situation we are in a better position to adapt to each other's concerns. We can follow up with questions and comments, try to explain our position in another way, pause to let the other person talk, and appreciate the fact that we are able to interact flexibly and competently with one another.

Interpersonal communication is shaped by social roles   When people are engaging in interpersonal communication, what they are saying—that is, *content*—can be interpreted only within the context of the roles that define their overall relationship.[10] For example, if we were to witness two individuals (whose role relationship was not known to us) arguing in the lobby of a hotel, we might attempt to analyze the situation by relying first on the content of the messages exchanged. The verbal content of the messages exchanged indicates that she wants some money from him and he's refusing to come up with it. Their nonverbal cues seem to indicate that their exchange is intense, serious, and evolving into an argument.

Without knowing anything else about the people involved, we could interpret their exchange as hostile or defensive, depending on the actual words employed by each party. However, to rely on *what* is said, verbally and nonverbally, is often insufficient for understanding the full meaning of such an argument. We have to understand the nature of the *relationship* between the two people—the role that each is playing and how their roles are interrelated. For example, the woman and man could be married; the woman could be the man's daughter or the man might be the woman's son. It is possible that the woman (or the man) works for the other person; the woman could be an undercover agent or policewoman and the man a suspect. Or the man might work for the hotel and the woman is a guest. Notice how the interpretation of the underlying meaning of the argument changes from one set of role relationships to another. Both content and relational messages, then, interact together in determining the meaning of any interpersonal exchange.

Interpersonal communication is uniquely irreversible   We pointed out the irreversible nature of communication in Chapter 1. This is a particularly significant feature of messages in an interpersonal context. There is no way to erase a regrettable message the way we erase unwanted sounds on an audio tape so that we can substitute something different. (If we could do that, it certainly would be a "kinder and gentler" world.) All too often we find ourselves afflicted with "foot in mouth"

disease—wishing we could "take back" the harsh words and labels that hurt someone in the heat of an argument. We can say we're sorry, but unfortunately, they remember the unkind words spoken earlier.

Interpersonal communication is unrepeatable   All of us can recall a special event with someone in which we communicated in such a special way that we occasionally wish we could experience it all over again. You may have heard your parents talk sentimentally about how they first met and fell in love. What they said to each other, at least as they recall it, had such special meanings. Others are convinced that their high school (or college) years were the best times of their lives when they communicated in rewarding ways with their friends. And yet, we all know that we cannot go back and attempt to relive the exact same communication experiences again. Even if we had one of those wonderful machines, of which science fiction writers are so fond—one that can both transcend space and travel backward to our pasts—we would find ourselves viewing it all with changed perspectives, altered feelings, and new interpretations. Inevitably, we would communicate differently.

Overall, then, interpersonal communication is in one sense simply one form of the human communication process that we described in Chapter 1. However, it does have the above six characteristics that *taken together* distinguish it from other forms.

Reasons for Initiating and Maintaining Relationships

What is missing from our analysis thus far are the *reasons* for which we initiate and try to maintain close relationships through this process. Clearly, such relationships require a great deal of time and effort accompanied by many potential stresses and emotional costs, but they can also yield very satisfying rewards. There is, in other words, in this complex and uniquely human activity, a kind of "cost/benefit ratio" that results from forming and maintaining close personal ties with another individual by means of continuing interpersonal communication. As we will see, the nature of that ratio will influence the formation and the stability of the relationship.

We noted in Chapter 1 that all forms of human communication begin with intended goals that are set by particular sociocultural situations. Such goals are our "blueprints" for defining the content and structure of the messages we initiate. They define the responses we desire

Interpersonal communication is the foundation on which intimate human bonds are developed and maintained over long periods of time. Since most of us need close personal relationships with significant others, the cost/benefit ratio is highly favorable. Such bonds can provide the most important of all human experiences, but they must be maintained through skillful interpersonal communication.

from others and the strategies of message construction that we will use to arouse the meanings needed for influencing those responses. We can ask, then, what are the goals of interpersonal communication?

Perhaps the most important answer to this question is that we want and truly need close personal relationships—life is a lonely and shallow experience without them. *Interpersonal communication is the foundation on which intimate human bonds are built.* This is true of every kind of close personal relationship. Such affiliations characterize the ties between devoted family members, trusting friends, and loving members of the opposite sex. There are many other kinds of one-on-one human bonds, perhaps less intimate, that are nevertheless important, and these too are founded on effective interpersonal communication. They include such ties as a mutually respectful relationship between employer and employee, professor and student, neighbors, and valued associates at work.

Basically there are three broad reasons for engaging in lasting interpersonal relationships.[11] As we will explain below, one major goal of establishing such ties is to obtain much-needed information about *ourselves.* Another reason is more pragmatic—friends, family members, and other intimate associates help us solve a long list of *problems* of everyday living that would be difficult to handle alone. Finally, close personal relationships are developed

with people whose company and behavior are least punishing for the *rewards* that they provide for us.

Constructing and maintaining a positive self-image   The first characteristic of interpersonal communication that we discussed earlier was that it *begins with the self.* That aspect of the process was emphasized because it is one of the most significant of the "benefits" (from the "cost/benefit ratio") that are derived from interpersonal communication.

Almost all of us love to tell others what a good person we are, and we especially enjoy hearing others say nice things about us. This may appear to be nothing more than a comment on the egocentric and vain nature of the human individual. However, it points to deep psychological needs that we all have concerning the *origins* of the self-image and how it is *maintained* by each of us. We noted earlier that the self is a set of beliefs we entertain about our physical, psychological, and social characteristics. We noted also that the self was derived from a social process in which we form an image of what we are like, based on the reactions of others toward us. What we have not yet explained is why we urgently *need* positive responses from others as we tell them in hundreds of subtle ways about ourselves through a process of interpersonal communication.

Every clinically normal person wants, needs, and enjoys a positive self-image. It is a difficult and miserable situation if we have to accept a negative one, even on a temporary basis. To gain a positive self-image, early in life we develop sensitive skills in locating people who will supply us with favorable evaluations of our behavior and characteristics. While we cannot choose our family, we can respond coolly toward those members who fail to give us the responses we need and warmly toward those who do. Above all, we can choose our close friends. Actually we screen them carefully, often without even thinking about it deliberately. That is, from the available pool of individuals we encounter, we find some who seem to respond to us in a positive manner. They are the ones we value because they respond to and evaluate us in positive ways. Those who are critical or negative can be rejected. Such "unimaginative clods" can be discounted as of little worth and denied our friendship. Thus, by careful screening and by recruiting accommodating associates, we can build and maintain a satisfying self-image.

At the same time, those with whom we affiliate need positive feedback from us. They have their own self-images to construct and maintain. A part of the "cost" in the "cost/benefit ratio," then, is that we have to make continuing efforts and spend time providing our valued family members, friends, lovers, or whatever, with supportive and positive evaluations that will fulfill *their* needs. All of this, needless to say, makes up a large part of the goals for which we initiate and continue the process of interpersonal communication.

Such considerations explain in large part why we find *ourselves* to be our favorite, our most engrossing and completely captivating topic. We are anxious to share with others the details of our day—how we cleverly outwitted the professor, received approval from the boss, or put the clerk at the store in her or his place. We show what a noble and long-suffering person we are when we describe the crowded subway, the unbearable freeway traffic, or the other pressures we have had to endure. We offer personal testimony to our cleverness and good taste when we discuss the outstanding meal we have planned for dinner tonight, and our generous intention to take the other person to a movie that week. We then look for signs of approval and appreciation.

Of course, we like to hear what happened to the other individual too, but if our friend, spouse, lover, or relative talks too long about his or her positive qualities and behavior, we are likely to become bored. We are willing to provide feedback that shows sympathy, approval, subtle applause, or commiseration as needed by the other—up to a point. After all, it is a part of the cost we pay for the rewards of the relationship. But soon we will attempt to turn the conversation around again to those topics *we* feel reflect favorably on *us*—to those issues and events that best meet our needs as topics of discussion.

One of the most important reasons for entering into relationships with others, then, is that we learn more about how others perceive and feel about us. However, one of the built-in problems of constructing a self-concept on the basis of evaluations and assessments offered generously by mothers, sweethearts, or good friends, is that they have inherent problems of "validity." That is, such intimate associates seldom offer a balanced system of reality checks. Their reactions to us are usually positive, and only infrequently negative. This distorts the persona we construct.

If we want to understand our selves in a more objective perspective, we have to look beyond our immediate circle. People in close relationships with us usually tolerate too much of our shortcomings—or in some circumstances they might be overly critical of our behaviors, which can produce a different set of problems. Either way, we are deeply dependent on the reactions and implied evaluations of others for constructing and maintaining our self-image. Anyone who wants to develop a realistic, if not always flattering, self-concept needs to rely on many sources, not just on those who provide positive responses.[12]

Coping with daily problems While we rely heavily on others to help with our self-image, we also need them for many kinds of practical reasons. Consider how difficult your life would be without the cooperation of others. If you have ever moved from one apartment to another, you may have counted on all your friends showing up to help pack, lift, and move. In the unlikely event that no one came, you might have found yourself unable to transfer the couch from the living room onto the truck! Many of us rely on someone for routine assistance, such as taking the car in to get it worked on. Rather than wait around at the shop for hours, we hope to have a friend or family member drive us back home again. Individuals close to us supply information we need, work with us on projects, and even clean the bathrooms while we do the dishes. In short, we rely heavily on others to help us cope in a pragmatic manner with the realities of day-to-day life.

We are especially dependent on those close to us in times of stress or grief. Our friends and family members serve a **cushioning function**—supplying emotional support when we are anxious or afraid, when tragedy strikes, or even when we are just feeling down. They stand between us and an uncaring world providing an emotionally safe haven when events beyond our control make life difficult. In many ways, both practical and emotional, we need and want their assistance in our efforts to control or adapt to the constraints of our environment.[13]

Maximizing rewards and minimizing punishments This is one of the older ideas in the study of human nature. In 1789 the British philosopher Jeremy Bentham (1748–1832) published *An Introduction to the Principles of Morals and Legislation* in which he developed a complete explanation of human political, social, and personal behavior, called **utilitarianism.**[14] It was based on the ratio of pleasure to pain to be derived from our actions. We act, he maintained, according to the *principle of utility,* which means that we choose to engage in those behaviors that maximize pleasure and avoid those that result in pain. This idea laid the foundations for more contemporary psychological theories of learning that stressed rewards (pleasure) and punishment (pain) as the basis for establishing stable habits for responding to our

The importance of close relationships developed through intimate interpersonal communication becomes particularly apparent during times of stress and grief. Those with whom we have close affective ties cushion us at such times from an uncaring and impersonal world. Their concern sustains us through difficulties with which it would be difficult to cope alone.

surrounding environment. Today, we no longer subscribe to Bentham's particular formulation of utilitarianism, but it remains as the basic framework, a **cost/benefit ratio,** along with more contemporary psychological interpretations, within which we think about the relationship among reward, punishment, and specific forms of human action.

Generally, then, the part played by rewards and punishments in shaping interpersonal relationships remains important. For example, spending a major holiday all alone is a dismal (punishing) experience. It is simply more fun, more rewarding, and more pleasurable when we can share such a time with those we love. Similarly, celebrating a new job, graduation from college, a birthday, winning big in the lottery—all are events that we don't want to experience alone.

Just being with certain people is rewarding in itself. We simply "feel good" whenever we are with those special friends or loved ones. By the same token, we all know of persons who make us "feel bad" about ourselves. Whenever we are with them, it turns out to be a punishing experience. As we noted earlier, in terms of constructing a self-image, in an effort to minimize negative evaluations, we actively avoid spending time with them

if we can. It only stands to reason that we will not associate frequently, if at all, with those who ridicule us, find us distasteful, or perceive us unworthy of their affection or attention. A number of research studies support this modern form of utilitarianism.[15]

For all of these reasons—constructing a positive self-image, coping with daily problems, and maximizing pleasure while minimizing pain—we initiate or develop interpersonal relationships with others. We need and want others to like us, talk with us, and share life experiences with us. However, such benefits do not come without cost. As we will see in the next section, once we decide to enter into a relationship with another person, in order to obtain those advantages in the long run we must pay a price, at least initially, by following a number of fairly rigid communication rules.

Engagement: The Decision to Encounter

Moving from the very first moments in the history of an encounter to the decision to try to develop a closer relationship involves a set of relatively regular stages.

The first stage is the initial assessment of the person on the basis of physical appearance and his or her opening remarks. Then, as we will see, if the relationship survives those critical first moments, the next stage will be "small talk."

The Critical First Moments

As we will discuss in more detail in Chapter 9 ("Presenting Oneself Effectively"), our first, even momentary, impressions of someone new can influence dramatically our decision to move forward into the relationship. Unfortunately, those initial impressions are often based on trivial details about the person we have just met. In fact, the first information we receive about such a person usually consists of *nonverbal* cues—the person's overall physical appearance, clothing, and other "packaging." Yet, it is these initial data that will determine to a considerable degree whether we want to move to the next stage in the relationship.

If we do decide to go on, the next form of information we receive about the "candidate" comes during the first few minutes of interpersonal exchange, and it is based on a relatively superficial and nondisclosing kind of conversation. Nevertheless, both the first impression and the stage that follows can be critical in establishing a new relationship.

When people strike up a conversation with someone new, they rely on well-established routines. These are often called **scripted** conversations because they are like lines rehearsed from a play. They can also be called **stereotypic** in that they are highly standardized and predictable.[16] Conversations can be classified as stereotypic if they follow clear, even rigid, rules in certain well-defined situations.

Scripted or stereotypic exchanges are easily illustrated by what we almost always say when we are introduced to someone we do not know. Our initial "Hello" is usually followed by their "How are you?" Most of us understand that we are not expected to answer such questions factually or at any length. The normative reply is "Fine." In reality, you may be feeling rather poorly because you had an accident an hour earlier, or you've been fired from your job, or your pet dog just died. Still, the expected answer is "Fine" and "How are you?"

Why do this? Why shouldn't we just say whatever we want to say? The fact is, there are very good reasons for not violating the norms of "getting together." First, it is customary—that translates into predictable and comfortable. Research shows that new acquaintances almost always exchange factual, nonopinionated, and relatively superficial information.[17] Second, few of us are willing to disclose to a new acquaintance our deep, personal feelings about sensitive issues. Not knowing the stranger, we cannot trust that she or he will interpret our disclosures in the "right" way.[18]

Generally, then, initial conversations with others tend to center on "safe" topics. It is for this reason that in such situations we often find ourselves discussing such trivia as the weather and sports, while we scrupulously avoid issues and topics that would disclose more significant attitudes and beliefs. Obviously, there are exceptions to this pattern. Under some circumstances we may reveal our whole life story to people we have just met and whom we never expect to encounter again. For example, in his classic essay, "The Stranger," sociologist Georg Simmel noted in 1908 that because a stranger is both distant and near at the same time that person will often be called upon as a confidant. That happens because he or she is there and available, but intimate disclosures to a stranger will not have the same consequences as making such revelations to individuals with whom we have significant social ties.[19] Modern writers sometimes call this relaxation of the norms against initial disclosures to new acquaintances "the stranger on the plane" phenomenon.[20]

Moving to the next stage, if the potential relationship survives beyond initial impressions and early assessments based on the scripted conversation of getting acquainted, it can shift to a stage where the messages exchanged by the parties consist of **small talk**—discussions that focus on topics of general interest and have little emotional or personal significance. While this may sound trivial, it can be a subtle and complex part of establishing a closer relationship.

Small Talk as Big Talk

It may seem strange to maintain that small talk may be the most important communication skill we can possibly master! We can say this in all honesty because every dyadic social relationship, to some degree, *develops through a stage of small talk.* After we form our earliest impressions of a person, we usually get to add additional assessments based on her or his initial small talk. This gives us a somewhat more extended image of what that person is like. Without this kind of exchange, we would have a difficult time moving through the early stages of getting to know the other person. In fact, small talk can be so important in establishing a relationship with a new acquaintance that it should probably be called "big talk."[21]

The ability to engage in small talk may be one of the most important skills that we can master in contemporary society. It is through such seemingly trivial exchanges that we get a chance to audition and assess others for potentially closer relationships. Small talk allows us to identify those with whom we may want to continue and to screen out others without extensive self-disclosure or embarrassing consequences.

In spite of the importance of small talk, many people seem to dislike it. We've all heard comments like, "I hate small talk; it is so superficial" or "I went to the party and all they did was blab about trivialities." The final put-down of a person in the minds of many is something like, "He can go for hours and not say a single meaningful thing!" and so on. We could find wide agreement that small talk consists of little more than meaningless chatter.

Auditioning for friendship   What is missing from such negative interpretations is that small talk serves critical purposes. Therefore, let us look at small talk more closely so as to see beneath the apparent superficiality in order to understand how this kind of conversation can be important in the development of interpersonal relationships.

One function of small talk is to provide what communication researcher Mark Knapp calls an "audition for friendship."[22] Individuals assess one another in an effort to determine whether or not a relationship is worth establishing. Obviously, not all new acquaintances audition well, and in many cases no relationship forms or it remains purely at the small talk, acquaintance-only stage and dies on the vine later.

Controlling self-disclosure   Small talk also allows us

to reveal a bit of who we are to others cautiously and in a safe way. Because we are all so multidimensional, we have at our disposal a variety of "faces" to expose to someone who knows us hardly at all. We can display our humorous side, or we can do an "about face" and show our serious, highly critical profile instead. At the same time, the other person in the interaction is providing us with similar information. Consequently, both individuals involved in the interaction are attempting to reveal limited personal information—while simultaneously struggling to decipher who the other *really* is! In these early stages, we have little more to go on than superficial communication exchanges. Nevertheless, it's the only information we have.

Painless interaction   Another function of small talk is to serve what Knapp refers to as an "interpersonal pacifier." For many of us, small talk is easy and relatively painless. It neither requires a lot of brain power nor makes stressful demands on new relationships. As such, small talk can provide a welcome alternative to discussions about more significant topics, allowing us to approach dialogue and debates about complex and important themes at our own pace. Good manners dictate that we rarely leap right into heavy discussions with new acquaintances or even those we know well but whom we haven't encountered for a while. Think about it: The last time you called an old friend you probably initiated the conversation around light and effortless topics. Perhaps you followed the greeting with a brief discussion of the weather, a recent basketball game, or a concert you just attended. All of this small talk may have served as a prelude to revealing information of a more important nature—your latest job, your progress in school, a new friend, recent child, divorce, new car, or death in the family.

This "feeling-out" period associated with small talk has been well documented. What researchers have identified from studies of conversations between new acquaintances is an exchange of very basic biographical data.[23] People in such circumstances tend to reveal simple demographic or biographical information, such as "My name is Dianne," or "I'm from St. Louis," or "I divorced Ted last year." Moreover, such disclosures are reciprocal. Dianne should be able to predict that a new acquaintance will reveal her name and hometown too, or that a former friend will provide basic data on changes in his life. Importantly, both persons will tend to avoid heavier topics because neither wants to risk disclosing their true feelings about such matters as the abortion controversy or their feelings about lawyers.

In total, small talk makes it possible for each party to continue sizing up the other, adding to first impressions formed on the basis of primarily physical appearance. It enables them to begin developing a biographical "data-bank" from which to round out their impression of each other. In this way it provides a basis for determining whether or not they would like to see the relationship continue. Because small talk serves these functions, it simply cannot be dismissed as too trivial and superficial to merit serious consideration and analysis. On the contrary, as we noted earlier, it may be one of the most important communication skills a person can master.

The Skills of Small Talk

Perhaps one reason why some people dislike small talk is simply because they lack skills in handling this type of encounter. Some of us may have no idea what we can add after we say hello. We may worry that what we say is trite and that others will find our attempts at conversation boring. Worse yet, we may be concerned that we will "fail the audition" and that others will find us unworthy of further contact. These are not flattering interpretations.

Unfortunately, researchers have not been particularly interested in understanding the skills that comprise successful small talk. No single study or book chapter exists that addresses specific verbal and nonverbal communication strategies that distinguish effective from ineffective small talk. Nevertheless, some helpful guidelines drawn from our previous chapters can be followed in attempts to evaluate, monitor, and improve one's own small-talk skills.

The importance of eye contact   First, eye contact is mandatory for effectively initiating encounters with others. As discussed in Chapter 3 (pp. 83–84), eye contact is typically interpreted as a sign of interest. Most people are pleased and appreciative when someone appears to take great interest in what they have to say. Eye contact is a clear and standard nonverbal means of communicating just that. Consequently, those who are successful at small talk rely heavily on looking earnestly at their partner. Note, however, that direct eye contact may be considered rude by some people. The Japanese, for example, are taught to avoid staring directly into someone's eyes. Instead, they concentrate on the lower part of the face during direct conversation

Providing nonverbal immediacy   Other nonverbal cues connote interest as well. Recall from Chapter 3 that head-nodding, forward-leaning, smiling, and open body positions all suggest interest and liking. This is what we described earlier as *nonverbal immediacy* (pp. 90–92). Using such techniques is one way of establishing physical and psychological closeness with your partner that is likely to lead to greater perceptions of attraction.

The importance of names   "What's in a name?" In *Romeo and Juliet* Shakespeare claimed that names have little importance because "That which we call a rose . . . By any other name would smell as sweet." He could not have been more wrong! Above all, and without fail, be sure to remember and use the other's name! Names are an individual's most personal identification tag. It is a symbolic extension of themselves and a label for everything they are. So important is our name to us that it is the first piece of information we deliver about ourselves. Unfortunately, it's also the most likely bit of information that is misused, overlooked, or forgotten by others. People quickly become offended when we misspell, mispronounce, or worse, forget their name. It signals loud and clear that we regard the individual as *not worthy* of the effort.

Small-Talk Scale

Instructions   The following statements were obtained from actual conversations between strangers. Indicate how frequently you might say these or use similar statements in your initial encounters with strangers or new acquaintances. Use the following scale:

5 extremely likely   **2** unlikely
4 likely   **1** extremely unlikely
3 maybe/unsure

____ **1.** I'm from New York.

____ **2.** I hate lying in bed at night listening to the clock tick.

____ **3.** I wish my church was more relevant to my life.

____ **4.** I may be stubborn but only because I'm right.

____ **5.** I really liked the movie *Bugsy.* I saw it three times.

____ **6.** I go to the ocean for relaxation.

____ **7.** I've been married and divorced twice.

____ **8.** I have two cats—one is named Philip Howard and the other, Mary Elizabeth.

____ **9.** I enjoy going to outdoor concerts in the summertime.

____ **10.** Do you celebrate Cinco de Mayo?

____ **11.** I'm 45 pounds overweight.

____ **12.** How old were you when you had your first sexual encounter?

____ **13.** Have you ever considered fooling around on your spouse?

____ **14.** How much money do you make?

____ **15.** Do you own your own home, or do you rent?

____ **16.** Have you read the book *Sleepwalking Through History,* by Haynes Johnson?

____ **17.** Are you a Republican or a Democrat?

____ **18.** My name is ____. What's yours?

____ **19.** Do you like to go to beach parties?

____ **20.** Where do you like to shop for clothes?

Calculating Your Score

1. Add your responses to items 2, 3, 4, 7, 11, 12, 13, 14, 15, and 17 = ____.

2. Add your responses to items 1, 5, 6, 8, 9, 10, 16, 18, 19, and 20 = ____.

3. Complete the following formula:

SMALL TALK = 60 − Total from step 1 = ____.

Then, + Total from step 2. YOUR TOTAL SMALL TALK SCORE = ____.

Interpreting Your Score

Possible range of scores for the Small-Talk Scale: 20–100. (If your own final score does not fall within that range, you made a computational error.)

The ideal score is 100. The higher the score, the more others will want to continue a conversation with you. Moreover, others will find you interesting, attractive, and socially appropriate. Items from Step 2 (1, 5, 6, 8, 9, 10, 16, 18, 19, and 20) are all intended to draw out others or to provide a positive image of yourself to others. In short, these and other statements of this type ensure prolonged interaction with others.

The lower the score, the more likely others will pull away from you and hurry to end the conversation. That is, we would expect to ask questions and provide information that is generally "safe" for ourselves and others. Items from Step 1 (2, **3**, 4, **7**, 11, 12, 13, 14, 15, and 17) all reflect statements that are potentially risky or unsafe. In addition, several of those statements are worded negatively. Remember: Accentuate the positive! These types of comments or questions can be shared more easily between friends or intimates—but not between strangers or new acquaintances. Do you understand why?

Reference

A number of these statements were obtained or updated from the following source:

Berger, C. R., Clatterbuck, G. W., & Shulman, L. S. (1976). Perceptions of information sequencing in relationship development. *Human Communication Research, 3,* 34–39.

There are effective ways to remember someone's name. One is to rehearse it several times "in your head." Another is to use it right away. Writing it down is very effective. Using it frequently also makes it sink in better. If you are unable to catch the name when introduced, feel free to ask for it. Asking the person the correct spelling can be a good strategy because it implies that it is important to you. (If the name is "Smith" forget that step!) When you see the same person a day or two later and you cannot remember her name, ask for it again. It is better than not knowing it at all.

Drawing out the other person   A great small-talk skill to try to develop is how to get the other person to talk about himself or herself. Keep in mind that everyone's favorite topic is typically themselves. Capitalize on that notion by asking your small-talk partner a lot of questions. Good examples are: "Where are you from?" "What do you enjoy doing in your spare time?" "What brings you here to this event?" and so on.

Indicate further interest and active listening with follow-up questions. Pursue their responses with directed questions or comments. When your partner indicates that she or he is from Peoria, Illinois, you can develop the conversation by asking, "What brings you all the way here to (wherever)" or "Do you miss Peoria? I'll bet life was different there than it is here." So as not to turn the conversation into an inquisition, you might comment that "I like small cities. In fact, I have grandparents who still live in a rural community. I love to visit them because the people are so friendly." Be sure that your comments and questions evolve either directly or indirectly from what the person just said. Try to avoid random topic switching; you'll just end up talking about what *you're* interested in as opposed to what the *other person* might want to talk about.

Keeping it light   An important rule is to keep the conversation light. Should you plunge too quickly into heavy issues early in the relationship, the other individual is likely to feel threatened. No one wants to hear about your latest scrap with your parents, your financial difficulties, or your philosophical convictions at this point.

Accentuate the positive   Finally, you are better off making most of your talk *positive.* Even minor negative complaints, such as the weather is awful, your workload is too heavy, the professors are unfair, or the team is unsuccessful, are commonly perceived as "downers." In particular, commenting negatively about others in the room or mutual acquaintances can lead very quickly to some rather destructive, disagreeable interactions, particularly if your partner finds those same individuals attractive.

Generally, then, skillful small talk is not all that difficult. The rules we have suggested by no means exhaust the possibilities, and they may or may not work in specific cases. But once a small-talk conversation has been managed successfully, the next experience is more likely to be rewarding and enjoyable.

Management: The Decision to Linger

Movement toward greater intimacy, closer friendship, and generally more intensity in a relationship depends to a large extent on the *rewards* versus the *benefits* we think we have gained or suspect we will gain from the affiliation.[24] Crudely put, some theorists claim that we (perhaps unconsciously) take some kind of mental "inventory" to determine the relative rewards and costs that we potentially can derive from a relationship before we commit ourselves to it. This interpretation is based on a formulation called **exchange theory,** which was originally developed by sociologist George Homans to try to explain *all* forms of human social interaction.[25] (Exchange theory itself was derived from Jeremy Bentham's utilitarian philosophy.)

Exchange theorists argue that we implicitly count up the history of rewards received from interacting with the other person, weigh that against the history of costs, and make an estimate of the worth of the relationship to us. According to this explanation, when the cost/benefit ratio has been calculated, we make our decision. That is, when rewards outweigh the costs for both individuals, then the relationship is likely to survive and gain momentum. Conversely, if one or both partners perceive the relationship as too costly, the relationship is likely to terminate.

Many current theorists argue against this utilitarian, cost/benefit approach to relational development. In its elementary form, it is probably oversimplified. Nevertheless, it still may have something to offer. Granted, we are not likely to take a systematic inventory regarding each and every good versus bad action that we think our partner has performed. By the same token, we are unlikely to be consciously aware of all that *we* do in a positive or negative way that might influence the cost/benefit ratio for the other person in our everyday efforts to maintain a relationship. Yet, most of us can conveniently manufacture, at least in the back of our own mind, some idea of the rewards versus costs that we believe represents our relationship. Furthermore, we can express (at least to ourselves) some idea of what that ratio might be in the relationship at a later time.

Thus, the reasons we feel that the old cost/benefit principle has some merit are simple: We know for a fact that most of us prefer to be around individuals who make us feel good. Such people *do* provide us with rewarding experiences as we relate to them. Similarly, we do not like to be around persons who make us feel bad. They provide us with punishing experiences that, in a psychological sense, cost us a great deal. Generally, then, the classic idea of costs versus benefits—the balance of rewards and punishments in an exchange—is still a viable idea that can predict the fate of a relationship.

Assessing the Rewards and Costs

If the "exchange" concept has merit, it should be reflected in reality. For example, when you examine your current relationships, you should find that most of your good friends, over the long haul, have provided you with greater benefits and rewards than they have costs or punishments. It is not always easy to decide, but there are at least some clear signs: They probably tell you in many ways that they like you. This shows up in their behavior as well: They may laugh politely at your bad jokes, call you when you are sick or feeling depressed, lend you money when you're broke, and tell you what a great person you are even though others may feel you are a slob. Sure, these same individuals may be burdensome from time to time, and you may not like some of the things you have to do to retain them as friends. Over time, however, it should be clear that you gain more from these relationships than you lose. If that is not the case, either you are very strange or the exchange formulation is simply wrong!

This ratio of costs and benefits is a long-term matter. That is, in lasting interpersonal relationships with friends or family we find that the individuals involved are likely to have accumulated a kind of "reservoir" of rewards that can be drawn upon in troubled times. It is these rewards that maintain the relationship. True, they have built up a reservoir of costs as well, but keep in mind that the rewards continue to outweigh the costs. This accumulation process is critical for relational management. In times of temporary crisis, when costs tend to be very high, we can turn to that reservoir of rewards to help us through. Without it, the relationship can be in big trouble.

There is, however, an important exception to the preceding principle: We can put up with an incredible amount of costs as long as we can also predict that significant rewards will follow.[26] This is the so-called **principle of delayed gratification** that is so important to middle-class Americans. It keeps millions of college students with their noses firmly pressed to the unpleasant grindstone of boring degree requirements in the expectation that it will all "pay off" after graduation.

In interpersonal relationships, rewards that seem reasonably certain in the future allow us to endure the more immediate costs of continuing the bond with the other person. Such costs may involve financial strain, isolation, career interruptions, or even physical or psychological abuse. However, such arrangements may not always work out. Consider the often repeated story of the couple who married very young while they were both still in school. But alas, they couldn't make it financially, so the wife dropped out and took a full-time job. Her reasoning at the time was that her husband would get a good job after graduation and then it would be her turn to finish school. In the meantime, the wife accumulated a lot of costs, fully expecting the husband to deliver to her the rewards of financial solvency, loving gratitude, and other forms of "interest on her investment." In reality, many such couples do not live happily ever after when there is such a high level of "balance due." Husbands may resent having to "pay off" the debt, and in many cases, they simply leave with younger women. Or wives may find that they cannot endure the costs, and they simply give up the idea of collecting at a later date. In such cases, the relationship terminates (usually with considerable malice).

Overall, this process of assessing and cataloging the ratio of rewards and costs in a relationship is important. The outcome appears to determine whether it will move forward or backward toward greater or lesser intimacy. Individuals moving from casual, impersonal contact to more meaningful, interpersonal communion are likely to put a lot of energy into filling one another's reward reservoir and, at the same time, they try to avoid adding to each other's costs. However, as the relationship develops, problems can arise that may have a significant influence on its future. One thing that can determine its future fate is the degree to which the individuals involved put themselves "at risk" by revealing core information about themselves.

Revealing Core Information About Self

When a particular relationship is rewarding, that is, when both parties seem to make each other feel good, they usually become closer and closer. Soon, they find themselves sharing very private information with each other that is usually reserved only for a few individuals that each knows very well. Such "core" information involves risks because it requires disclosure of very personal matters.[27]

Testing the water: self-disclosure As we begin this process of mutual **self-disclosure,** we may test the water by revealing something about our family or friends that affects us only indirectly. For instance, we might disclose the fact that Great Aunt Wilma had an out-of-wedlock child who died at birth. We dangle that family skeleton and then wait to see what kind of reaction such a "secret" will provoke. If our partner responds sympathetically, we might conclude that he or she has passed our test, and perhaps we can reveal more sensitive information. However, if the response is critical, our partner has failed. After all, Great Aunt Wilma was a favorite relative and her unwanted pregnancy wasn't her fault!

Once a sensitive self-disclosure has been received negatively, we generally keep the other person at a safe distance. We choose not to expose further information about our family, friends, or self simply because we now have evidence that the person is unlikely to be understanding and supportive. But if the person passed the test, we have at least initial confirmation that it is safe to make a more significant self-disclosure or expose even more sensitive family information.

It all comes down to the process of establishing *trust.* Can we trust the other to respond sensitively to our personal attributes, our secrets, and our deep feelings? Can we be confident that the other will continue to like us after we've disclosed both positive *and* negative information about ourselves? If we can answer yes to all of the above with conviction, then we can assume that the relationship will move toward greater intimacy.

This movement toward greater intimacy generally occurs after the initial experimental or test phase of the relationship.[28] Satisfied that our partner will remain sympathetic and supportive, we intensify the relationship. The partner has similarly established trust. We have also been tested and have passed. In other words, this is a reciprocal process. For each party, self-disclosure increases as we tell each other more and more about ourselves. We begin to reveal not just more positive information, but

Moving to a close and intimate relationship in interpersonal communication requires a gradual establishment of mutual trust founded on increasingly extensive self-disclosure. That trust requires that each of the parties respond sensitively to the individual attributes and personal history of the other.

also more *negative* information about ourselves. And we risk disclosing information that few others may know. ("I was caught shoplifting when I was 8 years old. I swiped a candy bar and my folks were really mad.")

Labeling the relationship   Before long we perceive our relationship to take on a life of its own. We provide our relationship with a *label.* In heterosexual social settings, persons of the same sex call themselves "buddies" or "best friends." A male and a female become a "couple." This labeling process is important because it attaches specific and culturally shared *meanings* to the relationship that it did not previously have. Labeling identifies the relationship as a specific instance of a generally understood concept (Chapter 2, pp. 50–59). Once

we have a symbol or label with associated and shared meanings for a relationship between two people, it greatly changes their self-conceptions. Suddenly the pronoun "we" becomes far more significant than either "me" or "you."

In the male-female case, this welding of two people into a single labeled entity has significant implications. Because of the labeled concept, it controls everyone's perceptions of the persons involved. This, in turn, alters the responses of other people to them. They come to be seen not as two separate, unique persons but as a single entity—a *couple* that has to be thought about, responded to, and dealt with socially as such.

This change in meaning and behavior by friends, family, and others has many consequences. For one thing, it brings different kinds of responses from others that make it necessary to reconstruct the self-images of the individuals who make up the couple. This external social process, along with an increase in self-disclosure, reinforces the movement toward intimacy.

Another consequence is that as we become a two-person dyad, in the eyes of others as well as ourselves, we find that we have established mutually accepted expectations for relating to each other. This imposes a division of labor, with roles that define the separate parts we will play. All of these rules for social relationships make up a fairly complex and mutually held set of guidelines that define how each is "supposed to" communicate with the other.

At each stage in this movement toward intimacy, the individuals employ "secret tests" to check out the level of commitment each feels to the other.[29] For instance, we might test our partner's commitment by suggesting that it's time to meet our parents—and we all know what *that* means! Or we might mention a chance meeting with a former boyfriend or girlfriend the other day (in hopes that our partner will act possessive and jealous!).

Achieving full disclosure   Assuming all goes well, our relationship moves forward to greater and greater levels of intimacy. Throughout this entire experimenting stage, we take risks by exposing more and more about ourselves. Then we observe carefully how our partner responds to that disclosure. The more consistently our partner responds in a supportive, understanding manner, the more likely we are to trust that person, gaining confidence that she or he won't hurt us, no matter what we do or say. In short, once the foundation of trust is established and we reach a state of full disclosure, we have become an *intimate pair,* who are seen as such by ourselves and others.[30]

Communicating with an Intimate Other

Once two individuals believe they are in an intimate relationship, a transformation takes place in the way they talk to and behave toward each other. We noted earlier that during the process of coming together, a pair develops norms for their friendship or marriage. Some of those rules are common to almost any set of intimate communicators. For example, in their study of intimate dyads, researchers Michael Argyle and Monika Henderson found that very good friends share several rules such as "Don't nag" and "Don't criticize a friend in public."[31] However, many of the communication norms that develop between intimates are unique to the specific relationship between those two particular individuals. For example, a couple may develop a communication norm that ensures an easy escape from late-night social events. They share an agreement that when one or the other feels it's time to go home, that person signals the desire to the other by exclaiming, "Well, the kids sure get up early in the morning." The other quickly agrees, and they then begin the process of leave-taking.

You probably can think of special understandings that you share with an intimate partner concerning what messages are or are not appropriate. Some couples have norms about fighting, such as that they agree never to call each other "ugly" names when they are angry. Others insist on discussing any conflicts *before* they go to bed at night. You may know of couples who avoid any open communication of affection, even refusing to hold hands in public. Whatever they may be, such rules tend to be both personal and private to the relationship. Some may be quite explicit and a consequence of negotiations between the partners. Others are often implicit and are simply "assumed" by one another.

Another characteristic of participants in close relationships is their use of "intimate idioms" and "inside" humor.[32] That is, special friends or lovers generally share words, nonverbal gestures, and meanings for situations that others may not quite understand, recognize, or know about. You may have friends who talk "baby talk" to each other when they are alone. Should they slip and reveal that talk in public, others may laugh or feel embarrassed for them. You may know of a couple in which one partner calls the other "pet" names such as "Sweetie-pie" or "Babycakes" when they are alone. Or you and your best friend may use a common phrase, such as "That's nice," to signal boredom when interacting with "outsiders." Inside humor, in the form of private jokes, is another example of an intimate and private dialogue. It is

not uncommon to see a couple crack up over a remark, when no one else around thinks it is funny.

In this section we have traced how movement toward greater intimacy generally occurs. Obviously, while some relationships follow the stages we have described, others do not. Some move forward quickly overnight into intimacy; others may take years to reach that stage. Even less predictable is whether or not any given relationship is likely to be successful. Life would be far more comfortable if we could determine our probability of success or failure in the long run *before* developing an intimate relationship with another person. Unfortunately, too many different factors, situations, and events can go wrong so as to disrupt any human relationship.

Disengagement: The Decision to Leave

So far, we've focused primarily on relationships in which both partners choose to move forward toward greater intimacy and eventually to a stable pattern of companionship or loving affiliation. In this section, we will discuss the opposite kind of process, in which the intimate qualities of the relationship erode, become a problem, and are eventually disrupted to a point where one or both decide to leave.

How do people disengage, or withdraw, from an intimate relationship in which the costs greatly exceed the benefits? The reasons or the causes for disengagement vary widely, but one important factor is what each partner *believes* to be the problem. Some answers can be found in the study of alienation between husbands and wives and disruption of marriages: According to a *Redbook* magazine survey of marriage counselors, the 10 most common causes of marital breakup include (in order of frequency): (1) communication problems, (2) no longer sharing common interests or goals, (3) sexual incompatibility, (4) infidelity, (5) no more fun in the marriage, (6) money, (7) conflicts involving the children, (8) alcohol or drug abuse, (9) women's equality issues, and (10) the in-laws.[33]

Assuming that such a poll has validity, these are what people *say* were the reasons leading to their separation or divorce. It probably matters little whether the "real" causes of these disengagements were something else, such as unfulfilled unconscious needs or other unfathomable psychoanalytic factors. Whatever the "true" reasons may be, it is clear that the people in the survey *thought* their marital breakup was due to the problems they indicated in the preceding list.

What people *believe* guides what they *do*. Shortly after the turn of the century, social psychologist W. I. Thomas developed the principle of the **definition of the situation,** which essentially states that if people believe something to be real, they will act as though it were real.[34] People's beliefs, in turn, are derived from their interactions with others, which is another example of the "social construction of reality."[35] Because of these principles, both members of a couple undergoing disengagement often go through a process of creating, as a result of communication with others, their own individual interpretations of what they believe to be the *real* causes of the disengagement—what went wrong, who is to blame, what they were justified in doing, and so forth. These constructed definitions of reality, then, become the basis for their subsequent actions.[36]

Causes of Relationship Disengagement

Whenever we finally determine that a friendship, marriage, or any other type of serious intimate relationship is coming to an end, we need to explain *why*. In particular we feel a need to attribute "blame." Blame is an important concept in our culture. It provides simple explanations of human behavior that are easy to understand and that "make sense." That is, most people interpret the causes of human behavior within a "good guy/bad guy" framework, where bad outcomes are due to bad people (and vice versa). It is too difficult for most people to try to probe more deeply and to understand human decisions and actions as consequences of complex impersonal forces and factors.[37]

The pressure for an explanation   Even if we try to avoid labeling anyone as the "bad actor," others invariably will ask, "So tell me, why did you two break up?" (Read: What did he [or she] do?) We can be flippant in our response, but then people think we're being cold-hearted and cruel. They may speculate further that we were never really committed to the relationship in the first place. And so it goes. Friends and family need, want, and expect us to give them an *accounting* of what happened. Furthermore, not just any interpretation will do—only a certain kind of causal explanation will be met with their approval.[38]

If the intimate and trusting qualities of a relationship begin to erode, the nature of interpersonal communication undergoes predictable changes. Each party begins to see the other person in a different and less positive perspective, and a process of distancing, disassociation, and ultimate disengagement begins. If that process cannot be reversed, each individual has to create an account that is acceptable to themselves, and to others that they care about, as to who was to blame for the collapse of the relationship.

Ideally, in an accounting there has to be blame. So, for the sake of others as well as ourselves, we have to create an explanation—a plausible "theory" of what went wrong—that our friends and family will find acceptable. Most of us do this by identifying the bad motives and misconduct of the other person that led to the problem.

Acceptable assignments of blame   One of the first requirements of such a story is that our family and friends must believe that somehow, in some way, we were justified in leaving (not to blame). In other words, we need an explanation in which we ourselves are seen as occupying the moral high ground. For example, if we were the one that "got left," we must be careful to spin a tale that does *not* warrant his or her leaving us!

Ideally, the story we construct should lead us to think, and should compel the sympathetic listener to exclaim, "You made a rational decision; and you are definitely better off without such a person!" We need to convince both ourselves and others that we are still worthy candidates for future relational ties.[39] It could do us great harm, both personally and socially, to provide a story in which we assume blame and identify ourselves as the culprit. By the same token, it may be risky to create a version that blames our partner entirely. If that is done, the individual probably will attempt to justify his or her actions by laying all of the blame on you. You become the villain in the partner's construction of reality.

Another important requirement for a story explaining a disengagement is that it should reflect a sense of emotional maturity and recognition that it "takes two" to make and to break a relationship. Consequently, a well-created story that will be received sympathetically by those we care about might include just a little bit of self-blame. It can have a lot of other-blame as long as we indicate some degree of understanding of our partner's behavior.

The explanatory story, then, provides for an accounting that should satisfy the needs and expectations of others, and if well constructed it provides a "true" version of what happened for consumption by friends and family. And, of course, it is one that we ourselves can firmly believe. Ideally, it lets us accept a minor part of the blame, but it must dump the lion's share on the other so that we can feel better about our part in the disengagement.

Saying Goodbye

Just as the language of intimate communicators differs significantly from that of new acquaintances or strangers, the language of individuals involved in disengagement reflects a dramatic change. Obviously, couples going through disengagement are unlikely to call each other "Sweetheart" or "Honey." They revert back to first names, and once again use some of the more stylized, stereotypic language of strangers. Their conversations become hesitant and awkward as they hold back disclosure. They have trouble sharing their feelings because predictable responses of support are no longer evidenced.

Couples begin to disengage by a two-fold process called *distancing* and *disassociation*.[40] What this means is that in their interpersonal interactions they begin transmitting messages designed to increase both physical and psychological distance and to disassociate themselves from their partners.

Establishing distance   Messages designed to achieve the goal of **distancing** can take both verbal and nonverbal forms, but the goal is always the same. For example, one of the simplest and most obvious ways that a person can begin to disengage is by spending more and more of his or her time away from the other. He or she may work late at night, take weekend trips to visit friends or relatives without the partner, or go to plays, concerts, or movies with friends. Increasing physical distance can also be achieved at home. When one partner is in the living room watching television, the other reads alone in the kitchen. At some point, one partner may sleep in their bedroom, while the other takes to the guest room or the couch.

Psychological distancing can be achieved in many subtle and indirect ways. The partners may look at each other less, touch less often, put up such barriers as folded arms, or experience more uncomfortable periods of silence, and they may employ colder vocal tones in exchanges. Psychological distancing can also be accomplished by close control over the content of their messages. That is, as disclosure begins to shut down, one partner may be unwilling to volunteer a lot of personal information to the other. When this happens, the responses of one toward the other become less supportive and sympathetic. By any of these strategies and patterns, then, both physical and psychological distance replace the close association that had been developed and maintained earlier. Distancing is a very clear and necessary aspect of the disengagement process.

Disassociation   The term **disassociation** refers to reducing the use of the unit-implying pronoun "we" and reverting back to the individualistic "you" and "I." Unwilling or unable to vest any further interest into the relationship itself, couples are likely to become concerned with their own feelings, costs, and benefits rather than those they shared earlier. Typically, one begins to hear such messages as, "You only care what happens to you. What about me?" Where they once referred to "our" furniture and "our" dishes, they now talk about "my" chair and "your" mother's china. Messages about the future become transformed into messages about the past.

Throughout the disassociation process, differences, rather than similarities, are emphasized. Even though such differences may have existed throughout the entire relationship, they now are seen as divisive and the couple begins to communicate and complain openly, sometimes bitterly, about those differences. The other side of this coin is that discussions centered on common likes, dislikes, and mutual interests are now understated or ignored altogether. Partners experiencing disassociation come to believe that they never really had anything in common with the other person and they wonder why they failed to see that before. Or if they see that they did earlier, they conclude that they've "developed" and "grown" while the other has "failed to change."

Obviously, neither distancing nor disassociation contributes to relational bonding. To some degree, however, even healthy intimate relationships occasionally experience both communication processes. We cannot (and will not) spend every waking and sleeping moment with our partner. All of us need personal space and time away from each other. We cannot (and will not) hide or suppress our likes and dislikes, either, simply because our attitudes and beliefs differ from our partner's. Unlike intimate communicators, though, disengagers spend an increasing amount of time and energy avoiding contact and stressing dissimilarities. While intimates talk about togetherness, coupling, and attachment, disengagers frequently communicate separateness, autonomy, and detachment.

"Fifty Ways to Leave Your Lover"

Popular musicians Simon and Garfunkel maintained in a song that "there must be fifty ways to leave your lover." Nevertheless, most people find it awkward and difficult to make it through even one. In fact, the majority of attempts to disengage from relationships can be characterized as *nondirect*. People don't like to confront each other. They much prefer to just let the relationship "pass away" over time.

In an effort to determine the most common strategies that people use to disengage from relationships, researcher Leslie Baxter had college students describe those termination attempts they had used in actual friendships or *close* friendships.[41] She categorized their accounts into four main strategies: (1) withdrawal/avoidance, (2) ending on a positive tone, (3) Machiavellianism, and (4) open confrontation.

Withdrawal/avoidance This first strategy parallels our discussion of distancing and disassociation. Rather than confront the partner with a direct statement that the relationship is over, individuals who use this strategy rely on a more indirect approach. They are likely to telephone less frequently, be "too busy" to get together this weekend (or any weekend anytime soon!), and avoid making any definite future plans to spend time together. This could be called the "Don't call me, I'll call you" approach. The outcome (if it works) is that the couple see less and less of each other without the strain of confrontation. Before long, the relationship simply "fades away."

Obviously, this strategy may work well in terminating unwanted friendships, but it would be difficult to employ when you're married. For one thing, a marriage is a relationship involving the community as well as the couple, and the legal constraints defining the relationship generally require that all loose ends be tied. The partners can't just drift away and let the relationship fade. Nevertheless, we do know that some form of avoidance and withdrawal precedes almost all disengagement attempts.

Ending on a positive tone This strategy represents a "socially appropriate" means of ending relationships. Couples who use this strategy show concern and regard for one another. They try to avoid major conflict or attempts to malign or slander the relationship. In short, they are "nice" about the breakup! In rare instances, some of these couples may revert to a less intense relationship by remaining friends. There are couples who are divorced, but still celebrate holidays together and may even attend each other's second weddings. Positive-tone strategies are strongly encouraged for couples with children. Divorced parents who are able to resolve their differences amicably may also be those who can focus on providing their children with a secure, stable (although separate) environment.

Machiavellianism This is clearly the most unusual strategy.[42] That is not to say it is infrequently used. Students in the Baxter study reported a variety of ways to use this technique. What makes it so unusual is the manipulation and deception involved. Specifically, the Machiavellian strategy seeks to convince the unwitting partner that relational termination was his or her idea and is in the partner's own best interest! The person being convinced may not have wanted the relationship to end.

This strategy incorporates the principle of the *definition of the situation* noted earlier. If one partner can define the breakup as the preference of the other, then that other will act on the basis of the new definition. For instance, a woman may intentionally go out with the man's best friend, knowing that he will be angry. Then, when he does express his disapproval, she exclaims, "Go ahead. Leave me. You deserve somebody better than me." Or a man may intentionally provoke his partner into a fight. At the height of the brawl, she gets very angry and shouts, "Go ahead. Just leave. See if I care!" When he quickly takes advantage of the situation and does leave, the woman is left wondering what happened.

Obviously, there are ethical questions involved in using a Machiavellian strategy. No one likes to be tricked or deceived. And yet, we know that people justify their use of this technique by claiming their partner really *is* better off without them. Perhaps they are right. Furthermore, some who use the technique argue that because the partner initiates the disengagement, he or she is likely to get over the relationship a little easier than if the tables were turned. That is, it's more dignified to leave than to be left.

Open confrontation   This strategy contrasts sharply with Machiavellianism. It is for understandable reasons the least used of the ways to "say goodbye." As we noted earlier, no one likes to face the partner, disclose that the relationship is over, explain why this is so, and cope with the resulting emotional uproar that will follow. First the partner expresses shock or disbelief, then anger, and finally, hurt. Individuals using the open-confrontation approach should be prepared for an emotional roller coaster.

In reality, the disengagement of a particular set of partners may involve more than one, or perhaps all, of these strategies for termination. One may try withdrawal/avoidance only to discover that it doesn't work. Positive tone sounds nice, but there is no guarantee of success. Machiavellianism may be distasteful, but it may be effective. If all else fails, there is always open confrontation. In any case, breaking up a close relationship that started on a casual basis and then slowly, step by step, developed over time into a stable affiliation is never an easy process. The bonds of love, affection, deep concern for the other, and the mutual attachments that were once in place are not easily cast off. Disengagement leaves people drained, sad, and often bitter. At the same time, the personal and emotional ratio of costs versus benefits may make it the only viable option.

One of the more dramatic and least pleasant ways to end a relationship is through open confrontation. When interpersonal communication follows this pattern, the factor of irrevocability is especially important. Although such confrontation may produce an emotional roller coaster, it is likely to result in permanent disengagement and a total disruption of the relationship.

Chapter Review

- The study of interpersonal communication looks at the kinds of messages people use when they want to develop close ties to others, when they try to keep valued relationships going, or when they seek to disconnect themselves from attachments that they no longer want.

- The various kinds of settings in which communication takes place have strong influences on what is said, by whom, and with what effect, regardless of who is communicating and about what. Communicating parties are simultaneously influenced by their *physical surroundings,* the *social situation* in which their interaction takes place, and the *social relationship* that exists between them. It is precisely these three features of communication settings that identify what is meant by the *context* of their communication.

- Interpersonal communication is a process of transmitting messages between people through the use of language and actions designed to arouse meanings intended by sources. In that sense, it is no different from any other form of human communication. What does set it apart is that it is focused on interactions between two people.

- As individuals come to know one another better through interpersonal communication, their relationship tends to move from impersonal to personal. That is, they become increasingly close and intimate.

- There are six key characteristics of interpersonal communication: It begins with the "self," it is fully transactional, participants share physical proximity, their messages are shaped by social roles, interpersonal communication is irreversible, and it is unrepeatable.

- Patterns of interpersonal communication change during the different phases of relationship development. During the initial period, people rely on scripted and stereotypic conversational rules. Because all relationships begin with small talk, these communication skills are among the most important we can master.

- A number of specific skills can help in making effective small talk: steady eye contact, occasional head-nodding, forward-leaning, and smiling. These behaviors imply nonverbal immediacy indicating to the other that we are interested in and enjoy what she or he is saying.

- To the extent that we find our initial and subsequent encounters with another rewarding and interesting, we are likely to move toward greater intimacy. Much depends on the cost/benefit ratio of rewards versus punishments we think we will gain by going forward in the relationship.

- Communication during the management or intimacy phase of the relationship involves testing the degree to which the other person is open and supportive. This process requires disclosing selected sensitive information about ourselves and waiting to see how the other responds. Assuming the partner responds positively, we increasingly engage in disclosure. After we trust our partner, we negotiate unique rules to govern our relationship. We generate a private language system, perhaps calling each other pet names, using baby talk, and sharing private jokes.

- In terminating a relationship, we have to construct a "true" account of why it went wrong that will satisfy ourselves, our friends, and our relatives. It has to earn us some degree of social credit so that we are still perceived as having the potential for a good relationship in the future. We construct a plausible story that assigns blame to the "bad actor" and puts the best "face" on the disengagement.

- Breaking up a relationship that has yielded warm and satisfying rewards is never easy. Terminating the relationship generally involves both distancing and disassociation. We avoid spending time together and begin the uncoupling process by referring to "I" and "me" instead of "us" and "we." The strategies for "saying goodbye" and leaving include withdrawal and avoidance, showing concern for the other, the Machiavellian tactic of manipulating the partner into believing that the disengagement was his or her idea, and the sudden, open confrontation.

Key Terms

Controls (social)   Words or actions used by senders for the purpose of influencing a receiver to follow a group's norms, to abide by their expectations of how his or her role should be performed, or to recognize the ranks of authority, power, and prestige of others in the group.

Cost/benefit ratio   The ratio of the efforts that have to be made in establishing or maintaining a relationship to the rewards that the relationship brings. (See **utilitarianism.**)

Cushioning function The benefit derived from having friends or family members who provide emotional support when events beyond our control in an uncaring world make life difficult.

Definition of the situation W. I. Thomas's principle of behavior stating that if people believe something to be real, they will act as though it were real.

Disengagement Communication strategies people use when they are attempting to withdraw gracefully (or not so gracefully) from a close association with another.

Disassociation A strategy of transmitting messages to another person aimed at achieving a reduction in the use of the unit-implying pronoun "we," and reverting back to the individualistic "you" and "I."

Distancing A strategy of transmitting verbal and nonverbal messages to another person with the goal of increasing both physical and psychological distance between the two partners.

Dyad Two persons in a relatively enduring social relationship.

Engagement That communication process by which people try to move their relationships from an impersonal to a personal basis.

Exchange theory A formulation originally developed by George Homans to try to explain *all* forms of human social interaction. Applied to communication, it argues that we implicitly count up the history of rewards received from interacting with the other person, weigh that against the history of costs, and make an estimate of the worth of the relationship to us. If rewards outweigh the costs for both individuals, then the relationship is likely to survive and gain momentum. If not, the relationship is likely to terminate.

Interpersonal communication Communication that takes place between two people who come to know one another better as their relationship tends to move from impersonal to personal.

Machiavellianism A strategy for ending a relationship in which a manipulative individual desiring that goal is able to convince an unwilling partner, who is unaware of the strategy, that termination was the partner's idea and is in his or her best interest.

Management (communication strategy) The communication strategies people use to maintain valued interpersonal ties.

Norms In general these are shared convictions about what kinds of behavior are approved within a group or society. In the case of communication, norms are rules understood and accepted by the parties that define both the content and the style of messages which are appropriate or inappropriate in a particular situation.

Personal idea (persona) A set of beliefs, meanings, and understandings that an individual develops about another person as a result of communicating with her or him. (This is an older name for what social scientists later called "implicit personality.")

Principle of delayed gratification A belief that accepting costs or guarding resources in the present will pay off in significant long-term rewards.

Rank The level of social honor, status, or prestige assigned to a member of a group by the other members. Those with higher authority and power, or sometimes wealth, are accorded higher rank.

Roles In general, these are specific activities that are expected from each participant who performs a specialized part in a group. In interactive communication, roles are rules that govern who can say what to whom in a particular relationship.

Scripted or **stereotypic (conversations)** Conversations that are like highly standardized and predictable lines rehearsed in a play. Conversations can be classified as scripted or stereotypic if they follow clear, even rigid, rules in certain well-defined communication situations.

Self (self-image or self-concept) That pattern of beliefs, meanings, and understandings each individual develops concerning her or his own personal characteristics, capacities, limitations, and worth as a human being. In other words, our personal conceptions of *who* we are, *what* we are, and *where* we are in the social order.

Self-disclosure Communicating messages to another that reveal the nature of one's past, private thoughts, personal views, or deep feelings.

Small talk Discussions that focus on topics of general interest and have little emotional or personal significance, such as the weather, sports, or other matters not requiring self-disclosure.

Utilitarianism An explanation of human behavior formulated by 18th-century British philosopher Jeremy Bentham, in which actions are decided on the ratio of pleasure to pain that can be derived. He maintained that we choose to engage in those behaviors that maximize pleasure and avoid those that result in pain. This is similar to the **cost/benefit ratio.**

Withdrawal/avoidance A strategy of indirect distancing and dissociation in which parties telephone less frequently, are "too busy" to get together and avoid making any definite future plans. The couple sees less and less of each other without the strain of confrontation and their relationship simply "fades away."

Notes

1. For a more extensive analysis of the distinctions between the situational and developmental perspectives, as well as in-depth discussion between impersonal and personal relationships, see: Miller, G. R., & Steinberg, M. (1975). *Between people* (pp. 7–29). Chicago: Science Research Associates: Miller, G. R. (1980). Interpersonal communication. In C. L. Book (Ed.), *Human communication principles, contexts and skills* (pp. 109–114). New York: St. Martin's Press.

2. Although it may seem a bit strange, this term specifies rather precisely the idea of two people in a system of repetitive social interaction. It was first brought into the study of human social behavior by the 19th-century German sociologist Georg Simmel. See: Simmel, G. (1902). The number of members as determining the sociological form of the group (A. Small, Trans.). *American Journal of Sociology, 8,* 158–196. For more recent discussions of the dyad and dyadic communication see: Wilmont, W. W. (1979). *Dyadic communication* (2nd ed.). Reading, MA: Addison-Wesley.

3. Pearson, J. C. (1987). *Interpersonal communication: Clarity, confidence, concern* (pp. 7–14). Dubuque, IA: Wm. C. Brown.

4. The term *self* derives from turn-of-the-century social psychology in which theorists were trying to understand how a person develops personal understandings of his or her social, psychological, and physical characteristics, and the value placed on them by the society. Generally, such understandings were said to be obtained in a process of social interaction with others. See: Charles Horton Cooley's discussion of the "looking-glass self," in: Cooley, C. H. (1902). *Human nature and the social order* (pp. 81–263). New York: Charles Scribner's Sons. For a more contemporary discussion of the role of the self in interpersonal communication, see: Barnlund, D. C. (1970). A transactional model of communication. In K. K. Sereno & C. D. Mortenson (Eds.), *Foundations of communication theory* (pp. 98–101). New York: Harper and Row, 1970); and Pearson, op. cit., pp. 7–9.

5. This self and multi-image conception of interpersonal communication was first set forth by Charles Horton Cooley in his classic work *Human nature and the social order* (pp. 81–263). New York: Charles Scribner's Sons.

6. From the ancient Greek word *persona,* which means "mask." Masks were used by actors to indicate the character being portrayed. We continue to use the term today in our word *personality* to imply the major psychological traits and social characteristics of an individual. Thus, our "self" image is our imagined "personality."

7. Cooley believed that these personal ideas were the foundation of the social process. "The imaginations people have on one another," he said, "are the solid facts of society." See: Cooley, op. cit., p. 121. The same general idea was later developed by psychologists around the term *implicit personality.*

8. In a very general sense, we alluded to this process of "reading" the reactions of the other in Chapter 1 (pp. 16–20) when we discussed role-taking and feedback. The same kind of activity has been called "taking the role of the other" by classic social psychologists in the symbolic interactionist tradition. See: Mead, G. H. (1934). *Mind, self and society: From the standpoint of a social behaviorist* (Charles W. Morris, Ed.) (p. 254). Chicago: University of Chicago Press.

9. Laing, R. D., Phillipson, H., & Lee, A. R. (1966). *Interpersonal perceptions.* Baltimore: Perennial Library; Wenberg, J., & Wilmot, W. (1973). *The personal communication process.* New York: John Wiley and Sons; Wilmot, W. W. (1979). *Dyadic communication* (2nd ed.) (pp. 10–13). Reading, MA: Addison-Wesley; and Miller, G. R. (1990). In-

terpersonal communication. In G. L. Dahnke & G. W. Clatterbuck (Eds.), *Human communication: Theory and research* (pp. 91–122). Belmont, CA: Wadsworth.

10. Bateson, G. (1958). *Naven* (2nd ed.), Stanford, CA: Stanford University Press; Watzlawick, P., Beavin, J. H., & Jackson, D. D. (1967). *Pragmatics of human communication* (pp. 51–54). New York: W. W. Norton.

11. Pearson, op. cit., pp. 42–44.

12. For a complete discussion of the importance of the family in interpersonal communication see: Fitzpatrick, M. A., & Badzinsk, D. M. (1985). All in the family: Interpersonal communication in kin relationships. In M. L. Knapp & G. R. Miller (Eds.), *Handbook of interpersonal communication* (pp. 687–736). Beverly Hills, CA: Sage.

13. Burke, R. J., & Weir, T. (1975). Giving and receiving help with work and non-work related problems. *Journal of Business Administration, 6,* 59–78; Roloff, M. E., Janiszewsk, C. A., McGrath, M. A., Burns, C. S., & Manrai, L. A. (1988). Acquiring resources from intimates: When obligation substitutes for persuasion. *Human Communication Research, 14,* 364–396.

14. For a summary of utilitarianism, see Chapter 19, Bentham: Principles of morals and legislation. (1954). In W. Ebenstein (Ed.), *Great political thinkers* (pp. 484–499). New York: Rinehart and Company.

15. Byrne, D. (1971). *The attraction paradigm.* New York: Academic Press; Byrne, D., & Nelson, D. (1965). Attraction as a linear function of proportion of positive reinforcements. *Journal of Personality and Social Psychology, 1,* 659–663. For discussion of related research see: Bowers, J. W., Metts, S. M., & Duncanson, W. T. (1985). Emotion and interpersonal communication. In M. L. Knapp & G. R. Miller (Eds.), *Handbook of interpersonal communication* (pp. 500–550). Beverly Hills, CA: Sage.

16. Originally, a "stereotype" was a rigid cylinder of cast type that fit over a large roller in a newspaper press. Repeatedly, it turned out the same pages of print. Journalist Walter Lippman applied the idea to human thinking and behavior that is rigid and unchanging. See: Lippman, W. (1922). *Public Opinion.* New York: Macmillan. The term has been widely used since the 1930s to identify rigid beliefs of a negative sort about a particular category of people. It can also be used to describe communication behavior. See: Knapp, M. L. (1984). *Human communication and human relationships* (pp. 149–176). Boston: Allyn and Bacon. Knapp, M. L. (1978). *Social Intercourse: From greeting to goodby* (pp. 105–124). Boston: Allyn and Bacon.

17. Berger, C. R., Gardner, R. R., Clatterbuck, G. W., & Schulman, L. S. (1976). Perceptions of information sequencing in relationship development. *Human Communication Research, 3,* 29–46; see also: Knapp, *Social Intercourse,* p. 116.

18. Rosenfeld, L. B. (1979). Self-disclosure avoidance: Why I am afraid to tell you who I am. *Communication Monographs, 45,* 63–66.

19. The original essay is contained in: Simmel, G. (1908). *Soziologie.* Leipzig: Dunker and Humbolt. For a summary of the idea in English, see: "The stranger." In K. H. Wolff (Ed. and trans.), *The sociology of Georg Simmel* (pp. 402–408). New York: Free Press, 1950.

20. Miller, G. R., & Steinberg, M. (1975). *Between People.* Chicago: Science Research Associates. P. 314.

21. Knapp, *Social Intercourse,* pp. 111–112, and *Human Communication,* pp. 166–169.

22. Knapp, *Human Communication,* p. 168.

23. See, for example, Knapp, *Human Communication,* p. 168; Berger et al., op. cit.

24. Altman, I., & Taylor, D. A. (1973). *Social penetration: The development of interpersonal relationships.* New York: Holt, Rinehart, and Winston.

25. Homans, G. C. (1961). *Social behavior in its elementary forms.* New York: Harcourt, Brace & World.

26. Altman & Taylor, op. cit., p. 33; Homans, G. C. (1950). *The human group.* New York: Harcourt, Brace Jovanovich; Thibaut, J., Kelley, H. H. (1959). *The social psychology of groups.* New York: John Wiley.

27. Altman & Taylor, op. cit., pp. 27–29; Knapp, *Human Communication,* pp. 208–215.

28. Knapp, *Human Communication,* pp. 36–39.

29. Baxter, L. A., & Wilmot, W. W. (1984). Secret tests: Social strategies for acquiring information about the state of the relationship. *Human Communication Research, 11,* 171–202; Duck, S. (1986). *Human relationships: An introduction to social psychology.* Beverly Hills: Sage. P. 50.

30. Prager, K. J. (1989). "Intimacy status and couple communication. *Journal of Social and Personal Relationships, 6,* 435–449.

31. Argyle, M., & Henderson, M. The rules of friendship. *Journal of Social and Personal Relationships, 1,* pp. 211–238; Duck, op. cit., p. 96,

32. Duck, ibid, p. 95; Knapp, *Human Communication,* pp. 225–228.

33. Safran, C. (1979, January). Troubles that pull couples apart: A *Redbook* report. *Redbook,* pp. 138–141.

34. See: Volkhart, E. H. (1951). *Social behavior and personality: Contributions of W. I. Thomas to theory and social research* (pp. 7–8). New York: Social Science Research Council; also: Thomas, W. I., & Znan-

iecki, F. (1927). *The Polish peasant in Europe and America* (Vol. 1). New York: Alfred Knopf

35. This concept has ancient roots, extending back to a number of early philosophers. For an extended overview and summary of such social construction of reality theories and how they are important in the study of all forms of human communication, see: DeFleur, M. L., & Rokeach, S. B. (1989). *Theories of mass communication* (5th ed.) (pp. 228–271). White Plains, NY: Longman.

36. For an examination of the descriptions people give of current and dissolved relationships see: Hortalsu, N. (1989). Current and dissolved relationships: Descriptive and attributional dimensions and predictors of involvement. *Journal of Social and Personal Relationships, 6,* pp. 373–383.

37. Ibid.

38. La Gaipa, J. J. (1982). Rules and rituals in disengaging from relationships. In S. Duck, (Ed.), *Personal relationships 4: Dissolving personal Relationships* (pp. 189–210). London & New York: Academic Press.

39. Ibid.

40. This analysis incorporates a number of the ideas of Knapp, *Human Communication,* pp. 263–267, and *Social Intercourse,* pp. 189–193.

41. Baxter, L. A. (1982). Strategies for ending relationships: Two studies. *Western Journal of Speech Education, 46,* pp. 223–241; Cushman, D. P., & Kahn, D. D. Jr., (1985). *Communication in interpersonal relationships* (pp. 96–97). Albany: State University of New York Press.

42. The name comes from the Italian writer Niccolo Machiavelli, who in the 16th century elaborated rules for maintaining power through intrigue, cunning, and deceit. Machiavelli, N. (1947). *The prince* (T. G. Berger, Ed.). New York: Appleton-Century-Crofts. (First published 1513)

Additional Readings

Duck, S. (1987). *Human relationships: An introduction to social psychology.* Beverly Hills, CA: Sage.

> This is an interesting book on human relationships. Duck effectively integrates the social psychological and communication literatures on the initiation, maintenance, and demise of interpersonal relationships. Important topics of discussion include: communicating with families and friends and dealing with strangers and acquaintances. This book will pose few difficulties for the introductory student.

Knapp, M. L., & Miller, G. R. (Eds.) (1985). *Handbook of interpersonal communication.* Beverly Hills, CA: Sage.

> This edited book is an advanced text on interpersonal communication. It provides an excellent contrast to Miller's 1976 edited collection of essays. Selected scholars discuss basic positions and issues in interpersonal communication, fundamental units, basic processes, and interpersonal contexts. This text offers an insightful review of contemporary research.

Miller, G. R. (Ed.). (1976). *Explorations in interpersonal communication.* Beverly Hills, CA: Sage.

> This is a collection of early essays by a number of authors

on selected issues in interpersonal communication. It effectively brings together a group of well-known scholars in this area. Each essay provides both diversity of thought and an extensive review of research on a particular topic in interpersonal communication.

Miller, G. R. (1978). The current status of theory and research in interpersonal communication. *Human Communication Research, 4,* 93–101.

> This article sets the stage for what over the past 15 years has become the study of interpersonal communication. Interpersonal communication is conceptualized as a developmental phenomenon. Law and rule-governed approaches are also considered. Based on the perspectives discussed, a number of conclusions are offered regarding the future of research in this area.

Miller, G. R. (1990). Interpersonal communication. In G. L. Dahnke & G. W. Clatterbuck (Eds.), *Human communication: Theory and research* (pp. 91–122). Belmont, CA: Wadsworth.

> This recent statement on interpersonal communication defines this area from several perspectives. It distinguishes the stages of interpersonal relational development and discusses important communication issues in interpersonal encounters.

Chapter 6

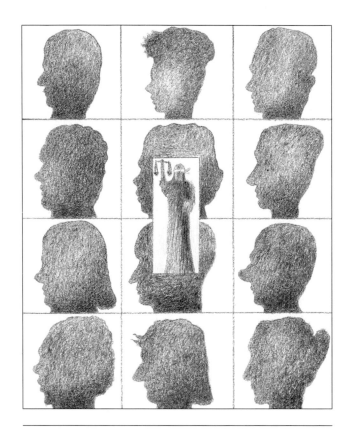

Communicating in Small Groups

Contents

The Nature of Small Groups
Basic features of a Group
The Influence of Group Size
Types of Small Groups
  Intimate groups
  Task-oriented groups

Sociocultural Situations: Why People Communicate in Small Groups
Communication Goals in Intimate Groups
  Communicating in family situations
  Communicating in peer group situations
Communication Goals in Task-Oriented Groups
  Conducting discussions
  Helping people improve themselves
  Reaching important decisions

Social Relationships: Rules for Communicating
Stages in Group Development
  Forming: The stage of initial orientation
  Storming: The stage of emerging conflicts
  Norming: The stage of stabilization
  Performing: The stage of task achievement
Informal Rules for Communicating in Intimate Groups
  Communication norms in intimate groups
  Communication roles in intimate groups
  Variations in social ranking

Subtle social controls
Rules for Communicating in Task-Oriented Groups
  Communication norms in task-oriented groups
  Leadership and other communication roles
  Communicating power and authority
  Enforcing the communication rules
Communication Codes in Formal Decision-Making Groups
  Official requirements for communicating
  Clearly delineated communication roles
  A hierarchy of power in controlling communication
  Explicit messages designed for control

Group Cohesion and Disorganization
Distinct Bases of Cohesion
  Sentiment-based cohesion in intimate groups
  Reward-based cohesion in discussion groups
  Assignment-based cohesion in decision-making
    groups
Communication Breakdown and Group Disorganization

Chapter Review

Key Terms

Notes

Additional Readings

Key Questions

- Is there any real difference between communicating in a group and communicating with just one other person? What difference does it make whether there are just two or two dozen people in a group? Isn't it just the same process?

- Why is communicating in a group such a big deal? What do people get out of groups anyway, other than the fact that it can be fun to take part in some groups? Also, isn't one small group just about the same as any other one? Is there any real difference between a group of close friends and one made up of acquaintances who get together for some purpose?

- How can groups have "rules" that supposedly govern the way their members communicate together? It is hard to believe that my close friends and I follow any kind of rules. We just talk to anyone we like, about any topic we want, and when we feel like it—or do we?

■ What is it that holds a group together? Why do people keep coming back and participating in a group? What do they get out of it anyway? Also, why do some groups just seem to come apart and the members stop wanting to be with the others?

By primary groups I mean those characterized by intimate face-to-face association and cooperation. They are primary in several senses, but chiefly in that they are fundamental in forming the social nature and ideals of the individual.

Charles Horton Cooley
1909

Miriam wondered why she had agreed to take part in a discussion group devoted to the problem of homeless people in Center City. There was no doubt in her mind that it was a serious problem and that people were suffering in the community. But what could be done? She really had no idea—probably nothing—and it was all a waste of time. She realized that she had been asked as a prominent and active citizen with deep concerns about civic affairs. Even so, her mood was not a happy one as she sat down with the six others like herself to see what they could recommend to the city council.

She looked around and realized that although she had met most of the people present, she really had never had an opportunity to discuss anything serious with any of them. She didn't quite know what to expect. Did any of them know anything about what they were supposed to do or how they were to proceed? Could they come up with anything of value? Others must have felt the same hesitancy, because for a few minutes they just introduced themselves and engaged in small talk.

Then Phillip, whom she could see was going to be something of a bore, began telling the others that he knew a lot about the issue, implying that he was an authority. She was about to challenge something he said when Bernard, who seemed to be quietly competent, said that perhaps they should try first to define clearly what they were to do, and then each take turns outlining their background and understanding of the scope of the problem in the city. Betty, who seemed to have a pathological compulsion to talk without ever really saying anything, objected and maintained that everyone should say whatever they wanted whenever they wanted to. Miriam realized that they were bickering over who was to lead the group and what the rules should be concerning who would talk about what.

After an initial half-hour of discussion that at times got a bit heated, they began to settle down. They had sized each other up and worked out ways in which they wanted to fit into the group. Woodrow had a lot of good ideas. Juanita seemed to have a unique facility for making

soothing comments that calmed down those who were getting a little emotional. Bernard had slowly taken over the role of moderator, indicating when it was time for each to talk. Miriam had agreed to keep a kind of running account of the important things that were said.

By the end of the session, the group had come up with three good proposals. They were going to suggest that the city convert an unused but very serviceable warehouse into an emergency shelter for homeless people. They were going to recommend that modest funds be allocated to several charitable groups; these funds would provide homeless people with needed basics, such as food and medical attention. Finally, they were going to meet again and try to identify a federal program that might be called on to provide funds for more permanent solutions. They saw that the city needed to provide assistance for temporarily displaced families and for the more unfortunate individuals who probably would never be able to fit into normal society.

The preceding discussion is typical of the first meeting of what communication scholars call a *task-oriented* group. In this case its "task" or goal was to try to identify and recommend solutions to an important local problem. As its members participated in the discussion, they moved through several stages, finally working out a set of rules for communicating and then settling down to move toward their goal. In addition to task-oriented groups there are many other kinds of small groups, and this chapter discusses both their differences and their similarities as contexts for communication.

In the simultaneous transactions model of communication developed in previous chapters we included *context* as an important component. We also saw that the *dyad* was the significant context of interpersonal communication. In this chapter and the next we will show how different types of groups are also communication contexts with unique features. In many respects, every act of human communication that takes place in a group is based

159

on exactly the same concepts and principles we have examined in previous chapters. However, communicating with other people in a group is not the same experience as doing so in a dyadic context consisting of only two persons. It requires different skills; it follows different patterns; and it has different consequences.

The Nature of Small Groups

A context, you will recall, includes three components: a *physical setting* in which communication takes place, a *sociocultural situation* in which the participants are engaging, and a set of *social relationships* that prevail among them. In considering a group as a context we will use these contextual factors as our central organizing framework. However, in the study of small groups we must add two factors: (1) the basis and size of membership and (2) an explanation of group *cohesion*—that which holds a group together as a functioning unit. Therefore, this chapter will show how the simultaneous transactions model—along with considerations of basis and size of membership and the nature of cohesion—aids in understanding how peo-

Groups come in many sizes and are organized in a great variety of ways. Communicating in the context of a group permits people to pursue goals and obtain satisfactions that they could not achieve by individual actions alone. In any group context, members communicate according to a set of agreed-upon rules that regulate who talks to whom, in what order, and about what topics.

ple communicate in different types of small groups and the consequences of their exchanges.

Basic Features of a Group

What is a group? Communication scholars have provided many answers to this deceptively simple question.[1] While there is little need for a complex answer, for the sake of clarity we can set forth a brief definition: Most **groups** consist of *two or more people who repeatedly interact together, regulating their conduct and communication within some set of rules that they mutually recognize and follow.* While most groups extend through time, certain kinds have members that meet on a one-time-only basis for purposes of orderly discussion or decision making. However, even these groups follow generally recognized rules and procedures.

People become members of groups, and maintain their membership, for many reasons.[2] Basically they participate in groups in order to accomplish goals they could not achieve by acting alone. In some cases they *voluntarily* seek individual satisfactions that cannot be met in solitary behavior (e.g., by marrying, finding friends, or even campaigning to become a member of the city council). In other cases, they may become members *involuntarily* (e.g., by being born into a particular family, by being drafted, or even by being sent to prison.) In still other cases, people may become members because someone *assigns* them the task and it is in their best interest to take part (e.g., serving on a jury or being asked by the boss to serve on a committee). In involuntary or assigned situations, members usually work toward some collective goal that is important to a large group or social system.

Communication scholars traditionally divide the study of groups into two broad classes on the basis of size: small groups and (larger) organizations. As we will see, there are important differences other than size between these categories, but looking at the influence of the number of participants is an appropriate beginning point for a study of communication in small groups.

The Influence of Group Size

In the study of small groups, how is communication influenced by the sheer number of people who participate in the process? Is this really an important issue? The answer is that it is not only important but essential to understanding the dynamics of communication in a group. To understand why this is the case, we need to return to our linear model, which analyzed the basic act of communication in terms of a series of steps or stages by which messages are organized, transmitted, and interpreted within a dyad (Chapter 1, pp. 12 21).

When one considers communication as simultaneous transactions that take place within a group, one must *still* consider what happens between individual senders and receivers. That is, in the ongoing and complex exchanges that take place between members of a group who are actively discussing some question or issue, messages still pass from source persons to receivers, back and forth, just as in the case of a dyad. The *pair,* consisting of sender and receiver, therefore, remains as an important unit of analysis.

The difference between dyadic and group communication is that in the latter a number of pairs may be involved at the same time. For example, consider a group with only three participants. At any given moment one sender may be transmitting a message to two receivers. While they may be simultaneously formulating their replies and providing ongoing feedback, the basic process is still there, taking place between what looks like two sender/receiver pairs involved in the exchange. However, if one looks more closely, there are actually *three* pairs involved. To be sure, only one person is talking to two receivers, but still another transaction is taking place between the two receivers. Even though they are not talking at the moment, they are influencing each other in subtle ways through posture, facial expressions, and other nonverbal signs and signals. In this sense, then, there are in fact three pairs to consider when one person talks to two others.

Three members with three pairs in a situation of simultaneous transactions is easy to understand. But what happens when the number of participants is greater? How does this have a qualitative influence on the communication processes that take place? Insights into this question can be gained from considering the number of pairs that can exist between groups of different sizes. The fact is that as the number of dyads or pairs that can be formed in a group grows, the more difficult it is to maintain a full flow of communication among all of the members. This is a very important consideration. For example, in our group with only three potential pairs, there would be little difficulty in "turn-taking," reading nonverbal cues and understanding potential nuances of connotative meanings. Role-taking would be more difficult than with a single receiver, but it would not be all that complex. Also, each member could recall fairly accurately who said what to whom in prior communication. Generally, then, in such a three-member situation, even with relatively full participation by all members, achievement of accuracy in any given exchange would not be difficult.

Now, let us consider larger groups. Simple calculations show that adding only one more person to a group of three *doubles the number of pairs to six.*[3] This makes turn-taking, role-taking, keeping track of what each person has already said to each of the others, and so on, considerably more difficult. A group of 10 would have 45 possible pairs, and one with 20 members has a startling 190 potential dyads! Thus, it is easy to see that as the number of group members gets larger, the number of potential pairs producing patterns of role-taking, feedback, turn-taking, prior communication, and nonverbal communication gets incredibly complicated very quickly.

For such reasons, many communication specialists maintain that an optimal size for discussion and getting decisions made in a small group, with all members participating fully, is something like *five* (with ten pairs). This brings at least *some* diversity of views to the exchanges, but it still permits a relatively full flow of reasonably accurate communication. While there are no hard and fast rules, when a group grows beyond that size individual members have an increasingly difficult time communicating fully and accurately with each other in the increasingly elaborate pair structure.

If the group gets up to, say, 20 or so, some members simply stop trying to participate and sit quietly on the sidelines. Others break up into small cliques, and a few dominant talkers "hog" the discussion. Thus, as size increases, communication patterns in a group undergo significant qualitative changes, and groups that exceed about a dozen members or so do not provide the same communicative experiences as those that are smaller.

Types of Small Groups

Our simultaneous transactions model specifies that people come together in specific sociocultural situations to pursue particular kinds of goals. This basic feature of all communication contexts permits an understanding of many different types of small groups in which communication patterns differ considerably. In this chapter we will focus on two general categories of small groups—*intimate* and *task-oriented*—each of which includes several subcategories and types that are particularly important in our society.

Intimate groups One significant classification is made up of **intimate groups,** a category that includes both the human family and **peer groups** of close friends. Both the family and the peer group are often referred to as "primary" groups, both because they are earliest in the experience of the human individual and because they play a critical part in the person's psychological and social development.[4]

In many ways, the previous chapter on interpersonal communication dealt with human relationships that developed into intimacy over a period of time. We were able to show how people sort out and select each other, and then become involved in increasingly disclosing and uninhibited communication. In the present chapter we need not take a developmental approach; we can look at intimate or primary groups that already exist in terms of the rich functions they serve and the objectives they achieve for their participants.

Task-oriented groups   A second broad category includes a number of **task-oriented** groups. Here, people participate in order to get something done through group participation—that is, to achieve some goal that they have mutually set as an objective. Some groups in this category are devoted to either formal or informal *discussions* of various kinds. Examples can range from a group of friends who get together to discuss ways in which they might plan a surprise birthday party for a buddy to highly structured discussions following formal rules, such as the case of a panel, colloquium, or symposium.

Some discussion groups are private, others are open to the public. A *private* group of this type is illustrated by a business conference within a particular company, where systematic discussions take place about confidential policies and problems. A *public* discussion group is illustrated by a situation in which audiences observe proceedings, such as the case of panels or symposia.

Another type of task-oriented discussion group with quite different goals is sometimes called the **experiential** group. Here, the principal goal of participation is to make people "feel better." Some are devoted to group therapy, in which people reveal their problems and concerns to others who have had similar difficulties, such as drug abuse, alcoholism, or excessive gambling. Through self-disclosing discussion, participants gain new perspectives.

A similar type of group tries to accomplish sensitivity training, where participants learn to understand the points of view of people unlike themselves. Such groups have been effective in police departments, where officers learn more effective ways of handling many kinds of situations, such as how to limit the use of violence, relate to rape victims, communicate with members of minorities, or resolve domestic conflicts.

Consciousness-raising groups are another type of task-oriented discussion group. They use discussions to help participants realize that they face mutual problems, such as sex discrimination, and how these problems should be defined and dealt with.

Another very important kind of task-oriented group is devoted to formal *decision making*. In **decision-making groups,** the goal is to make orderly judgments achieved on the basis of discussion. Many of these groups communicate in private settings—allocating scarce resources, evaluating people's performance, and achieving consensus about what is or is not true. Such groups often have highly formalized procedures, and they are usually organized within some large organization or social system. In this category are such groups as standing university committees, corporation boards of directors, politically appointed panels, and permanent councils in religious groups. Perhaps the classic example is the jury within the justice system.

In each of the different types of groups just noted, the norms, roles, ranks, and social controls that define the rules for communicating in permissible ways will be quite different. The reasons such rules are important were set forth in our discussion of the basic features of a communication context (Chapter 5, pp. 130–132). As we look at the different kinds of communication that take place in intimate groups and in various kinds of task-oriented groups, it will be clear that the rules designating who can transmit what messages to whom differ greatly from one setting to the next.

Sociocultural Situations: Why People Communicate in Small Groups

Human beings spend far more time communicating within small intimate groups than in any other context. Furthermore, such groups are much more important to all of us personally than any other kind. There are two reasons for this. One is that we derive our major satisfactions and gratifications from our families and our friends. The second is that these two groups make the earliest and most important contributions to our personal development compared to any other type of group in which we participate.

Communication Goals in Intimate Groups

It would be difficult to overstate the importance in our lives of the communication processes that take place in small intimate groups. The messages transmitted and received within both family and peer groups serve as critical sources that provide us with our deepest understandings of other human beings and how to relate to them. It is not always easy to see that communication occurring in such groups has very basic goals. Most people simply carry on their activities within such groups without consciously thinking about them in terms of communication and its consequences. Nevertheless, those consequences are very real and very important—so important that we could not develop as fully functioning members of our community and society without deep involvement in the communication processes of small and intimate groups. More specifically, our family and our innermost cliques of friends share the goal of shaping our psychological and social development in a variety of ways. In this sense they are truly "cradles of human nature," and this can be identified as one of their most important purposes.[5]

Communicating in family situations   Even at the dawn of human existence the family was already in place as the most basic of all human groups. It was the context within which the first steps toward communication as we know it took place—when language was being developed and human beings began to live and communicate very differently from animals. The family became the great teacher of the symbols and rules of meaning that were the foundations of social life. Thus, the family has always been the principal source for learning vocabulary, the linking of symbols, meanings, and referents so that new members of society could take the first steps in communicating. Today, it is within the family that the complexities of grammar and syntax are sorted out and mastered by all of us—crudely at first, but with an increasingly sophisticated command as the individual matures.

The acquisition of language allows the child to begin participating in the mainstream culture of the larger group and to start internalizing the beliefs and understandings of the physical, spiritual, and social world that are shared within it.[6] Language acquisition also allows the child to participate in the more specialized cultures of the ethnic, racial, or national-origin group with which the family is identified. Thus, we can truly say the family is the **primary group** in the communication experience of the human individual.

But learning the language as a child in family situations is only a necessary condition that permits one to participate more broadly in the entire communication process of a society. Taken together, all of these cultural

The family is the oldest of all human groups. Its basic organization was already established in prehistoric times. The family is the context within which virtually all human beings begin the process of communication. It prepares the new members of society with a fundamental command of speech and language, as well as knowledge of the basic rules for socially accepted behavior. This enables the young to cope with a growing number of groups they will encounter outside the family.

and group influences, plus all additional learning experiences that take place as the person is maturing, can be discussed together under the broad concept of "socialization." **Socialization** refers to *those long-term processes of communication within which deliberate or indirect lessons are internalized, enabling the person to become a unique human being, a functioning member of society, and a participant in its general and specialized cultures.*

Three aspects of human development are involved in this definition. These are that communication in family situations represents our intitial sources of *personality, social expectations,* and *enculturation.* All three of these terms need brief explanation because they are central to understanding both the process and the consequences of communication, especially in small and intimate groups.

The term *personality* in the sense we are using it—and will be using it in later chapters—is different from the common word used in everyday life to describe whether someone is pleasing or a bore. Technically, **personality** is an inclusive concept that refers to the individual's *more or less enduring organization of meanings, motivations, emotional patterns, orientations, skills, and other attributes that make that person different in psychological makeup from all others.*[7] Personality, in other words, is composed of "the individual's distinctive, consistent, patterned methods of relating to the environment."[8]

Individual differences in personality can be described in everyday terms: All of us understand that each person is unique and different from others. Some of us are serious and others are happy-go-lucky; some individuals are driven to succeed while others are lazy; some are smart but others are stupid. There is, in other words, an enormous list of psychological attributes or **traits** on which people differ.[9] Long before there were psychologists, people learned to identify such traits with common labels, such as "stingy," "generous," "smart," or "lively," that describe observable features of a person's behavior over time. Psychologists have developed less familiar trait names, such as "introverted," "anal-retentive," or "atavistic," but the idea is the same. People exhibit more-or-less enduring patterns of behavior.

As our discussion of family communication suggests, personality is not inherited. We must acquire—that is, *learn* it, through participating in social experiences in many kinds of group situations. The people around us communicate (either deliberately or without intending to do so) a great variety of *lessons* as to what we should think, how we should express our emotions, what should be valued, despised, accepted, rejected, understood, and so on. That entire process—including the presentation of lessons, their content, the act of learning, and the resulting shaping of our personality—is what is meant by socialization.

Socialization is also the source of *social expectations,* that is, our insights into how people expect us to behave in group situations. It is through participating in communication processes in social situations that the individual comes to understand the norms, roles, ranks, and controls of various groups. This development of internalized social understandings is one way in which socialization makes the individual *similar* to others—the opposite of the idea of individuality. If this seems contradictory, common sense tells us that all kinds of people, regardless of their individual personality differences, learn to conform to the everyday requirements of social life. By communicating in a variety of social situations, they learn what others expect them to do in many kinds of groups—sports teams, families, friendship cliques, stores, schools, factories, and so on. Thus, socialization produces both uniqueness and similarity.

Finally, the process of socialization is one in which **enculturation** takes place. This reduces individuality even further. To be accepted as members of a society, individuals must be keenly aware of the way of life—the general or mainstream culture—followed by the people to whom they must relate. This includes not only the language skills required but also the shared beliefs, emotional orientations, attitudes, values, and everything that makes a person an accepted member of the society who "fits in."

The total enculturation of the individual in this sense is a part of the complex process of socialization. It has long been one of the principal goals of the family, although in modern society other groups, such as schools, the church, political parties, and even the mass media, play a part. Overall, enculturation represents a very basic transformation of the individual. As anthropologist Ruth Benedict put it (using the language style of the 1930s) in her classic analysis, *Patterns of Culture:*

> By the time [a child] can talk, he is the little creature of his culture, and by the time he is grown and able to take part in its activities, its habits are his habits, its beliefs are his beliefs, its impossibilities his impossibilities.[10]

By the same means, children learn the basics of specialized cultures in which their families participate—distinctive languages, values, styles of dress, diets, and many other practices that are different from those of the mainstream culture. These may be associated with race, religion, ethnicity, region, or even socioeconomic level in the society.

In short, the rich communication processes that take place within family situations provide the foundations for developing our individual mental processes—equipping us to engage in self-communication. They also provide our initial exposure to shared social understandings and cultural rules that will enable us to engage in goal-oriented activities with other individuals in a collective way of life.

Communicating in peer group situations   While personality, social expectations, and cultural acquisition begin their development within the context of the family, it is not the only primary group. Each individual's insights into the requirements of the physical and social world are improved substantially by communication among *peers*. This communication experience begins within the intimate groups of friends that are formed outside the family during early childhood. Through communication in peer groups, individuals improve their *role-taking* skills and their ability to interpret *feedback*.

In the context of young children's groups—on street corners, in schoolyards, and on playgrounds—individuals gain deeper understandings of how the messages they initiate will influence others, and what their companion's responses imply about the meanings they are recon-

structing. Critical skills are sharpened in message construction, in nonverbal communication, and in understanding meanings intended by others. Thus, in the communicative exchanges within this peer group society-in-miniature, the individual receives basic lessons in what words, gestures, and actions make others angry, what causes them to smile or laugh, what messages bring respect or convey dishonor, what establishes one person as a leader or defines another as a follower. These are critical consequences of intimate communication in small groups that prepare children to take their place later in the society of adults.

The influence of peer groups does not stop with childhood. During the entire life cycle, people communicate in peer groups to achieve goals they seldom articulate and may never have tried to understand. If asked, they probably would reply that they simply want to "enjoy their friends" or "have fun." Thus, the members of such groups communicate among themselves simply for the pleasures that the process provides, but this brings companionship and personal fulfillment that cannot be obtained in other ways. In such groups, communication provides a bonding between members that is its own re-

Every child is born into a family in which that person's long processes of socialization and enculturation begin. The new human being's basic personality is formed in this communication context. He or she learns accepted ways of relating to others, initial patterns of speech and language usage, and the general way of life that characterizes similar kinds of people. Later, communication in other contexts, at school, among friends, and in the community at large, can modify personality. However, the family provides the foundation of shared beliefs, attitudes, and values that have the strongest influence on life chances.

ward. The goals of such communication, then, are the satisfactions provided by communication itself.

Communication Goals in Task-Oriented Groups

Included in this category is a list of different types of small groups that are distinguished by a number of criteria. In some, members relate to each other in informal and spontaneous ways, meeting irregularly or perhaps only once. In others participants follow rigidly formal patterns and hold regularly scheduled meetings. Some task-oriented groups are private and their members address agendas of confidential issues behind closed doors. Others are public and the group meets before observers or even interacts with audiences.

All of these differences are related to the particular goals that these various groups accomplish for participants, and they allow us to identify at least three subcategories of task-oriented groups. The boundaries between these subcategories sometimes overlap, and a particular group may help people achieve more than one goal. Nevertheless, for purposes of discussion we can identify the following: One subcategory of the task-oriented group is devoted to conducting some type of *discussion;* another is aimed at helping people *improve themselves;* still another has the purpose of orderly *decision making.*

Conducting discussions   Many kinds of groups can be identified as having discussion-related goals. These range from informal to formal. Some conduct their affairs in private; others do so in public. To give an idea of the diversity among this category, we can list the following examples:

1. *Private, informal, and casual discussions.* A small group of friends may get together casually and find themselves discussing a problem that is troubling all of them. They talk about various aspects of the problem for a while and wind up agreeing on a solution. The participants may not even identify themselves as a problem-solving discussion group, but they have gone through the process even if unwittingly and spontaneously.

2. *Private, informal, but deliberate discussions.* A group of neighbors may see that they face a shared problem, such as an increase in crime in their area, and deliberately call an informal meeting at one of their homes to see what they might do. Here they understand that they have a

problem and that the specific goal of their discussion is to try to figure out a solution. They might achieve consensus on an informal solution, such as watching each other's homes, and end the process there. Or they might ask someone to coordinate the group (a leader), schedule further meetings, and ask particular individuals to accept specialized assignments (roles) for the next meeting. If so, they are on their way to becoming a more formally organized problem-solving group.

3. *Private and formal discussion group.* The same neighbors may decide to organize a homeowner's association on a formal basis. They elect a president, a secretary, and a treasurer. Then they design by-laws and formulate an agenda of long-range issues and problems that face the neighborhood and need to be solved. However, even though they have become a formal association, they are still a discussion group.

4. *The round table.* A familiar form of a discussion group is one where diverse views on a topic or issue are discussed among a small group of participants, who may or may not be either experts or representatives of special interests. In the round table, no audience is present and the participants usually arrange themselves in some sort of circular pattern. Communication proceeds informally, and many round-table groups conduct their discussion with no formal leader.

5. *The panel.* A panel resembles a round table, but it is public rather than private. Here the participants tend to be experts or representatives of special interests. The panel is usually coordinated in a more or less formal way by a moderator, and the discussion usually takes place before a live audience. Sometimes questions are taken from the audience after the members of the panel have commented on the problem and explained their positions. Panels can be presented to audiences via radio and television, sometimes with opportunities for those who are attending to call in with questions. Panels seldom reach firm decisions, but they present alternative interpretations and insights and their discussion may or may not help members of the audience understand the issues.

6. *The symposium.* This is a very formal and public kind of group. Furthermore, it is a "discussion" group only in a limited sense. Usually a symposium has some unifying theme—a problem or an issue that is being addressed. The participants are usually a small group of experts who are knowledgeable about the theme. They are individually introduced by a moderator, and each then makes a speech about the theme. During or even between the presentations, the participants seldom talk with each other and simply take their turn delivering their analyses or views. Sometimes questions are taken from an audience afterward. Commonly, the presentations of the participants are published in a set of "proceedings."

7. *The seminar.* This is one of the oldest forms of small discussion groups. It was used by Plato as a teaching format 400 years before the birth of Christ. As can be seen in his famous *Republic,* Plato and his students strolled through the grounds of his academy and each student took a turn at addressing a central question that was the focus of the discussion.[11] The mentor then drew out of various comments the important lessons. Seminars usually have regular meetings over a lengthy period of time, a clear organization, and an intellectual leader who coordinates the discussions of students.

8. *The forum.* A number of somewhat similar small-group discussion formats combine features of the round table, panel, and symposium. In the forum there is usually a brief presentation by a small group who are introduced by a chairperson. Their presentations are followed by a considerable amount of participation by audience members, again coordinated by the chair. This is a favorite format on college campuses because it allows a great deal of audience participation.

9. *The conference.* In a typical small-group conference, several participants are brought together, usually under private conditions. Their purpose is to share technical information or to discuss some problem in their area of expertise. Such conferences are common among people who work in a particular corporation or agency, where solutions to problems can be worked out together. They are also common among professionals such as physicians, lawyers, and engineers. Conferences can even be done at long range, with telephones or some other medium linking the participants. As we will see in Chapter 8, modern media technology is making possible the *video teleconference,* which incorporates many of the features of our simultaneous transactions model. This makes it possible for people to engage in reasonably full and accurate communication at a distance.

10. *Specialized small-group discussions.* We could add a long list of other rather specialized discussion groups found in one setting or another. Most are conducted in private for confidential purposes. Some are called "buzz" groups, others "brainstorming" sessions. Here, the participants are often middle managers or supervisors. The purpose of the discussion is to review a problem, issue, topic, plane, or policy in the hope that bright ideas for improvement or solution will emerge. In industrial settings, a favorite (adopted from the Japanese) is the "quality circle," where employees periodically get together in small groups to discuss ways in which they might do their work better. Their suggestions are passed on to management. Still another is the "focus" group that is widely used by the advertising and market research industries. Here, small groups of typical consumers are brought together to discuss a new product or package in the hope that insights can be gained into ways to make it more acceptable and profitable.[12]

The great diversity of these different kinds of groups indicates the importance of the small-group discussion format in our society. It is a useful context for pooling the intellectual resources of people with diverse exertise or different views. Often, insights and understandings come out of such discussions that could never have been obtained by individuals thinking through the issue on their own. Because the small-group discussion is such a valuable and important process, communication scholars have spent a great deal of effort trying to understand how people communicate in this context.

Helping people improve themselves   Another subcategory of task-oriented small groups includes two rather different but related specialized types. One is the small group in which people get together so as to learn to cope with a serious personal problem. They hope to gain insights into their problem and feel better as a result of their communication experience. Examples are the *therapy group* and the *encounter group.* The second type is devoted not to helping with a personal problem but rather to reaching a goal of personal or social improvement. Here we can include various educational or *training* groups, ranging from school-like lecture-discussion sessions to less formal sessions such as the study groups often used by students to provide mutual assistance in preparing for a difficult test.

1. *The therapy group.* Group discussions are widely used for assisting people who have personal problems. Here, participants meet with a coordinator who usually has some special insight into the problem. The underlying assumption is that if people who share a common problem get together and disclose their experiences, thoughts, and feelings to each other it will help them feel better. Usually, these disclosures are encouraged and coordinated by a leader who has coped successfully with those same problems or has specialized knowledge about them.

Discussions in the context of a small therapy group can be an effective way of helping people who have various kinds of problems, such as with substance abuse, compulsive behaviors, or even impending death due to an incurable health condition. With the aid of a coordinator, participants discuss their experiences and feelings, disclosing what happened to them and how they interpret it. Such disclosures can provide insights into the nature of the shared problem and help participants learn to cope with their difficulty.

The presumed benefits are that the participants will gain insight into their difficulty and learn to deal with it more effectively. There are many groups that follow this pattern for helping people cope with personal problems. Typical are therapy groups organized to assist people suffering from mental illness, alcoholism, drug abuse, or even smoking. Others help people solve problems related to excessive weight, bereavement due to the death of a loved one, advanced age, serious medical conditions (such as AIDS or cancer), and so on.

2. *The encounter group.* Many kinds of discussion groups are organized for the purpose of identifying and coping with difficulties experienced in daily life. A common example is the group of married people that is sometimes organized by a church. A number of couples go on a kind of weekend "retreat," away from the distractions of their daily environment. Here they tell each other about the problems they have faced in their marriages, the mistakes they have made, and the stresses they have had to manage. They learn from each other how to deal with such difficulties. The experience is said to make couples able to cope better and to strengthen the marriage bond. Other encounter groups can be more dramatic: People get to-

gether and engage in mutual touching and feeling, or embrace each other frequently, talking about their most private thoughts. Some of these groups encourage screaming or other unusual behavior. Some commercial versions charge large fees to convince people that they can take responsibility for their lives.

3. *The assertiveness-training group.* Training goals are often sought in the small-group format. An example is the assertiveness-training group, where participants learn ways in which they can stand up for their rights and be more demanding in ensuring that they are treated with dignity and respect. More specialized goals are pursued in training sessions where small groups learn a technical skill, such as word processing or how to handle hazardous wastes.

4. *The consciousness-raising group.* Another type of training goal is sought in groups by participants who feel disadvantaged in society. In the consciousness-raising group they present positions, exchange views, and gain insights into a topic of mutual concern. Typically, such groups focus on significant issues in the society about which they want others to recognize as important. The focus may be related to environmental issues, discrimination in the labor force, sexual harassment, or the negative feelings members feel toward war or capital punishment. In any case, participation sharpens thinking about the issue and raises it in the consciousness of those who take part.

Reaching important decisions   While the goals of some task-oriented groups can be difficult to describe, those of formal decision-making groups are much easier to identify, define, and discuss. Furthermore, the manner in which this major kind of small group is formed helps to identify its goals: Formal decision-making groups are *deliberately* formed to serve decision-making needs of an organization or larger social system within which they operate.

The members of formal decision-making groups are not selected by chance or for convenience. Usually, they are requested, assigned, or even ordered to participate after some sort of screening. More specifically, a board of directors, a jury, a committee, or a council is usually made up of members who have significant qualifications related to the goals for which the group is formed.

Anyone who has participated in, or observed first-hand, the process of selecting members to serve on a jury

has seen the importance of specific personal and social characteristics as criteria of group membership. Potential jurors are questioned extensively about various attributes that lawyers feel might influence their judgment. On the basis of such attributes, final selections are made. The same is true of the selection of participants for other important decision-making groups.

But once members have been selected, what are the various kinds of goals pursued in the context of formal decision-making groups? Essentially they are all related to making orderly judgments. Generally, the kinds of judgments that are made fall into four categories: *allocating scarce resources, evaluating performance, formulating or changing policies,* and *weighing facts to reach truth.* Each of these decision-making tasks is usually performed within the context of a small group.

1. *Allocating scarce resources.* Designating who should get resources that are in short supply is a thankless task. Virtually all large groups, such as corporations, communities, or universities, have to designate who can command space, time, effort, money, or some other valued commodity. Only in rare situations are such resources avail-

Most small and formal decision-making groups are deliberately formed with members appointed to reach goals that serve the needs of some larger organization. The members communicate to develop recommendations, or make judgments, concerning such matters as the allocation of resources, credentials of applicants, performance of people, application of policy, or other courses of action.

able in abundance. Far more frequently, there are fewer resources than there are demands for them. To handle such problems, committees are formed. These small, deliberately designed groups are formally charged with the goal of making recommendations or reaching decisions regarding such matters as budget allocations, making research grants, approving loans, providing scholarships, or admitting students to educational programs.

A good example of a scarce resource is *space.* In any large organization, people require space in which to do their work. Space also has nonverbal meanings of prestige and power within the organization. There will be far more people who covet additional space than there are available square feet to accommodate those desires. In some organizations, one person is assigned the task of allocating space. In such a system, only a few individuals at the top can command the best. This can make life difficult for the single decision maker, and it is a source of tension and potential conflict. A convenient solution is to appoint a committee to consider requests for more or better space. While the end result may be an identical set of decisions, at least the claimants can feel that their appeals were examined fairly by qualified individuals. Presumably, those who made the decisions exercised "universalistic" criteria and did not just grant special favors to their friends.

Does it always work? Obviously not! People can still distrust committees because such groups can either act stupidly or conspire to act in ways that are less than fair. However, decisions made in such a group context have a higher *probability* of being objective, fair, and intelligent than do those of a single individual. This is because it is really rather difficult (but not impossible) to assemble an entire group of truly stupid people or to get several individuals to misuse their power in exactly the same way (also not impossible).

2. *Evaluating performance.* A very difficult kind of decision that must be made in larger systems is deciding who meets designated standards of performance to what degree. No issue has more emotional significance than assessing merit. Such judgments lead to the granting and withholding of rewards, such as salary raises, tenure, promotion, and in some cases, lead to termination from one's job. Even awarding lesser perquisites—like a good parking space, access to a special dining room, or a key to a restricted bathroom—provoke emotional reactions.

3. *Policy formulation or change.* Establishing or changing the formal rules that guide how organizations do things is still another task often assigned to formal decision-making small groups. This may involve planning the objectives, strategies, and directions that a large organization will take. Truly powerful policy groups of this kind are found at the top of the power structure within large organizations. For example, the military services have the Joint Chiefs of Staff. The President has his Cabinet and his White House Staff of close personal advisors. At more local levels, every bank and corporation has a board of directors who are responsible for major decisions, new policies, and changes in directions that will have consequences for their organization. A local church will have a committee of laypersons who advise the clergy; and even the smallest business, if incorporated under the laws of most states, must have a named board of directors that hold an annual meeting. Therefore, small and formal policy-making groups are not the exclusive realm of the powerful. They are found in many walks of life.

4. *Deciding what is true.* Our society could not operate without small groups that weigh facts and reach truth. The most obvious example of a task-oriented group whose goal is to make orderly judgments about truth is the *jury* in the American court system. Coming from an ancient tradition, the use of such a small group to weigh evidence and decide guilt or innocence has proved to be relatively effective. Truth becomes *what a jury says it is*— after discussion—even if it is wrong! It is not foolproof, but it is the most acceptable to Americans among available alternatives. The organization of juries is well understood; the communication processes by which they reach decisions are less so. While there have been a few studies of actual juries in action, these are no longer permitted by the courts.[13] Therefore, most research on juries has been conducted in experiments, where people act "as though" they were reaching the goal of deciding the truth, or in "after the fact" observations where people recall what they did while serving.

There are other kinds of fact-reviewing and truth-seeking small groups that are formally designed to reach decisions. Many operate within branches of the federal government, such as in the Department of Transportation. If a major train wreck or an airplane crash occurs, fact-finding experts are assembled. They sift the evidence supplied by many kinds of technicians and attempt to determine the cause of the accident. Others review evidence concerning new drugs, insecticides, and even land-use proposals.

Small task-oriented groups, then, are as much a part of society as are small intimate groups. They play critical roles in virtually every activity that people pursue. With this great variety of goals in mind, we can turn to an examination of the *rules* that govern the flow of communication within the two broad categories of groups. This discussion will reveal those rules that influence who says what to whom.

Social Relationships: Rules for Communicating

Social relationships between members of a group are controlled and defined by its rules of communication. Such rules become a part of the group's established culture in several different ways. Once in place, they serve as guides as to whether those relationships are informal and spontaneous, or formal as part of a deliberate design. But whatever their origins, the rules for communicating in a group identify who can transmit what kind of content by formal or informal channels to whom and for what purpose.

Stages in Group Development

The rules for communicating in some groups can be designated before members are recruited (e.g., formal decision-making groups like juries). However, many of the task-oriented groups we have discussed undergo a series of *stages* after the members first come together, during which the organization of rules for communicating emerges and becomes stabilized. A great deal of attention has been devoted by communication researchers to understanding these stages.[14]

One of the most influential researchers in the study of emerging communication systems in spontaneous groups has been sociologist Robert F. Bales. His classic experiments on "interaction process analysis," conducted during the late 1940s, showed that in an informal group discussion the members of small groups do achieve a considerable degree of *specialization* in the kinds of messages they communicate.[15]

Because there has been such a large amount of research devoted to the issue of development, many names have been applied to the stages that take place as participants come to know each other, confront various problems, and achieve the goals for which their group came together in the first place. Perhaps the easiest to remember and certainly the most colorful of those names are those that were proposed by social psychologist Bruce Tuckman during the mid-1960s.[16] He reviewed many studies

One of the most important of the many small task-oriented groups serving our society is the jury. It is a prototype of a formal decision-making group. Its goal is to seek the truth through organized deliberation and decision-making within a specific structure of evidence. It works so well that most people accept the decisions of juries with relatively little suspicion or complaint.

on the issue that had been published up to that time and came up with four distinct phases. He called them *forming, storming, norming,* and *performing.* These names are still entirely appropriate.

Forming: The stage of initial orientation As our example at the beginning of the chapter suggested, when people come together to confront a task or try to solve a problem, they face many uncertainties. This is especially true if they do not know each other and are not able to predict how each will respond to what is said. Thus, there is a stage of "orientation," both toward the task for which the group has been formed and toward each other. Sizing each other up, in other words, is one of the first things that has to take place in a task-oriented group. A considerable amount of the early communication involves exchanges designed to determine who responds in what way to what kinds of messages. The forming stage, then, is one of uncertainty, probing, and trial.

It is in this stage that the rules which will govern communication are first tried out: The **norms** of how ideas can be expressed and what can be said begin to be defined. Will a sophisticated vocabulary be the norm? Is poor grammar acceptable? Are comments to be expressed in a witty or a serious style? Can one use four-letter words?

Depending on the nature of the group, communication **roles**—that is, specialized parts to be performed—may also start to take definition in the forming stage. Here, the need for a group leader may become clear, and some individuals may start to take on that role. Others may try out for the part of group "clown," offering funny anecdotes or witty sayings. Still others may begin to play the role of "pourer-of-oil-on-troubled-waters"—a role as a social-emotional facilitator who tries to soothe the feelings of others.

Status and power ranking within the group is another factor that starts to emerge in the communication patterns during the forming stage. Some members begin to transmit messages intended to define their special status or expertise in the topic or subject. These messages start to identify the levels of prestige that will exist within the group. If these definitions are accepted, they will identify those members whose contributions are to be interpreted as having the most weight and authority. Other group members may feel intimidated by these emerging indicators of rank and begin to see themselves as low in the system and having less to offer to the discussion.

Communication at this stage also begins to identify the signals of control. Who will transmit messages of reward or punishment, and how will they do this? Will they use ridicule or merely a frown or raised eyebrow to transmit meanings of disapproval? Will the others reward a good comment with eye contact, nonverbal immediacy, or a smile, or will they be more verbal? Many of the messages of control will be those used more generally by people communicating in other contexts, but some system will characterize the group, and its dimensions are defined in the forming stage.

Storming: The stage of emerging conflicts   The orientation activities of the forming stage shift almost inevitably into one where conflicts emerge. Some participants may not accept certain individuals as qualified or competent. Others may find one or more of the fellow members as boorish or disgusting. Still others may object to participating at all, or they may want to shift topics, go about achieving the goal in a different way, and so on. Resentments may develop over perceived rank, and negative feelings can be aroused when controlling messages are transmitted. Of special importance at this stage is the emergence of a leader and a *style* of leadership. Several different patterns can develop, and we will discuss these more fully in a later section.

Norming: The stage of stabilization   After the group works its way through whatever conflicts arise, the members will have worked out at least the initial "images" they have of each other (Chapter 5, pp. 133–134). They will have achieved definitions of self that will be applicable within the group. This brings greater accuracy in role-taking and more predictability as to how particular kinds of messages will be received. Members can then turn away from the process of sizing one another up and start resolving the conflicts that were generated in the earlier stages. Once this has been handled, they can deal with the group as an existing and reasonably predictable pattern of social relationships and turn to the task that must be accomplished.

Performing: The stage of task achievement   With the group now stabilized in terms of its rules of communication, the task for which the participants came together in the first place can be addressed fully. That is, the members can work productively to get the job done. As we suggested in our chapter's opening example, participants at this stage have examined various proposed solutions and they come together in consensus about the ones they believe to be best.

Not all groups go through these stages. They are particularly useful, however, for understanding communication in small groups whose participants do not know each other well and have been brought together to accomplish some purpose or goal. Many of the types of task-oriented groups we have described will undergo some set of similar transitions, and they may be found in greater or lesser degree in more formal decision-making groups.

Informal Rules for Communicating in Intimate Groups

If an intimate group is to achieve its goals, or even to survive, communication among its members must have certain critical characteristics. By that we mean its members must communicate frequently and in ways that help, rather than hinder, both the goal achievement of the group as a whole and the satisfactions of individual members. It is not difficult to understand the characteristics of messages that can lead to both of these outcomes.

In this section, we describe the rules of **informal communication** that develop within intimate groups. These rules guide and limit the spontaneous and unrestrained transmissions and receptions of messages that take place between members. By "informal" we mean the absence of deliberately designed barriers, or constraints—communication that is spontaneous and unrestrained. When communicating informally, people feel relatively free to say what they feel and do not constantly worry that their meanings will be misunderstood or that they will arouse hostile responses. It is the kind self-disclosing communication that takes place between good friends, family members on good terms, or even associates at work who have become friends.

The fact that informal communication is relatively uninhibited does not mean its social pathways are random. Even in the most intimate groups, rules dictate who can communicate to whom about what. There are always topics that are not to be discussed and times when it is not acceptable to bring up certain issues. However, those restraints are simply "understood" in a broad and general way; they are not deliberately designed prior to the entry of people into the group. On the contrary, the members work them out as they go along and revise them as need be.

Communication norms in intimate groups   As we have explained, communication norms are general rules that each member is expected to follow concerning what issues, topics and modes of transmission are acceptable within the group. For example, few families or even peer groups permit members to discuss gross bodily functions before the others at mealtimes. Sexual experiences and related topics may also be taboo. Name-calling has obvious risks, tattling or "ratting" on a member is often regarded as truly deviant behavior, and interrupting others with loud talking or shouting is seldom tolerated. Even in very spontaneous and uninhibited primary groups, then, there are a surprising number of limitations on what, how, when, and in what manner specific messages can be transmitted.

Communication roles in intimate groups   A second set of rules centers on who has the right to transmit particular kinds of messages and who must pay attention to them. Most of us do not thoughtfully study and analyze the role system regulating communication in our own family, but it can be a very revealing exercise. By careful observation, and perhaps even a bit of surreptitious note-taking, the role pattern of any family can be described. Adult family members are seldom coequal partners in *every* area of family concerns, no matter how democratic they try to be. One person will usually talk and make decisions about certain areas of concern while another will initiate more messages about others. These areas may be automobiles, food, child rearing, income, recreation, and so forth. On the other hand, while one may initiate more suggestions and proposals, another may be the one who gives final approval.

Communication scholars have studied role systems in intimate groups extensively.[17] The roles of husband, wife, child, or even of relatives, in the contemporary family are more than simply a matter of agreements among members as to who will be permitted or expected to say what to whom. Cultural traditions backed by legal requirements prepare people, long before marriage and parenthood, as to what specialized part they will be expected to play in the communication patterns of the family. In fact, our culture sets forth a kind of *general model* of family communication roles that broadly define the permissible communication patterns of each member. (There are variations on that model, of course, within various specialized cultures.)

No particular family fits the general model exactly. It becomes modified into a *de facto* system of communication roles. That is, when unique human beings come together to act out the parts of husband and wife to communicate about family matters, they modify the general model by developing consensus around their own definitions. These, then, become shared within the new group. Thus, partners bring with them not only their shared understandings of general or specialized cultural traditions but also their own personal definitions of how they want to communicate and how they expect others to communicate within the family system.

A major point here is that each new family can work out its own communication role requirements, or even change them if they are already established and are judged to be unsatisfactory. If this is done, it can head off conflict and increase the harmony of interactions within the group. If criticizing the mother-in-law is by mutual agreement defined as "off limits" for the husband, and griping about "too much attention to sports" taboo for the wife, these are less likely to be the sources of continuing arguments. Getting family communication under control with clear rules of who can say what can reduce potential conflict.

The roles of our most familiar small group were deeply influenced by our cultural traditions. For uncounted generations, the role of the wife in most cultures around the world centered on domestic tasks, child-bearing, and emotional support. Today, in American society family roles are being redefined. In contemporary families, each works out its own division of labor and its general rules for decision-making, power-sharing, and other forms of communication.

The role system existing in a particular family, then, is an adaptation of the cultural model that has been shaped, modified, extended, and adapted to the needs of the unique individuals who make up that group. Unlike the "one size fits all" garment that one occasionally finds in a clothing store, one role system does not fit all families. Each group must to a considerable extent work out its own pattern of communication rules. Very clearly, each does so in an extended process of informal communication.

In many ways, the role expectations that develop among intimate friends follow parallel patterns. All cultures define how friends are expected to communicate with each other, and these serve as general guides for individuals in small groups of close associates. There is vast latitude in the way that one individual can communicate to another in intimate ways. Thus, peer roles are the most flexible of all communication rules found in intimate groups.

Variations in social ranking   Enormous variations exist in social **ranks**—hierarchies of authority, power, and privilege that govern communication within families. Their nature depends on the specialized culture of the people involved. In one family the husband may be sternly dominant, constantly transmitting orders, with the wife meekly receiving them and communicating feedback messages of submissiveness. In another the male

may be a hen-pecked wimp and the female a blustering bully. In still another a true partnership may evolve in which both husband and wife communicate fully and openly about sharing power, cooperating on domestic chores, and earning income in the labor force.

Until relatively recent times in the United States (post–World War II), the kinds of messages socially approved for males and females were governed by a kind of generally approved system of family ranks. By long tradition, the male had more power, authority, and prestige than the female had. He was not only allowed but *expected* to issue orders, to demand compliance, and to have the final word concerning problems, plans, and questions. These expectations even carried over onto the offspring, with the male child faring better than the female.

When many women entered the labor force during World War II, the foundation for change in this traditional system of ranking was set into place. A national women's movement began which challenged that traditional pattern. Today, complex social and cultural changes are still in progress that are redefining ranking within the family. The power and authority of the male has clearly been reduced, at least in most middle-class families. However, the exact position of the female in the system has yet to be clarified fully.

In some families, especially among those low in education and income, the *authoritarian* pattern of clear-cut ranks continues to prevail. The husband clearly communicates that he is the boss; the wife responds by accepting her definition as the domestic helpmate; and the children are deferent in their messages to both. Fewer and fewer such families are left. They can still be found among recent immigrants who have brought such cultural models with them, among poor families in rural areas, and among lower-income blue-collar workers in urban areas. However, an emerging general model is the *democratic* pattern, in which the ranks of husband and wife are the same and each has an equal voice in the decisions affecting the family. The position of children is less clear. In some cases they are allowed to have considerable voice in family affairs; in others they remain silent and subordinate. In any case, every family works out some structure of ranks that govern how their messages are received and interpreted.

In friendship groups, the communication rules related to ranks tend to be far more subtle. No member of such a group can transmit messages aimed at "lording it over" others through the blatant exercise of power and authority. People resist the idea that their close friends can order them around. Nevertheless, there is a pattern of ranks in every group that governs who transmits what to whom and how those messages are interpreted.

The need for ranks in peer groups comes from the problem of coordination. Even close friends have to decide what activities to get involved in. For example, if they all decide to go to a football game, there is the problem of where they will meet, whose car will be driven, and what they will do together afterward. Usually, one individual will suggest a plan and the others will agree to it. This is leadership in a very subtle form. Or, if a party is to be held there are the questions of where, who will bring what, at what time to meet, and if others will also be invited. Again, one individual is likely to emerge as the person in control.

It is important to understand such ranking and power in the context of the intimate group of friends as it illustrates the broader problem of *authority*. If no member of a group accepts the orders, commands, or even suggestions of any other member as proper guides to their action, then chaos and anarchy prevail. It is far more convenient to look to some particular individual, in whom the members have confidence, as a source for direction. If a particular individual is established in such a position, he or she is informally and even unwittingly *vested with authority*. That is, there develops a shared conviction among the members that they "should" look to that individual for messages that provide direction. The commands, orders, or even suggestions for action communicated by that person are seen as *legitimate* directives that should be followed.[18]

Subtle social controls The rules for communicating in small intimate groups are maintained through messages that provide "sanctions"—that is, rewards for compliance and punishments for deviance. Sanctioning or **control** messages can range from nonverbal signals of approval or disapproval to shouted praises or shrieking verbal abuse. Mainly, however, the communication of social controls in intimate groups tends to be subtle.

Communicating so as to establish or maintain social control in the family can be a complex process. In the traditional family it often became very physical. If measures were needed to control the behavior of an errant child, the father got out the razor strap, took the offender by the ear to the woodshed, and soundly communicated a physical message to the posterior. In most families today, especially among middle-class and more educated people, verbal and nonverbal messages are substituted for woodshed controls. Violence is not approved, and if it is used, everyone's feelings tend to be hurt. Instead, a frown or smile may be sufficient. If that fails, children are scolded or praised. Sometimes, valued freedoms are withheld with messages indicating "grounding," no TV, confinement to room, and so on. The strongest message of all indicates that "love" is being withheld. On the reward side, approval may be communicated through gifts, access to special privileges, or increases in allowances.

Adult members of families also use special categories of verbal and nonverbal communication as rewards and punishments. Simply ignoring another individual, or looking at the person with a stony stare, can arouse meaning. A raised eyebrow, or a glare, can speak volumes under some circumstances. A "headache" can send a powerful message on certain occasions. On the other hand, such rewards as pats, strokes, hugs, special meals, flowers, candy, and many other kinds of nonverbal communication express approval and elicit emotional responses. Members of families develop sensitive skills at reading the intent and meanings of social control behind such transmissions.

In the peer group, transmitting messages for purposes of social control can be equally subtle. Groups of friends do not resort to violence to enforce their rules and requirements. Most positive and negative sanctions in such intimate groups are expressed in very subtle ways. But whatever modes of communication the group uses—verbal or nonverbal, violent or gentle, subtle or blatant—messages expressing approval and disapproval stabilize its communication rules.

Rules for Communicating in Task-Oriented Groups

The rules for communicating in task-oriented groups involve the same concepts we have already identified. They have norms that define appropriate topics, styles, and sequences, and some are highly structured into differentiated roles. Some participants enjoy greater power, status, and authority than others within such groups. And, of course, each has its own types of messages and meanings for purposes of control—to ensure that the rules will be followed to an acceptable degree.

Communication norms in task-oriented groups
Because there are so many different kinds of task-oriented groups, no single set of norms governs the kinds of messages that are appropriate for transmission. The rules for communicating in each kind of group are set by the sociocultural situation; that is, those rules are defined broadly by the goal or purpose for which the group was organized. In such forms as the round table, panel, and symposium, the norms are usually *predesigned,* which means these groups have requirements for communicating that are derived from traditions. When participants are recruited and asked to take part in such groups, they are expected to follow those traditional forms.

On the other hand, each person is an individual and will bring his or her own personal style and interpretations to those rules as they are carried into practice. One may joke and have a lighthearted style, while another will be more serious. Thus, the communication norms that are adopted and used within a particular task-oriented group will be some mix of the traditional patterns applicable to that type of group (panel, seminar, therapy group, or whatever) and the personal styles of each participant.

Leadership and other communication roles   Many kinds of communication roles in task-oriented groups have been studied, and a host of different kinds have been identified. The classic analysis of such roles is that of communication researchers Kenneth Benne and Paul Sheats, who in 1948 proposed three general categories.[19] These depend on what members tend to do in more or less repetitive ways. Some are *group task* roles, such as "opinion-seeker," "initiator," and "energizer." Another set is concerned with *group building and maintenance.* These include such roles as "encourager," "harmonizer," and "gatekeeper." A third category concerns *individual* roles, such as "aggressor," "help-seeker," and "recognition-seeker."

Of particular interest to communication researchers has been the role of *leader* in discussion groups. Typically, in the task-oriented type of discussion group (that we illustrated with our opening chapter example) a leader *emerges* during the periods of initial orientation and conflict.

The problems of how leaders emerge, what kinds of characteristics they have, and what styles result in what consequences are of profound importance. These issues go beyond what happens in small groups. In fact, the question of how power is achieved and used to control the behavior of others is one of the truly critical issues of human civilization. It has been studied since the time of Confucius, and it came under special scrutiny by social and behavioral scientists in the 20th century.

Interest in the relationship between communication and leadership sharpened during World War II, when despots like Hitler, Mussolini, and Tojo used propaganda and other persuasive techniques to gain popular support that eventually led the entire world into chaos. Leadership remains a critical concern in government, the military, industry, and education. Effective leadership can have very good results—or, sometimes, dreadful consequences. For example, answers are urgently needed as to how a person like Jim Jones, who began life as a poor white boy in Indiana, could lead hundreds of followers to commit suicide in Guyana in 1978; or how a dictator like Saddam Hussein could rise to power in Iraq and lead a rich nation to devastation.

Obviously, answers to such questions will not be found in the study of task-oriented discussion groups, but intriguing insights do emerge from looking at leadership in that context. For example, classic research suggests that three basic styles of leadership can be found in task-oriented discussion groups: the authoritarian, democratic, and laissez-fair styles.[20]

In the *authoritarian* style, policies and steps to implement them so as to achieve goals are determined solely by the leader. Assignment of companions or work partners is made by the leader. She or he is "personal" in praise and criticism, but tends to remain somewhat aloof. Other members remain uncertain about future plans and steps. Essentially, this type of leader sets the goal, decides on who will do what to get there, and defines the techniques or methods by which success will be achieved.

In the *democratic* style, group members discuss prospective policies and then determine them by vote. Technical advice on how to proceed is provided when needed by the leader, but members are free to choose companions in the division of special tasks. The leader is balanced and objective in praise and criticism, tries to be like other members to some degree, but does not do much of the actual work. Basically, the democratic leader takes people where they already want to go: He or she helps them determine what that is and the best steps to take to get there—and then coordinates their efforts so that the goal will be achieved.

The *laisezz-faire* leader is "laid back" and does little to interfere with the choices or activities of members. She or he lets the group go whatever way it wishes, even if this leads to mistakes. Little in the way of visible authority or power is exercised, and the leader does not provide much in the way of criticism or reward. Basically, all he or she does is answer members' questions and give advice when asked for it.

In assessing the implications for these styles of leadership in small-group discussions, real differences emerge. Cohesiveness tends to be greatest in the democratic group because the experience results in greater member satisfaction (see "reward-based" cohesion, pp. 181–182). On the other hand, less actual progress toward achieving solutions tends to be the case under democratic leadership. It is the authoritarian group that accomplishes the most in the shortest time, but members tend to achieve their goals in a less original way and there is much less member satisfaction. The laissez-faire style is less efficient than either of the other two, and it tends to produce the lowest levels of member satisfaction.

What factors result in a particular person becoming a leader? Essentially, there are two answers. One is that the person has special qualities—leadership *traits*. These are personal characteristics that people admire and respect, attributes of personality that are the basis of leadership. The trait theory of leadership has been widely studied, and there seems to be merit in the idea.[21]

A second answer is that *situations,* rather than traits, determine leadership and that different types of people will be successful leaders in distinctive social circumstances.[22] This interpretation also has merit, because, as we have seen, the sociocultural situations and goals of groups vary greatly from one type to another. A dramatic leader with a lot of "charisma" (attractive personal traits) may be just what is required in one situation, but would be entirely inappropriate in another. A different situation might best be served by a technically proficient but relatively inconspicuous individual. Thus, the best answer to how and why leaders are defined seems to be that commanding personal characteristics do determine leadership in some situations, but in others such factors as technical competence, insight into how work can be best organized, and other aspects of the situation are far more important in different settings.

The nature of leadership has received a great deal of attention from communication and other scholars. One conclusion is that some people become leaders because they have "charisma," attractive and special personal qualities. Another view is that the situation determines leadership. That is, regardless of whether personal attributes seem positive or negative, individuals with technical competence in a particular situation can serve effectively as leaders.

Communicating power and authority   Because there are so many different subcategories and types of task-oriented groups, one set of observations will not "fit all" in terms of how communication patterns are determined by social ranking. In more formally organized groups, such as panels and symposia, members with formal roles of leadership and coordination are obviously in a position to control the flow of messages. Ranking is less clear in the discussion group, in which members presumably start on an equal basis.

What often happens is that the social position and prestige of the person *outside,* in the larger society, plays a significant part in determining rank within a discussion group. Thus, a person who is a physician will almost automatically be seen as having greater authority in a small discussion group than an individual who is in a less prestigious occupation.

Sargent and Miller Leadership Scale

Instructions   We are interested in the things that are important to you when you are leading a group discussion. Listed below are seven pairs of statements. Read each pair of statements and place a mark in front of the one you believe to be of greater importance. On reacting to the statements, observe the following ground rules:

1. Place your check marks clearly and carefully.
2. Do NOT omit any of the items.
3. Never check both of the items.
4. Do not look back and forth through the items; make each item a separate and independent judgment.
5. Your first impression, your immediate feelings about the statements, is what we want.

Again, which of the following statements in each pair do you believe to be of greater importance in your role as group leader?

1. ____ To give everyone a chance to express his/her opinion.
   ____ To know what the group and its membership are doing.

2. ____ To assign members to tasks so that more can be accomplished.
   ____ To let members reach a decision all by themselves.

3. ____ To know what the group and its membership are doing.
   ____ To help members see how the discussion is related to the purposes of the group.

4. ____ To assist the group in getting along well together.
   ____ To help the group see what you think is their best answer.

5. ____ To get the job done.
   ____ To let the members reach a decision all by themselves.

6. ____ To know what the group and its members are doing.
   ____ To let the members reach a decision all by themselves.

7. ____ To get the job done.
   ____ To assist the group in getting along well together.

8. ____ To help the members see how the discussion is related to the purposes of the group.
   ____ To assign members to tasks so that more can be accomplished.

9. ____ To ask questions that will cause members to do more thinking.
   ____ To get the job done.

10. ____ To let the members reach a decision all by themselves.
    ____ To give new information when you feel the members are ready for it.

Calculating Your Score

1. For each pair of 10 items, there are two possible responses. One response represents a "democratic" orientation; the other is "autocratic" or authoritarian. Label the democratic responses "D" and the autocratic responses "A" according to the following key:

Item 1:   Choice 1 = D   Choice 2 = A

Item 2:   Choice 1 = A   Choice 2 = D

Item 3:   Choice 1 = A   Choice 2 = D

Item 4:   Choice 1 = D   Choice 2 = A

Item 5:   Choice 1 = A   Choice 2 = D

Item 6:   Choice 1 = A   Choice 2 = D

Item 7:   Choice 1 = A   Choice 2 = D

Item 8:   Choice 1 = D   Choice 2 = A

Item 9:   Choice 1 = D   Choice 2 = A

Item 10:   Choice 1 = D   Choice 2 = A

2. Next, score a "1" for each "D" and a "0" for each "A." In other words, you get no points for A responses, but 1 point for each D response you made.

3. Finally, add together your total points across all 10 items.
   YOUR TOTAL LEADERSHIP SCORE = ____.

Interpreting Your Score

Possible range of scores for the Leadership Scale is: 0–10. (If your own final score does not fall within that range, you made a computational error.)

The higher your score, the more democratic your own group leadership behavior should be. In particular, if your total score was 8 or better, your leadership style is more egalitarian. That is, democratic leaders encourage more group participation, ask for individual input or feedback, and ensure that everyone has an equal opportunity to be heard. Group members feel greater cohesiveness, are more committed to the group decision, and appreciate working within the group.

Lower scores, 3 or below, reflect more of an autocratic or authoritarian leadership style. If your own score reveals an authoritarian style, you can expect group members to like you less, feel much less satisfaction toward the group, and show less commitment to the group outcome. On the other hand, authoritarian leaders "get the job done" quickly and efficiently. These leaders are more interested in the outcome than they are in people's input or feelings.

References

Rosenfeld, L., Goldhaber, G., & Smith, V. R. (1975). *Experiments in human communication: A laboratory manual and workbook* (pp. 98–103). New York: Holt, Rinehart, and Winston.

Sargent, F., & Miller, G. R. (1971). Some differences in certain communication behaviors of autocratic and democratic group leaders. *Journal of Communication, 21,* 233–252.

Unfortunately, much the same can happen with respect to personal characteristics or attributes that are defined as lower in prestige ranking in the community. Thus, in discussion groups males often have an edge over females; small people are listened to with less conviction than tall and imposing people; the elderly may be at a disadvantage; messages transmitted by minority individuals may receive less deference than those from persons in dominant groups. The principle even extends to attractive versus unattractive people.[23]

Enforcing the communication rules   The principles of verbal and nonverbal communication outlined in previous chapters govern the enforcement of who can say what in a task-oriented group. The rules are enforced with feedback and with verbal comments and nonverbal signs, just as in any other type of communication. Here, signals of nonverbal immediacy can encourage a person to keep talking, while sneers, rolled eyes, frowns, and slumping posture can discourage message transmission. Thus, various kinds of messages are transmitted to those who transgress the norms on what topics or meanings are appropriate, perform their communication roles poorly, or fail to show appropriate deference to those who hold and exercise the power.

Communication Codes in Formal Decision-Making Groups

While there is great variation in the rules for communication in the many kinds of task-oriented discussion groups, the formal decision making group is another matter. There are a number of key features that characterize communication rules in almost any small, formal decision-making group. Those features reflect the fact that decision-making groups are almost always formed within a larger organization, whose purposes they are designed to serve. Small groups are necessary for reaching orderly conclusions about resources, performance, policies, proposals, and other important matters, within corporations, churches, schools, government agencies, and every other kind of large organization that characterizes contemporary life.

The most obvious feature of small decision-making groups is that they are not spontaneously formed but are deliberately designed. That is, they use carefully defined codes as rules of communication. Thus, communication is in many ways formal in such groups. (The term *formal* implies "forms.") Those forms consist of the coded rules and definitions for communication that dictate who can communicate to whom about what topics in what way.

Formal communication can be defined as *controlled communication between parties who are allowed or required by the group's coded rules to transmit particular kinds of messages to specific receivers using officially designated rules and restrictions.* Thus, the social pathways for the exchange of formal messages are confined and limited by the group's precisely delineated norms, well-specified roles, clearly differentiated ranks, and explicit system of social controls.

There are several "official" versions of rules for formal communication in existence, but the most widely used are those developed originally by Henry Martyn Roberts, a 19th-century engineering officer in the regular American Army. Following the Civil War, he was active in civic affairs and found himself presiding over debates in a number of nongovernmental groups. At the time, such debates were chaotic because there were no coded rules for formal discussion and collective decision-making, other than those used by government bodies. Roberts made a careful study of the formalized rules for communication used in such official groups as the British Parliament and the U.S. Congress. He adapted and simplified them and produced a short set of guidelines for conducting formal meetings, both large and small. They seemed to work rather well, and he had them printed up in 1876 under the title *A Pocket Manual of Rules of Order for Deliberative Assemblies.* Everyone wanted a copy, and it soon became difficult for him to keep up with demand. Shortly thereafter, he sold the rights to his book to a small publishing firm, Scott, Foresman and Company, and it was brought out in 1896 in an expanded form as *Roberts' Rules of Order.*

To say that the book caught on would be a gross understatement. It quickly became the world's standard. Robert's rules for decision-making groups have acquired a kind of "official" status all of their own. Over the past century, the work has been revised and expanded many times, not only by the original Henry Roberts but also by his son and then grandson. It is now in its eighth edition, having sold more than 3 million copies.[24]

Official requirements for communicating   Many small decision-making groups follow Roberts' rules only loosely. The discussion that follows shows what happens when they use them to control their communication: First, if "official" requirements are followed, only an agreed-on list of topics (the agenda) can be discussed of-

ficially during a meeting. The entire manner of transmission of messages about those topics by group members is sharply restricted. That is, close regulation of the formal communication process significantly restricts the latitude of decision-making, focusing it on certain specified issues and dictating a limited number of outcomes.

In truly important meetings of city councils and the like, if these restrictions and constraints are not followed, the decisions reached by the group can be challenged, even in the courts. Individuals who are not satisfied with the decisions reached by such groups sometimes do contest them on the basis that they were not reached using *due process* rules governing deliberations within the group.

In other words, what started out as convenient guidelines have become quasi-legal restrictions that not only govern communication behavior in certain kinds of decision-making groups but also have implications for the *quality* of the conclusions that are reached. Anyone who plans to participate in such a group, even a small one, should be very familiar with such norms.

Clearly delineated communication roles   In decision-making groups following formal rules, the role of leader is termed "the chair." Others in the group are "delegates" (of some other body) or "representatives" (of some constituency). If the group is very small, they are more likely to be just "members." Formal terms of address related to these roles are deemed appropriate. One doesn't say to the group "Hey, can I talk now?" Roberts' rules require that a plea for the group's attention be phrased as a formal request to "have the floor." The member can speak only if "recognized" by the chair. While he or she speaks, others cannot simply blurt out casual remarks. If they do, they will be ruled "out of order" by the chair.

Proposals for action, or possible solutions to problems, must be communicated to the group in the form of "motions," after recognition by the chair. Comments can be offered, or discussion regarding a motion can take place, only after the motion is "seconded" and the chair indicates that discussion is appropriate. The official rules, then, tightly control both the nature and the flow of messages between people in specific roles.

A hierarchy of power in controlling communication   Ranks in a formal decision-making group are well defined, and power in the group is not uniformly distributed. At the bottom, below the regular members, is a rank that may include nonvoting members, such as a "secretary," who does not participate in debate but is responsible for keeping the "minutes" (an accurate record of all transactions). There may also be a "sergeant at arms," whose duties are restricted to controlling unruly members if that should be necessary, although this seldom exists in small groups.

The largest stratum is made up of voting members, and they do have both power and authority. For example, they can offer motions, or amendments to motions, that are persuasive and that capture votes. And, through effective presentation of arguments, they can create consensus or conflict regarding a particular issue.

The greatest power is vested in the chair. For example, under formal rules, the chair controls the agenda. Issues and topics can be placed on the list, kept off, moved up for earlier consideration, or delayed. Debate can be restricted or extended, remarks can be ruled out of order, and certain members can be recognized ahead of others. Finally, the chair has the sole power to break a tie if votes are evenly divided.

Explicit messages designed for control   Official codes make ample provision for controlling their members with the use of explicit messages. For example, if a member performs a task for the group particularly well, a "resolution" commending the member may be brought to a vote. If it passes, it is entered into the minutes. Special symbolic awards are sometimes provided in the way of names on "honor roles," the presentation of "certificates of achievement," or special plaques for members to hang on their wall.

On the negative side, critical messages about a motion or a participant's conduct can be offered by an irate member. A member judged to be deviant may be criticized in a specifically worded motion of "censure," which if passed by vote is placed in the official minutes. Beyond that, resignations are sometimes requested. Or, if communication completely breaks down and, for example, a fist fight erupts, a sergeant at arms may have to eject the offenders physically from the meeting.

Decisions made by such small groups may range from very good to very bad. Recommendations for allocation, evaluation, policies, and so forth, emerging from such a communication context may be objective, insightful, and practical, or they may be self-serving, unjust, and unrealistic. For the most part, however, group decision-making, achieved within a formal pattern of rules that control communication, produces decisions that are likely to exceed in quality those made by individuals alone. Thus, the discovery of orderly decision-making in formal groups was a genuine breakthrough in human life.

Group Cohesion and Disorganization

Our final question is: what keeps groups together? The reverse, of course, is equally important—what causes them to break down? In every kind of group, large or small, intimate or formal, there is some set of factors that move the participants to maintain their membership and to perform the activities required of them. That binding condition, which we will call **group cohesion,** can range from very strong to very weak. As long as the basis of that cohesion is present, members will maintain their memberships and try to achieve whatever goals they are collectively pursuing. If the basis of that cohesion erodes, the group will begin to break down. Thus, group disorganization often stems from "bad communication processes" rather than from "bad people."

Distinct Bases of Cohesion

Four distinct bases of cohesion can be found in different types of groups. The one that is fundamental to intimate groups can be referred to as *sentiment-based* cohesion. A second, which characterizes the small task-oriented group, can be designated *reward-based* cohesion. Still a third basis is found in the formal decision-making group, and it can be called *assignment-based* cohesion. Finally, a fourth variety is what we will label *dependency-based* cohesion. This latter is not typical of small groups but is a condition that is found in large impersonal organizations where a complex division of labor provides interdependency among the system of roles.[25] (We will review the characteristics of this fourth type of cohesion in the next chapter.)

Sentiment-based cohesion in intimate groups   This type of cohesion is based on bonds of affection generated *within* the group; it cannot be imposed from without. Thus, by sentiment-based cohesion we mean that *members of a group are tied to each other by their feelings.* In a highly cohesive group, the members feel a deep sense of loyalty and obligation to each other. They willingly set aside their personal interests, modify their expectations if the welfare of the group is at stake, and are ready to make personal sacrifices for the sake of the other members. In such groups each member is valued not just for a role that he or she can play but as a person in an entire sense. Disruption of the group by illness, death, or other circumstances is a matter of deep emotional concern. In such a group, cohesion is high indeed and commitment to the group's goals is very strong.[26]

Such powerful cohesion is not universal in small intimate groups. In some, individuals can be tied to the other members, but less deeply. This can be true in either families or peer groups. In such cases, individuals may *like* the group and value their membership, but they do not feel their bonds so intensely. It is for this reason that we need to think of sentiment-based cohesion as a "variable"; that is, it can be present in different amounts.

Reward-based cohesion in discussion groups

Discussion groups are seldom held together because of the strong feelings participants have for each other. Here, *member satisfaction* of a personal or individual nature is the key factor. People continue in therapy or weight-loss groups, panel discussions, symposia, and consciousness-raising or encounter groups because they derive personal benefits—rewards—by maintaining membership. By participating they feel better, learn important things, or gain beneficial skills. If such personal rewards are not present, it is very likely that participation will be terminated. Common sense tells us that if people do not want what the group is trying to achieve, and find they are getting little out of membership, they are not likely to remain.

Assignment-based cohesion in decision-making groups

Clearly, people who happen to wind up on the same committee or board of directors are not necessarily bound to the group by their strong feelings for each other. In fact, they may be relative strangers or even actively despise each other. Furthermore, they may see no personal benefit in participation. Yet, it is possible for them to work together effectively to accomplish the group's goals. The reason is that members of small deliberative groups normally participate as a result of some "assignment" process. That is, they have been asked (or ordered) to serve by their boss, are voted into membership by a valued constituency, or must serve for some other valid reason.

Thus, member behavior in small decision-making groups is more likely to be cooperative than disruptive; their members seldom deliberately generate problems. The fact is that the social control system of the larger organization served by the group carries into the smaller context with powerful influences on its members. People's careers, raises, promotions, and reputations are at stake. It is reasonably safe to assume that for the most part they will behave in a constructive manner. Assignment-based cohesion, then, is a condition binding a person to a group based on a willingness to work with others to accomplish goals because that has been defined as one's *duty*.

At the same time, people who have been assigned to work together in a decision-making group may genuinely come to like each other, and some level of sentiment-based cohesion can develop in such a group. Thus the two types of cohesion can coexist, and they are not mutually exclusive.

Communication Breakdown and Group Disorganization

We have shown why a group within which formal or informal communication takes place following well-defined, deeply understood, and completely agreed-on rules for communicating probably will experience few difficulties in achieving its goals. However, the very same factors that produce cohesion in a group can sometimes be sources of confusion, disequilibrium, and distress.

Whether a group is large or small, intimate or impersonal, spontaneous or deliberately designed, a loss of cohesion can occur if members of a group are unclear about its communication *norms*. If these have not been effectively clarified, or if consensus breaks down about what kinds of messages, topics, or issues are approved and disapproved, **normative confusion** is the result. This can be a serious condition, and it can quickly result in group disorganization. In such a situation, individuals lose effective guidelines, conflicts arise, and group disintegration becomes increasingly likely.

Another source of potential disorganization is **role confusion.** Like norms, consensus concerning the communication requirements of the various roles in a group is achieved when members agree on who can appropriately say what to whom in what manner. If these shared understandings are inadequate, ineffective, or unclear, confusion about who should transmit what kinds of messages to whom is certain to result. Whatever the type of group, ranging from a family to a vast corporation, role confusion can be a major factor leading to a loss of cohesion.

Failure to clarify and gain consensus about the *legitimacy of ranks* is another obvious source of potential group disorganization. Thus, if the members of a group come to believe that the messages transmitted by those in positions of power and authority lack legitimacy or credibility, a condition of **rank ineffectiveness** will exist. Under such a condition, coordinating the activities of the

A loss of cohesion in a group can occur for a variety of reasons. Due to inadequacies in communication between members, the group's norms may be confusing; conflicts between roles may occur; there may be a failure to understand the distribution of power; or the social controls used to keep members from breaking the rules may become ineffective. Under any of these conditions, members of a group may exclude an individual who does not conform to its expectations.

group will be impossible. Thus, the very basis of *effective control* over communication behavior in a group lies in shared beliefs accepted by group members that breaking the rules will bring disapproval and rejection and that conforming to them in an exemplary manner will result in approval and honor.

Generally, then, communication breakdown in a group is the reverse side of cohesion. Thus, one need not always attribute group disorganization to "bad actors" with problem personalities, although such individuals obviously exist. In trying to understand why a given group does not function well, it may be more effective to begin by analyzing the degree to which its rules of communication are understood and accepted by its participants.

Chapter Review

- Groups consist of two or more people who repeatedly interact together, regulating their conduct within some set of rules for communication and social activity they mutually recognize and follow. People participate in groups in order to accomplish goals they could not achieve by acting alone. Communicating with other people in a group is not the same experience as doing so in a dyadic (two-person) context. Different types of groups provide distinctive communication contexts with unique features.

- Communication scholars traditionally divide the study of groups into two broad classes on the basis of size—small groups and (larger) organizations. Size is not only important but essential to understanding the dynamics of communication in a group. As the number of dyads, or pairs, that can be formed in a group grows, the more difficult it is to maintain a full flow of communication among all of the members. Many communication specialists maintain that an optimal size for discussion and getting decisions made in a small group with all members participating fully is something like *five*.

- Intimate groups include both the human family and peer groups of close friends. These are sometimes called "primary" groups because they are earliest in the experience of human beings and because they play a critical part in the individual's socialization, enculturation, and personality development. There are many kinds of task-oriented groups, and their characteristics vary greatly. They may be formal or informal, private or public. Their goals include holding discussions for various purposes, helping people feel better or improve themselves, and making orderly decisions within a larger organizational context.

■ Social relationships between members of a group are controlled and defined by its rules of communication. Those relationships may be very informal and spontaneous, or they may be formally specified as part of a deliberate design. In many kinds of discussion groups, the rules dictating who can transmit what kinds of messages when and to whom emerge through a series of stages. In more formally structured decision-making groups, most of the rules are in place before the members are chosen.

■ Of particular interest to communication researchers has been the role of *leader* in discussion groups. Classic research suggests that three basic styles of leadership can be found in task-oriented discussion groups: the *authoritarian, democratic,* and *laissez-fair* styles.

■ There are essentially two kinds of factors that result in a particular person becoming a leader. One is that the person has special personal characteristics (traits) that people admire and respect. Another view is that the *situation* determines leadership and that different types of people will be successful leaders in distinctive social situations. Overall, both views have merit.

■ In every kind of group, large or small, intimate or formal, some set of factors moves the participants to maintain their membership and to perform the activities required of them. That binding condition, called *group cohesion,* can range from very strong to very weak. As long as the basis of that cohesion is present, members will maintain their membership and try to achieve whatever goals they are collectively pursuing. If the basis of that cohesion erodes, the group will begin to break down. Thus, group disorganization often stems from "bad communication processes" rather than from "bad people."

Key Terms

Assertiveness-training group   A specialized discussion group in which participants learn ways in which they can stand up for their rights and be more demanding in ensuring that they are treated with dignity and respect.

Assignment-based cohesion   A type of cohesion based on the fact that members of a group have been asked (or ordered) to serve by their boss, are voted into membership by a valued constituency, or must serve for some other valid obligation or duty.

Cohesion (group)   That set of factors in every kind of group, large or small, intimate or formal, which moves the participants to maintain their membership and to perform the activities required of them.

Consciousness-raising group   One in which people engage in discussions that help them realize they face mutual problems such as sex discrimination, and help them define and deal with these problems.

Controls (communication)   Messages that provide sanctions—that is, meanings of rewards for complying with and punishments for deviating from the communication rules shared in the group.

Decision-making group   One in which the goal is to arrive at orderly judgments, usually through a process of formal communication and discussion.

Encounter group   One in which participants come together for discussions in which they identify and seek ways of coping with difficulties they experience in daily life, such as discrimination, harassment, or other problems.

Enculturation   The process of acquiring understandings of the general culture of a person's society, including not only language skills but also shared beliefs, emotional orientations, attitudes, values, and everything that makes a person an accepted member of society who "fits in."

Experiential group   One in which the principal goal of participation is to make people feel better.

Formal communication   Controlled communication between parties who are allowed or required by the group's coded rules to transmit particular kinds of messages to specific receivers using officially designated rules and restrictions.

Forum   A type of discussion group usually based on brief presentations by each member of a small group who are introduced by a chairperson. Their presentations are followed by a considerable amount of participation by audience members, again coordinated by the chair.

Group   Two or more people who repeatedly interact together, regulating their conduct within some set of rules for communication and social activity that they mutually recognize and follow.

Informal communication Communication that takes place in the absence of deliberately designed barriers or constraints—communication that is spontaneous and unrestrained. When communicating informally, people feel relatively free to say what they feel and do not constantly worry that their meanings will be misunderstood or that they will arouse hostile responses.

Intimate group People who make up either a human family or a peer group of close friends. The key factor is that communication is extensive, self-disclosing and uninhibited.

Normative confusion A basis of group disorganization that takes place when communication norms have not been effectively clarified, or it occurs if consensus breaks down about what kinds of messages, topics, or issues are approved and disapproved.

Norms (for communication) General rules that each participant in a group is expected to follow concerning what issues, topics, and modes of transmission are acceptable to the other members.

Panel A more formal type of discussion group in which participants are often experts or representatives of some sort. The panel is usually coordinated by a moderator, and the discussion usually takes place before a live audience.

Peer group A small group of close and intimate friends, often of the same general socioeconomic characteristics, age, and gender.

Personality The individual's more or less enduring organization of meanings, motivations, emotional patterns, orientations, skills, and other attributes that make that person different in psychological makeup from all others.

Primary group Intimate groups that are earliest in the experience of the human individual and which play a critical part in the person's psychological and social development. Essentially these are the family and early peer groups. Peer groups in adult life can also be considered primary groups.

Rank (communication) Rules that define communication patterns based on authority, power, and privilege within a group. For example, who can issue orders, who must always listen to whom, who has a right to speak first or last, and whose messages are regarded as more or less important?

Rank ineffectiveness A situation in which members of a group come to believe that the messages transmitted by those in positions of power and authority lack legitimacy.

Reward-based cohesion A type of cohesion based on the personal satisfactions or rewards that flow to individuals because they participate in a group. This leads them to maintain membership and work toward the goals of the group.

Role confusion A situation in which shared understandings are inadequate, ineffective, or unclear about who should

transmit what kinds of messages to whom. Such role confusion is a basis for group disorganization.

Roles (communication) A cluster of rules in a group that define who has the right to transmit particular kinds of messages and who must pay attention to them.

Round table A common format for informal discussion groups in which no audience is usually present and the participants arrange themselves in some sort of circular pattern.

Seminar One of the oldest forms of small discussion groups, now commonly used in advanced study in universities. Usually, each student takes a turn at addressing a central question that is the focus of the discussion, and the mentor draws the important lessons out of various comments.

Sentiment-based cohesion A type of cohesion based on bonds of affection that exist between members of a group.

Small group One in which the number of members can vary from two to perhaps a dozen or more, but optimal size with all members participating fully in communication is *five* members.

Small-group conference A small discussion group in which several participants are brought together, usually under private conditions, to share technical information or to discuss a problem in their area of expertise.

Socialization Long-term processes of communication within which deliberate or indirect lessons are internalized, enabling the person to become a unique human being, a functioning member of a society, and a participant in its general and specialized culture.

Symposium A very formal type of discussion group whose participants are usually a small group of experts. They are individually introduced by a moderator, and each then makes a speech about the theme. During or even between the presentations, the participants seldom talk with each other and simply take their turn in delivering their analyses or views.

Task-oriented group One in which people participate in order to get something done through group participation that they have mutually set as an objective. There are many kinds.

Therapy group A specialized discussion group in which participants who share a common difficulty meet with a coordinator who usually has some special insight into the problem. The underlying assumption is that if such people get together and disclose their experiences, thoughts, and feeling to each other it will help them feel better.

Trait (personality) A relatively stable and predictable pattern of behavior that characterizes a person; a feature of an individual's personality that makes her or him different from others. Examples are "stingy," "honest," "smart," "happy-go-lucky," and so forth.

Notes

1. Homans, G. C. (1950). *The human group* (p. 1). New York: Harcourt, Brace & Jovanovich; Brilhart, J. K. (1978). *Effective group discussion* (pp. 20–21). Dubuque, IA: W. C. Brown; Shaw, M. E. (1981). *Group dynamics: The psychology of small group behavior* (3rd ed.). New York: McGraw Hill. Weaver, R. L., II, *Understanding business communication* (p. 200). Englewood Cliffs, NJ: Prentice-Hall; and Goodall, H. L., Jr. (1990). *Small group communication in organizations* (2nd ed.). Dubuque, IA: W. C. Brown.

2. A number of explanations have been advanced as to why people choose to become members of (voluntary) groups. For thoughtful reviews of theories and other relevant issues related to the determinants of such membership, see: Trenholm, S. (1991). *Human communication theory* (pp. 188–191). Englewood Cliffs, NJ: Prentice-Hall; and Shaw, M. E. & Gouran, D. S. Group dynamics and communication. In Dahnke, G. L. and Clatterbuck, G. W. (Eds.) (1990). *Human communication: Theory and research* (pp. 123–155). Belmont, CA: Wadsworth.

3. The number of pairs (*p*) in any group of people can be calculated as the number of "twos" that can be drawn from *n* (the number of members). The formula is *n* times (*n* − 1) divided by 2. If we care to consider combinations of more than two, such as "triads," or even larger coalitions that can exist in a group, the numbers become astronomical. Here, the algebraic formula is that for "combinations," which is typically given as:

$$_nC_r = \frac{n(n-1)\,(n-2)\,\cdots\,(n-r+1)}{r!}$$

Where: *n* = the number of people in the group.
　　　 r = the number of people in a given coalition of, say, 3, 4, etc.

4. The term is an old one. It was introduced into the study of communication in groups by Cooley early in this century. See: Cooley, C. H. (1909). *Social organization* (pp. 23–31). New York: Charles Scribner's.

5. For a classic statement of this function of small and intimate groups, see: Cooley, C. H. (1909). Primary groups. In *Social organization* (pp. 23–31). New York: Charles Scribner's.

6. There are many theories that attempt to explain how children acquire internal understandings of objects, space, time, causality, and other complex aspects of the universe that are shared in their culture. One of the most seminal approaches is that of the Swiss psychologist Jean Piaget. See, for example, his classic: (1954). *The construction of reality in the child*. New York: Basic Books. Also, for an excellent discussion on the influence of family interaction and communication on child development see: Pearson, J. C. (1989). *Family communication: Seeking satisfaction in changing times*. New York: Harper and Row.

7. No single definition of personality has found acceptance among all social scientists or communication scholars. The one advanced here was adapted from a classic formulation developed by a team of psychologists, psychiatrists, and social anthropologists. See: Adorno, T. W., Frenkel-Brunswick, E., Levinson, D. J., & Sanford, R. N. (1950). *The authoritarian personality* (p. 5). New York: Harper and Row.

8. This is a typical contemporary definition. See: Houston, J. B., Bee, H., & Rimm, D. C. (1983). *Invitation to psychology* (2nd ed.) (p. 490). Academic Press. A variety of studies have been published over the years which suggest that an individual's personality influences behavior in groups. See, for example: Beckwith, J., Iverson, M. A., & Render, M. E. (1965). Test anxiety, task relevance of group experience, and change in level of aspiration. *Journal of Personality and Social Psychology, 1,* 579–588; Cattell, R. B., & Strice, G. F. (1960). *The dimensions of groups and their relations to the behavior of members.* Champaign, IL: Institute for Personality and Ability Testing; Haythorn, W. (1953). The influence of individual members on the characteristics of small groups. *Journal of Abnormal and Social Psychology, 48,* 276–284; Mann, R. D. (1959). A review of the relationships between personality and performance in small groups. *Psychological Bulletin, 56,* 241–270; and Plax, T. G. & Rosenfeld, L. B. (1976). Dogmatism and decisions involving risk. *Southern Speech Communication Journal, 41,* 266–277.

9. The seminal work on the nature and origins of personality traits is: Allport, G. W. (1937). *Personality: A psychological interpretation.* New York: Henry Holt. See especially Chapter 11, "A Theory of Traits," and Chapter 12, "The Nature of Traits," pp. 286–342.

10. Benedict, R. (1934). *Patterns of culture* (pp. 2–3). Boston: Houghton Mifflin.

11. (1941). *The Republic of Plato* (Francis MacDonald Cornford, Trans.). London: Oxford University Press.

12. For a thorough discussion on focus-group communication see: Plax, T. G., & Cecchi, L. F. Manager decisions based on communication facilitated in focus groups. *Management Communication Quarterly, 2,* 511–535.

13. One of the best known of such studies was reported before observation of actual juries in action was prohibited by courts. See: Strodtbeck, F. L., & Mann, R. D. (1956). Sex role differentiation in jury deliberations. *Sociometry, 19,* 3–11.

14. A classic early study is that of Bales, R. F. & Strodtbeck, F. L. (1951). Phases in group problem-solving. *Journal of Abnormal and Social Psychology, 46,* 485–495. Notable recent research on group decision development includes: Fisher, B. A. (1970). Decision emergence: Phases in group decision making. *Speech Monographs, 37,* 53–66; Poole, M. S. (1981). Decision development in small groups I: A comparison of two models. *Communication Monographs, 48,* 1–24; Poole, M. S. (1983). Decision development in small groups II: A study of multiple sequences in decision making. *Communication Monographs, 50,* 206–232; Poole, M. S. (1983). Decision development in small groups III: A multiple sequence model of group decision development. *Communication Monographs, 50,* 321–341; Poole, M. S. & Roth, J. (1989). Decision development in small groups IV: A typology of group decision paths. *Human Communication Research, 15,* 323–356; and Poole, M. S., and Roth, J. (1989). Decision development in small groups V: Test of a contingency model. *Human Communication Research, 15,* 549–589.

15. Bales, R. F. (1950). *Interaction process analysis: A method for the study of small groups.* Cambridge, MA: Addison-Wesley.

16. Tuckman, B. W. (1965). Development sequences in small groups. *Psychological Bulletin, 63,* 384–399.

17. For introductory-level overviews of research on communication with family and friends and in close relationships see: Pearson, op. cit.; and Galvin, K. M., & Brommel, B. J. (1982). *Family communication: Cohesion and change.* Glenview, IL: Scott, Foresman. For more advanced reviews of these literatures see: Blumstein, P., & Kollock, P. (1988). Personal relationships. In Scott, W. R., (Ed.), *Annual review of sociology* (pp. 467–490). Palo Alto, CA: Annual Reviews, 1988; Clark, M. S. & Reis, H. T. (1988). Interpersonal processes in close relationships. In Rosenzweig, M. R. & Porter, L. W. (Eds.), *Annual*

review of psychology (pp. 609–672). Palo Alto, CA: Annual Reviews; and Perlman, D., & Duck, S. (Eds.) (1989). *Intimate relationships: Development, dynamics, and deterioration.* Newbury Park, CA: Sage.

18. This is, of course, a miniature version of the "social contract" theory of the origins of roles for behavior (laws), discussed by Thomas Hobbes in the 17th century. See: Hobbes, T. (1950). *The leviathan.* London: J. M. Dent and Sons. (First published 1651)

19. Benne, K. D. & Sheats, P. (1948). Functional roles of group members. *Journal of Social Issues, 4,* 41–49. For reviews of both classic and contemporary studies on group roles see: Moreland, R. L., & Levine, J. M. Newcomers and oldtimers in small groups. (1989). In P. B. Paulus (Ed.), *Psychology of group influence* (pp. 143–186) Hillsdale, NJ: Erlbaum; Levine, J. M., & Moreland, R. L. (1990). Progress in small group research. In M. R. Rosenzweig & L. W. Porter (Eds.), *Annual review of psychology* (pp. 585–634). Palo Alto, CA: Annual Reviews; and Shaw & Gouran, op. cit., pp. 134–136.

20. A classic small-groups study that focused on these styles was done in 1938 under the direction of Kurt Lewin. See: Lippit, R., & White, R. K. An experimental study of leadership and group life. In Maccoby, E. E., Newcomb, T. M., & Hartley, E. L. (Eds.), *Readings in social psychology* (3rd ed.). New York: Holt.

21. For example, see: Stogdill, R. M. (1974). *Handbook of leadership: A survey of theory and research.* New York: Free Press.

22. Fiedler, F. E. (1967). *A theory of leadership effectiveness.* New York: McGraw-Hill.

23. For an excellent review of the classic investigations of personal characteristics and attributes that influence perceptions of social ranking and leadership see: Gibb, C. A. (1969). Leadership. In G. Lindzey & E. Aroson (Eds.), *The handbook of social psychology* (2nd ed.) (Vol. 4, pp. 216–228). Reading, MA: Addison-Wesley. Also, for an excellent discussion of research examining the relationship among physical attractiveness and various social rewards see: Schneider, D. J. (1976). *Social psychology* (pp. 471–476). Reading, MA: Addison-Wesley.

24. Historical details about this important work were supplied by the publisher. See: Roberts, H. (1981). *Roberts' rules of order* (Newly rev. ed.). Glenview, IL: Scott, Foresman.

25. The concept of dependency-based cohesion was derived by the authors from the underlying theory of "mechanical" versus "organic" solidarity set forth by Emile Durkheim for describing "social solidarity" in contrasting types of societies. Our application is not to societies as a whole but to the kinds of groups included in our analysis. See: Durkheim, E. (1947). *The division of labor in society* (G. Simpson, Trans.). New York: Free Press. (First published 1893). Sentiment-based dependency was derived from the contrast between two distinctive types of social bonds that bind people to simple and complex social systems. See: Tonnies, F. (1957). *Gemeinschaft und Gesellschaft* (C. P. Loomis, Trans.). East Lansing: Michigan State University Press. Reward-based and assignment-based cohesion were developed by the authors for this text.

26. The classic study was of the intense loyalty to peers shown by common soldiers in units of the German Army in World War II. The members of such groups were so intensely loyal to each other (but not to Nazi political ideology or to the German high command) that they resisted surrender and fought on even when the odds became hopeless. See: Shills, E. A., & Janowitz, M. (1948). Cohesion and disintegration in the Wehrmact in World War II. *Public Opinion Quarterly, 12,* 280–315.

Additional Readings

Cathcart, R. S., & Samovar, L. A. (Eds.). (1988). *Small group communication: A reader* (5th ed.). Dubuque, IA: W. C. Brown.

This is an excellent compilation of basic articles on group communication. Now in its fifth edition, this reader has remained popular for over two decades. Essays include discussion-group environments, decision making, messages, performance, leadership, and evaluation. Each article is well written and easy to read. This text is a valuable supplement to any course in group communication.

Goodall, H. L., Jr. (1990). *Small group communication in organizations* (2nd ed.). Dubuque, IA: W. C. Brown.

This introductory text provides a straightforward overview of small groups in American organizations. In simple language the author discusses the basics of small-group processes, as well as participation and communication in small groups plus leadership in the small group. Numerous examples help the student work through the material.

Levine, J. M., & Moreland, R. L. (1990). Progress in small group research. In M. R. Rosenzweig & L. W. Porter (Eds.), *Annual review of psychology* (pp. 585–634). Palo Alto, CA: Annual Reviews.

This article represents a state of the art review of the contemporary social psychological literature on small groups.

Literature is reviewed and analyzed around group ecology, composition, structure, conflicts, and group performance. This is a somewhat advanced treatment of this area.

Perlman, D., & Duck, S. (Eds.). (1989). *Intimate relationships: Development, dynamics, and deterioration.* Newbury Park, CA: Sage.

This edited reader considers topics and issues that are pertinent to the study of group communication. It brings together essays that discuss the development and dynamics of relationships plus the deterioration and reorganization of relationships. All of the readings deal with communication in intimate relationships of one type or another.

Shaw, M. E., & Gouran, D. S. (1990). Group dynamics and communication. In G. L. Dahnke & G. W. Clatterbuck (Eds.), *Human communication: Theory and research* (pp. 123–155). Belmont, CA: Wadsworth.

This article blends the psychological and communication literatures on groups into a comprehensive review of this area. The authors consider all basic issues and concepts as well as make recommendations about the future of this important area. This is a thoughtfully written report that makes a good source for additional study of group communication.

Chapter 7

Communicating Within Organizations

Contents

Sociocultural Situations: Why People Communicate in Organizations
Society's Need for Organizations
Bureaucracy as a Prerequisite

The Classical Theory of Bureaucracy
The Emergence of Rational Society
Weber's Principles

Management-Oriented Approaches to Organizational Communication
Human Use Perspectives
    Wage formulas from classical economics
    The era of "scientific management"
    "Universal principles" of management
Human Relations Perspectives
    The Hawthorne studies and their legacy
    The decline of the human relations perspective
Human Resources Perspectives

The Flow of Messages Within Large Organizations

Formal Communication Through Official Channels
Vertical transmission
Message content in formal communication
Accuracy versus distortion up and down the line
Informal Communication in Organizational Settings
    Socially validated constructions of meaning
    Capacity, flexibility, and speed
Distortion of Messages in the Grapevine
    The embedding pattern
    The compounding pattern
Consequences of Organizational Communication
    Specialized organizational cultures
    Conflicting specialized cultures
    Organizational cohesion

Chapter Review

Key Terms

Notes

Suggested Readings

Key Questions

- Why is it so important that I understand communication processes in organizations? Is there something different about them, or are they the same as the communication processes that occur in any other kind of setting?

- There are an enormous number of organizations in our society. They are devoted to everything from selling hamburgers to manufacturing high-tech space satellites. How did we get so many organizations, and what do they really do for all of us?

- There are a lot of jokes about "faceless bureaucrats" and the horrors of the "red tape" involved in "bureaucracy." Is it all a big joke? Is bureaucracy one of society's mistakes? Or, if one looks closer, are there very serious and socially beneficial aspects of bureaucracy?

- How have management styles in organizations changed over the years? Are they any better than they were generations ago? Or did people in earlier years have a better understanding of how to motivate people by communicating effectively within organizations?

- What is this "grapevine" that we hear about? How does it work within an organization? What kinds of messages do people pass along by this means, and does this kind of communication have positive or negative consequences for people who participate or work in organizations?

We are born in organizations, educated in organizations, and most of us spend much of our lives working for organizations. We spend much of our leisure time playing and praying in organizations. Most of us will die in an organization, and when the time comes for burial, the largest organization of all—the state—will grant official permission.

Amitai Etzione
1964

It was 4,600 years ago when Pharaoh Khufu (Cheops) decided to build a great pyramid near the Nile that would demonstrate his power and authority to all future generations. The pharaoh understood well that time was of the essence: Life expectancy was short, and he needed to get the project completed. The goal, then, was to complete the huge physical structure, using human and material resources efficiently, and to the highest standards of quality.

Now suppose that you have been transported back in time as a pharaoh and are determined that your pyramid will be completed before you die. How will you organize the labor and materials to get the job done? Constructing a gigantic monument is a formidable task, because you have no machinery as we have today. Fortunately, you have an excellent site near a quarry and a large river, and you have at your command talented engineers, architects, masons, artists, and craftsmen plus a virtually inexhaustible supply of peasants to do the labor.

How do you begin? How can all of the thousands of activities that are needed be directed in a team effort? One strategy would be to talk, individually, to each of the thousands of specialists whose skills are needed, explaining what each has to do. However, such an approach would take a lifetime to communicate the explanations to such an army of workers one at a time. You would be dead before construction even began.

A far better way is to divide the work up into several broad but interrelated areas of responsibility. Then administrators can be selected and placed in charge of each area, and they can select whatever subordinates they need. Suitable workers can then be placed under the supervision of these managers. For example, one team can design the structure while another prepares the site; a third can cut stone blocks; and a fourth can drag the blocks to the site and up temporary ramps to the various levels. Organizing the work into such areas of responsibility means that thousands of laborers can work under management teams with efforts coordinated by a hierarchy of supervisors and managers. To achieve such coordination, procedures for communication are devised for transmitting orders up and down the chain of command and for receiving reports of progress through carefully designed channels.

After all personnel have been recruited, the project actually begins. From dawn to dusk, year after year, the work goes on. Everywhere is evidence of careful and deliberate planning. Every specialized activity fits into a pattern with every other one. Communication flows up and down the line through many channels.

Finally, the pyramid is built. The organizational communication system that you designed made it possible to coordinate and control all of the talent, technology, labor, and materials at your disposal in an efficient manner. With your goal attained you know that you will be able to rest peacefully in your great monument with the world forever in awe of your enormous power and prestige.

As our example suggests, the use of large groups of people who coordinate their work in a well-devised plan to accomplish an important goal is as old as civilization itself. By the time literate societies developed in Africa, Europe, the Americas, and Asia, deliberately designed groups characterized by formal communication systems were common. Today, thousands of years later, our society is almost totally dependent on relatively large groups of many kinds whose goal achievement depends on organizational communication.[1] It is difficult to imagine a single activity that can be performed in our time, short of becoming a hermit, without depending in some way on communication within an organization.

Communication patterns within any organization include all of the verbal and nonverbal processes, both linear and transactional, that we have already discussed. Within an organization people communicate both formally and informally within the interpersonal and small-group contexts we have described in previous chapters. However, an organization is a distinctive communication context in its own right. That is, it includes forms and processes of communication that are not found in the other contexts we have examined.[2] Those unique communication processes will be discussed in the present chapter.

Simply put, an **organization** is a human group that has been deliberately designed so as to achieve a desired objective. Usually it has a large number of participants, at least compared to the small groups we discussed earlier. As we saw, a large group requires complex rules for communication so that the activities of its participants can be coordinated. This is usually handled by a hierarchy of managers who transmit and receive various kinds of messages, upward and downward to and from the rank and file, and in a few situations, laterally among themselves. These messages, whether linear or transac-

tional, formal or informal, are what make up "organizational communication."

There are many kinds of message transmissions that scholars in various disciplines call "organizational communication." For example, each of the following is discussed as organizational communication in one field or another:

- *Internal communication* (between workers, supervisors, and managers in the day-to-day operation of the organization)
- *Advertising* (in the case of groups that produce goods to sell in the marketplace for profit)
- *Public relations* (for organizations that need to maintain a positive image in a community or population)
- *Consumer relations* (for organizations that need to retain positive relationships with people who buy and use their products)

We could easily add to the list. Some organizations need to communicate with government officials; others with parents, religious followers, welfare recipients, retirees, convicts, and so on. This is too large a territory to cover

In contemporary societies, many kinds of large organizations provide goods and services. Communication within such organizations follows both formal and informal channels. Formal channels have rigid rules, specifying who can say what to whom about what topic. Informal channels, commonly called the "grapevine," are complex social pathways through which people pass on gossip, rumors, or other unofficial messages by word-of-mouth.

in a single chapter. Therefore, for purposes of this text, we will define organizational communication rather specifically. In terms of the preceding list, we will be concerned mainly with the first category. However, our focus will be on communication patterns and processes that are found in many kinds of organizations, whatever their goals and products. For present purposes, then, **organizational communication** can be defined as *the transmission of messages through both the formal and the informal channels of a relatively large, deliberately designed group, resulting in the construction of meanings that have influences on its members, both as individuals and on the group as a whole.*

To understand this vital form of communication, we will look briefly at an intellectual background that helps explain why there are so many organizations in our contemporary society and what they do for us. That intellectual background is drawn from interdisciplinary sources which include economics, management, psychology, sociology, and speech communication. As will be clear, organizations are critically important to all of us because they serve us in countless ways.

Sociocultural Situations: Why People Communicate in Organizations

In terms of the linear and transactions models we developed in earlier chapters, every organization in modern society can be regarded as a "sociocultural situation." That is, people get together in organizations not in random assemblies but in carefully organized patterns so as to accomplish certain goals that could not be attained in alternative group settings. Our first task, therefore, is to understand the *purposes* for which people communicate in organizational contexts.

One way in which the goals of the thousands of large organizations existing in contemporary society can be understood is to view them within a framework of economics. For example, as societies became more complex with the advance of the Industrial Revolution, more and more of the goods and services that their populations wanted and needed had to be provided by organizations. The era of individual craftspersons and small "mom and pop" operations that once supplied people with what they wanted and needed declined sharply during the late 20th century. Larger and increasingly complex organizations were developed to produce and distribute consumer products and to satisfy growing markets for services. Organizations served needs efficiently in the public sector, and at higher profit levels in the private sector.

In a somewhat parallel manner, the needs of a population are provided not only by an economic system but

also by what social scientists call "social institutions." The great growth of organizations in modern society, then, can be traced to significant changes in its institutional structure.

Society's Need for Organizations

The basic needs of a population in any society are met by its social institutions. A **social institution** can be defined as *a rather broad configuration of closely related cultural elements and organized social activities that are essential to fulfilling a perceived basic need of the social order.* At first glance, this definition may seem somewhat technical and difficult to understand. However, its basic ideas can easily be illustrated. For example, we can look at the *educational* institution. It is one of the five *basic* institutions, and one exists in every society—without exception. That is, organized social life requires that new members born into the society be systematically introduced to its ways and requirements. In traditional societies without formal schools, that task is usually assigned to parents or other relatives, such as grandparents, aunts, and uncles. These individuals have the responsibility to teach children the skills they need and generally how to behave in a socially acceptable manner. In our society today, those functions are still located partly in the family, but many aspects of education are now handled by organizations, such as schools, sometimes churches, and even leisure organizations like the Girl Scouts and Boy Scouts.

All societies have four additional basic social institutions. For example, we all have a deep need for order, predictability, and security in social life, so the institution of *government* has been developed. A *religious* institution has been organized around the need to understand and try to influence the supernatural. An *economic* institution evolved to handle the production and distribution of goods and services. Finally, the *family*—the oldest and most fundamental institution of all—was established to regulate bearing and rearing children within responsible and stable groups. In modern urban-industrial societies there are many others in addition to the basic five. Medicine, science, spectator sports, and mass media are examples that come easily to mind.

Against that intellectual background, the relationship between *societal needs, social institutions,* and *organizations* becomes clearer. It is quite easy to see this relationship with respect to the economic institution. Business enterprises, industries, banking, and commercial establishments that meet our economic needs are obviously structured around organizations. However, it is also true of the other social institutions. Religion, for example, is not just a matter of individual belief and action. Our religious needs are satisfied in part by established faiths, churches, and denominations, some of which have been with us for centuries, plus more modern organizations—such as the "electronic churches" that depend on highly trained and professional personnel who bring religious messages to millions of people via television.

One reason we are emphasizing this relationship between societal needs and social institutions is that scholars who specialize in the study of organizational communication have typically been more narrowly focused. They have been preoccupied with assisting *management* in solving problems of worker control and productivity in business and industrial environments.[3] In this chapter we will of necessity address that issue because it is a traditional concern of the discipline, and management's need for effective communication techniques to use to control workers and raise their efficiency is undoubtedly important. However, there is more to understanding organizational communication than that narrow perspective. Thus, we will also present perspectives that apply to *all* organizations, regardless of their location within a particular social institution.

Bureaucracy as a Prerequisite

The basic organizing principle of organizations is *bureaucracy.* If our imaginary account about organizing work to build the pyramid was easily understood, the idea of bureaucracy will not be difficult to grasp. The term has a number of sometimes rather funny connotative meanings of "red tape," "mindless rules," and "bumbling inefficiency." However, the idea of bureaucracy has important technical meanings that have little to do with such common connotations. Those meanings are essential to understanding the link between an organization and the rules for communication that make it work. Therefore, we will focus on a technical meaning of **bureaucracy** as *a deliberately designed plan of the goals, norms, roles, ranks, and controls in an organization.* Simply put, it is these features that control an organization's patterns of formal communication, and they will provide our framework for analysis.

As we will see, the need for bureaucracy (as an organizational plan that controls the formal routing of messages within any large-scale group) comes about for two reasons: One is group *size,* and the other is the *complexity* of the tasks a group must pursue to achieve its goals. We saw in Chapter 6 that as the number of members of a group increases by a few, the problem of maintaining face-to-face communication among its members grows

It was the German sociologist Max Weber who recognized the critical contribution of large organizations to modern societies. He contrasted their type of leadership, based on legal-rational principles and formal organizational design, with other types based on charismatic qualities or tradition. Weber's analysis provided an important foundation for the systematic study of formal channels of communication within organizations.

very rapidly. This means that communication cannot take place frequently between all members of a group larger than about 20. Clearly specified and restricted channels of communication must be defined, if for no other reason than to avoid having everyone spend the entire working day just trying to greet each other!

One of the critical features of a design for an effective organization, then, is provision for a *formal communication network* that will both maintain cohesion in the group and make it possible for it to attain its goals. In the sections that follow, we will look closely at the nature of bureaucracy, as this concept helps in understanding formal communication within a large and complex group.

The Classical Theory of Bureaucracy

While organizations have been with us since ancient times, the systematic study and analysis of the basic *principles* of their design did not begin until the early part of the present century. A concise theory of bureaucratic organization was developed by Max Weber, a German social scientist.[4]

Weber developed his theory of bureaucracy because he wanted to understand the broad changes in society that he saw resulting from the Industrial Revolution that had been taking place during the 19th century. The underlying change was a movement away from *traditional* forms of society. These were relatively homogeneous and overwhelmingly rural societies held together by cohesion based on sentiment, on shared values and beliefs.

The emerging *urban-industrial* society was quite different in that it was far more heterogeneous and impersonal. In other words, the new society was made up of many different kinds of people who did not have meaningful social ties to each other and who did not share the same set of values and beliefs. Nevertheless, they were able to live and work together in a coherent social order. Weber believed that one reason they were able to do so was that they made effective use of bureaucratic organization.

The Emergence of Rational Society

Weber began his analysis by asking an important question: If a population is heterogeneous and impersonal, how is the social order held together? That is, what is the basis of social cohesion in society itself? Weber believed that it was an outcome of the urban-industrial society's trend toward *rationality.* That is, increasingly, the new society was developing around *thoughtfully designed organizations* that provided for the needs of their populations. He saw that there were two factors underlying this trend: One was society's increasing ability to design organizations along rational lines, and the other was an increasing understanding of the nature of the leadership that made such organizations work.

Weber wanted to understand the basis of leadership in the emerging rational order. This led him to an analysis of *authority* and the exercise of power in different types of societies. Understanding leadership in society as a whole and in its organizations, he felt, would provide an important clue as to the basis of their social cohesion. He saw that in earlier times, authority was often based on *tradition.* In some societies it was based on *charisma.* In urban-industrial societies, however, authority tended to be based on *legal-rational* organizational designs. Each of these needs brief explanation.

The idea of "tradition" as a source for legitimizing the authority exercised by leaders is evident at almost all levels in many earlier societies. At the family level, the power exercised by the father was virtually absolute. He had the undisputed, that is, "legitimate," right to approve or disapprove of the actions of all family members. Similarly, the local lord of the manor had the legitimate authority to assign work to serfs and peasants and to decide whether they could live on his lands. At the top of the society, the political sovereign's power was based solidly on tradition. An example is the Japanese society's traditional beliefs about the divine origins of the emperor. This was also the case among monarchies in other parts of the world.

A second source of legitimate power can come from **charismatic authority,** based on the personal qualities of the individual exercising power. Weber maintained that in such situations authority is grounded in *charisma*—a unique personal attractiveness that makes an individual exercising leadership power seem very special to those who are led.[5] For example, throughout history, strong personalities emerged in many parts of the world. They gathered emotionally devoted followers and brought their followers together into a remarkably cohesive whole. Powerful military leaders have often done this. To his followers, Ghengis Khan must have seemed to have extraordinary personal qualities. At the time of World War II, this personal type of authority characterized Hitler's Germany and Mussolini's Italy. Later, this type of social cohesion characterized Ghandi's India, and Iran as it was led by Ayatollah Khomeini.

Weber saw, however, that neither tradition nor charisma accounted for leadership legitimacy and authority in modern urban-industrial societies. Here the exercise of power is far more likely to be based on what Weber called **legal-rational** authority. That is, leaders in the (bureaucratic) organizations that provide for institutional needs are usually selected or appointed because they possess technical managerial skills, and they are permitted to exercise power within a limited sphere that is narrowly defined by "official" definitions and rulings.

Weber's Principles

To describe the essential characteristics of a well-designed bureaucratic organization, Weber set forth a number of basic principles that should be present in its operation. His description was both lengthy and complex, and it cannot be presented in full. However, we can focus on the central factors with which he was concerned. These help in understanding the nature of formalized channels of communication.[6] That is, Weber maintained that a bureaucratic organization should have:

1. *Fixed rules.* This means stable and explicit norms for all forms of behavior (including communication) that apply equally to everyone and that can readily be learned and followed. (In our time such norms would include standards for relationships between male and female workers, between the races, and so forth.)

2. *A rationally defined division of labor.* This means that each position within the organization is mapped out in a formal (written) plan. The jurisdiction and official duties of the individual carrying out the specialized tasks of such positions should be set forth in "official" rules, laws, and regulations. These govern not only the ex-

The organizing principle of large organizations is bureaucracy. This is a kind of social design that calls for fixed rules, a clear division of labor, a graded hierarchy of power and authority, and uniformly applied rewards and punishments. It permits people to handle specific categories of tasks on a routine basis. Despite jokes about bureaucracy, it is a highly efficient design.

act activities to be performed but also what messages the occupant can transmit to whom about what.

3. *A clear and graded hierarchy of power and authority.* This means a "chain of command" in which the ranking system is formally set forth in an official plan. This shows that every worker has a supervisor, and every supervisor has specified subordinates. The official rules state who has authority to transmit what orders to whom, who must comply, who must communicate reports to whom, and so on.

4. *A fixed and "universalistic" system of sanctions.* This means that workers should be hired, promoted, rewarded, reprimanded, or fired solely on the basis of their competence and performance. The criteria should be made explicit and equally applicable to all ("universalistic"). That is, everyone should be judged by clear and uniform standards, and personal factors such as likes or dislikes, family ties (or in today's world, such factors as race, age, gender, and ethnicity) should not enter the exercise of social controls. Such a system requires clear and accountable communication and records of all decisions concerning those rewarded or punished and the reasons on which such decisions were based.[7]

On reflection, it can be seen that in the United States, these conceptions have evolved into an organizational

"model" toward which we are moving—if sometimes slowly and painfully.

While Weber was the pioneer in the systematic study of bureaucracy, thousands of research studies concerning many aspects of organizational design are now published every year by scholars, especially from fields related to management.[8] As a result, a massive body of knowledge has accumulated about the relationship between types of organizations, various strategies of management, and the kinds of communication problems they engender.[9] In fact, so many different approaches, theories, and perspectives have been advanced that one scholar, Harold Koontz, has characterized the situation as the *management theory jungle.*[10] Obviously, we cannot hope to cover such a body of knowledge in the present chapter. However, in the next section, we will provide at least a brief outline of several alternative ways of looking at organizations and some of the types and problems of communication that take place within them.

Management-Oriented Approaches to Organizational Communication

As we noted above, the study of organizational communication today focuses heavily on problems of *management* and the design of production-oriented groups.

This is perfectly understandable, because factories, corporations, and other work-related organizations are at the heart of the economic institution in our industrial society. In this section we will review three distinct theories of how communication in work-related organizations is managed. Each was originally developed as a means of promoting efficiency, raising productivity, and increasing output. These goals, of course, are important keys to higher returns on investment—a deeply approved value in a capitalistic society. Thus, the study of organizational communication today is preoccupied with designs for the flow of messages and influences by which management can manipulate various beliefs and activities so as to get more output from both themselves and their employees.

We will consider three such theories that have been developed during the past two centuries. These can, for simplicity, be called: (1) *human use* theories (developed between the early 1800s and the late 1920s), (2) *human relations* theories (dominant between the early 1930s and the 1960s), and (3) *human resources* theories (which began to be important starting in the 1960s and are still popular today).

Our reason for reviewing these perspectives on organizational communication and management strategies is *not* to provide lessons on how to squeeze more work out of employees. It is to provide an important intellectual foundation that will give additional meaning to our look at the communication patterns existing within the context of organizations. As we will see, each of these theories reveals a different part of the organizational picture and the communication problems existing in each. Hopefully, our brief review will lead to a better understanding of both the nature and some of the consequences of communication within large organizations.

Human Use Perspectives

In the first decades of the Industrial Revolution, those who established and managed factories or other organizations had little to guide them but their personal intuition, prior experience, hunches, and common sense as to how to communicate with or relate to employees. They often made serious mistakes. They lacked insights into the social and psychological nature of workers, or how they could be motivated by effective messages so as to achieve efficient production. Workers were not thought of in humanitarian terms, but simply as one more thing that had to be "used," along with machinery, and "exploited" like raw materials. It was this kind of thinking that was at the heart of the **human use perspectives.**

Early in the 19th century, some owners and managers actually considered using slaves to work in the newly established factories, but public sentiment was against it. About the only other example they had of an efficient use of labor was the army and navy. In the armed forces of the time, a "big stick" type of communication was used to control common soldiers or sailors. They could be flogged, clapped in irons, or even shot if they disobeyed orders, shirked on the job, or even talked back to their superiors. Such measures for communicating power were looked upon wistfully by early factory owners. However, there was no way they could use the big stick methods of the military for maintaining discipline among workers and ensuring that orders they transmitted were strictly followed by those at the bottom.

Nevertheless, lacking other means, communication within 19th-century organizations often seemed like military commands. Orders were given and they were not to be questioned. Workers were often bullied into high levels of performance. Iron-fisted foremen drove them with blows and kicks. Or workers were threatened with being fired, at a time when no unemployment benefits or welfare programs were available and termination meant serious deprivation for their entire family.

Wage formulas from classical economics   A far more acceptable answer to the problem of communicating the need for productivity to workers was another human use perspective that emerged from the classical economic theories of the time. That answer involved careful designs of formulas for *wages.* In 1776, Adam Smith published his *Wealth of Nations*—one of the most influential books ever written.[11] As Smith's political ideas, and especially his "economic man" theories (as they were called), spread they totally dominated management-worker communication during the early decades of the Industrial Revolution.

In particular, Smith's conceptions of the relationship between wages and the demand for labor shaped the thinking of managers about the use and control of workers. Smith maintained that if labor was scarce, higher wages would have to be paid—but a labor glut would permit them to be lower. Generally, he maintained, wages in balance with performance are the proper return for work. Thus, their level is not to be set by humanitarian considerations but solely by the *demand* for and the *supply* of labor, plus considerations of individual productivity. What this meant was that wages were virtually the only means thought to be available to motivate employees. Thus, it was assumed that if ways to earn more money could be communicated to workers, they would rationally decide to work harder.

Early in the 19th century, then, the major form by which managers communicated motivating messages to workers was through the design of **wage incentive systems.** Piecework formulas were developed so that wages were tied to personal output. That is, earnings for a worker in a production shop were determined by the number of "units" the individual produced in a given time period. Production norms were established for a standard day's work, and bonuses were added as motivating controls to stimulate workers to exceed those norms.

By the end of the 1800s, this approach to job design and to social control on the factory floor was in wide use. However, it had many problems. For one thing, workers hated it. They had discovered that if they really speeded up their work to increase personal output and get bonuses, management would simply raise the norm to force their wages back down. Then, they had to work harder than ever just to get the same wages as they had before. As a result, workers intelligently developed ways of subverting the piecework formulas to keep the norms down. As we will see later, it was *informal communication* among workers that subverted these human use designs.

The era of "scientific management"   During the late part of the 19th century, Frederick W. Taylor developed a startling refinement of the human use approach for controlling workers. Taylor started his career as an apprentice pattern-maker and machinist in a Philadelphia foundry. Later he worked his way up and became a chief engineer in a large steel mill.[12] In 1881 he began to make careful studies of conditions of work in the mill. He was appalled at the inefficiency he found. Poorly qualified and ill-trained workers were left to figure out for themselves how to perform their jobs. The wage incentive formulas in use led workers deliberately to restrict their output (which he called "systematic soldiering") so as to keep management from raising workload norms.

Taylor decided to make detailed observations on how each worker actually performed his individual task in the mill. With a stopwatch he painstakingly timed the various movements workers made while performing such mundane tasks as shoveling coal and lifting blocks of pig iron. He was able to simplify, standardize, and control the ways in which each worker actually did his task. His results showed ways to rearrange work stations, control rest periods, and redesign the flow of the work through the mill. As a result of his innovations, the workers were less fatigued at the end of the day, but they were able to increase their pay by an astonishing 60%! Furthermore, their increased efficiency raised the profit margins of the

mill significantly, which guaranteed the support of management.

It was with these "time and motion" studies plus his other innovations that **scientific management** was born. Essentially, it was a system for managing an organization by communicating rules to workers concerning wage incentives, the flow of work, and patterns of authority. These ideas made Taylor famous.[13] He went on to develop his theories more elaborately, and by the turn of the century his principles were widely applied in various industrial settings. In fact, Taylor's theories of scientific management swept the industrial world. It was the first time that experiments, systematic observation, and detailed studies had been used to achieve rational designs in production-oriented large organizations.

Later, his approach was made even more exact by time and motion experts such as Frank and Lillian Gilbreth, who used motion pictures and other techniques to find the most efficient ways to perform work activities in every task performed by a worker.[14] Even the laying of a brick was reduced to standardized movements of hands and arms. Unfortunately, Taylor's humane approach was not always followed by those who adopted his scientific management strategies for creating efficient designs of large organizations. Workers were often regarded as little more than mechanical cogs in the machine. Many were shamelessly manipulated in dehumanizing ways as the drive to boost efficiency and maximize profits surged.

During the Great Depression years, Taylor's open communication system between workers and managers was abandoned. However, even today, the old "human use" perspective has not entirely died. Views have changed, but many of the innovations introduced by Taylor remain as standard communication strategies for the efficient management of product workers in large organizations.

"Universal principles" of management   Another important organizational design theorist was Henri Fayol, a French engineer and manager of a large mining enterprise who in 1919 published an important book setting forth "universal principles" of management.[15] His ideas were also concerned with the rational design of organizations. Actually, Fayol was less of an abstract theorist than an individual with a depth of experience as a manager and a keen analytical mind. He did not publish his book until he was 75 years old, and it reflects his many years as a practical administrator.

The most important contribution of Fayol for present purposes was the **organization chart.** Such a chart communicates graphically the chain of authority and com-

Behavior Alteration Techniques (BATs) and Messages (BAMs)

Instructions   Below you will find a series of statements that a supervisor might use to encourage her or his employees to change their behavior. These are grouped into 18 categories. Please read all of the statements in each category before responding to that category. Then indicate how frequently your boss or supervisor has used statements of that type for each of the 18 categories to influence you to change *your* behavior in interactions with you. Indicate how frequently your supervisor has used each of these or similar messages by referencing the following scale:

5 very often   **2** seldom
4 often   **1** never
3 occasionally

____ **1.** You will enjoy it. You will get a reward if you do. It will make you happy. It will help you. You will benefit if you do. (We call this category, REWARD FROM BEHAVIOR.)

____ **2.** Others will think highly of you if you do. Others will like you if you do. Others will respect you if you do. (REWARD FROM OTHERS)

____ **3.** I will punish you if you don't. I will make it miserable for you if you don't. I will continue doing bad things to you if you don't. (PUNISHMENT FROM SOURCE)

____ **4.** This is the way I always do it. People who are like me do it. People you respect do it. (REFERENT-MODEL)

____ **5.** Do it, I'm just telling you what I was told. It is a rule, I have to do it and so do you. I don't know why, you just have to do it. (LEGITIMATE-HIGHER AUTHORITY)

____ **6.** If you don't, others will be hurt. If you don't, others will be unhappy. Others will be harmed if you don't. (GUILT)

____ **7.** I will give you a reward if you do. I will make it beneficial to you if you do. I will continue to reward you if you do. (REWARD FROM SOURCE)

____ **8.** Everyone else does it. We voted, and the majority rules. Society expects you to do it. All of your friends (or coworkers) are doing it. (NORMATIVE RULES)

____ **9.** It is your responsibility. It is your obligation. There is no one else that can do it. People are depending on you. (PERSONAL RESPONSIBILITY)

____ **10.** From my experience, it is a good idea. From what I have learned, it is what you should do. This has worked for me, it should work for you too. (EXPERT)

____ **11.** You will lose if you don't. You will be punished if you don't. You will be unhappy if you don't. You will be hurt if you don't. (PUNISHMENT FROM BEHAVIOR)

____ **12.** You will feel good about yourself if you do. You are the best person to do it. You are good at it. (SELF-ESTEEM)

____ **13.** You owe me one. It's your turn. You promised to do it. I did it the last time. (DEBT)

____ **14.** I will dislike you if you don't. I will lose respect for you if you don't. I will think less of you if you don't. (PERSONAL RELATIONSHIP-NEGATIVE)

____ **15.** If you do this, it will help others. Others will benefit if you do. It will make others happy if you do. (ALTRUISM)

____ **16.** I will like you better if you do. I will respect you if you do. I will think more highly of you if you do. I will appreciate you more if you do. (PERSONAL RELATIONSHIP-POSITIVE)

____ **17.** Your group (or team) needs it done. Our group depends on you. Our group will be hurt if you don't. (DUTY)

____ **18.** Because I told you to. Just do it. You have to do it, it's required. You don't have a choice.   (LEGITIMATE-PERSONAL AUTHORITY)

Calculating Your Score

1. PROSOCIAL strategies: Add your responses to items 1, 2, 10, 12, 15, 16, and 17 = _____.
2. ANTISOCIAL strategies: Add your responses to items 3, 4, 5, 11, 14, and 18 = _____.
3. TOTAL BAT USE: Add your responses from all 18 items = _____.

Interpreting Your Score

Possible range of scores for the PROSOCIAL strategies: 7–35.

Possible range of scores for the ANTISOCIAL strategies: 6–30.

Possible range of TOTAL BAT USE: 18–90.

(If your own scores do not fall within those ranges, you made a computational error.)

Behavior Alteration Techniques (BATs) and sample messages (BAMs) refer to those strategies or statements that people use to get others to do things they might not otherwise do. The first score you computed refers to how frequently your manager uses reward-based or prosocial strategies to influence your behavior at work. The second score refers to your manager's use of punishment-based or antisocial technique, or BATs. The higher the obtained scores, the greater the frequency with which your manager uses each BAT type.

We would expect employees to report greater satisfaction or liking of those supervisors who use prosocial, rather than antisocial, techniques in the workplace. While that may be true in some contexts (such as with teachers in the classroom), we find that employees resent their managers' use of *any* BAT type—regardless of whether it's prosocial or antisocial. According to researchers Richmond, Davis, Saylor, and McCroskey (1984), almost all of the BATs are negatively associated with employee satisfaction. Thus, the more frequently your supervisor uses strategies to get you to change your behavior, the less satisfied you will be with that person. Examine for a minute your TOTAL BAT USE score—how often does your boss attempt to influence you? And why do you suppose that higher TOTAL BAT USE scores are negatively associated with employee satisfaction?

Even though your boss's use of any given BAT is likely to be negatively correlated with your satisfaction at work, the fact is that certain BATs can contribute to our negative attitudes more than others. In particular, we find that employees are intolerant of supervisors' use of ANTISOCIAL BATs (step 2). When in a management position yourself, then, we recommend that if you should have to use an influence technique, you should rely primarily on prosocial BAT types (step 1).

References

Richmond, V. P., Davis, L. M., Saylor, K., & McCroskey, J. C. (1984). Power strategies in organizations: Communication techniques and messages. *Human Communication Research, 11,* 85–108.

This scale can be modified to assess employees' behavior toward supervisors, supervisors' behavior toward employees, or supervisors' and employees' perceptions of each other's behavior. Designed to measure teacher perceptions of their own behavior in the classroom, the original scale can be found in:

Kearney, P., Plax, T. G., Richmond, V. P., & McCroskey, J. C. (1985). Power in the classroom III: Teacher communication techniques and messages. *Communication Education, 34,* 19–28.

A revised and extended 22-item scale can be found in:

Kearney, P., Plax, T. G., Richmond, V. P., & McCroskey, J. C. (1984). Power in the classroom IV: Alternatives to discipline. In R. Bostrom (Ed.), *Communication yearbook 8* (pp. 724–746). Beverly Hills, CA: Sage.

In early factory production, organizational communication was simple. Little thought was given to the idea that the psychological well-being of workers might be a factor in efficient production. They were seen as an impersonal resource to exploit, along with machinery and raw materials. The theories of Adam Smith insisted that wages be just enough to keep them working and to permit them to raise their children so that there would be replacement workers.

mand, and thereby the flow of formal messages. It is especially helpful in understanding the vertical flow of communication—up and down the organization. Fayol maintained that between supervisors and their subordinates, communication should be easy and uninhibited, but that it should be *restricted* to the tasks or operations related to the work being done. Furthermore, in normal operations it was essential for communication to follow rigidly the channels mapped out in the organizational chart. At the same time, he recognized that during times of crisis it might be necessary and helpful to "bridge" or bypass those formal channels. Thus "Fayol's bridge" concept provided for the rapid transmission of vital messages when they were critically needed. This was, of course, a necessary *informal* communication process that Fayol had identified through his long experience as a manager.

Both the work of Taylor and that of Fayol added to Weber's classic bureaucratic theory in focusing attention on the essential nature of *deliberate planning* in the design of communication systems in organizations. Their norms, roles, ranking patterns, and systems of control (govern-

ing who should transmit what to whom) were not matters to be left to chance, spontaneous development, tradition, or common sense. People could work best in achieving their goals in organizations only if the activities and communication channels of every one of their members were deliberately defined. Few would quarrel with that generalization today.

Human Relations Perspectives

During the first two decades of the present century, American industry grew enormously. During the 1920s, for example, cheap immigrant labor, raw materials, abundant capital, weak unions, and seemingly insatiable markets brought great prosperity to manufacturers. It was a time when scientific management was in vogue. Business leaders were determined to obtain a maximum amount of production by standardizing, organizing, and controlling all aspects of work—materials, space, pay incentives for workers, and any other factor that they could think of to achieve top efficiency and profits.

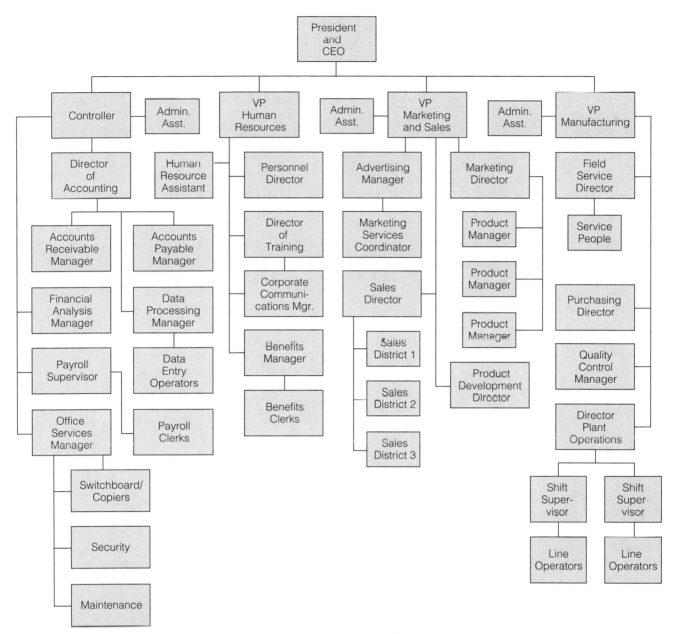

An important feature of an organizational design is a chart that displays graphically the pattern of linkages of power and authority in the group from top to bottom. It is also a map of the formal channels of communication, indicating clearly who must report to whom as well as give or receive orders from whom.

The Hawthorne studies and their legacy It was against this background that a number of scientific management experiments began in November 1924. They were conducted in Cicero, Illinois, at the Hawthorne Plant of the Western Electric Company.[16] These large-scale experiments were a joint effort between the huge Western Electric Company and the National Academy of Sciences. They have become classics in the study of organizational communication because they caused a radical revision of thinking about how people communicate at work.

The first group of experiments in the series might seem to have little to do with organizational communication. As we will see, however, they did. Rather accidentally, they yielded important insights. The first studies focused on the effects of *illumination* on worker output. In the tradition of scientific management, their purpose was to see if there were some particular level of lighting that would promote maximum worker efficiency. In the second set of experiments the focus was on varying *conditions of work,* such as number and length of rest periods, length of the working day, and number of days worked in a week.[17] To pursue this goal, the efficiency experts set up what they called the "Relay Assembly Room." This was almost like a laboratory setting in which observations were made on a small number of workers performing a repetitive task. Other experiments in the series continued into the early 1930s, confirming many of the findings from both the illumination studies and the Relay Assembly Room experiment.

As we will see, in this setting the experimenters got some very strange results that they simply could not explain, at least at first. In the end, they did figure out what happened, and the explanations turned out to have significant implications for understanding important aspects of organizational communication. The reason why these experiments remain important is that they touched off a sweeping change in management philosophy. It was a shift from the perspectives of "scientific management" to what came to be called the **human relations theory.**[18] This new theory became predominant in the 1930s. Today, although still newer ideas have been developed, the findings from the Hawthorne studies continue to offer insights into the relationship between organizational communication and the design of large work groups throughout the business and industrial world.

Strangely enough, the illumination experiments were, at least from the point of view of the scientific management experts, total failures! However, their seemingly inexplicable results provided the major evidence that the *personal and social characteristics of workers as individual human beings* are often critical factors in the work process. The scientific management perspective had regarded assembly-line workers as basically interchangeable—easily replaced "units" that merely needed to be controlled and motivated by communicating simple economic incentives or by other measurable factors.

The illumination experiments were based on that perspective. The industrial engineers conducting the studies were convinced that output per worker was closely related to the level of lighting in the workplace; that is, the more light the more work, at least within limits. They began by gathering *base-line* data. They recorded the output of three sections of workers in the plant who were

assembling telephone equipment. The workers were fully aware of the nature of the experiments. They had been told that the effort was being made to find the best level of illumination that would make their work easier and more efficient. Since pay was tied to productivity, via a piece-rate system, that seemed fine to the workers.

After the initial base-line output levels were determined, the engineers began systematically to *vary* the level of lighting in the work areas, always keeping track of levels of output. During one period of a week or so they would increase it slightly. Then, the next week it would be lowered a bit. This would be followed by a high increase in illumination. That, in turn, would be followed by a return to a very low level of lighting. All of these conditions prevailed over a long enough period so that accurate measures of per worker productivity were obtained in each. The engineers confidently expected that production per worker would *increase* with level of illumination, at least up to a point.

The problem was that the experiment yielded strange results! Every time the level of lighting was changed, output per worker went *up,* regardless of whether the illumination was increased or decreased. No matter what the condition, the workers just kept on getting more productive. Baffled by this, the engineers gradually *lowered* the lighting to a level where the workers could barely see what they were doing. Even that did not slow their productivity! At that point the engineers threw up their hands and declared the experiments a total loss.

What they had failed to realize was that the workers were human beings and that they had their own personal feelings and shared beliefs about the experiments. The workers had informally *discussed the situation among themselves,* and generally they liked the idea that management was concerned about them. They thought it was fine that management had sent the nice engineers to experiment and find the best level of illumination so that they could do their work better and make more money. The workers had decided to do a good job so that the experiments would be a success. Those positive feelings motivated them to increase output, even when the lights were low. Obviously, their enthusiasm altered the results and made the experiments meaningless in terms of their original plan.

The Relay Assembly Room experiments led to even stranger findings. Six female assembly-line workers were placed in a special room with an observer. Their task was to put together small electrical components called relays. The parts were brought to them, and their output was mechanically recorded when each completed relay was dropped into a chute. The observer did not interfere but simply took notes on the activities of the women as they went about their work.

The women were anxious at first. They did not know each other and were nervous about the observer. As time went on, however, they settled down, got acquainted, and began to perform well. At that point the experimenters began collecting base-line data on normal work output. The women understood that they had been placed in the special room for experimental purposes. They were aware that the goal was to try to find out how best to reduce fatigue and to make for a more pleasant work situation in which productivity would be at its greatest. They collectively decided that this was a good idea and were quite willing to serve as "guinea pigs."

After the base-line data had been gathered, the first experimental condition was introduced. The piecework formula was altered so that pay for the Relay Assembly Room workers was based solely on what they produced within the room, rather than using the quota of the factory as a whole. This arrangement seemed fine with the women, and their output (and pay) went up. (The experimenters were pleased.) After this had stabilized, two 5-minute rest periods were introduced. Again, output went up. (The experimenters were delighted.) Then the rest periods were increased to 10 minutes each. Again output went up. (The experimenters were elated.) Then a snack was served at mid-morning. Output rose again. The women got Saturday morning off (that was a normal work period at the time). Output still went up despite the reduced hours of work. The experimenters couldn't believe it! They concluded that they had found long-needed keys to increasing efficiency.

Then, just to be sure, they returned to the older, more oppressive work conditions—no rest periods, no snack, no Saturday morning off. Incredibly, output went up to *new heights!* The experimenters were dismayed—the whole experiment had blown up in their face. Output should have gone *down*—back to the base-line level. They then went back to try other conditions, but it seemed that no matter what they did, output still went *up*. Again, the experiments were termed a colossal failure.

What was going on here? The best efforts of scientific management had failed dismally in this setting to find keys to increasing worker output. Finally, data from the observer in the Relay Assembly Room, plus extensive interviews with the women and other workers, revealed what had actually happened. The women in the experimental room had become friends, and because of that they enjoyed their work. Also, they were happy that man-

agement was treating them in a special way, and they felt a sense of excitement at being part of an important experiment. It didn't matter to them what conditions were introduced.[19] It was the overall nature of the experience and the friendly small group itself that was important. They liked the experiment; morale was high; and they tried to do their best.[20]

More important for present purposes, the Hawthorne experimenters had discovered that workers are complex human beings. *Through processes of informal communication* they develop peer groups. These are important to them, and they come to be influenced by the shared social meanings they find on the assembly line—and indeed in *any* work setting. In other words, while working, people do not act as identical, interchangeable, or easily replaced "units," motivated solely by thoughts of economic gain. Each is a unique personality who participates in complex systems of informal communication and develops a pattern of human relationships. Within these systems, individuals collectively develop *social constructions of meaning* to interpret the work environment, their supervisors, the tasks they perform, and each other. All of these factors can have a profound impact on their work performance. Thus, informal communication is as much a part of an organization as are the formal channels.

Given those new understandings about human relations on the job, management set out to design new ways to increase worker efficiency. What they had to do now was to find messages that would *motivate, encourage,* and *foster* performance by taking advantage of factors in individual personality and human relationships. This is the **human relations perspective** in a nutshell. Styles of supervision changed. New efforts were made to promote high morale and loyalty to the organization. Ways in which workers could obtain personal satisfaction and subjective fulfillment had to be built into the design of work organizations. Overall, the new gospel was that it was the responsibility of managers to design communication systems in organizations that would produce *high job satisfaction.* The assumption was that such satisfaction would lead to *high work performance.*

In reality, sometimes it worked and sometimes it didn't. Certainly it was better than either the big stick and economic carrot assumptions of the earlier theories. However, the human relations approach to organizational management would not prove to be a universal guarantee of worker efficiency. One thing the human relations theories *did* make clear was that social ties between workers and their patterns of informal communication were critical factors in tying the worker to the organization. Based on the feelings the members have about one another, such informal communication links the individual to the group as a whole. *Sentiment-based cohesion,* in other words, was alive and well deep within the seemingly impersonal organization.

Thus, the early theories of Weber, Taylor, Fayol, and all the rest were fine as far as they went. However, they were dreadfully incomplete. The de facto organization was made up of some combination of the deliberately designed bureaucratic rules and the spontaneous peer group communication that emerged as people worked with each other on the job. Human beings at work developed complex networks of likes, dislikes, friendships, and animosities. These provided the basis of deeply established channels of *informal* communication that had nothing to do with the organization chart of carefully designed routes for transmitting messages. The discovery of the importance of informal communication within the larger work organization, then, was largely a result of the rather curious Hawthorne experiments. The study of informal networking and the kinds of communication that occur within this part of the organization was then pursued with vigor by communication scientists and management specialists alike.

The decline of the human relations perspective   Overall, the human relations concept remained the dominant perspective until the 1960s. However, managers slowly lost much of their initial enthusiasm for its principles because it was extremely hard to implement. Furthermore, in some cases it produced unforeseen and very undesirable consequences. For one thing, in practice it proved to be difficult to communicate freely with the rank and file. Supervisors who tried to be "caring" and "sympathetic" to workers sometimes found themselves at risk of being seen as weak and indecisive by both workers and higher-level managers.

One requirement of the perspective proved to be particularly difficult. That was involving workers in decision-making, policy-formation, and power-sharing. Even though they might feel better, people who lack expertise often made bad decisions. Effective policy-making usually demands solid knowledge and experience—it is not for amateurs. Furthermore, those who have status and power seldom want to share it with those lower in rank. These are central activities of management, jealously guarded by those with driving ambition. They are often the center of political tempests in organizations as competition for promotion becomes keen. Mixing rank-

Out of research like the Hawthorne studies, a realization came that workers were people with complex personalities and deep feelings. They also developed patterns of friendship and informal communication with co-workers. It became clear that these were important influences on how well they performed their jobs. The human relations perspective on worker-management communication was based on these insights.

and-file workers into such activities often created an up-roar of unwanted tensions and conflicts.

Gradually, then, the initial glow of the human relations perspective dimmed. For many managers it began to seem unrealistic—the kind of utopian idea dreamed up by starry-eyed professors and other idealists who championed the "dignity of labor" and the "inherent sensibility of the worker." While the idea that a happy worker is a productive worker sounded wonderful at first, it frequently failed in the tougher environment of the factory and corporation.

In more recent years, new perspectives have developed. Among them is one that seemed to be remarkably successful, at least in some settings. The Japanese, in particular, have made use of a *human resources perspective* in their organizational designs. This has helped their nation to become one of the most productive in history.

Human Resources Perspectives

Although it is not widely known in the United States, most of the fundamental principles of industrial production that have made Japan the economic envy of the world were *not* invented by the Japanese. They were brought to their shores and taught to Japanese industrialists by a remarkable American, W. Edwards Deming, just after World War II. Deming, a statistician and management consultant, had developed a complex philosophy of industrial production that stressed *quality* above all else.

At the close of World War II, Japan was in ruins. But President Truman and other leaders in the United States decided that rather than punishing the nation for its misdeeds, it would develop a reliable ally against the new threat of the Soviet Union. This was to be done by assisting the Japanese in recovering and rebuilding their lost industrial base. Deming was brought to Japan to help train postwar industrial managers in techniques that would establish a solid manufacturing basis for the rebuilt economy. Few people even dreamed how well his teachings would succeed.

Deming insisted that the primary objective which would ensure a place for Japan in the postwar industrial world was to produce goods of *maximum quality.* That was a drastic change from prewar Japan, when the emphasis was on cheap goods of low quality. Nevertheless, Deming taught Japanese industrialists to emphasize the production of goods manufactured to the highest possible standards. He provided them with a very clear program as to how to achieve this goal from a technical point of view. He believed fully that because they were, so to

As Japan was rebuilding its manufacturing industries after World War II, it was statistician W. Edwards Deming, (shown here about 1950) who persuaded their industrialists to stress quality above all else in the goods they produced. His complex philosophies of production were adopted by Japanese industries, along with their own form of worker-management communication. The result was the human resources perspective on the design of production organizations.

speak, starting from scratch, the Japanese could become a major industrial power within a relatively short time. To say that he was right is to understate the situation indeed. By the 1960s, Japan was well on the way to becoming one of the world's great economic powers.

Perhaps no one was more surprised at their success than the Japanese. They had listened politely to Deming, and equally politely, they followed his program. The end result was the incredible rise of Japan as an industrial power producing goods renowned for their high quality. As one Japanese executive wrote in his diary in 1950:

> Here was this tall American telling us that we would be an important force in five years if we listened to him. We really didn't believe him, but in order not to lose face, we did what he told us, *and it worked![21]*

By 1970, it was clear to the entire world that Japan was doing something different and remarkable in the way of designing production-oriented large organizations. The fact was that they had not only adopted Deming's guidelines regarding statistical bases for quality control and management, but they also had developed production organizations that were very different indeed from those used in the Western world.[22]

Essentially, Japan had implemented the **human resources perspective** in their design of production organizations. It was a theory of management based on the belief that bonds of loyalty and attitudes of dedication to work can be created among employees by selective patterns of management-worker communication. The Japanese implemented this perspective in a way that was totally consistent with their culture and equally consistent with the principles of management brought to them by W. Edwards Deming. For example, many Japanese workers are virtually assured of lifetime employment in the same firm, and they are promoted solely on the basis of seniority. This is clearly contrary to Weber's principles, but it eliminates cutthroat competition between employees that can threaten the goals of the larger group. For example, managers have no reason to feel threatened by competent and successful subordinates. Those subordinates can communicate their ideas, which can then be incorporated into production processes.

Since Japan's population is racially and ethnically homogeneous, there are a minimum of barriers to communication of the sort that are typical in the more heterogeneous multicultural population of the United States. Senior members of a Japanese firm can listen to and understand ideas suggested by those farther down in the power structure, which also makes training and indoctrination much easier. Bonds are created between workers and management that would be more difficult to establish in a racially and culturally diverse labor force.

The Japanese realize that workers on the line have insights and a grasp of the production process that cannot be developed by executives far removed from day-to-day operations. For that reason, they created small groups of workers called **quality control circles,** which are composed of individuals from particular units right on the line whose members all face the same production task. They meet weekly as discussion groups and are coordinated by their supervisor. Their objective is to find ways in which their particular assembly work can be done more efficiently and at a higher level of quality. Their solutions are taken *very* seriously by management, and if implemented, the group earns cash bonuses and awards.

This is quite a contrast from the American tradition, where jobs are designed by remote "experts" and where worker suggestions are often unwelcome. Under such conditions workers seldom care about quality because they have no personal stake in the outcome. The Japanese quality control circles, on the other hand, effectively use the human resources—the insights, talents, skills, and loyalties of workers—to improve efficiency of production and to maintain very high standards in products. In other words, the channels of communication between workers and management are studiously and deliberately kept flexible and open and workers' messages come through loud and clear.

In summary, the human resources approach is related to the human relations theory, but there are important differences. In particular, the former is more complex. Essentially, it sees employees as a major potential resource for the organization in terms of *talent, energy, dedication,* and *pride in work.* If the ideas of these human resources can be communicated effectively and incorporated into the manufacturing process, the result will be both efficiency in production and high quality in products. The task of management, then, is to design a system that will *minimize communication barriers* and lead to high performance by workers, while maximizing factors that will motivate them to work at a high level of quality. The end result is that millions of people in the world now drive Japanese cars, view Japanese television sets, listen to Japanese radios, take pictures with Japanese cameras, and enjoy Japanese VCRs, stereo sets, and hundreds of other products whose quality is often higher than that which can be obtained from other sources.

American managers largely ignored Japan for years, and had neither knowledge of nor interest in W. Edwards Deming, the human resources theory, or new perspectives on quality control. They woke up only when exported goods produced in the United States began to be considered *inferior* by other countries. That finally got their attention, but not before it cost the United States dearly. In recent times, American managers have been scrambling to apply both Deming's ideas and Japanese organizational communication ideas to production processes in this country. However, because of differences in culture and tradition, the ideas do not always fit.

The Flow of Messages Within Large Organizations

One of the most important of all the kinds of behavior constrained by an organizational design is *formal* communication. That is, an important function of the social plan of any organization is to direct the way in which messages can flow through the system. In our definition in Chapter 6, we stressed that formal communication takes place only within a set of carefully defined rules between certain designated parties. We can add that its messages concern only a range of topics relevant to the organization; they are transmitted and received via prescribed media; and their purpose is to accomplish goals set by the organizational design. That rules out all forms of personal messages transmitted for reasons other than the official business of the organization. A simple way of describing formal communication in an organization is to say that the design for the content, transmission, and reception of messages dictates:

who
can say *what*
to be received by *whom*
about specific kinds of *topics*
by communicating with what *medium*
in order to achieve specified types of *goals.*

Stated in that way, it will come as no surprise that formal communication in an organization is very tightly controlled and constrained.

Because official channels of formal communication are rigid, and because they can be used for only a restricted range of topics, more flexible and open channels for *informal* communication develop. People working in groups have a need to communicate in a variety of ways about a host of issues and topics. For that reason, the "grapevine" and other similar systems and networks develop and are used to convey a great many messages to and between large numbers of people about a variety of topics without noticeable restrictions on their transmission.

Formal Communication Through Official Channels

Four issues need to be considered in describing the flow of official messages through an organization. One is the nature of the *channels* themselves—who is allowed or required to communicate with whom. The second concerns the kinds of *topics* that make up most of the message content. The third is the *quality* of communication. Finally, we need to understand the *consequences* of both the restrictions and the limitations on accuracy produced by the formal communication system.

Vertical transmission   As can be seen in almost any organizational chart, the hierarchical structure almost automatically implies *vertical* communication. That is, in a group with clearly graded levels of power and authority, communication must by definition flow either up or down in the system. Although it does happen, there is usually no formal provision for messages to jump across organizational compartments. If they follow the design, employees at the bottom in a given unit communicate formally only with their supervisors. Those supervisors,

in turn, communicate formally only with the individuals who command their particular division, and so on up to higher-level officials and ultimately to the top. No one is supposed to "short-circuit" these channels and "leak" important message content between categories or across lines of authority. Indeed, if they do so they risk reprimand.

Message content in formal communication   There is remarkable similarity in the topics, that is, the general kinds of message content, that flow both upward and downward through formal channels in almost all organizations, regardless of their goals. We need to look at their typical content as they move in both directions. First, then, what kinds of messages flow *upward* in a formal communication system? In reality there are many kinds, but in most organizations the majority will deal with the following four categories of content:

1. *Routine operational messages.* A large part of the upward flow of messages consists of technical details about materials needed, inventory completed, personnel issues, accounting data, cost estimates, and the like. These provide the day-to-day data used by managers to make routine administrative decisions.

2. *Assessments by experts.* These are messages regarding the best ways to accomplish certain kinds of goals or to do particular kinds of work. Employees at or near the bottom often have precisely the skills, knowledge, and experience that supervisors need to understand when preparing proposals or designing work roles. Consequently this type of content is sent up the line.

3. *Feedback on completion of tasks.* Reports on how well orders were carried out and on what results were obtained provide important insights needed at the top. Such details can be provided only in the form of reports that are initiated at the lower levels where the work is actually performed.

4. *Reports on problems.* It is critical for decision-makers at the top to have full knowledge about problems encountered either within the organization or in dealing with outsiders. Such messages provide vital input needed for the formation and change of policies that can limit or avoid such problems.

Top management makes many decisions. The quality of those decisions, obviously, will depend on the accuracy and timeliness of the message content that moves up in the system.

But looking at vertical transmission from the other direction, what are the categories of messages that flow *downward* in the formal system? Again, there can be a considerable variety. However, there is a remarkable similarity in the general categories or topics from one organization to the next, whether it is a factory, a university, or a military unit. They include the following four basic categories of message content:

1. *Requests* for routine operating data and related content. This is the counterpart of the first category of upward flow listed above.

2. *Specific orders and instructions.* These focus on particular individuals, such as new job assignments, promotions, or separations. They also include instructions concerning the production or processing of particular services or products (e.g., how many are to be ready by what time).

3. *Operating guidelines.* These are generally messages on long-term matters. They may concern ways to perform particular kinds of work, allocate space for particular functions, incorporate certain kinds of materials, package finished products in a particular way, handle clients in a certain order, and so on.

4. *Policy-shift directives.* These usually concern relatively broad changes in the way of doing things. They represent shifts in the goals of an organization, in its organizational plan, or in the general way in which work will be handled. For example, a shift from a paper-based to a computerized accounting system, with consequent personnel changes, would be a policy-shift directive.

A major point to be made in considering the flow of organizational communication, either up or down, is that messages moving within the formal channels can, and often are, *critically important* to both the people who send them and those who receive them. People's jobs can depend on what they receive in the way of orders, assessments, directives, reports, requests, and instructions. Their rewards can be linked to how accurately they interpret the meanings that the messages are intended to convey.

Given that high level of importance, it would seem to follow that people would make few mistakes, either as senders or as receivers in constructing or interpreting official organizational communication. But the fact is that errors are common. What, then, are some of the factors that can operate to create what we referred to in Chapter

1 as a low index of fidelity, that is, a loss of accuracy, misunderstanding, and other limitations on the degree to which the meanings aroused by such formal communication are similar in senders and receivers?

Accuracy versus distortion up and down the line   In Chapter 1 we stressed the issue of communication accuracy becomes a vital concern in formal organizational communication. What are some of the reasons why the *vertical transmission* of messages either up or down is subject to inaccuracy? Actually, as messages move both up and down a number of factors tend to distort the meanings that are encoded and decoded by those involved in the chain of transmission.

Viewed within both our linear and simultaneous transactions models, policy-makers, managers, and supervisors at every level have the problem of effective *role-taking.* That is, they must encode their messages in such a way that when transmitted downward their content will be both understood as intended and influential in shaping the behavior of the persons they are supervising. If either of these goals is not achieved, their messages are ineffective. As we have implied, there are many reasons to anticipate that role-taking problems will be encountered. Furthermore, managers and supervisors face the challenge of effectively interpreting *feedback*—interpreting the real meanings of messages that originate with subordinates and which may have undergone change as they traveled upward.

To understand how such a formal system can fail to provide for completely accurate communication, we begin with the fact that it is human beings who formulate the messages that move up and down the line and human beings who receive those transmissions and try to interpret their meanings. Unfortunately, no human being is a perfect sender or receiver. As we have pointed out in previous chapters, many factors can distort and limit the paralleling of meaning between communicating parties. This is as true in the organizational setting as it is in any other communication context. In fact, given the significance of work and career to the members of such groups, such factors may operate in this context with particular force!

Let us consider, for example, what can happen to a formal communication that moves up through a hierarchy of *rank* levels. What are some of the things that can happen to a message transmitted, even in written form in memos and reports, from persons below to those above? Such messages can be and often are:

1. *Condensed.* That is, messages tend to grow shorter and more concise as they move up from one level to another. For example, a written report explaining a mechanical breakdown or a complex personnel matter is likely to be a much briefer version when it lands on the desk of the chief executive officer than it was when formulated several levels below by an immediate supervisor. Even the term "to brief" (an executive) implies that subordinates supply condensed versions of what has actually taken place.

2. *Simplified.* This is a counterpart to condensing a message. Details are selectively dropped out of complex reports. They are then organized around the most *salient* details. Often this transforms the content into simplified categories such as "good," "bad," "all," or "none," where this was not the case in reality. This represents a loss of richness of detail that may seem to bring clarity but actually brings a loss of subtle interpretations that were in the original message. It can also mean exaggerating what were milder conditions at the bottom into more stark implications when they reach the top.

3. *Standardized.* Messages are couched in terms of standard terms familiar within the organization's special argot or jargon. The original events may be of such a nature that the official language is really not adequate to describe them accurately. For example, a soldier who, despite his or her best efforts, was unable to get back to base on time (e.g., canceled flight) may be classified in official jargon as AWOL—Absent Without Official Leave—which implies a deliberate moral transgression that should be punished. Thus, meaning is changed.

4. *Idealized.* A message transmitted to a higher level may be rephrased to cast the person below in the best possible light. People want their supervisors to believe that they acted wisely and within organizational guidelines. Thus, they may leave out certain details and modify others almost unwittingly so as to idealize their own behavior.

5. *Synthesized.* The transmitted message may be combined with additional details to form a more understandable overall picture—even when the added meanings were never part of the original event. For example, a report on an individual who behaved in an unusual way may have included as additional comment that the person was "in the care of a psychia-

trist" several years earlier. That fact may have had absolutely no bearing on the incident, but it could obviously introduce distortions in the interpretations made by those above. The person may come to be seen as a "nut case."

Messages coming *down* the line can also undergo characteristic changes, and their intentions are sometimes subverted. A number of factors can produce such a result. They are the same general factors that operate in *any* form of communication to limit the degree to which senders and receivers achieve completely parallel meanings, or the degree to which messages modify the behavior of a receiver. For example, individuals receiving formal messages from supervisors above can fail to interpret them correctly because of:

1. *Selective exposure.* That is, they may not read or hear the entire message for a variety of reasons, including fatigue or just plain chance circumstance. Messages get misfiled, misplaced, and even accidentally thrown away.

2. *Selective attention and listening.* Even if a person hears a message in full, attention can wander and listening can deteriorate. Busy persons can be distracted by the presence of others, and attention to a formal communication can lapse. People are often surprised later when they reread a written message and find meanings within it that they simply never noticed the first time.

3. *Selective perception.* We have shown repeatedly that the psychological process of organizing incoming message symbols into associated meanings is a complex activity that is fundamental to the communication process. Assigning meaning to formal messages in an organization follows the same general principles we set forth in our earlier chapters. In addition, formal messages coming down from high places are a particularly important kind of transmission that may have implications for a person's welfare. Therefore, perception and interpretation will take place within a system of personal attitudes, beliefs, values, and expectations that can influence reconstructed meanings. To a considerable extent, those psychological factors can reshape the interpretation to fit with what the receiver hopes, wants, fears, or likes.

Along those lines, a situation in which meaning in a message is transformed by a receiver in a way that minimizes a potential threat is commonly referred to as a *perceptual defense.* Another kind of transformation

Messages flowing up through an organization's formal channels can undergo many changes. They often grow shorter and are simplified in various ways so that important details may be left out. They may be encoded into symbols with meanings that make senders seem to be performing better. Comparable problems arise when messages flow down through formal channels. The resulting distortions and inaccuracies can pose significant problems for those in leadership positions.

of meaning can occur because of *perceptual set,* where a receiver is expecting a particular meaning to be implied in a message. While these are subtle psychological reactions, the general principle is that selective perception does operate to modify meanings received, even via channels of formal communication that have been carefully designed to minimize misinterpretations.

4. *Selective retention and recall.* No one's memory is perfect. Receivers tend to remember complex meanings in important messages in very selective ways. For one thing, people tend to remember good or rewarding parts of a message and "repress" (unconsciously forget) those parts that seem stressful, punishing, or difficult. For that reason, a message coming down the line may be well understood at the time of reading, but a short time later it may be remembered in a distorted way.

5. *Selective action.* Even if a message is perceived and interpreted accurately and remembered fully, this does not mean it will be fully acted on as requested or ordered. Circumstances at the time may require that some of the ordered actions be postponed, carried out in a modified manner, or simply ignored. Subordinates quickly learn how to sidestep or avoid difficult or unrewarding actions requested by supervisors, or to develop logical reasons why the orders cannot be followed exactly as specified.

6. *Vocabulary differences.* Well-educated managers and less-educated lower supervisors do not always have the same vocabulary, or they may not have the same meanings for words that they do share. Furthermore, as we saw in Chapter 2, in a multicultural society, language usages can vary among people from our many racial, ethnic, and other specialized cultures. All of these factors can distort interpretations of a message due to the ways that different kinds of people establish conventions linking words, realities and subjective meanings.

Informal Communication in Organizational Settings

The major reason informal communication is so important in understanding organizations has already been made clear. Not only is the *de facto* organization made up of its deliberately designed structure, but it also includes the social ties existing among the many small and intimate groups of peers found in any large group. Thus, messages flow not only through the official channels prescribed for formal communication but through **grapevines** as well—complex social pathways in a network of intimate groups.

Socially validated constructions of meaning   It is through this network that rumors are passed on, gossip is exchanged, and word-of-mouth diffusion of important news is transmitted. In many ways, the fate of an organization can rest or fall on message content within this network and how well it works. If communication within the grapevine continuously contains meanings defining management as negative, uncaring, or callous to workers, or that it is exploiting them for its own advantage, then these are the socially constructed meanings about management that workers will share. That sharing *validates* such meanings—gives them social legitimacy. Individuals use these meanings to build or rebuild their personal beliefs about the organization. If this happens, a very different organizational culture will develop than one derived from more positive conditions of informal communication. For such reasons, studies of informal communication within organizational grapevines can be very important.

Capacity, flexibility, and speed   Generally speaking, informal communication networks within an organization convey a great number and variety of messages on a day-to-day basis—possibly exceeding the total number carried in the formal channels. These networks are very flexible, which is exactly the opposite of the channels for formal communication. In the informal process, messages flow not only by word-of-mouth but by telephone, computer, and written notes as well. They move without restriction both up and down the ranks, and horizontally within a given stratum. Certain "centers" for the exchange of messages facilitate the process. These include restrooms, the coffee machine, the cafeteria or lunch room, and even the parking lot. Indeed, any point or place where employees frequently encounter one another or get together can serve as a message center. Furthermore, people call each other at home and continue the process even after working hours.

The kinds of messages carried on the grapevine are not easy to classify into categories. Generally, they consist of *rumors* of one sort or another, *gossip* about individuals or events within the organization, *speculation* about what is going to take place as a result of some planned or sus-

pected change, and *interpretations* of the nature and meanings of actions taken by those in power.

Because of these conditions of few barriers, many channels, and virtually no restrictions on content, informal communication can flow very swiftly to surprisingly large numbers of people. In that sense it is a very efficient form of communication in that it can bring messages and meanings about a variety of topics to a large number of participants in a relatively short time.

Distortion of Messages in the Grapevine

While an organizational grapevine may provide for swift communication to a large number of people, the accuracy of this type of communication can be very low. That is not always the case, however—especially with very short messages (e.g., "the boss has just quit," "Jane has been promoted," etc.). In more complex messages, a number of specific patterns of distortion have been found by social scientists studying this kind of word-of-mouth communication.

Two general patterns of distortion characterize the spread of rumors, the movement of news from one person to another, and similar interpersonal transmissions of verbal messages. These two patterns will be described separately, but in reality they tend to occur together in the same setting when a particular message is transmitted by word-of-mouth along an interpersonal grapevine. The first has become known as the *embedding pattern,* which has been widely studied by social scientists and communication specialists interested in the flow of messages through certain kinds of social pathways.[23] The second is the *compounding* pattern, which appears to characterize rumors transmitted within communities or large groups, such as military organizations.[24] Both are found in almost every organizational setting.

The embedding pattern   The **embedding pattern** refers to a particular set of distortions in a message that may occur when it is transmitted orally from one person to the next in a kind of serial pattern. That is, a person learns "firsthand" of some event or condition and then passes on a message about it by word-of-mouth to another. The receiver lacks access to whatever realities prompted the first person to formulate the story but passes on a new version of the message to a third. From there it continues in a chain of tellers and retellers, none of whom have actually seen or heard the facts that were the basis of the original account.

Such a system is typical of what often happens along a grapevine, and it simply invites several kinds of distortions. In fact, a considerable amount of research has identified three specific forms of distortion that often characterize the content of a message as it moves along a chain of tellers and retellers. These are *leveling, sharpening,* and *assimilation.*

Leveling refers to a general shortening of the original account, rumor, or story. As it travels from one person to the next, limitations of attention, perception, and memory (much like those discussed in distortions of formal communication on pp. 209–210) quickly reduce the message to fewer words and ideas. If the original account is relatively long, it can lose as much as half of its details as it is retold by the first person in the chain. The second will forget additional details and pass on a still shorter account. The story or rumor continues to shrink in number of words and details as it passes on through additional individuals until only a short (leveled) version remains. This brief version is then passed along more or less intact as it continues to move from one person to another.

Sharpening is the counterpart of leveling. That is, as the story or account shrinks, it becomes organized around its more central or "salient" details. The version becomes increasingly concise until it is only a kind of summary of the original message. This is a result of the way human beings construct meanings and store them in memory. In Chapter 1, in our discussion of the basics of human communication, we discussed the concept of *schema* in terms of the memory patterns used psychologically to organize meanings that make up a message. It is that cognitive process which is at work when an individual hears a rumor, stores it in memory, and then recovers it from storage to pass on to another person. As each person builds a schema for the transmitted message, it becomes increasingly organized in a kind of standardized way around the most salient details. Inevitably, this results in a dropping away of original richness of detail, and consequent distortions creep in as the message is successively repackaged into briefer and briefer versions.

Assimilation is a process by which the message is reshaped by the psychological characteristics and culturally learned habits of the person who hears it. This is what most people would call "distortion" in that meanings are changed and the story undergoes transformations in content. These transformations can be pronounced. They occur because of selective perception, memory, and recall based on individual attitudes, values, and other personality factors. They also occur because people of a particular culture tend to think about topics in characteristic ways. To illustrate, a male and a female who are married, but not to each other, can be reported in a casual conversation as having "been seen in a lengthy and private conversation." The next person, with romantic orientations, may interpret this as a "possibly amorous encounter." A third, using our common cultural definitions of male-female relationships as potentially implying intimacy, speaks of the couple as "lovers," and a juicy scandal sweeps the organization.

Through leveling, sharpening, and assimilation, then, the embedding process can produce many unexpected and unusual changes in the content of a message as it moves by informal word-of-mouth communication through the grapevine of an organization.

The compounding pattern   The second major pattern of distortion in word-of-mouth networks that has been identified is the **compounding pattern.** When a message transmitted along a grapevine is of such a nature that it is of especially high interest to a group, it can move very swiftly and can undergo a pattern of distortion that is quite different than that described by the embedding process. A substantial body of research has revealed a pattern whereby an original message passed by informal communication in a grapevine gains additional details and interpretations that were never a part of the original. This tends to happen under two conditions: first, if the original message is relatively brief, and second, if it is of a threatening or disturbing nature.

To illustrate, assume that a short rumor is transmitted along the grapevine to the effect that "the factory will be closed and everyone will be laid off." Such a tension-producing message is likely to travel its social itinerary through the informal network very swiftly indeed. However, as it moves along, individuals are likely to add elements that they believe are relevant and which help "explain" what is happening. One may have heard that some government agency was planning an investigation. Another might have heard that accountants were seen working overtime. These elements could be compounded into the idea that the factory was going to close and everyone would lose their job because the owners were going bankrupt as a result of someone mismanaging the funds. On that base the story could grow even more with the retelling. Speculation would arise as to who would be fired first, when the closing would take place, and what benefits would or would not be provided for those let go.

In reality, the embedding and the compounding patterns tend to work together in the actual transmission of rumors through a grapevine. A story can grow one day and get smaller the next. It can be shortened, assimilated, and compounded at the same time. No single pattern characterizes the flow of messages in a process of informal communication in an organizational grapevine. What can be said with certainty is that messages transmitted in this manner are very likely to result in reconstructions of meaning by receivers. Their indices of fidelity, even from one person to the next, tend to be low.

Consequences of Organizational Communication

As this chapter has shown, communication processes in organizations are extraordinarily complex. They include both formal and informal communication, and each provides the basis for different forms of social organization and social pathways for the flow of messages.[25] This rich flow has at least two major consequences we need to note. The first is the development of a **specialized organizational culture,** and the second is the development and maintenance of two kinds of *cohesion* binding the members of the group to the whole.

Specialized organizational cultures   The concept of specialized cultures was discussed in Chapter 2. In the discussion of conventions of meaning that link symbols, reality, and their referents, we saw that various kinds of specialized cultures exist in complex societies in addition to the general culture that is more or less shared by all members. Specialized cultures are those beliefs, attitudes, values, and patterns of behavior shared within some segment of a society (e.g., a racial or ethnic minority, a religious group, or even a socioeconomic level) that make it different from the general culture of the society.

The idea also applies to organizations. Within each, an internal culture develops that is unique to that particular group. Thus, IBM has a specialized internal culture that is different than that of the Ford Motor Company. Similarly, each university, government agency, church, prison, bank, and any other organization has its own specialized internal culture. It includes all of the physical objects, attitudes, values, beliefs, sentiments, rules, special language, and everything else produced and shared by its members. In short, the internal culture makes the organization a unique context.

We can add that within any organization, there are even many *micro* cultures. These are miniature versions of specialized cultures that are developed by particular

branches or divisions—or even small groups of peers. An example is that developed by the women who worked in the Relay Assembly Room of the Hawthorne experiments (pp. 202–203). They became friends and shared a number of special meanings, beliefs, attitudes, and other orientations.

Specialized organizational cultures develop from two basic sources. One is obviously the official organization as it functions with its carefully defined channels of formal communication. The other is the informal network from which micro cultures develop among many spontaneously formed peer groups that are present among work associates at all levels of the ranking structure. In some organizations, the group's overall internal culture may support the organization and help it achieve its goals. In others, conflicting micro cultures can develop and become the basis of serious conflict. An important question is: How are specialized cultures related to communication channels in the group?

Conflicting specialized cultures   Earlier, we noted the vertical nature of the formal channels of communication in large organizations. For example, in a typical production-oriented industrial organization, within the engineering division formal messages flow up and down the line. They do the same within the manufacturing division, and they do so in a similar manner within the sales division. However, few formal messages cross these boundaries, so engineers seldom communicate extensively with sales specialists or those who manufacture the product. The consequence is a somewhat separate communication structure that fosters specialized cultures within each of these divisions. Thus, engineers, sales personnel, and manufacturing specialists develop and use their own language and habits of perception. This brings them to share distinctive attitudes, values, and beliefs that are not the same as those of the other divisions.

There is always a danger that these qualitative differences between specialized cultures within a diverse organization will become the basis for low communication fidelity. That is, the language of one may become incomprehensible to the others. If that happens, barriers to effective communication, even of the formal type, exist and limit the degree to which the group can achieve its goals.

Such cultural differences can become a basis for conflict. We noted that even small groups of work associates can develop a micro version of a specialized culture. A small group on the day shift and an equally small group on the night shift, who do exactly the same work on the same machines, may have different micro cultures. One

A specialized internal culture emerges from the formal and informal communication activities that prevail within every organization. It includes not only the particular physical artifacts used by its participants but also the beliefs, attitudes, and values they share. Some specialized cultures are positive and supportive of the organization; others can be negative and hinder it in reaching its goals.

may share favorable views toward management; the other negative views. In such circumstances one such group has been known to quietly "sabotage" the other.

Sometimes the disruptive impact of specialized cultures can be devastating. As an example, in 1989, Eastern Airlines found that its mechanics and baggage handlers (who belonged to a union) shared a set of beliefs that was completely hostile to management, who had a different culture. For a variety of reasons, these differences became irreconcilable. The two groups in Eastern Airlines, each with its own specialized culture, fought each other bitterly. The end result was that the airline went bankrupt and eventually went out of business altogether. Tens of thousands of employees were without work, and the airline shareholders lost million of dollars.

Organizational cohesion   If some form of cohesion did not exist within an organization, there would be no way to keep its members performing the often unpleasant tasks needed to accomplish its goals. We saw earlier how various management-oriented approaches have tried to find policies and strategies to enhance motivation so as to keep workers performing at a high level of efficiency. These approaches were based on the necessity to

provide *personal* goal satisfaction so as to maintain the loyalty and dedication of the individual members of the group.

Organizational cohesion is different from personal satisfactions, such as one might derive from a good salary, a secure job, or high status. It is also different from that which keeps other kinds of groups together. For example, we saw earlier that it is sentiment-based cohesion that binds members to small intimate groups, such as families and peers. However, it is reward-based cohesion that ensures participation by members of discussion groups, whereas assignment-based cohesion characterizes small formal decision-making groups.

Cohesion in an organization is not easily explained by any of those. Such a group is kept together as an organized whole by what we will call **dependency-based cohesion**.[26] This type of cohesion is a product of the complex division of labor that produces a strong pattern of dependencies between individuals (and even units) within an organization. To illustrate, the worker on the assembly line is "dependent" on clerks in the payroll division who process his or her wages into a check. In turn, those clerks would have nothing to do if it were not for such workers. In the same manner, every person per-

Organizational cohesion is a product of relationships of dependency that exist between people performing a multitude of specialized roles. Those who work in a clean-up crew may not even know those who prepare their paychecks or those who negotiate contracts for the company's services. Yet, all individuals in these specialized roles are bound to each other and to the organization through relationships of interdependency. It is the formal channels of communication that link them together.

forming a task in the entire division of labor produces a product or service on which others depend. Such people may not even know each other—or if they do they even may actively dislike each other. Nevertheless, they are in a relationship of mutual task dependency that holds the overall group together so that it can function as a unit.

Obviously, what coordinates the activities within this division of interdependent labor is *formal communication.* For example, the payroll department would have no idea how much workers should receive without formally communicated data regarding pay scale, hours worked, and so on, for each individual. Similarly, throughout the system, a flow of formal communication provides vital

instructions that coordinate subgroups and individuals performing specialized tasks within the structure. Thus, formal communication is the basis on which dependency-based cohesion is established and maintained. That was true at the time the pyramids were built, and it remains true today. If that formal communication becomes disrupted, distorted, or even late, serious consequences follow.

Realistically, however, we must look at all four types of cohesion to explain fully what holds an organization together, enables individual members to satisfy their needs, and makes it possible for the group to attain its collective goals. That is, the bonds that link members to the whole in the de facto organization are based on a *combination* of sentiment-based cohesion within small groups of work associates, reward-based cohesion in more temporary groups, assignment-based cohesion among members of decision-making groups within the organization, and dependency-based cohesion that is a product of task interlinkages in the overall structure. Throughout, however, *communication* in all of its various forms holds the organizational system together.

Chapter Review

- An organization is a human group that has been deliberately designed so as to achieve a desired objective. The use of formal communication to coordinate the activities of organizations is as old as civilization itself. Today, our urban-industrial society is almost totally dependent on these relatively large groups to fulfill the needs of our population. Modern society's needs for organizations grew out of the changes in its social institutions that took place over the past two centuries.

- Communication patterns within any organization include verbal and nonverbal processes, both linear and transactional. In an organization, people communicate both formally and informally within the interpersonal and small-group contexts. However, an organization is a distinctive communication context in its own right.

- Any large group requires complex rules for communication so that the activities of its participants can be coordinated. This is usually handled by a hierarchy of managers who transmit and receive various kinds of messages, upward and downward, to and from, the rank and file and, more rarely, laterally among themselves.

- Organizational communication can be formally defined as: the transmission of messages through both the formal and the informal channels of a relatively large deliberately designed group, resulting in the construction of meanings that have influences on its members, both as individuals and on the group as a whole.

- The basic organizing principle of organizations is bureaucracy, which can be defined as: a deliberately designed plan of the goals, norms, roles, ranks, and controls in an organization. It is these features of an organization that control its patterns of formal communication.

- Leadership in organizations is based on what Max Weber called "legal-rational" authority. That is, such leaders are usually selected or appointed not on the basis of tradition or charisma but because they possess technical managerial skills, and they are permitted to exercise power within a limited sphere that is narrowly defined by "official" definitions and rulings.

- Three general theories that focus on strategies of organizational design, management, and communication have been developed during the past two centuries. These are the human use theories (developed between the early 1800s and the late 1920s), the human relations theories (which were dominant between the early 1930s and the 1960s), and the human resources theories (which have been in vogue since the 1960s).

- Formal communication takes place only between certain designated parties; it concerns only a range of organization-relevant topics; and it is transmitted and received via prescribed media. Formal communication dictates who can say what to be received by whom about specific topics making use of what medium. As messages move up and down the line they are subject to a number of factors that may bring about inaccuracy and distortion.

- Messages flow not only through the official channels prescribed for formal communication but through grapevines as well—complex social pathways in a network of intimate groups. Through such networks rumors are retold, gossip is exchanged, and word-of-mouth diffusion of important news is transmitted.

- Two general patterns of distortion have been found that characterize the spread of informal messages through organizational grapevines. One is the embedding pattern, in which leveling, sharpening, and assimilation can distort messages. The second is the compounding pattern, in which a message grows larger and more elaborate.

- A specialized internal culture develops within any organization. Its shared language patterns and orientations set it apart from other similar groups. Furthermore, within the organization micro cultures can develop in various units and divisions or even among small groups of work associates. Specialized cultures can support an organization, or they can be the basis of serious conflicts.

- The bonds that link members in an organization are based on a combination of sentiment-based cohesion within small groups of work associates, reward-based cohesion in more temporary groups, assignment-based cohesion among members of decision-making groups within the organization, and dependency-based cohesion that is a product of task interdependencies in the overall structure.

Key Terms

Assimilation   A feature of the embedding process by which a message is reshaped into new interpretations (distortions) by the psychological characteristics and culturally learned habits of the receiver.

Authority   The basis of legitimacy for the exercise of power.

Bureaucracy   A deliberately designed plan of the goals, norms, roles, ranks, and controls in an organization.

Charismatic authority   Unique personal attractiveness that makes an individual exercising leadership seem very special to those who are led and thereby willing to accept his or her exercise of power.

Compounding pattern   A pattern of distortion whereby an original message passed by word-of-mouth through a grapevine grows larger and more complex, gaining additional details and interpretations that were never a part of the original message.

Dependency-based cohesion   A type of cohesion characteristic of organizations with a complex division of labor. Members are bound to the organization and to each other because all members perform specialized tasks that are in some way linked to and dependent on the tasks performed by others.

Embedding pattern   A particular set of distortions—leveling, sharpening, and assimilation—that may occur in a message when it is transmitted orally from one person to the next in a kind of serial pattern.

Grapevine   Complex social pathways in a network of intimate groups within an organization through which informal messages are transmitted by word-of-mouth.

Human relations perspective   A theory for managing organizations in which the personal and social characteristics of workers as individual human beings are critical factors in the work process. Managers try to motivate, encourage, and foster worker performance by taking advantage of human factors that make work more tolerable, under the assumption that this will increase output.

Human resources perspective   A theory for managing organizations based on assumptions that bonds of loyalty can be created between worker and employer and that workers have insights into production processes which offer valuable clues as to how both quality and efficiency can be improved.

Human use perspective   A theory of management in which workers are not thought of in humanitarian terms but simply as one more thing that can be "used," along with machinery, and "exploited" like raw materials.

Legal-rational authority   The basis of legitimate authority in organizations in which leaders are selected because they possess technical managerial skills that qualify them to exercise power within a limited sphere narrowly defined by "official" definitions and rulings.

Leveling   A general shortening of a message, such as a rumor, story, or other verbal account as it travels by word-of-mouth from one person to the next through a grapevine.

Organization   A human group that has been deliberately designed so as to achieve a desired objective. Usually it has a large number of participants whose activities are coordinated by complex rules for communication.

Organization chart   A graphic representation of the chain of authority and command in an organization, which also provides a guide to the flow of formal messages. It is especially helpful in understanding the vertical flow of communication—up and down the organization.

Organizational cohesion   That which binds members of an organization to each other and to the group as a whole. Realistically, it is based on a combination of sentiment-based cohesion within small groups of work associates, reward-based cohesion in more temporary groups, assignment-based cohesion among members of decision-making groups within the organization, and dependency-based cohesion that is a product of task interdependencies in the overall structure.

Organizational communication   The transmission of messages through both the formal and the informal channels of a relatively large, deliberately designed group, resulting in the construction of meanings that have influences on its members, both as individuals and on the group as a whole.

Quality control circles   Small discussion groups composed of individuals from a particular unit in an organization (usually devoted to manufacturing) whose members all face the same production task. They meet with their supervisor to find ways in which their particular assembly work can be done more efficiently and at a higher level of quality.

Scientific management   A theory for managing organizations in which managers themselves look systematically at the design of their group and its processes to try to communicate to workers ways in which incentives, the flow of work, and the exercise of authority can operate most effectively and profitably. Early versions were concerned with time and motion studies.

Sharpening   The counterpart of leveling in the embedding process: A verbal message shrinks as it is passed on by word-of-mouth. With each retelling it becomes increasingly organized around its more central or "salient" details, becoming more and more concise until it is only a kind of summary of the original message.

Social institution   A broad configuration of closely related cultural elements and organized social activities that are essential to fulfilling a perceived basic need of the social order.

Specialized organizational culture   The total pattern of all the shared beliefs, sentiments, attitudes, values, sentiments, rules, special languages, and everything else produced and shared by the members of an organization. These cultural elements set it off from other organizations and the society as a whole.

Vertical transmission   The flow of formal messages either up or down in an organization with clearly graded levels of power and authority.

Wage incentive system   A formula for paying workers in production settings in which wages are tied to personal output. That is, earnings for a worker in a production shop are determined by the number of units the individual produces in a given time period.

Notes

1. For excellent elementary discussions of the importance of groups and communication in groups in organizations see: Goodall, H. L. Jr. (1990). *Small group communication in organizations* (2nd ed.) (pp. 1–21). Dubuque, IA: Wm. C. Brown; and Richmond, V. P., & McCroskey, J. C. (1990). *Communication in organizations* (pp. 1–10). Edina, MN: Bellwether. Also, for more advanced discussions see:

Jablin, F. M., Putnam, L. L., Roberts, K. H., & Porter, L. W. (Eds). (1987). *Handbook of organizational communication.* Newbury Park, CA: Sage; Jablin, F. M., & Sussman, L. (1983). Organizational group communication: A review of the literature and model of the process. In H. H. Greenbaum, R. L. Falcione, & S. A. Hellweg (Eds.), *Organizational communication: Abstracts, analysis and overview* (Vol. 8, pp. 11–50). Beverly Hills, CA: Sage.

2. For excellent discussions of both the historical roots and the distinctive aspects of organizational communication see: Jablin, F. M. Organizational communication. In G. L. Dahnke & G. W. Clatterbuck (Eds.). (1990). *Human communication: Theory and research* (pp. 156–182) Belmont, CA: Wadsworth; Redding, W. C. (1979). Organizational communication theory and ideology: An overview. In D. Nimmo (Ed.), *Communication yearbook 3* (pp. 309–342). New Brunswick, NJ: Transaction; Redding, W. C. Stumbling toward identity: The emergence of organizational communication as a field of study. In R. D. McPhee & P. K. Tompkins (Eds.). (1985). *Organizational communication: Traditional themes and new directions* (pp. 15–54). Beverly Hills, CA: Sage; Putnam, L. L., & Cheney, G. (1985). Organizational communication: Historical development and future directions. In T. Benson (Ed.), *Communication in the twentieth century* (pp. 130–156) (Carbondale, IL: Southern Illinois University Press; and Richetto, G. M. (1977). Organizational communication theory and research: An overview. In B. D. Ruben (Ed.), *Communication yearbook 1* (pp. 331–346). New Brunswick, NJ: Transaction.

3. Contemporary examples of research that has focused exclusively on assisting management in their control of workers include: Richmond, V. P., Davis, L. M., Saylor, K., & McCroskey, J. C. (1984). Power in organizations: Communication techniques and messages. *Human Communication Research, 11,* 85–108; Richmond, V. P., McCroskey, J. C., & Davis, L. M. (1986). The relationship of supervisor use of power and affinity-seeking strategies with subordinate satisfaction. *Communication Quarterly, 34,* 178–193; and Richmond, V. P., Wagner, J. P., & McCroskey, J. C. (1983). The impact of perceptions of leadership style, use of power, and conflict management style on organizational outcomes. *Communication Quarterly, 31,* 27–36.

4. See: Weber, M. (1947). *Wirtschaft und Gesellschaft,* Part I of which has been translated by A. M. Henderson and Talcott Parsons as: *The theory of social and economic organization.* New York: Oxford University Press, 1947. A good secondary source is Gerth, H. H., & Mills, C. Wright (Eds./Trans.). (1946). *From Max Weber: Essays in Sociology.* New York: Oxford University Press.

5. Perhaps the ultimate example of charismatic power was that of the Reverend Jim Jones, who in the 1960s established a religious group called The People's Temple. In the early 1970s, the group developed an agricultural community in Guiana (in northeastern South America). In 1978 the Reverend Jones called on his more than 900 followers to join him in committing suicide. The world was horrified when these people unthinkingly followed his command.

6. Weber's analysis of the nature of bureaucracy was not focused exclusively on problems of communication. In fact, it dealt more centrally with components of formally prescribed social organization (which, of course, depend on well-defined channels of communication). For purposes of this text we have adapted his analysis somewhat so as to emphasize communication issues.

7. This list is a composite drawn from: Henderson and Parsons, op. cit., pp. 333–336. See also Gerth & Mills, op. cit., pp. 196–204.

8. Kreitner, R. (1983). *Management* (p. 38). Boston: Houghton Mifflin.

9. For representative reviews of the contemporary research on organizations and organizational behavior see: O'Reilly, C. A., III. (1991). Organizational behavior: Where we've been, where we're going. In M. R. Rosenzweig & L. W. Porter (Eds.), *Annual review of psychology* (Vol. 42, pp. 427–458). Palo Alto, CA: Annual Reviews; Ilgen, D. R. & Klein, H. J. (1989). Organizational behavior. In M. R. Rosenzweig & L. W. Porter (Eds.). (1989). *Annual review of psychology* (Vol. 40, pp. 327–352). Palo Alto, CA: Annual Reviews; House, R. J. & Singh, J. V. (1987). Organization behavior: Some new directions for I/O psychology. In M. R. Rosenzweig & L. W. Porter (Eds.), *Annual review of psychology* (Vol. 38, pp. 669–718). Palo Alto, CA: Annual Reviews; and Rothschild, J., & Russell, R. (1986). Alternatives to bureaucracy: Democratic participation in the economy. In R. H. Turner & J. F. Short, Jr. *Annual review of sociology* (Vol. 12, pp. 307–328). Palo Alto, CA.

10. Koontz, H. (1961). The management theory jungle. *Academy of Management Journal, 4,* 174–188.

11. Smith, A. (1976). *An inquiry into the nature and causes of the wealth of nations.* Chicago: University of Chicago Press. (First published 1776)

12. Copely, F. B. (1923). *Frederick W. Taylor: Father of scientific management* (p. 3). New York: Harper & Brothers.

13. See: Taylor, F. W. (1919). *Principles of scientific management.* New York: Harper & Row.

14. Gilbreth, F. B., & Gilbreth, L. M. (1917). *Applied motion study.* New York: Sturgis and Walton.

15. Fayol, H. *Administration industrielle generale,* which has been translated by Constance Storrs as: *General and industrial management.* London: Isaac Pitman & Sons, 1949.

16. Mayo, E. (1966). *Human problems of an industrial civilization.* New York: Viking Press. (First published 1933)

17. Pennock, G. A. (1930). Industrial research at Hawthorne: An experimental investigation of rest, working conditions and other influences. *Personnel, 8.* The entire series of the Hawthorne studies are discussed in detail in: Roethlisberger, J., & Dickson, W. J. (1939). *Management and the worker.* Cambridge, MA: Harvard University Press.

18. For a concise overview of human relations theory and the human relations school see: Pace, R. W., & Faules, D. F. (1989). *Organizational communication* (2nd ed.) (pp. 40–42). Englewood Cliffs, NJ: Prentice-Hall; and Goldhaber, G. M. (1990). *Organizational communication* (5th ed.) (pp. 43–48). Dubuque, IA: Wm. C. Brown.

19. This type of outcome, where the conditions of the experiment itself foster motivations and behavior among the subjects that can interfere with the results, has come to be called the *Hawthorne effect.* It is a standard research hazard to which social scientists of all kinds are alert when they study human behavior in experimental settings.

20. Our account of these experiments is necessarily a simplified one. In recent years they have become more controversial than our discussion would make it seem. Various post hoc interpretations have been offered in later years as to why the results were obtained and what they really mean. Some of these are quite different than those offered in the original reports. See, for example: Carey, A. (1967). The Hawthorne studies: A radical critique. *American Sociological Review, 32,* 403–416; and Frank, R., & Kaul, J. (1978). The Hawthorne experiments: First statistical interpretation. *American Sociological Review, 43,* 623–643.

21. Roth, J. (1985). The stuff that quality is made of. *Industrial Management, 9* (7), 18–19.

22. McMillan, C. J. (1982). From quality control to quality management: Lessons from Japan. *Business Quarterly,* Spring, 32.

23. The seminal study is that of Allport, G. W., & Postman, L. (1947). *The psychology of rumor.* New York: Henry Holt.

24. For a summary of classic studies on these issues, see: DeFleur, M. L. (1962). Mass communication and the study of rumor. *Sociological Inquiry, 32* (1), 51–70.

25. For additional discussions of formal and informal communication see: Shockley-Zalabak, P. (1988). *Fundamentals of organizational communication: Knowledge, sensitivity, skills, values* (pp. 47–51). New York: Longman; Daniels, T. D., & Spiker, B. K. (1991). *Perspectives on organizational communication* (2nd ed.) (pp. 92–101). Dubuque, IA: Wm. C. Brown; and Kreps, G. L. (1990). *Organizational communication* (2nd ed.) (pp. 195–221). New York: Longman.

26. This is a version of what Emile Durkheim called "organic solidarity" in his classic analysis *The Division of Labor in Society,* trans. George Simpson (New York: Free Press, 1947); originally published in 1893.

Additional Readings

Goldhaber, G. M. (1990). *Organizational communication* (5th ed.). Dubuque, IA: William C. Brown.

> This text definitively outlines the materials that should be included in the upper-level undergraduate course in organizational communication. In its fifth edition, this book is both comprehensive and clear in the integration of relevant issues and theories in this area.

Jablin, F. M. (1990). Organizational communication. In G. L. Dahnke & G. W. Clatterbuck (Eds.), *Human communication: Theory and research* (pp. 156–182). Belmont, CA: Wadsworth.

> This source presents a contemporary discussion of the history and current status of organizational communication. It traces the development of research in this area while elaborating on the role that communication plays in the four major schools of organizational theory.

Jablin, F. M., Putnam, L. L., Roberts, K. H., & Porter, L. W. (Eds.). (1987). *Handbook of organizational communication.* Newbury Park, CA: Sage.

> This handbook of selected essays presents an advanced overview of important topics within the general area of organizational communication. Each chapter presents a thoughtful elaboration of the published research on a particular topic coupled with a discussion of potential directions for further inquiry. This text tends to be somewhat technical.

Kreps, G. L. (1990). *Organizational communication* (2nd ed.). New York: Longman.

> This text presents a comprehensive introduction to organizational communication. The examples and case studies that appear throughout are based on the author's real-life industrial experiences. These descriptions make the chapters particularly informative. This book deviates substantially from more traditional introductory texts in its emphasis on utilization and application of important principles and theories.

Richmond, V. P., & McCroskey, J. C. (1990). *Communication in organizations.* Edina, MN: Bellwether Press.

> This is a brief but excellent introductory text for students as well as for managers and supervisors. Materials are presented as issues that can help managers in their attempts to survive effectively in contemporary organizations. The book's clear and concise style makes it a welcome addition to existing introductory works on this subject. This book is recommended for the beginning student.

Chapter 8

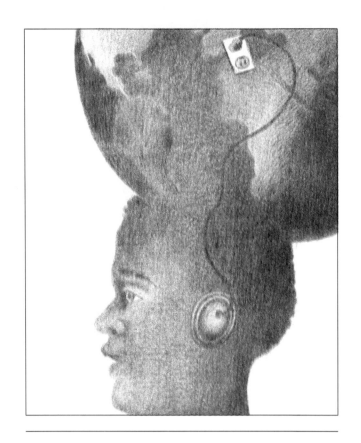

Communicating with Media

Contents

Face-to-Face Versus Mediated Communication
Why Media Matter
   Media limit effective role-taking
   Media limit the adequacy of feedback
The Personal and Social Influences of New Media

Traditional Written Media
Letters
   Advantages
   Disadvantages
Memoranda
   Advantages
   Disadvantages

Telephones and Related Systems
Using the Phone
   Telephone norms
   Answering machines
   Voice-mail networks
Using Fax

Computer Networks
Types of Networks
   Local area networks (LANs)
   Large-scale networks
   On-line information services
Electronic Mail
   Advantages
   Disadvantages
   E-mail norms

Teleconferencing
Computer Conferencing
Audio Conferencing
Video Conferencing

Chapter Review

Key Terms

Notes

Additional Readings

Key Questions

- Why is communicating with a medium, such as a telephone or even a computer, any different from just talking with someone? Doesn't communicating with media follow the same principles? Are any special problems introduced into an exchange of messages just because media are used?

- Many businesses and industries make use of the memorandum as a means of communicating within their own organization. What is a memorandum, and how does it differ from a regular letter? Also, why are memoranda needed when people can just call each other on the phone and exchange messages?

- Is the telephone so commonly used that everyone knows how to use it effectively? Are there any "rules" that should be followed when calling people? If so, what are they and how do they improve one's uses of the telphone?

- Using computers to communicate with other people seems cumbersome when it is so easy just to call them on the phone or write them a letter. How do these computer networks work, and why should anyone take the trouble to learn how to use them?

- How does "teleconferencing" work? How can this be a better way to get together and have a small group discussion than just having a face-to-face meeting? Are there any real advantages in using a telephone, computer, or video system for such a purpose? If so, what are they?

Private Leroy Williams stared out across the desert from his well-concealed forward observational post. There was no moon, but his special night binoculars showed sand dunes stretching to the horizon. It was like seeing a green-shaded fuzzy movie. He knew he had to remain very alert because his entire Marine company was depending on him to note any movement that might indicate the activities of the enemy.

Suddenly, he detected something several miles away in the distance. Although the greenish light in the glasses was poor, he could distinguish at least six vague shapes—some sort of machines—moving from left to right. He couldn't make out any details or tell exactly what they were; they could be trucks, but they might be tanks. His adrenalin level shot up. Was the enemy starting an offensive?

Quickly he checked his global position indicator, a hand-held device called a Trimpak, about half the size of a cigar box. Using satellite-transmitted signals, it indicates within 50 feet one's position anywhere on the surface of the earth. Seconds later Leroy had the lid of his portable laptop computer open and the power switched on. Earlier, he had placed its omnidirectional antenna into position and checked to see that it was working properly.

Leroy expertly typed in his identifying code and a brief message that tersely explained where he was and what he had seen. He hit "enter," and while he continued to search with his binoculars his computer silently encoded and transmitted his message to several destinations in the local area network. His message was received and instantly decoded by his company commander's computer a few hundred yards to the rear.

Private Williams's message was also received at the same instant at battalion headquarters, at regimental headquarters, and at division headquarters, some 3 miles back of the lines. Elapsed time, including Williams observing the machines, checking his position, entering the message in the transmitting computer, and having it show up on network screens was about 30 seconds. At division headquarters, Williams's e-mail was quickly integrated by special computer software into an overall graphic summary of enemy activities that were being observed all along the front. It was clear that something was going on out there. Tanks in motion had been observed across a wide segment of the line. It was clear that the enemy was preparing to attack.

General Summers, the division commander, immediately ordered his communication specialists to do two things: One transmitted a previously prepared e-mail message warning of the attack simultaneously to all regimental, battalion, and company commanders, including artillery, airforce teams, and tank units in the extensive area command computer network. The other specialist, using the portable satellite dish at the general's headquarters, transmitted a summary of the situation, and a strategy of response, to the general's superiors at the Pentagon so as to keep them on top of the field situation. It was received almost immediately by their computer system in Washington, D.C.

All of this may sound like something out of a science fiction movie, but it is not. American forces in Kuwait and Iraq made use of laptop computers, global position indicators, local area networks linked by radio, and larger systems that transmit and receive via satellites. This kind of communication is virtually instantaneous, even in temporary networks where forces are deployed in remote areas. (If the author of the biblical quotation in our epigram were alive today, he would believe that "lightenings" had indeed been sent to be used as the basis of communication.) Such computer-based e-mail systems and other **technologies** are incredibly more efficient and secure than the older phone and voice radio systems used in previous conflicts.

The computers and other hardware components of military systems operate in exactly the same way as those currently found in the computer networks of thousands of American business, educational, and government environments, where various electronic media are changing not only the speed at which people can communicate but also the very process itself.

It is obvious to all but the most unobservant that we are living in an age of rapidly developing and changing communication technology. For example, a mere decade ago, virtually all business letters and memos were dictated to secretaries who took messages down in shorthand. They typed them up with carbon copies, submitted them back to the originator for approval and signature, and sent them via surface mail. Several days later they arrived at their destinations. Today, only a few neanderthals still use typewriters, carbon paper has almost disappeared, and shorthand is a lost art. While letters and memoranda are still sent via surface mail, computers with word-processing software have greatly accelerated message preparation, and transmission of electronic messages via networks has greatly reduced the need to send paper documents of any kind. If they are needed they are likely to be transmitted by special (fax) machines over phone lines. Even meetings of small discussion groups are held via audio and video conferencing with the participants widely dispersed.

The purpose of this chapter is to examine the human communication process as it takes place with the use of several types of media. These include not only traditional written media—letters and memoranda—but contemporary electronic systems that move information almost instantaneously from message senders to receivers. The discussion will show that important differences exist between face-to-face communication and that which takes place when any kind of medium is interposed between the sender and the receiver. It will also show that the widespread adoption of any new communication technology brings about significant changes in the social, economic, and cultural life of those who use them.

Face-to-Face Versus Mediated Communication

In Chapter 1 we discussed human communication as a process that can be conceptualized in both linear and transactional terms. Our linear model indicated that a source person begins with some purpose or goal that can be achieved with a message. He or she then selects a pattern of symbols to represent intended meanings. Those same initial stages characterize *any* linear form of communication, whether media are involved or not. But once the message has been formulated, the transmission stage requires that the distance (and in some cases time) between the message sender and the intended receiver be conquered. Obviously, it is at this stage that media are used, both to increase the distance the message can travel and to reduce the amount of time required.

But what do media actually do? In terms of our analysis in Chapter 1, they simply transport **information**. To review this concept briefly, we noted that in face-to-face conversations or in public speaking, neither symbols nor their meanings actually span distance or become frozen in time. To move a message from a source to a re-

Increasingly, computers are being used as communication devices providing for rapid transmission and receiving. A journalist in a distant country, where important events are occurring, can type a story into a portable computer, use its internal modem and a telephone connection to make contact with a satellite uplink, and transmit the story in a matter of seconds to another part of the world. There, it is downloaded into a newspaper's video display terminal system so that an editor can process it to be a part of the paper's next edition.

ceiver, symbols are transformed into some type of physical event. Examples of information are the sound waves produced by human vocal chords or the variations in light patterns that travel between a transmitting person's written message and a receiver who reads and interprets the symbols. Indeed, such information can range from simple agitations of air molecules to radio waves relayed through space by satellites.

But whatever the means of transmission, in the final stages of the communicative act, the physical stimuli are perceived and reconstructed into symbols by one or more receivers who then interpret them within their own personal frameworks of meaning. And, as we noted earlier, accuracy in communication is attained if the "decoded" meanings of such a receiver have reasonable correspondence with those intended by the original message sender.

Why Media Matter

A **medium** is simply a device that moves information over distance so that people who are apart can communicate. (Media also store information through time.) The simplest medium that might be imagined is one that many of us played with as children. It consists of a string stretched tightly between the bottoms of two tin cans. When the message sender shouts into his or her tin can, the bottom acts as a diaphragm and sends vibrations (information) along the string. The bottom of the can at the other end vibrates sympathetically and reproduces the sound, which is then interpreted by the receiver. It is not much of a medium, and it really doesn't work all that well, but the communication principles are there. Like the tin cans and the string, all of the media that are in wide use today are designed to move information. They may be as common and familiar as a handwritten letter, or they may be at the cutting edge of sophisticated microchip technology. But they all function as information-movers.

A key question is whether or not the process of using media to move information alters the correspondence in intended and constructed meanings. As this section will indicate, the answer is a definite *yes*. Each medium places its own demands on both the source and the receiver, and mediated communication is both similar to but different than that which takes place when people are face-to-face. Some media alter the process greatly while others do so only in a minimal way.

The major similarity between mediated and face-to-face communication lies in the fact that there are people at each end. Just as in the example of the tin cans and the string, a source person transmitting via any medium has to formulate a message at one end and a receiver has to interpret it at the other. Thus, contemporary media systems, such as cellular telephones, answering machines, facsimile, and computers linked by satellite relays, continue to make use of the basic features of human communication that we have discussed. These features are

A medium is any device that moves information over distance so that people who are apart can communicate. While it can conquer distance, the use of any medium alters the communication process itself to some degree. Depending on the nature of the medium, both instantaneous role-taking and feedback may be reduced. Nonverbal communication may also be more difficult, and influences of context can be limited. For these reasons, mediated communication more closely resembles a linear process than one of simultaneous transactions.

verbal and written symbols based on language, at least some nonverbal cues and signals, transactional constructions of meaning, and all the rest.

Despite the similarities in the underlying principles of all forms of human communication there are also important differences. Some have to do with the modification of the social relationships that link senders and receivers in face-to-face versus mediated situations. Others have to do with the technical features of various kinds of media themselves that often impose their own behavioral demands on those who use them. Furthermore, some media can be used to transmit messages capable of subtle and sensitive interpretations, whereas others are severely limited to relatively concise denotative meanings.

Media limit effective role-taking One of the alterations in the social relationship between sender and receiver that occurs when media are used is the limitation on *role-taking*. This activity on the part of the message sender is especially critical in direct face-to-face communication between two people. If the sending person knows the receiver well and can anticipate subtle ways in which she or he will interpret a given message, then role-taking is at a maximum. The basic idea is that the sender mentally plays the part of the receiver (assuming his or her role) to try to predict how that person will interpret and respond to particular kinds of messages.

Role-taking is also an important consideration when a speaker addresses a group, where at least some anticipation of the audience's understanding and response is possible. In this case it may be based on nonverbal cues visible among the audience (age, gender, mode of dress, etc.) or on their actual behavior (clapping, yawning, or booing). However, effective role-taking is far less possible where persons who transmit a message cannot observe or are not well acquainted with their receivers.

Role-taking can be accomplished reasonably well with some media, such as a private and confidential letter between people who know each other intimately. However, it is far less possible to anticipate the responses of others in many of the communication contexts where media are used. For example, in the case of the typical internal memorandum that goes to a number of readers in an organization, it is simply not possible to forecast the potential reactions of each person who will read the message. Role-taking is an even greater problem with other media, particularly if the receivers make up a heterogeneous audience of many kinds of people who are not identifiable by the message sender. The extreme case occurs in mass communication, when huge numbers of

strangers are in an audience and a message source (such as a news anchorperson) can make only the most tenuous predictions as to how each member of the audience will react to his or her message.

Media limit the adequacy of feedback A second problem in using media centers around the process of *feedback*. Here, more depends on the nature of the medium than on the existing relationship between the communicating parties. For example, in a telephone conversation, some immediate feedback is possible—nonverbal cues such as voice tones, long pauses, audible yawns, or giggles convey back to the speaker the manner in which his or her message is being received. However, at least some cues that would otherwise be visible are missing. That is, one never knows in a telephone conversation, even with an intimate other, if that person is smiling, frowning, slumped down looking bored, or listening intently with an enthusiastic expression. Thus, a conversation via telephone is not as rich in nonverbal feedback as one where the two parties are face to face, even if accurate role-taking can be accomplished.

From the above we derive the important principle that *accuracy* in communication—what in Chapter 1 we called the "index of fidelity"—is almost automatically reduced by limitations imposed by the use of media. It is for this reason that face-to-face communication is the mode of choice for people who want to get a valid understanding of someone's feelings or views or who are trying to gain their cooperation, sell them something, or otherwise influence them. Nothing beats face-to-face communication—whether it is a conversation among peers, an interview, a personally presented sales pitch, or even a talk before a group—when accuracy is desired or influence is an important goal.

Despite these disadvantages, mediated communication is critically important to us all. Indeed, it was a part of civilized life long before modern media were developed. The history of humankind has been one in which increasingly sophisticated media have been used—from carvings on stone to systems using computers and satellites—to preserve information over time or to send it over longer and longer distances at an ever-faster pace.

The Personal and Social Influences of New Media

The current revolution in our nation's communication processes is more than just replacing traditional paper-based media with computer screens or other technological marvels. It is also a set of significant modifications in the way we collectively relate to each other. That is, the transition to new communication technologies has both personal and social consequences.

The widespread adoption of new communication technologies has always altered the communication process itself. This is because each new medium: (1) imposes its own special requirements on the ways in which messages are formulated, (2) governs the speed and convenience with which message transmission takes place, and (3) influences the ways in which receivers reconstruct meaning from what is sent to them. In addition, new media have always created significant changes in the social, economic, and cultural processes within which they are used. That was as true following Gutenberg's invention of the moveable-type press as it is today when much more sophisticated media are coming on line.

The ways in which new communication technologies influence both the communication process and the people who use them can be well illustrated by noting the changes that took place during the last century after the introduction of the telegraph. The new technology made it possible to send words at a mind-boggling 186,000 miles *per second*—literally the speed of lightning. Before 1844, when telegraphy started, the fastest way of moving a message was on a train, which could reach the (then) frightening speed of about 40 miles an hour.

But the changes the new "lightning lines" brought were far more extensive than just increasing the speed of message transmission. Because we have the advantage of a historical perspective we can use the example of the telegraph to gain an appreciation of what happens when a significant new medium of communication quickly comes into wide use in a society. This may help us to forecast what changes lie ahead as we increasingly use newer media.

The telegraph came very rapidly. The first message, "What Hath God wrought?" was sent in 1844 along a copper wire between Washington and Baltimore. Within a mere 3 years, New York had been linked by wire to New Orleans, nearly 2,000 miles away, and a network of the magic wires connected every major city in the United States.[1]

How did this new medium change the communication process? For one thing, a message via telegram took on meanings for both sender and receiver that other forms of communication did not. The implication was one of urgency and importance. Families quickly learned that a message sent to them via the wires implied emergency or crisis. Telegrams brought news of illness or even the death of a loved one, and opening the envelope within which the message was delivered was a traumatic event. For business and commerce, the great increase in speed provided by the wires enabled the stock market to develop, and the economic system of the nation accelerated its activities greatly.

The new means of communication served many users, but it was especially helpful to journalists, who gleefully adopted it almost overnight. The telegraph enabled them to get their stories to their editors very swiftly. But it also changed their writing style. Up to that time, newspaper correspondents at out-of-town locations were accustomed to writing long, elegantly phrased accounts of events they were covering. They dispatched them by post to their editors. When they eventually arrived, they were often shortened by the editors, but newspaper stories of the time tended to be much lengthier than they are today because much less news flowed into the typical newspaper.

When using the telegraph reporters were charged by the word, and a long story could be very expensive. Under pressure to keep costs down, they soon developed a new message style, consisting of short, terse sentences with all the flowery adjectives and nonessential words left out. In reconstructing the meaning, the editors could add such details and embellish the accounts as they wished. But the new way of communicating permanently changed journalistic writing in the United States.

Communicating by wire had broader and often subtle effects on the entire society. For one thing, it greatly expanded the consciousness of Americans concerning events beyond their local area. Prior to the telegraph, newspapers concentrated on news from their own community. There was some national and international coverage, of course, but it was often delayed and limited. In the spring of 1848, however, the Associated Press was formed for the purpose of transmitting news stories over the magnetic wires.[2] Within a decade it had expanded nationwide, and even the smallest newspaper got a daily flood of wire stories from beyond their local area, reporting relatively trivial happenings such as fires, robberies, and murders. When local papers published these accounts, it offended many critics, who thought the press should serve a more noble purpose. For example, in 1854, Henry David Thoreau dismissed most of the content of the newspapers of his day as mere *gossip:*

I am sure that I have never read any memorable news in a newspaper. If we read of one man robbed, or murdered, or killed by accident, or one house burned, or one vessel wrecked, or one steamboat blown up, or one cow run over on the Western Railroad, or one mad dog killed, or one lot of grasshoppers in the winter—we need never read of another. If you are acquainted with the principle, what do you care for the myriad instances and applications? To a philosopher all news, as it is called, is gossip.[3]

However, while the flood of crime stories and other negative news was seen by some as potentially harmful to the moral condition of the public, others saw great benefits from this expansion of communication. Charles Horton Cooley, looking back in 1909 at the newspapers that had developed during the 19th century, saw their effects as an "enlargement" of the human mind—a fundamental change in the human condition brought about not only by the telegraph but also by the telephone, mass newspapers, and other media that had altered America's communication processes during the century. As he put it, "The individual is broadened by coming into relation with a larger and more various life, and he is kept stirred up, sometimes to excess, by the multitude of changing suggestions which this life brings to him."[4] Thus, anticipating McLuhan, turn-of-the-century analysts of the new communication media saw that the world was becoming what they called a "global village."[5] But those who believed that this flow of messages would result in a degradation of human sensitivity called this unfortunate condition "newspaperism."[6]

Thus, the introduction of the telegraph as a new medium of communication was far more than just a technological advance. It brought about significant changes that touched the lives of every citizen and altered the functioning of some of the most basic institutions of our society. What lesson can be drawn by our brief look back at that history? We are now living in a period of accelerating change in communication media that will bring about changes even more sweeping than those of the 19th century. During the 21st century, our ability to communicate with each other will grow to a degree that has never before been experienced. The specific ways in which this will influence all of us, both individually and collectively, are difficult to forecast. But one thing is certain—our lives will be different than they are now.

Traditional Written Media

Communication in written form has been a part of human life for thousands of years. We continue to use writing both in traditional ways and as part of our newest media. However, our present analysis will not be concerned with the print mass media—books, magazines, and newspapers. These are very complex and worthy of intensive study in their own right, but the present section focuses on written transmissions that originate with a single individual who wants to transmit a message to one other person, a small group, or a large number of receivers. This kind of written communication takes place when people write letters or send memoranda. Later sections will include written communication that makes use of technologically sophisticated media, such as facsimile, and various forms of computer-based electronic mail.

Letters

Letters remain the medium of choice for many kinds of message transmissions. These include private correspondence between friends or family members and messages from individuals to an organization, between officials in different organizations, and from an organization to clients or members of the public. In an organizational context, there are many different categories of letters that have special requirements. Letters are sent out for a host of purposes—to request donations, solicit business, ask for voters' support, respond to specific inquiries, provide notification, build good will, invite or reject applicants, and for many other reasons.

We need not define a letter. People have been exchanging them since writing began. Indeed, until very recent times, this was the only way that people could communicate at a distance. Letter writing as we know it began after the use of light and flexible media spread in society. Earlier media were either slabs or walls of stone, which to say the least were difficult to move around, or clay tablets, which were perhaps somewhat easier. However, when portable media became available—in the form of papyrus, parchment, or vellum (and later paper)—the transportation of written documents over large distances became feasible. In fact, communication scholars such as Harold A. Innis have maintained that the great empires of classical civilizations could not have come into existence, or have been effectively administered, without portable media that permitted the swift transportation of messages over long distances.[7]

The great problem of letters in earlier times was, of course, just getting them to their destinations. The process was neither reliable nor cheap. Letters were used mainly by the rich and powerful. Even in the United States up to about 1850 it was very costly to use the mails, and they were dreadfully undependable. While Congress

Communication Technology Avoidance Scale*

Instructions   We are interested in your orientation toward using the various types of high-tech media in your daily life. Listed below are 10 pairs of statements. Read each pair and place a mark beside the media choice that best reflects your own personal preference for using that particular medium or technology.

Never check both of the items. Do not look back and forth through the items; make each item a separate and independent judgment. Your first impression, your immediate preference for each medium, is what we want.

Again, which communication technology from each pair do you prefer to use in your own life?

1. ____ A videocassette recorder (VCR) with multiple programming and memory capabilities
   ____ A VCR with single programming/recording capability
2. ____ Cordless phone
   ____ Regular telephone with cord attached
3. ____ Typewriter
   ____ Wordprocessor
4. ____ Write a letter
   ____ Talk on the telephone
5. ____ Rely on an answering machine or service to screen or record telephone calls
   ____ No answering machine or service
6. ____ Use voice mail or e-mail to send and retrieve business messages
   ____ Use the telephone or sending a letter through interoffice mail
7. ____ Go to the library
   ____ Use your own on-line computer service (Prodigy, etc.) to access reference material
8. ____ Send a business letter or memo through the mail
   ____ Transmit a business letter or memo by fax
9. ____ A computer fully loaded with modem, extended RAM, and hard disc memory, software organizer (e.g., WINDOWS), mouse, graphics, etc.
   ____ A simple wordprocessor
10. ____ Rely on teleconferencing or video conferencing to talk to several people at the same time
    ____ Telephone each person one at a time

*Copyright © by Patricia Kearney and Timothy G. Plax, California State University, Long Beach.

Calculating Your Score

1. For each pair of 10 items, there are two possible responses. One response represents an "avoidance" of communication technology; the other is an "approach" orientation toward the use of high-tech media. Label the avoidance responses "A" and the approach responses "B" according to the following key:

Item 1:	Choice 1 = B	Choice 2 = A
Item 2:	Choice 1 = B	Choice 2 = A
Item 3:	Choice 1 = A	Choice 2 = B
Item 4:	Choice 1 = A	Choice 2 = B
Item 5:	Choice 1 = B	Choice 2 = A
Item 6:	Choice 1 = B	Choice 2 = A
Item 7:	Choice 1 = A	Choice 2 = B
Item 8:	Choice 1 = A	Choice 2 = B
Item 9:	Choice 1 = B	Choice 2 = A
Item 10:	Choice 1 = B	Choice 2 = A

2. Next, score a "1" for each "A" and a "0" for each "B." In other words, you get no points for B responses, but 1 point for each A response you made.
3. Finally, add together your total points across all 10 items = ____.

Interpreting Your Score

Possible range of scores for the Communication Technology Avoidance scale is: 0–10. (If your own final score does not fall within that range, you made a computational error.)

The higher the score, the more avoidant you are toward the use of high-tech communication media. There may be a number of reasons you wish to employ low-tech over high-tech media, but one important reason is typically because people are afraid of change. After all, sending a letter has worked perfectly all right for us for a very long time; why switch over to fax? Second, as avoiders, we may experience anxiety about trying out the new technology because we fear evaluation from others. That is, we assume others already know how to use it (like voice mail or video conferencing), and we fear revealing to others that we do not know how to use it ourselves. Third, we may think we'll damage or break the technology (like the computer). Just because the technology appears more complicated, we often assume that it is also more fragile.

Low scorers on the Communication Technology Avoidance Scale, particularly those with scores 2 or below, approach the use of technology with anticipation and enthusiasm. They look forward to their use because they are sure the new technology offers them advantages, such as speed, simplicity, and convenience. Approachers are anxious to enter the media age and be on top of all the latest advances in communication technology.

A word of caution: Communication technology approachers are not necessarily those who are also media literate. Approachers may boast owning the new technology but may fail to learn how to program their VCRs; have trouble changing the message on their answering machines; have difficulty entering new software onto their computer hard disc; or never learn how to program telephone numbers into memory storage. Whereas approach/avoidance reflects a personal orientation or preference, communication literacy or media competency requires skill.

established an official postal service as early as 1790, it was not until the middle of the 19th century that a reliable and inexpensive system was fully operational, making use of improved roads, trains, and steamship lines.

Even today, the mail can be very slow. For example, in 1990, Price Waterhouse (a consulting firm) tested the system by sending 425,000 pieces of mail to 5,000 recipients in 286 ZIP codes. Less than three quarters arrived within the number of days claimed by U.S. Postal officials.[8] For such reasons a number of private and public services have developed over the last decade so that (for hefty fees) a letter or parcel from virtually any city in the United States can get to any other city overnight.

But how well can letters achieve that "complete and accurate" communication discussed at a theoretical level in Chapter 1? What are the factors that lower the index of fidelity when a letter is used rather than verbal and nonverbal communication in a face-to-face context? On the other hand, are there features of this medium that give it an edge in certain situations?

Advantages   One of the nice features of a letter is a quality that it has had since its beginning: It is not based on a complex technology, and it is truly portable. All the sender needs is a pen or pencil, writing paper, an envelope, and a stamp. After delivery it can be read almost anywhere. A letter does not have to be plugged into a wall socket; it does not require that either party use a complex machine that demands technical skills.

Another distinct advantage of a letter is that it is "hard copy." That is, it can be placed in a file—which can be important in a context of official correspondence. That same hard copy can be lugged around in one's pocket, or saved as a treasured message from a loved one, and it can be read or reread at the recipient's own pace.

A third advantage of a letter over either a conversation or a phone call is that it implies the recipient should "do something"—make a decision, take some action, or at least send a written reply. Verbal communication often lacks this implication of required action. Conversations can conveniently, or accidentally, be forgotten. The same is true of a phone call, which leaves no permanent trace. A letter, however, is a physical object, and it sits there on the desk of the receiver until it is dealt with.

Another positive feature of a letter is that it can be composed thoughtfully at the writer's own convenience and pace. When writing to a loved one, words and phrases can be selected with care. The same is true of business or official communication, where the words used can have significant legal implications. In these ways, letters as a medium share a distinct advantage over the face-to-face

Traditional written media have several important advantages over those that are more technologically sophisticated. Their messages can be encoded thoughtfully and reshaped until the communicator is satisfied. The receiver can read them over and over, decoding and interpreting the message at his or her own pace. They are very portable, needing no complex machine plugged into the wall for either transmission or reception. Their main disadvantage is that they can be agonizingly slow in bridging the distance between communicators.

mode, where one can sometimes regret immediately irretrievable messages formulated and transmitted in haste.

Finally, letters sent through the U.S. mails have one clear advantage not found in other written media. That is *privacy*. Strict federal laws forbid tampering with a person's mail or even their mailbox. While these laws do not totally deter a highly motivated snoop, they certainly reduce the temptation people may have to take a look at messages someone has sent or received via letter. As we will explain, other written media, such as memoranda and especially electronic mail, lack these legal protec-

tions. To have someone make public confidential messages one has sent by unprotected media can prove to be embarrassing at best and disastrous at worst.

Disadvantages   The disadvantages of letters lie mainly in the matters of inconvenience, limitations on length, and slow speed. Composing a letter thoughtfully, getting each phrase and sentence in a logical sequence and spelling every word correctly, can be a vexing task for the impatient. One has to locate stationery, something to write with, an envelope, and a stamp. Furthermore, the letter has to be taken to a mailbox. For many people, these steps seem like a lot of bother, and it is far easier just to pick up the phone and call.

Writing a good letter requires intellectual capacity and some skill with words. Both may be in short supply. Even if the intended receiver is a loved one or close friend, drafting a letter requires creative composition. Too often there is simply nothing to write about because many of us lead dull and routine lives and have few matters of interest that can be described in a letter.

The norms for writing letters are complex, and they cannot adequately be reviewed in a single section of a chapter. However, a number of basic guidelines can help in the preparation of any business letter so that it will be more favorably received and better understood:

1. *General features.* Needless to say, in business correspondence there is an absolute requirement for meticulously correct grammar, spelling, and punctuation. Such letters must meet the highest possible standards of neatness, and most should be written on formal "letterhead" stationery that identifies the organizational source of the communication.
2. *Format.* There are a variety of acceptable business-letter formats for positioning the address, the salutation, the body of the letter, and the signature. These are to some degree a matter of personal preference, although many organizations insist on a common style. A host of manuals and stylebooks set forth various business letter formats in use today.[9]
3. *Formulating an appropriate message.* A vast number of considerations enter into the formulation of effective messages for business and professional purposes. Selection of appropriate strategies will depend above all on the goal the letter-writer is trying to achieve. Such goals can range from applying for a job to persuading a receiver to buy a product. Some letters bring happy news about promotions and raises; others bring unwelcome news about denials, refusals, and unfavorable decisions.

Whatever the purpose, effective letters must express sincerity and concern and they must be readable and concise. They must adequately emphasize the main points in the message but have at least some pleasantries. Such messages must always be couched in diplomatic terms, especially if they bring bad news. Finally, they must never contain discriminatory language. The inappropriate use of masculine pronouns (women make up half of our labor force) is perhaps the most frequent error made in business letters today.

Memoranda

A **memorandum** (from the Latin *memoro,* meaning "to call to mind") is very different than a letter, and it serves a relatively restricted purpose.[10] It is a widely used medium for written communication between members within an organization, particularly where a permanent record seems desirable. There are some organizations that use them to communicate to readers outside their group, but the "memo" is seldom or never used for communication between friends, family members, or other private parties.

The memorandum is a very stylized medium. That is, it follows a standardized format that has evolved as a form of organizational communication over many decades. Some organizations supply preprinted forms for convenience on which the information needed can be entered. While minor variations can be used, the memorandum format usually looks something like the following:

Within an organization, this medium is used for a number of different purposes. In Chapter 7 we discussed vertical communication, up and down the levels of organizations. The memorandum is one of the principal media used for this purpose. Supervisors send orders to their subordinates via memoranda. Those lower in the system use memoranda to transmit requests and brief reports up the line. Some memoranda also flow between segments or divisions of an organization. Sometimes memoranda are very widely circulated—for example, when a head of an organization wants to transmit an official message to all employees or when a supervisor needs to send a message to those within a particular unit.

Advantages   As the Latin origins of its name suggest, one of the most important features of the memorandum is that it leaves a "memory"—that is, a "paper trail"—in an organization. A memorandum, like a letter, is hard copy that can be placed in a file. Such files often develop around sensitive transactions. (An example would be evaluations of someone's competence, performance for purposes of granting or withholding of rewards such as salary or promotion). If that file needs to be reviewed, proof is there that communication took place and the nature of the messages transmitted or received is clear. Thus, memoranda are often used in situations where there can be any kind of later dispute as to who transmitted what to whom. For that reason, even though it is much quicker and more convenient to call someone on the phone, or to send them a quick note via electronic mail, the memorandum preserves messages through time in an effective way.

```
                    Memorandum

   TO:        (receiver's name)

   FROM:      (sender's name)

   DATE:      (month, day, and year)

   SUBJECT:   (concise statement of topic)


        (The body of the message goes here,
     seldom exceeding one or possibly two
            8 1/2 x 11 inch pages.)
```

Most memoranda are brief and concise. This makes them convenient for both senders—who need not compose a long message—and receivers, who do not have to plow through long documents. A sort of rule of thumb is that if it cannot be said in a single page, then some other way to transmit the message should be used.

Disadvantages   While memoranda serve important purposes in an organization, they do have a number of limitations. For one thing, they lack legal protection. In addition, they can be interpreted as unimportant. Further, they suffer from the same limitations on role-taking and immediate feedback as do other media.

While memoranda are sometimes marked as secret and confidential, a determined snoop can manage to get hold of a copy. If that happens, there are no sanctions that can be invoked—other than what an organization can exercise through its own rules. In other words, memoranda lack the official protections and deterrents applicable to letters sent through the U.S. Postal service.

Certain kinds of memoranda tend to be seen as unimportant, which can limit the attention people pay to their contents. For example, those that are addressed to such collective receivers as "staff," or "all personnel," in organizations may actually contain very important information. However, this is so impersonal that they may be seen as just another form of "junk mail." When this happens, people either throw them away after only a quick glance or just leave them unread. To avoid this, some organizations use computer systems that generate personal labels for each member of the group, in the hope that this will increase attention to content. However, people soon catch on to this and once they see an automated label, they mentally classify the communication as unimportant. Such constructions of meaning by receivers obviously reduce the accuracy of the communication.

Finally, memoranda suffer from numerous limitations on role-taking and feedback. Because they need to be concise, with their messages formulated in official language, they are composed of phrases that might not characterize a conversation or even a lengthier and less formal written document. This is especially true of memoranda that are sent to multiple receivers. People at different levels and in various specialties in an organization have differing abilities and personal psychological resources with which to construct interpretations of the intentions and meanings of the transmitting person. This can significantly limit the fidelity of the communication.

Despite these disadvantages, however, the memorandum remains an important medium in organizational communication. In particular, it retains the advantage of leaving a "memory record." For that reason it is not likely to be easily replaced. In recent years, however, newer media have reduced the need for paper-based memoranda, at least for quick and noncritical messages.

Telephones and Related Media

The basic instrument and technology by which we telephone each other was invented in 1875 (and patented the following year) by Alexander Graham Bell.[11] And, despite the incredible growth and remarkable changes in telephone technology, we still use the basic principles that he developed. The telephone, like the telegraph before it, was one of those new media that had a powerful influence on the human communication process during the 19th century, and it certainly introduced great changes in our society and culture.[12] Today we have not only become a nation of very frequent telephone talkers, but our worldwide system has made other media possible. Long-distance and oceanic telephone lines and satellite relay systems provide the basic carriers for related media, such as facsimile, computer networks, and audio conferencing.

Using the Phone

By 1990 there were approximately 400 million telephones in use worldwide, with 155 million in the United States alone. We can dial directly to virtually any phone in the world. Furthermore, with the advent of cellular phones, we can do so without being connected to a wire system. Soon, with new types of phones transmitting to each other directly via a set of satellites that are about to be put into orbit, direct wire long-distance lines will no longer be needed and every phone in the world will be on one gigantic system. Thus, the telephone continues to be, and will remain, one of our most important media.

Today, we all use the telephone so often, and it is so ubiquitous, that it is almost entirely taken for granted. Americans make an astonishing 800 million telephone calls a day—over three for each member of our population—but we seldom take time to plan a telephone message or worry whether we are following the best procedure. We simply grab the phone, dial our number, and start talking. However, there is a reasonably well understood set of norms that thoughtful senders and receivers follow. That is, there is a set of rules to be observed when using the phone so as to make it a more effective medium.

A set of norms govern the use of every communications medium. One governing telephone usage is that almost any kind of activity should be interrupted to answer its ring. Other norms concern the hours during which it is acceptable to initiate calls, and how much time should be spent tying up another person on the phone. Less well understood are such matters as to whether a young child should be allowed to answer the phone; this can be especially annoying for a long-distance caller.

Telephone norms   Much depends, of course, on who is talking to whom for what purpose. We can divide telephone calls into two general categories that are reasonably well understood—business calls and personal calls. Sometimes the lines between the two become blurred when people who work together become good friends, but it is a useful distinction nevertheless.

What are some of the norms of telephone etiquette that separate the thoughtful business call from the rude and objectionable? Perhaps the following list comes close:

1. Business calls should be restricted to business hours. Many people are annoyed when called at home for business purposes, even though they may say it is all right. Such calls interrupt other activities that are important to people.

2. Nothing is more thoughtless and offensive than a call that interrupts a meal. It is bad enough when business associates or even friends make this mistake; it is even worse when aggressive salespersons catch people at home during this period. Evening mealtime is a favorite for hucksters who want to sell insurance, photo portraits, or other goods and services over the phone.

Some pretend to be taking some sort of "survey" so as to gain the receiver's attention and cooperation. For many people, such intrusive phone solicitations rank near the top of their list of annoyances.

3. Do not let a telephone call take priority. In some business settings, the telephone seems to take precedence over any other form of communication. We have all been in an office, or waiting in line trying to conduct important activities, when the phone rings. Everything else is dropped so as to accommodate the caller. Such calls should not be allowed to intrude.

4. Return telephone calls promptly. There may be very good reasons you have been unable to return a call promptly. In that case, have someone else call and indicate that you will personally call back as soon as possible. Of course a failure to return a call, or delaying a callback extensively, is a message in itself. Perhaps that is the interpretation that is desired.

5. Identify who you are when calling; do the same as a receiver. Some people call and just start talking, assuming that the listener will instantly recognize their

voice. Busy people who contact many others during a day may fail to do so or make mistakes. Telephones are not hi-fidelity instruments, and they sometimes distort voices. It is so easy for a caller to simply say "This is Mary Jane," or a receiver to indicate "Ed Stevens here." Why embarrass the other person?

6. If you want to chat, ask if the receiver has time. Don't just keep talking. Time is a precious commodity to many business and professional people. They may continue to be polite to the person who extends a conversation after the business has been conducted, but they are often thinking "when will this boring person stop blabbing so I can hang up and get back to work?"

7. Keep in mind that business phones are not always private. Someone may be in the receiving person's office, or the phone may be located where others can hear his or her side of the conversation. When in doubt, ask whether others can hear.

There are also telephone norms that apply to personal calls. Some are obvious, but it is suprising how thoughtless people can be. For example:

1. Think carefully before letting young children answer the phone. It is exasperating for some callers to have to ask "Is your mommy or daddy at home?" This can be especially annoying if it is a long-distance call.

2. Callers should consult their watch before calling. Phone calls before 8:00 A.M. or after about 9:00 P.M. can be considered rude. Pay particular attention to time zones. A call initiated at 8:00 A.M. in New York will wake up a person in California at 5:00 A.M. (not a good idea).

3. Many of the norms applying to business calls also apply to personal calls. For example, even personal callers should identify themselves. It is not always easy to recognize someone, even a good friend, from the sound of their voice over a telephone.

Answering machines   These devices are becoming increasingly adopted for both business and home use. They serve the obvious purposes of recording messages so that calls can be returned. However, many people use them to "screen" calls, listening to see who is there as they leave a message before they pick up the receiver.

There is great variation in the types of recordings one hears when a person's home phone is answered by a machine. The simplest merely indicate: "You have reached (the phone number). Leave a message at the sound of the beep." That type of message provides at least some se-

curity in that the caller is given only minimal information. Others like to indicate that "the Smiths are not home right now" (nice to know if you are a burglar) and that they will "return your call as soon as possible." Some owners get carried away and try to entertain their callers. Particularly tacky are those who put "cute" messages on their answering machine with which to greet people who call. These may include hearing some well-known voice (such as Ronald Reagan or Donald Duck) or a musical greeting that sings or chants the message in a style that may range from Beethoven to heavy metal rock. Such curiosities send their own nonverbal messages.

Voice-mail networks   An elaborate extension of the answering machine in organizational settings is a central computer-operated answering machine that serves everyone on a **voice-mail network** of users. The system can be used directly through each individual's telephone. By dialing the number of another person in the organization, a machine will answer if he or she is not there. By pressing appropriate keys, a voice message can be left for that person. When she or he returns, and calls the central answering machine, the recorded message will be played. Messages can be archived on the system for later reference or simply erased at the user's command. Another advantage is that users can call the system from home or elsewhere and hear all their messages, leave information for others, or even dictate self-directed reminders. It is a convenient and "user friendly" system.

Using Fax

A telephone-based medium of great significance is facsimile transmission—or "fax" as it is more popularly called. Like many other electronic devices, it is an American invention that has become a Japanese success story. As a technology it has been available since the late 1940s, but it has come into very wide use both in business and in homes during the last several years—after the Japanese developed small and relatively inexpensive machines.

Facsimile is a telecommunication system by which exact copies of a document or even a photograph can be sent via phone lines. A fax machine usually has its own phone number, and the user simply feeds documents (typewriter size) into it, dials the party to whom the material is to be sent, and presses the transmit button. The machine quickly scans the document, using an array of photodiodes that convert it into very fine horizontal lines of electronic picture elements (pixels). These are trans-

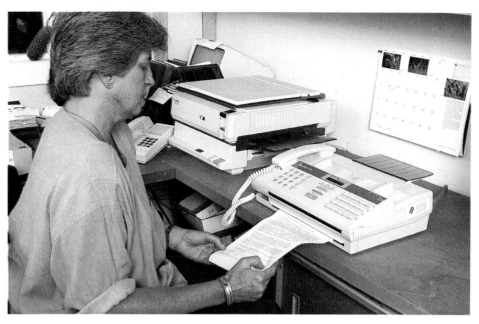

Facsimile transmission by telephone line (fax) is a 1940s communications medium that has recently been widely adopted both in the business community and in homes. It has some of the advantages of the letter, but it can be cumbersome for longer documents. Fax has a great advantage in speed over regular mail and has a very low cost compared to Express Mail services. However, in business settings it may not be particularly private, and more intimate messages may prove embarrassing.

mitted in the form of digital pulses via the phone lines to the receiving machine, where a reverse transformation takes place and a "facsimile" of the document is printed out. The technology is sophisticated, and a good-quality fax machine can even reproduce photographs with impressive fidelity.

Like all other forms of telecommunication, fax has advantages and disadvantages. There are also norms for using the system. The advantages are, as we have already suggested, speed and cost. Fax is remarkably cheap to operate (once the machine has been purchased). Sending a typed page by fax from New York to Los Angeles, for example, would require from 15 to 20 seconds on a long-distance line. Depending on the machine, a two- or three-page document can be transmitted in a minute (currently 24 cents during the day). That is even less than first-class postage, and it arrives immediately. In regular mail the document would arrive 3 to 5 days later. Sending it by Express Mail would cost $6 or $7, and it would get there the next day at best. Because of these speed and cost advantages, fax is rapidly overtaking mail as the most effective way of transmitting printed messages that need to arrive quickly.

One of the limitations of fax is that it may not be very private. It is not a good medium for sending love letters or other messages that one may wish to shield from unwanted eyes. Usually, the fax machine at the receiving end is operated by a secretary or someone in the mail room who can read any of the documents that come off the machine (although some can be programmed for security). Also, it is cumbersome to send long documents. About 15 pages or so in a single transmission is the upper limit. If a document is much longer, it may take several separate stages of transmission.

Fax transmissions should always include a cover sheet, indicating clearly the number of pages being sent, who originated the transmission, to whom it is addressed, and the telephone number of the sending fax machine. Above all, it is essential to indicate the full identification of the intended receiver. Typically in an organizational context, a single machine serves a number of users, and the receiving operator may not know to whom the message should be delivered.

For a while, fax systems were plagued by unsolicited messages. Everything from the menus of nearby food services to jokes and advertisements were sent to networks of fax machines. It became such a problem that an appeal was made to Congress to bar unsolicited messages on fax networks. The lesson here is that someone's fax machine should not be tied up or otherwise improperly used for trivial purposes.

If Alexander Graham Bell were alive today, he would be astonished at the uses to which his device was being put. Millions of conversations criss-cross the nation daily, along with an increasing number of digital signals related to facsimile and other kinds of telecommunication systems. Thus, the telephone lines are one of our most important media.

Computer Networks

We noted earlier that both the telegraph and the telephone changed many features of our nation's communication processes and had significant influences on our society and culture. Today, networks of computers, linked together in local, national, and international systems, are once again creating a quiet but profound communication revolution. That revolution is taking place with breathtaking rapidity and has already brought remarkable modifications in the ways by which people communicate in our society. Many observers have noted that these computerized communication technologies have changed the United States into an "information society" (where more labor-force time is spent in communicating and processing symbols than in agriculture or manufacturing).

Because those changes have taken place so recently and are in many ways invisible, they are only now coming under systematic study by communication specialists. As yet, only scattered studies exist that identify the special problems, norms, limitations, accuracy, and behavior patterns associated with computer communication networks.[13] In this section, we examine the nature of such networks and ways in which they are used for both interpersonal and organizational communication in virtually every type of private and public enterprise.

Types of Networks

Before 1960 computers were large, difficult to use, very expensive, and (by today's standards) severely limited in capacity. A "large" computer might have had as much

4K RAM. That means a temporary, random access or "working" memory of about 4,000 characters, such as letters or numbers. By contrast, a common IBM desktop today will have a working memory capacity of 1,000K RAM (1,000,000 characters) or more. Also, before 1960 there was no such thing as "word processing" for using a computer like a typewriter. Computers accepted only cumbersome decks of cards, which the machine read one-by-one. It then processed the information and printed out the results on paper. There was no screen on which either input or output could be viewed. Although such machines worked well enough for calculating large amounts of numerical data, only one person at a time could use them. They were not connected to other computers, so they had no communication applications.

In 1960 a significant advance was made in computer hardware. It was to provide the technical foundation for both word processing and the communication networking revolution we are now in. The advance was the first commercially available "interactive" computer—where an operator can type words or numbers on a keyboard and see them displayed on a screen as they are entered into the computer's working memory. It was developed that year by Digital Equipment Corporation. Then a rather simple software program was written by Dan Murphy at MIT. It allowed the person using the computer to write programs on a screen and edit and correct them on screen before they were run. It was the forerunner of the familiar interactive screen-displayed word-processing programs that many people use today.[14]

Once a computer could be used in this way, the idea of linking several of them together to provide a means for rapid communication was a logical next step. Scientists and engineers who were in different locations could work together far more effectively if they could exchange messages by some means other than talking on the phone or sending things through the mails.

Out of this need came the first **computer network.** By the late 1960s, a small community of computer scientists, with the backing of the Defense Department's Advanced Research Projects Agency (ARPA), came together to determine how scientists and engineers could communicate and share technical data quickly and easily, even if they were widely dispersed.[15] They designed a system by which computers could be linked by long-distance phone lines. By this means, scientists in one location would be able to send data and messages from their desks to their counterparts in another part of the country, as if both were right there in the same room.

With several universities linked together in this way—via a computer network—rapid communication between researchers would be possible. This was a revolutionary accomplishment.

Only one additional step was needed to create a new medium of communication. This was how to "package" information electronically for efficient transmission. Paul Baron, of the Rand Corporation, found the solution. He realized that digital messages (where each letter or character is coded into a distinct pattern of electronic impulses) could be sent by one computer over phone lines in "packets" to another. This was exactly what was needed to make the network serve efficiently as a communication medium. In 1968 a contract was awarded to a group of scientists and technicians to design the network.

The original ARPAnet was very slow by today's standards, but at the time it was a marvel. It was designed to use smaller computers to handle the phone connections and more sophisticated ones to pass along the messages. All were connected through a network of dedicated leased phone lines. In 1969 the first ARPAnet site was installed at the University of California at Los Angeles. By 1970 facilities were completed at Harvard and the Massachusetts Institute of Technology.

Today people use vast computer networks to communicate back and forth across the nation at speeds 20 times faster than the original system—transmitting complex information in a few seconds that would have taken days or even weeks in the pre-computer-network age. Furthermore, one does not have to be computer sophisticated to use such systems. In fact, many are designed for use by people who know absolutely nothing of computers.

For example, in Los Angeles a woman uses her VISA card to buy a new leather briefcase for $395. The sales clerk puts the card through a credit verification terminal and enters information into the cash register about the purchase. The information travels by phone lines, or sometimes by satellite or microwave, to National Data Corporation's computers in Cherry Hill, N.J. From there it is instantly routed to National Data Corporation's headquarters in Atlanta for processing. A computer there determines that the purchase amount exceeds $50 and sends the request to VISA's computers for verification that the account is valid. The card is from a San Francisco bank, so the VISA computer sends the transaction there to determine whether or not there is $395 in available credit remaining on the purchaser's card. The bank's

computer gives an OK and transmits the authorization back to the Atlanta VISA center, then to Cherry Hill, and finally back to the merchant in Los Angeles. No human being has intervened, but the transaction is approved. Total elapsed time: 15 seconds.[16]

The information transmitted in this commercial system was relatively routine. The clerk really did not have to compose a complex message. However, there are many other kinds of networks in which messages of almost any kind can be transmitted and received. Here, both senders and receivers must play their usual active roles in formulating their messages or reconstructing their meanings. In these contexts, using a network as a medium still depends on the principles of all human communication that we have discussed in previous chapters. As we will see, however, technological features of this medium influence the communication process.

Local area networks (LANs)   A local area network is a set of linked computers (usually of the desktop variety) that are confined to a limited physical area, such as an office or group of offices. This allows individuals at each "station" to send and receive messages; to share programs, software, data files, storage space, and expensive equipment.

Networks obviously vary greatly in size and complexity, which can be an important feature in how they are used. For example, in its smallest and most basic form, two personal computers in the same office may be wired to each other and to the same printer. This means that their users not only can type and send messages to each other, but they also can both use the printer, avoiding the expense of a second machine. In a somewhat larger system, several computers may be linked to a "server" (a small computer that coordinates the system and stores files). Here, computers on different floors or even in different buildings may share the same network. Or, in an even more complex LAN, dozens or even hundreds of desktop machines may be linked to a mainframe computer with massive storage space for huge data files and records. Each person on the network, wherever he or she may be, can access all of these components through a personal computer.

Information is passed through the network in "packets," or chunks of data (such as a single message). Each packet contains the necessary coded identification of both sender and individual (or multiple) receivers to ensure that the packet arrives at the correct destination computer. The LAN is programmed to act as a traffic cop to

Local area networks (LANs) of desktop computers are increasingly the communications medium of choice in business and industry. The use of e-mail (electronic mail) has proved to be extremely efficient and has largely replaced paper media in many office contexts. Larger-scale networks, such as BITNET and INTERNET, are used for communicating via e-mail between senders and receivers at sites in various parts of the world.

see that data are passed in an orderly manner. This prevents several computers from simultaneously sending information when other messages may already be traveling down the line.

At present, most local area networks use wires of one sort or another. That will soon be obsolete. The newer fiber optic cable, which will be increasingly common as its price declines, can relay an enormous volume of data through bundles of glass fibers thinner than a human hair.[17] Even newer systems do not use wires at all. They link computers by a wireless technology called spread-spectrum radio transmission. The network essentially is a broadcast system, and each computer is a miniature transmitter and receiver. The radio signals can travel through office partitions and sheet-rock walls (but not through concrete or steel).

Wireless networks will be the next generation in business and other organizational applications. Because there are no wires, a PC on this network can very easily be moved from one office to another. Therefore, wireless networks such as this are ideal for companies that are growing rapidly or have to reconfigure office designs frequently. We described one such wireless network in

our opening vignette, illustrating a military application. Although most will be at permanent sites, these "instant" networks are also ideal for any kind of temporary situation, such as coordinating rescue efforts after a large-scale disaster or news media covering a convention.

Large-scale networks   Large "super-networks" are also in place. These are networks linked to other networks through **gateway** computers. BITNET is an example. This system connects the local area networks of hundreds of universities and research organizations in the nation into a single system. Its use is growing very rapidly. An even larger example is INTERNET, which brings together 2,000 other networks in 35 countries. The military services operate MILNET, which provides for communication in both the United States and abroad to and between thousands of installations. Special computers called "gateways" connect users on one of these various super-networks with users connected to a different one.

Despite their obvious advantages sometimes things go dreadfully wrong with super-networks. For example, in a recent case a spy, who was secretly breaking into computers for espionage, originated his searches in Hamburg, Germany. For over a year he used his desktop computer at home, linking it via a simple local phone call to DATEX, the German national network. From there he connected by satellite to TYMNET, an overseas and long-distance phone service, which easily routed him through gateways and large-scale networks in the United States, such as ARPANET, MILNET, and others, to a variety of local networks. Before he was finally caught, he figured out how to get by security systems and passwords to gather information freely from computers at universities, research institutes, Defense Department installations, and businesses all over the United States and even as far away as Okinawa.[18]

During the years ahead, the present rather patched-together system of networks linked to other networks in the United States will be superceded by one gigantic "mega-network." The National Science Foundation recently awarded $15.8 million for research into the development of a huge national network that will connect every business, organization, government agency, university, office, and even every home in the nation, into one gigantic system! Government officials estimate the cost of building this national network at more than $200 billion. Experts expect that this will create another communication revolution and a technological transformation as profound for America in the decades ahead as that created by the telegraph and telephone since they became available.[19]

On-line information services Of increasing importance in the United States are various on-line information services provided for both organizations and consumers by commercial vendors. Supplying such services to computer owners was a $50 million industry in 1986. By 1991 it had grown to over $571 million, and it is increasing rapidly. Examples are CompuServe, Inc., which in 1991 claimed to be the largest with a customer base of some 740,000 users, and Prodigy with some 550,000 subscribers.[20] For various fees, a user can subscribe to such a service, access it from a desktop computer equipped with a modem, and obtain information from hundreds of databases containing an incredible variety of information. Some, such as BRS, specialize in providing information on scientific publications. Others, such as Prodigy, provide information on everything from stock market reports to airline schedules. Still others, like Lexis/Nexis, are devoted to the needs of specialized professionals, such as lawyers or journalists.

Many of the on-line systems provide electronic "bulletin boards," where users can leave messages for others to read. These often result in debates and controversies, occasionally in marriages between people who get acquainted in this way—or even in legal actions where feelings are ruffled by electronic messages. The rules and proper uses of these new forms of public communication are a subject of considerable controversy today. It is entirely unclear what rights individuals have when they originate a message, what restrictions the network owners can place on such electronic transmissions, and how the First Amendment applies to such communication.[21]

Electronic Mail

While networks originated to make it easier for scientists to communicate, they are now widely used for routine business and even personal correspondence in virtually every context where computers are in use. One of the most commonly used applications is electronic mail (e-mail). **E-mail** is the name given to messages sent from one computer to another by combining word-processing software with the nearly instantaneous transmission speed of computers linked by phone-line networks.

Advantages E-mail allows people to send various kinds of print messages—what in an earlier time might have been sent via a paper document—without having to stuff and address an envelope or wait several days for delivery. Instead, the message is typed on a computer screen, along with the receiver's electronic address on a local or national network. The source's computer transmits the information along the network directly to the recipient's computer. The receiver can respond immediately if she or he is "on line." If not, the message is stored in the receiving computer's memory so that it can be called up and read later. Messages do not have to filter through secretaries and administrators before reaching the intended person. Copies of a message can be sent to a single receiver, several people at the same time, or everyone on an entire local area network. Such messages can be sent through gateways to receivers in other networks, even to receivers in other countries via international systems.

Computer-based e-mail maintains its own archives. That is, almost all systems have both a temporary "reader file" for recent messages that have not been read by their recipients and a "notebook" file where all past messages that have been sent or received are permanently stored on disc or tape. These storage systems replace the old idea of file cabinets with folders of correspondence. If a hard copy of any particular message sent or received is needed, it can be printed out.

From these characteristics it can be seen that e-mail has great advantages. It is incredibly fast and efficient. That alone justifies its cost for many organizations. It permits decision time to be significantly reduced, which can mean a great deal of money and greater efficiency in operations. And, although computers and software are not cheap, network e-mail saves labor costs. This is because e-mail communication within an organization does not require a large typing pool, filing clerks, and secretaries. In addition, once a group has learned to use the hardware, they spend far less time in processing documents for in-house communication.

Disadvantages   With e-mail one need not ask for whom the bell tolls, because it doesn't toll at all! That is, in most systems, when an e-mail message is transmitted it does not signal its arrival, as is the case with a telephone call. If the receiver's terminal is off, the message simply reaches its electronic destination and is stored temporarily in the receiver's "reader file" until he or she connects to the mainframe computer to see if it contains any "mail." Thus, the sender is at the mercy of the receiver's schedule for reviewing e-mail messages.

Another problem with e-mail is that it is not totally private. Sometimes an e-mail address or user identification code actually belongs to a group of people, rather than just one person. An individual may have a personal code or address, but some are shared by everyone who is working on a particular project. There is no way for a message source to tell, without knowing the local situation in detail, whether or not a particular computer address belongs to an individual or to several people who will all read the messages. Even if the address is that of an individual, until that person "opens" his or her "reader" and then files a new message into his or her private "notebook" disc space, it is sometimes possible for others to read it. This means that one ought to think twice before transmitting highly sensitive or potentially embarrassing personal information.

E-mail norms   It must be kept in mind that, as in all forms of communication, e-mail provides clues about the person sending the message. That is, even when communicated by an electronic medium, message content and style play a part in the "presentation of self" by which receivers form opinions about and assessments of the personal qualities of the transmitting person. Thus, application of the principles of accurate communication, along with those of effective self-presentation, provides e-mail norms or "etiquette."[22]

To illustrate some of the problems of e-mail, two brief examples can be examined. Because e-mail is transmitted so rapidly, and because e-mail messages tend to be short, people who use electronic mail sometimes mistakenly assume their messages can be casually—even carelessly—composed. Electronic messages are typed on the computer keyboard and the letters appear on the screen. Since they are not on paper, they can "feel" informal, somewhat like telephone calls to a friend. The potential for trouble is that, like paper memoranda, electronic messages also leave a trail. As long as they are stored in the computer's memory they are permanent records. It can be difficult to predict when or under what circumstances someone else will have occasion to examine them. Therefore, e-mail messages should be as thoughtfully and carefully constructed as a letter.

Electronic mail messages do not smile, chuckle, cast knowing glances, or easily forgive. Nonverbal cues, in other words, are very limited in the technological environment of an e-mail message. It is mainly the denotative meanings of words that come through. Without nonverbal cues and feedback, those words can be misunderstood. For example, the computer itself may add nonverbal cues with a potential for misunderstanding. Some people (or even some computer terminals) routinely compose messages with the keyboard locked in the "all caps" position, which means that everything that is typed will be in capital letters. Electronic messages typed in all capital letters may imply connotative meanings never intended by the source person.

Say, for example, that an individual is working at his or her desktop computer and it is linked by network to a mainframe computer. Now suppose that she or he needs to use data that are stored on a particular computer tape. In most systems a tape must be attached to a device on the mainframe computer by a live computer operator. To get this done, the user has to send an e-mail message to the mainframe operator requesting that a certain numbered tape be "loaded." After several minutes, however, the tape has not been attached and the user thinks the request may have been overlooked. The user is in no hurry but wants to get started—so he or she sends the following e-mail message to the mainframe operator:

MSG OP1 : IS TAPE 10215 READY

This message (MSG) simply asks "operator 1" (OP1) if the requested tape (number 10215) has been loaded yet.

It is intended as a polite inquiry and as a gentle reminder if it has been overlooked. However, its terse content, all in capital letters, leads the computer operator to misinterpret the message to mean that the sender is angry and impatient. At that point she or he does what all sensible computer operators do under such circumstances—they let the sender wait and stew as long as possible! Perhaps the message would have been more kindly received and quicker action taken if the user had sent this message instead:

MSG OP1 : Hi! Is tape 10215 ready? Thanks.

Correct spelling and punctuation are as important in e-mail as they are in a letter or memorandum. Some e-mail users thoughtlessly assume that it is acceptable to use abbreviated writing styles. For example, consider the following (actual) e-mail message:

peggy we need to schdule mtg 2day or 2morrow let me know what times u are free. need to know what u want to discuss so i can put on agenda for mtg.

Such cryptic messages may serve well enough if they are going to a close friend. On the other hand, they may imply that the receiver is not important enough for the transmitter to have to bother with correct grammar and spelling. That in itself is a message.

The very speed of electronic messages can create problems. Because of the ease of e-mail, message originators are sometimes quick to type and send what might be regretted only a few minutes later. It is possible, for example, to undergo some annoying experience, compose a quick and hasty note about the incident, perhaps using ill-advised epithets or four-letter words, and then press a key to send it. A few moments later, after a little reflection, and after the receiver has read it, the sender may feel quite differently. But it is too late—like all other forms of communication, e-mail is irretrievable.

Finally, e-mail users must consider the issue of privacy. As mentioned earlier, it is possible to read or intercept the e-mail of others before the intended receiver "opens" his or her mail. In fact, some large corporations routinely read the e-mail of unsuspecting employees. Such intrusions into one's e-mail may be discourteous, but they are not necessarily illegal.

Ownership is another murky problem. The legal ownership of e-mail has not yet been fully resolved. This became an issue during the Iran-Contra hearings of the late 1980s, which investigated the sale of arms for the exchange of hostages during the Reagan administration. Congressional investigators wanted to learn to what ex-

tent President Reagan was involved. They wanted him to turn over all electronic mail messages between himself and his staff. The administration argued that this was privately owned communication. The special prosecutor, on the other hand, claimed that the e-mail messages were public records. Legal cases dealing with these matters are working their way through the courts, but clear answers remain elusive.

In overview it seems clear that electronic mail making use of computer networks has become thoroughly entrenched in most of our social institutions—economic, educational, government—among groups sharing a common need or interest. It allows for types of communication locally, across the nation, and even around the world that could be achieved no other way. Communication processes making use of this medium have yet to be widely studied, but there is little doubt that, like other media before it, the computer network will both alter the communication process between individuals and have significant influences on our society and culture.

Teleconferencing

The term **teleconferencing** comes from the Greek word *tele*, meaning "at a distance." Today, it refers to the use of several different media systems to overcome distance and to link spatially dispersed people together for the purposes of conducting a formal or informal meeting. Thus, telecommunication is relevant to our discussion of small-group communication (Chapter 6) because it enables participants to communicate in ways that, in greater or lesser degree, approximate a face-to-face discussion context.[23]

There are a number of ways to accomplish this goal—some far more effectively than others. The medium used can vary greatly in complexity and richness of verbal and nonverbal exchanges. The more the medium is able to duplicate the conditions of face-to-face exchanges, the greater its cost. The most limited in this respect are the computer networks that we described in the previous section. These provide only typed messages on a screen, but they are the least costly. Audio conferences make use of voice telephone lines that link people together so that they can hear each other and converse. Here, long-distance telephone charges are the major cost. Video conferencing provides the closest approximation to face-to-face communication, but until recently, this has been very expensive. The most sophisticated video systems use satellites to provide instantaneous transmission and reception in full color between participants.

Telecommunication technology is developing at a very fast pace. Video teleconferencing was once very expensive, requiring teams of technicians and specially equipped rooms. Much simpler and less expensive systems are now coming into use permitting senders and receivers to use desktop computers to see several persons on their screens at the same time. Such new technologies will have significant consequences, not only for coordinating work more efficiently but also for travel, hotel, and restaurant industries now serving people traveling to face-to-face meetings and conferences.

In addition to variations in the richness of the verbal and nonverbal information that can be transmitted and received, various configurations also characterize teleconferencing. Some systems merely permit one person to communicate to many in a point-to-multipoint pattern. Others are more complex multipoint-to-multipoint systems in which messages can flow back and forth in a transactional manner between individuals at various dispersed locations. We can briefly compare several different systems.

Computer Conferencing

From our earlier discussion it can be seen that a quick, simple, and limited form of conferencing can be based on e-mail exchanges through computer networks. If the software and the equipment are suitable, two or more people can communicate with each other in a kind of conference. That is, by prior arrangement they can all be at their computers at a particular time. Each participant can type and send messages to all the others. This is cumbersome in many systems because e-mail messages are routed to each individual receiver's "reader" for later retrieval. In some systems, however, short messages can be coded and transmitted in such a way that they immediately appear on all of the receiving screens of the addresses at the same time, providing a way in which people can communicate in a more-or-less interactive manner.

Computer conferencing is not particularly flexible (being restricted to typed messages). It is both linear and cumbersome in that participants have to wait until others type and send their messages. And it obviously provides for only minimal role-taking and feedback because senders and receivers neither see nor hear the others.[24] Thus, a computer conference would be unsuitable where sensitive discussions are needed and in situations where parties have to be persuaded to reach consensus through the use of subtle arguments. Examples of efficient and effective use of computer conferences would be in a situation where a quick vote needs to be taken, where rapid solicitations of opinions are needed, or where an immediate short report is required from the various locations. Not only can participants provide whatever information is requested, but the system keeps a stored record that can be printed later if hard copy is required. Furthermore, a computer conference can be arranged with a very short lead time and with the participants remaining at their regular work station without having to go to a special facility. In addition, it has the great advantage of being cheap.

Audio Conferencing

An older and familiar form of teleconferencing is **audio conferencing.** Anyone who has arranged for a "conference call," in which people at several locations can use telephones to engage in a group discussion, has experienced a simple form of audio conferencing. More formal audio conferences often take place in special rooms, one at each site, with participants seated comfortably around tables communicating via telephone lines. Such rooms are usually equipped with speakers and microphones for high-quality voice transmission.

While they are more expensive than simple computer conferences, they provide for a richer communication experience. For some purposes they can be used in lieu of face-to-face meetings. Here, audio conferences have a number of clear advantages over alternatives. The most obvious are comparative costs and time. Air travel and related meals, lodging, and taxis are very expensive, and if people can accomplish their goals in group discussion through an audio conference, it is far cheaper to pay the telephone charges than to move people around. Furthermore, an audio conference can be set up with only minor lead time. Thus, people can get together far faster, and with less disruption to work schedules, than would be the case in a face-to-face meeting.

On the other hand, audio conferences suffer all the limitations of any other form of telephone communication. In our chapter on nonverbal communcation we discussed the use of both actions and artifacts to arouse meanings in others. In an audio conference, such visual nonverbal signals cannot be received. It matters little whether the source person is well groomed or sloppy, is immaculately dressed or carelessly attired, uses an expensive pen or a drugstore throwaway, or draws papers from an impressive leather briefcase or a tattered paper bag.

The ability to "read" one's audience so as to engage in effective role-taking is also limited, as is the availability of immediate visual feedback. Even if the participants know each other well and can anticipate how their messages will be received and can detect feedback signals from voice tones, pauses, role-taking, and feedback are still far more difficult than in a face-to-face situation.

Despite these limitations, audio conferences provide a comparatively inexpensive and flexible system per-

mitting people to engage in group discussion. Such conferences may not be suitable for the attainment of some goals, but they will continue to be used for many purposes.

Video Conferencing

One of the fastest-growing forms of mediated communication is **video conferencing.**[25] In its most sophisticated form, it brings together video cameras, interactive satellite transmission, and television receivers. An example can be observed during week nights on the MacNeil-Lehrer *Newshour* on public television stations. These broadcast journalists frequently present groups of several individuals discussing a current issue. While one or two may be in the studio with the moderator, others are brought in by satellite from studios in distant cities. Their faces appear on screens in such a way that they almost seem like they are in the same room.[26]

Video conferencing has been by far the most expensive of the various teleconferencing systems. However, many American businesses find it to be efficient and are increasingly using this technology. For example, video-based conferencing is widely used by large organizations with divisions and offices in many locations. Examples are J. C. Penney, Eastman Kodak, Hewlett-Packard, and Texas Instruments, to mention only a few. Similarly, a number of federal agencies use this form of teleconferencing (including the Food and Drug Administration, the Environmental Protection Agency, the Army, and many others). All such large organizations have frequent needs for unique kinds of conferences among managers and others. It is far cheaper to conduct them via video conferencing than to try to get people together face-to-face.

The advantages of the video conference over any of the other technologies lie in the fact that it provides richer messages with both verbal and nonverbal elements. That is, people can both see and hear each other in an approximation of what their experience would be if they were all face-to-face in the same room. Thus, relatively effective role-taking, feedback, and the use of nonverbal cues are possible. Also, a feature that is shared by none of the other teleconferencing media is that video permits people to see various kinds of graphics, film clips, or displays of physical objects. For example, if a new product is under discussion, it can be shown on screen. In a medical setting, even delicate surgery can be performed in such a way that it is entirely visible to receivers—sometimes in a better way than if they were right in the operating room. The video conference, then, is an effective system in cases where the issues under discussion are time-sensitive, where interactivity is both important and useful, and where the discussion can be significantly enhanced by the video.[27]

On the other hand, video conferencing has significant cost disadvantages. Expensive equipment and trained technical personnel are needed. The medium consists of special cameras, satellite modems plus uplinks and downlinks, special rooms, lights, complex receivers and transmitters. In some cases it is necessary to "scramble and unscramble" the signals—in legal, military, and industrial uses. That adds significantly to the cost of equipment and services. On the other hand, advances in technology are rapidly bringing all of these costs down, and the use of video conferencing will continue to increase very rapidly.

Video conferences are less convenient than those that are based on computer networks or audio systems. Not only must the participants assemble in a special video facility, but technicians need up to 3 hours to get everything properly tuned and working flawlessly. In addition, some of the transmission systems now in use can be sensitive to weather. Thus, a conference can be arranged, but a rain or snow storm may cause some of the signal to be garbled or even lost.

Despite these limitations, many large organizations have found that video conferencing provides a rich communication experience that cannot be duplicated using other media. They are particularly useful for universities with numerous campuses where video systems transmit courses, seminars, and special events. For example, the state of New York funded SUNYSAT, an interactive satellite network that links the 64 campuses that make up the state's university system. This facility greatly enriches the educational resources available to students and faculty in the entire state system. In Alaska, RATNET (Rural Alaska Television Network) reaches over 200 villages that are so remote they are not served by roads. However, they have generators and within-village television cable systems by which they not only can receive regular programs but can engage in teleconferencing as well. In such settings it would be very difficult to bring people together for a face-to-face meeting.

Even newer systems have been developed for displaying multiple photo images on a desktop computer screen. They promise to be much cheaper to use. The screen is divided into sections, and the face of each participant appears live in one section. Thus, a person sitting at a desktop computer, connected with phone lines, can engage in a small-group discussion with four or five others without ever leaving his or her desk. Graphs or other data can also be displayed in one section. The simplicity and limited cost of this system promises to revolutionize teleconferencing.

With the various media we have discussed now available to extend and enrich the means by which we can communicate quickly and over large distances, we must ask how these will have an influence on the human condition. Given the hardware, and the ability to cover the costs, we can now choose among several ways to communicate easily with most people on our planet. As we move into the next century, the media we use will become more efficient and effective in enabling us to share meanings with even larger numbers of people. Will we be brought closer together by that ability, or as some critics fear, will the new communication technologies enable a minority of human beings to become information rich while the vast majority remain outside these systems and information poor? Furthermore, as teleconferencing becomes commonplace, the airline, hotel, and restaurant industries will suffer and travel to attend conferences will decline significantly. Thus, new media will again bring significant changes to our society.

Chapter Review

■ We are living in an age of swiftly changing and developing communication technology. Among these changes is an increasing use of rapid communication devices for both interpersonal and public communication. At the same time, traditional written media—letters and memoranda—remain important in our society.

■ Communicating with media is a different experience than doing so face-to-face. While message formulation and the reconstruction of meaning through the use of language are still involved, some elements of the communication process are absent or severely curtailed when people use media to communicate. The most obvious are opportunities for role-taking and the availability of feedback.

■ New media of communication alter the communication process itself. Each new medium imposes special requirements on the ways in which messages are formulated; it controls the speed and convenience with which information is transmitted or recorded; and it influences ways in which receivers reconstruct meanings from the messages they receive. New media also lead to significant changes in the social, economic, and cultural features of society.

■ Letters and memoranda remain the traditional media of choice for many communication needs. The letter is a simple and portable medium which allows for careful formulation of messages that can be read at the convenience and preferred pace of the receiver. The memorandum is mainly a medium of organizational communication, where a permanent record seems desirable. Both letters and memoranda have specific advantages and disadvantages.

■ The telephone, along with associated devices such as answering machines and voice-mail networks, continues to be one of the most widely used and important media in our society. It is so familiar that people often fail to follow appropriate norms of usage—procedures that can make it a more effective means of communication. An old medium (fax) using long-distance lines is now gaining in popularity as a means of transmitting written messages quickly and inexpensively.

■ Increasing use is being made of computer networks of various sizes and complexities for the transmission of many categories of information. Electronic mail is typed into a sender's computer, sent over a network, and recorded by the receiver's computer to be read on screen at his or her convenience. E-mail is very fast and convenient, and it is beginning to replace slower, paper media for many purposes. As larger networks become available, people will soon be able to exchange written messages even more rapidly on a worldwide basis.

■ Teleconferencing refers to the use of media to overcome distance and link people so that they can communicate with each other in ways that approximate a face-to-face discussion or meeting. This can be done with the use of computer networks, by audio conferencing with telephone systems, or by video conferencing that closely approximates the conditions of a face-to-face meeting with people in the same room. Each method has its advantages, disadvantages, and effective uses.

Key Terms

Audio conferencing   Connecting people by long-distance telephone lines (sometimes with the parties in special rooms where they can make use of good-quality speakers) so that they can talk to each other to hold a conference or meeting.

Computer network   A number of computers linked together by wires or a radio system so that their users can transmit files of data or other information and messages from one to another. Some are local and serve a given organization. Others are large-scale and reach many sites in a country.

Computer teleconferencing   Using a computer network for the purpose of enabling people at diverse sites to communicate in the manner of holding a meeting or conference. This permits them to type messages for each other that can be read on each of their screens.

E-mail   A system for sending and receiving typed messages on a computer network. It consists of software that permits word processing and hardware that allows a message to be displayed on the screen of a sending person and to be sent to a receiver's computer (where it can be displayed on his or her screen and be stored in the memories of the computers at each end).

Fax (or facsimile)   An electronic device for reading, transmitting, and reproducing documents, graphics, or photographs over long-distance telephone lines.

Gateway   A computer that receives transmitted information from one network, reformats it if necessary, and feeds it into another network in a form that it can accept.

Information   Physical events that span distance, such as sound or light waves, electronic impulses, or electromagnetic radiations, into which symbols or other signs are encoded when source persons speak, write, or use electronic media to transmit messages to receivers.

Medium   Any device, simple or complex, that extends the distance or time over which people can communicate. Media carry or store information into which symbols are encoded by senders and decoded by receivers.

Memorandum   From the Latin *memoro,* meaning "to call to mind." A stylized written document, widely used in organizational communication for the purposes of transmitting significant messages to one or more receivers.

Technologies   The application of physical, electric, or electronic principles so as to produce working devices that accomplish some purpose. In communication, the use of such principles to produce media that extend the ability of human beings to communicate swiftly over long distances.

Teleconferencing   From the Greek word *tele,* meaning "at a distance." The use of media to link spatially dispersed people for the purpose of communicating in ways that to some degree approximate the conditions of a face-to-face conference or meeting.

Video conferencing   The use of video cameras, long-distance cables, or satellite relays and television screens so as to enable people to see and talk to each other in a close approximation to having them face-to-face in the same room.

Voice-mail network   A telephone-based system in which a network of users share a sophisticated answering machine so that they can leave and store messages for others and themselves.

Notes

1. Czitron, D. J. (1982). *Media and the American mind* (p. 6). Chapel Hill: University of North Carolina Press. This book offers valuable insights into the social and cultural impact of three new media: the telegraph, motion pictures, and radio.

2. Stephens, M. (1988). *History of news* (p. 259). New York: Viking.

3. Thoreau, H. D. (1854). *Walden, or life in the woods* (pp. 148–149). Boston and New York: Houghton Mifflin.

4. Cooley, C. H. (1909). *Social organization: A study of the larger mind* (p. 63). Boston: Scribner's Sons.

5. (1889). The intellectual effects of electricity. *The Spectator, 63,* 631–632.

6. Pallen, C. B. (1866). Newspaperism. *Lippincott's Monthly, 38.*

7. Innis, H. A. (1950). *Empire and communications.* London: Oxford University Press. The major thesis of this classic work is that Rome was able to coordinate large military conquests and maintain control over a vast empire with centralized bureaucratic administration because written orders, reports, and other documents could be sent to colonial centers in written form via portable media.

8. *The Syracuse Post Standard,* Dec. 1, 1990, p. A-6. In New York City, overnight deliveries arrived on time in only a dismal 46.94% of the cases. For the whole northeast it was 71.12%. Nationwide the figure for all categories of delivery was 80.61%.

9. For an extended treatment of the art of writing effective business and professional letters, see: Treece, M. (1986). *Communication for business and the professions* (pp. 50–101). Boston: Allyn & Bacon.

10. The word *memorandum* derives from the Latin *memor,* which means "with a good memory." Two spellings for the plural of memorandum are widely used. One is the Latin *memoranda,* and the other is formed in the English manner by simply adding an "s" to make *memorandums.* Either is considered correct, and the choice is a matter of personal preference.

11. For a detailed history of the early years of the telephone see: Casson, H. N. (1910). *The History of the Telephone.* Chicago: McClurg & Co.

12. de Sola Pool, I. (1977). *The social impact of the telephone.* Cambridge, MA: MIT Press.

13. Parker, E. S. (1991). Computer conferencing offers boundless geography, time. *Journalism Educator, 45,* 49–55.

14. Markoff, J. (1990). Digital fetes the "germ" that began a revolution. *The New York Times,* Dec. 16, Bus. sec., p. 11.

15. This brief history of the development of networks is based on an article entitled "Creating a Giant Computer Highway," by J. Markoff, that appeared in *The New York Times* business section, Sept. 2, 1990.

16. This example is based on the following: (1990). Taming the wild network. *Business Week,* Oct. 8, p. 144.

17. Mirabito, M. M., & Morgenstern, B. L. (1990). *The new communications technologies* (pp. 48–49). Boston: Focal Press. See also: Greenfield, D. (1989). Chasing the light: Fiber optic LAN's for today and tomorrow. *LAN* Magazine, Aug., 63–78.

18. Stoll, C. (1990). *The cuckoo's egg: Tracking a spy through the maze of computer espionage* (New York: Doubleday, 1990). This remarkable book is highly recommended as both entertainment and as a means of understanding the scope of computer networks in use today.

19. Markoff, J. (1988). Sharing the supercomputers. *The New York Times,* Dec. 29, sec. D, p. 1.

20. Shapiro, E. (1991). Can Prodigy be all things to 15 million PC owners? *The New York Times,* June 2, Bus. sec., p. F4.

21. Lewis, P. H. (1990). On electronic bulletin boards, what rights are at stake? *The New York Times,* Dec. 23, Bus. sec., p. 8.

22. Anderson, A. (1988). The etiquette of electronic mail. *Perspective, 12*(3), pp. 1–5.

23. Rice, R. E. (1984). Commentary. In F. Williams, *The New Communications* (pp. 207–208). Belmont, CA: Wadsworth.

24. Rogers, E. M. (1986). *Communication technology: The new media in society* (p. 51). New York: Free Press.

25. This section has benefited greatly from an unpublished paper entitled "Interactive Systems Via Satellite," by Shannon Connors. The authors are grateful for her assistance.

26. Such "talking heads" are the most frequently used format for a video conference. However, they are also the least interesting. Many authorities advise using displays, charts, graphs, or other visual material to relieve this monotony. See: Widner, D. (1986). *Teleguide* (p. 48); Washington, DC: Public Service Satellite Consortium.

27. Ibid., p. 3.

Additional Readings

Hiemstra, G. (1982). Teleconferencing, concern for face, and organizational culture. In M. Burgoon (Ed.), *Communication yearbook 6* (pp. 874–901). Beverly Hills, CA: Sage.

This article reviews the literature on interactive technologies and reports the results of an investigation into the use of politeness in communication mediated by interactive information technologies. Results of the study indicate that interactive technologies influence perceptions of politeness and that these media appear to impact the culture where they are employed.

Komsky, S. H. (1991). A profile of users of electronic mail in a university: Frequent versus occasional users. *Management Communication Quarterly, 4,* 310–340.

This article reports the results of an investigation of factors that differentiate among frequent and occasional users of electronic mail. Results indicate that users are characterized by: preference for telephony and electronic mail, perception that users are required to use electronic mail in their jobs, degree to which use is for oneself or to send or receive messages for others, perception of system problems, and the ease of teaching someone else to use the system.

Parker, E. S. (1991). Computer conferencing offers boundless geography, time. *Journalism Educator, 45,* 49–55.

This is an excellent discussion of current computer conferencing opportunities. The author clearly overviews the state of the art in conferencing, electronic mail, file transfers, and on-line databases. In explaining these alternatives careful consideration is given to free services, sending messages, interactive uses and media bulletin boards.

Williams, F., Hudson, H. E., & Stover, S. (1990). Communication technologies. In G. L. Dahnke & G. W. Clatterbuck (Eds.), *Human communication: Theory and research* (pp. 70–86). Belmont, CA: Wadsworth.

This essay on contemporary communication technologies describes how new media move signals, store information, and interact with users. The discussions outline basic theories for explaining technologies and trace the history of advances in this area. This essay also considers how theory and research are affected by media technology.

Williams, F., & Rice, R. E. (1983). Communication research and the new media technologies. In R. N. Bostrom (Ed.), *Communication yearbook 7* (pp. 200–224). Beverly Hills, CA: Sage.

This is an excellent review and discussion of the new communication technologies. The authors compare new and more traditional media. The emphasis of the discussion is on the personal dimension of various media. Personal qualities and group and organizational considerations are used to illustrate media differences.

Part Three

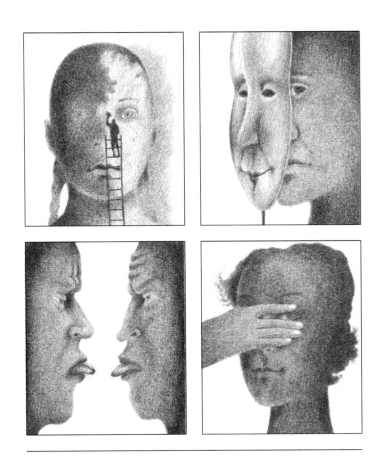

Managing Personal Communication Processes

Part 3 of this book focuses on four important problems with which everyone must cope as a communicator in daily life. In these chapters the book moves from a more theoretical and analytical discussion to a more applied orientation. It discusses how to present oneself effectively, ways to influence other people, how to manage and cope with such problems as stereotypes and conflicts, and how to overcome shyness and apprehension.

Chapter 9 brings together a large body of research and theory from which practical guidelines are derived to tell us how people form initial impressions of us. The chapter suggests a number of ways to help us present ourselves positively so that other people will form favorable initial impressions of us.

In Chapter 10, the important area of persuasion is reviewed. A large body of theory and research is analyzed to obtain guidelines as to how we can effectively influence others. This speaks to the ever-present problems of changing people's beliefs, attitudes, and behavior about issues or topics that we regard as important.

One of the inescapable features of dealing with other people is that, in a society of diversity, conflicts are sure to rise. Chapter 11 examines the nature of conflict, many of its common causes, and a number of strategies for dealing with it once it has occurred. A systematic set of guidelines is offered that can reduce tensions and conflicts between people.

Chapter 12 recognizes that communicating with others may be distressing in almost any context. Overcoming shyness and apprehension about communicating is a common problem to everyone, regardless of their gender or other personal characteristics. It is a particularly significant problem when an individual has to make a formal presentation before a group.

Chapter 9

Presenting Oneself Effectively

Contents

The Impressions We Make in Initial Encounters
What Research Tells Us About Initial Impressions
  The process of presenting one's self
  The principle of rapid impression formation
  The principle of the salient characteristic
  The labeling principle
  The "implicit personality" principle
Problems in Initial Encounters
  Common difficulties when meeting people
  Meeting one person versus several
  Familiar versus unfamiliar places

Presenting Yourself in Encounters That Really Matter
Goals in First Meetings
Preselecting Your Impressions
  The significance of selective perception
  Developing a preliminary game plan
Sizing Up People
  Attributing motives to others
  "Typical" behavior as a basis for attribution

Social constraints as factors in attribution
Getting People to Like You
  Affinity-seeking strategies
  Selecting strategies

Deciding What to Say
Self-Disclosure in Initial Encounters
Talking with New People
  Greetings
  Small talk
  The main topic

Changing Old Impressions
The Inflexible Nature of Preexisting Impressions
Resistance to Change
Constructing New Realities

Chapter Review

Key Terms

Notes

Additional Readings

Key Questions

- What really happens when someone meets you for the first time? Do they try to understand what you are like deep inside; or do they just form a quick impression of you and then relate to you on that basis?

- When you meet someone for the first time, do they observe some obvious feature of your appearance or behavior and then use that to construct a larger set of impressions of what you are like? If so, is the result likely to be flattering or demeaning?

- What kind of clues do you use when you first meet someone and initially "size them up" so as to relate to them appropriately? Are these particularly reliable as guides to what people are actually like? How can you do a better job at these initial assessments?

- What are some reliable ways you can use to get people to like you when you first meet? Are there communication strategies that will result in people forming a good impression of you and wanting to continue to relate to you in positive ways?

■ How can you change an unfortunate impression people have of you from previous encounters? Are there communication strategies that can dispel a negative image they may have formed and then get them to have a better opinion of you?

When an individual enters the presence of others, they commonly seek to acquire information about him. . . . They will be interested in his general socio-economic status, his conception of self, his attitude toward them, his competence, his trustworthiness, etc. . . . Information about the individual helps to define the situation, enabling others to know in advance what they may expect of him.

Irving Goffman
1959

Jim was nervous about meeting Maria's parents. Ever since they had become serious about their relationship, and especially after he proposed, Jim knew that this day would come. Now it was actually here because they were about to arrive. All during the 3-hour drive from the city, Jim thought about ways he could make a good impression on them from the start. He understood completely that what he looked like, how he acted, and what he had to say in the first few minutes of this important meeting, were likely to influence her parents' judgment of their future son-in-law for a long time to come.

In planning for the meeting, Jim had considered a number of factors that could influence the impression he would make. For one thing, he anticipated (correctly as it turned out) that Maria's parents would be different from most of the people they knew in the city and that their ideas about language, dress, and appropriate behavior between males and females would be based on an older and more conservative set of values. Jim did not want to misrepresent anything, but he agreed with Maria that they should not disclose they had a premarital relationship of complete intimacy. He agreed that he would occupy a guest bedroom and that Maria would sleep in her old room.

From what Maria had told him about her parents, they were quite religious and not exactly liberal in their political views. Jim decided to be cautious about discussing both his own rather thin religious background and his liberal political beliefs. The best strategy, he decided, was to avoid too much self-disclosure too quickly.

Jim knew also that physical appearance was going to be important, so he had made certain that his hair was neatly trimmed. He had dressed carefully for this first meeting. His clothes were casual, but his shoes and indeed everything about him looked very neat.

Suddenly they were there. Maria introduced him to "mama" and "papa," and he told them with a broad smile how much he had been looking forward to meeting them. He could see right away that they were "sizing him up," very carefully, and that they seemed to have formed at least an initially favorable impression. After they went inside and sat down, they talked a while about the trip up. Jim said how nice it was to get out of the city and how pleased he had been when they invited him. After a little small talk, he and Maria took their luggage to their separate rooms. Then lunch was ready, and they all sat down together as a family for the first time.

The lunch went well. Maria and her parents had a lot of catching up to do, and Jim did not have to carry much of the conversation at first. When it did turn to him, he was able to explain clearly the kind of work he did and how he and Maria had met. They both discussed their future plans. Both parents smiled a lot, and everyone seemed happy.

That night, when he and Maria were alone briefly, she told him that he had made a "big hit" with her parents and that they were both delighted that they were going to have such a nice son-in-law.

In today's multicultural world, the meeting between Jim and Maria's parents is hardly a unique situation. Whatever our background, we all face the problem of communicating a positive first impression every time we meet another person with whom we might want to have more than a fleeting relationship. First impressions are important when we meet someone we might want to date, make a presentation in a class, give a speech to a group of strangers, or interview for a new job.

While initial encounters proceed within the framework of the simultaneous transactions model that we discussed in Chapter 1, they also have a number of other important features that need detailed discussion. Therefore, in this chapter we will answer four major questions: First, how do people form impressions of other individuals when they are meeting them for the first time? Second, how can we influence the impressions others form about us when we have just met? Third, what specifically can we communicate, both verbally and nonverbally, to make the impressions others form about us more favorable? Finally, what can be done to change unfavorable impressions that people already have about us?

A good place to begin is with a review of communication research that has examined the general process of getting to know others and forming initial impressions. With the guidelines provided by such research in the background, we will then focus on what is involved in presenting ourselves to others in everyday life.

The Impressions We Make in Initial Encounters

It is very important to understand the whole process of how people get to know one another, both initially and in the longer term. Such understanding provides a foundation for developing skills for effective self-presentation. As we will see, this is not a simple process, and it involves a number of steps and considerations. Fortunately, scholars have spent decades studying what is involved when people undergo the process of getting to know each other. A number of practical guidelines can be derived from what those efforts have revealed.

What Research Tells Us About Initial Impressions

The broad area of investigation that focuses on the general stages people pass through when they first meet and develop initial impressions of each other is called *person perception*. A simple definition of the concept has been advanced by Renato Tagiuri. He maintains that person perception refers to "the processes by which a person comes to know and to think about other persons, their characteristics, qualities, and inner states."[1] This brief definition is so broad that the concept of person perception covers more than we need to consider for our present purposes. We do not need to review the entire body of

knowledge that has been developed on all aspects of person perception. For our purposes we will focus more specifically on the steps involved in what has been called *presentation of self.*

The process of presenting one's self   The term *self* was explained at length in Chapter 5. Generally, it refers to the pattern of beliefs, meanings, and understandings each of us has developed through communicating with others concerning our own nature and worth as a human being. The idea of **presentation of self** refers to formulating and transmitting verbal and nonverbal messages *to* other people about what kind of person we are. It is therefore a communication process that proceeds acording to the linear and simultaneous transactions models that we set forth in Chapter 1.

Our transmissions concerning ourselves may be deliberate or completely unwitting. In other words, as we talk, dress, or act in various ways we communicate *meanings* about our personal qualities. Thereby we "present" that information about our inner nature to others. From these messages those others construct interpretations or impressions as to what we are "really like." It works both ways, of course, as we form impressions of other individuals during our initial encounters with them. It is, as we will see, a universal and inescapable form of human behavior.

In our initial encounters, we do not always intend to get other individuals to evaluate us in a particular way. However, if we want to do so it is certainly possible to *plan* a communication strategy and transmit verbal and nonverbal messages that are deliberately designed to create a particular set of impressions. Irving Goffman referred to this process as **impression management.**[2] In this chapter, we refer to such management as "effective self-presentation." Such messages are effective insofar as they cause others to evaluate us in ways we desire. In later sections, we will address specific strategies for accomplishing this goal.

There is little doubt that what an individual says and does during an initial encounter leaves lasting impressions. In other words, the verbal and nonverbal messages we transmit as we are getting to know someone can strongly influence what that person comes to believe about us. There is also little doubt that those early impressions may be very difficult to change. For these reasons, presentation of self can be a serious business on which both personal and social success can depend.

To develop an understanding in greater depth of the relationship between initial encounters and person perception, some of the classic experiments on how people

In our initial encounters with people we are meeting for the first time, such as new neighbors or other associates, they will immediately form an impression of what we are like as a person. These first impressions are very important for future relationships and are difficult to change later. People's earliest interpretations of what we are like are based on the meanings we encode in what we say, how we dress, and how we act, and they provide the basis for the other person to like or dislike us from the beginning.

form impressions of others provide important insights. A brief review of some of the principles discovered in early research on the topic can show us how the process works. This in turn suggests several important guidelines we need to use in order to improve our ability to manage our impressions—that is, to present ourselves effectively to others.

The principle of rapid impression formation   Of the pioneering research on impression formation, the work of Solomon Asch in the 1940s was by far the most significant.[3] At the time, Asch was conducting experiments to try to find out how a person infers *unknown* things about another person from a limited amount of *known* information. (Obviously, this is related to the idea of forming impressions of a person one has just met.)

The method Asch employed to conduct his series of landmark experiments was quite innovative. It focused directly on the problem of examining how a person forms first impressions of other people. The typical investigation in Asch's research program was set up so that each participant or subject received a list of *descriptive words* said to characterize a "target person"—an individual whom the subject had never actually met. All the subject had was the list of words said to describe the otherwise un-

known person. However, after reviewing the words, each subject was asked to write a paragraph describing their *first impressions* of what that target person was like. Then each subject was given a *second* list of descriptive terms and asked to indicate those they felt would also be likely to characterize the person they had already described. Each did so, thereby revealing in greater detail their overall impressions of the target person.

Thus, in this second step, Asch was able to gather each subject's early impressions of the target person formed on the basis of very limited information supplied in the first step. Since early impressions in real life are formulated during initial meetings, this simple experiment represented that process. What was revealed was that subjects quickly formed relatively elaborate impressions of the target after receiving only very limited information about that individual.

In another of Asch's classic experiments, additional aspects of the process were shown. Again, subjects were provided with lists of descriptive terms and asked to form an impression of a target person. This time, however, the list described the target quite positively as intelligent, skillful, industrious, determined, practical, and cautious. Each of the subjects was then asked to write their paragraph about the target person. After these paragraphs were completed, the subjects were asked to assess that same individual in terms of *four additional attributes:* generosity, happiness, good-naturedness, and importance.

The results of this experiment were striking: More than half (55%) of the responding subjects reported that the target person would be "generous." An even larger proportion (71%) felt that the target person would be "happy." The target was also rated high in terms of being "good-natured" (69%) and "important" (88%). Thus, the experiment seemed to show that if the target was thought to have one set of favorable qualities, subjects believed that he or she had others.

The principle of the salient characteristic   In still another experiment of this type, Asch inserted the descriptive word *warm* in the middle of his first list of characteristics (used by the subjects to write their descriptive paragraphs). What happened was that their initial impressions were different because of the word *warm.* Subjects who received this characteristic rated the target person much more favorably. They overwhelmingly reported that the target would be "generous" (91%), "happy" (90%), "good-natured" (94%), and "important" (88%). Thus, adding a single known **salient characteristic** sharply altered initial impressions of the target person to a considerably more favorable image. This "principle of the salient characteristic" from the Asch experiments is important, and we will come back to it later in this chapter.

Asch was concerned that this substantial change in impressions would occur only when an emotionally positive quality, such as "warm," was introduced. Therefore, as a check on this, he did still another experiment using the same procedures. However, this time he substituted the opposite word, *cold,* in place of *warm.* The favorability of the final ratings of the target dropped sharply! Only a very small number (8%) of the subjects rated the target person as "happy." About a third (34%) thought he was "generous," and fewer (17%) indicated that he was "good-natured," but virtually all (99%) thought the target was "important." Thus, this final experiment strongly confirmed the principle of the salient characteristic.

To interpret these differences in the ways his subjects perceived the person under these various conditions, Asch concluded that the words *warm* and *cold* had served as strong focuses of attention for the subjects. That is, these rather emotionally meaningful terms did indeed become salient characteristics around which the subjects organized their overall impressions of the target person. The more bland words, used in the first step to describe

target persons, implied a rather positive general impression of temperament and social acceptability. But when the more powerful words *warm* and *cold* were introduced, the resulting impressions were restructured considerably.

All in all, the results of Asch's research provide us with valuable hypotheses as to how people form impressions of others. While we cannot conclude that such experiments represent real-life situations, their findings imply that when individuals meet a stranger they quickly bring together a kind of initial configuration of impressions of that person on the basis of the information they have. However, a single bit of significant information—particularly a salient characteristic—can alter that pattern considerably.

These principles make a lot of sense. All of us quickly form initial patterns of impressions of individuals whom we have just met. We do not base these impressions on single facts, but on all of their verbal and nonverbal messages—what they say, their actions, and their appearance. However, even a single additional message can rapidly alter our total first impression of another during the critical initial stages of getting to know that person.

This principle does operate in real life. When we meet someone who seems to have many attractive qualities, our initial pattern of impressions is positive. Then a single additional revelation suddenly changes the picture rather drastically. Such salient characteristics might be that the person has a serious disease, uses drugs, or has a criminal record. Upon fitting that into the configuration, our impressions switch immediately to a negative pattern.

The labeling principle   Researchers who study deviant behavior have extensively discussed the "salient characteristic" phenomenon. They have observed it not just in terms of experiments with words but also through observations of the way people in real life respond to individuals who transgress accepted moral norms. They call the principle the **labeling theory.**[4] It is essentially the same idea as the Asch principle. For example, if you learn that Johnny, your son Eddie's friend down the street, was picked up by the police and charged with swiping candy bars, he has suddenly become a "problem child," or worse, a "juvenile delinquent." Such labels identify new salient characteristics that bring with them emotionally charged meanings.[5]

The label "juvenile delinquent" in our culture is associated with switch-blade knives, mugging old people, early drug and alcohol use, and the like. Perhaps Johnny had never before done anything bad, and never will again, but his 10-second act of shoplifting can label him in a very serious way. It is no doubt very unfair. But one thing is certain, after hearing that Johnny has become a "juvenile delinquent," your son Eddie will now be forbidden to play with him!

The basic idea, then, is that one critical piece of information about a person can communicate a powerful message. Labels often supply such information, regardless of whether they are right or wrong. Any pejorative label, such as "former mental patient," "suspected sex offender," "unfair professor," "cheater," or "plagiarist," can have a dramatic and negative influence on the impressions people form. The label is like a magnet bringing people to dump on you the cultural meanings associated with it whether you deserve them or not.

The "implicit personality" principle   During the 1950s and 1960s, social scientists continued to use the experimental strategy developed by Asch. They followed up his study of the strong influence that can be exerted by a small amount of information on shaping or reshaping people's overall impressions of others.[6] They tried to determine just *how* people combine different kinds of information about a person into an overall configuration of beliefs about that individual—moving from one kind of information to another. In particular, two issues came under close investigation: (1) What kinds of overall *patterns* of impressions do people construct about individuals whom they have just met? and (2) What kinds of characteristics are *central* to such a pattern of impressions?

Thus, they were concerned about how people put together their early patterns of impressions about a person, quickly making a set of assumptions about the nature of the individual on the basis of what they know up to that point. They were also concerned with the way in which some readily observable (salient) characteristic comes to be seen as more important or central and how others are interpreted as less essential. In other words, how do people "construct" a personality for someone they have just met, and on the basis of limited data, project it onto an individual to form a pattern of impressions?

This line of investigation came to be called **implicit personality theory.** When we discussed the general meaning of the term *personality* in Chapter 6, we explained that it refers to a pattern of psychological attributes that makes each individual human being different or unique and that those traits are thought to shape people's responses to their physical and social world. Thus, the reason we form impressions of another person, constructing our interpretation of their "implicit" personality, is that we are trying to predict in our own mind how they will behave toward us and others.

An investigation by John Wishner clearly illustrates

The principle of the salient characteristic indicates that some unusual feature of another person will be the first thing we notice about someone we meet for the first time. That salient characteristic will then provide the central organizing feature for the immediate development of an overall impression of what the person is like. If the salient characteristic seems positive, we generally will like the individual. If not, a more negative initial impression may be formed.

implicit personality research.[7] Using Asch's approach directly, he reasoned that when responding to a target person, the central characteristics of "warm" and "cold" would have the greatest influence on those personal characteristics that were most related to the personality traits that they imply. For example, the characteristic "strong" is not particularly related to either "warm" or "cold." In contrast, the attribute of "friendly" is definitely related to "warm." That is, warm and friendly fit together very well, but cold and friendly do not. Thus, adding warm to the list of terms about a person should raise estimates of friendliness, whereas adding cold could be expected to reduce them.

To test this hypothesis, Wishner had a group of college students rate their professors on a list of personal characteristics. The terms *warm* and *cold* were added, as in the Asch experiments. An examination of the students' evaluations of their professors showed that the characteristics which were most strongly affected when warm or cold were added were those traits in the list which the students perceived to be most highly related to the general idea of warm and cold. Also important, the results indicated that for characteristics that were not related to each other, impressions of the target person were not influenced.

The results of Wishner's experiments imply that the overall pattern of impressions of a particular individual can be predicted from the *relationships* between the list of characteristics that the target person is first thought to possess. In other words, people construct a relatively well organized pattern of what they think is important about someone on the basis of very few facts. Furthermore, certain kinds of characteristics have a truly powerful in-

Labeling theory indicates that authorities often apply negative labels to people that can have very serious consequences. Such terms as "shoplifter," "drunk," or "prostitute" may or may not accurately describe the behavior committed by an individual. However, such terms can permanently stigmatize the person with culturally defined meanings. If that label comes into use in the individual's community, the person becomes "damaged goods" whether or not the label accurately describes what happened.

fluence on the "implicit personality" that they project onto the target person. This is important because that quickly constructed "personality" will strongly influence both their subsequent evaluations of and their actions toward that individual.

The findings of studies like those of Asch and Wishner are consistent with extensive observations of people in everyday life. It may not be particularly comforting to realize that certain of *your* salient characteristics will be observed very quickly by people when they first meet you. They will then use these characteristics as the central features of a rather elaborate set of assumptions about your nature and probable behavior. Those salient characteristics may be visible indicators of racial, ethnic, or cultural differences. Or they may be mannerisms, speech patterns, labels, modes of dress, hair length, or some other prominent and visible feature.[8] Obviously, one must wonder, what are my salient characteristics? Are they flattering or demeaning? Furthermore, what kind of implicit personality do others project onto *me* on the basis of a few central attributes? Is it one that truly represents me, or is it some grossly distorted image of me? Above

all, can I control or "manage" the kind of personality assumptions that others make about me?

These are truly important questions. They suggest that if it is important to us that others evaluate us positively, close attention must be paid to the *management* of initial impressions. If one is concerned at all, self-presentation cannot be left to chance. If little attention is paid to the initial impressions we make, people may make a host of incorrect and perhaps even grossly unfair assumptions about us. Furthermore, as we will see, these assumptions will be difficult to change.

Before turning directly to specific ways in which self-presentation can be managed more effectively, we will review briefly several additional features of initial encounters that research has clarified.

Problems in Initial Encounters

We need to look closely at three additional considerations that have an influence on the outcome when people meet and undergo the process of getting to know each other. The first consideration is *common problems* that people face when they meet for the first time. Any of these are likely to have an influence on the presentation of self. Some are obvious and widely understood, whereas others are so subtle that the participants may not even be aware they exist, let alone how they can influence the outcome of their encounter. Second, the *number of people* present in an initial encounter can be an important consideration. Whether we meet one person or several changes the factors that can make first meetings more or less difficult to handle. Finally, the *context* or setting in which people meet can play a significant role in determining both their strategies and the probability of success in their presentations of self and the impression they make in initial encounters.

Common difficulties when meeting people   If we were to worry about all of the potential problems that can come up during first encounters, we would no doubt be left with a feeling of hopelessness about ever successfully meeting anyone. In fact, there is such a long list that if we really thought about it, we might very well want to consider being hermits![9] For the sake of keeping our optimism high, we must assume that it is possible to learn to handle effectively the difficulties associated with initial encounters. In order to learn how to do this, let us consider a list of common problems that are encountered when meeting people for the first time:

- Finding things in common with strangers
- Finding things to say to strangers

- Not knowing how to say things appropriately
- Meeting people you just don't like
- Meeting people who just don't like you
- Adjusting to language differences
- Adjusting to different backgrounds of experience
- One- or two-way communication apprehension
- Feeling generally awkward
- Feeling self-conscious
- Feeling alienated from others
- Worrying about saying the wrong thing

Now let us place these potential difficulties into the context of a "worst case" first meeting. The scene is a party: Pedro and Elisa have just been introduced. Pedro is from a small town in Texas, and Elisa comes from Los Angeles. Both are new to the area, and so they really want to make some friends. Each is anxious to make a positive first impression. During the first few moments of their meeting they both react positively and are even physically attracted to each other. Each sees the other as about the same age, obviously intelligent, about right in height, with the same hair and skin color. Neither has acne, bad breath, dirty fingernails, a detectable body odor, an unfortunate label—or any other salient characteristic around which an unfavorable implicit personality can be instantly organized. So far, so good! All things considered, Pedro and Elisa should be able to get along just fine. So, rather than politely disengaging and moving on, each decides to try to carry on a friendly conversation—engaging in effective self-presentation, hoping that it just might lead to a pleasant outcome.

Unfortunately, as their conversation begins, things begin to go downhill. The first problem they encounter is that they really don't seem to share much of anything. They have difficulty in finding things to say to each other, and there are a lot of long and noticeable pauses in their conversation. The more difficult the meeting becomes for each, the more frustrated they are by the whole situation. Yet they do not give up. Each continues to try to find things out about the other. Both ask questions and probe as best they can, but it doesn't work. The encounter is falling on its face.

After a few more minutes of discomfort, it becomes apparent that they are both being very careful about how they are communicating with each other for fear of saying the wrong thing and being misunderstood. Neither Pedro nor Elisa want to prejudge the other. That is, each is obviously trying to avoid not being liked.

The more they talk, the more they discover that because they both come from very different backgrounds, they have had a variety of very different experiences.

Many commonly experienced difficulties can arise when meeting another person for the first time. Sometimes it is hard to find things to say; it can be difficult to decide what topics are appropriate; each party might feel self-conscious and awkward; there is always the danger of saying the wrong thing. Fortunately, most of these difficulties have been studied by communication researchers who have developed guidelines that can help in such initial encounters.

Moreover, they even seem to be using language differently. It sounds like they are both speaking English, but the words that are being used appear to be arousing very different connotations of meaning in each other. Each has to explain and apologize for meanings that were not intended. Although they both have parents of Hispanic origin, Elisa's language is from urban Southern California and Pedro's is from rural Texas.

By this time, each has constructed a pattern of impressions about the other. This now strongly influences how they speak and act. To Pedro, Elisa seems to be a very sophisticated city girl, probably with a lot of boyfriends, and he is afraid she will think he is just a dull country boy. To Elisa, Pedro seems very sincere but a bit old-fashioned and shy. She is afraid to say anything that will make her seem to be putting him down.

It also has become clear that both are apprehensive. Moreover, their apprehensiveness seems to be accentuated by having to communicate with a total stranger.

In other words, each feels awkward and self-conscious. So, the more they try to talk to each other, and the harder they try to get together, the worse they feel.

At this point, things are not looking good. It is obvious to each that there will be no lasting relationship between them. In fact, after about 20 minutes both Pedro and Elisa decide to give up. Their conversation just sort of dries up, and the noisy confusion of the party allows them to drift apart physically. Interestingly, if we were to ask either Pedro or Elisa who had the problem neither would be likely to accept fault.

It should be obvious from this vignette that Pedro's and Elisa's chances for a second meeting, let alone a lasting relationship, are near zero. In fact, about every problem in our earlier list was present. At the same time, it is important to point out that both had very good intentions. Both sincerely wanted to make an effective and positive presentation of self. However, "things just happened" that derailed what started as a promising encounter.

The fact is that things "just happen" in so many of our sincere efforts to communicate a good first impression to others. The bottom line of all this is that presenting ourselves effectively is a difficult job. It is not easy to communicate our preferred pattern of positive first impressions.

Returning to Pedro and Elisa, a fair question to ask about this first meeting would be: What (if anything) would have been different if more than the two people had been present? That is, what happens to the process of getting to know others when more than two individuals are involved in an initial encounter? In particular, how would this influence both the presentation of self and the resulting formation of impressions? Would it have helped the situation or made things worse?

Meeting one person versus several   Many situations involve more than two people meeting in an initial encounter. Examples are students and teachers walking into their classrooms for the first time, a recently hired employee going into an office full of people on the first day of work, or indeed any situation where people meet in groups.

We discussed the influence of group size in Chapter 6. This is also important in the context of a first encounter. As opposed to just two people, the dynamics of the situation are very different. For one thing, additional potential difficulties typically enter the picture.[10] This is not to say that encounters where more than two people are present are all negative. In some ways they can be easier. However, as we will try to show, the inclusion of additional individuals in the situation can have an influence on perception, evaluation, and the messages that are exchanged.[11]

To begin our analysis, let us first consider some of the typical problems that are created when more than two persons are present:

- Fragmenting participation and focuses of attention
- The problem of "you can't please everybody"
- Individual differences that create difficulties
- Perceptions of favoritism
- Speaking generally versus specifically to one person
- Coalitions among pairs
- Conversational intrusions and interruptions

With this list in mind, let us replay the scene with Pedro and Elisa. But this time we will assume that they encounter each other not in a pair by themselves but in a trio that includes Susan. They have all just been introduced at the party. In such a situation, the energies and focuses of attention will be spread across three people rather than just two.

In the new scene, Pedro and Elisa are introduced along with Susan, who is of about the same age. During the first moments of appraisal all three size each other up and reach the same conclusions. Initially, each is impressed favorably, and all is "go" for trying to get to know each other better. Therefore, each thinks that it is a good idea to try to engage in favorable presentations of self, just on the chance that a meaningful, long-term, friendly relationship might develop.

So, there they stand in a trio, surrounded by other people at the party. Just as Pedro begins to open the conversation with a question of where Elisa is from, Susan interrupts and asks Pedro's opinion about the latest football game, a topic about which she seems quite enthusiastic. After they spend a few moments listening to his negative opinions about spectator sports, Elisa tries to present a positive self-image to Pedro by telling him of her impressions of a recent symphony performance she had attended. Before he can comment favorably, Susan begins explaining *her* devotion to the latest rock group. It is clear that Susan's tastes are quite different. Both Pedro and Elisa now seem somewhat bored. They begin looking around the room to see what other possibly interesting people there might be at the party. However, they decide to try once again to learn more about each other. They begin discussing what restaurants each knows in the area. Susan, who also has been somewhat taken with Pedro, now senses that he has less interest in her than in Elisa. She feels a bit slighted, with just a twinge of jealousy. At this point she asks Pedro if he would mind getting her a fresh drink. Pedro, always the gentleman, agrees to do so. He leaves the trio to go to the bar. When he returns with the drink, Elisa is gone. She is now talking animatedly with another man in the far corner of the room. Pedro is disappointed and feels that he has been rejected. He decides he doesn't like the party and soon leaves.

This account illustrates several of the limitations inherent in trying to communicate positive impressions of self in conversations that involve more than two people. First, it is difficult to maintain a central focus on "getting to know you" when a third person introduces topics that derail such an effort. In Pedro's case, with two individuals interested in him, he could not be equally pleasing to both. Furthermore, it seemed that none of them had the same tastes. In such a situation, Elisa and Pedro could not concentrate on personal matters but had to discuss general topics (football, restaurants, music), rather than each other. In spite of all these difficulties, there was an inevitable "coalition of the triad" into an obvious pairing.[12] Susan, who was left out, perceived that to be favoritism and took action to disrupt it. Thus, with all the interruptions and intrusions, Pedro and Elisa never did get to know each other, and each went their separate ways.

Could anything have been done to improve the chances that what took place between Pedro and Elisa would have resulted in a more positive outcome? For example, if they had met in a different *place,* would the dynamics of this initial meeting have been altered and would the outcome of their encounter have been different? It is this contextual issue of *where* people meet that is the third and final contingency which we will consider among the factors that shape initial encounters.

Familiar versus unfamiliar places   The idea that *where* we meet people can influence the outcome of a meeting is scarcely new.[13] In Chapter 5 we discussed physical settings as part of communication contexts in our transactions model (p. 130). However, when this idea is linked to implicit personality theory, it becomes meaningful in terms of understanding what factors influence effective self-presentation.

There is little doubt that we feel more comfortable—physically, emotionally, and intellectually—in some places than in others.[14] Generally, we are more at ease in *familiar* surroundings. The importance of location, then, is that the physical surroundings where a person meets others can have a dramatic effect on how *capable* and *confident* the individual feels during that meeting. When manifested in behavior, those feelings can serve as salient

characteristics that help observers organize the pattern of personality characteristics they project onto the individual. Thus, persons who are seen as at ease, capable, and confident are also perceived in more positive terms overall than those who are thought to be inept and nervous. In this rather direct way, then, physical settings can help or hinder the outcome of self-presentation.

To illustrate this principle, let us refer once again to the initial encounter between Pedro and Elisa, but this time in terms of a different location. Earlier, we indicated that the initial meeting occurred in the unfamiliar context of a party—a place in which neither was particularly at ease. Suppose now that Pedro and Elisa had just met in a quiet lounge at the dorm where both were living. In such familiar physical surroundings they would have had something in common from the very start of their encounter. Clearly, that would have provided them with a basis for more easily finding out the many other things they had in common. In this way, their concern about liking or not being liked by the other would have been far less significant. In all likelihood, neither would have been guarded about talking to each other, and Elisa and Pedro would have had a basis for more easily dealing with their differences. Factors like their regionally associated languages would have become less central.

Unfortunately, people cannot always count on meeting others on familiar ground. When they do, however, it provides a sense of assurance about having successfully negotiated a complex social context. In other words, a familiar meeting place often has associated memories of previously successful self-presentations. The lessons learned from those efforts help greatly to communicate favorable impressions in the same surroundings the next time the need arises.

Presenting Yourself in Encounters That Really Matter

Thus far, this chapter has concentrated on several factors that are pertinent to getting to know other people and forming first impressions. What has been covered is by no means the whole story. However, we have purposely concentrated on essential issues that can enhance or limit the effectiveness of a person's presentation of self to others. Put simply, we now know that people tend quickly to form impressions of others based on a limited amount of information. Often, some central characteristic has a strong influence on that overall pattern of impressions. The number of people present can make a difference. Finally, physical settings often complicate the formation of first impressions.

These principles provide a good basis from which to develop *practical strategies* for the effective presentation of self. Our next task, therefore, is to move from a concentration on what researchers have concluded to a consideration of what is actually needed on an everyday basis to achieve the goal of managing people's impressions. We begin our discussion of those practical strategies by focusing first on the reasons for initiating a first meeting and how setting the stage properly for self-presentation can lead to positive results.

Goals in First Meetings

First, meetings can be either intentional or accidental. Furthermore, they can be organized as either very structured or completely open-ended. As was discussed previously, whether we like it or not, the social situation that we happen to be in defines the purpose of meeting people for the first time. That purpose might be a job interview, getting to know someone interesting that you have just seen across a crowded room, getting acquainted with the parents of a close friend, or giving a talk before a group. But whatever the nature of the encounter, having a clear idea as to *why* the meeting has been initiated can help in the selection of strategies, content, and style of delivery. In particular, in those meetings that can have an effect on our future, understanding every aspect of impression management in self-presentation can truly be important.

We have all had the experience of arranging to meet someone for the first time, and after leaving the encounter realizing that we did not present ourselves very effectively. This kind of failure can occur in any social context, but wherever it happens, at least part of the reason is often *poor planning*. Many people fail to realize how important it is to map out a deliberate strategy of self-presentation before an important meeting. Others sense the value of planning but feel that first meetings should be spontaneous and "fall together naturally." However, if the encounter is a critical one, planning in advance for self-presentation can lead to a more favorable outcome.

Obviously, in many social situations where we meet people little is at stake. If so, systematic and deliberate strategies for controlling the impressions of others probably are not needed or may even be out of place. Going to the supermarket and meeting the checkout clerk, or dealing with the waitress in a restaurant, is hardly an occasion that calls for strategic consideration of effective self-presentation. Similarly, when we are among people close to us—peers and family—we can indeed just "be

ourselves" and let it all fall together as it will. However, it is crucial to approach *those encounters that really count* with a thoughtfully formulated plan.

Developing a strategy for initiating and engaging in a social encounter is not as difficult as it may sound: First, before the encounter takes place, we must clarify for ourselves the goals to be achieved as a result of our presentation of self. Second, attention must be given to setting the stage to accomplish those goals. This means selecting strategies of self-presentation ahead of time that are most likely to accomplish those objectives.

What are the goals to be achieved in an important encounter? If we want that outcome to be favorable, there are three. Each is an important part of the self-presentation process, and the strategies we use to achieve them are all related to gaining greater *control* over the outcome. That is, we plan ahead to achieve effective control over:

1. The *earliest impressions* formed during initial moments of the contact. We explained earlier the critical nature of the first qualities others attribute to us. We need to ensure that some salient characteristic which can turn people off right away does not immediately spoil our identity.
2. The *expanding configuration of impressions* organized as our presentation of self unfolds. This is a result of systematic impression management, and it needs to be done with grace and style so as to produce a positive image of our qualities in the minds of observers.
3. The *lasting pattern of impressions* that the other party finally takes away. This is, of course, the "bottom line"—the more-or-less permanent "implicit personality" that observers attribute to us. It is the most important goal of all.

A very effective way to gain control over these outcomes is to know your objective ahead of time. Simply ask yourself: "What is it that I really want out of this meeting?" The answer may be obvious, like "getting the job." Or it may be something very different, such as entre into a particular social group, an experience with a member of the opposite sex, wanting to be assertive, or perhaps even getting paroled.[15] In any case, knowing clearly what you want in the first step makes that goal easier to attain. For one thing, defining the goal of an encounter ahead of time contributes to the design of the self-presentation strategy needed to attain it. Goal clarification, in other words, helps us identify the impressions that are most likely to contribute to success. Stated more simply, knowing what you want helps identify what it is that people need to believe about you.

Preselecting Your Impressions

In some first meetings, what you really want and how you want to be perceived may be virtually the same thing. For example, if you are running for public office, and will be speaking to groups of potential voters, you will want the audience to feel positively enough about you to cast their vote in your direction and to convince others to do the same. As you can see, what you really want (get elected) and how you want to be perceived (be liked) are closely linked.

It is important, then, to communicate those characteristics that count in the situation so that they will be quickly and unmistakably perceived and understood by those on the receiving end. We see politicians do this all the time. A candidate will don a farmer's cap and an informal jacket and use a "country folks" speech style when addressing a rural audience. The next day, when addressing a group of bankers, the same candidate will be dressed in a conservative suit and will use a different vocabulary. Still later it will be hard hat, blue shirt, and macho talk when making a speech to factory hands. Few of us need to go to such lengths in our personal presentations of self, but the principle is there. Strategies can be used in a more subtle way to preselect certain kinds of impressions that we want to create so as to achieve our goals. As we will discuss later, this can be done through selection of clothing, vocabulary, message content, demeanor, and many other alternatives.

There are two major reasons why preselection of qualities that can create positive impressions is not particularly difficult. The first is that *everyone has many positive qualities*. Each of us, no matter what our gender, race, ethnic identity, cultural background, age, body shape, educational background, and so on, has a long list of favorable characteristics that will be of genuine interest to others. The real task is to understand those attributes and to demonstrate them in appropriate ways through verbal and nonverbal communication. At the same time, pitfalls do exist. All of us have dull, unimportant, and undistinguished characteristics that if arbitrarily communicated in the wrong situation, can be boring or misread in such a way that they will contribute to a negative and inaccurate impression. An important part of the task of effective self-presentation is to minimize such potentially negative influences.

The second feature of the process of meeting someone for the first time that works in favor of creating positive impressions is the simple fact that *most people tend to like other people*. Unless there is something obvious that quickly turns them off, the cards are stacked *for* a favorable impression at the outset in most encounters, rather than *against* such an outcome. The real trick is to identify and maximize the impact of our positive features and to minimize those potentially troublesome salient characteristics that are so important in initial impression formation.

From the principle of salient characteristics and implicit personality theory, we know that first impressions tend to be lasting. However, lasting or not, it is difficult to explain just how people immediately pick out some particular characteristic from an individual's presentation of self that they decide is salient and then organize other attributes or qualities around that factor. What we are referring to is the universal tendency of *selective perception* that is at the heart of impression formation.

The significance of selective perception   The term *perception,* explained in Chapters 1 and 2, refers to "making sense of" or "attaching meaning to" some aspect of reality that has been apprehended by the senses. Perception is a critical process in forming impressions of other people, and there are easily understood reasons why it is inevitably a "selective" activity. We all have different memories of meanings linked to signs, signals, and symbols, and even to human characteristics stored from our lifetime of experience. No one's associated meaning patterns for those "stimuli" are exactly like the meaning patterns of anyone else. Thus, no one's stored denotative and connotative meanings used to interpret a *particular* thing or event are an exact duplicate of those of others. The consequence is that when we search for an interpretation of something we see or hear, we cannot avoid putting our own personal stamp of meaning on it. This is the basis of **selective perception.**

The process is heavily influenced by what we like and dislike. This occurs because each of us has a stable organization of **predispositions** (to approve of some things and disapprove of others). These are shaped by our attitudes, values, opinions, preferences, and so on. These factors modify our perceptions and interpretations of things that take place around us, because they lead us to like some stimuli and dislike others.

Even our temporary states, such as emotions and needs, can alter the way we interpret something we see or hear at a particular moment. Things just don't seem the same when we are angry or afraid as they do when we are happy and relaxed. Or we see some things differently when we are hungry, like a big juicy piece of apple pie, as compared to seeing the same piece just after

Experienced communicators understand the need to preselect the impressions that they will make on others whom they are meeting for the first time. For example, politicians who want farmers' votes carefully plan on appearing in a context surrounded by nonverbal cues and wearing clothing that suggest they have the farmers' best interest at heart. While such tactics may not get these politicians elected, they do help in limiting other kinds of less helpful impressions.

we have finished pigging out on Thanksgiving dinner. Thus, every person perceives and experiences the world through her or his own internalized meanings, dispositions, emotional states, and needs. Selective perception, then, refers to the unique way people interpret what they observe.

The importance of selective perception for present purposes is that *we know it will happen*. It is a fundamental part of person perception that takes place in initial encounters. We also know that it is the basis for the selection of a salient characteristic around which an observer can create a complex initial set of impressions about what we are really like. It may not be easy to detect when another person is perceiving us in some selective way, but you can be certain that it will take place.

Knowing the consequences of selective perception, and that it is inevitable, it is obviously very important to try to control it. That may be easier said than done. However, one good way to plan ahead is to organize a flexible *preliminary game plan*. This will go a long way toward limiting the display of negative salient characteristics. By the same token, presenting positive ones is an obvious part of such a strategy.

Developing a preliminary game plan   Strategies of effective self-presentation are not hard to identify. Basically, they consist of using such nonverbal forms of communication as clothing, mannerisms, gestures, posture, and demeanor, plus verbal messages with specific content delivered with a particular style and level of vocabulary. The problem here is that the best combination can be difficult to identify. Furthermore, we can never be sure exactly what people might pick out as salient characteristics. In one context, shaggy hair, sloppy clothing, and scruffy shoes, plus a laid-back speaking style, sprinkled with four-letter words, might be a basis for very negative selective perception (as in a group of conservative businesspersons). In another context, a tailored suit, neatly trimmed hair, well-polished shoes, plus a sophisticated vocabulary and a well-organized speaking style, might make exactly the wrong impression (e.g., among a group of construction laborers).

How does one tell in a general way which strategies to use so that personal characteristics might be perceived selectively in ways one desires? Perhaps the best guide is *common sense*. Do not do, say, or otherwise communicate, either verbally or nonverbally, *anything* that those whom you are meeting might perceive selectively and use as a basis to construct a negative implicit personality to impose on you.

It is not possible to develop a "one size fits all" checklist that will serve as a preliminary game plan for all people in all situations. Yet certain principles can be used in preselecting the kind of impression that one may want to create during a particular initial encounter. For example, consider the following:

1. Size up the *people* to whom you are making a self-presentation. Who are they? What criteria will they probably use in judging you? This is another way of saying that you should engage in accurate role-taking.

2. Appraise the *physical setting* carefully. Where will the encounter take place? What factors in that environment might be important in your self-presentation?

3. Above all, do not try to *misrepresent* yourself. People can spot a "con job" very quickly. Even a minor falsehood discovered will be blown up into a negative salient characteristic!

4. Use all *communication channels* open to you to get your positive qualities across. This means both verbal and nonverbal messages that communicate your positive characteristics.

5. Look very closely for *feedback* messages of a subtle nature from those involved. Use them to shift strategies if necessary or to follow up ones that seem successful.

Generally, what we are suggesting is that we need to be very deliberate in our pre-encounter planning, and specific in the selection of the self-defining characteristics we decide to present, and intentional in the strategies we plan to use. Our presentation must be honestly communicated, while focusing attention away from anything that might result in negative evaluations. Careful assessment of the people, the situation, the channels of communication available, and the nature of feedback messages transmitted during the encounter is far more likely to result in an effective self-presentation than a strategy that consists of just "letting things proceed naturally."

Sizing Up People

The central factor in any encounter is, of course, the *people*. All of the planning in the world will make no difference at all unless it is done in conjunction with an understanding of the individuals to whom you will be presenting yourself. You must have enough knowledge about them to engage in effective role-taking and to have a pretty good idea about how they are going to interpret your presentation and how they are likely to respond to you—particularly in terms of what they may perceive as favorable or unfavorable.

Fortunately, there are many role-taking guidelines that have emerged from research and common experience for making educated guesses about people. Furthermore,

most of us have already learned to make certain assumptions about how and why people from different groups in society will think and behave. While these can sometimes prove very wrong, they are certainly far better than mere guesses. Nevertheless, we need to take a close look at what social scientists have discovered, not only about how people think others are likely to behave in certain situations but also about the *causes* to which they attribute such behavior. It is an interesting picture indeed.

Attributing motives to others   An important part of the study of person perception is what social scientists call the **attribution process,** which can be defined as *the selection and assignment to another individual various personal qualities, conditions, or dispositions that we believe are the causes of or influences on some aspect of that person's behavior.*[16]

Some of those assigned or "attributed" causes or influences are seen as within or *internal* to the person (e.g., attitudes, values, and motivations). Other influences are seen as *external* to the individual (e.g., requirements of norms or roles, or other aspects of group organization).[17]

Obviously, the attribution process is related to the idea of implicit personality that we discussed earlier. The difference is that in an encounter where attributions are made as to *causes* of a particular form of behavior, we are not considering the entire personality. We are concerned only with selective characteristics that can explain *why* we think a person will engage in a particular action. For example, we may assign (attribute to) the other person the specific traits of being "mean" and "malicious" if we believe the individual will be likely to refuse us a raise or a promotion.

Thus, when we "size people up," we are making inferences about them in two ways: (1) *how* they are likely to react to us and (2) *why* that probably will be the case. In so doing, we base our predictions on either internal factors that we believe will influence their action (e.g., personality traits) or external conditions (e.g., norms, roles, social controls) that we see as limiting or shaping what they will do. Either way makes us feel better because it makes their behavior more predictable.

We have already looked closely at ways in which personality traits are attributed to others in initial encounters. We know that as part of the communication transaction our audience will form their assumptions about what *we* are like during the early part of an encounter. What we are now noting is that in an additional transaction we must also form our impressions of what *they* are like before the action begins. But how can we make judgments about either internal personality traits or external influences on action? One way is to examine the *social categories* to which the individuals belong; another is to grasp the *social constraints* (norms, roles, etc.) within which they are performing.

"Typical" behavior as a basis for attribution   We cannot invent attributions about probable behavior or its causes out of thin air. One source of information that can be used for attributions about other people is their membership in significant **social categories** (e.g., males, children, educated people, working class, farmers). Often, people in such categories are said to be characterized by certain regularities in their behavior. What we are referring to are generalizations about behavior thought to be "typical" of people from particular walks of life. For example, if we want to make a good impression on an elderly person who has little schooling and a low income, our initial small talk with that individual probably would not be based on the merits of the local symphony orchestra or a particular fine year for French wines. We could be wrong, of course, but it would seem safer to discuss alarming increases in the cost of medical services or possibly the local baseball team.

As a normal part of living in a complex society, we all learn to make such predictions on the basis of "typical" interests of people in specific social categories. However, there are certain dangers in such forecasts. As we saw in Chapter 2, rigidly held assumptions, categorical attributions, and unfounded forecasts become **stereotypes**—especially if they attribute socially undesirable qualities to the target group. Still, there are topics of interest typically associated with people of a particular age, occupation, gender, region, social class, religion, ethnic and racial identity, and so on. Knowing the category memberships of individuals to whom we will make a presentation of self, then, provides at least *some* information for making attributions about their tastes, beliefs, values, attitudes—and therefore their probable behavior.

Social constraints as factors in attribution   External to the individual, but very influential on behavior, are social constraints that dictate at particular times how the individual has to evaluate and respond to your self-presentation, regardless of their inner feelings and attitudes. For example, a person who is acting as a recruiter for a company may be all business in such an encounter. The same individual would be different at a cocktail party with peers or at home with the family. Similarly, individuals in positions of power and authority *have* to think and act according to the mandates of those positions at

times. If they did not, they would lose their jobs. Response to our self-presentation, then, may be strongly influenced by external factors, stemming from the demands of socially imposed constraints, as well as by a person's inner psychological traits.

What, then, are some practical techniques for assessing others so as to try to understand how and why they probably will respond to our verbal and nonverbal communication about ourselves? The following list includes seven simple and effective steps that can assist, both in the gathering of personal information about others and in reducing uncertainties about their probable reactions and behavior:

1. Look carefully at people so as to identify any obvious verbal or nonverbal behavior that communicates *psychological characteristics* (attitudes, intelligence, emotions, etc.).
2. Observe people interacting to see how they respond *to each other* (aggressively, politely, formally, warmly, etc.).
3. Ask questions about your potential audience, in advance if possible, so as to understand as much as you can about *who* they are and *where* they come from, both geographically and socially.
4. Compare the people with individuals you know. If they seem *alike,* they may think and behave similarly.
5. Gather whatever information you can about social category membership (education, occupation, age, race, ethnicity, religion, etc.) that can provide clues to probable normative behavior.
6. Review carefully the social constraints that are on these people at the time of the encounter, or other requirements they have to meet, and assess what they require them to do.
7. Review everything you have learned and try to put together a *composite*—an organized prediction—of how they will respond to various aspects of your self-presentation and why.

Thus far, we have stressed (1) considering carefully what we want to achieve in a first meeting, (2) preselecting the impressions we want people to perceive, (3) analyzing what information we have about the individuals to whom we will be presenting ourselves, and (4) anticipating how they will react to verbal and nonverbal messages that communicate our characteristics. Each of these activities is an essential part of the development of a sound design for self-presentation. The final step is to consider, choose, and incorporate the actual techniques and strategies that we will use to create the impressions we prefer. If the plan

In our complex and heterogeneous society, we often must make quick decisions about what a person is like on the basis of whatever is readily visible as cues. The way someone is dressed is one of the most obvious nonverbal indicators of such matters as occupational role, which is an important indicator of socioeconomic status. This can provide the basis for stereotyped attributions about such a person's tastes, intelligence, values, and beliefs.

works, this means communicating well-designed messages through all available channels in such a way that the people receiving them immediately begin to like you.

Getting People to Like You

In recent years, social scientists have done extensive research on strategies that people use to try to get others to like them. A more precise, and widely used, term for that process is **affinity-seeking.**[18] A number of strategies have been investigated.

Affinity-seeking strategies   The search for effective affinity-seeking strategies has turned out to be almost unbelievably complex. The main problem is that there are literally dozens that seem to work, at least sometimes. To provide an idea about how complex this process can be, we can look first at a table that summarizes in a single list most of the affinity-seeking strategies that have actually been identified.[19] The box on page 268–269 shows no less than 25 *specific* strategies from which people can choose to get other people to like them.

While 25 may seem like a large number, the selection gets much more complex when it is realized that in a given situation, people can use more than one from the list. They might use two, three, or some larger number in combination. If so, the number of available *patterns* has to be added to the original 25. If we take these 25 in pairs, then three at a time, then four at a time, and so on up to all possible combinations, and then add up all the possible patterns, a staggering number (over 40 million combinations) is produced.[20]

It is clear, then, that a great many strategies and huge numbers of combinations of strategies can be used to get people to like you. The problem is not one of whether affinity-seeking strategies are available; the problem is which to select.

Selecting strategies   There is no possible way to set forth a simple set of rules for the selection of strategies. Certainly, the rule of "one size fits all" cannot apply. A particular person's selection of a strategy, or some combination of strategies, must be based in part on that individual's gender, cultural identity, personal preferences, and familiarity with the situation, plus a combination of personality characteristics.

Affinity-Seeking Strategies*

Altruism. The affinity-seeker strives to be of assistance to the target in whatever she or he is currently doing. Example: The affinity-seeker is generally available to run errands for the target.

Assume control. The affinity-seeker presents him- or herself as someone who is in control over whatever is going on. Example: The affinity-seeker takes charge of the activities engaged in by the target and her- or himself.

Assume equality. The affinity-seeker strikes a posture of social equality with the target. Example: The affinity-seeker avoids one-up games and behaving snobbishly.

Comfortable self. The affinity-seeker acts comfortable and relaxed in settings shared with the target. Example: The affinity-seeker ignores annoying environmental distractions, seeking to convey a "nothing bothers me" impression.

Concede control. The affinity-seeker allows the target to assume control over relational activities. Example: The affinity-seeker permits the target to plan a weekend that the two will share.

Conversational rule-keeping. The affinity-seeker adheres closely to cultural rules for polite, cooperative interaction with the target. Example: The affinity-seeker acts interested and involved in conversations with the target.

Dynamism. The affinity-seeker presents her- or himself as an active, enthusiastic person. Example: The affinity-seeker is lively and animated in the presence of the target.

Elicit other's disclosures. The affinity-seeker encourages the target to talk by reinforcing the target's conversational contributions. Example: The affinity-seeker queries the target about the target's opinions regarding a significant personal issue.

■ *Facilitate enjoyment.* The affinity-seeker tries to maximize the positiveness of the relational encounters with the target. Example: The affinity-seeker enthusiastically participates in an activity that the target is known to enjoy.

■ *Inclusion of other.* The affinity-seeker includes the target in the affinity seeker's social groups. Example: The affinity-seeker plans a party for the target at which numbers of the affinity-seeker's friends are guests.

■ *Influence perceptions of closeness.* The affinity-seeker engages in behaviors that cause the target to perceive the relationship as closer than it has actually been. Example: The affinity-seeker uses nicknames and talks about "we," rather than "you and I," when discussing their relationship with the target.

■ *Listening.* The affinity-seeker listens actively and attentively to the target. Example: The affinity-seeker asks the target for frequent clarification and elaboration, and verbally recalls things the target has said.

■ *Nonverbal immediacy.* The affinity-seeker signals interest in the target through various nonverbal cues. Example: The affinity-seeker smiles frequently at the target.

■ *Openness.* The affinity-seeker reveals some social insecurity or fear to the target. Example: The affinity-seeker reveals some social insecurity or fear to the target.

■ *Optimism.* The affinity-seeker presents him- or herself to the target as a positive person. Example: The affinity-seeker focuses on positive comments and favorable evaluations when discussing mutual acquaintances with the target.

■ *Personal autonomy.* The affinity-seeker presents her- or himself to the target as an independent, free-thinking person. Example: The affinity-seeker demonstrates a willingness to express disagreement with the target about personal and social attitudes.

■ *Physical attractiveness.* The affinity-seeker tries to look and dress as attractively as possible in the presence of the target. Example: The affinity-seeker always engages in careful grooming before interacting with the target.

■ *Present interesting self.* The affinity-seeker presents her- or himself to the target as someone who would be interesting to know. Example: The affinity-seeker discreetly drops the names of impressive or interesting acquaintances in the presence of the target.

Reward association. The affinity-seeker presents him- or herself in such a way that the target perceives the affinity-seeker can reward the target for associating with him or her. Example: The affinity-seeker showers the target with gifts.

Self-concept confirmation. The affinity-seeker demonstrates respect for the target and helps the target to "feel good" about her- or himself. Example: The affinity-seeker compliments the target frequently.

Self-inclusion. The affinity-seeker arranges the environment so as to come into frequent contact with the target. Example: The affinity-seeker plans to have afternoon cocktails at the same time and place as the target.

Sensitivity. The affinity-seeker acts in a warm, empathic manner toward the target. Example: The affinity-seeker sympathizes with the target regarding a personal problem the target is experiencing.

Similarity. The affinity-seeker seeks to convince the target that the two of them share many similar tastes and attitudes. Example: The affinity-seeker often points out things to the target that the two of them have in common.

Supportiveness. The affinity-seeker supports the target in the latter's social encounters. Example: The affinity-seeker sides with the target in a disagreement the target is having with a third party.

Trustworthiness. The affinity-seeker presents her- or himself to the target as an honest, reliable person. Example: The affinity-seeker consistently fulfills commitments made to the target.

---

*This table was originally reported in: Bell, R. A., & Daly, J. A. (1984). The affinity-seeking function of communication. *Communication Monographs, 51*, 91–115.

One's final selection and eventual use of any of the available strategies needs to occur in conjunction with all the other issues relevant to planning for self-presentation. That is, the effectiveness of a decision to employ a particular strategy or set of strategies within a unique social context depends in large part on our knowing what we want, how we want to be perceived, and as much as possible about the people to whom we will be presenting ourselves.

For example, let us say that we are a real estate salesperson and have a selection of houses we want to sell. We have scheduled a meeting this afternoon at our local real estate office with a young married couple interested in purchasing their first home. Our objective for this first meeting is the successful initiation of a relationship with the couple that will (hopefully) lead to their purchase of a house. After assessing the situation, we believe that the best way to maximize the chances of meeting our objective is to communicate as quickly as possible the impression to the couple that we are a very *honest* and *credible* businessperson.

Considering the time available to us, we have gathered as much information about the couple's social categories as possible. We know that the young man and woman are (1) in their mid-twenties and (2) both have college degrees. We also know that (3) they do not have children and (4) together they make just over $50,000 a year. With this information, we can choose from the impressive number of available affinity-seeking strategies listed in the box at left. To be realistic, of course, we need to consider in our selection whether we can reasonably employ some of them within this particular context. Additionally, we must also consider whether we have the ability to communicate a given strategy effectively.

After evaluating all of these issues, we decide that our best alternative is to go with a combination of five strategies from the box. Our selection is (13) *nonverbal immediacy,* (19) *reward association,* (23) *similarity,* (24) *supportiveness,* and (25) *trustworthiness.* There are of course others that might work. However, we have concluded from our planning and evaluation activities that we might risk reducing our chances of communicating a positive impression if we attempt to employ too many.

Deciding What to Say

At this point, the time for background data-gathering and preliminary planning is over. Now we need to decide very specifically what we intend to *say* in our self-presentation. This is in many ways the most critical point of any encounter. It is here that sitting and thinking about what we want to do stops and actual performance begins. We need to move easily from plan to performance without a hitch. What are some of the guidelines for making this transition?

One pitfall we want to avoid is to get to the point of communicating with someone for the first time and then have what we actually say have little to do with anything we had intended. A very effective way to minimize either having nothing to say or saying the wrong thing in initial encounters, is to begin by talking about a topic that we know a lot about. In fact, it is a good idea to select a subject that you know better than anyone else. What is that topic? Actually, what we are most qualified to talk about is *ourselves!* Furthermore, it is a most suitable subject matter for beginning a self-presentation. Almost by definition, self-disclosure (revealing information about ourselves) is an important part of what goes on in any self-presentation. Let's look at that idea more closely.

Self-Disclosure in Initial Encounters

What we are considering here is the idea that disclosure of information about ourselves both dictates how others will perceive us initially and how they will formulate impressions about us. It is important to note that by self-disclosure we do not mean gushing on about intimate details about our lives. That is not an effective strategy.

The actual content of our self-disclosure will depend on both the *depth* and the *breadth* of what we communicate about ourselves.[21] The depth of self-disclosure refers to the *intimacy* of what we say about ourselves. Breadth refers to the *amount* of personal information we communicate. Appropriately, deciding what to say about ourselves in a particular situation is tied to all of our planning decisions and, in that way, to the overall development of our design for self-presentation. That is, as we consider what it is about ourselves that we should incorporate into our presentation we must keep in mind our objective for the meeting, how we want others to perceive us, what we know about the individuals we will be communicating with, and what we have selected as our affinity-seeking strategies.

In light of the above, let us go back to our real estate example to illustrate what is involved in "appropriate" self-disclosure. Because the salesperson and the young couple had never met before, it would be inappropriate

for the realtor to present either intimate details or vast amounts of personal information in this initial encounter. When strangers provide intense self-disclosure it tends to make their listeners feel very uncomfortable. Consider for a moment how you would feel if a real estate agent you had never met before disclosed a lot of intimate information, such as personal finances, sexual interests, and life history. Obviously, disclosures of such breadth and depth would be inappropriate.

What would be more acceptable in this situation would be the disclosure that the salesperson and his or her spouse had made a similar choice when they purchased their first home. Then the salesperson could further indicate that they had felt terribly uneasy with this first purchase, but that later they saw it had been a wise decision. In other words, two additional revelations of personal information would appropriately follow from the disclosure of the salesperson's similar family decision. First, information about the uneasy feelings could be disclosed—obviously similar to what had been disclosed by the young couple. Second, information about the long-term wisdom of the choice could be disclosed. That would definitely be perceived as supportive of the clients' decision to buy a house. Any other topics would need to be carefully prescreened before being disclosed.

We have good reason for being very cautious about what we advocate saying about oneself during self-disclosure in an initial encounter. Because of the factor of selective perception, early disclosures communicated to strangers are highly susceptible to misinterpretation. We also know that elaborate attributions are made to people on the basis of very limited information. Thus, the risks are especially high during the early phases of an encounter. Putting this idea a little differently, we would argue that self-disclosing information that is (1) other than what is obvious, (2) likely to be misinterpreted, or (3) too intense and revealing for strangers, is both *undesirable* and highly *risky.* For these reasons, we suggest that effective self-disclosure aimed at creating positive impressions must be provided carefully, gradually, and systematically.

Talking with New People

Three kinds of messages create opportunities for self-disclosure in initial encounters. For the purpose of explanation, we divide them into *greetings, small talk,* and a broad category that we will refer to as the *main topic* of the encounter. Each is very different from the other; all are important.

Greetings Under the heading of *greetings* we can include all the salutations that are employed when individuals recognize and acknowledge each other. They can be verbal, nonverbal, or both. Regardless of which of these we employ, the specific salutation we communicate to others at a first meeting can have important implications for how we are perceived from that point on. Thus, even our greeting can influence receptivity to what we say later.[22]

For example, let us assume that you are going to meet for the first time a group of individuals with whom you hope to maintain a very formal and long-term professional relationship. Greeting this group with a "Hi there; how ya doin?" is likely to be less helpful to the impression they form of us than a simple "Good morning." In fact, employing the "Hi there; how ya doin?" salutation with such a group would almost certainly lead them to form a negative impression of you. As a general rule, then, we must consider initial salutations very carefully.

Small Talk In addition to the careful choice of a greeting, what we discussed in Chapter 5 as "small talk" typically has an important place in our presentation of self to others. We noted that what makes this type of communication important is that individuals getting together for the first time can maintain social distance and do not have to discuss immediately topics that they are not yet ready to talk about.

Consider the possible small talk that could have occurred between the salesperson and the young couple in our real estate example. We can assume that in addition to the self-disclosure the salesperson engaged in, a number of totally unimportant topics were introduced and discussed. Engaging in small talk while showing the couple neighborhoods and homes would create a more relaxed climate. Moreover, such small talk could contribute to the impression that the realtor was a nice person from whom to buy a home.

Generally, then, integrating small talk into the situation helps people feel more at ease in a first encounter. If the salesperson in our example had been all business, providing only carefully monitored self-disclosure, the meeting would have been somewhat strained. Introducing small talk on such nonessential topics as the weather, the quality of a local restaurant, the recent football game, or whatever fit the occasion, on the way to the showing of a particular house, could stimulate relaxed discussion. Important business issues could be inserted gradually and naturally into the encounter. The only caution is that small talk must be perceived as sincere and believable as well

Managing appropriate levels of self-disclosure in various stages of encounters is an important strategy in planning for effective self-presentation. It is inappropriate to reveal intimate details about one's private life during the initial phases of encounters because this makes others feel uncomfortable. Personal information can be gradually disclosed at appropriate times as a relationship develops so as to continue making a positive impression on others.

as spontaneous. If that can be achieved, there is every reason to use small talk deliberately in a well-designed game plan to enhance the effectiveness of self-presentation.

The main topic. If the occasion of an encounter is informal there will be no main topic to discuss. That is, when people are at parties or in other social gatherings, self-presentations typically do not extend beyond greetings, small talk, and perhaps a limited amount of self-disclosure. In contrast, in a formal encounter (such as an interview, a sales presentation, or a committee meeting) the stages are different. After greetings and a certain amount of small talk, the participants must "get down to business" and communicate about the subject matter that brought them together in the first place.

However, there are several kinds of formal situations, and the stages of the encounter differ in each. For example, one common situation is the initial meeting where the primary objective is to present information to an audience. Although the individual delivering the information does make a presentation of self to members of

General Disclosiveness Scale

Instructions   Please mark the following statements to reflect how *you* communicate *with other people in general.* Indicate the degree to which the following statements reflect how you communicate with people by marking whether you:

7 strongly agree   3 moderately
6 agree   disagree
5 moderately agree   2 disagree
4 undecided   1 strongly disagree

Record the number of your response in the space provided. Work quickly and just record your first impression.

_____ 1. When I wish, my self-disclosures are always accurate reflections of who I really am.

_____ 2. When I express my personal feelings, I am always aware of what I am doing and saying.

_____ 3. When I reveal my feelings about myself, I consciously intend to do so.

_____ 4. When I am self-disclosing, I am consciously aware of what I am revealing.

_____ 5. I do not often talk about myself.

_____ 6. My statements of my feelings are usually brief.

_____ 7. I usually talk about myself for fairly long periods at a time.

_____ 8. My conversation lasts the least time when I am discussing myself.

_____ 9. I often talk about myself.

_____ 10. I often discuss my feelings about myself.

_____ 11. Only infrequently do I express my personal beliefs and opinions.

_____ 12. I usually disclose positive things about myself.

_____ 13. On the whole, my disclosures about myself are more positive than negative.

_____ 14. I normally reveal "bad" feelings I have about myself.

_____ 15. I normally express "good" feelings about myself.

_____ 16. I often reveal more undesirable things about myself than desirable things.

_____ 17. I usually disclose negative things about myself.

_____ 18. On the whole, my disclosures about myself are more positive than negative.

_____ 19. I intimately disclose who I really am, openly and fully in my conversation.

_____ 20. Once I get started, my self-disclosures last a long time.

_____ 21. I often disclose intimate, personal things about myself without hesitation.

_____ 22. I feel that I sometimes do *not* control my self-disclosure of personal or intimate things I tell about myself.

_____ 23. Once I get started, I intimately and fully reveal myself in my self-disclosures.

_____ 24. I cannot reveal myself when I want to because I do not know myself thoroughly enough.

_____ **25.** I am often not confident that my expressions of my own feelings, emotions, and experiences are true reflections of myself.

_____ **26.** I always feel completely sincere when I reveal my own feelings and experiences.

_____ **27.** My self-disclosures are completely accurate reflections of who I really am.

_____ **28.** I am not always honest in my self-disclosures.

_____ **29.** My statements about my own feelings, emotions, and experiences are always accurate self-perceptions.

_____ **30.** I am always honest in my self-disclosures.

_____ **31.** I do not always feel completely sincere when I reveal my own feelings, emotions, behaviors, or experiences.

Calculating Your Score

The Self-Disclosure scale allows you to compute five different scores that measure your disclosure in five different ways: (1) intentional or unintentional self-disclosure, (2) amount of self-disclosure, (3) positive/negative nature of the disclosure, (4) control of general depth of intimacy of the disclosure, and (5) honesty/accuracy of the disclosure. Consequently, you need to compute five different scores. Follow the procedures below.

1. Intentional/Unintentional =
Add scores for items 1, 2, 3, and 4 = _____.

2. Amount =
(a) Add scores for items 5, 6, 8, and 11 = _____.
(b) Add scores for items 7, 9, and 10 = _____.
Compute the following formula:
32 − Total from (a) = _____;
Then, + Total from (b) = _____.

3. Positive/Negative =
(a) Add scores for items 13, 14, 16, and 17 = _____.
(b) Add scores for items 12, 15, and 18 = _____.
Compute the following formula:
32 − Total from (a) = _____;
Then, + Total from (b) = _____.

4. Depth/Intimacy =
Add scores for items 19, 20, 21, 22, and 23 = _____.

5. Honesty/Accuracy =
(a) Add scores for items 24, 25, 28, and 31 = _____.
(b) Add scores for items 26, 27, 29, and 30 = _____.
Compute the following formula:
32 − Total from (a) = _____;
Then, + Total from (b) = _____.

Interpreting Your Score

This scale measures your general level of disclosiveness or openness toward people in general. To interpret your personality orientation, we will need to examine each factor or score separately. For the intentional/unintentional factor, your score should fall between the range of 4 and 28. Higher scores reflect more control over your willingness or intent to self-disclose. The more control or awareness you have over your disclosures, the more you can regulate whether or not it's appropriate to self-disclose to others. With new acquaintances, for instance, we may want to refrain from revealing a lot of intense information about ourselves in our efforts to manage a good first impression. With intimate friends, however, we may need to consciously share our private thoughts and feelings.

(continued)

continued from page 273

Your second score should fall between the range of 7 and 49, with higher scores indicating greater amounts of self-disclosure. With strangers or people we have known only briefly, we should avoid disclosing a lot of intimate information about ourselves too soon. Others might perceive us as abnormal when we go on and on about ourselves. Pay attention to others' feedback during disclosure: Do they continue to be interested, or do they look absently around the room?

Your third score should range between 7 and 49, with higher scores revealing more positive, rather than negative, disclosures. Receivers appreciate us more when we self-disclose positive information. In terms of impression formation, we want to carefully manage what others think of us. Consequently, revealing negative information could lead to a bad first impression. At the other extreme, "bragging" about our accomplishments could be hazardous as well.

Your fourth score should range between 5 and 35, with higher scores revealing greater depth or intimacy of self-disclosure. Ideally, we ought to be able to share our deepest, darkest secrets with others. However, we know that much of our disclosure relies on our feelings of trust toward the other person. With new acquaintances, we have not yet had the opportunity to fully learn to trust; consequently, we need to carefully monitor just how intimately we reveal ourselves to others. With people we have known a long time, we can afford to be more open.

Finally, your fifth score should range between 8 and 56, with higher scores suggesting greater honesty. Others rely on us to be sincere, open, and honest with them when we reveal intimate information about ourselves. To lie or distort will negatively impact their eventual and long-term impressions about us.

Reference

Wheeless, L. R. (1978). A follow-up study of the relationships among trust, disclosure, and interpersonal solidarity. *Human Communication Research, 4,* 143–157.

the audience, it occurs as an almost secondary activity. Examples of this type of situation include lectures, informative talks, narrations, and the public reading of factual material. In these situations, audience attention may be devoted more to the specific subject matter than to the individual presenting the material.

Another common situation occurs when an individual is presenting a message to one or more others and it is that person's specific interpretation of a situation that is the concern of the audience. Examples would be testimony on a witness stand, responding to questions during job interviews, presenting one's personal analysis to a decision-making group, or explaining to a professor why you missed the final examination and should be excused. In these kinds of situations almost everything that is transmitted is used to assess the presenter. In other words, the presentation of self is much more relevant to the audience than are the specifics of the message. It is not uncommon for the members of an audience in this type of situation to hang on every word of the speaker. Here, **credibility** can be a critical factor. That is, the information that is communicated may be judged within a framework of important dimensions—as valuable or worthless, critical or trivial, true or false—depending on the presenter's perceived sincerity and honesty as evaluated by the audience. Thus, perceived personal credibility can have a strong influence on the interpretation of the main topic under discussion.

In overview, whatever the specifics of the situation, an effective strategy for talking with new people begins with a greeting appropriate to the situation and the audience. It moves through just the right amount and kind of small talk that puts people at ease. This provides an opportunity for beginning a planned, subtle self-presentation. Above all, personal credibility must remain high, or subsequent efforts to present ideas about the main topic will be discounted and the entire encounter will end in failure.

Our entire analysis of the bases of effective self-presentation includes all of the issues discussed up to this point in the present chapter. As understanding of these issues grows, we should be able to present ourselves to others with increasingly positive results. At the same time, such a command cannot be achieved overnight. And, as we have emphasized, it is not true that "one size fits all." In other words, our suggested strategies do not provide a neat formula. These suggested procedures and techniques *must* be adapted to each individual's unique personality and to the specific requirements of any particular encounter. Nevertheless, they offer useful guidelines for making self-presentation more effective.

Changing Old Impressions

There is one additional issue to consider before we bring this chapter to a close. More specifically, if you have not yet been confronted with the effects of someone's old and lingering impression of you, sooner or later you will be. Unfortunately, such impressions can be based on earlier unfavorable attributions. In other words, someone may still be evaluating you in a negative way from an earlier encounter. The problem is, how can the strategies, techniques, and analyses already described in this chapter be used to change such old impressions?

It should be emphasized immediately that changing someone's entrenched convictions about a person is a formidable task. However, there are a number of similarities between the steps needed to do this and those required to communicate a *new* impression. However, if we were to work back through each of the areas we have discussed so far, we would have only partially considered what is involved in altering an unfortunate impression that someone may already have.

The reason why it is so much more difficult to change a person's previously formed impression is that there are more steps involved than in creating a new one. The individual has to "erase" the existing impression and then recreate a new one by effective communication of fresh messages while disregarding older, well-remembered, and entirely "workable" views of you as a person. That is a complex task.

To aid in understanding why it is difficult to make the transition, we need to recall two principles that we learned earlier from the Asch experiments on person perception. One was that individuals quickly form impressions of others when they meet them for the first time. A second was that they formulate those impressions on the basis of a limited amount of data.

It should not be surprising that these two principles should turn out to be so important. Actually, each of us *has* to adapt to people we have just met in these ways. We really have no choice. That is, when we encounter someone new, we must have *immediately ready for use* a kind of "filter" for selectively perceiving the target person. We must be ready to respond to that person in an appropriate way from the beginning. Therefore, we have to make quick attributions and assumptions about the individual. However, in doing so, errors are likely. Because each human being is an immensely complex phenomenon, it is not possible to take in and understand *every* aspect of a person all at once. We have to work first with incomplete data (which can lead to inaccurate impressions). Nevertheless, we project onto that person a general framework of attributions as quickly as possible. These enable us to respond in what we think is an appropriate manner.

Thus, right or wrong, we quickly form impressions on the basis of the first indicators that we perceive. These tend to become entrenched right away because once we have formed an initial impression about a particular individual, we have *reduced our uncertainty* regarding how we should relate to that person. Reducing uncertainty makes us feel more comfortable. From then on, any attempt to change our framework for selective perception will threaten to bring back that uncertainty and consequent discomfort. Therefore, the energy and inconvenience required to abandon an existing impression and create a very different one will be resisted. Nevertheless, people who entertain older negative impressions about us *can* be retrained, even though it is not easy.

The Inflexible Nature of Preexisting Impressions

A plan to extinguish a preexisting impression begins with an understanding of the way that we make attributions about *ourselves*. This process differs from the way other people attribute personality characteristics to us. This is an important difference indeed. Specifically, research indicates that when we engage in an activity we perceive as unacceptable to others, we tend to attribute the causes of that behavior to *external forces* beyond our control, rather than to our own *internal* preferences and desires that we can control. However, when other people observe us engaging in that unacceptable activity, they make just the opposite attribution. They tend to believe that we have deliberately chosen this course of action because of internal motivations. In other words, in interpreting the causes of our own behavior judged unacceptable by others, we feel we are driven by outside forces, but others believe we deliberately choose to be bad.

This fascinating difference between how we see ourselves and how others see us is particularly relevant to attempts to change the impressions others have of us. For example, if we meet someone who has been told by another person (who claims to know us) that we are *untrustworthy,* then our new acquaintance will have a preexisting negative impression of us coming into a first encounter. In fact, that person is very likely to perceive us negatively and to make biased and unfavorable attributions about the causes of our actions. In short, we have a problem.

What can we do to change such an impression? The first thing would be to begin planning *what* you are going to say and *how* you are going to say it. The basic goal is to suppress the existing impression and help the target individual in rebuilding a new one that includes greater credibility and more favorable attributions to you. Objectively speaking, your preparation in this instance would follow the same sequence of activities that we described for all self-presentations. However, because the purpose of the presentation would be to change rather than create an impression, the specifics of your plan would have to be different. The question is, how do we proceed?

Important guidelines can be drawn from researchers who study the attribution process. According to one well-known investigator, attributions concerning our behavior are a function of three factors: the *distinctiveness* of our behavior, its *consistency* over time, and the *consensus* regarding the behavior among attending persons.[23] Research on such factors has uncovered what is called the **principle of covarying attribution.** This is a kind of general rule, and it goes like this: If a person engages in a repetitive pattern of behavior, observers will attribute it to either an internal or external cause with which it seems to be consistently related over time. For example, suppose you are excited about having been accepted at a particular university (distinctive behavior) and you continue to be so over a period of time (consistency). Now assume that none of your friends are the least bit positive about that university; in fact, they are uniformly negative (consensus). Under these conditions, an attribution concerning the causes of your behavior is likely, and it will be made directly to *you.* That is, you probably would be perceived as *lacking good judgment*—which is an internal cause. If, however, under different circumstances, where you are fascinated with the idea of attending this particular university, and all of your friends believe it to be a good one, an attribution probably would be made to a different cause of your behavior, namely, to the *high quality of the university*—an external cause.

These conclusions offer a possible strategy for attempting to change the impressions people have of us by altering their attributions. Let us return to our problem of the person who has a preexisting impression of us as untrustworthy. We now design a strategy that will communicate effectively to that person that our behavior was acceptable to many people (consensus), that such acceptance has been in effect for a long period of time (consistency), and that such a behavior pattern (distinctive) is typically expected of people in our circumstances—that is, externally caused. If the self-presentation is effective, the initial unfavorable impression of us might begin to change.

Resistance to Change

We suggested earlier that people tend to resist attempts to modify existing impressions of an individual. In fact, it is difficult for people who have constructed internal meanings for almost *any* object or situation to shift to new ones. There are clear reasons why this is the case, and they are embedded deeply in the psychological processes people use to cope with the complexities of their physical and social environment. Specifically, all people, everywhere, construct "pictures in their heads"—*meanings* for various aspects of the world they live in. They do this in a process of communication with others.[24] Those constructions include their meanings, impressions, and interpretations not only of physical objects and situations but of specific individuals as well, such as each of us. We saw in Chapter 2 how meanings are shaped and how they serve us well as our major means of interpreting and adapting to our environment. Our meanings, then, are tools of perception and adjustment by which we negotiate through the daily world of stimuli that we encounter or that are thrust upon us. Because they serve such essential purposes, attempts to change them will be resisted.

Generally, then, attempts aimed at restructuring constructed realities of others will inevitably have to cope with resistance. One typical situation where resistance to change is very likely is one in which a person has privately formed a negative first impression of us. A different case would be a long-term negative impression passed on by a trusted third party. In effect, the outcome of either of these situations is that we will be consistently and selectively perceived negatively. What do we do?

Because long-term habits of meaning can be so deeply established, the first question we recommend considering is whether it is realistically possible to change such a person's impression of us. Second, is it worth the effort? Here we have to consider what we referred to in Chapter 5 as an assessment of costs versus benefits. There are going to be situations where the effort involved in changing someone's impression greatly outweighs the value associated with any change. If that seems to be the case, don't even try! In addition, there will be occasions where a negative impression is so robust that it is virtually impossible to change. Again, don't even try. Part of being successful at presenting self to others is learning to evaluate effectively such costs versus benefits.

Constructing New Realities

Let us assume that you feel change is possible and worth the considerable effort. You have decided to move ahead. The process of reconstructing a person's impressions and attributions by self-presentation should begin by careful consideration of the objectives. Obviously, if you are being perceived in a negative way, your overall goal is to change it to a positive one. But what beyond that? Do you have specific kinds of personal qualities of which you want that person to be aware? Furthermore, what are effective strategies for successfully communicating them so as to alter the person's existing impression?

We saw in Chapter 2 that the specific reality people perceive for any particular object is made up of subjective or internal meanings aroused by the perception of that object (or by a symbol that stands for that object). We will see in later chapters that in the case of human beings, such realities are constructed from the variety of experiences the person has with the other individual. Finally, in the present chapter we showed that early experiences are especially influential in forming that construction of reality.

Given all of that, the task of restructuring is to communicate unmistakably favorable (distinctive) meanings that are shared by others (consensus). This needs to be done over-and-over (consistency) without belaboring the message. By actions and comments, skillfully communicated, it can be made clear that others regard you favorably, respect your judgment, believe you to be trustworthy, and so on.

In addition, the individual's impression of you may lack depth. That is, you may have additional distinctive characteristics that can simply be *added* to what that person already thinks he or she knows. For example, if you are active in charities, play an instrument, have a special hobby, own an interesting pet, or have other positive qualities, communicating this new knowledge may improve the impression another entertains. If such information can be linked to the interests of the target person, so much the better. It may open new channels of communication that can be used to *displace* or at least *minimize* the unfavorable impressions that already exist.

To achieve such change, you have both verbal and nonverbal communication at your disposal. The meanings associated with words, gestures, and actions are the bricks and boards with which we can assist people in constructing new realities. The use of verbal and nonverbal communication for the restructuring of realities to achieve a positive impression follows the same general sequence of design activities we have outlined in previous sections. We note again that self-presentations must never be false or misleading. Phony presentations are a sure route to disaster.

Our final word of caution regarding the effective use of verbal and nonverbal symbols and signs when presenting self to others is to communicate *only that which contributes to the creation of a supportive climate for interaction.* In many ways that is the most important principle and the hardest lesson of all. Because we are human beings, we have the standard set of human emotions ready to be aroused. People can make us mad, and we feel a normal need to express our feelings in no uncertain terms. People who are "wrong" clearly deserve to be punished. However, it is a losing game and can only bring unfavorable consequences. Defensive or hostile words and phrases fired off in the heat of the moment cannot be withdrawn or erased. They do not contribute to either a positive impression or a supportive communication climate. It is perhaps this factor of achieving thoughtful *control* over emotional responses that most clearly sets apart the person in complete control of self-presentation from those who are content to just let it "fall together naturally."

Chapter Review

- Our skills at effective self-presentation can be enhanced greatly by understanding a number of basic principles of person perception. These have been drawn from extensive observations of people in natural settings and from careful research. The process of presenting oneself effectively is based on communicating, verbally and nonverbally, favorable meanings of our personal qualities. The goal is to help others form as positive an impression as we can.
- Classic research indicated that people make elaborate inferences about others on the basis of relatively little information. Salient characteristics become particularly important in constructing an impression of what that individual is "really like." In fact, with limited

data, we put together an organized implicit personality that we feel can predict the behavior of the individual we have just met.

■ Labels are an important part of implicit-personality construction. If we have a convenient label—mentally ill, nerd, sexpot, jock, or whatever—we can load onto the person all of the connotational meanings such terms carry. They may be incorrect, and quite unfair, but they provide guidelines for action that seem at the time to be based on realities. This gives us confidence and comfort.

■ Self-presentations can be heavily influenced by a variety of factors. These include encounters with one person versus several, meetings in familiar versus unfamiliar places, or having difficulty with a long list of common problems when confronting people for the first time.

■ One of the problems in self-presentation is selective perception on the part of the target individual or group. There is no way to avoid this inevitable process. However, a well-designed preliminary game plan will try to anticipate what selective perceptions people are likely to make and attempt to make sure that the ones perceived will be positive.

■ Another important process is attribution. People will tend to attribute unacceptable behavior to our personal shortcomings and praiseworthy behavior to causes beyond our control. An important part of planning for effective self-presentations is the forecasting of attributions and anticipated behavior patterns on the basis of social category memberships.

■ An important aspect of effective self-presentation is deciding what to say and how much self-disclosure is most desirable and at what pace. Too much, too quick, may be counterproductive. However, in talking with new people, a natural sequence usually takes place. It begins with greetings, moves to small talk, and then proceeds to the main topic.

■ Finally, changing embedded impressions that people already have of you is very difficult. They tend to be comfortable with such existing impressions because they reduce uncertainty for them. It is possible to displace established beliefs about you and to reconstruct them along more favorable lines, but it may not be worth the effort. If it is, one must first deal with everyone's natural resistance to change. This means being prepared to communicate systematically those new and more favorable meanings that you intend as the reconstructed impression you wish to create.

Key Terms

Affinity-seeking   Using various communication strategies in attempts to get people to like you.

Attribution process   The selection of and assignment to another individual various internal or personal qualities, conditions, or dispositions or external social pressures that we believe are the causes of or influences on some aspect of that person's behavior. (See **implicit personality**.)

Credibility   The degree to which a message transmitted by a source (person, group, or agency) is judged to be valuable or worthless, critical or trivial, true or false. This will depend on the perceived sincerity and honesty of the source as evaluated by the audience.

Implicit personality theory   An explanation of how a set of assumptions are quickly formulated about a person one has just met. These are beliefs about qualities and motives which are projected on that individual on the basis of limited information obtained in an initial encounter.

Impression management   Transmitting verbal and nonverbal messages that are deliberately designed to create a particular set of impressions.

Labeling theory   An explanation of the way people reinterpret the nature of an individual's characteristics and social worth after that person has been given a negative "label" by some official agency. For example, the term *mental patient* causes people to assign numerous negative characteristics to an individual who is so labeled, whether the person has those attributes or not.

Person perception   The processes by which an individual comes to know and to think about other persons, their characteristics, qualities, and inner states.

Predispositions   Tendencies to approve of some things and disapprove of others that are shaped by attitudes, values, opinions, preferences, and so on. These factors modify our perceptions and interpretations of things that take place around us, because they lead us to like some stimuli and dislike others.

Presentation of self   Formulating and transmitting verbal and nonverbal messages *to* other people about what kind of person we are.

Principle of covarying attribution A general rule concerning the attribution of internal or external causes to a person's pattern of behavior. If the behavior is disapproved by others, they will tend to attribute it to negative personal qualities (an internal cause). If the behavior is approved, they will attribute it to external factors beyond your control.

Salient characteristic Some feature or aspect of an individual that stands out in an initial encounter with another person and serves as a dominant attribute around which that person constructs a pattern of initial impressions.

Selective perception An individual's assignment of a personally unique pattern of denotative and connotative meanings to some person, activity, situation, or thing. Such personal stamps of meaning come about because each of us has different memories of meanings linked to signs, signals, and symbols, and even to human characteristics, stored up from our lifetime of experience.

Self-disclosure Informing another person about our beliefs, attitudes, values, accomplishments, status, and other personal and social characteristics.

Social categories A number of people who share some common characteristic by which they can be classified. Examples are gender, age, education, occupation, race, and so on. Often, people in such categories are said to be characterized by certain regularities in their behavior.

Stereotypes Rigid and usually negative sets of assumptions about the personal and social qualities of people who are members of a particular social category. For example, a person may believe that all older people are confused, cranky, inept, poor, and in bad health.

Notes

1. Tagiuri, R. (1969). Person perception. In G. Lindsey & E. Aronson (Eds.), *The handbook of Social Psychology* (2nd ed.) (Vol. 3, pp. 395–449). Reading, MA: Addison-Wesley. For several excellent examples of contemporary communication research on initial encounters see: Beinstein, J. (1975). Conversations in public places. *Journal of Communication, 25,* 85–95; Berger, C. R., & Calabrese, R. J. (1975). Some explorations in initial interaction and beyond: Toward a theory of interpersonal communication. *Human Communication Research, 1,* 99–112; Berger, C. R. (1975). Proactive and retroactive attribution processes in interpersonal communications. *Human Communication Research, 2,* 33–50; and Berger, C. R., Gardner, R. R., Clatterbuck, G. W., & Shulman, L. S. Perceptions of information sequencing in relationship development. *Human Communication Research, 3,* 29–46.

2. Goffman, I. (1956). *The presentation of self in everyday life.* Edinburgh: Social Sciences Research Centre. For an excellent discussion on impression management see: Giles, H., & Street, R. L., Jr. Communication characteristics and behavior. In M. L. Knapp & G. R. Miller (Eds.), *Handbook of interpersonal communication* (pp. 205–262). Beverly Hills, CA: Sage.

3. Asch, S. E. (1946). Forming impressions of personalities. *Journal of Personality and Social Psychology, 41,* 258–290.

4. See Becker, H. S. (1973). Labeling theory reconsidered. In H. S. Becker, *Outsiders: Studies in the sociology of deviance* (2nd ed.). New York: Free Press. A classic in this field is: Goffman, E. (1963). *Stigma: Notes on the management of spoiled identity.* Englewood Cliffs, NJ: Prentice-Hall.

5. The salient characteristic and the labeling principles are also closely related to the concept of "stereotype" that was discussed in Chapter 2. There, we saw that pejorative labels are still used by insensitive individuals to "keep down" categories of people—some of whom have a "salient characteristic," such as skin color or some other visible feature. Prejudiced people try to dominate that category by using a slang label in such a way that very negative meanings are uniformly associated with all of its members.

6. Hays, W. L. (1958). An approach to the study of trait implication and trait similarity. In R. Taguiri and L. Petrullo (Eds.), *Person perception and interpersonal behavior.* Stanford, CA: Stanford University Press; Bruner, J. S., Shapiro, D., & Taguiri, R. (1958). The meaning of traits in isolation and in combination. In R. Taguiri & L. Petrullo, op. cit.; Wishner, J. (1960). Reanalysis of impressions of personality. *Psychological Review, 67,* 96–112; and Crockett, W. H., & Friedman, P. (1986). Theoretical explorations of the processes of initial interactions. *Western Journal of Speech Communication, 44,* 86–92.

7. Wishner, op. cit.

8. Diabase, W., & Hjelle, L. (1968). Body-image stereotypes and body-type preferences among male college students. *Perceptual and Motor Skills, 27,* 1143–1146; Secord, P. (1970). Facial features and inference processes in interpersonal perception. In R. Taguiri & L. Petrullo (Eds.), op. cit.; Verinis, J., & Roll, S. Primary and secondary male characteristics; the hairiness and large penis stereotypes. *Psychological Reports, 26,* 123–126. For an excellent and general discussion of the characteristics influencing impression formation see: Burgoon, J. K., Buller, D. B., & Woodall, W. G. (1989). *Nonverbal communication: The unspoken dialogue* (pp. 219–259). New York: Harper & Row.

9. For a complete discussion of the many difficulties of getting to know others see: Duck, S. (1987). *Human relationships: An introduction to social psychology* (pp. 155–186). Beverly Hills, CA: Sage.

10. Wilmot, W. W. (1975). *Dyadic communication* (2nd ed.) Reading, MA: Addison-Wesley.

11. Ibid., pp. 20–33.

12. Ibid.

13. Goffman, E. op. cit., pp. 106–140.

14. Knapp, M. L. (1978). *Social intercourse: From greeting to goodbye.* Boston: Allyn & Bacon.

15. Ibid., pp. 84–87.

16. An excellent introduction to this area of study is provided by: Shaver, K. G. (1975). *An introduction to attribution processes.* Cambridge, MA: Winthrop.

17. Attribution theory was originally proposed in: Heider, F. (1958). *The psychology of interpersonal relations.* New York: Wiley. It was refined by: Kelley, H. H. (1973). The process of causal attribution. *American Psychologist, 28,* 107–128. For reviews of the accumulated research, see: Kelley, H. H., & Michela, J. L. (1980). Attribution theory and research. *Annual Review of Psychology, 31,* 457–503. Also see: Harvey, J. H., & Weary, G. (1984). Current issues in attribution theory and research. *Annual Review of Psychology, 35,* 427–460.

18. Bell, R. A., & Daly, J. A. (1984). The affinity-seeking function of communication. *Communication Monographs, 51,* 91–115.

19. Ibid.

20. For example, if just two of the strategies were to be selected to use at the same time, the algebraic formula $(_{25}C_2)$, for the number of available pairs taken from an array of 25, shows that there are 300 possible pairs to choose from. If three are to be used in combination, 2,300 such patterns can be selected from the list. From there, with combinations of 4, 5, 6, and so on, the situation becomes ludicrously complex because the numbers quickly become astronomical.

21. For several excellent examples of contemporary research and writing on self-disclosure see: Bochner, A. P. (1982). On the efficacy of openness in close relationships. In M. Burgoon (Ed.), *Communication Yearbook 5* (pp. 109–124). New Brunswick, NJ: Transaction; Bradac, J. J., Tardy, C. H., & Hosman, L. A. (1980). Disclosure styles and a hint at their genesis. *Human Communication Research, 6,* 228–238; Pearse, W. B., & Sharp, S. M. (1973). Self-disclosing communication. *Journal of Communication, 23,* 409–425; Rosenfeld, L. B. (1979). Self-disclosure avoidance: Why I am afraid to tell you who I am. *Communication Monographs, 46,* 63–74; and Wheeless, L. R. (1978). A follow-up study of the relationship among trust, disclosure, and interpersonal solidarity. *Human Communication Research, 4,* pp. 143–157.

22. Krivnos, P. D. & Knapp, M. L. (1975). Initiating communication: What do you say when you say hello? *Central States Speech Journal, 26,* 115–125; Nofsinger, R. E. (1975). The demand ticket: A conversational device for getting the floor. *Speech Monographs, 42,* 1–9; and Schegloff, E. A. (1972). Sequencing in conversational openings. In E. J. Gumperz & D. Hymes (Eds.). (1972). *Sociolinguistics: The ethnography of communication* (pp. 346–380). New York: Holt, Rinehart & Winston.

23. Kelley, H. H. (1973). *Causal schemata and the attribution process.* Morristown, NJ: General Learning Press; also: Kelley, H. H. (1973). The processes of causal attribution. *American Psychologist, 28,* 102–128; Kelley & Michela, op. cit., pp. 457–503; and Harvey and Weary, op. cit., pp. 427–460.

24. For a detailed review of scholarly writings (from Plato to the present) and various contemporary theories about the process by which people construct meaningful and shared interpretations of reality, see: DeFleur, M. L. & Rokeach, S. B. (1989). Mass communication and the construction of meaning. In M. L. DeFleur and Rokeach, S. B., *Theories of mass communication* (5th ed.) (pp. 228–271). White Plains, NY: Longman.

Additional Readings

Brown, R. (1965). *Social psychology* (Ch. 12, pp. 610–655). New York: Free Press, 1965.

> This chapter reviews and analyzes early research on impression formation and person perception. The entire chapter makes interesting reading. However, most pertinent are the sections on first impressions, the central trait, accuracy in impression formation, and the self and impression formation. This material emphasizes the important part self-presentation plays in human communication.

Goffman, E. (1959). *The presentation of self in everyday life.* Garden City, NY: Doubleday Anchor.

> This is the classic book on self-presentation. It masterfully articulates in simple terms the essentials of the communication of both first impressions and information about the self to other people. This book outlines the skills involved when guiding and controlling the responses others make when meeting someone for the first time.

Knapp, M. L. (1978). *Social intercourse: From greeting to goodbye* (pp. 90–93). Boston, MA: Allyn & Bacon.

> This brief section in Knapp's interpersonal communication text describes concisely what is involved in the process of perceiving others. Person perception is shown to be linked to the way individuals make attributions about why others engage in the behaviors they do.

Shaver, K. G. (1975). *An introduction to attribution processes.* Cambridge, MA: Winthrop.

> This introductory text provides an excellent discussion of the role of impression formation in the attribution process. Impression formation is considered in terms of information integration theory and primacy and recency effects. The text is written in a clear and understandable style.

Tagiuri, R. (1969). Person perception. In G. Lindzey & E. Aronson (Eds.), *The handbook of social psychology* (2nd ed.) (vol. 3, Reading, MA: Addison-Wesley, pp. 414–435).

> This chapter presents an advanced treatment of the original thinking and research on "the process of knowing others." The author traces the research in this area to the early studies on suggestion. The general properties of the person perception process are discussed in great detail.

Chapter 10

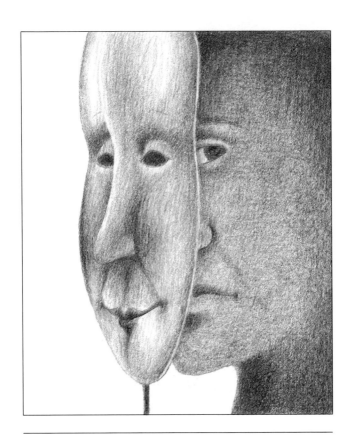

Influencing Others

Contents

The Importance of Persuasion in Everyday Life

Formulating a Definition
Linear Versus Transactional Views of Persuasion
  Persuasive messages as "magic bullets"
  Persuasion as communication transaction
A Formal Definition

The Dynamics of Influence
Using Coercion to Gain Compliance
Persuading People to Conform to Social Expectations
Cognitive Reorganization to Achieve
Behavioral Change
  Constructing or reconstructing meanings
  Shaping or altering beliefs
  Creating or modifying attitudes
  The relationship between attitudes and behavior

Understanding Resistance and Yielding
Resistance as Reaction to Persuasion Attempts
Types of Resistance
  Destructive resistance
  Constructive resistance

Types of Yielding
  Compliance
  Identification
  Internalization

Communication Strategies for Influencing People
Recognizing Receiver Characteristics
  Gender differences
  Personality characteristics
Features of Effective Messages
  Sidedness
  Message ordering
  Fear appeals
  Behavioral-alteration techniques
  Using nonverbal cues
Credibility of the Source

Chapter Review

Key Terms

Notes

Additional Readings

Key Questions

■ All of us are aware of advertising, political campaigns, and charity appeals for donations. The mass media are full of such attempts to manipulate or change us. But is persuasion actually something that we encounter every day among our friends and family in our private lives?

■ Isn't persuasion something that someone "does to us"? In other words, if a communicator is clever enough, isn't it possible to use subtle words and appeals that we can scarcely resist so that our feelings, needs, and behavior are manipulated by such messages?

■ If people are so set in their ways, how can groups like Alcoholics Anonymous or various weight-reduction programs actually succeed? The use of alcohol and overeating are difficult forms of behavior to change. Are there really any ways to achieve change here?

■ Isn't it true that our behavior is pretty much a reflection of our attitudes? In other words, if we have positive or negative attitudes toward some situation or even a category of people, doesn't that mean we will almost always act in ways that correspond with those attitudes?

■ Isn't it always important to "go along to get along"? Doesn't it seem wise to comply with what people want, or what those in authority tell you to do, so as to avoid unpleasant confrontations? What is to be gained by "fighting city hall" or "bucking the tide"?

Persuasion as an art has been practiced for centuries. The emergence of a science of persuasion is a product of the 20th century [but] "it is still too early to be sure" seems the most appropriate answer to the question "Has science created persuasive appeals that can control human behavior?"

Marvin Karlins and Herbert I. Abelson
1959

At first, Elva Garcia had been hesitant to represent Martin Symington because his situation looked like what fiction writers usually call an "open and shut" case. Finally, she had agreed to do so, and as the trial approached, she had been working on her presentation of evidence to the jury for days. From the outset she was determined to get a "not guilty" verdict if it was at all possible.

The problem was that Martin was charged with driving while intoxicated and with leaving the scene of an accident after injuring a child (a serious felony). The tough part of the case was that Martin had clearly been drunk when the police arrested him about 2 hours after the accident and several miles away. Not only had someone written down his license number as he left the scene, but the prosecution had the evidence of the breath test they had performed. It showed a level of alcohol in Martin's blood that was well over the legal limit.

Martin claimed that he was not drunk when it happened and that he had assumed he had hit a dog. It was a tough neighborhood, he said, and he was afraid of what might happen if he stopped. He had no idea, he claimed, that he had run over a child. His story was that he had been so shaken by the idea of hurting someone's pet, like his own dog "George," that he had stopped for drinks at the Happy Hour Bar, a couple of miles farther on, to calm his nerves before continuing to drive home. He had left the bar to get back into his car, he claimed, and the police had arrested him just as he was unlocking the door.

Elva knew it was going to be difficult to sell that whole line of defense to the jury. It just looked like some sort of phony story he had cooked up to cover his alcohol level. Even though she believed Martin, when she had checked it out, no one at the bar could remember him, and the bartender had left town. It did not look good.

Step by step, however, Elva questioned the witnesses as the trial began. She got the police officer to admit that the blood alcohol test had not been completed until more than 2 hours had passed after the accident. The fact that he was drunk at the time of the test, Elva told the jury, did not mean he had been intoxicated at the time of the accident. Furthermore, leaving the scene after striking someone's dog in a tough neighborhood, she argued, was an understandable decision, not a criminal act. She skillfully reminded the jury of the principle of "innocent until proven guilty," the legal concept of "criminal intent" (which was absent in this case) and that "proof" could not be based on guesses, assumptions, or mere conjunction of circumstances advanced by the prosecutor.

After 2 hours of deliberation, the jury filed back into the courtroom. Both Elva and Martin tried not to show their anxiety as they waited. Then the judge asked the jury if they had reached a verdict. Then he asked Martin to stand. Both Elva and Martin nervously faced the jury box. "We the jury," intoned the foreman, "find the defendant, Martin Robert Symington, *not guilty!*"

Most of us are familiar with the drama of the courtroom. Even if we have never personally been involved in a jury trial, hundreds of television shows and movies have shown lawyers in action. Their presentation of "the facts" to the jury is a classic example of persuasion. Both sides have available to them the same set of facts that they can place in evidence. However, the outcome is based on the winning lawyer's skill in influencing the way in which each individual making up the jury constructs his or her own personal meanings from those facts. The final decision will be based on consensus regarding those meanings among members of the jury.

In many ways, life is like a series of jury trials, where constant efforts are made to try to influence the beliefs, feelings, and actions of people. Sometimes we are like the lawyer, struggling to influence others whose decisions are important to us. At other times, we are like members of the jury, being bombarded by claims and counter-claims as we try to sort out the truth that we need to reach a decision. In both cases, we are participants in the process of *persuasion.*

In this chapter we will look at this process of influencing others within the perspective of communication. We will try to understand how such influence takes place; we will examine various strategies that are used to try to modify how people think, feel, or act; and we will discuss some of the barriers encountered in persuading others to change. As will be clear, the principles of communication underlying persuasion are those that we have outlined in Chapter 1 in the linear and transactions models and our extended discussions in other chapters.

The Importance of Persuasion in Everyday Life

We have already suggested that one of the most common goals of communication in modern society is to try to influence people's ideas, feelings, or actions. Almost everyone encounters such situations every day, either as a person who is trying to get someone else to make a change that seems desirable or as the receiver of another person's messages aimed at modifying *our* thinking or conduct. Almost from the time we get up in the morning until we retire at night, various kinds of people, groups, and agencies try to get us to attend to messages urging us to buy some commercial product, favor a particular political candidate, support a cause, modify our health practices, donate to a charity, or change some other way that we think and act. Such efforts impinge upon us from many sources—the world of advertising, politics, education, religion, and medical authorities, to mention only a few.

Efforts of this kind, to *change* us in some way by using strategies of communication, are collectively called "persuasion." It is one of the most pervasive communication processes in modern life—so pervasive, in fact, that people have to learn to ignore and resist most such efforts. However, there is no doubt that this form of communication is very important in modern industrial society. In fact, persuasion for a variety of purposes is so central to many of our social institutions that we could not continue our contemporary way of life without it. Persuasion for commercial purposes is used to sell and market a vast array of consumer products. It is a basic part of government; politicians use it in their campaigns for re-election and to establish support for legislative policies. Persuasion also plays a key role in religion, education,

and public health. In short, it is widely found in virtually every aspect of life where someone wants to shape or modify the ideas, feelings, or actions of someone else in a specific way.

Most of the persuasion processes that come immediately to mind are associated with mass communications. Such efforts make use of deliberately constructed messages designed to influence people to modify their ideas or actions in carefully defined ways. However, there is another, less obvious kind of persuasion that is even more important in our society, and it is one that each of us must deal with directly every day. That is, in almost every significant face-to-face human encounter, people initiate communication for the purpose of modifying the beliefs, attitudes, or behavior of someone else. The individual toward whom persuasive messages are directed may be a friend, neighbor, boss, professor, or family member. This kind of communication has nothing to do with the mass media. It is persuasion attempted and accomplished in many kinds of situations by individuals in all walks of life as they construct and present messages to each other for the purpose of influencing other persons in some way. This chapter will focus on that type of persuasion.

Formulating a Definition

Even when we focus our discussion exclusively on the kinds of persuasion that are a part of everyday social interaction, we still encounter a complex communication process. For example, in a single day, we might need to coax a friend into loaning us a few dollars, convince our parents that they should not be concerned with our low grade in chemistry, talk our way out of a speeding ticket, and persuade an instructor to let us into a closed class. At first glance, the goals involved in these influence attempts, and the persuasive communication process required to achieve them, all seem quite different and, in fact, there are differences. However, in the present section we will show that, on closer analysis, a great deal is *common* to most kinds of communication situations in which persuasion is a goal.

In order to understand the process of persuasion better, we can examine a situation where an individual constructs and presents messages to another person in an attempt to achieve influence, and in which the second party responds by changing views, feelings, or actions. (The example is a composite drawn from a number of actual transactions of a similar nature):

Tony was upset with his "D" grade on his test. He knew that he didn't do well on essay exams. However,

One of the most pervasive forms of communication in modern society is efforts to change us in some way by using strategies of persuasion. They include the advertising messages aimed at us daily, exhortations to become true believers, appeals for donations, requests for votes, and efforts to change our health-related behavior. Such efforts are so widespread that most of us have learned to ignore and resist them. Nevertheless, some strategies of persuasion can be effective in achieving results communicators desire.

he felt that his answer to the question about learning experiments contained all of the major points Professor Cheng had presented in her lectures and had mentioned when she discussed the test in class. If he could talk her out of just a few more points for that answer, he thought to himself, his test grade would become a C. Then he would not have an overall D going into the final. It would be tough to explain a low grade for the course to his parents. He decided to make an appointment and try to persuade her. He knew he could be pretty convincing and felt it was worth a good try.

Tony appeared at Professor Cheng's office at the appointed time. He was dressed neatly and had rehearsed all the points and arguments he was going to use to present his case. He felt he had a good chance. When she smiled and invited him to sit down and explain what he had in mind, his spirits rose.

Tony began his presentation by claiming that she really had not read his answer to the one question carefully enough. (He knew this was a form of *aggression* but thought it would place him in a strong position and her

on the defensive.) Then, to soften the attack, Tony outlined how really interested he was in the subject matter of her course and how much he enjoyed her lectures. (This, he knew, was *flattery,* but he thought most people liked it.) He then explained with great sincerity how hard he had studied for the examination. (This, he believed, would arouse her *sympathy.*) Tony concluded by explaining to Professor Cheng how badly he needed the grade. He pointed out that, because of personal problems he had earlier, his overall GPA was quite low and that he was working hard to raise it. If she did not give him a C for the course, he might have to leave the school. (This, he felt, would give her a sense of *guilt.*)

Professor Cheng listened carefully and then went over his written answer to the test question. She asked him to show her how he had addressed each of the major issues. She also asked a few questions, all of which were about the specific content of his answers. Then, for a time, she just sat there, looking at him a little strangely and drumming her fingers on her desk. Tony felt a growing fear that his effort to persuade her had bombed. But then to his surprise she said, "Well, Tony, I see that you really did include all five of the major points in your answer. I think that you have a good case, and I will give you an additional five points on your grade for the examination."

Tony could hardly contain himself; he left her office grinning. "It worked," he said to himself. "She really is a sucker for a sob story. I laid on a trip based on aggression, flattery, sympathy, guilt, and got her to change the grade. Wow, what a tear-jerker! I should have gotten an Academy Award."

As Tony was leaving, Professor Cheng thought, "What a con artist! He thought I would fall for his baloney about his burning interest in the course and how much he enjoys my lectures. His heart-wrenching story about how hard he had studied, and how he might have to leave school, was too much. I really had to try hard to keep from laughing." Professor Cheng smiled to herself and thought, "In spite of all the B.S., the fact is that his answer really was more complete than I first thought and it did merit an additional five points."

Did persuasion take place? Clearly, the grade was changed, and Tony's effort was successful in that sense. Yet, somehow it doesn't seem clear that Tony's messages *caused* Professor Cheng to comply with his goal. There are, in fact, two quite different interpretations as to what actually happened during the encounter: One is that Tony's cleverly constructed appeals based on interest, admiration, hard work, and deep need swayed Professor Cheng to comply. The other is that she was unmoved by Tony's appeals and that she had actually persuaded herself to make the change because of the factual content of his answer to the question. Which of these interpretations is correct will, of course, depend on how one defines *persuasion*. In fact, the major lesson to be derived from the little drama is that there are two ways to go in formulating a definition. Persuasion can be viewed either as a "one-way" process or as an "interactive" exchange between the parties.

Linear Versus Transactional Views of Persuasion

The way in which the process of persuasion has been viewed and interpreted by communication scholars has changed over the years. Earlier in this century, when research on the process first started, persuasion was something that one person "did to" another. That is, a person wanting to persuade another took an active role and used "tools" of persuasion—messages expressing "appeals" that could modify the thinking or action of a more or less passive receiver. Later, researchers began to realize that every person brings to every act of communication (whether persuasive or not) all of the personal attributes we have described in previous chapters. These played a critical part in forming the meanings people constructed in response to an incoming message. These two views of the persuasion process are obviously very different. One is a kind of linear "magic bullet" interpretation, while the other is clearly consistent with our simultaneous transactions model.

Persuasive messages as "magic bullets"   In this view, the message transmitted by the sender in the persuasion process is seen as aimed at the person selected as the target. The components of the message are seen as "magic bullets," impinging on the receiver and having an effect. That is, a source organizes a message with clever words, arguments, and appeals, then aims these at the person to be persuaded. Once the "bullets" arrive, the receiver undergoes the alterations desired by the source. Thus, the message organization and appeals *cause* some form of change of belief, attitude, or behavior. In this perspective, the change of grade made by Professor Cheng would be seen as a direct result of Tony's clever transmission of messages with meanings of aggression, flattery, sympathy, and guilt.

Persuasion as communication transaction   A second interpretation of the way in which persuasion works, and thus the manner in which it has to be defined, is based on the second view of what happened between Tony and Professor Cheng. That is, he presented his messages, including all of his carefully constructed appeals and arguments, and she listened carefully to what he was saying. However, in the end, she *herself* decided to make the change that Tony desired. She did not do so because of his clever "magic bullets" but because of her own decisions about the meaning of the situation and what response she should give.

This interpretation of persuasion indicates that the receiver of the message plays as active a part in achieving whatever changes take place as does the source or sender. It requires that persuasion be defined as a *transaction* that occurs between two parties in communication, rather than simply as a one-way action of one individual firing magic bullets at another so as to achieve desired change. This interpretation does *not* mean that the organization, appeals, images, and other features of persuasive messages are unimportant—indeed, they may have a significant influence on the transaction.

The view of the persuasion process as a transaction has now become the way in which most communication scholars think about it. Because of the importance of persuasion, and the *power* inherent in the ability to influence others, there is a continuing search for understanding as to how the process takes place. The heaviest emphasis in that search remains on the tools of persuasion—just the right kinds of symbols, images, and combinations of words that can arouse emotions, shape beliefs, sway attitudes, and hopefully shape actions as the receivers of the message play their part in the transaction.

The fact is, that kind of persuasion often works! Messages have been designed to which people have responded with great enthusiasm. This persuasion strategy has led large numbers of people at various times to buy things, vote for people, or take other actions that someone has wanted.[1] Even so, the strategy also often fails, and when it does no one is quite sure why. Nevertheless, given what potential power is at stake, it is little wonder the search for the effective appeals, message organizations, and other persuasive tactics continues with great enthusiasm even today.

A Formal Definition

In bringing these many ideas together, we will define *persuasion* in a way that is entirely consistent with our discussion of the two models of human communication we have set forth and expanded on in previous chapters. That is, although linear processes are involved, both parties engage in simultaneous transactions and play *active* parts.

What makes persuasion distinct from other communication transactions is that *change* takes place in the person interpreting the message. That change may be precisely what the originator of the message intended, or it may not, depending on the way the interpretation is constructed. However, if the desired change is in fact achieved, **persuasion** can be defined as *a communicative transaction in which a source constructs and transmits messages designed to influence a receiving person's constructions of meanings in ways that will lead to change (desired by the sender) in the receiver's beliefs, attitudes, or behavior.* If the attempt fails, the message is then just another piece of the vast communication clutter all of us experience every day.

As this definition implies, messages from a source can be very important, even though persuasion is a transactional process. A sender's messages can bring new facts, arouse feelings, and present logical arguments that lead receivers to form new conclusions. Sometimes they do not. And if they do, they may not always do so in ways intended by the sender. However, if no transaction takes place, no change will occur. In fact, in the example of

An older conception of the persuasion process was to use simple messages that worked like "magic bullets." Their powerful appeals were designed to capture the attention of virtually everyone and to arouse significant and persuasive meanings that would trigger direct action. This poster, from World War I, was thought to be very effective in getting young men and women to volunteer for military or other war-related service.

Tony and Professor Cheng, a transaction did take place that resulted in a change. Without a visit from Tony, she would never have awarded him additional points. Even though his linear-type "magic bullet" message structure and appeals fell flat, she did in fact review the situation and raise his grade, and in that limited sense it was a consequence of the transaction.

The Dynamics of Influence

It is not difficult to understand why people try to persuade others. They want them to comply with or conform to some planned change that is the objective of the persuasive attempt. Achieving compliance or conformity means getting someone to hold certain beliefs, have particular feelings, or engage in an action that seems desirable to the person orginating the message. It is more difficult to understand what takes place in the receiving person, the one who actually makes changes and complies to the suggestions or demands of the initiator of the message after engaging in a persuasive transaction.

To look more closely at why compliance occurs, we can contrast several important kinds of situations in which a person may modify his or her ideas, feelings, or actual behavior as a result of persuasive communication. One kind of compliance results from *coercive* message transmissions, in which people may have little choice but to change their behavior. A second, and very different, basis for compliance comes about because persuasive messages arouse meanings about what we will refer to as *sociocultural expectations.* When such messages are received and understood, people often modify their behavior to conform to the expectations or standards that operate in a group setting. A third kind of change comes about because of what we can call *cognitive reorganization* or restructuring, which is a fancy way of saying that people change the way they think or feel about the topic of persuasive messages.

Using Coercion to Gain Compliance

The term **coercion** refers to compelling someone to do something, or restraining them from acting in some way, by threatening them with consequences that they find unacceptable. Obviously, many kinds of goals are pursued by posing the prospect of force and bodily harm to alter someone else's behavior. At one extreme is the threatening statement of the mugger or rapist, who, with knife at throat, simply says, "Give me what I want or I will kill you!" That, of course, can be *very* persuasive. In fact, this type of persuasion fits the "magic bullet" definition very well. The statements of the sending person directly and immediately "cause" the receiver to behave in the manner demanded.

At the same time, messages that threaten force or bodily harm to modify the behavior of someone do not really fit with most people's commonsense idea of persuasion. The process implies a much more subtle kind of communication, in which the individual is "led" to make changes by some kind of clever message. For that reason, we will not address physical coercion as a form of persuasion by which one person can control another's behavior.

Persuading People to Conform to Social Expectations

As we pointed out in Chapter 5, almost all human behavior takes place in some sort of group setting. The organizing factors of all kinds of human social behavior (including communication) in group settings are the kinds of shared rules we have referred to as *norms, roles, ranks,* and *controls.* These general concepts are the heart of the kind of sociocultural persuasion that is based on clarifying **social expectations.** (Group members are expected to follow the rules.) The key here is that persuasive messages define the kind of behavior that is permitted and expected by members of a group. Messages that provide such definitions can be very effective in getting people to conform with the objectives of a source. This social expectations approach to persuasion has been far less studied than others, but it is very widely used in our multicultural society for the purpose of getting people from all backgrounds to behave according to some set of social rules.

Of particular importance is that such sociocultural persuasion can be an effective strategy in getting people to change their behavior in relatively *difficult* ways. The compelling nature of social expectations can sometimes bring about changes in people's behavior that probably would not occur as a result of lectures, pleas, appeals, or other conventional persuasion strategies. For example, people who urgently feel the need to lose weight often go to commercial groups that specialize in persuading people to drop pounds. Part of their process is to get such individuals on a weight-reduction diet and perhaps into some form of exercise. These are truly difficult goals. The task of convincing them to follow such regimens is a classic exercise in sociocultural persuasion. It works something like the following:

Lois is grossly overweight and has suffered from the condition for a number of years. She hates being fat and has tried many kinds of exercises and diets. Literally dozens of people have lectured her about her weight and tried to get her to reduce. Over the years she lost a few pounds from time to time, but they always seemed to come back. At one point she concluded that she was suffering from a "glandular disorder" and that she could not help being fat. However, after a complete examination and tests, her physician dismissed that explanation and insisted that she simply was eating too much and her problem was an excess of calories.

As something of a last resort, Lois decided to go to Pounds Ltd., an organization specializing in helping peo-

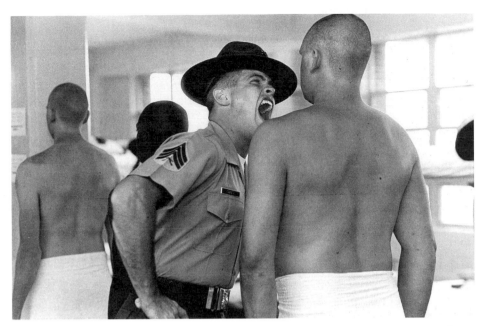

Coercive persuasion refers to compelling someone to do something, or to refrain from some form of action, by threatening them with dire consequences that they fear or would find unacceptable. While this type of persuasion fits the "magic bullet" model and is often very effective, it does not fit most people's conception of the process. More acceptable forms of persuasion take place in a transactional process leading people to interpret messages in such a way that they willingly change their beliefs, attitudes, or behavior.

ple with weight-reduction. She listened to their sales pitch, read their literature, and with the tantalizing vision of a slim figure to come, she paid her (rather substantial) fee. She started preparing her meals according to the plan and ate them without cheating, even though at first they left her hungry and unsatisfied.

A few days later, at her first *Pounds Ltd.* group meeting with the other clients, Lois had to get on a scale and be weighed by one of the "counselors." She was embarrassed when the trim young counselor said that she tipped the scales at 183 pounds. She was told that she would be weighed again for the record next week. Then the counselors and clients held a group "discussion" of different problems people were having in managing their eating. As part of the meeting, each person's weight was revealed to the others. For each participant, a history of where they had started was summarized along with details about their present weight. Those who were "success stories" were vigorously applauded. Even those who were still new to the program, but who had lost a pound or two, were given a round of applause. Those who had gained were given sympathy—along with looks of pity and thinly veiled smirks.

In the weeks that followed, Lois had mixed feelings about the program. She did get acquainted with some nice people like herself who were struggling with the same problem. She also had to admire those who had been fat and were now trim. It gave her hope. However, it was humiliating to have her weight revealed publicly. Most of all, she was in constant fear that she would not lose weight during the week and that she would be an object of pity and snickering when her weekly weigh-in was announced.

As the weeks turned to months, however, Lois did lose weight. Within 4 weeks she was down to 170; in 6 months she tipped the scales at a mere 150. She stayed with the program and finally broke the 130 mark in 16 months. She began to be asked out on dates. She had become accustomed to the smaller meals and felt that in time she would actually get down to 110, a normal weight for her height. Perhaps the most helpful thing about the program was the people she had met and their joint determination to get rid of their excess pounds.

What are the factors of persuasion here? Clearly, it was a difficult goal, and it was a long-range process. Equally clearly, it is far more than mere persuasive pep talks or lecturing by those in charge of the program. One key factor is the negative evaluation (norm) existing in society concerning being fat. That shared belief was most significant in getting Lois into Pounds Ltd. in the first place. Once she was participating, however, the functioning of the group itself played a central part in persuading her to continue. One factor was the norm constantly transmitted within the group, defining weight loss as approved and weight gain as *deviant*. Messages concerning *role* definitions within the group centered on personal responsibility for adherence to the diet and on continued weight reduction. When that role is played according to expectation, the applause received from the others is a well-appreciated social *reward*. Failing to lose, or gaining on the weekly weight report, results in a negative sanction of significance. Those who have achieved significant weight loss are *ranked* much higher in prestige within the group than those who have yet to do so. They receive messages of deference and are envied for their accomplishment. Along with all of these factors is the additional reward of forming friendships with others who are trying to cope with a similar problem.

Thus, the process of sociocultural persuasion based on social expectations is far more than simply a sender formulating a persuasive message and a receiver constructing some kind of meaning that will influence action. It is a complex process in which norms, roles, ranks, and social controls all play a part in defining what is acceptable versus what is deviant behavior.

Cognitive Reorganization to Achieve Behavior Change

The commonsense view of how behavior is determined and how it can be changed goes something like this: We all have a "mental" organization of understandings, feelings, beliefs, and preferences that are responsible for guiding our decisions about acting. Thus, our visible, or "overt," behavior is presumed to be shaped and determined by our mental organization. In other words, "mind" controls "action." From these assumptions it follows, logically enough, that if mental organization (feelings and beliefs) can be *changed*—by gaining the attention of receivers to persuasive messages, of course—overt behavior will be correspondingly changed.

Actually, that is not a bad way of thinking about certain kinds of persuasion, but the language is so old-fashioned. Therefore, some way of referring to these

mental phenomena is needed that brings greater precision and avoids old-fashioned labels. To handle the problem, such terms as *cognitive functions, cognitive organization, and cognitive processing* were invented and have come into wide use. Today, *cognitive functioning* is used to refer to what used to be called thinking, interpreting, and knowing. *Cognitive organization* refers to the structure of one's beliefs, attitudes, and values. Finally, *cognitive processing* includes perceiving, interpreting, remembering, and recalling. We will use them in those ways.

Cognitive organization (or structure) is important in discussing persuasion. The reason is that many communication scholars assume that persuasive messages can *alter* the components of that organization. That is, they believe that carefully designed messages can change the way people believe or feel about a topic and that such changes will result in modifications in the way they act toward the object of the communication.[2] We can call this the **psychodynamic strategy.** It is a traditional approach to persuasion, and it rests on the assumption that the route to achieving behavioral change lies in achieving cognitive reorganization.

Constructing or reconstructing meanings   One important way in which cognitive organization can be influenced is by providing people with *meanings* for objects, situations, and events that they have to interpret and react or respond to. This is most easily accomplished when the phenomena in question are not familiar to them. Through the clever use of symbols, message senders can sometimes get receivers to accept their desired meanings. Then, when those same receivers are called on to act toward whatever is at stake, those meanings can have a powerful influence in determining what they will do.

The nature of meaning was discussed in Chapter 1 (pp. 14–16), and the distinction between denotative and connotative meanings was made clear in Chapter 2 (pp. 58–59). These ideas are important in understanding the dynamics of influence, compliance, and change as these are achieved through the transmission of persuasive messages. The discussion of the meaning triangle in Chapter 2 showed that every symbol used in communication has associated with it, by conventional rules, both denotative meanings for the referent and a number of connotative meanings that are sometimes aroused. The important point here is that people trying to persuade others often make use of such connotative meanings to influence the interpretations that receivers make of a particular message. In that way, a sender can to some degree control the constructions of meaning that will take place as receivers of a message take part in the communicative transaction.

To illustrate how cleverly people can influence the meanings of others, we can refer to one of the most important historical events that took place in 1989. It was a year of political turmoil and upheaval all over the world, but one of the most remarkable episodes was the massive demonstrations that occurred in China as many thousands of people congregated and demonstrated in Tienanmen Square in Beijing.

Those demonstrations were, in fact, protests over corruption and misconduct by officials in the Chinese government. The students who led the protests were demanding certain reforms of their existing system. They were not by any means advocating that the existing Chinese government based on communism be replaced by democratic institutions modeled along the lines of those of the United States. At the same time, those student leaders urgently wanted international attention focused on their cause, particularly American attention. They were afraid (with ample justification) that without this scrutiny from abroad that the Chinese leadership would put down their demonstrations with military force—a traditional Chinese solution.

What did they do? One thing they did was to understand very well the cognitive organization of the average American citizen. Then they supplied the American public with a substantial number of symbols and images to be seen on television that would subtly structure what the demonstrators were doing so as to make it completely familiar and acceptable to people in the United States. They used a meaning-construction strategy to attract and hold the attention of Americans and to gain their sympathetic support.

To understand this strategy fully, it must be kept in mind that the entire upheaval was, as we have indicated, a Chinese event. Its causes and solutions were firmly rooted in the problems and the system of that country. However, by carefully selecting and presenting symbols whose connotative meanings are very powerful for Americans, they were able to *redefine* it into terms that had special significance for the people of the United States.

Howe did they do this? They accomplished this goal by focusing on slogans, sayings, expressions, and symbols that are at the heart of American democratic values. Then they made sure these were presented to the American public by television, newspapers, and magazines that

An effective strategy of persuasion is to try to achieve cognitive reorganization that will promote the behavior desired among those to whom the message is directed. This psychodynamic strategy of persuasion assumes that beliefs and attitudes shape behavior. Thus, if such cognitive variables are changed in desired ways, it is assumed that parallel behavior change will follow. Chinese leaders in the Tienanmen Square uprising used this strategy effectively to gain sympathy among viewers of television in the United States by linking their cause to symbols with powerful meanings for Americans.

were trying to show what was going on in Beijing. For example, many signs and banners with slogans in English were paraded before television cameras (who obligingly focused on them). These placards and banners displayed messages with which Americans are deeply familiar. An illustration is "Give me liberty or give me death!"—not exactly an ancient Chinese saying. Students were shown reciting the "Declaration of Independence," or talking about the importance of "freedom of the press," along with other American favorites. A big statue was built—

the "Goddess of Democracy"—carefully modeled after the Statue of Liberty. It was conveniently located where the television cameras couldn't miss it. Thus, a barrage of Fourth of July Americanisms were used to give the events in Tienanmen Square a special connotative meaning for Americans who tuned in.

The fact is that those American icons have little meaning for the average Chinese citizen. Indeed, the vast majority neither understand English nor know anything about the history of the American Revolution. Few would recognize the Declaration of Independence if they heard it in their own language. These *Americana* had little to do with the cause of eliminating corruption in government or the proposed reforms in the Communist system in China, which were the issues that actually brought on the demonstrations in the first place.[3]

We all know that the demonstrations ended in tragedy. Our purpose in using this example is not intended to be a criticism of either the demonstrations or the Chinese students who made use of this strategy. It was a very clever thing to do, and it very clearly accomplished its objectives. Americans were genuinely sympathetic with those who led the protests and were deeply disturbed when they were put down by the Chinese authorities with a great deal of bloodshed. Our purpose in citing Tienanmen Square is simply that it provides a very clear example of the meaning-construction strategy for redefining an event in terms that can be understood and approved by those to whom the messages were directed.

These same strategies of meaning construction and redefinition can be very effective at any level of communication and both within and across different cultural groups. A visit to any local automobile dealership can show how a mechanical object (an automobile) can be given new meanings of glamour, power, and even sexiness by a persuasive salesperson. Observation of the tactics of an effective trial lawyer can show how a body of factual evidence can be given new meanings by selective questioning, raising doubts, suggesting alternative interpretations, and so on. We are not implying here that this strategy is based on untruths or deception. Rather, it is a process of establishing, extending, substituting, and stabilizing meanings that are associated with particular words, concepts, events, or situations.[4]

Shaping or altering beliefs   One of the most important parts of our cognitive structure (the way things are organized in our heads) are our *beliefs*. Few people have difficulty understanding such a basic concept, but it is so fundamental that it is not all that easy to define. For our purposes here, a **belief** will be defined as *a kind of "statement of truth" that an individual accepts about some object, situation, or event.*

Each of us has thousands of truth statements in memory, such as "the world is round," "the sun rises in the east," and "water runs downhill." But for many objects or situations we have none. One strategy that is widely used in persuasion is to provide people with preshaped beliefs about events, issues, or situations where they have not yet formed any. Or, if they have, the strategy focuses on modifying the beliefs they already have but hold lightly.

Some beliefs are simply *factual*—like the three listed above. They do not involve any kind of positive or negative judgment, or imply any kind of emotional orientation, on the part of the person holding the belief. Other beliefs are *affective*—they do have an evaluative or emotional quality that implies such feelings as like, dislike, acceptance, rejection, approval, or disapproval. For example, it is one thing to believe that San Francisco is a *large* city. It is—and that is factually correct. Such a statement of truth about San Francisco implies no evaluative judgment. However, it is quite another thing to believe that San Francisco is a *beautiful* city. That kind of belief does have an affective component. It is a statement of truth (for the person holding the belief) revealing a positive affective orientation toward San Francisco.

The psychodynamic strategy of shaping or altering beliefs focuses mainly on *affective* truth statements. The reason is that they are closely linked to the kinds of actions often sought in persuasion—that is, accepting or rejecting something, or acting positively or negatively toward it in some other way. It is important to understand that people who hold beliefs rarely make the above distinction between factual and affective beliefs in their own minds. For a person who truly believes that "Detroit is a mean city," the negative character of that belief is simply a part of the statement of truth about that particular community. It seems as correct as "Detroit is a large city." In other words, our affective beliefs seem as valid and compelling to us as do those that incorporate only emotionally neutral facts.

The reason that altering beliefs is so often sought as a goal of psychodynamic persuasion is that beliefs—both factual and affective—are fundamental to every one of us as guides to *action*. Long ago, Plato, in his "Allegory of the Cave," showed that if people believe a situation to be real, they will act as though it is real.[5] In the 1920s,

Walter Lippman stated the principle in a much simpler way: The "pictures in our heads," he said, guide our actions toward things in "the world outside."[6]

That principle—that *beliefs are guides to action*—is amply illustrated thousands of times every day. People regularly punish others who they *believe* have transgressed the acceptable norms. Fist fights break out when one individual *believes* that another has insulted or ridiculed him or her, even if that was not the other's intent. Even more serious, every year some police officer regularly shoots an innocent person when he *believes* that the individual is "going for a gun." In each of these cases, reality is not the basis of action; it is beliefs about reality—that is, the "statements of truth" held by people—that make up the "pictures in their heads."

This link between beliefs and behavior provides the foundation for one of the most important assumptions underlying the entire field of persuasive communication: It is assumed that *persuasive messages can be designed to alter people's beliefs*—factual or affective—at least under some circumstances. If the messages do indeed achieve that objective, and people do modify their beliefs, then it follows that their *actions* may also change.

This assumption of a dynamic relationship between beliefs and action is the guiding principle of the psychodynamic strategies for achieving changes in someone through cognitive reorganization. Stated in the simplest terms, messages are designed to change beliefs, which will then (presumably) serve to modify behavior.

Does such a persuasion strategy work? The answer is a hesitant yes . . . but only sometimes. It can often be an indirect, accumulative process. It seldom works dramatically in a short-run and immediate sense. A very large body of research studies have focused on this issue. How does one bring about a change in beliefs in people through the use of persuasive message content? Traditionally, in the social sciences, changing people's beliefs has been seen as a *learning* process. Thus, belief changes have been brought about by lectures and exposure to training films, through group discussions, by asking people to read different kinds of materials, by having them listen to radio presentations, or through viewing material on videotape. Through any of these forms of communication, beliefs can be changed, but not easily. We will review some of the relevant research on these issues in a later section.[7]

Creating or modifying attitudes   Most research on persuasion has focused not on beliefs, in the basic sense we have discussed, but on configurations or structures of beliefs that we call *attitudes*. The term attitude is a very old one that predates all of the social sciences. It was adopted by the social sciences from previous meanings. Actually, the word came into the English language during the early 1700s. Originally, it derives from the Latin words *aptitudinem* and *aptus*. When it became a part of both French and Italian during the 15th century, it was as an important term in the world of art and design—meaning the physical positioning of an object in *space*. In England, in the 1830s, it became associated with the positioning of the *mind*. However, it did not become an important concept in the behavioral sciences until 1918, when it was used in its present form by W. I. Thomas and Florian Znaniecki to denote a person's affective beliefs about an object that lead to particular forms of action toward that same object.[8]

Today, the term *attitude* is perhaps the most widely used concept in the social sciences, and it has been studied in research for nearly three quarters of a century. Unfortunately, during that long period it has been defined in dozens of different ways, providing many different interpretations of what the term is supposed to mean.[9] However, we can avoid all of these controversies by dealing with it in a way that is completely consistent with our previous discussion of beliefs and their relationship to behavior. First, we can reject the notion that an attitude is some mysterious "force" that lies latent in our psyche and that becomes activated only when we have to form intentions to act. That is too complicated. A much simpler approach is to view attitudes as an extension of what we have already analyzed in the way of beliefs. That is, an attitude can be thought of as a "package" or "configuration" of beliefs of an affective nature. (A configuration is any set of interrelated elements.) For example, we may hold an attitude (set of beliefs) about a particular category of people. These beliefs will be related to each other. For example, if we believed these people to be undesirable, we probably would also think that they were stupid, cruel, lazy, and immoral. Alternatively, if we believed that category of people to be attractive, we probably would also believe that they were smart, virtuous, hard-working, and trustworthy. Thus, we have a configuration of affective beliefs about our attitude "object." When confronted with individual members of that category of people, either directly or indirectly, we use those affective beliefs to shape our thoughts or actions toward them.

But how closely do our actions match those beliefs? Common sense also tells us that our behavior seldom takes place in a "social vacuum." Furthermore, whatever is present in a situation of action can influence our behavior, regardless of our inner feelings. For example, we may feel quite negatively toward some topic, but if we are among friends who feel quite the opposite, we may refrain from saying or doing anything that we know they would resent. Thus, while our negative attitude can increase the *probability* that we will act negatively toward the object, various factors in our immediate situation of action can greatly reduce that probability.

While the above gives a kind of commonsense explanation of what is meant by attitude, and the relationship of attitude to behavior, it is such an important term that we need to set forth a carefully formulated definition. In this way, the part that attitudes can play in cognitive reorganization and behavioral change—using the pychodynamic strategy of persuasion—can be better understood.

We begin by reaffirming that an attitude is a configuration of affective beliefs about an object. In the previous section we gave a great deal of careful attention to the meaning of the term *belief* because it is so central to the meaning of attitude. "Affective" beliefs, as we explained, are "truths" (for them) that people embrace—implying such feelings as good/bad, like/dislike, acceptance/avoidance, and approval/disapproval.

The attitude "object" (that we think about, evaluate, and respond to) can in fact be almost anything. However, they are usually thought of as "general" rather than "specific." That is, they are broad topics or issues, as opposed to narrowly focused concerns. Examples are categories of *people* (like those who are addicted to drugs or people who litter beaches), *policies* (like capital punishment or disarmament), *practices* (like abortion or child abuse), or *issues* (like animal rights or welfare reform). We do not use the term *attitude* for people's affective beliefs about very specific objects (like left-handed saxophone players who have blue eyes, vanilla ice cream, or brown dogs with long ears).

Two additional features of an attitude must be a part of a formal definition. One of them is that attitudes are presumed to be a relatively *enduring* part of a person's cognitive structure. Many are learned early in life, and they remain as a more or less permanent part of the individual's psychological makeup. What this implies, of course, is that they are not easy to change. The second feature of attitudes is the assumption that they play a significant part in shaping or determining *actions* toward whatever is the object. This follows logically from the principle that we set forth earlier—that beliefs shape ac-

tions. That is, if attitudes are organizations of beliefs, they should also provide a basis for influencing the ways we will act—in a manner consistent with those beliefs. With these features in mind, we can define **attitude** in a more formal way as *a relatively enduring organization of affective beliefs about some broad object (such as a policy, social category of people, or situation) that increases the probability that an individual will respond to that object in a manner consistent with those beliefs.*[10]

Where do attitudes come from? The fact is that we *learn* them. Like beliefs of any kind, our attitudes are developed through experience. That is, from the experiences we have with objects, people, and situations we acquire complex patterns of affective beliefs that define our liking or disliking of those things. For example, we can develop a negative attitude toward the elderly by having a number of negative experiences with older people. These can then influence our behavior toward senior citizens.

As we suggested, when people talk about influencing others by using persuasive communication, they are typically talking about *changing* attitudes. It seems axiomatic to many people that if a person's attitude toward a particular topic or object is changed, then corresponding changes in behavior will also take place. This is a very important issue. We have suggested that attitudes (as organizations of affective beliefs) do provide guides to action. However, we have also implied that assuming a *close* correspondence between attitudes and behavior may be unwarranted.

The relationship between attitudes and behavior   If we are successful in influencing others to change their cognitive structure, can we automatically assume corresponding changes in related behaviors? In studying this issue, research on the relationship between attitudes and behaviors has been extensive.[11] Decade after decade, researchers continue to probe the question of whether attitudes are related to behavior or not.[12] Although a substantial controversy exists among researchers who continue to study this issue, there is general agreement that, in fact, *there is often little direct association between attitudes and behavior in most real-life situations.*[13]

Why, then, does interest in this particular psychodynamic strategy continue? The answer is that the relationship between attitudes and behavior is not yet fully understood, and it is far too early to dismiss changing attitudes as a means of bringing about changes in behavior. A far better alternative is to ask *under what conditions* are attitudes and behavior related, and what factors in a

The public generally believes that people's attitudes control their behavior in a direct one-to-one relationship, where positive attitudes lead to positive behavior and vice versa. That seemed to be the case with traditional attitudes of prejudice that were closely linked to discrimination in the past (that is, before 1960). A more contemporary view recognizes that social and cultural norms prevailing in a population can control people's actions, even if their private attitudes are contrary to that behavior. Thus, assuming a close relationship between attitudes and behavior is unwarranted.

situation of action reduce this relationship? In this section, we will examine at least some of the reasons for which the correspondence between attitudes and behavior may be limited.

Social scientists first faced the reality of inconsistencies between attitudes and behaviors in the 1930s when an early study challenged the assumption of a direct relationship.[14] Prior to that a direct relationship was almost universally assumed.[15] However, investigations of the degree of correspondence between attitudes and behavior have shown that any number of situations can have an influence on that relationship. That is, if some factors are present, the link between attitudes and behavior may be strong indeed. If other factors are in the situation, the relationship may be weak or even nonexistent. What these statements imply is that the *probability* of acting in accord with one's attitude (see the formal definition) depends on the presence or absence of several limiting and facilitating factors. Therefore, a solid understanding of such factors is critical where attempts are made to manipulate behavior by changing attitudes.

In the sections that follow, we describe three considerations that are critical to understanding the relationship between attitudes toward a topic and the probability of consistent behavior toward that same topic. Each must be considered in any communication strategy designed to change people's attitudes under the assumption that their behavior will then be changed in a parallel way. These three considerations are *topic importance, social pressures,* and *action constraints.*[16]

One reason why attitude change does not necessarily lead directly to corresponding behavior change has to do with the *importance* (to the person) of the *topic* that is the basis of the influence attempt. Some topics for which we hold attitudes simply have very little influence on what we actually do. If a topic is not of much importance to us, our attitude toward it is not likely to be strongly held. In other words, it is relatively easy for someone to get us to change our attitudes toward topics that either are unimportant to us or have no real consequences in our lives. Such topics probably include issues like programs for farm parity supports or federal regulation of programmed trading on the stock market. Typically, young adults do not hold deeply entrenched views about such issues, and they seldom resist changing attitudes toward them. Furthermore, whatever their attitudes on such topics, they may have no relationship to their behavior if ever confronted with a need to act in some relevant way.

On the other hand, a variety of topics are truly significant and consequential for the individual. It is unlikely that behavior toward them will be easily changed by exposure to a few persuasive messages. For example, people are often deeply committed to their positions on such matters as abortion, capital punishment, the dangers of radioactive waste, and smoking.

The beliefs people hold about such topics are likely to be deeply entrenched. Thus, both attitudes and behavior toward such topics are very difficult to change by any means. People work out their configuration of affective beliefs about such matters after long experience, and those patterns of convictions remain very durable. Having a well-entrenched position on a controversial issue is very *functional* (making decision-making uncomplicated) be-

cause such topics come up all the time and the person can simply respond with behavior consistent with his or her attitude. There is no need to work it all out over and over again, with endless considerations of new facts and new appeals for change. In that sense, then, an entrenched and well-defined attitude toward a personally significant topic is *efficient* in providing immediate guidelines for action.

Another critical factor in shaping our overt and visible behavior is the pattern of **social pressures** we encounter in the situation of action. These are our needs and desires to comply with social rules for behavior that are expected by others whose approval we seek. As we have indicated throughout the present book, action and communication always take place in a some *context* that includes a sociocultural situation and human relationships. Thus, what we *say* and what we *do* is usually observable by other people. The context of our actions then almost always include all the rules for social behavior which played a part in our example about Lois and Pounds Ltd.

Thus, while attitudes are "invisible" because they are inside heads, overt behavior is "visible" and therefore

People are often deeply committed to their positions on socially controversial topics. It is unlikely that their beliefs and attitudes will be changed by exposure to a few persuasive messages. Such positions are often embedded in values they acquired as children during long-term socialization. Moreover, their orientations are usually reinforced by family and peers in adult life. While the actions of demonstrators against such positions may make the protesters feel better, the messages they present are unlikely to result in significant change.

subject to scrutiny by others. This poses a set of social pressures on us that can cause attitudes and behavior toward the same topic to be very different (inconsistent).

Generally, then, the relationship between attitudes and behavior is unpredictable if that action takes place in a public context. If we know that the people in that context hold the same attitude and expect corresponding behavior, then there probably will be a close relationship. However, if people, whose opinions we value, would be appalled by behavior consistent with our privately held attitude, then it is entirely unlikely that our behavior will correspond.

To take a simple example, suppose that Jim, a college senior, came from a conservative business-owning family in which there has been a longstanding anti-union tradition. Jim has held anti-union attitudes since childhood. At the home of Sandra, his fiancée, however, he finds that her parents are not only union members, but her father is an officer in a large local. The father invites Jim to accompany him to the union meeting that evening. What will happen? One scenario would be that Jim's attitude would guide his behavior and he would decline. Another would be that social pressures would prevail and Jim would accept the invitation so as to please Sandra and avoid a strained relationship with her parents. In other words, it would be difficult to predict whether his attitude and behavior would be consistent.

In the real world, there is a diversity of such social pressures on each of us. They come from social expectations at work, at school, in family relationships, and so on. Regardless of how we may feel, we may or may not act in accordance with our attitudes. The importance of the topic may carry the day, but social pressures in the context of action can all influence our behavior.

There are also many **nonsocial constraints** on our actions. That is, there can be many occasions when an individual is inclined to act in accordance with his or her attitudes, and there are no social pressures to inhibit such behavior, but the correspondence is still not there. One simple reason can be that a number of physical and personal difficulties would have to be overcome for the action to take place in a corresponding manner. Action constraints of this type can sharply reduce the consistency between attitude and action. For example, the act may be *inconvenient*, perhaps requiring the person to travel a long distance to perform it. The behavior may involve potential *financial loss*. There may be *risks* or unwanted *trade-offs*. The act may be *physically difficult to perform*. There may be no real *opportunity*, or the individual may lack *competence* to engage in the behavior.

Generally, then, even if a person has a strongly held attitude toward a topic he or she regards as important, and even when inhibiting social pressures are completely absent, there may still be numerous factors in a real-life situation that will prevent corresponding action from taking place. For any or all of these reasons, then, it is unwise and unrealistic always to expect close correspondence between attitudes and actions toward a topic in the real world. It is even more unrealistic to expect that if persuasive messages *do* succeed in bringing about attitude change, there will be a corresponding change in behavior with attitudes and actions remaining in accordance.

Understanding Resistance and Yielding

Attempts to change our beliefs, our attitudes, and our behaviors are everywhere. We live in a society in which we are the targets of an almost unlimited number of message sources who seek to control our behavior in some way. Whether it is to change the product we typically buy at the grocery store, shape our vote intentions, solicit our contributions to worthy causes, uplift our minds, or instruct us in relating to the supernatural, an army of persuaders seem determined to alter our lives. As human beings, however, we are universally *resistant to change*. In fact, if there is a single consistent and totally defensible prediction that can be made about people, it is that they will resist change.

Resistance as Reaction to Persuasion Attempts

Only a limited amount of research has focused directly on resistance to change. It may be that there has been so much research effort devoted to trying to find ways to influence people, the study of resistance has been neglected. Furthermore, the information that is available explaining people's universal tendency to resist change is only indirectly related to the issue of persuasion. However, one particular perspective, Jack Brehm's *theory of psychological reactance,* does provide valuable insight into our universal inclination to resist change.[17]

Psychological reactance occurs when a person is motivated to "rebel" when his or her freedom to choose a particular way of acting is threatened by persuasion. Consequently, those who demand compliance from us may actually activate feelings of determination in us to

Student Resistance Scale

Instructions   Below you will find a series of statements that students have reported saying or doing to avoid going along with a teacher's request or demand. For the purpose of this survey, please consider these statements assuming you want to avoid going along with a teacher's demands. In other words, recall an incident or imagine a situation where a particular college teacher wanted you to do something and you didn't want to do it. For example, imagine that your teacher wants you to come to class more prepared from now on, or imagine that your teacher wants you to participate more in class discussion.

Please read all the statements that are grouped together into each category, and then indicate how likely you would be to use statements of this type in an effort to resist your teacher's demands to come to class more prepared or to participate more in class. Indicate your likelihood of using each group of statements by using the following scale:

5 extremely likely   **2** unlikely
4 likely   **1** extremely unlikely
3 maybe/undecided

_____ **1.** I would offer the teacher advice by saying something like the following: "Prepare yourself better so that you give better lectures." "Be more expressive; everything will work out to your advantage." "You should relate more with students before trying to give any advice." "If you open up, we'll tend to be more willing to do what you want." **(Teacher advice)**

_____ **2.** I would resist by claiming that "the teacher is boring." "The teacher makes me feel uneasy." "It is boring; I don't get anything out of it." "You don't seem prepared yourself." "If you weren't so boring, I would do what you want." **(Teacher blame)**

_____ **3.** I would simply drop the class. I won't participate as much. I won't go to class. I'll sit in the back of the room. **(Avoidance)**

_____ **4.** I'll do only enough work to get by. Although I would comply with the teacher's demands, I would do so un-

willingly. I'll come prepared but not be interested at all. Grudgingly, I'll come prepared. **(Reluctant compliance)**

_____ **5.** I won't come prepared at all. I'll leave my book at home. I'll continue to come unprepared to get on the teacher's nerves. I'll keep coming to class, but I won't be prepared. **(Active resistance)**

_____ **6.** I'll act like I'm prepared for class even though I may not be. I may be prepared, but play dumb for spite. I might tell the teacher I would make an effort to comply, but wouldn't. I'll make up some lie about why I'm not performing well in this class. **(Deception)**

_____ **7.** I'll go to the teacher's office and try to talk to him/her. After class, I would explain my behavior. I would talk to the teacher and explain how I feel and how others perceive him/her in class. **(Direct communication)**

_____ **8.** I'll disrupt the class by leaving to get needed materials. I'll be noisy in class. I'll ask questions in a monotone voice without interest. I'll be a wise-guy in class. **(Disruption)**

_____ **9.** I would offer some type of excuse like: "I don't feel well." "I don't understand the topic." "I can remember things without writing stuff down." "I forgot." "My car broke down." "This class is so easy I don't need to stay caught up." **(Excuses)**

_____ **10.** I would simply ignore the teacher's request, but come to class anyway. I probably wouldn't say anything; just do what I was doing before. I would simply let the teacher's request go in one ear and out the other. **(Ignoring the teacher)**

_____ **11.** I would tell the teacher I had other priorities, like: "I have other homework, so I can't prepare well for this class." "I have kids and they take up my time." "I'm too busy." "This class is not as important as my others." "I only took this class

for general education requirements."
(Priorities)

____ **12.** I would challenge the teacher's authority by asserting: "Do others in class have to do this?" "No one else is doing it, so why should I?" "Do you really take this class seriously?" "If this is such a good idea, why don't you prove it?" **(Challenge the teacher's basis of power)**

____ **13.** I would rally up student support. For instance, I would talk to others in class to see if they feel the same. I would tell my classmates not to go to class. I might get others to go along with me in not doing what the teacher wants. **(Rally student support)**

____ **14.** I would talk to someone in higher authority. For instance, I might complain to the department chair that this instructor is incompetent and can't motivate the class. I would make a complaint to the dean about the teacher's practices. I would talk to my advisor. I would threaten to go to the dean. **(Appeal to powerful others)**

____ **15.** I would indicate to the teacher that I would participate more if she/he were more enthusiastic about what she/he was doing. Or I might say, "You aren't enjoying it, so how can I?" "If you're not going to make the effort to teach well, I won't make an effort to listen." "You don't do it, so why should I?" **(Modeling teacher behavior)**

____ **16.** I would tell the teacher that he/she doesn't seem to care about us as students, why should I care about what he/she wants? Or I would say, "You don't seem to care about this class, why should I?" "You have no concern for this class yourself." **(Modeling teacher affect)**

____ **17.** I'd take a more active stance and tell the teacher that "I'm old enough to know what I should do in this class." "Right or wrong, that's the way I am." "I'm

surprised you even noticed I'm in your class." "Lead your own life!" "My behavior is my business." **(Hostile defensive)**

____ **18.** I would argue that "I know what works for me; I don't need your advice." "I don't need this grade anyway." "I'm doing just fine without changing my behavior." "We'll see when the test comes up." **(Student rebuttal)**

____ **19.** I'll get even by expressing my dissatisfaction with the teacher/course on evaluations at the end of the term. I'll write a letter to put in the teacher's personnel file. I'll steal or hide the teacher's lecture notes/tests. **(Revenge)**

Calculating Your Score

1. Add your responses to items 1, 2, 14, 15, and 16 = _____.

2. Add your responses to items 6, 10, 11, 17, and 18 = _____.

(Don't worry about responses to the rest of the items; we don't include them in your two final scores.)

Interpreting Your Score

Possible range for each of your scores is 5–25. (If either of your two scores falls outside that range, you have made a computational error.)

Our research on student resistance in the college classroom reveals that students often blame or attribute reasons for their resistance on one of two sources—either the teacher "owns" the problem or the student does. In other words, college students are able to discriminate between problems of their own making from problems attributed to their teachers.

We call your first score "TEACHER-OWNED" resistance techniques. Five categories or groups of statements represent this dimension of student resistance: Teacher Advice (#1), Teacher Blame (#2), Appeal to Powerful Others (#14), Modeling Teacher Behavior (#15), and Modeling Teacher Affect (#16). No

(continued)

(continued)

tice how all the items that make up this dimension refer to teacher blame or ownership. Students who report a greater likelihood of using TEACHER-OWNED techniques are likely to perceive their teacher as behaving inappropriately or inconsistently with their notions of what teachers should or should not do. Most of the messages reflected in these strategies refer to the teacher as "boring," "unenthused," and "unprepared." No wonder students feel justified in their resistance with teachers of this type. And, no wonder they select strategies that place blame squarely on the teacher.

We call your second score "STUDENT-OWNED" resistance techniques. Once again, five categories make up this dimension: Deception (#6), Ignoring the Teacher (#10), Priorities (#11), Hostile Defensive (#17), and Student Rebuttal (#18). These strategies reveal that students frequently assume responsibility for their own behavior. With these techniques, students claim the right to make their mistakes and to assume control over their own lives. They make up excuses, claim to have other more important responsibilities, and may even resent the teacher trying to tell them what they can or cannot do. When selecting these strategies, students are more likely to blame themselves, not the teacher, for their own resistance decisions.

The rest of the strategies fall somewhere in-between the two problem ownership types. For the most part, our research on college student resistance indicates that students are more likely to avoid open and aggressive confrontations with their teachers; instead, students prefer to give excuses, try to change the teacher's behavior, or grudgingly comply. In most cases and with most of your teachers, how do you fit this profile yourself?

References

Burroughs, N. F., Kearney, P., & Plax, T. G. (1989). Compliance-resistance in the classroom. *Communication Education, 38,* 214–229.

Kearney, P., Plax, T. G., & Burroughs, N. F. (1991). An attributional analysis of college students' resistance decisions. *Communication Education, 40,* 325–342.

resist persuasion, causing a *reaction* against the attempt. Brehm expresses this idea by suggesting that the target of the influence attempt feels that "he can do what he wants, that he does not have to do what he doesn't want, and that at least in regard to the freedom in question, he is the sole director of his own behavior."[18]

Thus, our need to be in *control,* plus our strong desire for a stable and balanced life, provide the foundation for reactance. That is, as adults we expect and like the freedom to choose and control most of our own behaviors. This expectation of freedom, the importance of that freedom, and many other closely related issues, all motivate us to resist particular influence attempts.[19]

We agree with Brehm's perspective for several reasons. First, it "makes sense." We do generally react negatively to people who openly attempt to get us to do things we don't want to do. No one likes to believe that they are being "talked into" doing something against their better judgment. Moreover, because we are bombarded with a daily barrage of messages attempting to get us to change, we have to develop a "thick skin"—a strong tendency to resist—just to get through the day.

A second reason why we like Brehm's explanation is that it compliments our conceptions of beliefs and attitudes, including our position on the relatively unpredictable relationship between attitudes and behavior. Brehm's perspective strengthens an important part of that discussion. While our explanation focused on social and nonsocial factors, Brehm's adds a psychological perspective to our understanding of attitude/behavior inconsistency by noting people's universal tendency to resist changing their behavior as a result of exposure to persuasive communication.

Finally, the third reason we like Brehm's explanation is that it serves as a useful point of departure for discussing additional areas that are important in learning how to influence people. Specifically, before we can consider how a variety of available influence strategies can be used, we must know more about the nature of *resistance* to change through persuasion.

Types of Resistance

Discussions of resistance to persuasion often characterize any kind of opposition to persuasion as negative or destructive.[20] Furthermore, the idea of people resisting to a limited degree has seldom been addressed. This is unfortunate because when we view resistance as essentially destructive we limit our ability to understand effectively those people who resist to some degree, but do not entirely reject, influence attempts. Furthermore, some kinds of resistance are entirely justified and serve constructive purposes. Thus, it is more realistic to maintain that there are essentially two types of resistance—destructive and constructive—and to assume that people resist in varying degrees.[21]

Destructive resistance   Extreme **destructive resistance** is characterized as disagreeable, negative, subversive, or even rebellious behavior. From this perspective, resistance is *misbehavior*—disobedience or corruption of authority. This type of resistance clearly illustrates a contempt for an authority figure or for authority itself. That is, people who resist the requests and influence attempts of legitimate authorities for no other reason than that they *are* authorities, are destructive.

For example, if a manager directs an employee to engage in a legitimate work task and the employee refuses to comply, the employee is being destructively resistant. In this situation, the employee is being openly disobedient and is undermining the manager's rational-legal authority. Assuming that the order does not involve immoral or illegitimate behavior, the fact that it is a designated superior who is making the assignment requires the employee to comply. In this case, the employee's refusal illustrates destructive resistance. This type of resistance normally contributes nothing to a situation. Indeed, it is just what the label implies.

Constructive resistance   There are numerous ways that **constructive resistance**—refusing to comply when the behavior being solicited is against ethical norms—can contribute to a situation. For example, in the experiments of Stanley Milgram, subjects were ordered to administer dangerous levels of electric shocks to other individuals. Only a few subjects resisted their orders. Fortunately, there were no other human beings actually receiving the shocks, even though the subjects thought there were.[22] Refusing to engage in such behavior, in spite of "orders," provides an example of constructive resistance.

In real life, the boundaries between constructive and destructive resistance can be very murky indeed. What seems constructive to one group may be interpreted as destructive by another. The problem of deciding whether a particular form of resistance is one or the other can cloud many circumstances. For example, members of certain religious groups have for generations refused to consult physicians when a member of their family becomes ill.

They hold deep convictions that prayer will provide healing and that turning to conventional medicine amounts to a rejection of their faith. From a legal standpoint, such resistance can be a violation of law. Some see such resistance as unacceptable when lives are at stake. Others, however, see a need in a society that respects religious convictions to make provision for such resistance.

The debate as to what is constructive or destructive may be impossible to settle. Today, at least some people feel morally compelled to resist laws supported by the majority of society which they deem improper. One example is the animal rights groups that throw blood on women wearing fur coats or break into laboratories to free animals used in medical research. Another example is the so-called right-to-life activists who block the paths of women seeking legal abortions at clinics, even though they know they will be arrested for their resistance. In their own minds, these individuals are engaging in constructive resistance. Others in society see their behavior as destructive resistance to legitimate norms and laws.

Two important implications follow from what we have just considered: First, and most obvious, is that when trying to persuade someone to change his or her views or behavior, it is almost certain that resistance will be encountered. This implies that provision must be made for reducing that resistance if at all possible. Second, to develop a strategy for reducing resistance, it is important to understand whether, from the standpoint of the person, it is seen as constructive. If this is the case, the task of persuasion may be difficult or virtually impossible because constructive resistance is often based on deep commitments to ethical, moral, and culturally based positions. Such beliefs are particularly difficult to overcome. It would not be an easy task, for example, to persuade an animal rights advocate that wearing fur coats is a positive form of behavior, or a right-to-life advocate that abortion is an acceptable concept. Thus, viewing resistance as constructive from the subjective viewpoint of the person to be persuaded changes the way we think about it, and it certainly has a bearing on the strategies that might be used to circumvent it.

Types of Yielding

Although the most predictable reaction to an influence attempt is resistance, sometimes it is neither possible nor appropriate. There are many occasions when people either consciously or unconsciously need to submit to influence. That is, there are a variety of circumstances in which we might want to yield in a particular situation where someone is attempting to influence our beliefs, attitudes, and behaviors.

In a now-classic article on social influence processes, Herbert Kelman has described three types of yielding.[23] These are what he calls *compliance, identification,* and *internalization.* Although these three concepts can and frequently do overlap, each follows from a particular set of conditions.

Compliance   Kelman's first type is consistent with our previous discussion of compliance. It refers to yielding publicly or observably to an influence attempt—but in this case without actually accepting the change privately. A number of questions arise in discussions of this kind of compliance. The first is: Why would anyone publicly appear to change while not having some corresponding private change? The answer is that we frequently find ourselves in situations where it is better to "go along to get along." That is, it is more *expedient* not to challenge what is being said by an individual or a group than it is to speak out in opposition or to resist.

Most people simply comply in situations like this, either to receive a reward or to avoid being punished. For example, suppose you are driving on the highway and a police officer drives up alongside and directs you to slow down. Even though you are not exceeding the posted speed limit, you slow down. The issue here is that you accept being influenced because this individual controls certain punishments that can be imposed (e.g., a ticket). When the police officer is down the road and out of sight, however, you are likely to resume your original speed. Compliance in this situation is solely public or observable; it lasts only as long as the influencing agent is visibly present. Compliance as a form of yielding, then, is based on our expectation of gaining rewards or avoiding punishment.

Identification   Kelman's second type of yielding to influence occurs because of our desire to emulate a particular individual or group. Yielding of this type is based on our wish to gain satisfaction in being "like" some individual or group that we want to imitate or that we admire. For example, suppose that we became acquainted with a young man we would like to have as a close friend. The primary reasons we like this individual include the fact that we feel good about ourselves when we are around him and that he has a positive influence on our behavior in ways that please us very much. We admire, and want to be like, this individual.

Now suppose that this person we admire is zealously committed to an anti nuclear-power position—an issue that we find boring or feel the opposite about. Our new friend frequently attempts to get us to accept his position. Although our natural inclination is to resist change, based on what we have described, it is likely that we will yield to his attempts to influence us. We will become more negative toward nuclear power. This probably would not come all at once, but if our relationship with this individual continued to develop, we probably would eventually yield.

Why do we end up yielding in these kinds of circumstances? The answer is that there are *rewards* in having this individual as our close friend and in feeling that we are like this person. He makes us feel good about ourselves, and that in itself is very rewarding.

Internalization   Kelman's third type of yielding to influence indicates that we do so because it is personally rewarding or useful. But more important, people yield in this manner so as to be consistent with their values. By "values" we refer to whatever an individual *deeply believes to be important in life.* Thus, values (like attitudes) are configurations of affective beliefs. Unlike attitudes, however, they do not have clear-cut "objects." Furthermore, they are much more general because they are *goals* or end-states that people seek, rather than objects. For instance, a person may value (and seek) as a major goal such end-states as a moral life, happiness, freedom, service to others, power, or even wealth. Such broad and general goals help to determine many of an individual's attitudes and beliefs as well as actions.[24]

The basis of Kelman's internalization, as a type of yielding, is how much intrinsic value a specific change actually provides for the person. It is no simple task to influence people to internalize a change. They must have an incentive—that is, making the change must be worthwhile. This type of yielding is the result of a rational decision to do so because the change fits into the individual's system of values. In this way, such change is interpreted as consistent with the person's innermost convictions of what is important in life.

Communication Strategies for Influencing People

Most of our attempts to influence people typically won't extend over a long period. However, even immediate or short-term influence encounters can and should be handled as if we intend to develop a long-term relationship.

That is, prerequisite to making *any* one-shot or long-term influence attempt successful is our approaching the encounter as we would approach the development of a lasting relationship.

This long-term perspective is critical. Regardless of the cultural or ethnic groups to which we belong, all of us like to feel special, attended to, and cared about. It is impossible to create the impression that you care about someone you want to influence unless you sincerely approach your encounters with them as if you would like to develop a lasting relationship. Convincing people that you care in this way contributes to the style and affect of your influence attempt.

In addition to the influence processes and changes already discussed, several specific communication strategies can contribute to the success of attempts to influence people. Our use of the term *communication strategy* refers to a specific message technique, or a series of such techniques, for influencing change. These strategies focus on characteristics of receivers, messages, and sources of persuasive messages.

Recognizing Receiver Characteristics

As in all communication, persuasion strategies require some knowledge of the receiver targeted for change. If an individual is identified as possessing a particular attribute or a set of characteristics, then that knowledge can be part of a planned communication strategy. There are a variety of ways we can acquire information about people we want to influence. Our discussion in Chapter 9 on sizing up people (pp. 265–267) describes the acquisition of relevant information following six simple and effective steps.

Rather than repeat what we have described earlier, we focus very specifically on areas that are pertinent to the use of persuasion strategies. The first of these is receiver **susceptibility**: the degree to which an individual's personal characteristics make him or her either more or less easily influenced by others. Such attributes are important in deciding the best ways to influence receivers. Any person in the role of receiver possesses a number of identifiable attributes that make him or her more or less susceptible to influence attempts.

Gender differences   One of the more widely investigated, and certainly the most controversial, of the attributes related to susceptibility is whether a person is male or female. The reason for the popularity of gender among investigators conducting susceptibility research is obvious. So many differences exist between males and females that many people just assume differences exist in susceptibility to influence as well. This popular belief has stimulated a great deal of research over the years. Early studies supported the assumption that females were more easily influenced than males.[25] By the late 1970s, however, researchers had concluded that there probably are no *major* gender differences in susceptibility to persuasion. Contemporary investigations indicate that certain things about more culturally "traditional" males and females probably do affect the degree to which they are susceptible to influence. Attributes like emotionalism, expressiveness, and assertiveness that were part of the definitions of traditional male and female roles in decades past do seem to be related to persuasibility.

Personality characteristics   Large numbers of researchers have investigated whether differences in personality characteristics among human beings are related to susceptibility to persuasion. One particular study provides us with insights into which receiver personality characteristics should be considered in the selection of communication strategies. This study examined a number of receiver attributes as a way of determining susceptibility to certain topics of influence.[26] As an initial step, college students completed an extensive battery of personality tests. Their attitudes toward several topics of communication were also assessed.

Later, on a different occasion, the investigators asked randomly selected groups of these same students to engage in a "counterattitudinal activity." This required them to act *as if* they believed in one or more of the originally assessed communication topics. Attitudes toward these topics were assessed again at the end of this second session. Analyses of the results enabled the researchers to define receiver *personality profiles* of students who showed high and low levels of yielding. Results indicated that high and low amounts of change were clearly tied to particular receiver personality profiles. Specifically, large amounts of change occurred with receivers who were obliging, changeable, dependent, and unstable. Minimum change occurred among those who were aggressive, unchanging, forceful, efficient, and well informed.

Features of Effective Messages

As we noted earlier, for decades researchers have tried to discover the "magic keys" (words, appeals, message structures) that can be used to influence people. Of all the potential keys examined in thousands of studies, only a few come close to working that way, and few universal prescriptions for influencing people with messages exist.

With this caveat in mind, we will discuss several keys to changing people that have shown at least some results in research. These keys are more accurately called *features of effective messages* that have persuaded people in experiments and other kinds of studies. The degree to which these can be incorporated into influence attempts outside experimental settings is not entirely clear. However, for what they are worth, at least five such features can be identified:

Sidedness   Some of the earliest and most meaningful examinations of communication strategies were conducted in the 1950s by social psychologists Carl Hovland, Irving Janis, and Harold Kelley.[27] One of the factors they studied was called **sidedness.** Specifically, this is the question of whether to use a message that presented only one side of a persuasive argument, to include both sides, or to use both sides and refute the opposing arguments as well. Results from a number of studies supported the strategy of using the two-sided message, which refutes the other's position.[28]

Message ordering.   A substantial amount of research has examined whether the *first* side of an argument presented, or the most *recent* side, carries the most influence. This is what is usually referred to as the *primacy-recency* question. That is, is it more persuasive to put the arguments favoring a position early in a message, or does more change result when arguments are inserted at the end of the message? The safest recommendation we can make concerning this persuasion strategy is that there is no universal law of primacy-recency, and one's choice should depend on what conditions exist at the time of the influence attempt.[29]

Fear appeals   One of the more intriguing communication strategies available involves the use of fear-arousing appeals to influence change. The original research examining the effectiveness of this strategy indicated that large amounts of change are produced with *weak* fear appeals and little or no change results from *strong* appeals that aroused high levels of fear.[30] More recent fear appeal studies suggest that the opposite is the case.[31] That is, strong fear appeals do work, producing more yielding than weak appeals. The explanation of this seeming contradiction is that there appears to be a point at which too much fear in a message causes people to avoid, or to disregard, the message or to do both.[32] As with the other strategies described, our recommendation is to consider both the target and the situation carefully prior to trying this strategy.

Behavior-alteration techniques   This refers to a set of message techniques rather than a single persuasion strategy. Each of these **behavior-alteration techniques** is represented by a set of messages of a particular kind. For example, one of these techniques, called "Reward from Behavior," includes messages like "You will enjoy it," "You will get a reward if you do," "It will make you happy," "It will help you," and "You will benefit if you do it." Investigations of these techniques indicate that using several behavior-alteration procedures appears to be effective in motivating a person to yield in a particular influence attempt.[33]

Recent examinations indicate that the original techniques are more appropriately categorized into two general types—*prosocial* and *antisocial.* For example, the "Reward for Behavior" technique is an example of the prosocial type. A technique called "Punishment from Behavior" is a good illustration of the antisocial type. Messages representative of this antisocial type include "You will lose if you don't," "You will be punished if you don't," "You will be unhappy if you don't," and "You will be hurt if you don't."

Using nonverbal cues   In Chapter 3, the nature of nonverbal cues in messages was discussed in detail. One of the principles from that discussion that is extremely important in influencing people is nonverbal immediacy (pp. 90–92). This can be the basis of an integrated verbal and nonverbal persuasion strategy, especially in cases where the goal of the persuasion is to create a lasting relationship.

Recall that the nonverbal immediacy refers to such behaviors as smiling, head-nodding, forward-leaning, eye contact, and standing close to someone. Also recall that the effects of immediacy are based on the principle of utility. In brief, we tend to approach people we like both physically and psychologically, and we tend to avoid behaving in these ways toward people we don't like. People understand this, and therefore, signals of nonverbal immediacy are an effective form of persuasive communication.

Credibility of the Source

The issue of credibility of the sender can be discussed separately because it is not always seen as a feature of an effective message. However, we will treat it as such. We also set it apart because it requires detailed explanation.

In its simplest form, **credibility** refers to "how believable a person believes a message source to be."[34] This simple definition says two very important things: First and most critical, credibility is something that is perceived—"in the eye of the beholder." Thus, we may think that we are a highly credible person, but if others don't think so we are not.

The second issue implied by the definition is that to be credible we must be *believable*. Believability means several things. Conversely, since the two concepts are defined in terms of each other, credibility means several things. In fact, after many years of investigating source credibility, researchers have come to define it as a combination of five separate dimensions: *competence, trustworthiness, extroversion, composure,* and *sociability.* In order for us effectively to get people to perceive us as credible sources, and thus use it as a communication strategy, we need to understand each of these dimensions and how they fit together.

The five dimensions of credibility can be explained very simply. The first, competence, refers to how knowledgeable or expert a source is thought to be in a given content area. The second, trustworthiness, refers to whether people believe us to be an honest person: To be credible we need to be perceived as honest. The third

dimension of credibility is extroversion. This refers to the degree to which we are believed to be talkative, bold, dynamic, and outgoing. Interestingly, if we are not perceived this way to some degree, we tend to be perceived as untrustworthy. The fourth dimension is composure. To be composed is to be in control of one's emotions; that is, reasonably composed people tend to be perceived as poised, relaxed, and confident. The fifth and final dimension is sociability, which refers to how likable and friendly we seem. If people interpret us in this way, they perceive us as the kind of person others would want to socialize with.

Taken together, all five dimensions interconnect to influence people's perceptions of credibility. It is important to note that too much extroversion can be perceived as oppressive; too much composure can be perceived as not caring, etc. All things considered, the best combination is to try to control how you are perceived so as to possess moderate to high levels of each of the five dimensions. If you are successful at getting people to see you in these ways, you will likely be seen as a *believable* person. If that can be done, you might be effective at changing a person's attitudes.[35] At least that is what is suggested by a considerable body of research.[36]

Chapter Review

- In modern society numerous individuals, groups, and agencies constantly try to influence people's ideas, feelings, or actions. We all encounter such situations every day, either as a sender trying to get someone to make a change or as the receiver of messages aimed at modifying *our* thinking or conduct.

- Earlier, persuasion was seen as something that one person "did to" another. The message sender took an active role and transmitted "appeals" that could modify the thinking of a passive receiver. Later, researchers saw that every person was influenced by numerous personal attributes that influenced the meanings people constructed for persuasive messages. The first of these views of persuasion is a linear "magic bullet" interpretation; the other is a simultaneous transactions model.

- If the sender's desired change is in fact achieved, persuasion can be defined as a transaction in which a message source constructs and transmits messages designed to influence a receiving person's constructions of meanings in ways that will lead to planned changes in the receiver's beliefs, attitudes, or behavior.

- The dynamics of compliance fall into three categories: One results from coercive messages, in which people may have little choice but to change their behavior. A second basis for compliance comes about because persuasive messages communicate meanings about sociocultural expectations. A third is based on cognitive reorganization in which people change the way they think or feel about the topic of persuasive messages.

- The assumption of a dynamic relationship between beliefs and action is the guiding principle of the psychodynamic strategies for achieving changes in someone through cognitive reorganization.

- Attitude can be defined formally as a relatively enduring organization of affective beliefs about some broad object (such as a policy, social category, or situation) that increases the probability that an individual will respond to that object in a manner consistent with those beliefs.

- Attitudes and actions toward the same object are seldom consistent. While an attitude can increase the *probability* that we will act in a consistent way toward the object, various social factors in our immediate situation of action can greatly reduce that probability.

- Human beings are universally *resistant to change*. In fact, if there is a single consistent prediction that can be made about people, it is that they will resist change. It is this factor that makes achieving persuasion especially difficult.
- Psychological reactance to persuasion occurs because of our need to be in control, plus our strong desire for a stable and balanced life. As adults we expect and like the freedom to choose and control most of our own behaviors. Desire for that freedom, and many other closely related issues, all motivate us to resist influence.
- There are essentially two types of resistance—destructive and constructive—that cause people to resist in varying degrees. Extreme destructive resistance is characterized as disagreeable, negative, subversive, or even rebellious behavior, clearly illustrating a contempt for an authority figure or for authority itself. In contrast, constructive resistance can be positive, especially when the behavior solicited is against ethical norms.
- Herbert Kelman has described three types of yielding: compliance, identification, and internalization. Compliance refers to yielding publicly to an influence attempt, but without actually changing privately. Identification is yielding to influence of a desire to emulate a particular individual or group. Identification is yielding because it is personally rewarding or useful.
- All persuasion strategies require knowledge of the receiver targeted for change so that they can be used as part of a specific communication strategy. One set of such attributes is receiver susceptibility, personal characteristics that make people either more or less easily influenced by others.
- Five features of messages have been widely studied as possible keys to persuasion. These are sidedness, message ordering, fear appeals, behavior-alteration meanings of reward and punishment, and nonverbal cues in persuasive messages to achieve immediacy. Some seem to bring results in some cases.
- Source credibility refers to the issue of whether a receiver believes the originator of the message to be a trustworthy sender who is transmitting truthful statements or claims. Researchers have come to define such credibility as a combination of five separate dimensions: competence, trustworthiness, extroversion, composure, and sociability.

Key Terms

Attitude   A relatively enduring organization of affective beliefs about some broad object (such as a policy, social category of people, or situation) that increases the probability that an individual will respond to that object in a manner consistent with those beliefs.

Behavior-alteration techniques   Including meanings in a persuasive message that are designed to arouse feelings of reward and punishment. These techniques are based on principles of behavior modification in learning.

Belief   A kind of "statement of truth" that an individual accepts about some object (thing, situation, or event). Some are "factual" in that they do not involve any kind of positive or negative judgment, or imply any kind of emotional orientation, on the part of the person holding the belief. Others are "affective," having a positive or negative component of feeling or judgment regarding their object for the person holding the belief.

Coercion   Compelling someone to do something, or restraining them from acting in some way, by threatening them with consequences that they find unacceptable.

Cognitive reorganization   A modification of the feelings, beliefs, attitudes, motivations, or other internal components of an individual's cognitive structure (as a result of persuasion in the present context).

Compliance   Yielding publicly or observably to an influence attempt without actually accepting the change privately.

Constructive resistance   Resistance to persuasion that contributes positively to a situation, especially when the behavior being solicited is against ethical norms.

Credibility (of a source)   Simply, the degree to which a receiver sees a source person (group or agency) as trustworthy and the messages transmitted as truthful. More technically, a perceived characteristic of a source based on a combination of beliefs about that source's competence, trustworthiness, extroversion, composure, and sociability.

Destructive resistance   Disagreeable, negative, subversive, or even rebellious behavior in response to legitimate attempts at persuasion.

Identification   Yielding to influence that occurs because of a person's desire to emulate a particular individual or group.

Internalization   Yielding to influence because it is personally rewarding or useful.

Message ordering   Often referred to as the *primacy-recency* question. That is, is it more persuasive to put the arguments favoring a position early in a message, or does more change result when arguments are inserted at the end of the message?

Nonsocial constraints (on attitude-related action) Nonsocial factors that reduce the consistency between attitude and action. For example, the act may be inconvenient, involve potential financial loss, pose risks, or be difficult to perform. Also, the person may lack opportunity or competence.

Persuasion   Basically, efforts to *change* us in some way by using strategies of communication. More formally: a transactional process in which a source or sender encodes and transmits messages designed to influence a receiving person's constructions of meanings in ways that will lead to changes desired by the source in the receiver's beliefs, attitudes, or behavior.

Psychodynamic strategy   A traditional approach to persuasion resting on the assumption that the route to achieving behavioral change lies in achieving cognitive reorganization. In nontechnical terms: based on the idea "mind" controls "action," it follows that if feelings and beliefs can be changed by persuasive messages (cognitive reorganization), overt behavior will be correspondingly changed.

Psychological reactance (against persuasion)   Strong feelings of determined resistance that cause a person to react against an attempt at persuasion.

Sidedness   A feature of a persuasive message concerning the degree to which the arguments it presents explain one side only or include and refute opposing arguments as well.

Social expectations   The shared rules that govern all kinds of human social behavior (including communication) in group settings. These are the *norms, roles, ranks,* and *controls* by which group members pattern their interactions with each other.

Social pressures   Our feelings of needs and desires to comply with social rules for behavior that are expected by others whose approval we seek in a situation of action (see: Social expectations).

Susceptibility   The degree to which a person is more or less easily influenced by others because of his or her personal characteristics.

Notes

1. A classic example is the case where Kate Smith, a popular singer and radio personality of the 1940s, sold $39 million worth of war bonds during an 18-hour marathon radio broadcast. See: Merton, R. K. (1946). *Mass persuasion: The social psychology of a war bond drive.* New York: Harper & Brothers.

2. Advertisers who strive to sell products with the use of persuasion communications mastered this formula decades ago. They call it the "learn, feel, do" approach. As far as they are concerned, it is not particularly effective. See: Jones, J. P. (1986). *What's in a Name? Advertising and the concept of brands* (p. 141). Lexington, MA: Heath.

3. This example was drawn from a seminar paper entitled "On Money and Meaning in the Popular Press," prepared by Lee Ordman for a graduate course at Syracuse University in the Fall of 1989.

4. Originally formulated by Melvin DeFleur and Timothy Plax as an explanation of certain kinds of effects of mass communication, meaning theory is equally applicable to persuasion at an interpersonal and group level. See: Lowery, S., & DeFleur, M. (1983). *Milestones in mass communication research* (pp. 28–30, 383–385). New York: Longman.

5. Cornford, F. M. (Trans. and Ed.). (1941). *The Republic of Plato* (pp. 227–231). London: Oxford University Press.

6. Lippmann, W. (1922). The world outside and the pictures in our heads. Chapter 1 in his *Public Opinion* (pp. 1–19). New York: Macmillan.

7. A large earlier literature is summarized in: Hovland, C. I., Janis, I., & Kelley, H. H. (1953). *Communication and persuasion.* New Haven, CT: Yale University Press.

8. Thomas, W. I., & Znaniecki, F. F. (1927). *The Polish peasant in Europe and America* (Vol. 1). New York: Knopf. (First published 1918)

9. DeFleur, M. L., & Westie, F. R. (1963). Attitude as a scientific concept. *Social Forces, 42,* 17–31. See also: Fishbein, M. & Azjen, O. (1975). *Belief, attitude, intention, and behavior* (pp. 5–13). Reading, MA:

Addison-Wesley; Bettinghaus, E. P., & Cody, M. J. (1987). *Persuasive communication* (4th ed.) (pp. 6–10). New York: Holt, Rinehart & Winston.

10. This definition is derived from: Rokeach, M. (1973). *Beliefs, attitudes and values* (p. 122). San Francisco: Jossey-Bass.

11. Seibold, D. R. (1975). Communication research and the attitude-verbal report-overt behavior relationship: A critique and theoretic reformulation. *Human Communication Research, 2,* 3–32; Cushman, D. P., & McPhee, R. D. (Eds.). (1980). *Message-attitude-behavior relationship: Theory, methodology, and application.* New York: Academic Press; and Cooper, J., & Croyle, R. T. (1984). Attitudes and attitude change. In Rosenzweig, M. R., & Porter, L. W. (Eds.), *Annual review of psychology,* (Vol. 35, pp. 395–460). Palo Alto, CA: Annual Reviews.

12. Ibid.

13. Ibid.

14. LaPiere, R. T. (1934). Attitudes versus actions. *Social Forces, 13,* 230–237.

15. DeFleur, M. L. & Westie, F. R. (1958). Attitudes and overt acts. *American Sociological Review, 23,* 667–673.

16. Plax, T. G., & DeFleur, M. L. (1980). Communication, attitudes, and behavior: An axiomatic theory with implications for persuasion research. Paper presented to the Western Speech Communication Association, Portland, OR.

17. Brehm, J. W. (1966). *A theory of psychological reactance.* New York: Academic Press.

18. Ibid., p. 9.

19. Most explanations of why people resist change follow from discussions of the human need for a comfortable, stable, and balanced life. In American society, middle-class children are told from early childhood that if they engage in the right forms of preparation, a comfortable life style will follow. In other words, if they work hard, go to school, get good grades, get a good job, and save their money, they will have stability, balance, and thus happiness in their lives.

That is, they will achieve the "American Dream." We are taught to make achieving this life style one of our highest priorities, and to do so we must attain *control* across a diversity of activities. Our natural and common reaction to threats to such control, with their possible suspensions of personal freedom, is to *resist both change and attempts to get us to comply.*

20. Burroughs, N. F., Kearney, P., & Plax, T. G. (1989). Compliance-resistance in the college classroom. *Communication Education, 38,* 214–229.

21. Ibid.

22. Milgram, S. (1963). Behavioral study of obedience. *Journal of Abnormal and Social Psychology, 67,* 371–378.

23. Kelman, H. C. (1961). Processes of opinion change. *Public Opinion Quarterly, 25,* 58–78.

24. The most frequently cited treatment of values is Rokeach, op. cit. For other interesting discussions of values see: Oskamp, S. (1977). *Attitudes and opinions* (p. 13). Englewood Cliffs, NJ: Prentice-Hall; and Simmons, H. W. (1976). *Persuasion: Understanding, practice, and analysis* (p. 20). Reading, MA: Addison-Wesley.

25. For a discussion of the early research on this topic see: Cronkhite, G. (1969). *Persuasion—Speech and behavioral change.* Indianapolis: Bobbs-Merrill. A large number of subsequent research studies have probed this issue, but the findings have been inconsistent. Some studies indicated that women are more susceptible. Other studies suggested that males are more persuadable. Additional studies indicated that there are no sex differences in susceptibility.

26. Plax, T. G., & Rosenfeld, L. B. (1977). Antecedent of change in males and females. *Psychological Reports, 41,* 811–824. For additional examples of research examining personal characteristics and persuasion see: Boster, F. J., & Stiff, J. B. (1984). Compliance-gaining message selection behavior. *Human Communication Research, 10,* 539–556; Hunter, J. H., Gerbing, D. W., & Boster, F. J. (1982). Machiavellian beliefs and personality: Construct invalidity of the Machiavellian dimension. *Journal of Personality and Social Psychology, 43,* 1293–1305. Also, for a review of research on locus of control and persuasion see: Cody, M. J., & McLaughlin, M. L. The situation as a construct in communication research. (1985). In M. L. Knapp & G. R. Miller (Eds.), *Handbook of interpersonal communication* (pp. 263–312). Beverly Hills, CA: Sage.

27. Hovland, C. I., Janis, I. L., & Kelley, H. H. (1953). *Communication and persuasion.* New Haven, CT: Yale University Press.

28. Allen, M., Hale, J., Mongeau, P., Berkowitz-Stafford, S., Stafford, S., Shanahan, W., Agee, P., Dillon, K., Dickson, R., & Ray, C. (1990). Testing a model of message-sidedness: Three replications. *Communication Monographs, 57,* 275–291.

29. Hovland, C. I., Mandel, W., Campbell, E. H., Brock, T., Luchins, A. S., Cohen, A. E., McGuire, W. J., Janis, I. L., Feierabend, R. I., & Anderson, N. H., (1957). *The order of presentation in persuasion.* New Haven, CT: Yale University Press.

30. Janis, I. L., & Feshbach, S. (1953). Effects of fear arousing communications. *Journal of Abnormal and Social Psychology, 48,* 78–92.

31. Higbee, K. L. (1969). Fifteen years of fear arousal: Research on threat appeals: 1953–1968. *Psychological Bulletin, 72,* 426–444.

32. McGuire, W. J. (1968). Personality and susceptibility to social influence. In E. E. Borgatta & W. W. Lambert (Eds.), *Handbook of personality theory and research* (pp. 1130–1187). Chicago: Rand McNally.

33. Kearney, P., Plax, T. G., Richmond, V. P., & McCroskey, J. C. (1984). Power in the classroom IV: Teacher communication techniques as alternatives to discipline. In R. Bostrom (Ed.), *Communication yearbook 8* (pp. 724–746). Beverly Hills, CA: Sage. For an excellent review of the research on compliance-gaining in other contexts see: Seibold, D. R., Cantrill, J. G., Meyers, R. A., (1985). Communication and interpersonal influence. In M. L. Knapp & G. R. Miller (Eds.), *Handbook of interpersonal communication* (pp. 551–614). Beverly Hills, CA: Sage.

34. McCroskey, J. C., Richmond, V. P., & Stewart, R. A. (1986). *One on one: The foundations of interpersonal communication* (p. 73). Englewood Cliffs, NJ: Prentice-Hall.

35. Plax, T. G., & Rosenfeld, L. B. Individual differences in the credibility and attitude change relationship. *Journal of Social Psychology, 111,* 79–89.

36. Bettinghaus & Cody, op. cit., pp. 84–94.

Additional Readings

DeFleur, M. L., & Dennis, E. E. (1991). *Understanding mass communication* (4th ed.) (Ch. 18, pp. 558–585). Boston, MA: Houghton Mifflin.

> This is a relatively comprehensive chapter on the influences of the media on society and culture. All of the material in this chapter is important to understanding persuasion. However, of particular relevance is the section on "media-created meanings as influences on behavior." This material will pose no difficulties for the beginning student.

Larson, C. U. (1989). *Persuasion: Reception and responsibility* (5th ed.). Belmont, CA: Wadsworth.

> Now in its fifth edition, this book provides the undergraduate student with an excellent survey of the persuasion area. The book covers all of the same issues, concepts, and theories as other basic texts. However, especially noteworthy are discussions of ethics, language, advertising, and propaganda. This text will not be difficult for the introductory student.

O'Keefe, D. J. (1990). *Persuasion: Theory and research.* Newbury Park, CA: Sage.

> This text provides a comprehensive examination of the theories and research surrounding the persuasion process. It covers both traditional and contemporary issues. Large sections of the book are devoted to the most recent research in this area. This book tends to be somewhat more advanced than those listed below.

Reardon, K. K. (1991). *Persuasion in practice* (2nd ed.). Newbury Park, CA: Sage.

This text provides an excellent overview of the persuasion area. The format of the book is structured to answer the most relevant questions concerning theory and application. The content covered in the book includes explanations of the most basic issues and theories as well as chapters on influence in organizations, the mass media, and the political arena.

Roloff, M. E., & Miller, G. R. (Eds.). (1980). *Persuasion: New directions in theory and research.* Beverly Hills, CA: Sage.

This book represents an excellent selection of essays written by well-known persuasion scholars. Each essay contributes in a significant way to an understanding of persuasion in society. Important issues covered include bargaining and negotiation, the trial process, marketing, and mass communication.

Chapter 11

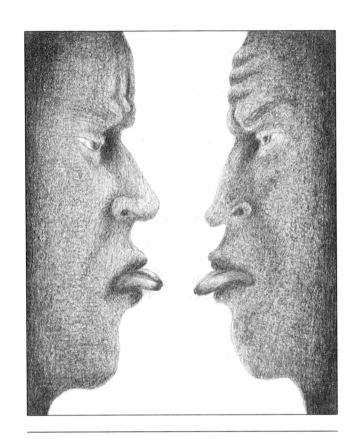

Coping with Conflicts

Contents

The Nature of Conflict
Formulating a Definition
Consequences of Conflicts

Personal Styles of Coping with Conflict
The Competitive Style
The Collaborative Style
The Compromising Style
The Avoidance Style
The Accommodation Style

Common Causes of Conflict
Meanings as a Primary Cause
Contextual Factors That Can Generate Conflict
   The sociocultural situation
   Social relationships

Successful Conflict Negotiation
Defining Negotiation

Guidelines for Negotiation
   Guideline 1: Don't bargain over positions
   Guideline 2: Separate the people from the problem
   Guideline 3: Focus on interests, not positions
   Guideline 4: Invent options for mutual gain
   Guideline 5: Insist on using objective criteria
   Guideline 6: Develop the best "fallback" position
   Guideline 7: Cope with resistance to negotiation
   Guideline 8: Deflect "dirty tricks"

Chapter Review

Key Terms

Notes

Additional Readings

Key Questions

■ Conflicts rarely occur between people of good will. Right? After all, adults think and act at all times like mature individuals. Right? Even when they disagree, intelligent people control themselves. Right? Responsible human beings don't act in irrational and vicious ways. Right? . . . Wrong! Wrong! Wrong! Wrong!

■ Why is it that conflicts are normal among people and as typically American as apple pie, motherhood, and the flag? Is it because most people have a dark and vicious side, or is it that certain forms of conflict are an established and approved part of the American culture?

■ Isn't it true that conflict is inherently bad? That is, how can anyone say that sometimes they have positive outcomes? Don't all conflicts have negative consequences, or is it possible that there can be advantageous outcomes, with benefits to the people involved?

■ Isn't it obvious that conflicts arise because of *flawed personalities*—that is, that bad people are responsible when conflicts occur? Or is it possible that parties to a conflict are decent people and that conflict is a result of contextual factors?

*The termination of a conflict is a special undertaking
. . . It involves more fundamental changes in social
relationships than the actual outbreak of a conflict.
The latter is usually merely an outburst of a latent
antagonism due to existing frictions and oppositions.
But the termination of a conflict involves fundamental [interpersonal] changes.*

Georg Simmel
1908

John and Loretta are both in the Personnel and Training Unit of a large computer manufacturer. They have
the same boss, and they must frequently rely on each
other to complete various tasks. Normally, they work
together very well and are well liked by the others in the
unit. Unfortunately, they are currently in serious disagreement over a specific assignment their boss gave
Loretta. In fact, they are engaged in a heated conflict that
has escalated to a point where it is keeping them from
communicating rationally to each other about their
work.[1]

Their mutual dislike has become obvious to everyone
around them. They glare at each other during meetings
and have gotten to a point where each seems to take
pleasure in finding ways to undermine the other. Other
people try to avoid talking with them about this dispute.
In fact, it has become difficult to talk to them at all, and
this situation is causing the productivity of everyone in
Personnel and Training to suffer.

Earlier, John and Loretta liked each other, spent time
together socially, and helped each other out on the job.
The problem started when Loretta was assigned a task
that would normally have been John's responsibility. She
was asked to evaluate the success of the company's
recently implemented program for recruiting and training new workers. It was a plan that John had originally
designed and developed. Loretta didn't really want to
make this evaluation because normally it would be John's
responsibility and she knew that John would be upset.
She had tried to explain John's probable negative reaction
to their boss, but her response was simple. "Loretta, I
gave you an assignment and I expect you to get it done.
I couldn't care less what John or anybody else thinks
about you doing this work. Just do it—understand?"

Loretta understood. On the one hand, she knew that
she was competent to handle the assignment, having
successfully completed numerous such evaluations

earlier. On the other hand, staffing plans were John's
responsibility, and she knew how possessive he was about
his job. Nevertheless, she realized that she really had no
alternative, short of resigning—so she went ahead with
the evaluation.

Several times, Loretta tried to tell John that it wasn't
her fault. Again and again she tried to explain to him how
she had no choice and how uncomfortable she felt, but
his reaction was as flexible as a brick wall. In fact, he
became more hostile each time she approached him.
Finally, Loretta began to get angry. The madder she got,
the more hostile he became toward her. She was furious.
Finally, resolving their conflict just seemed impossible.

After several weeks, the boss called both of them into
her office to try to settle the dispute. Her approach was
about as subtle as someone using a sledge hammer to
break an egg. John and Loretta sat stiffly and silently in
chairs in front of her desk staring straight ahead; neither
would look at the other.

Their boss moved right to the point. "You two people
have wasted a lot of this company's time over the last
several weeks. Your uproar over this evaluation is cost-
ing a great deal of money. It is interfering with your work
and everyone else's. I want both of you to put a stop to
this nonsense right here and now. So listen to me very
carefully! Your conflict is officially *over,* as of this minute.
Stop dreaming up ways to convince me and the rest of
us here that the other person is in the wrong, and stop
bad-mouthing each other. And quit screwing up our
work!"

"I am giving you two the rest of the day to get your
act together," she continued. "I don't care how you do
it, but do it! Tomorrow morning I expect you two to be
talking to each other just like old buddies. Let me remind
you both that no one—I mean *no one*—in this organization is indispensable. We don't have room for prima
donnas. Neither of you is going to waste one more

minute of this company's time. Do you two get the drift of what I am saying?''

John and Loretta both gulped, and reluctantly nodded yes to their boss. They "got the drift" loud and clear. It was time to resolve their differences.

Perhaps the conflict between John and Loretta sounds unusual—the kind of thing that rarely occurs between intelligent people. After all, such employees are adults, and they must surely think and act like mature individuals. Almost anyone can disagree from time to time, but intelligent people control themselves. Responsible human beings don't act in irrational and vicious ways, systematically trying to destroy each other's careers over some issue as insignificant as who evaluates a staffing plan. In fact, people who would *purposely* go out of their way to behave like John and Loretta may be emotionally unstable. Perhaps, what they really need is psychiatric counseling . . . right?

Wrong! Wrong! Wrong! Given the right set of circumstances, almost any one of us is likely to act *exactly* like John and Loretta. No one is immune. We all get angry when we perceive a threat to, or a potential loss of, something we value. We try to protect ourselves and to stop the person representing the threat. We feel it is natural to "get back" aggressively at anyone who tries to take something away from us that we feel is rightly ours. The result is often an unresolvable conflict.

Why does this happen? For one thing, it is a standard psychological principle that, regardless of what is at stake, we all tend to respond to frustration with aggression.[2] Hostility between people can occur anywhere, and for an infinite number of reasons. Conflicts occur between people of all kinds—strangers, friends, lovers, employees, spouses, relatives, teachers, parents, and so on. It is as common among the educated as it is among the untutored. Conflict is as characteristic of the highly intelligent as it is of the poorly gifted. In short, conflict is both *widespread* and a *normal* part of social life. Sooner or later we all wind up mad at someone.

Conflict can develop between people in almost any relationship. In fact, we could realistically rewrite the scenario of John and Loretta as employees into a description of John and Loretta as man and wife, as close friends, as landlord and tenant, or even as professor and student. Perhaps the only unique aspect of the conflict between those two is that they had a boss who forced them (albeit clumsily) to do something about their confrontation. Most people involved in conflict don't have

the luxury of a built-in controlling agent. They either have to negotiate their conflicts themselves or seek the help of some type of "referee" or mediating party. That seldom happens, because in most cases it is either inconvenient or impossible to find such a person. The majority of the conflicts that we will face in life, therefore, will have to be resolved by each of us as best we can.

Given all of the above, an important question to ask is *how* can people successfully deal with conflicts in which they will (inevitably) become embroiled? Understanding that question is the primary objective of this chapter. In order to provide insightful answers, the first section of the chapter discusses the nature of conflicts generally and provides a *definition* of what we mean by the term. After presenting our definition, we will distinguish between "productive" and "unproductive" conflicts, based on the *consequences* or outcome of a particular dispute. In the second section, we describe five common *reactions* to conflict. By reactions we refer to the more common styles of handling or trying to manage dissension. In the third section, we discuss common *causes* of conflict, focusing specifically on ways in which they begin as problems of communication and on the contextual bases from which controversies and confrontations arise. The fourth and final section moves directly into ways in which conflicts can be *negotiated,* which may be the only effective way to deal with them—short of shooting all the participants!

The Nature of Conflict

Each of us can confidently expect to experience many kinds of conflicts during our lifetimes. That is, conflicts are *inevitable, recurring,* and *normal* in human social life. Moreover, they come in many forms; they arise in virtually every type of social situation; and they can occur between people in all kinds of social relationships.

One of the first characteristics of conflict we need to recognize is that it can range from trivial, as in a minor competition, to a devastating clash that becomes brutal and destructive. However, we are not concerned in this text with violent conflicts, such as gang wars, police shoot-outs, barroom brawls, or others of that nature. We are concerned here with conflicts that occur between people in everyday walks of life, such as in the family, at work, among neighbors, or at school—the type illustrated by what happened between John and Loretta in the context of their work.

These kinds of conflicts are normal among people and as typically American as apple pie, motherhood, and the flag. That is, certain forms of conflict are an established

Conflict is as normal among people as is any other form of routine interaction. In any group where members associate with others frequently, disagreements will arise over many issues. As long as it does not become destructive, conflict can produce positive consequences as people learn ways to handle their differences, compromise unrealistic positions, and accommodate the needs of other members.

and approved part of the American culture. That is not to say that Americans blindly approve of violent or destructive behavior. They don't. However, ours is a complex society made up of many groups and categories, with distinctive specialized cultures and agendas, who are often in competition for power, privilege, or other scarce resources. This inevitably generates struggles—in other words, conflicts—among various segments of the society. Thus, Americans often see themselves in a "we" versus "they" perspective. Common examples are management versus labor, rich versus poor, males versus females, one racial or ethnic group versus another, farmers versus city-dwellers, or even the old versus the young.[3]

A second major characteristic of conflict can best be understood within this cultural perspective. That is, within limits, to be a "fighter" is commonly seen by Americans as *good*. To shrink from conflict is widely regarded as *bad*. People who typically go out of their way to dodge conflicts are sometimes referred to with pejorative terms, such as "wimp," "spineless," "yellow," and "soft." The American general culture, then, supports *a culturally approved readiness* toward engaging in conflict (that does not escalate to physical violence).[4]

There are other cultural roots of our readiness to en-

gage in conflict. In many ways, that orientation is an extension of our cultural mandates to *succeed in life*. Middle-class children in both the dominant and many minority groups are taught early-on that to be "happy," and above all, "worthwhile," they must be "successful." In childhood it means *winning* in various settings, ranging from sports contests to spelling bees. Later, it means "making it" by acquiring impressive material possessions and achieving upward mobility in a career. Thus, "getting ahead" is a very important value to many Americans, perhaps the majority.

But "getting ahead" inescapably means *getting ahead of someone else.* Thus, we share a conflict perspective on the so-called American Dream (of upward mobility). To act in ways consistent with this aspect of our culture, then, we literally must engage in a lifetime of competitive conflicts. To please ourselves and others, we compete at home, at school, on the job, and in whatever situation lends itself to such rivalry. Thus, our tendencies to be competitive and to engage in conflict are deeply embedded in our way of life. They are part of our mainstream cultural traditions, and they inevitably become a central part of our personalities as we participate and are socialized within that culture.

The American mainstream culture stresses getting ahead in competition with others for material rewards, power, and prestige. Such competition is a central feature of many of the professions and among managerial ranks in business, government, and industry. This cultural theme inevitably generates conflict with others who are in the same competitive struggle. Understanding how conflicts arise, their consequences, and ways of coping with them is an important part of mastering communications skills.

Formulating a Definition

We need to be very clear about what we actually mean by the term *conflict*. This will help us understand both our almost reflexive tendency to engage in conflicts and how we can go about resolving them when they occur. Although the idea of conflict may seem simple enough in a commonsense way, there is surprising disagreement among experts about what kinds of states, situations, and behaviors should be referred to by the term. Consequently there are a variety of definitions, each stressing different meanings. Unfortunately, most are either too narrowly linked to a specific scientific research project or are much too complicated and technical. Thus, few of these existing definitions fit our present purposes. Therefore, we will define the term simply. For the purposes of this text, then, we define **conflict** as *a dispute in which different values result in claims to rewards or resources that are in limited supply, and where the main objective of the people engaged in the process is either to neutralize or eliminate the prospects of their opponent to win what is at stake.*[5]

We recognize that our definition is a bit long. But it does set forth in a simple way the essential features of conflict. It notes the "object" around which conflict develops, the goals of the participants (to win, and keep the other from doing so), and the nature of their relationship

(as one of contention). A simpler, but reasonably adequate, definition would state that participants in a conflict are in *competition* with each other over something important to them.

Admittedly, this definition states a kind of "economic model" of the causes of conflict. As we will see, this is only one way to look at the causes of conflict, but it does provide a good beginning because it shows that conflicts develop over some "commodity" (reward or resource) that all the participants desire but not all can have. If a commodity is valued, and if it is possible for only a few people to have it, that commodity will appear to them to have great worth. This sets the stage for strong competition to attain it. The struggle can be over anything people want. It may be money, power, authority, prestige, immediate access to the boss, or an office with a nice view. It is the scarcity of the rewards and resources valued in the specific situation that serves as an important beginning point for the development of conflict.

We can see these principles in our example of John and Loretta. Their conflict represents one of the most common types found in the workplace—competition for such rewards and resources as status or power positions. Thus, the conflict began when part of what normally was John's authority became an object of competition—or at least he *believed* that to be the case. He felt that he had worked long and hard for the right to assess programs. After all, that fell within his job description. In his mind, that authority *belonged* to him as part of the status rewards of his job. John felt threatened because he thought that Loretta was attempting to usurp some of his status and power. It didn't really matter whether Loretta or his boss initiated Loretta's actions. To John, she was the direct and visible competitor.

Was John's interpretation irrational? Perhaps. But we each define our own interpretations of reality, and as we have explained in previous chapters, they become *the facts* on which we base our actions and decisions.

For Loretta, a very different set of facts seemed to be present. She knew that she did not ask for the assignment; indeed, she tried to avoid it; and she tried to explain to John that she had no intention of usurping his authority. When he was inflexible, however, she came to believe that he wanted to fight. When that happens in the American society, our general culture instructs us that only spineless wimps let others walk all over them! That, then, becomes a compelling guide for behavior. Thus, if John wanted a fight, it was OK with Loretta. She could give back whatever he "dished out," and then some. After all, career issues and *getting ahead* were at stake. At that point the conflict escalated and became a problem for everyone.

We indicated in our definition of conflict that the main objective of the protagonists is to either *neutralize* or *eliminate* the prospects of their opponent. Because middle-class Americans have a strong culturally based need to succeed, it makes sense that "beating the opponent" would be a primary goal in all types of conflicts. If we neutralize our opponent's efforts, we get what we want; if we eliminate his or her prospects altogether, we *guarantee* that we get what we want. Either way, we win the struggle and capture the valued commodity.

There are, however, other rules surrounding the goals and objectives of those in conflict. Specifically, they define limits on how we go about "winning"—that is, neutralizing or even eliminating the chances of the opponent to capture the commodity. It is not acceptable in our society to damage, destroy, or even discredit our opponent in some completely destructive way. Our general culture requires that what is done must be within ethical standards.

These seemingly conflicting cultural definitions are not incompatible. At first glance, what we have proposed may seem like a scene from Kafka in which bitterly opposing attorneys, locked desperately in a courtroom battle, enjoy a convivial lunch together. As we will point out, there are ways to neutralize one's competition in a conflict while remaining ethical and *constructive*. That is, the opponent does not have to be destroyed and end up with absolutely nothing. In some situations (and ideally in all situations), each of the parties in a process of conflict can and should *benefit* in some way when it is resolved.

Getting what we want, then, simply means that in a conflict we compete with someone in an ethical manner—and in the end gain at least some advantage (from our perspective). This implies getting a share of whatever value, reward, or resource is at stake, but in a way that allows both parties to gain at least something through the resolution of the conflict.[6]

These points about the process and meaning of "winning" are extremely important. Opponents in a conflict need not even be cold and distant—in fact, they can compete vigorously and remain friends. For example, friends and family members frequently train for and compete in activities ranging from athletic events to courtroom trials. Co-workers often spend time in conflicts that lead to formulating the best approach to such activities as marketing, employee relations, labor negotiations, hiring, and so on. In other words, viewed in these ways, conflicts are not *inherently* negative or adverse. In fact, conflicts can range along a continuum from positive through neutral to negative.

Consequences of Conflicts

What the foregoing indicates is that engaging in a conflict doesn't automatically mean we are participating in an intrinsically positive or negative activity. That is, conflicts are not, in and of themselves, either productive or unproductive. What is important is how people behave during a conflict and especially the specific *consequences* of the process. Moreover, it is the people who initiate and engage in a conflict who determine whether it will ultimately be productive or destructive; their specific personalities influence the kinds of outcomes that result from all forms of human interaction. Conflict is no exception.

Conflicts are followed by unproductive, negative, or even destructive outcomes when we enter the process with negative attitudes or hostile feelings toward our opponent. As we noted, these directly arouse needs for aggression. Therefore, as one might expect, conflicts that start on a negative note often end up that way. Fortunately, most of us are not normally antagonistic toward other people. And, unless provoked, we seldom go out of our way to be hostile toward each other. Because we aren't naturally antagonistic, most of our conflicts start out looking rather innocent. In some cases, however, things just "happen" and the conflict escalates.

Even though it may be uncomfortable, conflict can be constructive. There is no need to communicate in ways that leave both parties bitter and frustrated. Trying to understand the other's point of view, and being very careful not to send irrevocable messages can head off heated exchanges and explosions into ugliness and hostility. Handled properly, we can often get what we want in an ethical manner that leaves both parties as winners.

Conflicts that produce bad feelings and unproductive results tend to be those that just seem to get out of hand. One of the opponents gets hot under the collar, or the other gets angry, and the encounter explodes into ugliness and hostility. The case of John and Loretta provides an example. If it had been handled properly from the beginning, it might have had productive consequences. However, that was not the case, and having a third party end the situation was one of the few ways that was open.

Examples of conflicts that often end up being unproductive are those centering on divorce, child custody, job termination, disputes between members of a family over an inheritance, and union-management impasses. All of these frequently lead to bitterness, alienation, sabotage on the job, or even physical violence. In these kinds of cases, all of the parties involved lose even if they "win," because of the negative consequences they face, whatever the outcome.

Conflicts that have negative or unproductive consequences for the people involved seldom start out in a dramatically negative way. Often, the initial events seem minor, and the early exchanges seem little more than mild disagreements. In fact, what occurs between people during the early stages of a conflict can and often does dictate both what happens later in the encounter as well as its ultimate consequences. In particular, what happens initially usually determines whether a conflict will escalate or de-escalate so as to become unproductive or productive for the people involved.

It is important to keep in mind that the uncontrolled escalation of a competitive encounter can change an apparently minor disagreement into something resembling World War Three. Part of learning to handle confrontations effectively is acquiring the ability to distinguish between potentially good and bad conflicts during their early stages. Thus, we need to learn to recognize the *symptoms* of disagreements that potentially lead to escalating and unproductive conflicts. This is not always easy, but there are several obvious identifiers of potentially good and bad conflicts. One class of such identifiers is the characteristics of the people in the encounter. People who are likely to engage in unproductive conflicts are the easiest to spot.

Specifically, individuals likely to escalate a conflict and cause it to have unproductive outcomes often show signs of stress, even during the early stages. Such signs can include a conspicuous loss of energy or dedication, rapid conversation, noticeable indications of anxiety, and various forms of compulsive behavior such as overeating or sometimes the excessive consumption of alcohol, or even

Destructive Outcome of Conflict

drugs. If an unproductive conflict persists over a long period, other symptoms are likely to be evident. These might include spending inappropriate amounts of time, and the irrational use of resources, to undermine an opponent at the expense of getting important work done.[7] Many of the behaviors of John and Loretta fell into this category.

A variety of other identifiable indicators of unproductive conflicts exist as well. The effects of conflict on individuals tend to vary, both by person and by particular situation. It is important to be able to recognize the negative signs of either a useful and positive conflict or one leading toward counterproductivity. The bottom line on all of these signs is that if we recognize them in time it may be possible to redirect a degenerating communication encounter into one that yields productive consequences.

Productive conflicts can be identified by a different set of signs. As is the case with unproductive conflicts, the most important signs are the participants' characteristics and actions. The most obvious include friendly conversation between the opponents. At the nonverbal level, the signs are smiles versus frowns, friendly versus threatening gestures, and even how far apart the opponents have positioned themselves during their encounter. Most of the constructive signs are very obvious. Yet, typically, people who witness a productive conflict tend to see the encounter as negative.

The main reason why many obviously constructive conflicts aren't seen as positive is that people are committed to the idea that all conflicts are somehow destructive. As we indicated earlier, such a narrow interpretation is both incorrect and unfortunate. Certain types of conflicts can result in positive consequences that far outnumber any of the potential drawbacks.

For example, two individuals working together on the design of a sales campaign for a product with a profit potential are likely to engage in conflicts. Disagreements will inevitably occur over issues pertinent to the potential effectiveness of the campaign. These may focus on which media to use, how to phrase the advertising copy, what colors are best, what meanings to imply, whether personal endorsements are worthwhile, and so on. In such a case, some level of disagreement is a normal part of work relationships.

Conflicts of this kind provide a forum for deliberating and discussing important professional ideas. Depending on the profession, the result of such a conflict can be a thorough and critical analysis leading to a variety of ways to solve problems more effectively. Those solutions may be innovative legal strategies, more accurate medical diagnoses, more efficient production techniques, or better ways to present ideas in classes. Constructive conflicts of this type are common in almost all professional and business environments.

Similar to what takes place in business and industry,

conflicts can be productive in any setting where people communicate with each other. For example, conflicts of one degree of intensity or another constantly arise between husbands and wives, girlfriends and boyfriends, sisters and brothers, and so on. Most people find some mutually acceptable means of dealing with such disputes—they have to if they are to continue their social relationship over time. These solutions to continuing their relationship range from the congenial settlement of long-term disagreements to the mutual definition of acceptable ways to communicate during heated discussions over sensitive issues. To illustrate our point, let us consider some typical and potentially productive conflicts that were observed between (an actual) husband and wife.

Marla and Tom spent many years dating before they were married. Afterward, they found that living together brings a variety of problems, which if not handled constructively, can affect the stability of a relationship. They hadn't anticipated having conflicts over such issues as money, domestic chores, disciplining children, relating to friends, privacy, or pets, to list but a few that troubled the early years of their marriage. During the first year especially, it seemed as if almost every issue they dealt with provided a basis for disagreement. They often had difficulty understanding why they were so frequently at odds with one another.

Any number of things happen to people when they marry that can contribute to the occurrence of conflict. Ironically, when Tom and Marla were dating they seemed to agree on almost everything of importance. They truly believed that they had considered and worked through all of the potentially rough spots in their relationship. They were so sure that they were completely compatible, and that they agreed on everything important, that marriage seemed the natural next step.

Needless to say, it is in the first few years of marriage that people are particularly likely to experience conflicts. During this period, failures to resolve them often have negative outcomes. Statistics on divorce show that breakups are most likely within the first 10 years. If the marriage survives this critical early period, it is likely to last much longer.[8]

There is no way to simulate and work through the problems of marriage before the relationship becomes a fact. These include forming a family in a legal sense, merging resources into a single economic unit, changing relationships with friends, renting or buying a home, carrying on domestic activities, earning a steady income, and relating to in-laws. Living together can provide some indications about potential sources of conflict, but the marriage and family relationship is far more complex.

Moreover, many of the issues that new couples will face after marriage were poorly understood beforehand, or they seemed insignificant to them during the periods of dating and engagement. At that time, love and romance were the priorities in their lives.

Generally, then, the single most important issue for newlyweds is not where and how they will live, or even when they will have children and how they will raise them. The truly critical issue is how they will handle their conflicts. In large part, it is on that issue that the success or failure of their marriage will depend. If they allow minor disagreements over numerous problems that arise to escalate into negative and unproductive conflicts, they will soon be making arrangements with divorce lawyers. If they can deal with their disagreements, and keep their conflicts from escalating, they are more likely to continue their married life together.

Fortunately, when conflicts occur many couples try to direct their discussions toward productive outcomes, which is just what is required. Obviously, the actual nature of the effort depends largely on the specific causes of each conflict, but it also depends very heavily on the probable *reactions* of the people involved in the encounter. We need, therefore, to consider at this point a number of common ways in which people try to deal with conflict when they are confronted with them.

Personal Styles of Coping with Conflict

Much of human behavior is relatively predictable because it follows patterns of action and reaction deeply established in our culture. This is certainly true of reactions to conflict. That is, it is possible to predict with some degree of accuracy how people will try to deal with various kinds of conflict situations. These can be described in terms of what communication researchers refer to as personal *conflict styles.*[9]

By a **conflict style** we mean how an individual is likely to behave when anticipating or engaging in a confrontation. Typically, investigators determine an individual's conflict style by administering some type of self-report questionnaire. While the idea of common styles as copying strategies to deal with conflict has been examined in a number of ways, in our discussion we will focus on an assessment and classification system devised by Ralph Kilmann and Kenneth Thomas.[10] According to these investigators, our personal style of handling conflicts is based on our need to meet two interconnected yet competing objectives. One of these is our *concern for self* in a conflict situation; the other is our *concern for our opponent*. Although these appear to be different goals, they

Argumentativeness Scale (ARG)

Instructions   This questionnaire contains statements about arguing controversial issues. Indicate how often each statement is true for you personally by placing the appropriate number in the blank to the left of the statement. Use the following options:

5 almost always true for you   **2** rarely true
4 often true   **1** almost never true
3 occasionally true

_____ 1. While in an argument, I worry that the person I am arguing with will form a negative impression of me.

_____ 2. Arguing over controversial issues improves my intelligence.

_____ 3. I enjoy avoiding arguments.

_____ 4. I am energetic and enthusiastic when I argue.

_____ 5. Once I finish an argument I promise myself that I will not get into another.

_____ 6. Arguing with a person creates more problems for me than it solves.

_____ 7. I have a pleasant, good feeling when I win a point in an argument.

_____ 8. When I finish arguing with someone I feel nervous and upset.

_____ 9. I enjoy a good argument over a controversial issue.

_____ 10. I get an unpleasant feeling when I realize I am about to get into an argument.

_____ 11. I enjoy defending my point of view on an issue.

_____ 12. I am happy when I keep an argument from happening.

_____ 13. I do not like to miss the opportunity to argue a controversial issue.

_____ 14. I prefer being with people who rarely disagree with me.

_____ 15. I consider an argument an exciting intellectual challenge.

_____ 16. I find myself unable to think of effective points during an argument.

_____ 17. I feel refreshed and satisfied after an argument on a controversial issue.

_____ 18. I have the ability to do well in an argument.

_____ 19. I try to avoid getting into arguments.

_____ 20. I feel excitement when I expect that a conversation I am in is leading to an argument.

Calculating Your Score:

1. Add your responses to items 1, 3, 5, 6, 8, 10, 12, 14, 16, and 19 = _____.

2. Add your responses to items 2, 4, 7, 9, 11, 13, 15, 17, 18, and 20 = _____.

3. Complete the following formula:
   ARG = 60 − Total from step 1 = _____.
   Then, + Total from step 2. YOUR TOTAL
   ARG SCORE = _____.

Interpreting Your Score

Possible range of scores for ARG: 20–100. (If your own final ARG score does not fall within that range, you made a computational error.)

The average score or midpoint for the ARG is around 60. If your score falls below 50, you are among those who are low in argumentativeness, or what we call "avoiders." Avoiders try to keep arguments from happening and generally feel relieved when an argument is over. When compelled to argue, low ARGs experience unpleasant feelings before, during, and after the argument. If your score falls above 70, you are classified as high in argumentativeness, or what we call "approachers." Approachers find arguing an exciting intellectual challenge, a competitive event. High ARGs feel invigorated, satisfied, and delighted after an argument—even if they did not win. If you scored between 50 and 70, you are "moderate" in your argumentativeness orientation. Moderate ARGs neither like nor dislike arguing. In order for them to argue, they must feel that either there is something to gain or the probability of winning is high.

Reference

Infante, D. A., & Rancer, A. S. (1982). A conceptualization and measure of argumentativeness. *Journal of Personality Assessment, 46,* 72–80.

actually tend to overlap in terms of the way we make decisions about coping with confrontations. Kilmann and Thomas maintain that this struggle over goals is a reflection of our underlying desire to be either competitive or cooperative in dealing with opponents in a conflict situation. Our resolution of these two interdependent goals in a specific situation represents our predictable "style" of reacting to all kinds of conflicts. This formulation allows for the assessment of five distinct conflict styles based on *competition, collaboration, compromise, avoidance,* and *accommodation.* These five coping strategies are important because they point directly to alternative ways in which conflicts are typically handled by people caught up in them.

The Competitive Style

Although we generally define the term *conflict* to mean competition over something of importance, certain people are so predictably and strongly competitive that it is possible to describe this reaction as a separate and common style. Strongly competitive people narrowly view all conflicts as win-lose events. They believe that winning is their only goal and that having a concern for their opponent is both unnecessary and unimportant. Highly competitive people would agree with statements like "Once I get going in a heated discussion, I am unable to stop," and "I like the exhilaration of engaging in disagreements and conflicts." In short, such people are commonly "very aggressive" in the way they react to conflicts.[11]

Individuals who clearly illustrate a very **competitive style** are often found in jobs or professions where this may be an advantage. These include such jobs as courtroom lawyers, police interrogators, labor leaders, aggressive salespeople, or just about any type of work in which conflicts are defined as strictly win-lose encounters. For example, in labor-management negotiation meetings, where demands are being made by representatives from both sides, *every* issue is defined as a win-lose conflict. Opponents on both sides predictably act as if they are doing battle to their last breath. In some respects such competitive behavior is acceptable in sessions where union contracts are negotiated because they have become a tradition. These same behaviors can be far less productive in other conflict situations. However, they are typical of highly competitive individuals who tend to use this style as a means of resolving all of their disputes.

The Collaborative Style

Another common style of reaction to conflict is based on *collaboration,* which literally means working jointly or willingly in cooperation with an opponent. The **collaborative style** is characteristic of persons who are not only seeking self-related goals in a conflict situation but who also have a sincere concern for their opponents. People who use this style would endorse statements like "When I get in a conflict with someone, I try very hard to find mutually acceptable solutions," or "I like to assert myself, but I also like to cooperate with others." These kinds of statements communicate the idea that the person tries to find alternative solutions to conflict that will maximize reaching goals for both participants.

An example of collaborative styles of conflict would be the case of two members of a study group who have a conflict over the correct interpretation of what their professor meant in a particular lecture. Each disagrees with the other's understanding of the lecture. However, both parties feel that their personal objective in studying together is to get a better grade on the next test (self goal). At the same time, they also believe that by working together both parties can score higher than by studying alone (opponent's goals). Thus, in an attempt to maintain a productive relationship, they resolve their disagreements and work collaboratively toward a shared interpretation of the lecture.

The Compromising Style

A third common and predictable reaction to conflict is based on **compromise**—reaching agreement by making mutual concessions. People who use a compromising style fall somewhere on a continuum between competitive and cooperative types of people. The behavior of compromisers in conflicts is sometimes incorrectly interpreted by observers as "giving in."[12] In any case, individuals using this style would assent to statements like "I accept the fact that I can't always get my way," "I am thankful to get part of what I asked for," and "I know I am going into a conflict where I will have to give a little."

An example of a person using this style would be an individual who is brought in as a third party to help resolve a conflict. Neither of the protagonists is willing to reach an agreement, and all efforts to resolve their differences thus far have resulted in increased hostility. Finally, they agree to seek help. Typically, third parties in all such mediation situations try to get the participants to compromise. There really are no alternatives to getting each party to move toward a middle-ground position so that each of the opponents makes equal compromises.

The Avoidance Style

The typical reaction of individuals who are passive, subservient, and acquiescent in conflicts is **avoidance.** People using an avoidance strategy do not expect to attain personal goals from the conflict, and they are not sympathetic to those of their opponent. They just want to escape from the whole confrontation. Thus, they generally remain idle and refuse to engage in what we would normally expect from people in a conflict. Avoiders simply stay away from situations where conflicts are likely to occur. And, if they find themselves in a conversation which is beginning to sound like a disagreement that might lead to a conflict, they find some way to remove themselves from confrontation.

Conflict avoiders are easily recognized. Many are highly apprehensive individuals. Some are even reclusives who fear all interaction with other people. For example, people with high levels of communication apprehension experience fear and anxiety when they have to talk with others in a variety of social contexts. If they find themselves communicating with a stranger in a situation that might lead to conflict, they will either excuse themselves or find some reason to change the topic of discussion. They will not make any effort to pursue their side of a position on an issue.

At the same time, avoidance is a technique that is also used by a different type of person. Many times conflicts break out among one's fellow workers, associates, relatives, or friends. Often, taking part in such confrontations has no payoff for an individual. Indeed, it can easily result in significant losses. It may be far better to "stand on the sidelines" and watch the fight, rather than join the fray for no personal benefit. This is also a form of avoidance, but a mature and thoughtful one that does not imply some of the negative personality implications discussed above.

The Accommodation Style

The fifth and last style of handling conflict in the Kilmann and Thomas category system is based on *accommodation.* The people who use an **accommodating style** "give in" to their opponents. Thus, accommodators are the opposite of competitors. They tend to be passive in that they forego trying to reach their personal goal, preferring to let their opponents reach their objectives. Moreover, accommodators tend to go along with the position that is being argued by the majority of the individuals in the conflict. In other words, they exhibit no resistance and make every effort to yield to their opponents' decisions.

Examples of people who are accommodators in conflicts are employees who never want to be the leader of a group, individuals who commonly defer to authority, and those who place a higher value on relationships than on being a decision-maker. Trying to argue with accommodators is very difficult. They simply will not engage in too much disagreement over anything. Even if they initially take a position on a particular issue in a discussion they will only push their point to a limited extent. Their primary objective in all conflict situations is to conform to the majority position of their opponents.

While each of the above "styles" is used exclusively by some people, it cannot be assumed that a given person uses only one strategy all the time. A more likely situation is that a particular person will *shift* among these various styles, depending on the nature of the conflict and on the characteristics of the persons involved. In any given day, an individual may choose to compete vigorously with one person, collaborate with someone else, and compromise with still a third. Or the same individual may avoid a particular conflict but accommodate in another. It all depends on the circumstances, and much depends on whether the conflict is with a loved one, a stranger, a person in a subservient position, one's boss, or a child.

In any case, these conflict styles offer different models as to how we might want to try to defuse, escalate, or ignore a *particular* conflict. This implies, of course, that we are capable of shifting from one style to another. If that is not the case, and we do tend to use one to the exclusion of the others, understanding our likely reaction to all conflict situations can be helpful in a number of ways. First and most obvious, such understanding provides us with important information about ourselves that can help us in selecting conflicts in which we really want to engage. In this way, we can better assess which conflicts are likely to be productive for us and what strategy we want to use in managing our relationships with other people when they inevitably arise.

Finally, all of us get caught in conflicts in which we had no intention of getting involved. Usually, they are caused by factors over which we have little or no control.

Having a solid understanding of the styles we can use to cope with them can help us to monitor our behavior more effectively when we find ourself engaged in conflicts we had not anticipated.

Common Causes of Conflict

Aside from the five styles we have reviewed for keeping conflicts going or bringing them to termination, we need to comprehend some of the common *causes* of conflicts in social life. When we defined conflict earlier, we did so with an "economic" model of the basis of conflict. It stressed that conflicts arise when there is a scarcity of some value over which competition developed. That is still a good explanation, but two other major factors also play a part in generating conflicts between people. One is fairly obvious, consisting of the *meanings* constructed by each party for the messages transmitted and received during a process of communication. The other set is far less obvious. It consists of *contextual* factors—the physical settings, sociocultural situations, and social relationships in which people communicate. These can also be critical in the generation or escalation of conflicts in a number of ways.

Meanings as a Primary Cause

To say that the meanings people construct during processes of communication can be a primary cause of conflict is to state the obvious. Unless people communicate with each other, there is simply no way for them either to initiate or to engage in conflict. In that sense, the meanings aroused as people disagree, become competitive, or get angry are a "necessary" but not "sufficient" condition, and conflicts of all types are in some way an outgrowth of human communication.[13]

By the same reasoning, it is our ability to communicate fully and effectively that enables us to *resolve* conflicts. This gives an incredible advantage to human beings over other species. As we saw in Chapter 2, human communication is the foundation of culture and virtually everything that elevates our ways of life to levels far above those of other animals. Ironically, then, while communication skills enable us to show aggression and hostility toward each other, it is precisely the same skills that provide the foundation for peaceful resolution of conflicts.

Returning to our opening discussion of what happened between John and Loretta, their conflict started with a communicated work assignment by their boss. Loretta communicated her concerns to their boss about John's probable interpretations of the meaning of that assignment when it was given to her, but the boss ignored these messages. Then, every time Loretta attempted to clarify the meaning of the assignment for John, he became increasingly hostile. Eventually what John provided in the way of feedback to Loretta brought her to change from a patient compromiser to an antagonistic competitor. When that happened, both John and Loretta began communicating negative, malicious, and hateful messages about each other to other employees and to their boss. The meeting between them and the boss, where she demanded an end to their conflict, also depended on communication. Thus, from the beginning, the meanings constructed by each party for the messages they transmitted served to define, maintain and escalate their conflict.

Generally, then, problems of meaning are at the heart of virtually any conflict. Stated more systematically, one important principle is that the constructions of meaning by communicating parties assume a *primary instrumental role* in generating and escalating conflicts. Another is that a *low index of fidelity* (low accuracy, pp. 25–27) is likely to characterize messages transmitted and interpreted by senders and receivers who are in the process of conflict development. These two conditions work together as central causal factors in producing and intensifying controversies.

Contextual Factors That Can Generate Conflict

Although, as the previous section indicates, mismatches of meanings, or similar features of communication, may be primary causal factors in conflicts between most people, other conditions typically seem to the participants to be the "real" causes. In particular, many people who get involved in a conflict with someone come to believe that their opponent's *flawed personality* is responsible for what occurs. In fact, this is almost universal. To the participants in a conflict it seems obvious that "bad people cause bad relationships."

To those who look on and see people in conflict this is not at all obvious. In fact, it usually seems to neutral observers that both parties are decent people and that their conflict must be a result of other kinds of factors. This is, in most cases, far closer to the truth. The "flawed personality" explanation seldom holds up.

A very different set of factors that contribute to the generation of conflict can be found in the *context* within which communication takes place. Here, as our general transactions model suggests, both the *sociocultural situation* in which the communicators are involved and the *social relationships* that exist between them play parts in shaping the meanings they construct as they communicate (pp. 21–25). The physical setting can also play a part, but it is these two contextual features that contribute most significantly to the generation or escalation of a conflict, regardless of the personalities involved.

The sociocultural situation   It is not difficult to see how the sociocultural situation in which people pursue goals can be a factor in generating conflict. In the conflict that developed and escalated between John and Loretta, both parties were in a work situation. In that feature of their context, both were dedicated to the same overall group goals—doing a good job in carrying out the assignments of the Personnel and Training Unit. However, each had very different personal goals. One party (John) believed strongly that the goals of the unit could best be accomplished by having him pursue his personal goal, conducting all evaluations of new programs for recruiting and training. He felt strongly that it was his legitimate right to do so. The boss had another view, and she gave the assignment to Loretta. Although Loretta sympathized with John's position, she had her own personal career goals to think of, and she wanted the boss's approval. This kind of situation, where all the parties are basically good persons, but where all are convinced that they are in the right in pursuing such a mix of goals, is almost certain to generate conflict.

Counterparts to John and Loretta's situation are common in daily life. Every family in which a husband and wife both have jobs to which each is dedicated has many potential sources of conflict. Personal goals, work goals, and family goals can produce an unstable mix. Two common goal conflicts come easily to mind: If either the husband or the wife has a great opportunity for advancement, but one that requires moving to another city, should the partner sacrifice his or her career goals? Or, if one partner's job requires evening and weekend work for the person to be successful, should the other complain or make sacrifices to help achieve that goal?

Even achieving the mundane domestic goal of living together as a family provides bases for conflict. For example, whose job is it to do the shopping, run the vacuum cleaner, look after the cars, make the bed in the

Conflicts that turn out to have destructive consequences often start out as minor disputes. Increasingly negative messages from both parties produce hurt feelings that anger each participant and lead to frustration and higher levels of hostility. If the individuals do not understand how to defuse this escalating process, what began as a disagreement can end up producing a very negative outcome and a ruined relationship that can never be repaired.

morning, do the laundry, feed the cat, do the shopping, cook the meals, clean up the kitchen, and take out the garbage (to mention only a few domestic tasks)? Each of these may seem minor "assignments," but each poses the potential for a disagreement that can escalate into conflict.

Social relationships   Social relationships as basic features of communication contexts were discussed at length in Chapter 5 (pp. 130–132). We pointed out that the basic social rules for behavior in human groups—norms, roles, ranks, and controls—provide powerful definitions concerning who can legitimately communicate what kinds of messages to whom within a particular social situation. In Chapter 6 we discussed how misunderstandings or misinterpretations of those social expectations are often at the heart of breakdowns and difficulties in groups (pp. 182–183). We saw that serious problems of group cohesion and group disintegration can arise when confusion develops concerning any of those rules and expectations.

In precisely the same way, conflicts can arise. That is, conflicts between members of a group tend to occur when inaccuracies or inadequacies in communication lead to (1) normative confusion, (2) unclear definitions of roles, (3)

failures regarding the rules of power and authority (social ranks), and (4) ineffective messages of social control.

We can illustrate how difficulties with such rules can contribute to a conflict by referring again to John and Loretta's case. The social relationships between them in the workplace were defined by a large number of norms, role definitions, considerations of social ranking, and social controls. These placed many demands on them—dictating both their overall behavior in the group and the kinds of messages each could transmit to others. These rules were shaped by a number of policies, decisions, practices, and company politics.[14] Like all employees, John and Loretta constantly had to deal with all of these complexities and consider them when formulating messages and making decisions.

Looking more closely, a number of norms common to almost any work group were openly violated by both John and Loretta. For example, the boss pointed out that they had been "wasting time"—absolutely unacceptable in work settings. They had also been "interfering with the work of others" (again, unacceptable). Each had also apparently been "bad-mouthing" and "acting viciously" to hurt the career chances of the other (serious transgressions). But while these deviations of norms may have come about because each of the parties deliberately chose to behave in that way, other problems of norms were not under individual choice. For example, Loretta had to follow a compelling norm demanding that she satisfy the boss by doing a good job. At the same time, she had to cope with a different norm that required her to avoid hurting the feelings of her friend John. It was not possible to comply with both norms.

Another confusion in social relationships that contributed to their conflict was the conflicting role definitions that prevailed. Specifically, John was convinced that he was supposed to do what his *job description* stated. Such descriptions communicate clear formal definitions of an employee's rights, duties, and responsibilities. However, the boss "muddied the water" by assigning the evaluation to Loretta—communicating a different set of rights, duties, and responsibilities to both parties. Job descriptions (and even temporary assignments) of work roles indicate what employees are "supposed to do" (or not do) if they are to perform their work satisfactorily. Confusion can be experienced by workers when their roles are not clear or when they conflict with those of others.

In many respects, then, the social expectations prevailing in John and Loretta's work situation forced both of them into a no-win condition. Both may have behaved badly, but they were caught in a turmoil of confusing and even conflicting definitions of norms and roles created by the boss.

In the situation that developed, therefore, the boss must bear a special responsibility. An effective leader understands social relationships and takes steps to head off conflicts by appropriate communication before they begin. Instead of explaining to John ahead of time valid reasons for assigning the evaluation to Loretta, and gaining his approval and support, the boss let a serious conflict develop. Only after it escalated seriously did she step in and forcefully exercise social control by communicating her power and authority in strong terms. Gentler controls communicated earlier would have been far more effective. Therefore, if anyone was *most* responsible for the messy situation that developed it was the boss.

Generally, then, the social settings within which people communicate can be major factors in generating or escalating conflicts. Potentials for their development arise out of the general sociocultural situation (work, family, etc.) within which people interact, and especially when confusions and contradictions exist in the rules and expectations defining their social relationships. While conflicts can arise because of personality clashes, few are due solely to the bad actions of bad people.

Successful Conflict Negotiation

If one clear conclusion stands out from our previous sections, it is that understanding the sources of a conflict is not easy. Furthermore, as we indicated earlier, conflicts come in many forms from many causal conditions. Even more difficult is how to resolve them. Unlike certain items of clothing, one solution does *not* "fit all." That is, each and every conflict occurs in a unique environment of interconnected personal predispositions, exchanges of meanings, and contextual factors. For that reason, each requires its own mode of negotiation if it is to be brought to a productive conclusion.

Having seen, at least in overview, some of the more salient causes of conflicts, and how people try to cope with them with various styles, the remaining question to answer in this chapter is this: How do people successfully *negotiate* conflicts when they occur? Our approach to answering this question begins first by defining the term *negotiation*. And, second, our discussion of this important idea is an overview of a clear-cut set of principles and guidelines that have proved effective for negotiating many kinds of conflicts.[15]

Defining Negotiation

The effective negotiation of a conflict cannot begin until all of the individuals involved start to explore ways in which they can seriously propose and consider alternative solutions to their disagreement. This may seem like a strange way to explain such beginnings, because it says that the people involved need to settle on the *rules* for negotiation before they actually begin the process itself. Moreover, for negotiation to get off to a good start, the primary objective of the discussions that are to take place between opponents must be agreed upon. That primary objective is *to reach an agreement* as an end product of the negotiations. In other words, if people agree that they want to agree, and then set up rules for proceeding, they can then begin the process of working out the specifics. After that, discussions continue until communication between opponents results in an arrangement that is acceptable to everyone involved.

The idea of negotiation may need no formal definition. However, it is always helpful to set forth exactly what is meant by a concept. In a basic sense, then, **negotiation** refers to *a continuing set of transactions in which proposed solutions are communicated back and forth between op-*

It is not easy to resolve any conflict. One of the most successful approaches, however, is through a process of negotiation. This can work effectively only if each of the parties agrees to conduct discussions according to an agreed-upon set of rules. Each must want to find a solution, agree to engage in a series of communicative transactions in an ethical manner, and be willing to compromise in various ways until each party agrees that the dispute has been resolved.

ponents for the goal of reaching agreement on ways to resolve a conflict.

A principle that is evident in this definition is that the basis of negotiation is *carefully planned communication* whose goal is the mutual construction of similar meanings between opponents. Thus, communication plays two parts in conflicts: We noted earlier that communication is a primary cause of conflict, in the sense that it is a necessary if not sufficient condition. Clearly, however, it is also the principal means by which opponents negotiate conflicts.

As implied earlier, equally critical to being able to negotiate a conflict successfully is that opponents agree to communicate about potential solutions. Without sincere agreement by all opponents to communicate, efforts to negotiate will more than likely prove unprofitable. All the discussion in the world will not result in a successful resolution if the people involved do not agree that they want to air their grievances and try to resolve their differences. In fact, what usually occurs when opponents in a conflict are not serious about negotiating is further escalation of the controversy.

Guidelines for Negotiation

Over the past several decades, a group of researchers at Harvard University have studied the process of conflict negotiation extensively. The result of these efforts has been the identification of a number of specific guidelines concerning the most feasible way to negotiate conflicts through the use of carefully planned communication.[16] Their program has been widely recognized as one of the most effective approaches to conflict resolution. The section that follows is directly derived from that program. We will review the basic features of their suggested guidelines and illustrate how they can be used. Our objective is to present ways in which individuals can understand the process of successful negotiation better and hopefully negotiate their own conflicts.

Part of the popularity of this approach has to do with its demonstrated applicability. That is, it provides a practical and effective way to negotiate conflicts by using a specific set of guidelines for planned communication. The method, called "principled negotiation," is designed to help people get what they want from others in every conceivable type of conflict, from the simplest to the most complex—and to do so within an *ethical* framework, which is very important. For example, principled negotiation has been used successfully in a variety of legal situations (including sticky divorce cases), union contracts, and a host of political and organizational conflicts at local, state, national, and international levels.

The recommendations of the method boil down to eight points which, if applied correctly, lead to successful negotiation and thus conflict resolution. Each of the eight is a guideline that, if followed, can help resolve the problems that led to the conflict. Thus, each is a kind of "rule of thumb" as to what should and should not be done.

After discussing each of these eight guidelines, we will illustrate their use with John and Loretta's case. As we indicated, this was a real conflict between real people, and it provides a convenient setting for showing how the guidelines can be used. We will indicate what the two participants *actually* experienced during their conflict and also what they *could* have experienced had they followed the recommended rule. In the sections that follow, then, each of these eight guidelines is considered.

Guideline 1: Don't bargain over positions Applying this rule means that people trying to negotiate should never attempt to "bargain" over—that is, explain and try to justify—the different positions they hold on the issue of disagreement. Conflicts are seldom if ever negotiated when people try to bargain solely over the positions they initially advocate on a particular issue. If each party in a conflict takes a strong position on an issue, and if the positions are far apart, there is simply no way for negotiation to occur. People are never going to reach an agreement over an issue when they stubbornly maintain very different views. Moreover, trying to defend very different positions on a point or an issue can only contribute to opponents' greater and more heated separation on that issue.

We saw this kind of stalemate over positions very clearly in John and Loretta's case. Recall that Loretta approached John several times in an attempt to explain and justify her position regarding the work assignment. She wanted to stress and maintain her position that it "wasn't her fault" and that she was simply "acting under orders." John, on the other hand, wasn't buying that interpretation, and he wanted to defend his position that evaluations were "his turf."

The result was an early collapse of the relationship. Her bargaining attempts increased John's hostility toward her. Moreover, because Loretta was frustrated in her bargaining effort she ended up as antagonistic toward John as he was toward her. They held very different positions on the issue of who should be evaluating the staffing operation. It was not a viable issue for bargaining. It didn't even matter that Loretta's position was the result of their boss having directed her to do the assignment. As long as they narrowly stuck to their initial positions no concessions could be made.

Guideline 2: Separate the people from the problem This rule stresses firmly the need to get the participants to look beyond the personal characteristics and suspected motives of the people involved to the nature of the problem itself. That is, what led up to the conflict? What is at stake for both parties? How might it have happened to *anyone* in the same social situation and set of relationships? This makes a great deal of sense. Individuals engaged in conflicts often tend to build up more and more antagonism toward each other. The results of such antagonism typically include rampant misunderstanding, counterproductive communication, and irrational or overly emotional reactions between opponents.

This was clearly the case between John and Loretta. Each of them failed to separate the person they were dealing with from the problem. In fact, John and Loretta saw *each other* as the problem. As long as they continued to approach their conflict in this fashion no negotiation could occur. The more John and Loretta associated the issue of their conflict with their beliefs about the personal motives and characteristics of the other, the more they became each other's enemy. They forgot that they were working in the same organization. They forgot that they shared the same basic business goals. Their conflict became a personal vendetta—a search for ways to punish the other as a "bad" person.

Separating people and their personalities from the problems that cause conflicts implies that it is *relationships* between the people that are most important. Taking the position that relationships must remain constructive if at all possible changes the way opponents perceive, think about, and communicate with each other. Holding this position, they are less likely to overreact emotionally to what they say and do to each other. In the final analysis, what occurs when opponents separate people from problems is an increased willingness to negotiate compromises and solutions that may be acceptable to them.

Guideline 3: Focus on interests, not positions This guideline brings us back to the first—the recommendation that opponents refrain from bargaining over positions. Instead, opponents should focus on *interests,* looking beyond their positions to the personal goals and needs that must be served for each party. That is, in all conflicts opponents take positions because of personal interests that are at stake. In John and Loretta's case, John's primary concern was to protect all the rights, duties, and obligations associated with his job. Loretta's primary interest was to do what her boss directed her to do, so as to remain a valued employee.

Other interests probably were represented in the positions of John and Loretta, but the point is that if the two had been able to deal directly with what was at stake, they could have negotiated their conflict themselves. There would have been no need to involve their boss. They could have explained their interests, discussed alternative ways to solve their dilemma, and still found ways to satisfy their boss. For example, John could have worked *with* Loretta on the evaluation, which would have avoided the negative consequences of their extended conflict.

Guideline 4. Invent options for mutual gain An important part of resolving a conflict is to get to a point where each party gets something he or she values out of the process. One of the many incorrect assumptions that we make which can lead to the intensification of a conflict is that there is room for only one winner. This is by no means always true; and we indicated earlier in the chapter that just because people are engaged in conflict, they do not have to be enemies. We also indicated that, if handled properly, conflicts can actually be beneficial to everyone involved. This position is well represented in the recommendation that opponents work hard to invent options for mutual gain.

To illustrate, if John and Loretta had not acted as if there was only one solution to their disagreement, a variety of other possible outcomes could have been considered. From the start, the position of each was that "it's my way or no way." To make the assumption that there is only one possible solution simply precludes negotiation.[17] The opposite is to assume that there are alternative ways in which the problem can be resolved (so that everyone can gain). This is an important foundation for successful negotiation. If both John and Loretta had been open to communicating about options for mutual gain, they would have been able to negotiate their conflict without intervention by their boss.

Guideline 5: Insist on using objective criteria We noted at the beginning of this section that in negotiation it is important to have mutually agreed-upon rules within which to communicate about potential solutions. Estab-

lishing shared criteria for evaluating proposals from one side or the other is part of that process. If this is *not* done, in the heat of an intense conflict, opponents typically impose subjective criteria when evaluating proposed solutions. The phrase "subjective criteria" refers to personal or private standards for making such evaluations—standards not necessarily shared by others.

Subjective criteria seem fair only to the person using them; objective criteria seem appropriate to most people. When subjective criteria are used, conflicts escalate because they often seem unfair to the other party. Employing an agreed-upon set of objective criteria that both parties see as fair provides an important basis for successful negotiation.

Using subjective standards will almost always lead to such evaluations as "Your proposal is totally unfair to me" and, in response, "You are unwilling to make any concessions." These judgments are completely oriented toward only one side's feelings and interests. A more effective approach is for opponents to make every attempt to develop before negotiation even starts a mutually agreed-upon set of objective criteria for evaluation.

It was obvious that neither John nor Loretta even considered employing objective criteria for evaluating their positions in the conflict. If they had mutually generated a set of such objective criteria as their conflict was first developing, their handling of the disagreement would have been done on a much more rational basis. Also, if they had taken the time to do this, they would have been able to reach an agreement long before their boss called them into her office.

Guideline 6: Develop the best "fallback" position Even when people follow the five previous guidelines, things can still go wrong. In that case, several other issues need to be handled if a successful negotiation is ever going to occur. An important one is that a fallback position is needed that would be acceptable in case things do not work out to our entire satisfaction in negotiation. In other words, a good way of protecting yourself in a negotiation is by having already developed an acceptable alternative to what you see as the most desirable negotiated agreement.

This alternative refers to knowing ahead of time exactly what you would accept as a resolution to a particular conflict. It is the "bottom line" by which a particular conflict can be resolved. It has to be a *realistic* position. It may not be the most desirable, but one that you could agree to if all else fails. When a party to a conflict has such a position already in mind, he or she is in a much better position to ask for concessions from the opponent.

If both John and Loretta had gone into their disagreement with a solid grasp of their own best alternative to a negotiated resolution, the makeup of their conflict would have been very different. For example, although John normally had the power position in the staffing area, Loretta had more power because their boss had given her the assignment. John was in a no-win position to expect her to back away from that assignment. However, he could have developed an acceptable alternative that would have allowed him to gain at least some concessions from Loretta. For example, he could have agreed to assist her, which would have permitted him to provide "input" into the assessment of the staffing plan he had originally developed. This would not have been difficult because Loretta was initially open to communicating with John about the assignment and at that point would have accepted his help. Thus, John lost out completely by not having considered an acceptable alternative.

Guideline 7: Cope with resistance to negotiation   Like Loretta, we all run into people who simply stonewall all attempts to negotiate a conflict. This can bring things to a permanent halt. One must be prepared to cope with such a situation without abandoning the negotiation process. Fortunately, most people, even when in a resistant mood, can be persuaded to communicate and even to negotiate if it is done in the right way. If can be a complex and difficult task, but there are several ways it can be approached.

First, never attack the position a resistant opponent is advocating.[18] Look beyond the position to the personal values and interests that are motivating the individual on the issue. It is these that are leading to his or her unwillingness to change. By dealing directly with what is driving the resistance, it is much easier to weaken it. Proposed solutions can be based on those same values and interests. People have a difficult time resisting proposed solutions that are consistent with their own needs and orientations.

Second, try to minimize the time spent defending your own ideas during conflict, and solicit criticism and counsel from your opponent. This is a disarming tactic that seems to work especially well. When given the opportunity, people can rarely resist the chance to criticize and give advice. This, of course, changes their perspectives on the issues at stake.

Third, ask questions and pause for answers. This promotes a transactional process—a rather simple and obvious idea, based on our analyses of verbal and nonverbal communication in the early chapters. However, it is a very important tactic for lowering resistance to negotiating because it opens and promotes communication, and that in turn provides a basis for proposing mutually acceptable criteria, different perspectives, alternative solutions, and so forth.

Promoting a transactional process would have helped greatly in John and Loretta's conflict. Specifically, if during Loretta's initial attempts to communicate with John she had backed off and asked him a few simple questions, he might have responded differently. This is not to say that Loretta was "at fault" for John's early resistance. But if she had advanced questions respectfully, with each followed by a period of silence, John might have responded in a positive way. Creating the need for someone to answer a question sometimes brings him or her to do so.

Guideline 8: Deflect "dirty tricks"   Many conflicts are characterized by "dirty tricks" that opponents often play on each other.[19] These include using deception, using phony facts, invoking ambiguous authority, creating stress, and making personal attacks, to mention just a few. The final guideline is based on three steps to follow when an opponent appears to be employing a dirty trick. Specifically, these are: (1) "recognize the tactic," (2) "raise the issue explicitly," and (3) "question the tactic's legitimacy and desirability—negotiate over it."[20] These three steps can sometimes deflect further dirty tricks.

Overall, these eight guidelines derived from the Harvard Project provide a practical and effective way of negotiating a conflict. When viewed as an entire set, what we indicated at the beginning of this section makes more sense. The rules for achieving the goal of resolving a conflict are agreed upon before negotiation begins. That is, the first step is for participants to *negotiate the way they will negotiate*. If followed in good faith, these guidelines focus all concerned from the outset on communicating in a transactional mode about what will be acceptable and unacceptable behavior during the process of negotiation. Once progress is made toward this initial goal, the actual negotiations can begin. Proposals and potential solutions can be advanced, examined, discussed, modified, rejected, or accepted until solutions to the problems that brought on the conflict can be achieved to the reasonable satisfaction of all concerned.

Chapter Review

■ Every human conflict represents a unique and complex process encompassing a variety of interconnected activities and human predispositions. However, each of us has the potential of determining the kinds of outcomes that follow from most of the conflicts we will experience in our lives.

■ Because the sources of conflict are so much a part of most of our cultures, few of us will be able to avoid them. In other words, many of the conflicts in which we will engage are consequences of our shared cultural orientations regarding competition and the process of getting ahead of other people.

■ Conflicts are not inherently negative; many can have positive consequences. It is the people engaged in a conflict who dictate how productive or unproductive it will be. Knowing that individuals influence the outcomes of conflicts should make us more sensitive to signs which illustrate that something has gone wrong or that a conflict is moving in an unproductive direction.

■ At least some individuals respond to all conflicts in a more or less uniform style. For example, some people tend to be highly competitive; others are collaborative; still others are compromising or accommodating in the way they react to conflict. Still other people attempt to avoid all conflict at any cost. Finally, some individuals can shift from one of these styles to another as the occasion demands.

■ The primary cause of conflicts is problems in communication. However, other causes may also be involved. The context in which we interact can serve as the basis of conflict. Both the specific situation in which we pursue goals and the social relationships that prevail in that situation can include unique ingredients that cause conflicts between people.

■ The Harvard Group's recommendations for negotiating conflict include suggestions concerning bargaining over positions, separating people from the problem, focusing on interests rather than positions, indicating a need to invent options for mutual gain, using objective criteria for assessing issues, and developing a bottom line position for settling a conflict.

Key Terms

Accommodating style   A strategy for handling conflict in which people "give in" to their opponents. Accommodators are the opposite of competitors. They tend to be passive, foregoing their personal goal and preferring to let their opponents reach their objectives.

Avoidance style   A strategy for handling conflicts in which a potential participant chooses not to be a part of the confrontation but chooses to stay away from situations where disagreements and disputes are likely to occur.

Collaborative style   A strategy for handling conflicts in which people work jointly or willingly in cooperation with an opponent. The collaborative style is characteristic of persons who not only are seeking self-related goals in a conflict situation but also have a sincere concern for their opponents.

Competitive style   A strategy for handling conflicts in which people narrowly view all conflicts as win-lose events. They believe that winning is their only goal and that having a concern for their opponent is both unnecessary and unimportant.

Compromising style   A strategy from handling conflicts in which participants reach agreement by making mutual concessions.

Conflict   A dispute in which different values result in claims to rewards or resources that are in limited supply, and where the main objective of the participants is to either neutralize or eliminate the prospects of their opponents to win what is at stake.

Conflict style   The manner in which an individual is likely to behave when anticipating or engaging in a confrontation.

Negotiation   A process of communicating proposed solutions to a conflict back and forth between opponents for the purpose of reaching a joint agreement and thus resolving the dispute.

Notes

1. This is a real case drawn from the experience of one of the authors who served for several years as an executive in a large corporation. The names are fictitious but not the situation.

2. Berkowitz, L. (1964). Aggressive cues in aggressive behavior and hostility catharsis. *Psychological Review, 71,* 104–122; Berkowitz, L. (1965). The concept of aggressive drive: Some additional considerations. In L. Berkowitz (Ed.), *Advances in experimental social psychology* (Vol. 2, pp. 301–329). New York: Academic Press.

3. DeFleur, M. L., D'Antonio, W. V., & DeFleur, L. B. (1981). *Sociology: Human society* (3rd ed.) (pp. 93–94). Glenview, IL: Scott, Foresman.

4. At least some Americans stress the opposite—to avoid "standing out" or being "pushy." Native American groups, such as the Hopi and the Pueblo groups of New Mexico, share a strong orientation toward maintaining harmony and avoiding actions that imply one is trying to rise above others.

5. This definition is similar to Lewis Coser's. See: Coser, L. (1956). *The functions of social conflict* (p. 8). New York: Free Press.

6. A similar discussion of conflict is offered in: Jandt, F. E. (1985). *Win-win negotiating: Turning conflict into agreement.* New York: Wiley.

7. Ibid., p. 101.

8. Rollins, B. C., & Feldman, H. (1970). Marital satisfaction over the lifecycle. *Journal of Marriage and the Family, 32,* 20–28.

9. Frost, J. H., & Wilmot, W. W. (1991). *Interpersonal conflict* (3rd ed.). Dubuque, IA: Wm. C. Brown.

10. Kilmann R., & Thomas, K. (1975). Interpersonal conflict-handling behavior as reflections of Jungian personality dimensions. *Psychological Reports, 37,* 971–980.

11. Frost & Wilmot, op. cit., p. 29.

12. Frost & Wilmot, op. cit., p. 31.

13. Frost & Wilmot, op. cit., p. 10.

14. Koehler, J. W., Anatol, K. W. E., & Appelbaum, R. L. (1976). *Organizational communication: Behavioral perspectives* (p. 241). New York: Holt, Rinehart, & Winston.

15. Fisher, R., & Ury, W. (1987). *Getting to yes: Negotiating agreement without giving in* (p. 33). New York: Penguin.

16. This definition is similar to Fisher and Ury's position. See: Fisher, R., & Ury, W., (1988). *Getting to yes: Negotiating agreement without giving in* (p. 33). New York: Penguin.

17. Ibid., p. 61.

18. Ibid., p. 114.

19. Ibid., pp. 136–138.

20. Ibid., p. 135.

Additional Readings

Fisher, R., & Ury, W. (1987). *Getting to yes: Negotiating agreement without giving in.* New York: Penguin.

This book was a national best seller and is now considered a classic concerning conflict and negotiation. The authors present in simple terms the basics of bargaining successfully within many types of situations. The use of real-life anecdotes and examples in all of the chapters make it both interesting to read and highly informative.

Hocker, J. L., & Wilmot, W. W. (1991). *Interpersonal conflict* (3rd ed.). Dubuque, IA: Wm. C. Brown.

Now in its third edition, this book presents an excellent discussion of interpersonal conflict. The authors present the case that because we experience so much destructive conflict, we need to transform such conflict into a productive experience. The book covers the basics of conflicts and proceeds chapter by chapter to consider ways to make destructive conflict constructive.

Jandt, F. E. (1985). *Win-win negotiating: Turning conflict into agreement.* New York: John Wiley.

This text presents in simple terms the basics of managing conflict productively. The chapters cover what the author learned conducting professional development seminars in this area over many years. Numerous excellent experi-enced-based examples are included that make for interesting reading and clear explanations.

Likert, R., & Bowers, D. G. (1972). Conflict strategies related to organizational theories and management systems. In B. T. King & E. McGinnies (Eds.), *Attitudes, conflict, and social change* (pp. 101–121). New York: Academic Press.

This now classic article discusses the premise that "the nature of a society [and of all organizations] is reflected in its management of conflict." This premise is traced historically and through the findings of early research on management systems. The authors offer a theory of conflict management based on the actions of effective managers.

Swingle, P. (Ed.). (1970). *The structure of conflict.* New York: Academic Press.

This edited collection brings together essays by the founders of the study of conflict. Topics covered include conflict resolution and game theory, toughness, power, threats and promises, and personal influences on cooperation and conflict. Each essay reviews comprehensively and in complex terms the origins and early research on a particular topic.

Chapter 12

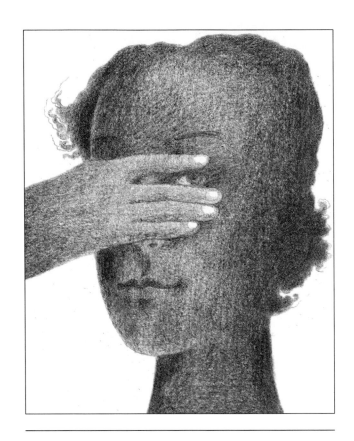

Overcoming Shyness and Apprehension

Contents

Communication Apprehension as a Common Reaction
Apprehension as a Personality Trait
The Influence of Apprehensive Experiences

Causes of Communication Apprehension
Common Contextual Sources of Anxiety
Communicating with unfamiliar or dissimilar others
Novel or formal situations
Subordinate rank
Conspicuousness and excessive attention
Undergoing evaluation
Repeated failure
How We Learn to Be Characteristically Apprehensive
Long-term socialization of the apprehensive person
Socialization includes learning
The importance of learning
Learning to fear by observing others
Learning as a consequence of reward and punishment
The resiliency factor
The consequences of inconsistency

Consequences of High and Low Communication Apprehension
Evaluations in the Classroom
Assessments in Interpersonal Encounters
The Reactions of People at Work
Influences on Careers

Dealing with Stage Fright
The Contributions of the Context
What the Speaker Brings to the Problem

Reducing Communication Apprehension
Systematic Desensitization
Cognitive Restructuring
Skills Training
Courses on skills
Limitations of the skills approach

Chapter Review

Key Terms

Notes

Additional Readings

Key Questions

- I have always been a bit afraid of getting up and talking before a group of people. Actually, it makes me a bit nervous just thinking about it. I suppose that most people are not like that. I guess that this makes me different from other people. Or does it?

- Some people seem very comfortable when they are talking to others, even to strangers. They don't even seem nervous and they can get right up and talk even without preparation, as though it is the easiest thing in the world. Is it possible that they are born with that ability?

- What is it that brings on "stage fright" when we are confronted with the necessity of talking to a group of people? Is it something that we learn to fear, or is it a natural reaction to the pressure of having to perform before people? Also, do those who do it a lot get over it?

- Is there any way in which a person can learn to cope with his or her nervousness about talking to groups? Is it just a matter of developing skills, or are there other ways in which people who are shy and tense can handle their fears?

When people fear flying, they can stay on the ground. . . . [However], there are a great number of human activities that cannot be avoided . . . death and taxes, daily greetings to people, dealing with tradespeople, asking and answering questions, and carrying on one's duties on the job. There are few people who can avoid talk during the course of a day, and there is no way to avoid being evaluated on the way you talk.

Gerald M. Phillips
1984

Craig sat outside the paneled board room waiting for his turn to be invited in to make his presentation. Having just been promoted to the post of Assistant Manager of the Transportation Department in the Distribution Division, he knew that he had a lot riding on the report he was about to make. In his earlier job he had never been invited to make a presentation to the board of directors, and frankly, he was very nervous. If he blew it, his career might well be over before it really got started.

Craig's anxiety had been growing over the past few weeks, ever since his boss had first told him that he had to make the presentation. He had spent nights and weekends putting together his report. He knew that he had only 10 minutes to bring the board members up to date on the latest trends and basic data in his Transportation Department, and he had polished and repolished his skills.

To make his presentation more effective, he had developed a set of charts, diagrams, and tables, all professionally prepared on the computer. He had ordered an overhead slide projector to use in displaying his visuals, and he knew they were impressive. To avoid mistakes, he had memorized his speech and knew it by heart. In fact, he had practiced it more than 10 times. His wife, Maria, had almost died of boredom.

Despite all these preparations, Craig was sweating as he sat waiting. Now he really felt that fear, like a hard knot in the pit of his stomach. His hands were trembling and his mouth was dry. Suddenly, he was convinced that he had forgotten his speech. He wanted to bite his fingernails, like he used to do when he was a kid.

He heard the sounds of laughter coming through the door of the board room. My God, he thought, are they laughing at Joe, who had gone in just before him? The very thought made him feel like he was going to be sick. Why did he ever consent to do this? He had always dreaded the idea of getting up and talking in front of a group. He remembered when he had to drop that public speaking course when he was in college. He just could not do it and had bailed out after only a single try. He had prepared a pretty good talk, but he had literally stumbled through it, gulping, turning red, and generally behaving like a perfect idiot. Now he wished fervently that he had controlled his anxieties and had completed the course instead of avoiding it.

Then he heard the door open. He saw the eyes of the board members turning to him. He tried desperately to think of some last-minute way he could get out of there. It was no use. Bud, the board secretary, was telling him, "Come on in, Mr. Anderson; it's your turn now."

Craig went to the front of the big table and looked around. His palms were sweating and his heart was racing. He fervently hoped that no one would notice. Everyone was looking at him in an expectant way. The moment of truth had arrived! He hoped that he would not faint.

In one degree or another we have all had Craig's experience. Even polished and accomplished communicators never quite get over a sense of nervousness and anxiety about getting up in front of a bunch of strangers to make an organized presentation. Anxiety and nervousness about communicating in a public setting are common and unavoidable.

Note that it was not that Craig lacked *skills*. He had a good report prepared; he knew it well; and he had prepared effective visuals to go with it. Craig's performance has relatively little to do with such matters. In fact, research reveals that all the skills training in the world may contribute only minimally to your effectiveness as a speaker. Furthermore, contrary to popular wisdom, "practice" does *not* always "make perfect." Performing over and over again may help some to communicate more effectively, but others may actually get worse.

The bottom line is our emotional state—which has little to do with skills. In fact, the results of over 200 separate studies reveal that a person's ability to perform well while speaking to a group is closely related to a condition called *communication apprehension*.[1] That condition, its causes, its consequences, and how to cope with it in various contexts, are the central topics of this chapter.

Communication apprehension is a condition most associated with *public* communication, especially when presenting a talk to a group. However, it can occur under other conditions, such as when it is necessary to talk to strangers. It is seldom a problem when people communicate within intimate groups, among family members and close friends. After all, those people are "safe." As we discussed in Chapters 5 and 6, we trust our friends and family to support us, encourage us, and generally make us feel good about ourselves. We don't share that same trust with people we do not know. We have no reason to believe that an audience of strangers will understand and sympathize if we forget part of what we were going to say, generally look stupid, and are forced to sit down in embarrassment. We have no reason to believe that any audience will easily overlook our "uhs" and "ums" and "you knows" as we stumble through our presentation. Clearly, then, we have very good reason to feel apprehensive whenever we consider communicating to an audience of strangers.

Many people—far too many—are convinced that competent communicators are *born* with the right performance skills or that speaking just naturally "comes easily" to some. There are no grounds for such a belief.

It ignores a large body of research findings that underscore a need for reducing people's fears of addressing audiences.[2] We know, for example, that skills training is likely to aggravate some peoples' anxieties and actually make their condition worse.[3] These individuals, unable to perform competently in front of a group, are exposed over and over again to their own failures. It doesn't take too many trials before they learn to *expect* failure—and that expectation only increases their fears about trying to do it again. Even if such persons are able to acquire all the necessary skills to give a good talk, anxieties about communicating before an audience can continue to interfere with competent performance.

This chapter has been designed to help you cope with communication apprehension and anxieties we all feel when talking to strangers or to a group. This is extremely important, as few people in complex roles in modern life can get by without having to present their ideas to others. It is at the heart of almost any occupation or profession you can list—doctor, lawyer, teacher, business executive, politician, and salesperson.

Communication apprehension is a condition associated with shyness and fear of speaking before a group. However, it can occur under a variety of conditions, such as when people must meet and talk with strangers. It is a learned condition, not something a person is born with. It is also quite normal; even veteran speakers feel some degree of communication apprehension before getting up in front of an audience. Too much apprehension can not only induce anxiety but also reduce communication skills. Understanding its nature and sources is an important way to begin coping with such apprehension.

Communication Apprehension as a Common Reaction

All of us have felt anxious about communicating at one time or another. For example, we might feel extremely uncomfortable when forced to interact with people we don't know well, engage in small talk, handle conflict, justify our employment in an interview, work productively in a small group, give a briefing, or simply participate in class discussions. All such situations can provoke anxiety. Because apprehension is such a widely found condition, no other aspect of communication has received more attention from scholars and researchers over the past 20 years. Defined simply, **communication apprehension** refers to *fear or anxiety associated with either real or anticipated communication encounters.*[4]

Note that this definition does not suggest that we have to be actually communicating at the time. We can dread having to communicate even when we think we *might* have to speak. A good example is the case when students realize that in a required course their grade will be contingent on participation in class discussion. Knowing that they will have to talk before an audience may trigger a threshold of anxiety inhibiting their ability to ask or answer questions. Similarly, anticipating the social demands of a dinner at the home of your new boss may stimulate communication apprehension long before you arrive. In other words, anxiety about communicating is a condition that can occur either prior to or during any particular encounter.

Some specialists regard communication apprehension as a special kind of *shyness.*[5] However, reasons for shyness can vary greatly. Some shy people may lack communication skills. Others may have the necessary skills to communicate effectively but may simply enjoy being unobtrusive or reflective. Certainly it is not true that all shy individuals experience communication apprehension. Looking at the population as a whole, about 40% report being shy, whereas only a little over 20% experience a truly significant degree of communication apprehension.[6] Therefore, about half of the people who are shy appear to be satisfied with avoiding interaction with others. The remainder, however, are probably shy because of some degree of fear about communicating. This is especially likely among those who lack communication skills. A kind of circular pattern can often be seen in the behavior of many shy people. It begins with a person being shy, which creates anxiety, which reduces communication skills, resulting in increased shyness, and so on.

The circular link between shyness and apprehension can manifest itself in many ways: Because such individuals are not good at small talk, they become anxious about engaging in it. Because they are not skilled at speaking eloquently in front of a group, they become fearful of doing it. Because they are not good at asking for dates, they become apprehensive about that. Then, because of limited experience, they become even more shy as time goes on.

Others dread communicating, not because of any skill deficiency but simply because they are afraid of the *act itself.* Even thinking about it ahead of time brings on fear.[7] People who are afraid to communicate may actually avoid interacting, even when it's in their own best interest to do so. For example, they are unlikely to approach a boss to ask for a raise—although they know they deserve more money. They may avoid answering a professor's question in class—even when they know the answer. In both instances, such individuals may know *how* to perform the required behavior: That is, they can utter the words necessary to request the raise, or they can comprehend and respond to the professor's demand. However, their emotional reactions to the situation often prevent them from doing so.

To understand further the nature of communication apprehension, we need to differentiate between two different categories of people in which this condition is present. The first is *apprehensive individuals* who, regardless of the situation, almost always feel anxious about relating to others. The second is people who have had *apprehensive experiences* that have incited fears about communicating. Both categories are widely found. But, while apprehensive individuals are troubled with a continual and pervasive condition, people who have had apprehensive experiences often suffer more temporary anxieties.

Apprehension as a Personality Trait

Apprehensive individuals fear communicating with almost anyone in any kind of situation. James McCroskey labels this type of more-or-less permanent and predictable apprehension, *trait-like.*[8] We saw in Chapter 6 that the term **trait** comes from the study of personality. It refers broadly to "any characteristic in which one individual differs from another in a relatively permanent and consistent way."[9] More specifically, we defined a trait as a relatively stable and predictable pattern of behavior that

Some people dread communicating in any context, even if there is no logical reason to feel that way. Those high in such apprehension may avoid interacting with other people even when they would be welcome and appreciated. The reasons for this form of anxiety and fear are not always clear. Some people seem to suffer from communication apprehension as a stable personality trait. Others become apprehensive only in specific kinds of situations on a more temporary basis.

we observe in an individual that is presumably due to a characteristic of his or her personality.

Social scientists do not assume that personality traits have genetic origins. That is, we do not inherit them. Individuals acquire their traits in processes of learning in a social and cultural environment. This takes place over a long period of time.[10] In terms of communication apprehension, learning from past experiences can contribute to an overall, generalized trait of anxiety about communicating.

Personality traits are not rigid. That is, individuals characterized by a particular trait may or may not exhibit the behavior in every instance. For example, an "honest" or a "jovial" person may not be like that in every circumstance. The same is true of an individual with a communication apprehension trait. Much depends on the context and the nature of the other party. For example, individuals who are high in communication apprehension report little or no anxiety in the context of interacting with their best friends or with family. Or, they may be comfortable communicating with a specific professor or employer. Thus, they can talk freely without anxiety under some circumstances. Overall, however,

persons high in the apprehension trait exhibit generalized avoidance toward *most* communication situations.[11]

At the other extreme, we all know of persons who actively seek out others and talk easily and sometimes endlessly. Some talk so much that it is hard to get a word in edgewise. We would classify such individuals as very low in the apprehension trait. In our society, being low in communication apprehension can have great advantages—as long as it is not *too* low. For the most part, we tend to approve of those who can give a good interview, easily stand in front of a crowd and entertain them, or meet new acquaintances with finesse and charm. In contrast to the chronically apprehensive who *avoid* communication encounters, those low in the trait *seek them out*. For example, a person low in communication apprehension will look forward to attending a party where he or she may not know anyone. On the other hand, an individual high in this trait would dread such a situation.

A number of studies reveal that persons with little fear of communication tend to talk more, to date a greater variety of individuals, to choose occupations that demand more social contact, to communicate more assertively, and to engage in more self-disclosure than do those who are more fearful.[12] In contrast, the accumulated research shows that the apprehensive person tends to be withdrawn, to engage in steady dating (versus "playing the field"), to select careers that allow them to work apart from others, to agree with the opinions of others (rather than express independence), and to be reluctant to reveal much information about themselves.

While people who are high or low in communication apprehension represent the ends of the continuum, most of us can be categorized as *moderately* apprehensive. In other words, having some fear of communicating is normal for most people. About 20% of the population falls into the high category, and roughly the same percent are at the other end of the scale. This means that the remaining 60%—the majority of us—are in between.[13] This in-between category experiences apprehension only when a particular situation arouses discomfort. For example, it is normal for most of us to experience some level of apprehension in situations where our behavior is being *evaluated.* That makes sense, because when we recognize that what we say and how we say it will make a difference in how a prospective employer or some other significant person views us, it is entirely normal to feel some anxiety or fear. Furthermore, it is highly likely that we will experience some stage fright before or during *any* kind of presentation. If we know we are ill prepared, or believe our audience will be hostile, that fear probably *will* increase.

The Influence of Apprehensive Experiences

There is probably no one who has not at one time or another temporarily experienced communication apprehension. The situations that trigger it vary greatly. Some people feel anxious whenever they have to talk into a tape recorder or on the radio. Suddenly, they can think of nothing intelligent to say! For others, particular individuals trigger apprehension, such as a person conducting a job or promotion interview or the parents of someone held dear. Most of us have encountered individuals who provoke a temporary case of near communication paralysis. It may be a boss, a police officer, our statistics professor, future in-laws, a strikingly attractive person whom we would like to know better, or even a special-delivery letter carrier.

When our communication capacity is temporarily reduced, we become like those who fear communication as a function of a personality trait. Like them, we will avoid apprehension-producing experiences. Thus, whether apprehension is one of our enduring personality traits, or is based on an experience producing temporary apprehension, our ability to communicate suffers in similar ways. We either become avoiders or ineffective communicators, unable to either send or receive adequately.

Causes of Communication Apprehension

No one who has been apprehensive about communicating has been particularly happy about it. We all would like to be in control—to be in full command of our own communication behavior. Unfortunately, our likes and preferences do not always coincide with what we actually do in the real world of behavior. Occasionally, we suffer from "foot in mouth" disease. That is, we forget what we were planning to say; we stammer in embarrassment; or we "clam up" just when we need to perform at our best.

Trying to explain why we develop forebodings that interfere with our ability to communicate competently is no simple task. Sometimes we improperly conclude that the individual with whom we are in a social relationship is the culprit. As it turns out, such interpretations and conclusions are usually wrong, and we have to look further for answers. Sometimes those answers can be found within the immediate context of communication. In other cases, they lie deep within the entire history of a person who continuously experiences apprehension while communicating with others.

Common Contextual Sources of Anxiety

As we suggested earlier in this chapter, certain contexts as well as certain individuals can lead us to be apprehensive. Sometimes there are good and logical reasons for concern. For example, if we are driving at 70 miles per hour on the freeway and a police car with a rotating red light and siren pulls up quickly behind us, adrenalin will undoubtedly flow! In such a situation we have real cause for anxiety.

At other times, however, we feel distress even when the situation does not realistically call for such feelings. Also, it often happens that we misinterpret the context. We believe there's reason for concern when, in fact, no objective grounds for worry exist. An example of how our imagination can provide us with unrealistic interpretations is provided by the following experience of a former student:

Terry developed a severe case of communication apprehension when his girl friend, Jill, announced that she had planned for him to meet her parents. Jill explained that her mom and dad were looking forward to meeting him. She knew that her parents were loving, sensitive, and warm individuals. Clearly, Terry had no basis in reality for fearing a meeting with Jill's folks. However, even though Terry is normally a personable and outgoing young man, his initial meeting with Jill's "mom and dad" revealed quite another side to his character. It was almost like a Dr. Jekyll and Mr. Hyde situation. At their first encounter, he seemed withdrawn; he mumbled responses to their questions; he spilled coffee on his pants and then retreated to the bathroom where he stayed for a long time. Jill was embarrassed (and furious). Afterward, Terry justified his behavior by arguing that he suffered great apprehension about the whole encounter. However, Jill contended that he distorted the situation and misread the entire context.

Both were correct. Understandably, Terry and Jill interpreted the situation differently. Each defined the meeting with Jill's parents from her or his own perspective. Jill believed that a meeting with her parents would be enjoyable; after all, they are such nice people. Terry, however, believed there was good reason to be nervous. He had concluded that her folks were interpreting the event as a commitment to an eventual marriage and that they were judging him to be unworthy of their daughter.

Whatever the contextual cues, factual or imaginary, we do know that people react to what they *believe* is real. Throughout this book we have stressed the influence on communication of contextual factors—both the situation in which it takes place and the social relationships between the people involved. The meanings that these contextual factors have are constructed in the mind of each participant.

Researchers have identified a number of contextual factors that heighten our apprehension and affect our ability to communicate effectively.[14] Stated briefly, these are: *unfamiliar or dissimilar others, novel or formal occasions, subordinate status, conspicuousness or excessive attention from others, undergoing evaluation* and *previous repeated failure.*[15]

Communicating with unfamiliar or dissimilar others

It is always easier to talk to people we know as opposed to those who are unfamiliar to us. Initiating conversation with strangers is in itself anxiety-producing. In such an encounter, where do we start? What do we say to people we don't know?

Correspondingly, persons who are different from us may generate some anxious moments. If you have in-

teracted at length with someone who dropped out of high school and who resents college students as "smart-alecks" who always "look down on others," then you know what we mean. Or, imagine a conversation between a person with strong convictions against abortion and one with exactly the opposite view. These individuals are likely to be hard-pressed to find common ground in order to communicate constructively with each other.

Novel or formal situations

Novel occasions tend to trigger communication apprehension because they are filled with uncertainty. We have repeatedly noted that *predictability* is a very important factor in social interaction. The norms, roles, and other features of stable relationships with others allow us to anticipate correctly what people probably will say, the actions they will take, and their expectations of us. This helps us to know what to say and do. When we can't make such predictions, we begin to worry. A good example is one's first date. The norms may not have been clear. No doubt, you felt much anxiety about what to say, what to wear, and what to do (or not do). Similarly, your first day at college, the first week of your new job, or the first visit to your in-laws—all presented you with some uncertainty. Communication apprehension tends to be very high in such unfamiliar and relatively unpredictable situations.

Extremely *formal* situations, such as elegant dinners, weddings, or other important ceremonies, are also likely to induce uncertainty and apprehension. Recognizing that such events require us to behave in "correct" ways, many of us feel uncomfortable because we may not be familiar with the etiquette others expect us to follow. Or, we may not know how to behave "casually" in a rented tuxedo or long formal gown. Again, the factor of unpredictability raises apprehension.

Subordinate rank

Certain kinds of situations are coupled with clear understandings of your lower status compared to others present. This kind of social relationship may cause anxieties. For example, attending a dinner party at your boss's home may serve to remind you of where you fit into the power structure, and intensify your realizations that you are really not sure how to behave in the presence of those who can control your destiny. Communication apprehension is sure to follow.

Conspicuousness and excessive attention

Any context in which you are singled out, with the attention of a crowd directly on you, can be a source of intense communication anxiety. More than any other aspect of a public speaking situation, *conspicuousness*—the belief that all

Communication apprehension may be especially high for some people in novel situations. One reason is that social relationships in such a context are not entirely predictable. The norms and role definitions among the strangers present are unknown and the person cannot anticipate how they will respond if they try to initiate a conversation. Fear of rejection due to saying the wrong thing easily inhibits any such attempt.

eyes are riveted on you, scrutinizing everything about you—can induce communication apprehension. This can happen in any occasion when you become the center of attention. Perhaps you've felt self-conscious when a professor held up your work to show the entire class that this was an example of what to do—or worse, an example of what *not* to do!

Similarly, *excessive attention* from others may give rise to communication apprehension. For example, we are likely to feel uncomfortable when an adviser or counselor seems determined to have us reveal private and confidential information. We may find it difficult to communicate in such circumstances. Another example is the discomfort we feel when someone monopolizes all of our time at a party. This may cause us to wish they would go away or that we were somewhere else. Most of us like some moderate level of attention from others but are ill at ease when someone wants to peer at us "through a microscope."

Undergoing evaluation   Being "checked out" or evaluated is almost certain to bring on communication anxiety. In situations where we know that our supervisor

at work, or a professor in class, is appraising us on the basis of an oral performance, we are likely to become anxious. Even though we may do well without their scrutiny, the idea that we're being assessed heightens our apprehension about what we say or do. Students often report that when they practice their speeches at home, they experience no problems. As soon as they see the professor with that grade book, however, they get nervous, forget their lines, and generally perform poorly.

Repeated failure   Finally, memories of previous failures in identical or similar situations are a common source of apprehension. For instance, if the last 12 times we tried to arrange a date with someone only to be repeatedly turned down, trying for the 13th time might be distressing, to say the least. Or, if we know from past experience that every time we have asked for a raise, the boss has listened impatiently and then sneered at our request, we might well be nervous and reluctant about going in and asking one more time.

Most of us can readily identify with such sources of communication distress. We all have found ourselves in circumstances that seemed to provoke a degree of such

A situation that is likely to create some degree of apprehension is one in which our communication skills are being assessed. Many people are much less nervous speaking before a group if they feel that no one is grading them or evaluating their performance. If judges of some sort are present, however, they forget their lines and generally perform poorly.

temporary or transitory apprehension. They are relatively easy to understand and explain. However, the problem becomes more complex when attempting to identify causes of communication apprehension as a persistent personality trait.

How We Learn to Be Characteristically Apprehensive

We do know one thing about people whose apprehension is a stable personality trait. They tend to *distort* their interpretations of the contextual factors discussed above. They selectively perceive events around them and interpret them in ways that are different from those who are not usually apprehensive. For example, those high in apprehension sometimes perceive a situation to be *more* novel or formal than it really is. Or, they feel *very* conspicuous and are convinced that *everyone* present notices a mistake they make and is laughing at them. Even if we try to persuade them otherwise, they don't buy it. Unfortunately, those with a high apprehension trait engage

in so much self-monitoring that they can be oblivious to reality or to the way other people interpret the context.

Long-term socialization of the apprehensive person   Earlier, we discussed the process of *socialization* and defined it as a long-term process of communication whereby a human being acquires a personality and becomes a functioning member of society. In this chapter we have made it clear that communication apprehension can be a personality trait—a label for a deeply established pattern of behavior. The importance of this view is that it identifies the trait as a product of long-term socialization.

It will help to compare the socialization process that produces communication apprehension to that which produces fear of going to the dentist. In our society, fear and dread—supposedly caused by pain and suffering—are indelibly associated with dentists. Children understand that early and well. Even if they have never gone to the dentist, they can tell you that it is a dreadful experience to be avoided! They have learned this from cartoons, old movies, lore in the street, jokes heard from others, and tales told by earlier generations. The fact is, going to the dentist today is virtually painless. It may be inconvenient, perhaps uncomfortable at times, and certainly expensive, but it is hardly an experience that leaves every person visiting a dentist racked with pain and suffering. In short, this is a culturally shared construction of meaning that people learn for "going to the dentist" rather than an objective reality. In a similar way, some people acquire convictions about the terrors of "speaking before a group," even if they have never done so.

Socialization includes learning The importance of noting the dependency of communication apprehension on the socialization process is that it includes *learning*. Socialization and learning are not identical concepts. Socialization is a very complex process, in which learning is but one component. It is a long-term set of influences on a person. Those influences result from activities not only of the individual but of others who function in the person's sociocultural environment. That environment defines the kinds of indirect lessons the individual will experience concerning meanings for particular terms and concepts (like "going to dentist" or "speaking before a group").

In the socialization process, such lessons are presented deliberately or unwittingly by **agents** of socialization (teachers, friends, parents, media, etc.) that play a key part in the process. As a result, over a period of time, repeated instances of learning take place in which specific meanings are acquired regarding the ease or difficulty of communicating. For some individuals those lessons will consistently define public communication as pleasurable. For others the lessons will repeatedly teach that it is frightening and to be avoided. For most of us it will be neither of these extremes. It is the content and pattern of these learning experiences, then, that shape the individual's beliefs, attitudes, and behavior regarding the pleasures or horrors of public communication.

The importance of learning A bright feature of focusing narrowly on the learning part of the socialization process is that it offers hope for changing people who have acquired excessive apprehension as a personality trait. There is little hope that their entire personality and all their meaning schemata regarding communication that have been acquired by socialization can be radically modified. But with systematic training they may be able to *unlearn* at least some negative beliefs and *change* troublesome meanings that promote communication anxiety. In other words, with adequate training, substitute beliefs, modified attitudes, and new behavior patterns can be ac-

quired that will make it easier for shy and apprehensive people to communicate. Such "relearning" processes have been successful in limiting people's fears of flying, in improving sexual adequacy, and even in reducing fears of snakes.

To gain a perspective that may help reduce excessive fears of communicating, we can look more closely at the process of learning itself. Social scientists have developed many theories of how learning takes place. We will consider only two relevant ones that are related, but which offer different accounts of the origins of particular behavior patterns. One is called *social learning theory*. The other is a broader approach called *reinforcement learning theory*. Each has a long history, a huge amount of associated research, and numerous applications to modifying many kinds of behavior.[16] However, we will focus narrowly on the application of these two learning theories to the acquisition of a communication apprehension trait.

Learning to fear by observing others Social learning theory, or as it is sometimes called, "observational learning theory," was developed originally by Albert Bandura as an extension of earlier, more general reinforcement theories.[17] It is a broad formulation that explains how we acquire many kinds of behavior that are important in our lives. As the name suggests, **social learning theory** was originally developed to try to explain how individuals could learn, not by performing actions themselves but by *observing* how other people coped with problems that confronted them. This idea can be applied to communication apprehension.

Essentially, social learning theory explains that we begin learning to be high or low in communication apprehension by observing the behavior and reactions of people who are important as models in our lives. As young children, our parents and siblings served as our primary models of how to behave. As we entered school, friends and teachers probably became significant models as well.

As Bandura and others have illustrated, we often learn how to do something by observing how other people do it. We watch another person perform an activity and then, under certain circumstances, we imitate that performance. We do this all the time with many forms of behavior. For example, from our earliest years we learn to talk and respond to others appropriately by copying many of the verbal and nonverbal patterns of others—especially those we admire and want to emulate. Looking to the behavior of other people is, after all, the main source from which we find out what our family, friends, and society at large expect of us. From the beginning, they serve as models for us and we emulate them.

The key to this modeling approach is trying out the observed behavior. That is most likely when we observe that those serving as our models are *rewarded* for particular kinds of behavior, in the sense that it solves some kind of problem for them. In other words, it is not enough just to imitate. Any new form of behavior copied from another has to be useful to us in some way. If it seems so, we may try it out. Then, as a result of such trials we may or may not adopt the new behavior as part of our own habit patterns. What leads us to adopt it more permanently is that the modeled behavior helps us cope with a problem that confronts us. If it does so successfully, we will experience a personal "reward" (i.e., "it worked, and the problem was handled"). Even removing a problem and feeling relief can be a reward.

Learning specialists refer broadly to the consequences of such rewarding experiences as "reinforcement," which can be defined as an increase in the probability that we will respond in that particular way again when confronted with the same circumstances. By this means the response is learned to become a lasting part of our overall behavioral patterns. On the other hand, if adopting the modeled behavior results in a bad or punishing experience, it is unlikely we will make it a permanent part of our repertoire.

Not only do we copy actual or overt behaviors, we are also good imitators of our models' fears and anxieties. For instance, some of us learned to fear spiders simply by observing the anxiety attacks of one of our parents. For example, an actual instance of such modeling occurred in the following way:

When Kerry was in third grade, her teacher owned a pet tarantula named Precious. The pet became Kerry's favorite. In spite of that early positive experience with Precious, Kerry, now a young woman, shakes in fear every time she faces even the tiniest spider. Something happened! Specifically, she was *resocialized,* and observational learning played a key part. Over the years, she was exposed to the repeated hysterics of her mother every time an uninvited spider, or indeed any unknown bug, entered the house. Her parent served as a model, and Kerry acquired her pattern of reacting with fear to the stimulus of a spider. Her mother was someone she wanted to be like, and emulating her was rewarding. That reward reinforced the bug-fear connection.

Similarly, children pick up on the subtle and obvious cues of their parents', siblings', or peers' anxieties about communicating.[18] Exposed at an early age to a number of important models who appear uncomfortable in communication situations, any one of us might have been unintentionally socialized to be high in apprehension.

Learning as a consequence of reward and punishment   Social learning theory is an attractive explanation that seems to make sense. By itself, however, it fails in one important respect: It does not explain fully why one individual raised in a particular set of circumstances acquires a communication apprehension trait while another, reared in exactly those same circumstances, does not. We know, for instance, that a child who is high in communication apprehension may grow up in the same family that also produces another child who is low in such anxiety. Presumably each has been exposed to the same behavioral models by the parents. Therefore, social learning theory may explain the problems of one but not the other. Furthermore, we know that children can be low in apprehension about communicating even when both parents (as models) are highly apprehensive. The same is true in reverse. Thus, while the modeling perspective may provide a reasonable account of why apprehension results in some people, it fails in others.

An alternative explanation that does not have the preceding shortcoming can be derived from **reinforcement theory.** According to this explanation, individuals "try out" a number of behaviors. Postponing for the moment the question as to *why* they try them out for the first time, these initial trials are followed by some sort of consequence. If the consequence is positive or rewarding (and thereby reinforcing), then the behavior becomes part of the individual's repertoire, to be repeated in similar circumstances.[19] Should the consequence be punishing, however, the behavior is likely to be dropped and replaced with some other response. Assuming that we prefer positive, rather than negative, consequences to our behavior, reinforcement theory explains why some of us enjoy social situations that require communication, whereas others will avoid them. More than any other explanation of communication apprehension, this perspective has received fairly consistent confirmation in research.[20] Basically, then, advocates of reinforcement theory claim that people high in communication apprehension have been punished for their communication, whereas those low in apprehension have been rewarded.

We temporarily set aside a problem associated with this approach—the question of *why* the individual tries out a new response in the first place. One answer to that question is provided by what are called "operant" versions of reinforcement learning theory. Essentially, this view holds that "chance" plays a part. The individual may need to cope with some sort of problem. To do so he or she randomly tries out many potential solutions—similar to random trial and error—and finally gets it right. In fact, hitting on a form of behavior that produces rewards need not be the result of a conscious decision. The individual may simply have unwittingly engaged in a form of activity that produced a rewarding experience. That response pattern then is reinforced—has a higher probability of being repeated. If rewards continue when the behavior takes place, it becomes a permanent habit pattern, perhaps without the person even realizing what has happened.[21]

Reinforcement learning of specific forms of behavior can be illustrated in the context of the typical elementary grade school classroom. Children are quickly taught to raise their hands to seek permission to speak. They are also taught that blurting out comments without prior recognition by the teacher brings sharp reprimands or simply results in their being ignored altogether.

But in this context, who gets reinforced for what? And what are the long-term consequences for communication apprehension? Much depends on prior socialization in the home. Those children who have an early history of being rewarded for their precocious behavior at home are likely to persist in gaining teacher recognition for "talk time." On the other hand, those who have been reared in environments where "children should be seen and not heard" are not likely to ask to be heard in the first place. Often these are the ones who are most ignored by the teachers. If they do decide they want to talk and try to gain the teacher's attention, they may be unable to do so. They may then just blurt out what they wanted to say anyway. However, the punishing consequences for such unrecognized interjections are likely to stamp out their efforts rather quickly. By this time, communication apprehension is well on the way to becoming an established trait.

The resiliency factor   Despite our learning histories, many of us have encountered negative consequences of our communication behavior at one time or another, and yet, we have not become crippled by communication ap-

Behavior that is rewarded can increase the probability that it will be repeated to become a permanent part of a person's way of acting. Children who respond bright and easily to a teacher are likely to be called on repeatedly and rewarded for their participation. This can reduce communication apprehension greatly. Other children who may be more reserved or who have been reprimanded when they gave inappropriate answers may fear the teacher's attention. This can raise their level of communication apprehension.

prehension. Fortunately, most of us are *resilient* enough to try again in our efforts to gain positive consequences. This resiliency is a product of our socialization or reinforcement history, which suggests that we can usually "expect" our communication to be well received. As a result, when an occasional interaction goes wrong, we are able to chalk it up as an unusual event—a mistake.

Those already high in apprehension do not share this resiliency. For them, success is not expected. On the contrary, such individuals have already learned to expect failure or punishment when they talk. A history of punishment for talking prompts those high in apprehension to *avoid* the behavior that typically results in negative consequences. Thus, fear of communicating and the expectation of negative consequences have become a deeply established personality trait—in short, predictable communication apprehension.

The consequences of inconsistency   A follow-up of reinforcement theory suggests that some individuals may experience *inconsistent* consequences to their behavior. If a youngster is rewarded for talking sometimes and punished at other times, she or he is likely to develop high communication apprehension. In our discussions of the nature of group life, we repeatedly noted the significance of *predictability* in producing stability in social relationships. Irregular or inconsistent consequences of behaving in a certain way over time can induce a condition of personal **anomie**—a feeling of anxiety or distress arising from confusion concerning the social expectations of others. This can be a serious condition, and it has even been linked to increasing the probability of suicide.[22] In the present discussion of communication apprehension, if we cannot accurately make reliable predictions about what will happen to us—whether we will be rewarded or punished when we attempt to communicate—we probably will develop fears and anxieties about it and stop attempting to do so altogether.

Another source of anxiety is the "no-win" situation. For instance, we may find ourselves always saying the wrong thing. If we greet the boss at work or the neighbor next-door, saying, "Good morning," she grumbles and claims that it isn't. If we change strategy and declare that "we've seen better days than this one," she argues that we should appreciate what we have. Finally, if we choose to ignore her altogether, she alleges that we are cold and unfriendly. This no-win situation, like the repeated failures condition, is likely to make us feel very apprehensive in subsequent encounters with her. We are helpless to initiate a successful communication. Should this experience

happen often in other contexts and with other individuals as well, we begin to see how **learned helplessness** would be aroused in almost all of our attempts to communicate with others.[23]

By now, we can readily see that by the time we are adults, we have confronted and assimilated a number of communication experiences that eventually result in differential levels of communication apprehension. Those of us who share a history of positive reinforcement for communicating are probably moderate to low in our apprehensions. While we may occasionally suffer from anxiety in a specific situation, as a rule we tend to be comfortable with people and enjoy talking with them and to them. Conversely, those who have experienced a very different history of socialization—with punishment or unpredictable consequences tied to attempts to communicate—are likely to be chronically apprehensive about approaching any communication task. We can illustrate the issues with an example drawn from extended observations of actual cases.

Consequences of High and Low Communication Apprehension

Suffering from high anxiety about—and avoiding—public speaking are not the only consequences of being chronically apprehensive. Over a hundred research studies demonstrate that individuals high and low in apprehension are *evaluated* differently by other people in many ways.[24] We can look at the consequences of these assessments at several stages in their lives. As will be seen, those who are low are evaluated positively for many kinds of behavior, whereas individuals who are high are regarded negatively in a variety of ways. These assessments can have profound and surprisingly long-term consequences for them.

The initial competitive arena of evaluation of people in terms of their communication habits and traits begins in childhood, and one of the earliest settings is the *classroom*. That process begins even when children are in kindergarten and first grade. These are important sociocultural settings for socialization in the area of communication apprehension, because what children learn in their early educational experience can carry over into later stages of life. As we will show, their schoolroom communication habits can have later influences on their experiences with higher education—how they are evaluated by their instructors—and even how they fare in making friends in college.[25] In addition, their communication traits follow them into the labor force and have

Personal Report of Communication Apprehension-24 (CA)

Instructions   This instrument is composed of 24 statements concerning your feelings about communication with other people. Please indicate in the space provided the degree to which you agree or disagree with each statement—by noting whether you:

5 strongly disagree   **2** agree
4 disagree   **1** strongly agree
3 are undecided

There are no right or wrong answers. Many of the statements are similar to other statements. Do not be concerned about this. Work quickly, just record your first impression.

_____ **1.** I dislike participating in group discussions.

_____ **2.** Generally, I am comfortable while participating in a group discussion.

_____ **3.** I am tense and nervous while participating in group discussions.

_____ **4.** I like to get involved in group discussions.

_____ **5.** Engaging in a group discussion with new people makes me tense and nervous.

_____ **6.** I am calm and relaxed while participating in group discussions.

_____ **7.** Generally, I am nervous when I have to participate in a meeting.

_____ **8.** Usually I am calm and relaxed while participating in meetings.

_____ **9.** I am very calm and relaxed when I am called on to express an opinion at a meeting.

_____ **10.** I am afraid to express myself at meetings.

_____ **11.** Communicating at meetings usually makes me uncomfortable.

_____ **12.** I am very relaxed when answering questions at a meeting.

_____ **13.** While participating in a conversation with a new acquaintance, I feel very nervous.

_____ **14.** I have no fear of speaking up in conversation.

_____ **15.** Ordinarily I am very tense and nervous in conversations.

_____ **16.** Ordinarily I am very calm and relaxed in conversations.

_____ **17.** While conversing with a new acquaintance, I feel very relaxed.

_____ **18.** I'm afraid to speak up in conversations.

_____ **19.** I have no fear of giving a speech.

_____ **20.** Certain parts of my body feel very tense and rigid while giving a speech.

_____ **21.** I feel relaxed while giving a speech.

_____ **22.** My thoughts become confused and jumbled when I am giving a speech.

_____ **23.** I face the prospect of giving a speech with confidence.

_____ **24.** While giving a speech I get so nervous, I forget facts I really know.

Calculating Your Score

The PRCA-24 allows you to compute both an overall, total apprehension score as well as four different subscores that measure your apprehension toward four familiar contexts: talking in groups, meetings, dyads, and public situations.

Group   = 18 + scores for items 2, 4, and 6;
              − scores for items 1, 3, and 5.
              YOUR GROUP SCORE = _____.

Meeting = 18 + scores for items 8, 9, and 12;
              − scores for items 7, 10, and 11.
              YOUR MEETING SCORE = _____.

Dyadic = 18 + scores for items 14, 16, and 17;
              − scores for items 13, 15, and 18.
              YOUR DYADIC SCORE = _____.

Public   = 18 + scores for items 19, 21, and 23;
              − scores for items 20, 22, and 24.
              YOUR PUBLIC SCORE = _____.

Overall Communication Apprehension (CA) = Simply add your subscores together: Group + Meeting + Dyadic + Public.

YOUR TOTAL CA SCORE = _____.

Interpreting Your Score

Possible range of scores: 24–120. (If your own overall CA score does not fall within that range, you made a computational error.)

High CA's (scores higher than 83) are characterized as low talkers, shy, withdrawn, fearful, tense, and nervous. Low CA's (scores lower than 55) talk a lot, seem to enjoy the company of others, are more immediate with people, and occasionally communicate even when others would rather they wouldn't. Moderates (scores between 55 and 83) are considered more "normal." They know there are times when they should talk and times when they should not. Moderates are apprehensive during important job interviews but feel little or no tension at all when talking to acquaintances over the telephone.

Reference

McCroskey, J. C. (1982). *Introduction to rhetorical communication* (4th ed.). Englewood Cliffs, NJ: Prentice-Hall.

significant influences on their career development for many years afterward.

Evaluations in the Classroom

The consequences of evaluations in the classroom of two persons who are very different in communication apprehension can be illustrated by comparing "Gail" and "Pat"—who represent "composites" of individuals whose experiences have repeatedly been revealed by research. In other words, these characterizations of "Gail," as an individual low in communication apprehension, and "Pat," as one who is high in that trait, are actually based on numbers of real individuals who have been studied extensively.[26] These composites will seem familiar because we all know people who fit each of these behavioral profiles:

Gail and Pat are best friends. At 14 years of age, they are both attractive and they both like boys, pizza, and rock stars (in that order). Gail is outgoing, popular, and captain of the cheerleading squad. Pat is more of a loner, reads a lot, and uses her home computer before school every morning. Gail is rarely, if ever, apprehensive about talking to anyone about anything. Even though Pat interacts regularly with Gail, she seldom initiates conversations with others at school.

If we could observe and record all the ways teachers respond differently to Gail as compared to Pat, we might be alarmed at what we would find. There would be disturbing discriminations in favor of the girl low in communication apprehension. For instance, extensive research shows that teachers would perceive Gail to be a better student than Pat (even if they are intellectual equals). This attribution would be maintained even when the objective evidence of their grades was similar and their IQ scores identical. It would still hold true if Pat finished the school year first in her class and Gail finished fifth!

How can this be? The answers lie within the patterns of communication with teachers established by the two girls. We would find that teachers talk more to Gail than they do to Pat. Of course, we know that Gail would be likely to raise her hand and volunteer to talk more frequently. However, even when both girls had their hands raised simultaneously, teachers would call more readily on Gail. Moreover, teachers would initiate conversations much more often with Gail than with Pat.

As we explained in Chapter 9, on self-presentation, attributions about personal qualities, such as academic ability, are based on *assumptions.* This type of assumption is made on the basis of communication "input" from the person involved. For example, when teachers ask Gail a question and she doesn't know the answer, they will assume the question was too hard or unclear. Consequently, they will follow up with prompts and hints to assist her. Should the same thing happen with Pat, teachers will assume that she doesn't know the answer because she's not too bright. Then they would move on to someone else. Teachers will readily interpret Gail's congeniality as a sign of an enthused, dedicated, and utterly delightful student. Pat's quietness will be construed as a sign of detachment, indifference, or even apathy toward school.

Clearly, students who resemble Gail are more likely to be seen as ones who do well in school, despite the fact that teachers often give them extra help and attention. Students like Pat have their work cut out for them. Teachers regularly underestimate their intelligence and misinterpret their quietness as an "attitude" problem. They waste little extra time on "cases of this kind" because these students do not seem to "appreciate" the teacher's efforts. This discriminatory behavior, of course, reinforces communication apprehension. Thus, the process of socialization of the person high in communication apprehension is seldom corrected by their experiences in school.

Assessments in Interpersonal Encounters

Let us assume that Pat, who is high in apprehension, and Gail, who is low, are now 19 years old and both in college. The problems for Pat and the advantages for Gail will have continued, both in the college classroom and in interpersonal relationships outside of school. Specifically, we would be likely to find that Gail has a date several times a week. She enjoys the company of several young men, who find her attractive, affable, and exciting.

Objectively speaking, Pat is just as physically attractive as Gail. However, for a variety of reasons, few men (or women) even notice her when she's in the same room with them. Like most people high in apprehension, Pat appears to "hide" or physically "contract" when others are around. She does date, but it is with the same young man pretty regularly. Actually, she doesn't find him all that interesting and would like to date others on occasion. Unfortunately, she seldom has the opportunity.

When men first meet Pat, their impression is that she is cold and distant. Her telephone seldom rings afterward.

The point is that interpersonal opportunities are much greater for individuals like Gail, who are low in communication apprehension. They seem approachable, and they are fun to be with. They give the appearance of being good listeners in conversations with others; they ask and answer questions; they are high in nonverbal immediacy; and they are generally personable. Those who are high, like Pat, give off the wrong signals. High communication apprehension sends a clear message of avoidance. Those with this trait look away, respond only when spoken to, and rarely ask questions about the other partner. Few people want to initiate or continue a relationship with someone who appears disinterested and unfriendly. Once again, the objective reality makes little difference: Pat, who is high in apprehension, may want and need our company, but her behavior communicates the opposite.

The Reactions of People at Work

What started as an early personality trait acquired through socialization in childhood often stays with a person through college and beyond to become a permanent characteristic during his or her subsequent years. Again we can illustrate the issues by drawing on our composite individuals, Gail and Pat. As we will see, their predisposition as either high or low in communication apprehension continues to have significant influences throughout their lives.

Right after graduation from college, Gail and Pat look for employment. Gail applies for career opportunities in public relations (in which she majored). Pat considers jobs as a data analyst and in developing computer software (she majored in computer information systems). Obviously, the communication demands of each career path differ dramatically. Typical of people low in communication apprehension, Gail chooses positions that require her to interact regularly with corporate clients. On the other hand, Pat, who is still highly apprehensive, selects opportunities that help her avoid such communication encounters.

Consider the major area of study *you* selected and the career decisions you have made thus far. Do these decisions reflect positive or negative feelings about communication? We know that an abnormally large number of those high in communication apprehension are likely to select such majors as accounting, computer science, pharmacy, and engineering. Correspondingly, we know that those low in apprehension are likely to pick such areas as speech communication, theatre, journalism, advertising, and public relations.

In understanding the relationship between anxiety about communicating and the impressions people form at work, we need to consider the effects of apprehension on job applications and interviews. All things being equal, those who communicate easily generally do much better in job interviews than those who are more anxious. Therefore, Gail will make a more positive first impression than Pat. Research indicates that employers are likely to form an impression of Gail as sociable, competent, responsible, and having leadership potential. Pat is much more likely to receive negative evaluations from her interviews. Employers will find her uncommunicative, restrained, aloof, and tense. At the extreme, they may conclude that Pat is really not all that interested in working for them.

Influences on Careers

What can we anticipate if we look in on Pat and Gail 7 years later? We are likely to find Gail in management and Pat still working at lower levels in the company. When it comes to promotions at work, those low in apprehension are promoted significantly more often than those who continue to be fearful and nervous about communicating. Apparently, those who communicate comfortably promote their own achievements to their bosses and assert their needs. Those reluctant to communicate hesitate to tell others about their successes. They just wait for good things to happen to them.

Job satisfaction is another area of difference revealed by research.[27] We would find Gail much more satisfied with her work than Pat is. Perhaps we are seeing reality here. That is, it may be that those low in apprehension report significantly more satisfaction than do their high counterparts simply because their jobs are more rewarding. After all, Gail's position probably pays more, includes greater work variety, and provides more flexibility than does Pat's lower-ranking position.

To summarize, the selective, distorted impressions that people construct on the basis of someone's apprehension about communicating can easily lead us to conclude that the world of the "easy talker" is much more positive than

that of the person who is shy and timid. In some ways it is. Overall, people who are more or less permanently apprehensive about communicating appear to be less likely to succeed in academic pursuits, social relationships, and career opportunities. In contrast, those who are not troubled by such anxieties seem to get more of what they want. Others form the impression that they are competent, sociable, popular, hard-working, attractive, responsible, and more qualified for leadership roles. It is a hard picture to resist.

At the same time, there are reasons to qualify these conclusions. Obviously, the preceding generalizations have many exceptions. They are *tendencies* documented by research but are by no means iron-bound laws. It would not be difficult to find children high in apprehension who do well academically (sometimes in spite of the teacher). As adults, many such people establish long-term successful marriages and friendships and even get paid handsomely at work. On the other side of the coin, there are certainly many people who are not at all apprehensive about communicating but have trouble graduating from school, can't seem to get a date, and fail to hold down any one job for long. Thus, no one needs to feel doomed simply because they're shy and somewhat uncommunicative. For one thing, as we will explain in some detail, change is possible. Even so, there is a lot to be said for privacy. The fact is, the majority of people who tend to be apprehensive about communicating have learned to live with their condition and have no desire to change their life style.

Dealing with Stage Fright

Everyone, at one time or another, has to make a presentation before a group. A common form of communication apprehension is **stage fright.** In fact there are few people who have failed to experience it. In this section we will look at this condition, understand its nature, and suggest ways of coping with it.

First, we need to keep in mind that stage fright is *normal.* In fact, it is even a *routine* experience for those who repeatedly perform before audiences. Almost all professional performers complain about feeling nervous just before they have to stand up and speak before an audience. It's no simple feat to march up, front and center, with all eyes on us, and speak fluently and meaningfully. Most of us hope just to get through the event as quickly as possible without making ourselves look foolish.

To understand stage fright we need to examine two of its potential causes: the apprehension-producing event itself and our own level of communication apprehension. Contrary to what you might think, we do not recommend ridding ourselves completely of stage fright. Like certain kinds of unpleasant medicine, in limited doses it serves us well! That is, stage fright is often a necessary condition for expert performances. What we do recommend is that we first understand *why* we suffer from it and what it can do to *help* or *hurt* our performances.

The Contributions of the Context

To discuss stage fright we will narrow our focus from communicating with people in general to the problem of public speaking in particular. That is, we will concentrate in this section on those specific occasions when we have to make a report, address an assembly, or otherwise speak to a group or audience.

Like all other aspects of communication, stage fright is partly a product of the context in which the activity takes place. That is, public speaking takes place in a physical place, in a social setting, and among persons in particular social relationships. Each of these factors can contribute in their own way to the development of temporary communication apprehension, even for the calmest among us. In addition, speaking before a group has many of the characteristics we referred to earlier as specific sources of apprehension. That is, it is a performance before *unfamiliar others,* in a *formal occasion,* that makes us feel *conspicuous,* and in such a way that everyone seems to be *evaluating* us in some way. It is little wonder, then, that this kind of communication generates anxiety.

But are these sources of apprehension real or only products of our imagination? The answer is that they are *very real!* Giving a talk *does* place us in a formal occasion before unfamiliar others where we are conspicuous and being evaluated! In fact, every audience rates a public speaking event much in the same way they judge ball games, soap operas, or movies. Because public events are subtly defined as "entertainment" by the prevailing practices of our culture, people often expect a speaker to be "amusing" or at least expect that she or he will inform them in some interesting, and hopefully fascinating, way. Their expectations seem to increase as a function of how much money, time, and effort is involved in attending the presentation. Unfortunately, then, everyone becomes a *critic* when they assume the role of audience member,

and they judge whether a speaker is good or bad, entertaining or boring. We have to recognize that fact. Fortunately, as we will see, there are ways of coping with the anxieties generated by that fact.

What the Speaker Brings to the Problem

Sometimes stage fright is not so much a product of the context as it is the speaker's personality. In previous sections we have showed that persons high in communication apprehension as a trait are likely to overemphasize the stress factors in almost any situation. Even though we all recognize the conspicuous situation of the speaker and evaluative factors inherent to the event, people who are chronically apprehensive will interpret the situation and the audience in a distorted way. They will conclude that the people truly are strangers, that they will be even *more* conspicuous, and that the audience will be even *more* evaluative than will those who are not so apprehensive. If you are not usually apprehensive, but think it's difficult enough to face an audience in a public speaking situation, consider how a chronically apprehensive person feels who is truly agonizing over the experience!

The chronically apprehensive will do almost anything to avoid having to speak before an audience. When given the option of taking any other course elective, students high in apprehension will choose not to enroll in anything like a public speaking class. Some universities require such classes. When that happens, seriously apprehensive students may enroll, drop the class, and enroll again. Sometimes they do not muster the courage to enroll or to finish the class until the last semester of their final year in college. In fact, there are students who have never graduated simply because they were unable to complete that one required course.

In contrast, easy talkers typically enjoy public speaking courses and despite experiencing mild and normal stage fright, they learn to perform quite well. For such individuals, and indeed for those who are moderately apprehensive, stage fright can be controlled. By practicing skills, they learn to channel their apprehension toward the event in productive ways. Specifically, a certain amount of stage fright generates motivation—enough drive so that those who are low or even moderate in general communication apprehension can excel on stage.

Unfortunately, many novice speakers, along with the chronically apprehensive, fail to manage their stage fright productively. Rather than using their anxiety to stimulate motivation, they allow it to inhibit their abilities. They don't act on their fears but give in to them. As a result, they cannot perform competently. The signs of that defeat are visible—physiologically, psychologically, and behaviorally. Physiologically, their palms become sweaty and their hands and knees shake. In severe cases, their skin blotches and their stomach cramps. On stage, they stutter and their memories fail. For these unfortunate people, the expectancy of failure overrides any chance for success. They "just know" they will perform poorly in front of everyone—and so they do.

At some point, however, even those who are very anxious will want to (or will have to) break away from that pattern. As we have already indicated, continued, habitual anxiety can result in serious consequences. For instance, we may find ourselves overlooked for pay raises at work, unable to defend our beliefs and convictions successfully, and powerless to express our ideas forcefully.

Reducing Communication Apprehension

None of us has to go through life avoiding events that require us to communicate. We can learn to control our apprehensions. In particular, we can cope with stage fright, and we can even modify a communication apprehension trait. That is not to say there is some easy way to transform an individual who is chronically high in apprehension into one who will henceforth be low. Nevertheless, strong evidence indicates that even those who are truly anxious can be moved to a moderate level where their apprehensions can be managed. If so, they can gain enough confidence to communicate with others effectively in both public and private settings.

A number of methods have been touted as potential cures for communication anxieties. We will consider only three that appear to be effective. All have impressive names, but as we will show, they are not that difficult to understand. The three are *systematic desensitization, cognitive restructuring,* and *skills training.* There are many other techniques, such as hypnosis, group counseling, and psychoanalysis. While these may have merit, they can be very costly. More important, none are as successful as the three noted above. Today, most colleges and universities offer at least two of the three techniques we discuss in this section as part of training in public speaking. After reviewing each, we urge you to consider examining a program if one is available and it seems suitable to your needs.

There is no easy way to transform a person who is high in communication apprehension to one who will communicate easily and comfortably in virtually any context. Most programs designed to aid people in reducing such fears have been associated with public speaking programs at colleges and universities. Some programs seem to work well with some people. None are universally effective. For most of us, some degree of communication apprehension is normal and probably helpful in motivating us to practice and prepare with care.

Systematic Desensitization

The process of *systematic desensitization* is the most widely used of all treatment programs for communication apprehension. There is good reason because it has one of the highest success rates.[28] Systematic desensitization, known commonly as *SD,* has been around since the early 1950s. It is a form of treatment that has been applied to many kinds of fears, not just communication apprehension. Therapists employ SD to treat clients' fears of flying, heights, driving, the water, school exams, and even snakes, bugs, and rats (if anyone really wants to warm up to them).

In the mid-1960s, research began on the effects of SD on public speaking anxiety. Over and over again, experimenters found that SD significantly reduced students' fears about communicating. In 1972 a university-wide SD program was initiated for students at Illinois State University. It included published guidelines that others have used to initiate similar treatment programs at universities and high schools across the country.[29]

Systematic desensitization reduces apprehensions through muscle relaxation techniques. We all become tense and tighten our muscles whenever we feel anxious—it is an "involuntary" response. If we have reason to be fearful, we unwittingly signal our bodies to be on the alert and get ready for action. Many people do the same thing with communication situations. If they anticipate that the situation will be apprehension-producing, they become taut and rigid. SD works on the principle that if an alternative response, such as relaxation, can be *substituted* for that tension and stress, we will be able to cope with the situation.

So, the big message of SD is *relax!* "Well," you say, "that's easier said than done." The fact is, it can't be done without learning *how* to do it. In SD treatment programs, individuals are actually taught how to relax. They get right down to basics and learn to manipulate every muscle so that on demand they can either tighten or release them. Moreover, they also learn to control their breathing so that on cue they can "let go" and exhale. Part of the treatment program, then, requires that the trainee become conscious of physical tensions, from whatever source, and practice methods of releasing that tension on command.

The next phase of SD introduces the anxiety-producing conditions for which the training is all about. In the case of communication apprehension, students are exposed *gradually* to a graded sequence of communication situations. At first, situations are presented that arouse relatively little apprehension. For example, while in a relaxed state, subjects are asked to imagine themselves talking on the telephone to their best friend. Next, with the level of potential stress in the situation increased somewhat, they may be asked to visualize themselves working on a group project or going on a blind date. If the program has progressed successfully, in later stages situations are confronted that would have produced a lot of stress before the therapy began. Subjects are asked to imagine themselves presenting a speech or being inter-

viewed on television. By the time they get to this level, they have developed the relaxation techniques to a point where they can handle the situation. Thus, the principle is that communication demands at each successive level become increasingly more likely to bring about apprehension. Meanwhile, those in the program practice their relaxation exercises. What finally happens is that they learn to associate relaxation, not tension, with communication situations.

Besides the obvious success rate associated with this method, SD is cost-effective. Each session lasts about an hour, and the entire program requires only about four or five sessions. Research shows that if students are exposed to SD at the same time they are enrolled in public speaking classes, where they learn specific skills, they are more likely to finish the course, perform competently, and report feeling less apprehensive about communicating. In short, SD is convenient, simple, and effective.

Cognitive Restructuring

An interesting and equally successful alternative to SD is "cognitive restructuring." While systematic desensitization focuses on muscle tension—the physiological effects of our apprehension—**cognitive restructuring** centers are psychological processes. It examines the individual's *interpretations* of the anxiety-producing situation itself. Again, this is a general therapy system and is not restricted to communication anxieties. Nevertheless, it is used to reduce temporary or chronic communication apprehension.

Proponents of this method argue that people *label* certain situations inappropriately and that they often evaluate events as more negative than they actually are. These negative evaluations are based primarily on specific *irrational beliefs* that underlie a lot of their emotions. Three irrational beliefs that individuals commonly entertain can be summed up in the following terms:[30]

- Everyone must love me all the time or I am a bad person.
- I must be competent or successful in all situations or I am a bad person.
- When life is not the way I want, it is awful and upsetting.

Cognitive restructuring focuses on changing these kinds of beliefs. The role of the trainer or therapist is to help individuals understand the basis for their anxieties. When irrational beliefs are exposed, the therapist challenges them, questioning each and arguing logically against them all. Then the therapist offers rational alternatives to replace those that have been discredited. In this way, troublesome beliefs are "restructured," or they are displaced and new convictions are established.

When cognitive restructuring is applied to communication apprehension, four major steps are involved. For present purposes, we will focus our discussion of each step on fears about one kind of communication situation that apprehensive people find particularly pernicious—public speaking, with its associated arousal of stage fright.

The first step in cognitive restructuring is called (logically enough) the "introduction." Here, the basic principles involved in the cognitive restructuring are brought out. The trainer (or therapist) explains that apprehension toward public speaking is *learned* and that anything which has been learned can be unlearned and replaced with new ideas and behavior. Apprehension can be reduced significantly when the individual becomes aware of the irrational beliefs or negative thoughts that he or she holds about public speaking. Alternative, and more rational, beliefs providing a foundation for coping with the problem are then substituted.

The second step requires that subjects identify *negative self-statements* that inhibit their speaking performances. These are derogatory convictions that anxious people often say (to themselves) about the situation or their activities in that situation when they have to confront it. The worried person is asked to consider three separate occasions for (silently) saying those negative statements—*before* the public speaking event, *during* the speech, and *after* the presentation. For example, a person just starting treatment might normally transmit to self the following kinds of negative statements before they begin their speech: "My topic is so boring. Why did I pick this one?" "I know I'll forget my second major point." "No one will like me or my speech." Later, while standing at the podium and speaking to the audience, they are likely to say to themselves, "No one likes what I am saying," "My hands are all sweaty," or "They don't think I'm funny." Finally, after the speech is over they conclude, "I blew it," "I can't do it again," or "I was as bad as I thought I was going to be!"

Each of these statements is then analyzed for errors in logic. Problems with overgeneralization ("*No one* likes what I am saying"), basing inference on limited data ("I *know* I'll forget my second major point"), and other logical errors are discussed. The idea is that the individual begins to see that she or he has been rehearsing an entire monologue of irrational, negative self-statements. These

are shown to have formed the basis for a kind of self-fulfilling prophecy—believing that they are failing, they wind up doing so. It is no wonder their attempts at public speaking have been so frightening and frustrating up to this point.

In the third step, the individual learns a new set of *coping statements* to communicate to self. The trainer helps them to generate these alternative statements and substitute them for the previous list of negative ones. Once again, the coping statements are generated for use at three stages—before, during, and after the communication event. The trainer encourages the person to replace their entire repertoire of negative expectancies and evaluations with positive self-directed statements. So, instead of saying to themselves, "My topic is boring," they substitute "My topic is really interesting." When a few audience members aren't paying attention to our presentation, they attend to those who are: "Almost the entire audience is hanging on my every word." And, rather than emphasizing the negative aspects of their performances, they learn to evaluate the positives. "I'm getting better every time I try this;" or, "I forgot my second major point, but I'm convinced that no one even noticed."

Finally, step four of cognitive restructuring requires that the individual *practice* the new coping statements. The trainer points out that when they think about the number of years they have been rehearsing negative self-statements, they realistically should not expect to replace them immediately with positive ones. Old habits are hard to break. A whole new tool-kit of coping statements has to be developed, lodged in memory, and be available for immediate recall when the occasion demands. Eventually, these begin to serve "automatically" to come to the aid of the individual and reduce communication anxieties. As we pointed out in Chapter 1, this kind of "automatic" behavior is common in such physical tasks as driving, typing, reading, and playing tennis, where we have learned not to monitor every move we make. Our responses to communication situations can also be reduced to this level by appropriate cognitive restructuring.

Like systematic desensitization, cognitive restructuring has a record of success in dealing with communication apprehension. Over and over again, we find that people's apprehensions toward communicating are reduced significantly with this technique. The emphasis of the treatment program, however, should be on the coping statements themselves and the practice of those statements, rather than understanding the principles. Mere insight into the negative self-statements is insufficient. At times, such insight can serve to increase our anxieties simply because we give excessive attention to the problem, as opposed to the solution.

Skills Training

The third and final method of reducing communication apprehension that we will consider differs sharply from the other treatment techniques. The major difference is in the assumptions underlying the procedure. Rather than assuming our apprehensions lead to problems in communicating successfully with others, **skills training** reverses the causal sequence. It assumes that people's skills limitations in communicating influence their apprehension levels. That is, those who favor this approach argue that a primary cause of fears of communicating is a *deficit in skills.* Gerald Phillips, the leading spokesperson for this mode of treatment, reasons that some people develop apprehensions partly because they find themselves inept in communication situations.[31] In other words, they have good and sufficient reasons for feeling anxious. They just do not know how to communicate effectively. Once they learn how to perform successfully, their apprehensions will be reduced. Thus, training programs based on these assumptions are designed to teach appropriate and effective communication skills.

Courses on skills   Training people in specific skills has long been the strategy of choice in the field of speech communication as an academic subject. Lower-division courses in persuasion, public speaking, interpersonal communication, interviewing, small groups, and oral interpretation are offered regularly. Occasionally, upper-division courses in these and other communication skills (e.g., conflict resolution, or management and leadership) are available as well. Off campus, in the business and professional world, organizational communication consultants and trainers provide instruction in skills to management and employees. Many kinds of community groups and voluntary organizations encourage their members to enroll in communication skills training programs.

In implementing skills training strategies in academic, business, and community organizations, the usual approach is to expose people to lectures, readings, and discussions of important communication concepts and principles. This exposure is usually followed by some form of behavioral rehearsal or performance of the ideas studied. Thus, those undergoing the training are first led to understand the specific communication behavior under study, and second, to engage in a public demonstration of that behavior. Whether the behavior consists of eliciting and responding to someone's self-disclosure, seeking and obtaining affinity, managing group and dyadic conflict, persuading others to adopt your ideas, or giving a speech in front of an audience, practice is seen as the key to success.

Limitations of the skills approach   Early in this chapter we maintained that ''practice'' does *not* make ''perfect.'' Yet the skills training method that is so popular holds that it does. There is little doubt that training in skills can result in learning more effective techniques and strategies for communicating in various settings. However, the degree to which it specifically reduces *apprehension* is another matter. The fact is, there is less agreement on this issue, and research evidence on the effects of skills training on apprehension remains equivocal. There are many clear instances where with specific training, amateur speakers have learned the requisite communication skills they needed to become effective public speakers. And, when they became more effective public speakers, they felt much less anxious about performing.[32] However, there is also evidence suggesting a different pattern. There are people who have learned exactly *how* to perform the necessary communication skill, but their apprehension continues to interfere with their ability to give a talk. In other words, skills training reduces apprehension in some situations but not in others. In fact, for those with chronically high communication apprehension, skills training can make them more anxious! Compared to SD and cognitive restructuring, skills training alone is probably the least effective approach to reducing apprehension. An evaluation of all these methods reveals that a combination of *all three* is more effective than any single treatment alone.[33]

Chapter Review

■ Some individuals suffer from a chronic personality trait of communication apprehension. In contrast, others tend to be low in that personality characteristic. Those high in apprehension tend to be shy and withdrawn; they are likely to select occupations that demand little or no interface with others; and they prefer a quiet evening at home with family and friends. In contrast, people who are low in apprehension are likely to be open and talkative, choose careers that require active interaction with the public, and look forward to an evening of parties and large get-togethers.

- The chronically apprehensive share socialization and learning histories that differ from those who do not have that problem. For many people apprehension is temporary or transitory. The factors in a context that temporarily affect our ability to communicate include unfamiliarity, dissimilarity, novelty, formality, subordinate status, conspicuousness, excessive attention from others, evaluation, and previous failure.

- Social learning theory and reinforcement theory offer alternative explanations of communication apprehension. The former suggests that individuals who are truly apprehensive acquired their anxieties by adopting the fears and behaviors of models that were significant to them in their early social development. Reinforcement theory explains apprehension by suggesting that those high in the trait may have tried out a variety of responses in social encounters and failed to be rewarded or reinforced for their efforts.

- People respond differently to individuals who are characteristically high and low in communication apprehension. Apprehensive people are often regarded as aloof, disinterested, and uncaring. These negative impressions influence their experiences in academic,

social, and work situations. In contrast, persons low in communication anxiety are seen as friendly, industrious, and warm, which gives them advantages in the classroom, at work, and in social life.

- One of the most common and frustrating forms of communication apprehension is stage fright. Moderate apprehension is not all negative because it helps people to channel their stage fright productively. Persons chronically high in apprehension are truly terrified of public speaking situations, and they often need help in overcoming this problem.

- A number of treatment programs are available to ameliorate communication apprehension. Those programs with the highest known success rate include systematic desensitization (SD), cognitive restructuring, and skills training. The SD method reduces communication apprehension through muscle relaxation techniques. Cognitive restructuring requires changing or modifying beliefs about the particular communication event and the substitution of positive self-statements for negative ones. Skills training assumes that apprehensions stem from poor communication proficiency.

Key Terms

Agent (of socialization)   Persons such as teachers, friends, or parents, or even mass media that deliberately or unwittingly present to us learning experiences or "lessons" that play a part in the development of our personality.

Anomie (personal)   A feeling of anxiety or distress arising from confusion concerning the social expectations of others.

Cognitive restructuring   A form of treatment for fears (which can be used to reduce communication apprehension). The process centers on a subject's personal interpretations of an anxiety-producing situation and seeks to change them through training.

Communication apprehension   A fear or anxiety experienced by a person when anticipating or during communication encounters.

Learned helplessness   A feeling of inadequacy and stress arising from an inability to communicate in a predictable way with a person who is completely inconsistent in their responses to messages.

Reinforcement learning theory   An explanation of how individuals acquire particular patterns of response to particular stimuli. Essentially, it states that individuals "try out" a number of behaviors (sometimes selected randomly) as responses to stimuli. If the consequence is positive or rewarding, the behavior becomes part of their repertoire, to be re-

peated time and again in similar circumstances. Should the consequence be punishing, however, the behavior is likely to be dropped and replaced with some alternative response.

Resiliency factor   The propensity of human beings to be flexible in their learning histories, and not be rigidly shaped by a few negative consequences of our actions.

Skills training   A form of treatment for communication apprehension based on the assumption that limitations in a person's skills in communicating influence their apprehension levels. To reduce the apprehension, the person receives training in skills through systematic courses.

Social learning theory   Sometimes called "observational learning theory," this extension of earlier, more general reinforcement theories was originally developed to try to explain how individuals learn, not by performing actions themselves but by observing the behavior and reactions of people who are important as "models" in their lives.

Stage fright   A special category of the more general condition of communication apprehension that specifically focuses on anxiety about a public performance or speech before a group or audience.

Systematic desensitization (SD)   A form of treatment that has been used to reduce many kinds of fears, including communication apprehension. Essentially it seeks to reduce apprehensions through muscle relaxation techniques.

Trait (personality) Broadly, any psychological characteristic in which one individual differs from another in a relatively permanent and consistent way. Many traits have common labels, such as "stingy," "happy-go-lucky," or "introverted." In the present context, communication apprehension can be a stable personality trait.

Notes

1. A number of studies indicate that skills training alone fails to reduce fears about communicating. If these fears aren't addressed and alleviated, performance may continue to suffer. For a review of relevant research, see: Allen, M., Hunter, J. E., & Donahue, W. A., (1989). Meta-analysis of self-report data on the effectiveness of public speaking anxiety treatment techniques. *Communication Education, 38,* 54–76.

2. For a review of these studies and more, see: Daly, J. A., & McCroskey, J. C. (Eds.) (1984). *Avoiding communication: Shyness, reticence and communication apprehension* (Beverly Hills, CA: Sage.

3. Ibid., pp. 13–38.

4. McCroskey, J. C. (1977). Oral communication apprehension: A summary of recent theory and research. *Human Communication Research, 4,* 78–96; McCroskey, J. C. (1982). Oral communication apprehension: A reconceptualization. In M. Burgoon (Ed.), *Communication yearbook 6* (pp. 136–170). Beverly Hills, CA: Sage.

5. McCroskey, 1982, pp. 142–143; McCroskey, J. C., Richmond, V.P., & Stewart, R. A. (1986). *One on one: The foundations of interpersonal communication* (pp. 41–42). Englewood Cliffs, NJ: Prentice-Hall.

6. Duck, S. (1986). *Human relations: An introduction to social psychology* (p. 19). Beverly Hills, CA: Sage; McCroskey, Richmond, & Stewart, 1986, pp. 41, 48.

7. McCroskey makes a distinction between communication competence (knowing and understanding the appropriate behaviors to engage in) and communication performance or skill (being able to adequately perform those behaviors). He argues that even competent communicators can be apprehensive about interacting with others. For a more intensive explanation of this distinction, see: McCroskey, J. C. (1984). The communication apprehension perspective. In J. A. Daly & J. C. McCroskey (Eds.). *Avoiding communication: Shyness, reticence, and communication apprehension* (pp. 13–38). Beverly Hills, CA: Sage.

8. McCroskey, 1984, pp. 14–22; McCroskey, Richmond, & Stewart, 1986, pp. 49–58.

9. Hilgard, E. R., Atkinson, R. C., & Atkinson, R. L., (1975). *Introduction to psychology* (6th ed.) (p. 368). New York: Harcourt, Brace, Jovanovich.

10. The seminal work on the nature and origins of personality traits is: Allport, G. W. (1937). *Personality: A psychological interpretation.* New York: Henry Holt. See especially Chapter 11, "A Theory of Traits," and Chapter 12, "The Nature of Traits," pp. 286–342.

11. McCroskey, 1982, p. 164; McCroskey, Richmond, & Stewart, 1986, pp. 58–63.

12. Between 1970 and 1980 alone, over 200 reported studies examined the causes and effects of communication apprehension and related constructs. For extensive reviews of these and more recent research, see: McCroskey, 1982, pp. 136–170; Richmond, V. P. Implications of quietness: Some facts and speculations. In Daly and

McCroskey, 1984, pp. 145–156. In addition, a complete bibliographic listing of relevant studies is available from: Payne, S. K. & Richmond, V. P. A bibliography of related research and theory. In Daly and McCroskey, 1984, pp. 247–294.

13. McCroskey, Richmond, & Stewart, 1986, pp. 49–50.

14. For a discussion of alternative interpretations of the causes of communication apprehension, see: Beatty, M. J., & Friedland, M. H. (1990). Public speaking state anxiety as a function of selected situational and dispositional variables. *Communication Education, 38,* pp. 142–147; and Beatty, M. J., Balfantz, G. L., & Kuwabara, A. Y. (1989). Trait-like qualities of selected variables assumed to be transient causes of performance state anxiety. *Communication Education, 38,* pp. 277–289.

15. Buss, A. H. (1980). *Self-consciousness and social anxiety.* San Francisco: W. H. Freeman; McCroskey, Richmond, & Stewart, 1986, pp. 56–58.

16. For a brief but comprehensive review of the origins and nature of learning theories and their relationship to both socialization and communication, see: DeFleur, M. L., & Ball-Rokeach, S. (1989). *Theories of mass communication* (5th ed.) (pp. 174–181, 212–219). White Plains, NY: Longman.

17. Bandura, A. (1977). *Social learning theory.* Englewood Cliffs, NJ: Prentice-Hall.

18. Beatty, M. J., Plax, T. G., & Kearney, P. (1985). Reinforcement vs. modeling theory in the development of communication apprehension: A retrospective analysis. *Communication Research Reports,* 80–85.

19. For a general explanation of the principles of operant conditioning or reinforcement theory, see: Skinner, B. F. (1957). *Verbal behavior.* New York: Appleton-Century-Crofts. For a discussion linking reinforcement theory to the development of communication apprehension more specifically, see: McCroskey, 1984, pp. 22–30; McCroskey, 1982, pp. 153–155.

20. Beatty, Plax, & Kearney, 1985, pp. 80–85; Daly, J. A. & Friedrich, G. (1981). The development of communication apprehension: A retrospective analysis of contributory correlations. *Communication Quarterly, 29,* 243–255.

21. One of the problems of such operant explanations is that they give little credit to the rational abilities of human beings to engage in analysis, planning, insight, and other thought processes. As we have explained in earlier chapters, human beings are able to use language as a basis for such rational and analytic mental activity. Psychologists, seeking universal laws of learning that apply to all organisms have generally been reluctant to bring uniquely human mental processes into their learning theories.

22. The term *anomie* was first introduced into the analysis of social life by Emile Durkheim at the end of the 19th century. See: Durkheim, E. (1951). *Suicide: A study of sociology* (J. A. Spaulding, Trans.,

and G. Simpson, Ed.). New York: Free Press. (First published, in French, 1897)

23. Early research on learned helplessness examined dogs' responses after inconsistent or random rewards and punishments were applied to their behaviors. After trying out a variety of behaviors, the dogs eventually gave up behaving altogether and, instead, retreated to a corner. See: Seligman, M. E. (1975). *Helplessness: On depression, development and death.* San Francisco: W. H. Freeman. For a more intensive application of learned helplessness to communicate apprehension development, see: McCroskey, 1984, pp. 26–30.

24. Daly, J. A., & Stafford, L. (1984). Correlates and consequences of social communicative anxiety. In Daly & McCroskey, 1984, pp. 125–144; Payne & Richmond, 1984, pp. 247–294; Richmond, 1984, pp. 145–156.

25. McCroskey, Richmond, & Stewart, 1986, pp. 63–66.

26. Payne & Richmond, op. cit., pp. 247–294.

27. For a review of the research that examines the impact of communication apprehension on job satisfaction and other work-related variables, see: Richmond, V. P. Implications of quietness: Some facts and speculations. In Daly & McCroskey, 1984, pp. 153–155.

28. Friedrich, G., & Goss, B. Systematic desensitization. In Daly & McCroskey, 1984, pp. 173–187; McCroskey, J. C. (1970). The effect of systematic desensitization on speech anxiety. *Speech Teacher, 19,* 32–36.

29. McCroskey, J. C. (1972). The implementation of a large-scale program of systematic desensitization for communication apprehension. *Speech Teacher, 21,* 255–264.

30. Fremouw, W. J. (1984). Cognitive-behavioral therapies for modification of communication apprehension. In Daly & McCroskey, 1984, p. 210. For a more detailed description of the steps involved in cognitive restructuring, see: Fremouw, W. J., & Scott, M. D. (1979). Cognitive restructuring: An alternative method for the treatment of communication apprehension. *Communication Education, 28,* 129–133.

31. Phillips, G. M. (1977). Rhetoritherapy versus the medical model: Dealing with reticence. *Communication Education, 26,* 34–43; see also the review by: Kelly, L., (1984). Social skills training as a mode of treatment for social communication problems. In Daly & McCroskey, 1984, pp. 189–207.

32. Kelly, 1984, pp. 201–205.

33. A recent analysis comparing the effectiveness of all three methods to treat public speaking anxiety reveals the relative superiority of both SAD and cognitive restructuring over the more popular (and also effective) skills training. For further information see: Allen, M., Hunter, J. E., & Donahue, W. A. (1989). Meta-analysis of self-report data on the effectiveness of public speaking anxiety treatment techniques. *Communication Education, 38,* 54–76.

Additional Readings

McCroskey, J. C. (1982). Oral communication apprehension: A reconceptualization. In M. Burgoon (Ed.), *Communication handbook six* (pp. 136–170). Beverly Hills, CA: Sage.

> Although now somewhat dated, this essay has been considered a state-of-the-art report on communication apprehension, presenting a clearly referenced review of this area. It offers suggestions for researchers interested in further investigating this topic. In addition, it presents a thorough discussion of the effects of apprehension on communication behavior.

McCroskey, J. C., & Beatty, M. J. (1984). Communication apprehension and accumulated communication state anxiety experiences: A research note. *Communication Monographs, 51,* 79–84.

> This research report is a good example of the hundreds of studies on communication apprehension that have been published in the technical communication literature. The findings of the study support the idea of a relationship between communication apprehension and situationally aroused anxiety. The results add to the accumulating evidence supporting the cross-situational nature of this construct.

McCroskey, J. C., & Richmond, V. P. (1987). Willingness to communicate. In J. C. McCroskey & J. A. Daly (Eds.), *Personality and interpersonal communication* (pp. 129–156). Newbury Park, CA: Sage.

> This essay addresses variations in people's willingness to communicate within a variety of interpersonal contexts. The issues are discussed in large part as products of communication apprehension. The authors provide an in-depth and upper-level explanation of the communication apprehension construct along with related issues.

Richmond, V. P., & McCroskey, J. C. (1985). *Communication: Apprehension, avoidance, and effectiveness.* Scottsdale, AZ: Gorsuch Scarisbrick.

> This short text provides excellent explanations of shyness, communication apprehension, and avoidance. Each of these pervasive communication problems is discussed in terms of communication effectiveness generally. Alternative approaches to helping people with these maladies are considered. The book is written with the practitioner in mind.

Zimbardo, P. G. (1977). *Shyness.* New York: Harcourt Brace Jovanovich.

> This book describes a body of research findings and theory dealing with shyness. A case is presented for conceiving of shyness as a serious social problem. It is clearly written so as to be easily understood. Although research findings are a central part of what is discussed, the author's objective is to explain what shyness is and what can be done about it.

Part Four

Communicating in Public Settings

Part 4 focuses specifically on planning, polishing, and delivering effective speeches before an audience. This is a critical skill that is required for success in our heterogeneous society. Only those who are content to remain in the most humble jobs are exempt from the requirement of presenting ideas to groups. Thus, public speaking is an essential part of human communication in virtually all walks of modern life. This final part of *Mastering Communication in Contemporary America* effectively uses all of the theoretical ideas and guidelines that have been derived in the previous chapters. It brings these forward into practical applications to the public speaking task.

Chapter 13 takes the reader through the steps needed to organize speeches designed for different purposes. Whether the speech is designed to inform, persuade, or entertain, it must be planned, researched, and outlined. Each of these steps is explained in detail with specific guidelines for preparing the content.

In Chapter 14, specific considerations are reviewed that will show the beginning speaker how to make an effective delivery before a group. The chapter offers concrete steps, rules, and strategies that will help in acquiring a comfortable and natural speaking style. It discusses the advantages and limitations of different modes of delivery, how to establish credibility, and how to deliver the speech in a well-organized manner.

The last chapter is unique to the present book. It focuses on how to polish and fine-tune a speech so as to make a good address into an excellent one. It offers strategies for the effective use of language, how to orchestrate and control responses from an audience, and how the beginning speaker can develop an effective personal style.

Chapter 13

Preparing the Content

Contents

Three Steps for Getting Started
Choose the Topic
Determine the Purpose
Analyze the Audience

**How to Research the Topic
to Find Supporting Materials**
Rely on Personal Knowledge and Experience
Make Use of What Others Know
Criteria for Selecting Evidence

Organizing a Speech to Inform
A Basic Format for Informing
    The introduction
    The body
    The conclusion
Outlining the Informative Speech
Six Rules for Increasing Effectiveness
    Rule 1: Keep it simple
    Rule 2: Keep it concrete
    Rule 3: Be repetitive and redundant
    Rule 4: Elicit active responses
    Rule 5: Use familiar and relevant examples
    Rule 6: Use transitions and signposts

Organizing a Speech to Persuade
A Basic Persuasion Format: Monroe's

Motivated Sequence
    Step 1: Gain the audience's attention
    Step 2: Identify unfulfilled needs
    Step 3: Imply satisfaction by offering a solution
    Step 4: Visualize what satisfaction will mean
    Step 5: Define specific actions
Outlining the Persuasive Speech
Seven Strategies for Persuading
    Strategy 1: Conceal the intent to persuade
    Strategy 2: Don't ask for too much
    Strategy 3: Avoid inflammatory words and phrases
    Strategy 4: Keep objections to a minimum
    Strategy 5: Use a "two-sided" message with
        refutation
    Strategy 6: Inoculate against counterarguments
    Strategy 7: Use fear appeals

Chapter Review

Key Terms

Notes

Additional Readings

Key Questions

■ The thing to be dreaded most in preparing a speech is selecting a topic. This is because there are so few topics to choose from, and almost any topic will be boring. There is simply no way to make most topics interesting to an audience . . . Right? Wrong! Wrong! Wrong!

■ To impress people when preparing material for an informative speech it is essential to base it on complex ideas, stress abstract issues, avoid repetition or redundancy, and use exotic or unfamiliar examples to hold attention . . . Right? Wrong! Wrong! Wrong!

■ It would be a mistake to develop a speech around some topic, issue, or experience with which you are already completely familiar. It would be much better to select, research, and present a talk on a topic that you know nothing about at the outset . . . Right? Wrong! Wrong! Wrong!

■ In presenting a speech intended to persuade an audience, little attention need be paid to their personal wants and desires. It is better to sweep them off their feet with clever anecdotes and well-chosen adjectives to convince them . . . Right? Wrong! Wrong! Wrong!

[The] best and most telling speech is not the actual impromptu one, but the counterfeit of it; . . . that speech is most worth listening to which has been carefully prepared in private and tried on a plaster cast, or an empty chair, or any other appreciative object that will keep quiet until the speaker has got his matter and his delivery limbered up so that they will seem impromptu to an audience.

Mark Twain
"On Speech-Making Reform"

In today's society effective public speaking is a requirement for success in virtually any field. Anyone wanting to do more than hum-drum work has to learn to speak informatively, persuasively, and humorously to audiences. It is the good speakers who get hired, promoted, admired, honored, and respected. In short, when good public speakers take the floor, *everybody* listens!

Learning how to give a speech is like learning to ride a bicycle. Before we could ride a bicycle easily we had to gain motor skills with training wheels. As we continued to practice, riding became easier and more natural. After a lot of experience, we could say, "Look Ma. No hands!" as we performed the activity with grace and style. Similarly, before we can stand up and give an effective public presentation, we need to acquire the necessary skills. While part of that process is managing shyness and apprehension, as we discussed in the previous chapter, we must also pass through additional stages when using the "training wheels" of public speaking. With practice and effort, most people are able to reach the "no hands" stage where they can do it easily, naturally, and effectively.

However, confidence and skills are not enough. We have to have something to say! That may seem obvious, but it is a critical aspect of effective public speaking. In fact, there is really no point in worrying about *how* to deliver a talk until we know *what* we plan to say. Many people who make presentations already have a topic related to their work or area of expertise. Often, however, that is not the case. Students in speech courses are an obvious example. Here, we cannot overemphasize the need to select topics that can be developed into a good presentation. In this chapter we set forth in systematic ways the steps required to identify and put together the content of an effective speech.

Three Steps for Getting Started

Preparing a speech is never easy. Few speakers can "wing it" in front of a group—unless they perform on a topic they have used time and time again. Even then, many professional speakers perform successfully with one audience but fail when they employ the same speech with another.

Getting started on the preparation of a speech is especially problematic for inexperienced speakers who often have no idea how to begin. However, certain questions come up immediately and provide a logical point of departure. For example, when one needs to prepare and deliver a speech, it is natural to ask the following three basic questions:

1. What topic should I choose?

2. What do I want the audience to believe or understand about that topic as a result of what I tell them?

3. What characteristics do these people have?

An effective way to begin is simply to try to answer each of these questions. In other words, we begin by selecting a *topic,* determining the *purpose,* and analyzing the characteristics of the *audience.*

Choose the Topic

In courses on public speaking, most students would rather have the instructor assign them a topic than go through the pains of finding one themselves. They agonize in their search for just the right subject, often spending more time selecting it than actually putting together the speech. Selection is never easy. Even when

In today's society, anyone who wants to be successful must acquire the ability to speak effectively before groups. In virtually any complex field or profession, it is usually those who can inform or persuade others with well-organized presentations who rise to the top. Regardless of one's technical competence in performing an occupational role, being an effective speaker will provide an important edge in the competition.

veteran public speakers are invited to talk, they are usually given only general (and often vague) guidelines, like "Oh, just speak on any aspect (of some topic) that you feel comfortable with." As a result, they have to narrow the subject matter considerably. For instance, Lee Iacocca, president of Chrysler Corporation, may be asked to speak on "foreign trade." Obviously, the issue is an extensive one, and Iacocca and his speech writers have to decide among many alternative aspects of such trade.

When topics aren't restricted to some general content area, we tend to find selection even *more* difficult. Why is that the case? After all, there must be a million things we can talk about. With complete freedom to pick and choose, we could talk about any of the following: the economy, religion, politics, dating and marriage, children, the American flag, profanity, gun control, the death penalty, evolution, Greenpeace, acid rain, computer software, the last novel we read, our favorite (or worst) movies, jazz and rock 'n' roll, health foods, holidays, vacation spots, foreign investments and trade, defense spending, clothing fads, designer earrings, or physical fitness. Clearly, we have an infinite number of topics available to us. Still, people complain, "I can't find a topic!"

The principal reason people have trouble selecting a topic is that they assume each topic that comes to mind has the unbearable potential of being *boring*. After all, how wildly exciting can the issue of health foods be? Or consider the entertainment value of a talk on aerobic exercises. And aren't we tired of hearing speeches on gun control, capital punishment, and illegal immigration? No, these won't do. It looks like a tough assignment. We need a topic that is *fresh,* but *interesting, compelling,* and *absorbing.* In fact, it looks like an impossible assignment!

Wait! Before we discard any of these topics or reject others on the basis of some arbitrary and self-imposed "dullness quotient," we need to recognize a little-known fact: *Topics aren't boring; people are!* Some individuals can make even the most mundane subject entertaining. An illustration of making a ho-hum topic seem interesting is what NBC's "Today Show" star, Willard Scott, does with the weather report. There's a man who makes talking about the weather amusing with his corny, inane comments and delivery. In fact, he has become something of a hero to many people by showing birthday pictures of senior citizens who are 100 years old. Neither the rainfall in Iowa nor seeing pictures of centenarians is likely to rate very high on most people's entertainment

One of the most important principles of public speaking is that topics are never boring but speakers often are. A well-organized presentation can make even the most mundane subject seem interesting and exciting. However, a truly stimulating topic can be made tedious and boring by a dull speaker. The key is to understand the topic well and to develop a style of delivery that will hold the audience's attention and keep them wanting to hear more.

meter. Yet, Willard Scott transforms these potentially boring issues into interesting and humorous presentations.

By the same token, we know of other speakers who can ruin almost any topic, no matter how potentially interesting. Everyone who ever went to college can recall professors who could make a lecture on sex practices among the rich and famous appear tedious. It is not difficult to find speakers who, regardless of the topic, are boring, monotonous, and clearly unimaginative. The important lesson here is that it is the *speaker* who makes his or her presentation fascinating, powerful, and gripping—it is not the topic itself.

A second important lesson in topic selection is to focus first on something about which you *already know,* which is what experienced speakers always do. Rather than select a theme you know nothing about, you will be better off choosing a subject with which you have had some experience. The benefits are obvious: Your knowledge will expedite the research process. Moreover, familiar topics are likely to be interesting to *you.* Topics that interest the speaker will also be likely to turn on the audience.

Once you've discovered a general subject area to use in your speech, you'll need to apply our final lesson: *Nar-*

row down the topic. All of those we listed earlier are much too broad. For example, take the issue of "marriage." It is hopelessly broad. How can such a broad topic be narrowed? There are dozens of ways. We could talk about predictors of marital satisfaction (or dissatisfaction), intimate communication between marital partners, resolving or managing conflict, planning a wedding, having children, dealing with in-laws, dual-career couples, and so on. Even these topics can be restricted further. To illustrate, let's examine potential topics under the subheading "dual-career couples": We can easily list: maintaining separate professional identities, retaining one's own last name, "commuter" marriages, and conflicting gender-role requirements. Narrowing the topic prevents us from wandering aimlessly and helps us to focus on specific information that we want to share with others.

Determine the Purpose

The next step in getting started is to consider what effect we want from our audience. Do we want to *entertain* them? Or is our purpose to *inform* them of the issues? Or perhaps we hope to *persuade* them to change their mind about something. Whatever the goal, we need to be clear from the beginning as to exactly what we want to accomplish, because the way we define our intentions and set our goals will result in very different decisions about the evidence we select to support our ideas. This in turn will define the way we organize the presentation itself. Furthermore, our presentational style will differ dramatically when our purpose changes from entertainment to information to persuasion.

Entertaining an audience is one of the more difficult goals in speaking. Fortunately, most speaking situations rarely require us to give speeches of this type. Nevertheless, many effective informative and persuasive speeches do demand that we amuse or at least create positive feelings to some degree. But when the overriding purpose is to amuse the audience, to make them laugh, we have our work cut out for us. We can amuse people by using humor and telling jokes, but fortunately we can also entertain them by describing an exciting adventure, place, or story. Whatever our approach, we need to make sure that someone other than our close friends finds our talk entertaining, too. Furthermore, we must make sure that our humor is in good taste, unoffensive, and appropriate for the occasion and the audience.

In speaking to inform, the goal is to change the audience's factual beliefs in some way. Perhaps we hope to extend what they already know about a topic; we may want them to think about the issues in a new way; or we might like them to learn something about an entirely new subject. In order to bring about any of these changes, we need to provide our audience with accurate details and clear facts about our subject. Moreover, we must be *credible;* the audience must be willing to "buy into" what we have to offer. Consequently, our task is twofold: First, we need to make sure our points are understood, and second, we must inspire our audience to have confidence in what we have to say.

The goal in a persuasive speech is not simple. After all, we know that people generally resist attempts to influence their beliefs or to persuade them to change their ideas. Nevertheless, many occasions require that we do exactly that. As we saw in Chapter 10, persuasion typically involves messages designed to change opinions, attitudes, beliefs, or even behavior. Speaking to persuade requires that we take a position on an issue and advocate a cause, policy, product, or idea. We may want to sell the latest-model stereo system, convince an audience to sup-

An important step in developing the topic of a speech is to decide the precise nature of the goal of the presentation. Is it to inform the audience, to entertain them, or to persuade them to change their thinking about something? Once this goal has been determined, planning for the overall organization of the speech, and deciding on the presentational style that will be most effective, are the next steps.

port farm relief programs, encourage them to maintain the 55 mph speed limit, or advocate that all American citizens read and speak English. Whatever the topic, our purpose is to get people to feel, think, or behave differently as a consequence of the speech.

As soon as we decide whether we want to entertain, inform, or persuade, we can narrow the purpose to a more specific goal. It can be helpful to write this down as a kind of "purpose statement." Purpose statements typically begin with the same introductory phrase: "To inform (or entertain or persuade) my audience about . . ." Then fill in the rest. Limit the purpose to one declarative phrase or sentence, keeping the statement simple and clear. For example, let's look again at the general topic of marriage. Recall that we could narrow the topic to dual-career couples and then further restrict the discussion to "commuter" marriages. Let's assume that the purpose of our speech is to persuade. To convert the general to the specific, we begin by stating that we want "to persuade the audience that commuter marriages are often necessary and feasible" or that "commuter marriages are hazardous to marital health." With such a specific purpose in mind, we can begin to develop the substance of our presentation. First, however, we will need to understand the nature and characteristics of the audience.

Analyze the Audience

The linear and simultaneous transactions models of human communication we developed in Chapter 1 make us realize that every receiver—every person in an audience in this case—listens to a speaker with her or his own personal framework for perception and interpretation. For present purposes, this means that each member of an audience will have a personal list of topics and ideas that seem more (or less) important, interesting, tasteful, amusing, and so forth.

People's motives for being in the audience are also an important factor. Even though your purpose may be to persuade or inform, the audience may or may not be interested in your goal. For example, they may have some special interest in the topic you are going to present and will wait eagerly to hear what you have to say. On the other hand, they may simply be there because their bosses required them to attend or because it is a class requirement. Therefore, we need to ask and answer three questions: "Who are these people?" "Why are they here?" "What will they be interested in?" If we can obtain answers, we can begin to tailor our speech to meet their specific needs and at the same time accomplish our own purpose.

The next question we need to ask is "What does the audience *already know* about my topic?" It is an important question because we could end up talking "down" to them or "over their head." Patronizing the audience by telling them what they already know perfectly well is an obvious mistake. Equally bad is attempting to sound bookish by spouting big words or too much jargon that is unfamiliar to them.

How an audience feels about an issue is also important. If they already agree with the position we will take, then we design a message that reinforces or strengthens that position. If we realize that the audience is likely to disagree with what we are going to say, we need to design ways of making our points that make our presentation appear to be closer to their point of view. The exception to such strategies is the case in which a speaker *must* present a particular topic with a particular point of view—as in debates where one group is required to take a positive stance and the other a negative position. It can be a tough assignment!

The next question is "*How do we discover* information about the audience to whom we will speak?" Few speakers have the resources available to politicians and advertisers to learn details about their audience from professional pollsters and market research groups. For example, as Yogi Berra, the well-known baseball player, put it, "You can observe a lot just by watching." Seriously, audience characteristics can be assessed just by observing them and making realistic assumptions. Moreover, an obvious advantage can be gained if the history of this audience is understood. What kind of speakers and speeches have they liked in the past? This can provide at least some guidelines.

One practical basis for making assumptions about an audience is to ascertain their *demographic* makeup. That is, into what kinds of social categories can they be classified? Analysis by social categories can reveal "typical" beliefs and orientations they are likely to share (Chapter 9, p. 266). For example, will both males and females be in the audience? Approximately how old are they (e.g., young adults versus senior citizens)? Does the audience represent primarily lower, moderate, or higher family income levels? Are they well or only modestly educated? Obviously, an audience composed of well-educated young adults from affluent families is going to share different frameworks for interpretation than one made up of older people with restricted economic means and limited educational attainment.

Audience Analysis Survey

The following items can be used to gather information about your audience in a systematic way. This survey can be administered to a "pilot" sample of audience members—or a small group of individuals who resemble your actual audience. While that approach may not be feasible for every occasion, you could also ask and answer the questions about your projected audience yourself. When you do make such guesses, however, try to be as informed as possible. Interview representative others for validation or clarification of your conclusions. Whichever data-gathering scheme you choose, the whole point of using a survey of this type is to determine the demographic makeup of your audience and to determine their attitudes, feelings, and beliefs about issues that may be extremely important to your topic selection and purpose. Remember: Preparing and planning a speech must be strategic.

So, with a particular audience in mind, have sample members complete the following items:

Demographic Information

____ 1. I am a:
   A. Female
   B. Male

____ 2. My approximate age is:
   A. 18–21
   B. 22–29
   C. 30–39
   D. Over 40

____ 3. My religious preference or background is:
   A. Catholic
   B. Protestant
   C. Jewish
   D. Other _____
   E. Not identified with any religious group

____ 4. My primary ethnic background is:
   A. Anglo
   B. Hispanic
   C. American Indian
   D. Asian
   E. Other _____

____ 5. My educational background is: (highest degree earned)
   A. Doctorate
   B. Master's
   C. Bachelor's
   D. Associate degree
   E. High school diploma
   F. Other _____

____ 6. My annual salary (or, if still a dependent, my parents'):
   A. Below $10,000
   B. Between $10,000 and $20,000
   C. Between $20,000 and $50,000
   D. Between $50,000 and $100,000
   E. Over $100,000

____ 7. My marital status is:
   A. Married
   B. Single
   C. Divorced

____ 8. I have:
   A. No children
   B. 1 child
   C. 2 or 3 children
   D. 4 or more children

____ 9. I live:
   A. In my parents' home
   B. In my own apartment or house
   C. In a dormitory
   D. In a fraternity or sorority
   E. Other _____

Psychographic Information (Attitudes, values, and beliefs)

____ 10. To what extent are you liberal or

conservative in your political orientation? (circle the number that most closely reflects your attitude)

Liberal   5   4   3   2   1   Conservative

_____ **11.** How involved or committed are you on this issue (insert topic of your presentation—e.g., the environment, financial security)?

Highly involved   5   4   3   2   1   Low involved

_____ **12.** How informed do you consider yourself to be on this issue (again, insert topic of your presentation)?

Highly informed   5   4   3   2   1   Low informed

_____ **13.** How interested are you in this issue (insert topic)?

Very interested   5   4   3   2   1   Not at all interested

[Finally, what other characteristics of your audience do you think are relevant to your presentation? Add additional items as needed.]

Calculating an Overall Audience Score

For each item, calculate the "average" audience score by summing across audience members' responses for that item and then divide by the number in your sample. You may also want to calculate percentages for some of the items, where relevant. For instance, the percentage or ratio of males to females in your audience may give you more information than would a simple mean. Obtaining mean scores or percentages for each item will give you an idea of where your audience "sits" in terms of their socio-economic status, religious preferences, degree of involvement in your topic, and so on.

Interpreting Your Audience's Scores

Answers to these and similar questions can give you valuable information that you can use in designing your own message. Let's consider responses to the demographic item #2. Suppose the average age of your audience is over 40 years old; you would want to make sure that the examples you select and the issues you address in your speech are relevant and familiar to them. In a speech on music, referencing the rock group INXS may not be particularly appropriate for this age group; but examining the contributions of the DOORS may be germane.

Similarly, responses to the psychographic or attitudinal item #8 may be extremely important to your selection of specific persuasive appeals. That is, we know from the research on persuasion that highly involved or committed audience members are extremely difficult to persuade. Consequently, you should be careful not to ask for too much change too quickly—this advice is particularly crucial for this kind of audience. As we discuss in this chapter, we want to avoid the boomerang effect and, instead, move our audience gradually toward our desired goal.

Given the specific topic or issue you select for your presentation, you may want to ask additional questions regarding your audience's demographic or psychographic characteristics. For example, you may wish to consider their college major; what area of the country they grew up in; their source(s) of financial support; grade-point average in school; career aspirations; degree of religious or political convictions; attitudes toward gun control, AIDS research, the Palestinians, the wealthy, the homeless, and so on. With answers to these or other pertinent questions, you can begin to tailor your speech to meet their specific needs and, at the same time, accomplish your own objectives.

Understanding the nature of one's audience is important in determining the goals and style of presentation that will be most effective. Will they already know what is to be presented? Will they respond favorably or negatively to certain kinds of humor? Will they understand references to contemporary popular culture or to historical events? A meaningful way to answer such questions is by understanding what social categories they represent in terms of their age, income, educational levels, and other socioeconomic characteristics.

It would be even better if more elaborate procedures for audience analysis could be used. With a great deal of time and planning, we could construct questionnaires to determine in greater detail the audience's motivations and feelings. Ideally, we could interview a representative sample of members of the audience beforehand. In any case, obtaining information about the audience's background, beliefs, and attitudes will increase understanding of their expectations about the speech and the occasion.

How to Research the Topic to Find Supporting Materials

When we use evidence in a speech to help prove or support a position we are better equipped both to inform and to persuade.[1] Gathering evidence or supporting material to use in a speech is like researching a term paper. We can draw heavily on what other people know by examining books, magazines, and other references in the library. This is perhaps the most used and most obvious source. Another possibility is to talk to experts by conducting phone or face-to-face interviews with persons who have special knowledge about the topic. Even better is to make effective use of our own personal knowledge about the subject. Of course, whether we depend on the experts or ourselves for information, we must evaluate the credibility and appropriateness of that evidence very critically.

Rely on Personal Knowledge and Experience

Earlier, we noted the importance of selecting a topic that is familiar and interesting to you. One of the great advantages of this approach is that it can eliminate a lot of headaches later on. For one thing, audiences are more likely to enjoy a topic that the speaker obviously understands and enjoys as well. For another, preparing a speech on a topic that we already know a lot about saves a great deal of time at this stage of speech development.

Unfortunately, many students simply ignore themselves as potential resource material. Perhaps they believe that their own experiences will be perceived as trivial and trite, or they may feel that no one will see them as credible or expert in the topic. Whatever the reasons for overlooking themselves as references, speakers should rely wherever possible on their own experiences. Failure to do so may imply to audiences that the speaker doesn't understand the realities of the topic being presented.

This failure to rely on one's self as a resource is well illustrated in an actual case of a speech presented by "Holly," a student speaker. Holly decided to develop a speech aimed at persuading her audience to become more involved in helping in the struggle against continuing racial discrimination. Her point was that we all need to become more active in efforts to help people understand and manage the problem.

It was an excellent topic. With good organization and delivery, Holly told her audience that, with a few exceptions, today's college students are identified as the most apathetic in history. She had done her homework in the library. In order to support her claim that today's students are apathetic about discrimination, she gathered and cited relevant statistics. And the expert sources she had consulted also gave her information supporting her claim. It was an impressive assembly of facts. However, she failed to make use of the most interesting and most dramatic piece of evidence of all—she made no reference to herself.

Holly could have told them about her own apathy toward racial discrimination, how she saw firsthand the consequences of such discriminatory practices where she had worked during the summer. She could have shown how that experience changed her views and made her want to support the efforts of minority groups on campus. By alluding to her own prior apathetic experiences, followed by her personal commitment to becoming more involved, Holly would have been far more persuasive. Audiences are more likely to empathize with, and eventually agree with, a speaker who demonstrates some personal connection with the issues. Consequently, we shouldn't be afraid to rely on ourselves as important reference material.

Make Use of What Others Know

Not only can speakers use their own past experiences for developing speeches, they also can ask experts and professionals for their opinions, interpretations, and recommendations. These people can be especially helpful in locating excellent sources of facts and findings. Colleges and universities are full of experts, most of whom are glad to help people organize a topic—as long as no unreasonable demands are made (like phoning them at home at 7:00 A.M. or intruding on their lunch hour). The same is true of business leaders. Most do not mind a phone call—and may even prefer it to a more time-consuming personal interview. However, most are willing to arrange a *brief* personal interview and will enjoy talking about subjects they know well. The most difficult to reach on the phone or get to agree to an interview are professionals, such as physicians and lawyers, who charge clients for their services by the hour (sometimes hundreds of dollars).

But even if a source readily agrees, conducting an interview requires a lot of planning and direction. Besides setting up the meeting time and place, and communicating a specific purpose to the person, it is important to know the right questions to ask. Even if the questions are obvious enough, there are still techniques to consider as to how to frame them. Finally, we need to consider the issue of time. Good interviewing strategy requires that a list of clear questions be prepared ahead of time, that they be posed in a straightforward way, and that every consideration is given to the time demands and needs of the source. Most intelligent adults can conduct a good interview, even if it is their first, with a little sensible planning.

One of the problems with contacting experts is that they aren't always available and willing to help when we need them. But one source is always there on a regular schedule and needs no appointment. The most used, and perhaps the most useful, source of information for developing speeches is the *library.*

For many of us, libraries can be intimidating. Just walking through the big and impressive doors can create anxiety. There are mysteries behind those doors, and many of us have had only limited experiences in finding information we need in such a maze. But the fact is, once one gets over the initial impression of apprehension, most libraries turn out to be remarkably useful and convenient places. The people who work there are almost always "user-friendly." They do not jealously guard their books and reference sources from intrusions by novices. In fact, they earn their living by bringing together just such people and the information they need.

Not everyone in a library will be able to drop what they are doing on demand and rush to your aid. Some have jobs other than helping users directly, and they cannot abandon their duties at a moment's notice. However, there *are* specialists in every library—people with the title "reference librarian"—who are extraordinarily knowledgeable and helpful. If you do not see one, ask where such a person can be found. At the same time, it is easy to learn the basics of library use yourself so that you do not have to depend on others every time. For example, libraries usually have pamphlets or displays telling where different kinds of information can be found. Many regularly offer orientation lectures or even tours.

If we give libraries a chance, then, we can quickly learn how to use the card catalog (or their computerized counterparts), the reference sections, government document sections, indexes to periodicals (magazines and technical journals), biographies, and newspapers. In many contemporary libraries, we can learn how to make computerized searches, which can save hours of work. Libraries will even go to a lot of trouble to get sources that are not on their shelves but that can be borrowed from others on "interlibrary loan." Impressive nationwide systems exist for this purpose. In fact, the library systems of American colleges and universities are incredible by comparison with what exists in other parts of the world. They never cease to amaze people coming from less developed countries.

But just what should one look for? When assembling information in the library it is best to start with the most general aspects of a topic. Until the major outlines of a topic are clear, it is hard to understand how more specific information fits in. For example, unless the world system for obtaining petroleum is broadly understood, it would be difficult to understand and speak to the important reasons *why* we need to continue (or discontinue) offshore drilling or the delivery of oil by tankers. Or, unless the role of animals in the development and testing of new medicines is understood, including what alternatives are or are not available, it could be difficult to develop a persuasive speech that would convince people that animal experimentation should be stopped. We may have our own personal reasons for speaking on these or other issues, but we still need to consider points and facts that the *audience* will think about and accept, or possibly use to reject what the speaker is saying. Consequently, we need to begin by reading as many general discussions of the subject as we can locate.

In addition, we should be looking for *facts* to use as evidence to back up our claims. When these are "statistical" data, they can sometimes effectively be presented with a projector, or in the form of charts, diagrams or tables as "handouts." However, it is important to find verbal examples or simple illustrations that will dramatize the main points. Such examples or explanations

should be presented before any statistics. In this way, audiences will be more readily predisposed to accept your evidence as true and typical.[2]

Sometimes we will need definitions that we can cite, eyewitness accounts, or "quotable" phrases that add punch to our pitch. When we find these potential sources of evidence, we need to record them for future use. Typically, we cite the complete reference on separate note cards, specifying the author's full name, the exact title of the article, document, or book, its date of publication, the publisher, and the page numbers. Moreover, we need to copy the quotation, facts, or figures *exactly* as written. (Obviously, copy machines come in handy for this.) We can paraphrase the wording later when we organize the speech itself, or we may decide to quote the reference exactly.

Criteria for Selecting Evidence

Not all references are usable. Also, among those that can be used, there are a number of reasons why some are better than others. Importantly, we need to sort through the material and information that has been gathered to decide which are appropriate and credible, and which are clearly not. Fortunately, several clear guidelines are available for deciding what evidence to use and what to ignore.

The most crucial criterion for judging the acceptability of material is *objectivity of the source.* Above all else, sources of facts and opinions should be "unbiased."[3] How can we tell? Truly objective sources have little or no vested interest in their position. A biased source stands to gain something from expressing certain attitudes, beliefs, or conclusions. Unfortunately, most biased sources have hidden agendas and seldom reveal them. Thus, careful attention to this possibility is necessary.

Most of us feel secure about using scientists as sources of evidence. We believe that they make every effort to maintain some level of objectivity in the research they conduct. In fact, there are rules that scientists must follow that help ensure that their data are truthful and unbiased. But even though it is rare, some scientists have been known to distort research findings—usually unintentionally. While most of us respect the words of a priest, minister, rabbi, or nun, they often have their own agendas. They can be subjective and biased—especially when it comes to morals related to their particular body of religious beliefs. Nevertheless, they do make excellent sources as long as they are identified as religious leaders. When members of the audience understand their credentials, they can decide for themselves whether or not to accept their conclusions as biased opinions or as facts.

The second criterion is that sources of evidence should be *competent* or credible in the given area.[4] For example, your mother may be very knowledgeable about issues related to her work. As the personnel director for a major corporation, she may be highly credible when it comes to employment interviews, how to prepare a résumé, and how to select people for specific jobs. But when the topic moves away from her work and turns to unrelated issues, her opinions and beliefs are no more competent than those of any other nonexpert. Often, people trying to persuade others will rely on a kind of "halo effect."[5] A person well known in one area may be used to convince others that they are competent in another. For example, during any election, television and movie stars speak in support of politicians. It is possible, but most unlikely, that these actors are experienced in the issues of the election. Nevertheless, they continue to champion this candidate or that cause, expecting us to value their endorsement because we recognize them as well known personalities.

The third criterion focuses on *ethical* standards. Whenever we include supporting materials in a speech, we need to make careful judgments of the appropriateness and truthfulness of the sources of the facts and opinions we use. Unfortunately, many speakers ignore ethical standards. Politicians and lawyers are famous for it. In their enthusiasm to win, they often distort the evidence they select. With little more than unfounded claims and carefully selected facts that arouse emotional responses (ignoring those that contradict their position), they try to sway juries and voters, to alter their beliefs and influence their decisions. We do not condone this approach.

Once the topic has been selected, relevant information has been assembled, and credible sources have been identified, the development of the actual speech can begin. In the next two sections, we look first at how to organize a presentation. We will concentrate first on an informative address, then on how to organize a persuasive speech. Each, as will be seen, is developed and organized differently to obtain the maximum possible effect.

Organizing a Speech to Inform

Probably no other communication objective has received more attention through the ages than has teaching and learning. It has been of deep concern on every continent, at all periods of history, among all people, and it continues to be very important today in schools at all levels.

But teaching and learning is not limited to schools and classroom situations. Almost everyone is interested in new and improved methods of informing others. Medical groups want to educate their patients to take their medication correctly. Consumer advocates want to inform us about the harmful effects of pesticides, the dangers of alcohol, and the nutritional content of foods. News reporters want to inform us about political corruption, corporate takeovers, and toppled regimes. The point is, many kinds of people are involved in the business of *informing*.

At first glance, we might suspect that teaching or informing people can't be all that difficult. It seems like little more than a matter of telling them what we want them to know, and once they hear what we have to say, then they will know it, too. Unfortunately, it doesn't work that way. Even the brightest people often fail to learn something that is explained to them on the basis of a single presentation. Yet, that is exactly the nature of an informative speech. The speaker is given one chance to explain, and the audience has one chance to learn. It is a tough assignment for both, so it is important to organize such a presentation into a basic format that will maximize its effectiveness.

A Basic Format for Informing

Every speech designed to inform, whether it's delivered as a lecture in a classroom or as a public service announcement over the radio, relies on the same basic plan. All informative speeches have an *introduction,* a *body,* and a *conclusion.* In this sense they are not much different than term papers or reports that we write. The organizational structure of an informative speech always begins with opening and introductory statements, followed by the main points and supporting materials, and it always reaches conclusions that include a summary. In other words, every speech designed to inform follows an ancient but effective pedagogical formula: First, *tell them what you're going to tell them;* then *tell them;* and finally, *tell them what you've told them!*

The introduction The introduction to a speech should be viewed as the preview of what's to come. Here, we alert the audience to the central idea or theme of our speech, and we provide them with an overview of each major idea—a kind of "road map" of the territory through which we intend to take them. This approach serves to orient the audience right away and gets them ready for all that follows. If done well, it is like an appetizer that tantalizes them and makes them hungry for the main course.

A first-rate introduction begins with an attention-gaining opener. Getting and holding attention is obviously important. How will the audience learn what we have to offer if they're not paying attention, or worse, if they seem bored and disinterested?

There are many ways to capture attention, and some work better than others. We might open our speech with a dramatic story, a humorous anecdote, a famous quotation, a startling statement, a demonstration, a vivid illustration, or an emotional account. Try to avoid the use of rhetorical questions and worn-out clichés, however. We are unlikely to make a hit with our audience if we begin our speech by asking, "Nice day, isn't it?" or if we drop a book on the floor and exclaim, "Now that I've got your attention."

The attention-gaining opener should be relevant to the topic as well. In one speech class, "Yanmin," a student speaker, used a knock-knock joke to begin her talk. Seven speakers before her had all chosen the same topic—abortion. So, Yanmin began by saying, "Knock! Knock!" Of course the audience played along by asking in chorus, "Who's there?" "Orange," Yanmin replied. "Orange who?" the audience countered. "Orange you glad I'm *not* going to talk about abortion?" The audience laughed. When they quieted down, they were ready to listen closely. Yanmin had obtained her initial goal; she had their attention. Unfortunately, the effect did not last. As soon as she began to talk about her main theme, which was all the different ways that color communicates meanings, the audience got bored.

Yanmin would have been better off if she had begun her speech with something related to her topic. For example, she could have set the stage by showing the audience two panels with different shades of red: One with a yellow tint to it and one with a blue tint. Next, she could have quizzed the audience by asking which of the two shades of red they preferred. She could then launch into a brief discussion of how males typically prefer the yellow-red, and females the blue-red. By so doing, Yanmin would have focused the audience's attention directly on her topic right from the start. The use of the panels would have made them curious enough to want further information.

Once we have the audience's attention, we need to move to our central theme and provide an overview of what we are going to say. Yanmin could have briefly explained her purpose: "I want to examine with you some interesting facts about *how* and *what* color communicates. We all use colors every day, but we may not realize what they communicate. So, let's take a closer look at how color influences our lives." Then, she should have given them the road map: "First, we'll look at how each of the primary colors communicates different *moods* and feelings. Next, we'll examine what our favorite colors say about who we are." In other words, once we have presented the attention-gaining opener, stated the central idea or purpose, and listed the main points, we are ready to move on to the body of the speech.

The body   Most classroom speeches are limited to somewhere between 5 and 10 minutes of actual presentation time. Consequently, the body of a speech can focus on no more than two or three main points. Even when speeches are much longer and extend to an hour or more, an audience will seldom tolerate more than a few main points. It is important to not make them suffer from "information overload." Too much information, organized around too many points, usually results in confusion and incoherence. For the audience that translates to boredom. Therefore, we need to be very *selective* when we consider the major points to be addressed. Earlier, we suggested two main points for a short speech on color. Restated as complete sentences, they are: (1) Each of the primary colors communicates different moods and feelings, and (2) Our favorite colors say a lot about our personal characteristics.

In organizing the body of a speech, the main points need to be arranged in a logical order. A variety of organizational patterns are available for this purpose. For instance, the body of the content can be arranged in a *spatial* order. Speeches that lend themselves well to this particular structure include descriptions of a scenic vacation spot, the route of an auto race, or the location of buried treasure. *Temporal* orders are used when a time sequence or chronology is demanded. For example, when we inform our audience how to make much better home-made chili than can be found anywhere in the State of Texas, we need to explain what to do first, second, and third when creating such a masterpiece. (We should also be prepared to escape from angry Texans.)

Another ordering pattern is the *causal* sequence. A speech can be arranged causally by demonstrating how a particular effect or outcome is a direct consequence of one or more causes. For instance, we might suggest that the effect of grade inflation on our college campuses is caused by two factors: Professors are teaching better than ever, and students today are both smarter and working much harder than they used to. (No one would have any problem believing that!)

Perhaps the topic calls for a *problem/solution* order: You may remember the wonderful old movie, *The Music Man,* in which the hero was a slick musical-instrument salesperson. In his opening scene he proclaimed, "We have trouble, folks, . . . *big* trouble, . . . and it's right here in River City! The kids are hanging out in pool halls and reading trash in the city library." The solution, presented by the Music Man, was "A band!" . . . "A band," the speaker claimed, "will keep the children off the streets and bring them back into our churches and homes."

Another good order for the body is one that fits Yanmin's speech on color. It is called a *topical* pattern. The two main points we identified do not fit any of the patterns mentioned above. They cannot be arranged in a spatial, temporal, causal or problem/solution sequence. What we have are two (or more) subtopics—two categories of information that divide the topic in some consistent way. This kind of topical pattern is often used in informative speeches. It requires that we have at least two main points that address different, but related, aspects of the central idea.

These and other ordering patterns for organizing the body of a speech are ready and waiting. All are intended to impose some logical, meaningful order on the body of the speech. Without some kind of organization, we might confuse the audience. However, one need not be overly concerned about a really tight organization. Research on audience responses to speeches organized in different ways clearly demonstrates that unless the speech is wildly disorganized, listeners are able to interpret and understand just fine.[6] Rather than force one's talk into a preset organizational scheme, then, it is perfectly acceptable to invent one's own. The basic requirement is to outline the presentation, think about *some* logical pattern that makes sense, and go from there.

Once the main points have been organized, the next task is to fill in the blanks with subpoints, to "flesh out the skeleton" with explanations, examples, and facts. Here is where one uses the supporting materials that were gathered and evaluated when the research was done. Now is the time to put those materials to good use. For example, if we had to organize Yanmin's speech, we would have read up on all the different moods that colors stimulate. We would then be able to identify some associations that are important to the first main point. The research would have yielded evidence that red stimulates and brown depresses; orange is disturbing and distressful; blue and green are soothing and calming; black com-

municates power, while purple conveys dignity and nobility.[7] And so on.

The research would also have yielded information relevant to the second main point. Specifically, some experts claim that the colors people like say something about where they come from and who they are. They say that people in southern countries with warmer climates seem to prefer bright colors and white. Those who live in more temperate climates are said to choose grays, browns, and other neutral colors, while individuals who grew up in the West or Midwest select warm, soft colors. We would have learned that color preferences also provide us with clues about personality. People who wear clothes that are predominantly yellow have been identified as confident, industrious, compulsive, and idealistic. Those who wear a lot of red are said to be extroverts, dramatic, competitive, and sensual. And how about blue? Such people tend to be highly educated, cultured, sensitive, loyal, and well respected.[8]

With all of this supporting material and more, we would now be able to fill in the rest of the body of the speech on color. We have to keep in mind that the two main points set forth in the introduction begin as mere declarations or assertions that we claim are true and that we maintain we know something about. By adding the evidence found in the research on color, we have documented these assertions and are in a better position to convince the audience that we know what we are talking about.[9]

The conclusion The basic format for any speech to inform always includes a conclusion, but we have to design it carefully. Once we've given the audience all the relevant facts and all the pertinent evidence, we need to wrap it up, but at this point in the speech, we certainly do not want to add any new information. In addition, we do not want to go over each and every subpoint again.

The conclusion serves two functions: (1) It succinctly spells out the main points, and (2) it "signs off," hopefully leaving the audience wanting more! To perform the first function, the conclusion repeats concisely what we just told the audience. We stated the main points in the introduction; we expanded on each in the body; and now we review them very briefly. The second and final function provides a graceful "sign-off," signaling to the audience that we have reached the end of the presentation.

Keep concluding remarks brief. A typical conclusion for a 5-minute speech should take only about 30 to 40 seconds. For an hour-long speech, 4 or 5 minutes is appropriate. Once the audience is aware that the conclusion has begun, they become impatient and are unwilling to stay and listen much longer. If the speaker drags on, people start giving nonverbal signals—looking at their watches, fidgeting, putting on their coats, and so on. It is far better to wrap it up neatly than to turn everyone off at the end.

On the other hand, when we start presenting the review, the audience typically is curious about how we will leave them. An effective way to conclude is to devise a conclusion that leaves the audience thinking, "Gee whiz! I didn't know that!" Jolt them if possible, or make it an "Ah ha!" experience. Be dramatic. Sometimes we'll want to tell a brief but relevant story. Or we may want to hook up with our opening remarks in some innovative, creative way. We might even use a clever quotation.

To wrap up the speech on color, for example, one might conclude with the idea that audience members should look closely at the next attractive person to whom they are introduced and want to know better. They can try to predict where he or she comes from and what he or she is like, based on the colors of the person's clothing or on a series of intriguing questions that can be asked about color preferences.

It is a good idea to consider a number of alternative closing remarks. One certain way to ruin a good speech is to just wind down the clock with something like, "Well, that's all I have to say," or even worse, to thank the audience "for being so patient" and apologize "for taking so long." It is far better to leave the stage with the audience satisfied, but intrigued. It's like providing guests with a good meal. Afterward, they may be full, but they wish they had room for more!

All of the parts of the basic format have to fit together smoothly. The introduction, the body, and the conclusion must work together to inform the audience in an effective and efficient way. Therefore, the next step in developing a speech to inform requires that we draft an outline that puts it all together, incorporating all the relevant main points and supporting subpoints.

Outlining the Informative Speech

A detailed outline is mandatory. President Lincoln may have been able to get away with just a few notes on the back of an envelope for his Gettysburg address, but don't try it! At minimum, the outline for an informative speech should include three major sections that we have already discussed: the introduction, the body, and the conclusion.

Every outline for an informative speech is preceded by a *purpose statement*. Immediately following the purpose statement, the introduction, body, and conclusion are major headings, labeled as Roman numerals I, II, and III. All main points under each heading are further classified as A, B, and C and subpoints as Arabic numbers 1, 2, and 3. Finally, all outlines end with a reference list or bibliography that documents all the sources used in the speech.

To illustrate how an outline is developed according to the foregoing format, consider the one that follows. It focuses on the influence of color and follows the suggested heading sequences.

COLOR ME BLUE

Purpose: To inform my audience about some intriguing if little-known facts about how and what color communicates about us.

I. INTRODUCTION
   A. Show two different shades of red and ask the audience to indicate their preference for each.
   B. According to color-research experts, most men will choose the red with a yellow tone; women will choose the blue-based red.
   C. We know that color can tell a lot about us, including our gender, where we live, even our personality type. Today I want to share with you some little-known, but important, facts about how color communicates!
      1. Each primary color communicates a different mood or feeling.
      2. Our favorite colors say a lot about who we are.

II. BODY
   A. Each primary color communicates a different mood or feeling.
      1. We know that people are affected a great deal by color.
         a. A color researcher, Birren, discovered that human beings react 12% faster when we see a red-colored light and we react much slower when we see a green traffic light.
         b. Another researcher, Knapp, reports that a city jail in Oregon was painted soft colors, pastel pinks and blues, in order to have a "calming effect" on the inmates. It seemed to work.

2. Studies show that people are able to identify certain moods with individual colors.
   a. Red = arousing, stimulating
   b. Blue – secure, comfortable
   c. Black = powerful, strong
   d. Orange = distressed, upset
   e. Purple = dignified, stately
   f. Green and Blue = calm, peaceful
   g. Yellow = cheerful, joyful
B. Our favorite colors say a lot about who we are.
   1. Geographic region
      a. People who live in southern, warm climates prefer white or bright colors.
      b. Temperate climates = Grayed or neutral colors
      c. West or Midwest U.S. = Warm and neutral colors
      d. Green or flat areas = Cool and neutral tones
   2. Personality type: Look at the predominant colors in your wardrobe.
      a. Red = extroverted, impulsive, sensual
      b. Blue = highly educated, cultured, introverted
      c. Yellow = philosophical, compulsive, intellectual, confident
      d. Orange = friendly, extroverted, athletic
      e. Green = fair, respectable, frank, wants to impress
      f. Black = vain, sophisticated, worldly
      g. Brown = earthy, conscientious, shrewd, dependable
      h. White = simple, decent, flirtatious
   3. Demographic characteristics
      a. Loud color preferences with a lot of variety = poorly educated, immature, lower socioeconomic status
      b. Subtle, delicate colors with little contrast = highly educated, older, higher socioeconomic status

III. CONCLUSION
   A. Summarize the two main points.
      1. Color communicates a variety of different moods and feelings, ranging from the calming effects of pastels, blue, and green to distress signals associated with the color orange.
      2. Our favorite colors, the colors we wear most often, the colors we use to decorate our homes, can tell a lot about us—including where we're from, our personality types, and how much money we make.
   B. Final "Gee whiz!" statement: (Alternative 1): "Go home; take a look at your closet. What's the predominant color? What does that say about you? Take a look at your living room or bedroom. Do the colors communicate a secure, comfortable environment? Or do the colors in your home seem to communicate a sense of strength, dignity, or perhaps, peace? If you had to pick a color for yourself, what color would you want to be?"
   (Alternative 2): "Study the next attractive person you meet; ask for color preferences; and then infer origins and personality traits; discuss implications with that person."

BIBLIOGRAPHY

Birren, R. (1965). *Color psychology and color therapy.* New York: University Books.

Burgoon, J. K., Buller, D. B., & Woodall, W. G., (1989). *Nonverbal communication: The unspoken dialogue.* New York: Harper & Row.

Compton, N. H. (1962). Personal attributes of color and design preferences in clothing fabrics. *Journal of Psychology, 54,* 191–195.

Knapp, M. L. (1978). *Nonverbal communication.* New York: Holt, Rinehart and Winston.

Wexner, L. B. (1954). The degree to which colors (hues) are associated with mood-tones. *Journal of Applied Psychology, 38,* 432–435.

Looking over the sample outline, the first thing you will notice is that the speech has a title, "Color Me Blue." Even though we are unlikely to announce the title ourselves, one will be needed for the person introducing us or for a printed announcement of our speech. Consequently, we may want to develop a clever title that captures the essence of what we will say. Next, you'll notice that the purpose statement leads the way for the speech that follows. We need always to keep in mind exactly what it is we intend to do with the speech; therefore, we identify our goal up front.

To tie the outline firmly to what we have discussed earlier, the Roman numerals I, II, and III identify the basic format of an informative speech—introduction, body, and conclusion. The introduction begins with an attention-gaining opener: I hold up the two shades of red, ask the audience to select their favorite, and then reveal the fact that males prefer one red tone while females prefer the other (see I, A and B). The introduction should also include the preview ("tell them what you're going to tell them"). The two main points are identified by Arabic numbers 1 and 2.

Notice how the body of the speech repeats the two main points under roman numeral II: A and B. Each of these main points is divided further in 1 and 2. These subpoints are still assertions and require supporting documentation. That's what the sub-subpoints provide in the series of (a) through (g) or (h).

The conclusion repeats the two main points, with some general, brief extension. The first "Gee whiz!" statement ties back to the title of the speech by asking the audience how they have colored themselves. Moreover, the conclusion asks the audience to identify personally with the topic in an effort to leave them with some meaningful, memorable experience. An alternative is provided in case a different closing gimmick seems to be needed. One or the other will need to be chosen.

The bibliography lists all the sources we used in the speech. We may have read others in the earlier stage of gathering materials, but only those references included as evidence or documentation should be listed.

Generally, then, the outline gives us a clear "road map" to follow when it's time to deliver the information to the audience. There is no other way, short of memorizing every word or reading the speech from a manuscript, to make an effective presentation. As we will explain later, memorizing and reading are not as effective.

Six Rules for Increasing Effectiveness

It is important to transfer the findings from teaching and learning research to the practical task of informative speaking. This is seldom or never done in textbooks on public speaking, but we intend to do it here. A number of practical guidelines can be borrowed from the findings of instructional communication and education research. In the following sections, we have condensed those major findings to provide six practical rules that speakers can use to inform their audiences efficiently and successfully.[10]

Rule 1: Keep it simple   This is the famous KISS rule (Keep It Simple, Stupid). The fewer points the speech presents, the more likely the audience will learn them. A related point is that too many numbers turn people off. The same is true with long lists, numerous points, or issues that have subdivisions. Thus, every aspect of our presentations, explanations, and definitions should be brief and easy to understand. Keep in mind that an audience rarely gets the opportunity to ask a speaker to back up and repeat explanations or anything else. Therefore, illustrations and reasoning should also be clear and simple.

Rule 2: Keep it concrete   Avoid abstract explanations. The more abstract the issues are and the more theoretical the explanations, the less likely the audience will comprehend the message. For instance, let us suppose we are talking about the issue of "reliability" in measurement. It can be explained abstractly by relying solely on textbook definitions of the idea. That is, we could say that reliability refers to the "test-retest consistency of a measure" and that "reliability is essential to validity," and so on, just as researchers discuss the term. It is not wrong to do this, but the audience may go to sleep. A much better way would be to explain the idea with everyday, concrete illustrations. For example, we might demonstrate the concept by asking why, when we've already stepped on a brand new scale to weigh ourselves the first time, we may want to step on it again a second or even third time. We answer the question by suggesting that we want to make sure the scale provides a "reliable" estimate of our weight—that it consistently yields the same results every time. Such a concrete example will make the idea clear.

Rule 3: Be repetitive and redundant   These are two different strategies. **Repetition** refers to explaining something exactly the *same* way over and over and over again. **Redundancy** involves explaining something more than once, but in a slightly *different* way each time. Both are extremely important strategies to ensure that an audience remembers certain points in a talk. Each is used for different purposes. Repetition is essential for lists of simple, but important, concepts. For example, there is good reason why we remember our ABC's, even though we learned them back in preschool. Most of us still mentally rehearse the list every time we look up a word in a dictionary or a name in the telephone book.

Redundancy helps audiences remember more complex ideas and arguments. For example, we noted that an audience hears a speech only once. This means that it is important to build in some degree of redundancy by the old formula we noted earlier: Tell the audience what we're going to tell them (introduction), then tell them (body), and finally, tell them what we told them (conclusion). The same general ideas are included in each, but in a slightly different way.

We can do more. Additional examples can be added to support or explain an issue. Key definitions can be repeated; explanations can be extended; main points can be covered again and connected to later points. Without repetition and redundancy, the audience may fail to understand or simply miss key issues and explanations.

Rule 4: Elicit active responses One way to increase understanding and retention is to stimulate the audience to *do something* in an open and public way. Using such an **active response** is an ancient technique. It was used by church teachers and educators for centuries in the form of "responsive reading," where the teacher read one passage from scriptures or some other book and those learning the material read the next passage in unison.

There are a number of techniques for eliciting active responses during the presentation of a speech, ranging from subtle to dramatic. A solid base of research shows that active responses greatly enhance both learning and commitment.[11] A simple example is to ask for a show of hands as a response to some question. At a more interactive level, a speaker might ask, "Pollution is a problem in Peoria. Isn't that right?" The audience is then encouraged to respond "Yes" in unison. The speaker can go on: "Pollution is a problem in America. Isn't that right?" By this time the audience has the idea and says, "Yes!" Finally, "Pollution is a problem all over the world!" At this point, the speaker's arms are open wide in a clear invitation for them to say "Yes" one more time. Audiences become involved when we have them answer the speaker in other ways as well: "We demand *more* from our government; we need *more;* and we deserve *more.* OK, now, what is it that we want?" And with that, the audience is encouraged to respond altogether, with a rousing "More!"

Eliciting such enthusiastic responses is far more effective when dramatic nonverbal gestures are used. When a speaker asks for a show of hands, his or her own hand must be held high. The "yes" request from the audience must be elicited by moving the hands rapidly upward and toward the speaker, drawing the response from the audience; the "more" request can be made effective by dramatically pointing at the audience. Since most audiences are trained to remain seated and silent, some may be surprised by such tactics. But even if that is initially the case, people generally enjoy playing their part.

Rule 5: Use familiar and relevant examples Audiences, like all human beings, need a framework to learn and recall information efficiently and effectively. We discussed human memory in terms of *schemata* as configurations of meaning in Chapter 1. This is a useful concept as it can help in getting an audience to understand an unfamiliar idea through the use of familiar and relevant examples that they will have stored in their memory schemata.

To illustrate, suppose we have to explain to an audience who have no background the idea of statistical *correlation*—a relatively sophisticated procedure used widely in scientific studies. The wrong way to go about it would be to define it as "the ratio between the covariance between two arrays of numbers and the geometric mean of their variances." While technically correct, the audience will long since have drifted off into inattention.

A far better way to explain correlation would be to pose two ideas that every member of the audience would understand and would be able to recover easily from memory schemata. One would be the average daily "outside air temperature" in a typical American city. The other would be the "crime rate" prevailing during particular days in that city. To explain correlation one could show that as the average outside air temperature went up or down in the city, the crime rate did the same thing. In other words, they rose and fell together. If the average temperature was high the crime rate tended to be high. When it was low, the crime rate tended to be low. The obvious explanation is that crooks don't like to go out when it is cold any more than the rest of us, and they prefer to commit crimes when the temperature is more comfortable.

Thus, new ideas presented can be related to examples and illustrations that are familiar and meaningful. This will enable the audience to store them in memory and recall them much better. Without linking them to an established set of ideas, however, the information is likely to be ignored, misunderstood or forgotten.

Rule 6: Use transitions and signposts That is, give frequent warnings. Let the audience constantly know when you're leaving an old point and moving on to a new one. Transitions are statements that link together prior issues or points with the next ones. Signposts are simple words or phrases that signal organization. Both serve to alert the audience to change or movement. For example, consider a transition that can be used to link up the first main point with a discussion of the second. (Wind up the prior part.) . . . "So, a color may depress us or it may cheer us up. (Now here comes the transition.) . . . But color can do more than that. (Now introduce the next point.) . . . Color can reveal a lot about who we are.'' Or signposts, such as a series of numbers (with nonverbal use of the fingers as cues), can be used: "First, we will consider . . ." or "The second reason we need to be concerned is . . ." Transitions and signposts help the audience to visualize the speech outline and to follow the presentation with little or no effort.

These six rules are by no means the only ones available to help induce audience learning and retention. In fact, a rich literature and entire texts examine such issues. For purposes of this chapter, however, the six we have discussed provide good examples of strategies that can enhance what an audience will learn from a speech. In the next section, we turn to an examination of the principles involved in persuading or influencing the audience.

Organizing a Speech to Persuade

The same three-part format that we have reviewed for informative speaking could be used to structure a persuasive speech. However, if we want to achieve the maximum possible effect, it is much better to use a different approach—one specifically designed for achieving persuasion. One reason for using a different format is that persuasion is unlikely to take place if we openly declare in our introduction that we want to influence the audience to change their beliefs or behavior in a particular way. As we noted in Chapter 10, people tend to become defensive the moment they suspect that our intent is to change what they think or do. This kind of reaction has been called the "un-uh" response—which translates roughly to "Not me, Pal!"

A second reason why a format organized around an introduction, body, and conclusion is inappropriate for a persuasive speech is that it fails to "set up" the audience for the proposed change. That is, it is important to get the audience to *want* to change. Unless the audience feels there's something wrong with what they're doing now—unless they feel a strong need for change—they are unlikely to go along with some new way of thinking or acting. In order to get them to change, we must speak first to their needs, wants, and desires.

In the sections that follow, we will review a basic format for organizing a persuasive speech that is designed to accomplish the goals noted above. We will also look in detail at a suitable outline. Finally, we will consider a number of persuasive strategies.

A Basic Persuasion Format: Monroe's Motivated Sequence

The most widely used **format** for organizing a persuasive speech is one developed by Alan Monroe early in this century.[12] The format is based on John Dewey's philosophical work, specifically his model of reflective thinking. It is also a product of Monroe's own early experiences in training sales personnel during the 1920s. Essentially, it is a working scheme for motivating people to accept and even welcome change. He first published his "Motivated Sequence" in 1935. Since then, speech instructors and textbook writers have relied almost exclusively on his scheme.

One reason Monroe's scheme has stood the test of time so well is that it is a practical application of the general "psychodynamic strategy" for persuasion based on cognitive reorganization, which we discussed in Chapter 10. In other words, it rests squarely on a sound and very general psychological theory of persuasion.

Specifically, Monroe's motivated sequence is a plan for organizing a speech into an **order** that identifies people's needs, wants, or concerns. Once those are specified, the speaker then tries to satisfy or fulfill them in some way. Consequently, the speaker gives the audience a solution, and they visualize their future with that solution. Finally, the speaker then tells them how to go about obtaining that solution. It can be a very effective way to proceed, but the entire speech relies heavily on the initial stages. That is, unless the speaker can isolate the audience's needs and establish that a problem of some kind currently exists, then no amount of persuasion will result.

To understand how the sequence works, let us take a concrete example and follow it through all the steps. We will assume for a moment that our speaker, "Travis," is interested in persuading his audience to purchase even more baking soda than the token box they now buy annually. Even though this example is targeted at product purchase, the same principles and steps are involved whenever we try to influence people to do something. "Doing something" can range from adopting the practice of flossing one's teeth regularly to supporting animal rights organizations. As will be clear in the outline immediately following this discussion, the steps remain the same whatever the goal of the persuasion. That is, the principles and issues involved are identical.

Monroe's motivated sequence consists of five separate steps: gaining the audience's *attention,* identifying unfulfilled *needs,* proposing a *solution* for satisfying them, visualizing the solution as *fulfilling* the needs, and identifying the concrete *actions* to be taken.

Step 1: Gain the audience's attention   Our speaker, Travis, must begin by ensuring that the audience is alert and interested in what he has to say. Consequently, he needs to employ some kind of attention-gaining opener, not unlike those referred to earlier in our discussion of informative speaking. In this case, Travis chooses to secure his audience's attention by complaining about all the different household cleaning products that seem to fill up his shopping cart every time he goes to the grocery store. He elaborates by listing very quickly almost 20 different products and brand names, ranging from Mr. Clean and Top Job, to spray disinfectants, like Glade and Lysol. He exclaims, "By the time I get through with the cleaning aisles, I have no room and no money for my food. Isn't there one simple, inexpensive product that can do it all?" At this point, the audience should be just a little curious as to the point of this whole presentation. Moreover, they should all be able to relate to this complaint.

Step 2: Identify unfulfilled needs   This second step cannot be emphasized enough. When preparing for his speech, Travis must put most of his energy into stressing the idea that the audience has clear, urgent, but unfulfilled needs, and expanding on each. Unless he clearly establishes in their minds that they have a problem which is not being met, his solution, baking soda, will not wash (no pun intended). Moreover, in the needs step, the solution (in this case, the product) should not be mentioned. Solutions that are identified at this stage, early in the presentation, are likely to stimulate the old bugaboo of resistance to change (Chapter 10). So Travis stays away from the product and sticks to the problem of identifying and clarifying the audience's needs.

To do this, Travis will talk about all the problems he and the audience both encounter—problems that he will later show can be eliminated by his solution. For instance, he could begin by identifying embarrassing *smells* that "all of us have experienced"—smells that originate from the refrigerator every time he stores onions, fish, or liver overnight. Travis might disclose the fact that guests quickly detect unfortunate odors that reveal he has both a cat and a dog in his home. And, "Have you ever noticed how your garbage disposal seems to take on a life of its own and breathe spoiled smells of leftovers all through the kitchen?" And so on.

In each instance, Travis speaks to a shared problem, a problem that seemingly has no one uniform solution. Remember, he has not mentioned his product, baking soda. Before too long, the audience should be anticipating that there must be a solution to these problems!

One way of gaining and holding audience attention in a persuasive speech is to use objects that fit the theme of the presentation. An accomplished speaker can use them to highlight a problem that needs to be solved and offer a proposed solution related to the object. The satisfactions to be gained from adopting the solution can then be made clear, along with the actions advocated to solve the problem and fulfill the need.

Step 3: Imply satisfaction by offering a solution   Just about the time the audience becomes anxious with concern, need, and desire, the solution is offered. In this step, Travis must show how the audience's needs can be satisfied. He does this by stating the solution, explaining how it works, relating it back to each of the needs identified earlier in step 2, and meeting any potential objections. Travis carefully and deliberately pulls forth his box of baking soda and declares, "What we need, folks, is *baking soda!* Here is the answer. Baking soda will solve the problem. Baking soda will satisfy our needs." He then goes on to explain how it works: "Baking soda can be used in its purest form by sprinkling it directly on spots, pouring it down the drain, or by simply leaving an opened box in the refrigerator. Baking soda can be used in liquid form by adding a half cup to each gallon of water."

When relating it back to the needs and problems identified in step 2, Travis must show how baking soda satisfies every one of those concerns. For instance, Travis needs to explain, "A little baking soda scattered throughout the cat's litter box will conceal unwanted pet odors. Sprinkle some on pet stains that linger in the carpet; you may still see the stain, but at least no one will smell it. And try leaving some dry soda in your garbage disposal overnight. By morning, no unfortunate reminders of last night's dinner will remain." And so on.

Importantly, the satisfaction step considers possible *objections* that audience members might raise. The audience may worry about financial costs, effort, time, or other issues related to the solution. Good speakers are able to empathize with their audience and then anticipate their objections. Travis needs to identify ahead of time and then speak directly to each objection or problem that an audience might pose: "I know what you're probably thinking: A product that does so much good in so many ways must cost a lot. Well, you're wrong. The largest container, which is the one you'll want, costs less than $2! Or maybe you believe that this particular product promises too much and it can't possibly deliver! At one time, I would have agreed with you, but that's before I tried it out for myself. It does what it promises. You have my word on that!"

Step 4: Visualize what satisfaction will mean   After the solution is offered and the audience's objections are met, Travis needs to intensify the audience's desire for the solution by getting each of them to visualize what their lives will be like once they've adopted the solution. Or he could ask them to imagine how bleak life would be without the proposed solution. Even better, he could do both: Have the audience picture a life with and then without the solution in an effort to heighten the contrast between the two worlds. "Suppose you went home today with a single box of baking soda in your hand. In no time, you'll be living in an odor-free environment. No longer will your children's friends complain about the smell from the litter box. No longer will your mother-in-law be able to guess what you had for dinner the night before." And so on.

Step 5: Define specific actions   It may seem like the speech is over, but now comes the most important part of all. It is time to close the deal. In the final or action step, the speaker should tell the audience specifically and concretely what they should do to secure the product and the benefits of the solution. Obviously, Travis needs to spell out exactly where to shop conveniently for baking soda (the campus drugstore, the local supermarket, and the nearby convenience store) and where it's located on the shelves (in the home baking aisle next to cake mixes and flour). In other kinds of persuasive speeches, the suggested actions will be appropriate to the goals. The speaker may ask the audience to volunteer to work with a shelter for the homeless, write to their local legislator about a pollution problem, or make a donation to a specific group. Or perhaps the speaker will implore them to see their dental hygienist today to find out how to floss their teeth correctly, or to stop by and pick up a brochure on safe sex.

Inexperienced speakers have a tendency to linger at this point and spend far too much time on the action step. If the steps involved are lengthy and complicated, the audience will not take the effort required to adopt the solution. Instead, be brief; end with a "Gee whiz!" statement—which is our modification of Monroe's sequence—and then sit down. Travis needs to conclude, then, with a catchy and memorable finish: "The next time you go to the grocery store, pick up a box of baking soda. Pick up several. After all, baking soda doesn't just bake anymore!"

All five steps—attention, need, satisfaction, visualization, and action—are designed to motivate people to change. When used systematically and sequentially, there is a good chance of influencing others. Even so, Monroe advises that we view his motivated sequence as a "flexible arrangement."[13] Sometimes speakers will be better off visualizing the future with the solution and omitting any reference to a future without the product, idea, or policy. Some solutions will require only a cursory explanation of how it works (like our baking soda example). Other, more complex solutions will demand lengthy demonstrations (for instance, a water purifying system). For these reasons, the kind and amount of supporting information may vary greatly from speech to speech.

Regardless of the particulars, the general principles are important. That is, Monroe advises us to spend more time and energy on establishing a need than on the product itself. He found that, too often, anxious salespeople leap to a lengthy monologue about the product features without first identifying the consumer's needs. For example, consider the last time you went shopping for a new or used car. If you had an ineffective salesperson, your experience may have been similar to that of "Alicia's" experience when she was considering a new car:

No sooner had she entered the dealer's showroom than a salesperson descended on her and abruptly asked, "Can I help you?" To most of us, this trite question translates into, "How can I make you spend your money?" So, like the rest of us, Alicia replied, "No, thank you, I'm just looking." To get away, she walked directly over to a small four-door sedan and peered inside. Undaunted, the salesperson followed her and immediately launched into a technical description of the car's horsepower, the fuel-injection system, and the entire electrical package. Alicia, bored with the monologue, turned away and left. She went down the road to another car dealer.

If, instead, the salesperson had bothered to assess Alicia's needs, she would have discovered that Alicia was not really interested in a modest four-door sedan. She had in mind a nice little convertible. In particular, she wanted a red one with leather seats and a great stereo system—including six speakers, disc player, and computerized equalizer.

Similarly, public speakers need to assess what needs are pertinent to their audiences and then respond to those needs. However, not all audiences have readily identifiable needs and wants that are pertinent to the speech topic. In that event, speakers have to *create* needs and wants for them. Once again, let's consider the topic of baking soda. Many of us may be unaware of the fact that our carpets smell. After all, how often do we get down on all fours and sniff the rug? Advertisers of rug-cleaning products have cleverly invented a need by claiming that *all* carpets smell after prolonged use. Naturally, those same advertisers were quick to provide us with their solution, Carpet Fresh, or some similar product. (If we look closely at the ingredients, we find that it is largely scented baking soda.)

After the preceding five steps have been carefully considered, the next step in designing a persuasive speech is to develop the outline. The next section provides a brief illustration of such an outline based on Monroe's five-step motivated sequence.

Outlining the Persuasive Speech

The sample outline illustrates an organized speech to persuade. Unlike the purpose of our baking soda speech, which was designed to sell a product, this sample speech was designed to sell people something less tangible, an idea. Most persuasive speeches we employ in the public arena require that we influence people to adopt an idea, policy, or practice.

In one important respect, selling an audience on an idea, policy, or practice is much more difficult than selling them a product. Audiences can't test drive an idea; they can't taste a policy; and they can't try on a practice. Consequently, they can never be sure that what the

speaker offers them is better than what they already think and do. When a speaker asks them to think in a new way or change their old habits, that speaker is asking them to do much more than part with their money. Sure, money is important, but our minds, our attitudes, and our traditions are often valued much more. In other respects, persuading people to buy a new brand of toothpaste is not that different from persuading them to sign a petition. For both, needs still must be identified and feasible solutions offered.

The outline presented here can be adapted easily to any persuasive speech outcome. It is designed around a particular goal in which "Carmen," the speaker, is deeply interested. All five steps from Monroe's motivated sequence represent the major categories (roman numerals I through V). Main points, in capital letters, reflect what each category should do. And, finally, subpoints in arabic numbers exemplify examples or extended illustrations. In the sample speech that follows, Carmen is intent on changing the audience's language behavior.[14]

NEUTRALIZING OUR LANGUAGE

Specific purpose: To persuade the audience to neutralize their language in an effort to eliminate sexist implications in speech.

I. ATTENTION
   A. What do the words *chairman, salesman, workman,* and *mailman* all have in common? Sure, they all contain the word *man,* but more important, they all exclude women.
   B. We've all been guilty of using these so-called generic words. After all, they seem harmless enough. But how harmless are they?
II. NEEDS
   A. Theorists have long agreed that how we view the world is closely tied to how we use language. In turn, language helps to shape how we perceive and understand the world. The way we understand something shapes our actions toward it. Therefore, how we use language influences how we act toward one another.
   B. Women are excluded when we use generic pronouns and man-linked words.
   C. Women are viewed as afterthoughts and put into subordinate positions when only man-linked words are used.
   D. Recent studies show that generic words and phrases do not, in fact, refer equally to men

One way of organizing and holding an audience's attention when delivering a speech that involves a series of points is to use an outline through which the audience can be systematically moved. Such an outline provides a visible map that will keep the audience from getting lost. It can be difficult for people to remember lists of points and steps that have already been discussed when they are hearing them for the first time. A clear visual outline allows the audience to see where they have been, where they are now, and where the next steps will take them.

and women. Instead, people are more likely to perceive "he" as referring to men only.

1. Women are likely to view job descriptions that use generic words/phrases as neither suitable nor appropriate for women.
2. Students who read textbooks that contained generic pronouns and man-linked words were 40% more likely to assume the passages referred to men, rather than both women and men.
3. Other research shows that children exposed to generic words assume that only males are being referenced.

E. In other words, what we once thought of as "harm*less*" speech turns out to be potentially "harm*ful*." Clearly, folks, we have a problem. We can no longer assume that generic pronouns and man-linked words refer to both sexes. And we can no longer assume that it makes no difference.

III. SATISFACTION

A. We need to provide alternatives to man-linked words and generic pronouns.
B. Rather than use third-person singular pronouns (he, she, him, and her), switch to first- or third-person plural (we, they, their).
C. Alternate male pronouns with female pronouns; use these forms in opposite-sex situations.
D. Use she/he and him/her when referring to both sexes.
E. Replace man-linked words with neutral ones (airline steward/stewardess vs. flight attendant; mailman vs. mail carrier).
F. Specific examples of change already implemented:

1. New edition of *Roget's Thesaurus* eliminates sexist categories ("mankind" is now "humankind").
2. English teachers beginning to accept alternatives to the generic pronoun "he."

G. Objections

1. We might agree that switching pronouns to include she and her is a hassle and awkward to do. But it's surprising how quickly we can get used to it. It was hard for me at first, too. Now it's become a habit.
2. Others might believe that we're making "much ado about nothing." The research findings tell us something quite different. Children and college students alike are affected. Simply put, sexist language encourages sexism.

IV. VISUALIZATION

A. If gender-based language were eliminated from our vocabulary entirely, we would be well on our way to establishing a world free of sexual bias. After all, language helps to shape how we view our world and one another.

B. But if we continue to insist that generic pronouns and man-linked words are harmless, then we can expect to go on as before, condoning and encouraging separatism and alienation between the sexes.

V. ACTION

A. Practice eliminating gender-based language in your everyday speech, in your conversations, and in your letters.

B. Give gentle reminders to others when they use these so-called harmless words and phrases. Suggest alternatives they can use.

C. We don't want to reverse sexism; we want to eliminate it. Let's begin now with ourselves, in our everyday speech. Neutralize!

BIBLIOGRAPHY

Bem, S. L., & Bem, D. J. (1973). Does sex-biased job advertising "aid and abet" sex discrimination? *Journal of Applied Social Psychology, 3,* 6–28.

Pearson, J. C., Turner, L. H., & Todd-Mancillas, W. (1991). *Gender and communication* (2nd ed.) (pp. 76–103). Dubuque, IA: Wm. C. Brown.

Todd-Mancillas, W. (1981). Masculine generics-sexist language: A review of literature and implications for speech communication professionals. *Communication Quarterly, 29,* 107–115.

An examination of Carmen's outline for her persuasive speech reveals some similarities with the earlier one developed for Yanmin's informative speech on color. Both have a title and begin with a purpose statement, and for the same reasons. That is, the title can be used when the host introduces the speaker to the audience. A title may also be necessary for printed announcements, posters, advertising, or other prespeech publication of the event. The specific purpose statement sharply defines for the speaker, not the audience, exactly what her intent is. Notice how Carmen could have specified other persuasive outcomes. Rather than neutralize language usage, she could have asked for extreme change; that is, substitute female pronouns for all generic words and convert all man-suffixes to woman endings to refer to both males and females (e.g., chairwoman, mailwoman, etc.). Knowing what the objective is up front helps the speaker stay on track as the speech is developing.

The first major step, attention (roman numeral I on the outline), includes only two main points—both of which are designed to trigger the audience's interest. Unlike the attention step employed in the informative speech, Carmen does not want to "preview" for her audience her central thesis or her main points. Instead, persuasive speeches bury the purpose until much later in the presentation.

As we indicated earlier, the need step, roman numeral II, should demonstrate clearly that a problem exists with the status quo and it's time for a change. Carmen reveals how language shapes our perceptions of reality. Then she shows how generic pronouns and man-linked words contribute to that distortion process by excluding and subordinating women. Next, she provides the audience with evidence to back her claims. She cites research findings that show obvious gender discrimination. Finally, she concludes that generic language is not all that harmless (referring back to the introduction) and that, in fact, such language is potentially harmful. She clearly states that we have a problem.

In the satisfaction step, roman numeral III, Carmen immediately and explicitly reveals her solution. Not until the satisfaction step does she disclose her persuasive intent. Before this point, the audience assumes that Carmen is informing, relating problems to the status quo. If she was successful, the audience should be sympathetic with the problem and ready and willing to accept some kind of solution. After all, they *need* satisfaction! So she offers several palatable solutions, shows specific instances, and provides examples of their use in respected publications and professions. All of this is accomplished in III, A through F. In III, G, Carmen poses two objections. She states the audience's potential problems with her solution, agrees with them, and then adds a "but." Once she was in their position, but now she's seen the light. She shows *why* she no longer shares those objections and why the audience shouldn't either.

In the visualization step, roman numeral IV, Carmen ties her proposed solution to the audience's desire by having them imagine a world free of gender-based language and contrasts that positive image with a version of the world remaining biased and discriminatory. Finally, in the action step, roman numeral V, Carmen calls for adoption of her proposal by specifying two courses of action. First, she asks them to practice neutralizing their own speech, and second, she tells them to remind others when they use gender-based language and to provide them with alternatives. Both action steps are brief and to the point. Before Carmen walks off stage, however, she needs to leave the audience with a "Gee whiz!" impression. So she concludes with a dramatic appeal and one final very positive command, "Neutralize!"

Like the outline for the informative speech, this one for the persuasive speech ends with a selected bibliography containing only those references that Carmen used to organize her speech.

Delivering a speech from this outline is more likely to accomplish a persuasive objective than is relying on alternative formats. Eliciting the audience's attention, establishing a need, providing them with a solution, helping them visualize a future with (or without) the solution, and specifying a course of action—all are designed to influence an audience to change their beliefs, and attitudes, or even their behaviors.

Seven Strategies for Persuading

We noted in Chapter 10, and earlier in the present chapter, that in a society like ours, where advertising and other appeals are ubiquitous, people become highly resistant to persuasion. From the start, then, persuasive speakers have their work cut out for them. Success in influencing others requires that speakers become sensitive to the dynamics of persuasion and resistance. What follows is a list of seven practical strategies that have been derived from a large body of theory and research on persuasion.[15] These strategies consider both attempts by speakers to influence and efforts by audiences to resist that influence.

Strategy 1: Conceal the intent to persuade   By now it should be clear why it is important to mask the objective to influence others. People are repelled generally whenever someone tries to pitch them a line or hustle a product. Their first response is to say, "No," and as soon as they do, they become committed to or entrenched in a resistant stance.[16] Don't give the audience the opportunity to say no. Instead, identify the need; spend an inordinate amount of time developing that need; and then, and only then, provide the audience with the solution.

Strategy 2: Don't ask for too much   This is the issue of "discrepancy." Simply put, it means that the speaker's message should not be overly demanding—too far from what it is realistic to ask in the way of change. A whole body of research on message discrepancy indicates that persuaders who deliver a message or speech that is too far afield from what their audience is willing to accept are doomed.[17] This does not suggest that persuaders should deliver only messages that appeal to their audience. What it does mean, though, is that speakers should only expect and ask for gradual, minor progress toward the changes that they want. Otherwise, the well-known **boomerang** effect will result, in which an undesired effect of a persuasive message "backfires." The idea of the boomerang effect can be illustrated by a simple example:

Rob wants to convince Jeanine that they should get married. If Rob had his way, they'd be married now, but Jeanine has resisted the whole idea. So, ignoring our caution against asking too much, he decided to try to persuade Jeanine to marry him within the next 2 weeks. If she says no, he plans to threaten to leave her. (We can all picture this scenario, can't we?) Sure enough, Jeanine resists. In fact, she's so put off by his attempt that she tells him not only will she refuse to marry him within the next 2 weeks, but she has no intention of ever marrying him—the relationship is over!

That illustrates the boomerang effect. The outcome is opposite what the persuader wanted to achieve. But suppose now that Rob had chosen to use strategy 2 in the first place and avoided asking too much. He already knows that Jeanine isn't particularly thrilled about the idea of marriage. So, putting a time constraint of 2 weeks is out of the question. He decides to avoid a lengthy discussion about marriage altogether; instead, he discusses an informal engagement. She agrees. Later in the relationship he asks her to formalize the engagement with a ring. She says OK and agrees to wear his ring. Still later, he suggests a possible wedding date. Jeanine rejects that appeal, but she is warming up to the idea. By reducing the amount of change requested at each stage, Rob avoids getting hit by the boomerang and stands a much greater chance of achieving his goal.

Strategy 3: Avoid inflammatory words and phrases   Unfortunate choices of words and phrases can also backfire. For example, we all know certain words that make us angry or phrases that we find disgusting. In addition, we all know how to push other people's emotional buttons by making use of offensive and provocative words.

Carmen's speech on neutralizing gender-based language could boomerang easily should she employ explosive terms during her arguments. Because the issue is a sensitive one for many people, Carmen must select words and phrases carefully so that they do not arouse negative feelings toward her. Rather than use words or phrases like sexist, feminist, women's-libber, man-hater, and chauvinist pig, Carmen should use substitutes that are relatively innocuous or even positive, but which have the same basic meanings—such terms as bias-free, gender based, democratic, genderless, exclusionary, and generic. By doing so, Carmen is not as likely to alienate large segments of her audience to a point where they will neither listen, learn, nor change.

Strategy 4: Keep objections to a minimum   We noted that in the satisfaction step of Monroe's motivated sequence, the speaker is supposed to identify and counter potential audience objections to the proposed solution. That's all well and good, but we can carry this suggestion too far. The number of audience objections dealt with, and the time spent on them, should be limited. At most, only a couple of objections should be raised. In a 5- to 10-minute speech, their recognition and refutation should not occupy more than 30 to 60 seconds.

The reason for allocating such a short time is that the purpose of the speech is to persuade the audience in a direction counter to possible objections to the solution. Thus, if too much attention is devoted to them, as opposed to advantages, the audience is more likely to be influenced by the objections. Moreover, the speaker risks exposing the audience to objections they had never thought of before. Once raised, those new objections may sound pretty convincing!

Strategy 5: Use a two-sided message with refutation[18]   Two-sided messages were discussed in Chapter 10 (p. 306). They give both sides of an argument a "fair" hearing (or at least appear to do so). Two-sided messages *with refutation* give both sides *and* refute or deny the validity or worth of the opposing side. Finally, one-sided messages give only the speaker's position on the issue and ignore the opponent's argument. Of the three message-sided options, audiences are most influenced when the speaker discusses both sides—and when the speaker takes the time to argue against the opposing view. What happens is that if the speaker does so, the audience believes in his or her credibility, intelligence, and objectivity. Such a presentation shows that the speaker is aware of all the issues at stake and is forthright about presenting them. At the same time, the best case can be made for the speaker's point of view. This is accomplished when audience objections are spelled out and counterargued. Importantly, it's not enough just to list the arguments on both sides. The speaker must be able to refute or deny the legitimacy of the opposing position. Moreover, the speaker needs to deal sensitively with the way in which objections are raised and argued.

In order to explain how this strategy can be applied, let's consider Carmen's speech on gender-based language one more time. She empathizes with an audience member who might object to switching pronouns to include *she* or *her*. The objection (III, G, 1. in the outline) is that it is "a hassle and awkward to do." Note how she plans to use the word *we* to show that she and the audience are connected on this issue. But if we look carefully at her text, we see that Carmen's plan is subtle. She will state that "we might agree" that it can be a hassle, but she will not agree that it is *too* much trouble. Next, she will tell the audience that switching pronouns "was hard for me at first, too. Now it's become a habit." Thus, she further empathizes with their position but will demonstrate how she was able to change without great difficulty. In this instance, Carmen's plan is carefully designed to avoid alienating the audience by a one-sided presentation—stating only her perspective. At this point, she is cautious not to denigrate other positions. She will state her side and then give theirs. However, she doesn't leave it at that. When she recognizes that their position may be counter to her own, she will be sympathetic but will downplay and then refute those objections. Throughout the speech, Carmen plans to create a *we/they* mentality. She and the audience will become one team, while "they" (the less sensitive) comprise the other. For example, she will note (III, G, 2.) that "Others might believe that we're making 'much ado about nothing.'" This will insinuate that the "others" are wrong and that "we," Carmen and the audience, are right.

For many years, researchers and teachers argued that there are occasions when a one-sided message is more appropriate than a two-sided refutational approach. Until very recently, we contended that a one-sided message should be used when the audience already agrees with your position. Today, we know that regardless of the audience's attitudes toward the topic, a two-sided refutational message is still the best bet. Second to a two-sided refutational message, however, is the one-sided message approach—with two-sided "without" refutation, a poor third choice.[19]

Strategy 6: Inoculate against counterarguments
Occasionally, a speaker may want to take the opportunity to "inoculate" the audience against possible counter-persuasive attempts. If a speaker has been preceded, or will be followed, by someone who advocates a contrary position, then a two-sided message with refutation becomes essential. In this case, the speaker knows that the audience already agrees with him or her but wants to make sure that they won't be swayed by the other speaker. Consequently, the speaker uses counterarguments to inoculate or "immunize" the audience against "counterpropaganda" by systematically destroying what the other speaker is likely to say or has already said. In this way, the use of evidence serves an essential role in the inoculation process.[20]

Strategy 7: Use fear appeals   As explained in Chapter 10 (p. 306), fear appeals can provide effective persuasion strategies. Some fear appeals are life-threatening (high), whereas others are mild or weak (low). In a recent review of over 30 persuasion and public speaking texts published and sold today, over half of the authors mistakenly recommend that moderate, rather than high (or low), amounts of fear should be used to influence others effectively.[21] These text authors reason that scare tactics that are too fearful are likely to be perceived as unrealistic or inapplicable and thus will be rejected by the audience. Similarly, they claim, audiences are likely to dismiss low fear appeals simply because little or no fear fails to incite or stimulate change. Moderate fear appeals, they say, are perceived as more reasonable and real and, at the same time, serve to prompt or motivate the audience to change. As we showed in Chapter 10, such conclusions are based on a single 1953 study and do not take into account a body of more contemporary research.[22] Today, it seems clear that, within reason, high fear is more likely to influence people than either moderate or low amounts of fear.

Using fear as a persuasive strategy in your speech, however, assumes that your topic allows you to do so. That is, speeches advocating stiffer penalties for people who drive drunk, consume drugs illegally, or fail to respect others' property all provide appropriate contexts for high fear appeals. Spokespersons for automobile safety, including advocates for seat belts and air bags, have been known to rely heavily on fear appeals to persuade people to "buckle up" or to influence Congress to pass a variety of auto safety bills. Some of these speakers show devastating films and slides that depict mangled, distorted bodies resulting from auto accidents; others cite catastrophic statistics or provide personal testimonials to the destruction that occurs when seat belts are ignored or when air bags are unavailable. Other examples of high fear-appeal use in modern media messages include campaigns against smoking, illegal drug use, eating foods high in fat or cholesterol, and the lack of physical exercise.

This list of seven strategies to use in persuasive speeches speaks only to some of the more relevant and interesting research findings that can be translated to practical use. Many others are available that will assist speakers in their efforts to influence an audience. Like strategies for informing, those for persuading are extensive and complex. While this chapter has covered only a limited number, it does reveal how complicated the art and science of public speaking can be.

Chapter Review

- The most difficult part of speech preparation is getting started, which means selecting a topic, specifying both a general and a specific purpose, and finally, analyzing the audience.
- Topics are not inherently boring, but speakers can be. If possible, speakers should select topics they already know something about; and once a general subject is selected, they must narrow it down and focus on one specific issue.
- The purposes for speaking are generally: to entertain, to inform, or to persuade. The purpose should be capable of being stated in specific terms and limited to one simple declarative sentence.
- An important phase of preparation is gathering research materials that can be used as evidence to support the specific purposes of the speech. Speakers should look first to themselves as credible sources of information. However, speakers most often rely on what others say. Expert sources are commonly obtained through library research. Interviews with experts provide another option.
- All informative speeches have three main parts—an introduction, a body, and a conclusion. The introduction serves the purpose of gaining the audience's

attention and previewing the substance of the speech. The body of the speech is usually limited to two or three main points, and it can be organized in a variety of ways. Spatial, temporal, causal, or problem/solution can be good choices, but topical order is used most often. The conclusion summarizes the main points and signs off so as to leave the audience with a "Gee whiz!" feeling.

■ An outline of an informative speech provides the "road map" or plan that helps the speaker systematically organize and deliver the presentation.

■ A speaker should keep the message simple and concrete; add repetition and redundancy throughout; involve the audience in active responses as much as possible; make examples and illustrations familiar and relevant to the audience; and use transitions and signposts to keep the audience organized and alert.

■ The most widely used persuasive speaking format is Monroe's motivated sequence. The first step is to gain attention. The second is to identify needs. The third step of proposing a solution is designed to get rid of the problem or satisfy the need. In the fourth step, the speaker asks the audience to visualize a future without the proposed solution. And finally, the speaker asks the audience to adopt the solution.

■ Finally, a number of research-based strategies for persuasion can help speakers optimize their influence attempts. Specifically, persuasive speakers should conceal their intent to persuade; resist asking the audience to change too much; refrain from using inflammatory words; avoid discussing too many of the audience's objections; employ a two-sided, refutational message; and use high fear appeals when the topic seems suited.

Key Terms

Active response   Getting an audience to engage in a form of behavior in response to a request or suggestion by a speaker. Examples are holding up hands, clapping on cue, saying yes or no in response to questions.

Boomerang   An undesired effect of a persuasive message (speech) that "backfires." That is, it creates an effect which is the opposite of that desired by the person originating the message.

Counterargument   A persuasive message in a speech that presents information intended to discredit a particular conclusion or position.

Format   A manner in which a lengthy message (like a speech, article, term paper, or book) is organized. Usually this is in terms of a number of major sections, each of which is divided into subsections.

Order (in format)   The sequence in which major points in a speech are to be presented. This can be in terms of space (a sequence of places where the events took place), time (the chronological sequence in which events happened), cause (which events brought on others as consequences), or by topic (which does not require a particular logical sequence).

Repetitive (vs. redundant)   Repetition is presenting the same message more than once with the same wording. Redundant means presenting the same message more than once, but with different wording each time.

Two-sided message   A persuasive message (speech) that presents both sides of a controversial issue.

Notes

1. For a comprehensive review of the persuasive effects of evidence, see: Stiff, J. B. (1986). Cognitive processing of persuasive message cues: A meta-analytic review of the effects of supporting information on attitudes. *Communication Monographs, 53,* 75–89.

2. Some research indicates that anecdotal stories may have greater impact on persuasion than the use of statistics—at least, in the short run. Over time, however, the use of strong statistical evidence appears to have persuasive effects. Importantly, the effective use of statistics relies on the speaker's ability to show that the data are "typical" and valid. For a thorough review of the persuasive effects of evidence, see: Reinard, J. (1988). The empirical study of the persuasive effects of evidence: The status after fifty years of research. *Human Communication Research, 15,* 3–59.

3. The research on source bias consistently concludes that biased sources are not particularly influential. The exception to this conclusion is when a biased source apparently speaks *counter* to her/his own position or vested interest. This exception also holds for "reluctant" testimony or evidence provided by individuals who are asked to support a position contrary to their own. See, for instance: McCroskey, J. C. (1986). *An introduction to rhetorical communication* (2nd ed.) Englewood Cliffs, NJ: Prentice-Hall; and Reinard, 1988, p. 34.

4. Overwhelmingly, the research indicates that highly credible sources of evidence are more persuasive than sources low in credibility. In turn, the use of high-quality evidence positively influences perceptions of speaker credibility. For a review of the credibility of evidence sources and the quality of evidence used, see: Reinard, 1988,

pp. 34–39. See also: Luchok, J. A., & McCroskey, J. C. (1978). The effect of quality evidence on attitude change and source credibility. *Southern Speech Communication Journal, 43,* 371–383.

5. This term was originally coined by L. L. Thorndike, who studied the halo effect of attractiveness or liking. (1920). A constant error in psychological ratings. *Journal of Applied Psychology, 4,* 25–29.

6. Darnell, D. (1963). The relation between sentence order and comprehension. *Speech Monographs, 30,* 97–100; and Kissler, G., & Lloyd, K., (1973). Effect of sentence interrelation and scrambling on the recall of factual information. *Journal of Educational Psychology, 63,* 187–190.

7. Wexner, L. B., (1954). The degree to which colors (hues) are associated with mood-tones. *Journal of Applied Psychology, 38,* 432–435.

8. Compton, N. H. (1962). Personal attributes of color and design preferences in clothing fabrics. *Journal of Psychology, 54,* 191–195.

9. Actually, all of these claims and conclusions about color are very controversial and are not all supported by evidence. That should be made clear in any speech on this topic.

10. For an overview of the research findings pertinent to these rules and others, see: Woolfolk, A. E. (1987). *Educational Psychology.* Englewood Cliffs, NJ: Prentice-Hall; Higbee, K. L. (1977). *Your memory: How it works and how to improve it.* Englewood Cliffs, NJ: Prentice-Hall; Eggen, P. D., Kavchak, D. P., & Harder, R. J. (1979). *Strategies for teachers: Information processing models in the classroom.* Englewood Cliffs, NJ: Prentice-Hall.

11. The classic example of how effective this can be is: Lewin, K. (1947). Group Decision and Social Change. In E. E. Maccoby & T. M. Newcomb, *Readings in social psychology* (pp. 197–211). New York: Holt.

12. Monroe, A. H. (1935). *Principles and types of speech.* Chicago, IL: Scott, Foresman.

13. Ehninger, D., Gronbeck, B. E., & Monroe, A. H. with L. Moore. (1984). *Principles of speech communication* (9th ed.) (p. 257). Glenview, IL: Scott, Foresman.

14. The content of this speech draws heavily from the textbook by: Pearson, J. C., Turner, L. H., & Todd-Mancillas, W. (1991). *Gender and communication* (2nd ed.) (Ch. 4). Dubuque, IA: W. C. Brown. For further information about the effects of gender-based language, we encourage you to select the Pearson et al. text, which provides the most comprehensive and most readable review of the current research and thinking on gender communication.

15. All of the proposed rules are based in research. Reviews of relevant investigations underlying these and other "rules" are available from a number of textbooks on persuasion and attitude change. See, for instance: Petty, R. E., & Cacioppo, J. T. (1981). *Attitudes and persuasion: Classic and contemporary approaches.* Dubuque, IA: Wm. C. Brown; Bettinghaus, E. P., & Cody, M. J. (1987). *Persuasive communication.* New York: Holt, Rinehart & Winston; and Reardon,

K. K. (1981). *Persuasion: Theory and context* (pp. 113–146). Beverly Hills, CA: Sage. Moreover, reviews of literature and meta-analytic reviews are also available and cited where applicable.

16. Psychological reactance theory speaks to the reasons why individuals typically respond with such resistance. See: Brehm, J. W. (1966). *A theory of psychological reactance.* New York: Academic Press.

17. Social judgment theory provides an extensive explanation of this phenomenon. See: Sherif, C. W., Sherif, M., & Nebergall, R. E. (1965). *Attitude and attitude change* (pp. 186–192). Philadelphia: Saunders, 1965. For further research support of this finding, see: Harvey, O. J., & Rutherford, J. (1958). Gradual and absolute approaches to attitude change. *Sociometry, 21,* 61–68; Hovland, C. I., Harvey, O. J., & Sherif, M. (1957). Assimilated and contrast effects in reactions to communication and attitude change. *Journal of Abnormal and Social Psychology, 55,* 244–252; and Petty & Cacioppo, op. cit., 105–106.

18. For a thorough, updated review of the literature on the effects of message sidedness, see: Jackson, S., & Allen, J. (1990). Meta-analysis of the effectiveness of one-sided and two-sided argumentation. Paper presented at the 1990 International Communication Association, Montreal, Canada. Also, see: Allen, M., & Preiss, R. W. (1990). Using meta-analysis to evaluate curriculum: An examination of selected college textbooks. *Communication Education, 38,* 103–116.

19. In an effort to update and sort out the research on message sidedness, Allen and his colleagues designed three critical studies to examine the persuasive impact of two-sided refutational, two-sided nonrefutational, and one-sided messages. Those results support the conclusions advanced from the meta-analytic review reported by Sally Jackson and Mike Allen, op. cit., and are reported in this chapter. See: Allen, M., Hale, J., Mongeau, P., Berkowitz-Stafford, S., Stafford, S., Shanahan, W., Agee, P., Dillon, K., Jackson, R., & Ray, C. (1990). Testing a model of message sidedness: Three replications. *Communication Monographs, 37,* 275–291.

20. McCroskey, J. C. (1970). The effects of evidence as an inhibitor of counterpersuasion. *Speech Monographs, 37,* 188–194.

21. Allen, M., & Preiss, R. W., (1990). Using meta-analysis to evaluate curriculum: An examination of selected college textbooks. *Communication Education, 38,* 103–116.

22. One of the first studies to examine the effects of fear appeals was done by: Janis, I., & Feshbach, S. (1953). Effects of fear-arousing communications. *Journal of Abnormal and Social Psychology, 48,* 78–92. More recent research failed to support their hypothesis that moderate fear appeals were more effective than either high or low fear. Instead, increases in fear are positively and linearly associated with increases in attitude and behavior change. For a comprehensive review and meta-analysis of that research, see: Boster, F., & Mongeau, P. (1985). Fear-arousing persuasive messages. In Robert Bostrom (Ed.), *Communication yearbook 8* (pp. 330–377). (Beverly Hills, CA: Sage.)

Additional Readings

Beighley, K. C. (1952). A summary of experimental studies dealing with the effect of organization and of skill of speaker on comprehension. *Journal of Communication, 2,* 58–65.

This research report describes a six-study investigation into the influence of organized and disorganized written material on reader retention. All six studies support the conclusion that organized material produces more receiver retention than does disorganized material. This early investigation provides good insight into the importance of effective organization in speech preparation.

Clevenger, T., Jr. (1966). *Audience analysis*. Indianapolis, IN: Bobbs-Merrill.

This short and somewhat older text still provides an excellent discussion of the audience dimension in all public speaking activities. It reviews in some detail the step-by-step phases of the audience analysis process. This book continues to serve as a helpful guide for students interested in effectively adapting to their audience.

Jensen, J. V. (1981). *Argumentation: Reasoning in communication*. Belmont, CA: Wadsworth.

This is a good standard text on argumentation. It covers all of the areas important to the argumentation and debate area. Most notable are the chapters on evidence, reasoning, receiver analysis, organization, and language. A great deal of care is taken to illustrate the application of each principle.

Reinard, J. C. (1988). The empirical study of the persuasive effects of evidence: The status after fifty years of research. *Human Communication Research, 15,* 3–59.

This comprehensive article reviews the development of research on the persuasive effects of evidence. Over 175 references are reviewed that either directly or indirectly address the use of evidence in persuasive communications. Conclusions drawn from the review indicate consistency in the effective use of evidence in the preparation of messages.

Smith, R. G. (1951). An experimental study of the effects of speech organization upon attitudes of college students. *Speech Monographs, 18,* 292–301.

This report describes a study of the effects of reordering the main part of a speech and variation in disorganization of content on persuasiveness and general reactions to the presentation. Results indicate that reordering the main points has minimal effect but that disorganization has some persuasive influence. Participants indicated that the well-organized speech was most effective.

Chapter 14

Speaking Before a Group

Contents

Public Speaking as Extended Conversation
"Planned" Spontaneity
Recognizing and Responding to Audience Feedback
Adapting to the Audience Through Collective
   Role-taking

Selecting a Mode of Delivery
Reading from a Manuscript
Delivering a Memorized Speech
Impromptu Delivery
Extemporaneous Speaking

Five Ways to Establish Credibility
Demonstrating Competence
   Using jargon
   Including oral footnotes
   Admitting your ignorance
   Appearing to be competent
   Arranging a socially validating introduction
Generating Trust
Exhibiting Composure
Communicating Sociability

Displaying Extroversion
Performing the Speech: Beginnings, Middles, and Endings
Act I: Managing Initial Impressions
Act II: Strategies to Keep the Plot from "Sagging"
   Making the plot more interesting
   Using redundancy and repetition
   Signaling transitions and signposts
   Using vocalics effectively
   Stimulating interest with oculesics
   Employing gestures and actions to hold attention
   Learning to handle hecklers
Act III: The Famous Final Scene

Enhancing Immediacy

Chapter Review

Key Terms

Notes

Additional Readings

Key Questions

- The best way to give a speech is to write it out carefully ahead of time and then simply read it word-for-word to the audience. That way there is no possibility of forgetting what you want to say or having any other problems. Right? . . . Wrong! Wrong! Wrong!

- An excellent way to give a speech is to write it out and then practice it over and over until it has been completely memorized. That way there is little likelihood that you will forget part of it or get into any other kind of trouble. Right? . . . Wrong! Wrong! Wrong!

- When giving a speech it is best just to be yourself, completely. Such tactics as dressing up, and trying to make the audience believe that you know a lot about your topic and that you are trustworthy, sociable, and composed, are poor strategies. Right? . . . Wrong! Wrong! Wrong!

- When delivering a speech, it is best just to get up and say what you have been thinking in whatever order comes to mind. Following some formal plan, with a beginning, middle, and end is artificial and the audience will be turned off. Right? . . . Wrong! Wrong! Wrong!

During the 1988 presidential election campaign, George Bush was faced with a serious image problem. Americans were used to a very different presidential speaking style. For many citizens, Ronald Reagan was a charismatic "Great Communicator." By comparison, candidate Bush often seemed awkward and lacking in self-confidence. Moreover, he frequently used gestures and phrases that the media defined as "prissy." For instance, he described the negative campaigning used against him by the Democrats as "naughty stuff."[1] He came across the television screen as "frenetic, nervous, and unsure of himself. He had a habit of speaking in incomplete sentences, and his penchant for slips of the tongue left an impression of one who was high-strung and at times almost silly."[2] At one point, *Newsweek* magazine showcased the (then) Vice President Bush on its cover with the caption "Fighting the Wimp Factor." It was far from a powerful image.

But despite those problems, Bush was able to effect an astonishing turnaround. After trailing his opponent, Michael Dukakis, in the polls (by 17 percentage points for much of the early part of the campaign), he began to close the gap. In fact, in less than a month, almost one person in four had changed his or her choice for president.[3] What happened in that short time to change the outcome of the election provides a powerful lesson for anyone studying public speaking.

For one thing, Roger Ailes, a communication expert, became Bush's speaking coach. Together, they watched videotapes of Bush's appearances. Ailes showed him how to make himself come across as more forceful and dynamic by using purposeful, slow gestures. Ailes had Bush take some of the shrillness out of his voice by having him practice more measured tones. Ailes deliberately goaded Bush into standing up to CBS anchor Dan Rather, in a now famous CBS interview. But prior to the interview, Ailes warned Bush that tough and aggressive Rather was going to try to "ambush" him and make him look bad. They planned ahead, and minutes into the interview, Bush firmly challenged Rather, who then became flustered, argumentative, and contentious. Bush continued the attack. The crafty Ailes, stationing himself right beside the camera, outside of Rather's view but within Bush's line of vision, supplied key phrases on a yellow legal pad every time Bush seemed to struggle for a response.[4] From the viewer's perspective it looked like Bush was able to match wits with a very tough and experienced newsman. In this widely viewed confrontation, the public saw a George Bush who looked strong and far from wimpy.

Soon after that performance, Bush presented the speech of his life at the Republican national convention in New Orleans. Instead of his usual awkwardness, he displayed a highly practiced, professional speaking style. His delivery was strong, even, and crisp. The training had paid off enormously. The crowd applauded enthusiastically. And it was all on national television.[5]

What can we learn from George Bush's experience? Obviously, there were factors other than speaking style that helped him win. For example, many analysts have concluded that the widely criticized television ads were very effective. An example was the brief Willy Horton campaign plug, showing how Dukakis had let a convicted murderer out of jail to kill again. Another was his strategy of linking himself to treasured American symbols—the flag and pledge of allegiance.

One clever *nonverbal* strategy was that Bush arranged to speak against interesting backgrounds that visually communicated subtle but important meanings. For instance, in a dramatic attempt to ward off criticisms leveled against the Republican administration's "do-nothing" policy on the environment, the networks showed Bush with the clean, crisp blueness of Lake Erie as a backdrop while he outlined his plans for environmental improvements. To provide a contrast, he took a well-photographed boat trip around the polluted Boston harbor. The networks showed him attributing "this mess" to his opponent.

His strategy also included providing a number of very effective "sound bites"—captivating one-liners—that the news media dutifully picked up. For example, at one point Bush told the media that Dukakis should "stop dodging the L-word (liberal)" and admit his anticonservative bent. He reinforced that strategy by calling Dukakis a "card-carrying ACLU member" in derogatory terms.[6] He also used humor. For example, later in the campaign, Bush explained to the media that because Dukakis was so "soft on defense," he "wouldn't be surprised if [Dukakis] thought that a naval exercise was something you find in Jane Fonda's workout."[7] Such colorful sound bites are eagerly seized upon by television and other media that are always hungry for interesting footage to show in the evening news.

Our purpose here is not to understand presidential elections better or to editorialize about George Bush. It is to see that it is possible to develop an *effective communication strategy.* In George Bush's case it was a keen awareness on the part of the candidate of how to handle himself in front of an audience and a camera. He learned how to present himself and talk in ways so that viewers saw him as credible, interesting, and even entertaining. In contrast, Dukakis did not learn those lessons well and often looked like a "talking head," standing stiffly at a podium with only a blue curtain as backdrop.

The major lesson to be drawn from this example, then, is that the way someone communicates can be as important as what they have to say. Therefore, while the previous chapter emphasized the importance of organizing the *content* of a speech, the present chapter focuses on *delivery.* A second lesson is that we need to be strategic in our planning for public speaking—focusing on long-range objectives. That is, we need to *plan ahead, organize our effort* carefully, and proceed with our presentation *step-by-step.*

In the section that follows, we begin that planning by examining a contemporary approach to public speaking that is easier and more effective than some of the older approaches. It is one in which speakers relate directly and openly with their audience, focusing on those delivery skills we use in everyday conversations with others.

Public Speaking as Extended Conversation

In order to understand what the contemporary study of public speaking does and does not emphasize, it will be useful to contrast it with what it was like at the beginning of the century. Then, teachers of "elocution," as the art of oratory was called, required students to rehearse their

speeches with special attention given to the voice, speech sounds, and pronunciation. Some textbooks on elocution advised new speakers to do breathing exercises regularly and to practice sample sentences known for their difficulty in articulation. Imagine having to say, "I fancy the first Frenchman fenced furiously," or "My weak words have struck but thus much show of fire."[8] A great deal of emphasis was given to deliberate structuring of nonverbal gestures. In 1893 a popular text on the *Practical Elements of Elocution* discussed the "law of pauses," which recommended 17 separate pause rules for students to use in their delivery. Even speakers' "elbows" were said to be important in expression.[9] One authority of the time set forth a remarkable "law of the feet"!

> The most natural position is for the weight of the body to rest mainly on one foot, the feet nearly at right angles and not wide apart nor touching each other. This gives the body such poise that the arm may be used with freedom of gesture, unity being preserved by employing the right hand in gesture when the weight of the body is on the right foot and changing the weight to the left foot when necessary to use the left arm.[10]

These early recommendations and drill procedures were designed to minimize annoying, nervous distractions that speakers often exhibit when they are tense. All such advice was preceded or followed, incidentally, by the (impossible) caution that gestures, emphasis, and voice should be "natural, not contrived"! The end result, unfortunately, was often a speaker who emerged as stiff as an oak board.

In contrast, today we teach public speaking as if it were an extension of *normal, everyday conversation.* We ask that speakers picture their audience as if they were talking one-on-one with each member. We jokingly refer to this approach as the "Mr. Rogers's method" of public speaking. On his syndicated television show for preschoolers, Mr. Rogers speaks directly to the camera and simulates an intensely personal relationship with the viewing child. The child becomes convinced quickly that Mr. Rogers exists on television just for her or him. This is a very good style for speaking before a group. All members of the audience can believe that you have a personal relationship with them. Once the audience members feel that you both share a special relationship, you can effectively proceed to influence, inform, or entertain.

Obviously, there is more to it than that. We know that public speaking isn't just a simple matter of conversing freely and openly with an audience. As will be seen, we still advocate the use of certain nonverbal behaviors. But to the extent that you can make your delivery *appear* as if you were casually interacting one-on-one with an entire audience, the more successful your effort will be. Therefore, let us turn to some basics of everyday conversation so as to demonstrate how to transform daily interactions into practiced, polished public speaking events. We can look briefly at three important issues—*"planned" spontaneity,* recognizing and interpreting *feedback,* and *role-taking* for the purpose of audience adaptation.

"Planned" Spontaneity

Our everyday conversations with others are usually unplanned and spontaneous. That is, they are not rehearsed ahead of time. We just talk—not thinking about some organized intent or agenda. Thus, we are natural, candid, and sincere. These are wonderful qualities with which to make a presentation before a group, and the importance of appearing to be spontaneous is well understood by the expert public speaker. Indeed, such speakers spend a great deal of time preparing their deliveries in an attempt to *look* as if they were speaking in a natural manner without self-consciousness.

Even though speaking before a group in a spontaneous way may seem natural, or at least easier, for some people than for others, we know that speaking skills are *learned.* No one is born either a "Great Communicator" or an inherently poor one. Furthermore, those skills can be learned by anyone. It is largely a matter of understanding what works and then learning to do it.

The first lesson is *planning.* In order to seem as though you are relaxed and spontaneous before an entire audience, you have to prepare for it fully well ahead of time. Such advice may appear to be incongruent. After all, how can we be both planned and spontaneous at the same time? You can't! However, you want to *appear* to be casual, relaxed, and unrehearsed before a group—to be at ease and in full command. This can be the case only if you have organized your message well, committed your main ideas and subpoints to memory, and practiced "looking" like the entire event is quite elementary—no problem at all! And, the fact is, when all of those steps have been taken, there really is nothing to be nervous about. As far as the audience is concerned, you are a competent speaker who with little or no anxiety can walk up to the podium, organize your thoughts, and deliver your presentation without slip or pause.

Recognizing and Responding to Audience Feedback

Our original linear and simultaneous transactions models of the human communication process, set forth in Chapter 1, provide the basis for a second critical skill. There, we discussed the importance to a source of *feedback* from the individuals who receive his or her messages. We elicit and receive an incredible amount of feedback during our everyday conversations with others. We watch their facial expressions and body movements in an effort to understand how well or poorly they are interpreting what we are transmitting. We also monitor verbal cues to assess how accurately we have communicated our points.

Obviously, the public speaking context does not allow for such open and free exchange between a presenter and each member of an audience. Most of the feedback received by public speakers takes the form of nonverbal communication, many features of which we reviewed extensively in Chapter 3. That is, in limited but visible ways, audience members express agreement or disagreement, approval or disapproval, and understanding or confusion during a speaker's delivery. They provide such feedback through facial displays, including yawns, smiles, and stares. They slump down in their chairs or press forward erectly. They occasionally raise their hands or interrupt; sometimes they turn away in silence; at other times their enthusiasm and interest is openly expressed in gestures. (For example, if they boo and hiss or throw tomatoes, this feedback suggests that the speaker has a problem!) All kidding aside, all experienced public speakers are able to read audience feedback with sensitivity.

The only way a speaker can effectively capture and interpret the more subtle nonverbal signals from the audience is to *look* for them. That seems obvious, yet this point is often the hardest to drive home to students of public speaking. No matter how logical and reasonable this advice sounds, novice speakers almost always try to *avoid* looking directly at anyone in the audience. Instead, they look up, down, around, and away—anywhere but directly at their audience. If they deliver their talk in this manner, and should they happen to glance accidentally at the audience, they are likely to see eyes glazing over.

Perhaps the best guideline is this: If members of the audience in your particular situation are (because of the prevailing social context) unlikely to interrupt, ask questions, or demand explanations, then you need to look at them especially closely and learn to read their more subtle nonverbal feedback cues. You need to be able to identify when they are confused, bored, surprised, excited, thoughtful, and/or convinced. Without that kind of feedback, it's difficult to know if you are communicating accurately.

More specifically, look at each and every individual audience member. Give eye contact. Scan the group, noting quickly what each person is wearing, who is in the back row, and what response you're getting from the center. Notice them as individual people. Try not to lump them all together as one big collective herd; instead, see them as unique participants in the event.

Finally, *acknowledge* them! That is, use what can be called "recognition strategies." Try to show every person that you recognize him or her—smile, nod, hold eye contact a moment, ask them their names and then use at least some of them. Any or all of these actions help to develop bonds with the audience. Before long, you and your audience will disregard the formality of the context and instead feel as though you are conversing naturally and openly.

Adapting to the Audience Through Collective Role-taking

Again, our models of human communication from Chapter 1 provide the basis for another skill that is important in public speaking. We pointed out that *role-taking* is an essential part of the communication process. In conversation we engage in role-taking in order to *adapt* what we are transmitting to receivers we are constantly assessing so as to maximize the chances that they will understand our intended meanings. We use feedback that the receivers provide to gain insights into ways we can modify our message or our delivery style so as to increase the level of accuracy with which they can reconstruct those meanings. Thus, role-taking and feedback are at the heart of the transactions of interactive communication.

In public speaking we cannot monitor each individual intensively. Therefore, the process of role-taking and adaptation to feedback are not the same as in one-on-one situations. Nevertheless, presenting a speech to an audience does involve *collective* counterparts of these same processes. The nonverbal cues coming from the audience as a whole tell us whether they are interested or bored, alert or lethargic. Seasoned speakers can easily determine whether an audience is already familiar with a point being

One effective mode of delivery in speaking before a group is to make it seem as though your remarks are unplanned and spontaneous. This requires that your speech has been well organized, with the main points, subpoints, and illustrations committed to memory. Speakers who are able to prepare in this manner appear to be casual, relaxed, and unrehearsed to their audience. This may be because they know their material so well that they really are at ease.

made, whether they did not understand an explanation, or generally whether the level of discourse needs to be revised upward or downward. This may not be easy for a beginning speaker, but it is important to be aware of the processes involved and to learn to assess audience behavior by collective role-taking and to adapt to the feedback they are providing.

Comparing everyday conversation with public speaking, then, provides us with valuable insights showing how formal presentations can be an extension of basic transactional communication in interpersonal interactions. Whether we are talking one-on-one with our friends or presenting a speech to an entire audience, we must keep in mind some of the essential communication principles that contribute to success in both contexts. Thus, formal speeches should appear as spontaneous and natural as casual conversations.

One of the key factors in effective delivery is continuous decoding of audience feedback. This is more difficult than interpreting feedback from a single individual in a one-on-one situation, but with nonverbal expressions, actions, and postures members of audiences show interest or boredom, approval or disapproval, and understanding or confusion. Any such feedback offers guidelines to the speaker that there may be need to adjust the delivery.

Selecting a Mode of Delivery

In an effort to converse effectively with an audience, we need to consider the appropriateness or inappropriateness of the different modes of delivery available to us. Specifically, we will examine the pros and cons of four such modes: *manuscript, memorized, impromptu,* and *extemporaneous.* The selection of which one to use in a particular occasion depends largely on the situation, the topic, and the speaker.

Reading from a Manuscript

The **manuscript** mode of delivery is the most popular presentational method among beginning speakers. The entire speech is written out beforehand and the speaker simply reads the speech aloud to the audience. The popularity of this method is based on the security it seems to provide. When reading from a prepared text, the speaker is unlikely to overlook any major point, to be at a loss for words, or to have to struggle to find the right phrase.

Furthermore, the manuscript can be used for other purposes. A text of a speech can be printed in an organization's newsletter or published in some other way.

The manuscript mode also has the advantage of completeness and precision. Facts and figures can be assembled and placed in the text where they are right at hand to be quoted. In more spontaneous modes of delivery, precision and completeness are often less possible. For example, numbers are especially hard to remember. Dates have to be approximated, and financial figures tend to become mere estimates. This can prove embarrassing. Imagine how would it look to a group of black citizens to hear from their mayor, in a spontaneous speech on civil rights, that Martin Luther King, Jr.'s, birthday is "sometime in January." Or what would be the credibility of a Defense Department budget expert, commenting spontaneously on expenditures for the coming fiscal year, who said that he thinks they are "somewhere in the millions, or maybe it's billions, of dollars"? In both cases, the manuscript delivery offers a more credible and convincing alternative.

However, despite the several advantages inherent in the manuscript mode of delivery, there are a number of

Reading a speech word-for-word from a manuscript is the most widely used mode of delivery among inexperienced speakers. This mode provides security for the speaker and ensures that every point of the speech is presented. However, if it is delivered in a monotonous manner, it can be very boring for the audience. With eyes focused on the manuscript, the speaker has no eye contact with the audience and can totally miss important nonverbal feedback.

drawbacks associated with this approach. These discourage most speakers from relying on it exclusively. For one thing, reading from a manuscript makes it difficult to approximate a natural conversation between the speaker and the audience. Even the most experienced speakers seem to read aloud in a way that differs from normal speech. For many people this becomes a kind of sing-song pattern. If that style of speech is used, audiences quickly get bored. Second, trying to read word-for-word from a text makes it difficult to look at the audience. In fact, when speakers do notice the people out front, they are sometimes startled; they lose their place, and even perceive the audience as a distraction. Third, attempts to gesture or move away from the podium are inhibited and awkward when you're holding onto a manuscript. Finally, a prepared text limits your ability to engage in role-taking to adapt to the audience even if feedback is abundant.

Thus, a manuscript delivery is like a train on a track. It goes along a fixed path, and chances for deviation are very limited or nonexistent. Above all, even planned spontaneity cannot be maintained. Questions from the audience are either ignored or perceived as interruptions. In other words, adequate role-taking, assessment of feedback, and effective audience adaptation rarely take place when a speaker chooses the manuscript mode.

Delivering a Memorized Speech

The memorized mode of delivery is the second most popular method for novice speakers, but it's also the most difficult. Stated bluntly, most experts warn speakers against memorizing their speeches for reasons we will explain. Even so, one student after another continues to try this approach. Almost always, they fail to deliver effectively.

The **memorized** mode requires that you write out the speech beforehand and practice it over and over again until the entire text is committed to rote memory. Obviously, this approach carries with it all the advantages associated with the manuscript mode. Perhaps the principal advantage memorizing has over reading a manuscript is that it allows the speaker to use gestures, to look at the audience, and to move around rather than remain before a podium.

The big disadvantage of the memorized mode is that few of us can commit an entire speech to memory. Even if you have the speech down perfectly at home in front of the mirror, the probability is high that your memory will fail in front of an actual audience. This is a constant source of worry that produces a great deal of anxiety. Unfortunately, if parts are forgotten, the whole effort tends to disintegrate. Trying to recover and remember major or minor points is problematic. Often, the only way to pick up the pace again is to recapture the exact next word in the memorized sequence. Because recalling just that word is unlikely, you may have to start the entire speech from the beginning, which is both embarrassing and a clear signal to the audience that you are depending on rote memory.

All too often memorized speeches sound exactly like what they are—memorized speeches. Like manuscript reading, the memorized mode often comes across as rhythmic and monotonous. In addition, speakers, anxious to get through the speech without a delay, tend to move rapidly through their lines at a speed that many in the audience are not able to follow. And finally, the memorized mode fails to allow for either feedback interpretation or effective role-taking for adaptation. Like reading a manuscript, it also resembles a train on an immovable track. A confused look from an audience member, a ripple of laughter, or a shudder of disgust may be overlooked in the interest of getting through the speech without interruption.

About the only situation in which the memorized mode may be appropriate is that of professional speakers who repeatedly perform standardized, stock addresses. Examples are politicians, certain management consultants, and evangelists. For them there is a considerable efficiency in committing a presentation to memory. They may have a number of such speeches ready to be summoned up as the occasion demands. By not worrying about content, these professionals can concentrate on their delivery. This can give the appearance of a fluent and polished speaker. Because they are evaluated primarily on the basis of their oratorical skills, these professional speakers often practice their use of gestures, vary their vocalic cues, and rehearse appropriate pause time for applause, laughter, or tears. They may even memorize applaudable or quotable phrases that predictably invite audiences to respond.

Impromptu Delivery

The third type is **impromptu delivery,** which is a speech that is delivered on the spot, with little or no lead time or formal preparation beforehand. This is, of course, what we all do in our everyday interactions with others. But even though it is our most common communication style in everyday life, it is dreaded by students in other contexts. They fear being called on in class to provide a brief overview of what has just been discussed, what their professor just said, or what the assigned readings covered. In the corporate world, too, employees and managers alike are often uneasy when asked to "brief" others on the problems they encountered or to explain the instructions required to assemble a product. In all of these cases, impromptu delivery is required.

You would think that with all the practice we have in delivering impromptu speeches in the form of everyday conversation, we would all be comfortable doing it by now. Unfortunately, when most people are asked to make impromptu remarks, they become inarticulate and suffer from an acute case of self-consciousness. Clearly, the luxury of having sufficient lead time to prepare a well-organized presentation far outweighs whatever benefits may be associated with impromptu speaking.

Extemporaneous Speaking

Most students in public speaking courses are required to deliver their speeches **extemporaneously**. This refers to making use of a well-organized, well-rehearsed speech outline, but not a complete text. In other words, instead of writing out the entire speech beforehand and reading or reciting it word-for-word, the extemporaneous speaker uses only an outline or notes as reminders of major points and issues. This does not mean that the preparation is any easier or less thorough. In Chapter 13 we discussed how to outline both a persuasive speech and an informative speech.

Rehearsing a speech from an outline produces a slightly different version every time it is practiced aloud. Yet it covers the same points in the same sequence and incorporates the same essential meanings. The examples may change; word usage and sentence structure will differ; and major and minor points may need to be extended or abbreviated. But the point is, the speech itself is not memorized or read. This provides a far less formal style of delivery, more closely approximating normal conversation. For many purposes this is a distinct advantage.

Perhaps the major disadvantage to the extemporaneous mode is that without a prepared text available to the press, "quotable quotes" may be overlooked and information may be distorted. Moreover, it's easier to make slips of the tongue, deviate from correct grammar, and fumble for words or phrases. Nevertheless, the advantages of the extemporaneous mode far outweigh any of these potential drawbacks.

Speaking extemporaneously enables you to gesture frequently and openly, elicit and maintain eye contact with the audience, and move freely around the stage or even among the audience. Not tied to a script and a podium, you are allowed to speak spontaneously and rely somewhat on your feelings as you go along. That is, it is much easier to make decisions. For instance, should you spend more time on this section? After all, feedback cues from the audience suggest that they are pretty interested right now. Should you skim over this next point—the audience appears to know all about this already. Role-taking adaptation suggests skipping it. Thus, speaking from an outline empowers you to adapt flexibly to audience feedback. And as long as you have your outline close by, you can deviate temporarily from what you were going to say and then return easily to your next point.

More than any other delivery mode, the extemporaneous approach is preferred by the audience. Audiences like speakers who apparently speak "off the cuff" and yet are sufficiently prepared to know where they are going and where they have been with their talk. Audiences like speakers who seem to converse naturally with them. They like knowing that they are not just another collection of bodies; instead, they are special enough for the speaker to acknowledge them as individuals. Without the restrictions of a prepared text, a speaker can comment on specifics associated with a particular audience. Their moods and responses can be recognized; confusion or boredom can be spotted easily; and laughter or tears can be rewarded. In short, the extemporaneous style allows the speaker to accommodate, adapt, and adjust to real people in the audience as he or she moves through the outline.

Five Ways to Establish Credibility

Regardless of the delivery mode that is used, how the audience perceives you as a speaker will have a good deal to do with your potential effectiveness. The interpretations they construct concerning your personal characteristics will determine whether they let you inform, persuade, or entertain them. Obviously, they do not have much time to develop their impressions, and they will do so on the basis of limited data. We reviewed the principles of effective self-presentation extensively in Chapter 9, and many are relevant to our present discussion of delivering a speech.

What is critical in delivering a speech is that the audience needs to find you highly *credible* if they are going to believe and be influenced by what you tell them. That principle is widely supported by research evidence.[11] When we discussed the concept of "source credibility" in Chapter 10, we saw that it refers to how much the audience feels that a speaker is *believable*. That is, it is a quality that receivers attribute to a speaker in a given set of circumstances. Thus, the degree to which credibility is imputed to any particular speaker can vary sharply from one person to the next. For one member of the audience, a given speaker may seem to be a totally reliable source of truth whose conclusions can be trusted. For another that same speaker may seem sleazy and untrustworthy. One of the real challenges facing every speaker, then, is to create an attribution of credibility from the majority of people in an audience.

In this section, we will examine some of the more obvious and subtle ways that credibility can be enhanced or significantly reduced. To do this we will examine five factors that are the basis of credibility: *competence*, *trustworthiness*, *composure*, *sociability*, and *extroversion*. Each is a dimension of the relationship that a speaker must establish with his or her audience in order to be judged in a positive way.[12]

Demonstrating Competence

The most important dimension of credibility for public speaking is perceived competence. Put simply, every audience demands that the speaker standing before them know more about the topic than they do. **Competence**, in the sense we are using the term, has little to do with intelligence. Instead, it refers to how much valid knowledge the speaker is perceived to command about the issue under discussion.

To be perceived as competent, the first prerequisite is to study and research as much about your subject as you can. A comprehensive background in the area requires that you exhaust the information available and then coherently and logically organize the relevant material essential for the content of your speech. In other words, you must have valid knowledge to offer. But even if you already know quite a bit about the area, you can still be perceived as incompetent. Sometimes speakers are guilty of creating such misperceptions of their own performances. In an effort to make the material interesting and themselves entertaining to their audience, they may make the material seem too easy. They simplify the information to the point of distortion and fail to address some of the more difficult, yet substantive issues. Several guidelines can help in avoiding this situation.

Using jargon   To be seen as competent, do not completely avoid the use of jargon. Use it, but use it sparingly. Even when defining a technical concept, make it sound jargonistic, but also make it clear. For example, speech communication experts often talk of the importance of establishing *homophily* with others. A good way to present such a term would be to go ahead and use the technical phrase "principle of homophily" but quickly add a clear definition. State that "homophily simply refers to attitude similarity, or how similar you and your partner perceive yourselves to be." Then add redundancy. For example, explain that "how much people are alike—how much homophily they share—will have a great impact on whether or not they continue with their relationship." Thus, using some jargon shows the audience that you know the scientific term. But, by defining and adding redundancy, you also demonstrate that you recognize they may not know the term, yet you give them credit for learning what it does mean quickly and easily.

Including oral footnotes   A second strategy in demonstrating your competence is to use "oral footnotes." In the previous chapter on preparation, we stressed the importance of relying on research evidence. Now that you have all of those wonderful sources and a storehouse of facts, you need to deliver some of them to the audience. Orally footnoting, that is, citing evidence in your speech, can increase your perceived competence and thereby your credibility. Use your evidence to support and verify your assertions. Use your references as testimony to show that other experts agree with your conclusions. Before long, audiences are likely to perceive you as one of those experts, too.

Admitting your ignorance   It is very important to admit ignorance when you don't know something. If an audience member asks a question and you don't know the answer, admit it! It is not clear why speakers often find this admission so difficult. Whatever the basis, it is

important to get over it. Audiences are very perceptive, and they can spot an evasion when they see one. The minute you try to sidestep the question, stonewall, or make up the data, they are likely to see right through you. If this happens, your entire presentation is discredited, even though you may have been in complete control of the facts until that point.

If you admit that you don't know the answer to a question, it can be helpful to add, "I'll find out for you and get back to you as soon as I can." Sometimes we do not know the answer because we're momentarily confused and unable to think of a response right away. Or perhaps our level of anxiety prevents us from thinking at all! When that happens, you might try asking the audience for their opinion: "I don't know offhand. Can anyone help us out?" Turning to the audience for input and support communicates to them that you give them credit too. At the same time, this strategy gives you a chance to get your own thoughts together. More often than not, an audience member will volunteer an opinion; in turn, that response will trigger an appropriate answer from you. An interesting side effect can occur when you occasionally admit to not knowing everything. That is, when you have already shown that you do know the facts pretty well, and have revealed them convincingly, the audience is prepared to believe you even more. In other words, admitting to a lack of expertise in one specific area can often increase perceptions of your competence in others.

Appearing to be competent   To make people believe that you are competent you have to "look" the part. We already know that people tend to be more impressed by the box than by the product. That may sound cynical, but the reality is that packaging is important. Faced with alternative soaps, soups, or sardines—all functionally equivalent—consumers are more likely to buy the ones that have the most attractive packages. Audiences, too, are more likely to be impressed with a well-dressed and well-groomed public speaker than one who is not. Our chapter on nonverbal communication discussed the implications of clothing and other artifacts that people use to send different types of messages. These may vary considerably from one audience to another, but the selection of the right combination that will signal competence to various kinds of audiences is an important aspect of delivery.

Arranging a socially validating introduction   Anybody who says, "This speaker needs no introduction," is dead wrong. Even the most prestigious speaker needs

Audiences can be very perceptive, and if it appears that a speaker doesn't know something when asked a question and is trying to bluff or evade the issue, credibility is lost and the entire presentation can be discredited. A far more effective way of handling situations of this kind is to be very open, admit your ignorance on the point being discussed, and offer to try to find answers for the person posing the question.

a well-organized introduction that testifies to his or her competence. Therefore, you should be introduced by someone who has competence in the topic or subject on which you will speak. When someone else tells the audience how great you are, they tend to be impressed. At the same time, you can afford to pretend that you are flattered and embarrassed. But if you try to tell the audience yourself how great you are, they will tend to be skeptical because in our culture people are not supposed to "blow their own horn." Your audience may conclude that you have a large ego! In both cases, the audience receives the same information, but when another person testifies to your credibility, it is a form of the "social construction of reality": The audience is more likely to accept socially validated expertise than self-proclaimed credentials.

To illustrate the point, you might think everyone knows that John Glenn was an astronaut in the early Apollo program, long before he was involved in politics. Yet many in an audience may recognize him only as a U.S. senator. If he was to speak on the space program, being a senator would not by itself provide him with credentials as a person competent in that area. The person introducing him should briefly summarize his accomplishments as an astronaut. Similarly, many people, even in his own city, may not realize that Tom Bradley was

the chief of police before he became mayor of Los Angeles. Without knowing his firsthand background in law enforcement, an audience might respond very differently to a Bradley speech on how to handle teenagers involved with gangs and drugs. A suitable introduction would testify to his competence in this area.

Speakers are usually introduced formally by an "emcee"—a master of ceremonies or host. Never just assume that your host will provide a suitable introduction that will establish your competence so as to enhance your overall credibility. She or he may not be familiar with your background or may not understand the importance of establishing speaker credibility. Consequently, *you must* supply that person with information about yourself (for which she or he will almost always be very grateful). You do not need a detailed life history. Just briefly list the most relevant issues from your background that will contribute to audience perceptions of your competence concerning the topic you will be addressing.

Generating Trust

Audiences appreciate speakers who seem **trustworthy**—that is, good, decent, and honest. After all, how can they interpret what you say as credible if they have little or no reason to believe you are an honest person? The prob-

One of the most effective ways of getting an audience to believe that you are competent in an area is to look and act the part. To do this, a speaker obviously must know something about the topic, but nonverbal communication can be very important in establishing the appearance of expertise. While the exact choices may vary considerably from one group and situation to another, the use of clothng, artifacts, grooming, and other nonverbal indicators can often make the difference.

lem is illustrated by the dilemma of the stereotyped car salesperson. They know that people do not trust them. National polls verify the fact that people rank the job of selling cars at the bottom of their list of honest professions. So, when a potential customer enters the dealer showroom, the salesperson can expect him or her to have serious misgivings as to trustworthiness. The first thing that such salespersons must do is to demonstrate openness and sincerity. Not until after they convince you of their own personal trustworthiness are you likely to believe that their sales pitch is credible.

What we suggest is that perceptions of trust, like those of competence, are *socially established* and validated. And as we have seen, in that process of social validation, it is the judgments of others that count, rather than objective facts about the person whose qualities are not yet clear.[13] For example, a speaker may be a rabbi or a priest, but even this objective fact may not be enough to bring all members of an audience to perceive that individual as trustworthy. Only when there seems to be consensus

among people whose judgment is respected that the individual is indeed trustworthy do most individuals believe that to be the case. Further, there are often ample grounds for withholding trust on the basis of objective facts alone. An example of a religious figure who illustrates the point is the former television evangelist Jim Bakker, who lied, stole, and committed adultery before he was prosecuted, found guilty, and sent to prison.

Once a relationship of trust is violated, it's very difficult to re-establish it. Trust is often the "bottom-line" for most long-term interpersonal relationships.[14] We require and expect our friends and family to be trustworthy. When they are not, we feel exposed and violated. Within the public speaking context, we similarly demand our speakers to be honest with us. Should we learn later that they lied to us, we often feel duped and misled.

How do public speakers generate perceptions of trust? The only advice we can give is to be consistently honest and sincere. Again, when you don't know the answer to a question, you should say so. If you try to fake an answer and are wrong (or the audience thinks you are wrong), they are likely to dismiss you as untrustworthy. If you are asked an embarrassing question and would rather not disclose the truth, it's better to avoid the question by responding, "That is rather personal; I'd rather not say," or "My personal views are irrelevant in this case." Then proceed quickly to the next issue.

Exhibiting Composure

A speaker who appears calm, cool, and collected before a large audience is easily admired by others. After all, every member of an audience can empathize with the perils of stage fright. Often, an audience anticipates that a speaker will be nervous, only to discover that is not the case and that he or she is perfectly capable of handling the situation. In such a situation, the audience is likely to regard the speaker with appreciation and respect. This is especially true when the speaker is supposed to be under a lot of pressure. Responding to a crisis with apparent confidence and control increases speaker credibility. Conversely, if the speaker is unable to control his or her fears and anxieties, the audience is likely to disregard what the individual has to say.

A good illustration of how a lack of composure can destroy credibility is provided by the case of a news broadcaster who was on the air during an earthquake in Whittier, California, in the fall of 1987. He was delivering his regularly scheduled program when the studio floor, the cameras, and the props all began to shake. Suspecting that this tremor was the forecasted "Big One" that would destroy all of Southern California (and make Nevada beach-front property), the newsman ducked under his desk—and remained there while the cameras stayed on! The poor man's nervousness and fear became objects of ridicule as one station after another replayed the scene during later broadcasts of the news. Realistically speaking, his response to the earthquake as an individual was entirely rational and appropriate. For a person in the role of a television anchor, however, audiences demand composure. His reaction under pressure failed to instill a sense of security or to provide much-needed assurance to an already frightened audience. Needless to say, the newsman's overall credibility suffered.

Maintaining composure can be difficult for inexperienced speakers, and even those who regularly engage in public speaking can have their composure disrupted. Hecklers in the audience can shake their confidence; people who stand up and leave during the middle of a pre-

sentation can rattle their nerves; and individuals who legitimately ask difficult questions can be a source of distress. Keep in mind that audiences *want* (and expect) you to maintain a sense of composure. Even during a difficult experience, they want to see you handle situations confidently.

You can appear self-assured (even when you're not) by being prepared. Once again, *know your material!* Next, *rehearse your presentation* over and over. Be careful to *omit* all "uhs, duhs, ums, you-knows," and other such fill-in grunts, words, or phrases. They really grate on an audience. Some listeners even count a speaker's overuse of distracting words or phrases. Instead of filling pauses with such utterances, just remain silent. Learn to appreciate silence during your presentations. We've all heard of "pregnant pauses"—brief periods of silence that can alert an audience that something of importance is to follow. Similarly, avoid nervous mannerisms. If you know that your hands begin to shake during a presentation, put them behind you for a minute; shift them to your side and then to your pockets; and finally, hold on to the podium or table.

Plan the use of purposeful but natural gestures. When you want to accentuate a point, do it like you would in an enthusiastic discussion with a friend—with a clenched fist or a dramatic sweep of your arm. However, it is important to vary your gestures. Punching the air in the same way, over and over again throughout an entire 10- or 15-minute presentation, is not likely to enhance your point. Your audience will see it as boring. Avoid dancing and pacing across the stage. When you want to speak directly to one side of the audience, walk over there, stop, and do it. After a few moments, return to center stage. Then, after a bit, walk to the other side and do the same. Too much pacing and fidgeting connotes nervousness and tension. Little or no movement at all can communicate a lack of composure as well; it can also suggest disinterest or apathy.

Composure does not just happen. A good speaker practices looking relaxed and confident. Give the audience eye contact; smile as though you are enjoying the experience. Slow down your speech rate from time to time, speaking deliberately and with conviction. Avoid the use of nervous gestures—what we called "adaptors," such as scratching your head, swinging your arms back and forth, picking lint off your jacket, twirling your hair, or fiddling with your glasses (see Chapter 3). Instead, use purposeful hand and arm movements that you would normally use in talking with friends to help you emphasize or clarify an issue. The whole point is to *look* confident. The best possible way to do this is to express confidence by your actions.

Communicating Sociability

Audiences greatly prefer speakers who appear to be friendly and warm. Perceptions of sociability are based on how congenial a person seems to be. When an audience finds the speaker likable, they are more willing to listen and to give him or her the benefit of the doubt. A good example is the presumed sociability ratings of former President Ronald Reagan. Even his political enemies had to admit that Mr. Reagan was a "likable guy." Congressional leaders quarreled bitterly over his policy issues on the floor of the House, but socially, they were able to appreciate and enjoy his company. As for the American public, they may not have always agreed with the president politically, or even thought he was all that sharp, but almost everyone believed he was a very nice man who was sincere and doing the best he could! For that reason, they listened.

Sociability, therefore, has the power to override or, at least, soften the blow of potentially alienating or disagreeable qualities. In other words, bad news is easier to take when the carrier is well intentioned, affectionate, and sincere. The point is well illustrated by the reverse: How likely would you be to work longer hours or willingly take a cut in pay from a boss who is cold, distant, and offensive? Wouldn't you be more likely to oblige when the source is apparently affable, pleasant, and good-natured? Whether a source seems sociable or not, then, can make a big difference.

As a public speaker, you will need to make every effort to appear sociable. Unfortunately, the "stage" often interferes with our good intentions. That is, how friendly can a speaker appear to be when almost hidden from the audience by a table or podium? How accessible can a speaker appear to be under bright lights, tied to a stationary microphone? Even worse, how endearing or likable can a speaker be who appears to be suffering from stage fright, forgets major points, sweats, and begins to develop red welts on the neck? Despite these potential obstacles, we need to recognize that audiences prefer their speakers to be sociable. Without such perceptions, speaker credibility can be seriously affected.

Communicating sociability to a group requires that you rely heavily on *nonverbal immediacy*. This idea was discussed at length in our chapter on nonverbal communication, and we will go into it more thoroughly later in this chapter. Essentially, it refers to perceptions of physical or psychological "closeness" based on nonverbal cues. We saw that some of the more relevant nonverbal behaviors contributing to those perceptions include eye contact, smiling, head-nodding, and decreased distance. These same cues may also contribute to audience assessment of the speaker in the public speaking arena. That is, a relaxed, comfortable posture coupled with a genuine, warm smile and frequent eye contact can communicate both composure and sociability. Consequently, some of the same strategies that can be used to show poise and confidence can also be used to demonstrate likability and friendliness.

Referring to the audience in some familiar or intimate way may affect their perceptions of your sociability. We know, for instance, that people appreciate it when you are able to remember and use their names. Similarly, audiences warm to speakers who make a point of saying something nice about their geographic location, history, or culture. In other words, they want to be sure that the speaker recognizes the uniqueness, the "specialness" of their particular group. An example of this technique can be seen in the speaking style used by Willard Scott, the weather man on the "Today" show. No matter from where in the country he is bringing us his national weather summary, he is apt to comment favorably on some local feature. It may be a good restaurant located in White Sulphur Springs, West Virginia, or the quality of the good folks he discovered living in Chenoa, Illinois. He may not always deliver a very good weather report, but clearly, no one questions Willard's sociability!

Displaying Extroversion

A personality characteristic somewhat similar to sociability is **extroversion,** which refers to the degree to which someone is "outgoing," that is, people-oriented, talkative, and gregarious. People low in communication apprehension (who do not seem nervous or anxious) are often perceived as extroverted. Conversely, shy individuals, those who are highly apprehensive about communicating, are generally believed to be *introverted*. As we indicated in the chapter on overcoming shyness and apprehension, typically negative attributes are associated with people who are high in apprehension, whereas positive qualities are often assigned to those who are low. Similarly, introverts are often thought (incorrectly) to be purposefully withdrawn, detached, and uninterested in others. People tend to assign low credibility to introverts because they are quiet and often withhold information from others. People who don't know them personally tend to doubt their basic intelligence and even question their trustworthiness.

On the other hand, extroverts talk a lot. Consequently, they reveal a great deal about themselves. They let people know how they think to a much greater degree than do introverts. Rather than assume incompetence or put ourselves on guard with extroverts, we give them the opportunity to demonstrate their credibility. Thus, we judge or weigh their credibility by what they say, as opposed to what they don't say. In a public speaking situation, extroverted speakers have a clear advantage. After all, the audience is captive, willing, and ready to let the speaker have their full attention. The introvert, by comparison, has some disadvantages. It is rare to find an introvert who is eager and anxious to talk in front of an audience. This reluctance is often seen to be a sign of low credibility and low trustworthiness.

There is a kind of "catch 22" here. If you are highly apprehensive about taking to the podium for the first (or hundredth) time, an audience may perceive you as introverted. In that situation, you can "act like" an extrovert. Expand your gestures by extending your arms. It will seem to enlarge your whole being. Despite your fears, you need to show enthusiasm, energy, and dynamism. Once again, you should smile, look directly at each audience member, walk up to people in the audience, and by all means, keep talking! What will happen is that the audience quickly relaxes and accepts you. Then you feel much more confident. When that happens, your credibility is on the way up.

We have spent a great deal of space going over a number of ways to enhance each of the five dimensions of speaker credibility. We have given these issues special attention for two reasons: First, we know that credibility is an important predictor of success as a public speaker. Second, we know that most speakers do not understand what they can do to get an audience to consider them credible.

We cannot leave this discussion of speaker credibility without a word of caution. Just as a speaker can be perceived as displaying too little competence, trustworthiness, composure, sociability, and extroversion, she or he can also be perceived as "showcasing" too much. Audiences who perceive the speaker as having too little or too much of any of the five dimensions can cause his or her credibility to suffer. A quick overview of each dimension will make this point clear. A speaker can use too much jargon, dress too formally for the event, pomp-

ously refer to a long list of books she or he has written, and talk "above" audience members. The end result is that the person is seen as *too* competent!

But what about being seen as too trustworthy? At first glance, we might conclude that no one can ever be perceived as too honest, but it is difficult to say. For example, audiences are sometimes embarrassed by personal disclosures that are intended to display honesty but which only show the speaker in a negative light. Confessing an indiscretion, a health condition, or some other situation, may be ill-advised. Unless they are highly relevant to the topic and strategy of the speech, some matters are better left undisclosed or, at the very least, revealed tactfully and graciously.

As for composure, a speaker who sprawls across a table, sits down in front of the audience, leans against a backdrop, never gets excited or rattled even when insulted, will lose credibility. Being too friendly, smiling constantly and inappropriately, and being too willing to agree with patently unfair audience dissension, may do as much if not more damage to credibility than being too unsociable.

Finally, there certainly is a case to be made against too much extroversion. No one likes a "ratchet-mouthed" speaker who demands center stage, draws constant attention to himself or herself, and blabs on and on. Such a person may be labeled a terrible bore rather than a great talker.

Performing the Speech: Beginnings, Middles, and Endings

As we explained in Chapter 12, the beginning and the end of the speech have similar content and in some ways similar purposes: The beginning previews what you're going to say, and the last section summarizes what you just said. Both are intended to stimulate audience enthusiasm and generate interest toward the content or body of your speech. The introduction should pique their curiosity and capture their attention. The conclusion should leave them wishing you would go on another hour! Beginnings and endings, then, are designed to arouse anticipation, interest, and approval on the part of the audience. Given these similar functions, we can expect some of the same techniques to work for both introductions and conclusions. As we will see, that is indeed the case.

A speech is like a three-act play. You are the playwright; the production has just one role; and you are the only actor. Your play will be presented in three acts, and your audience will respond differently in each. In the first act, your audience forms its initial impressions about you and how well you are going to be able to deliver what you promise. In the second act, the body of the speech is presented. Since it is much longer and covers far more information, techniques and tactics are needed to keep the audience interested and enthusiastic during the entire segment. Finally, the third act provides the wind-up—the punch line, the unforgettable ending. For each stage, we will offer a number of specific guidelines and recommendations that can be of great help.

The production of your play begins when the audience-to-be becomes aware of who the speaker will be and what the speech will be about. Such information is typically available through media reports, speech introductions, or even word-of-mouth. Therefore, as the speaker, you have an important stake in what kind of information is available to your audience prior to your actual presentation. Professional speakers handle this by disseminating "pre-game" information in the form of pamphlets, posters, and press releases—all of which are designed to entice the audience to attend.

Act I: Managing Initial Impressions

Once the occasion arrives and the audience is in place, a host or "emcee" should provide some opening remarks. We've already talked about the importance of the introduction. The audience needs to hear from a reliable source the speaker's credentials. Effective speeches of introduction validate the speaker's credibility, especially in the area of competence. Moreover, such introductions should arouse audience interest in the speech topic itself.

From then on, building and maintaining success with the audience depends entirely and directly on *you*. Overriding any advantages gained in the advertising or in the speech of introduction is the "package" in which you present yourself and your wares. Audience members are able to see you as a physical object as soon as you leave your chair and walk to center stage. All eyes are on you, and your audience is assessing what they see. It is a dramatic moment! What you communicate nonverbally during those first few seconds on stage can have a major impact on the audience's collective perception of your credibility.

An illustration of what should *not* happen during this brief period is provided by the experience of one of the authors of this text during a presentation she made before a professional group in Portland, Oregon. She was seated at the front table with four other persons waiting for her turn to speak, making every effort to suppress any visible sign of her very real stage fright. Finally, it was her turn to speak and her name was announced. She carefully stacked her note cards, pushed her chair away from the table, and began approaching the podium. All of a sudden there was a loud crash behind her. The folding, metal chair she had been sitting on had collapsed on the tile floor.

Confusion reigned! Everyone scrambled to be helpful and righted the chair. Eventually, but what seemed like hours later, the commotion ceased. Now at the podium, she could get on with her presentation. However, before she could speak her first line, she was told to adjust the microphone. Immediately, she discovered that the microphone had a life of its own. It refused to stay attached to the podium and fell to the table. After bouncing at least three times it ultimately came to rest on the floor in front. Needless to say, those first few agonizing moments did little to provide the audience with a positive initial impression!

Ideally, those first few seconds should have gone something like this: The speaker's name is announced and she nods and smiles at the audience. While doing so she gathers her materials inconspicuously and gets up gracefully. Dressed immaculately in subdued professional attire, she walks confidently to the podium, looking at all segments of the audience and smiling broadly. Setting her materials down, she moves a bit away from the podium and, after waiting just a moment to build a little suspense, she begins her presentation. From the beginning, her audience is with her. In fact, it almost always works that way, and one should not be concerned that a total disaster will take place or that the entrance will resemble a Laurel and Hardy slapstick.

As suggested earlier, we begin to set the stage with what we wear, and clothing sends powerful messages. Even if we feel that our physical appearance should have little or nothing to do with who we really are, we have to face the fact that first impressions are often based almost exclusively on how we look. We know, for instance, that dressing neatly in a professional style connotes meanings of credibility. Being well groomed shows that you made an effort to look "good" for the occasion. Even without thinking about it consciously, members of an audience sense the time and trouble you take to present the best possible you.

There are other ways to look good as well. Earlier in this chapter we discussed the importance of appearing composed and poised, especially when the situation is tension-producing. Your audience will be looking for signs of apprehension. They want to feel comfortable knowing that you can handle the situation easily and confidently. Looking composed, then, is critical to impression formation. As we noted, the more apparent signs of looking relaxed include smiling, head-nodding, leaning back, prolonged eye contact, and slow, deliberate movements. Concentrate on those behaviors before getting up to give your presentation. And then, once on stage and in place to deliver your opening line, pause for more than a moment. Look out at your audience. Sweep your eyes across the room, but be sure to take notice of actual faces in the audience. See them as individuals. Smile, nod, and say hello. Then, and only then, are you ready to proceed.

Without taking your eyes off the audience, even for a second, deliver your opening line—slowly, deliberately, confidently. Then deliver the rest of your opening. Tell your dramatic story, recite the perfect quotation, or recount the joke you practiced beforehand. Make every effort to relish those first few minutes of your presentation. Act as though this particular audience is eager to catch every word, every phrase, every nuance of your speech. Expect them to be aroused, rather than bored, by your presence. Assume that they will laugh, rather than groan, at your humor. Feel certain that they will appreciate, rather than discredit, what you have to say. When you expect the audience to be supportive and agreeable, you stand a much better chance of making that happen.

We cannot emphasize enough the importance of physical appearance, of nonverbal behaviors, and of delivery skills that initiate and reinforce the audience's first impressions of you as the speaker. You must carefully plan your attempts to lure the audience into paying close attention to what you have to offer. The time and energy you exert "packaging" yourself and your talk will pay off in audience response. You need to prepare the audience for an exciting, stimulating presentation. Thus, Act I, Managing Initial Impressions, can go a long way toward positioning yourself from the outset as reputable and worthy of audience attention.

Act II: Strategies to Keep the Plot from "Sagging"

Even speeches with great beginnings and wonderful endings can suffer somewhere in the middle. Speech experts Paul Nelson and Judy Pearson refer to this in-between lag as the "mid-speech sag"![15] Somehow the plot or storyline of the speech begins to drag. What is supposed to be the best part of the presentation gets bogged down in facts, data, statistics, examples, and references. These can bore even the most expectant and engaged audience member.

Too often, as Act II begins, audiences tend to settle in, lean back, mentally put their feet up and cross their arms. Then their eyes start to glaze over. If the speech is not lively and interesting they will remain semicomatose until they recognize the signs of an emerging conclusion (i.e., that longed-for phrase: "In conclusion" or "I've kept you long enough."). At that point a disinterested audience begins to look alive again, changing position and readying themselves for leave-taking. It is essential that steps be taken to avoid this "sagging middle." We suggest six specific strategies for doing this plus an additional one in case someone decides to be a heckler.

Making the plot more interesting   As repeatedly emphasized, it is important to make your topic interesting to your audience. We suggested a number of ways to do this in Chapter 13 (pp. 374–375). This is the best way to keep the plot from "sagging," and that is why we have given so much emphasis to planning. The content of your speech should be interesting and relevant to the audience's needs and interests. We recommend that during the planning stage you always keep your audience in mind when determining what points to make, what evidence to employ, and what issues are most appropriate. Here, your initial assessments of your audience pay off. In other words, you need to anticipate: "What does my audience need? What is important and meaningful to them?" Besides selecting information that is significant and related to your particular audience's needs and concerns, we also offer some additional suggestions on your mid-speech delivery or approach.

Using redundancy and repetition   Both redundancy and repetition contribute significantly to audience levels of attention and retention (Chapter 13, pp. 382–383).[16] Sometimes we forget that audiences are exposed to the words of the speech only one time. They don't have the advantage of hearing you practice the speech over and over again. Nor do they have the advantage of rereading certain portions of the speech they didn't hear or understand as you presented them. Finally, audience members are reluctant generally to interrupt or ask questions when they require clarification or forget an earlier point. Consequently, a speaker must build into the message both redundancy and repetition to help the audience keep track of and remember salient points and conclusions.

Signaling transitions and signposts   Similarly, transitions and signposts steer the audience in the direction you're heading so that they can anticipate what is coming. These are what speech communication specialists call rhetorical devices or stylistic expressions that provide "bridges"—follow-ups from former points and lead-ins to future ones. For instance, you may want to employ a transition when it's time to leave your first major point by showing how it relates to the next. To illustrate a transition, suppose your talk is about global warming and you have just discussed its implications for the future. Now you want to move to another major issue: its implications for the present generation. The transition might be made by saying: "Not only do we need to be alarmed with the evidence that global warming is a concern to future generations [first major point], we should be equally disturbed with the facts which suggest that global warming is an immediate concern to our own generation [second major point]." Such transitions provide the audience with a sense of smoothness and continuity between the parts of your presentation.

Signposts serve a different purpose. They are used to signal issue changes so that the audience knows what is coming. They act like oral paragraph headings within the text of your speech. The most commonly used signposts are numerical: "First, I'll define global warming for you. Second, I'll share with you the long-term hazards associated with global warming. And third, we'll look at some of the more immediate, short-term effects of this atmospheric condition." Other signposts include such familiar words or phrases as *next, at last, finally, in conclusion, subsequently, in closing,* and *following.* They help an audience follow your organization, so don't be reluctant to use signposts even if they seem trite and ordinary.

Using vocalics effectively   The most certain way to elicit and maintain audience attention is by adding variety to the way you use your *voice.* We have all listened to speakers who appear bored with their own presentation. They talk on and on endlessly, without any variation in their vocal quality, delivering their speech in a dull monotone. This type of delivery decreases audience attention and reduces what an audience remembers from a presentation. A number of studies demonstrate that monotone delivery interferes with audience comprehension and later recall of the information.[17]

Audiences also prefer speakers to vary their speech *rate.* In all likelihood, you have been told to "slow down" when talking before a large group. This is good advice, but sometimes it will be advisable to alternatively speed up and slow down your rate of speech. We know, for instance, that listeners are able to process information much more quickly than we are able to speak. Despite what we might guess, research indicates that faster rates of speech tend to increase, rather than decrease, listener comprehension and recall.[18] One problem of maintaining a slow or normal speech delivery rate throughout is that listeners tend to drift in and out in their attention to the presentation. Varying your speech rate will keep them alert and help them to stay in tune with your talk. Practice slower rates to use during your introductory and closing remarks. You might also reduce your speech rate when you want to emphasize or reinforce a main point. Otherwise, you should resume a normal speed or shift to a faster rate of speech in an effort to keep audience attention and promote recall.

Silence or *pause time* is another strategy that can be used to affect audience attention. A pregnant pause used before or after a phrase or line can add special meaning and emphasis to your message. Many new speakers find pause time very awkward and, as a result, often fill it with "uhs," "duhs," and "you-knows." When filled pauses are used, composure is adversely affected. As explained earlier, we have to learn to be comfortable with silence and use it to our advantage.

Stimulating interest with oculesics   Eye contact acts as a powerful stimulus for eliciting audience involvement in a presentation. We stressed its importance earlier, and as Chapter 3, on nonverbal communication, indicates, eye contact functions to increase involvement or arousal in all forms of communication exchange.[19] Consequently, the more you look at your audience while you talk, the more likely your audience will stay interested and attentive. It is very difficult for audience members to avoid a speaker who seems to be looking directly at them. Eye contact generally obligates a person to do something in return. More specifically, in the case of public speaking, audience response usually takes the form of nonverbal head-nodding, smiling, and reciprocated eye contact.

Employing gestures and actions to hold attention   A nonverbal form that can function either to distract or to enhance a presentation is *gestures.* When a speaker uses gestures that are "adaptors," such as pulling at a beard, smoothing the sleeve of a coat, or adjusting and readjusting eyeglasses, the audience assumes the speaker is nervous and unprepared. However, when that same speaker uses gestures that are "illustrators," intentionally designed to emphasize or demonstrate what is being said, the audience perceives the speaker to be decisive and committed. We often use illustrators in our normal, everyday conversations with others. We point to give directions; we hold up fingers to count aloud; we draw pictures to show size and shape.

On stage, these same illustrators can be effective, but you will need to exaggerate them. At first, you may find exaggerated illustrators awkward and unnatural. But in front of a large group, illustrators will go unnoticed unless you swing your arm wide, raise your hand high, and emphatically pound your fist in the air. Even gestures that are "bigger than life" will not appear peculiar and cumbersome to audience members in the fifth, tenth, or one hundredth row.

Finally (note the "signpost"), *overall body movement* can make a difference in how attentive or bored an audience will be. A speaker who strides confidently toward the podium to begin a speech is likely to come across as more committed and enthusiastic than one who shuffles along. A speaker who walks first to one side of the room, speaks directly to the group, and then walks purposefully to the other side will be perceived as friendlier and more open than one who paces nervously or wanders aimlessly. You can also signal your interest and involvement in your message with *posture*. Leaning forward into the audience can communicate concern and intensity toward the more meaningful, relevant issues that you present. Direct, face-to-face body posture also suggests active interaction and a sense of inclusion or belonging to the group.[20] Clearly, overall body movements help keep the audience attentive and involved in your presentation.

One way to gain and hold the attention and interest of an audience is through the use of gestures that serve as "illustrators." Using dramatic illustrators, if chosen carefully, can make a speaker seem dynamic, decisive, and committed. Many experts maintain that even "larger than life" gestures, such as raising the hands high or pounding the podium vigorously to illustrate a point, will appear quite normal to an audience and will add an important dimension to the speaker's presentation.

Learning to handle hecklers   Some forms of audience attention can pose serious difficulties. A speaker's worst nightmare is a handful of hecklers in an audience who are determined to disrupt the speech event itself and make the speaker look bad. It is natural to lose composure and attempt to fight back. The best advice we can give, but the hardest to take, is to simply *ignore hecklers*. By responding to their outcries and criticisms, you will end up giving them credibility and their message substance.

When your patience wears thin and their momentum continues to swell, however, you may find yourself in an awkward position: On the one hand, you cannot continue to talk and still be heard over their protests, and on the other, to respond to their objections is likely to give them credence they don't deserve. So, what do you do? We recommend that you begin by responding briefly and sincerely to the heckler's concern and then use a transition to get back into the text of your performance. You should not assume that the individual will be satisfied; however, you might assume that the rest of the audience is. Consequently, next you need to rely heavily on nonverbal behaviors of dismissal. That is, gradually walk

over in the direction of the heckler while continuing to talk. If it is physically possible, put your hand on the back of his or her chair. However, *do not give that person eye contact!* (The minute you do so, the individual will seize the opportunity to interrupt.) Instead, purposefully look away in the direction of the audience that continues to support you. And, above all, keep talking!

The middle stage of a speech, then, requires special consideration to avoid the pitfalls of mid-speech sag. Whatever the reason, speeches that get bogged down mid-stream can frustrate audience acceptance of your message. Whether your purpose is to inform, entertain, or persuade, you must systematically implement those verbal and nonverbal skills that will keep your audience attentive and responsive. However, Act II need not be a problem. Holding attention and preventing boredom can be achieved by selecting information that is relevant to your audience, being somewhat redundant and repetitious, inserting transitions and signposts, varying vocal rate, pitch, and volume, making effective use of pause time, maintaining eye contact, relying on purposeful ges-

Every speaker fears that some heckler will disrupt his or her speech and ruin the presentation. Experts maintain that the most effective strategy for handling such interruptions is simply to ignore them, neither giving hecklers eye contact nor answering their questions or demands. Responding to their statements or charges merely gives them credibility. Ignoring them defines them as out of order, and the audience who came to hear the speech, not hecklers, probably will turn on them and demand that they desist.

tures, and controlling overall body movement. All of these techniques will contribute to an exciting, dynamic, open, and attentive speaking style.

Act III: The Famous Final Scene

Besides summarizing the main points of your speech, the conclusion should leave the audience *wanting more*. In order to achieve that goal, you need to conclude with what in Chapter 13 we called a "Gee whiz!" ending. In other words, ideally you want your speech to be memorable, and your final scene as dramatic as you can make it. This is especially important when other speakers are yet to follow. You want your ending to stand out from all the others. Even after your audience members have gone home, you still want them to remember you and your

message. In chapter 13, we considered some strategies to do just that. For instance, we recommended employing closing lines that hook up with your opening remarks in a clever way, relying on a famous, relevant quotation, or relating a dramatic story. The point is illustrated by the following example:

Several years ago a student, "Julia," delivered a "famous final scene" that remains memorable even today. Her speech was on the state lottery system. She talked about lottery winners; how much money they generally won and sometimes lost; how a number of winners squandered their money and eventually lost even their cars and homes. Julia had the facts and explained how family, friends, neighbors, and even strangers came to the winners begging for and demanding handouts. After reviewing a number of actual cases supporting her contention that sudden money can bring lottery winners a great deal of unexpected sorrow and grief from jealous and greedy family, friends, and neighbors, Julia concluded with this startling disclosure: "Two and a half months ago my husband and I became lottery winners ourselves. After much thought, we decided to keep it secret from our family and friends. We hate the deception, but we love our friends and relatives more." It was an astounding admission that brought her point home.

She provided a wonderful illustration of how to end a speech. For one thing, she made very effective use of pause time. She also dropped her voice volume. She spoke so softly that the audience leaned forward in their efforts to hear each and every word. And they weren't disappointed. As soon as she announced that she, herself, was a lottery winner, the audience began to buzz: "When was that?" "How much did she say she won?" "She doesn't look like a millionaire!" And so she waited. She waited until they became silent and attentive again. Just when they thought she was wrapping up, she astonished them once more with her second revelation. Anticipating another audience hum, she paused again, looked around the room, and finally delivered her exit line. She was hiding this information from her relatives and friends! Seemingly unperturbed by audience reaction, she calmly walked away from the podium. Julia's message, both verbal and nonverbal, gave the audience much to think about. She succeeded in making us all appreciate and remember her "good fortune."

Unfortunately, few of us are likely to win big in the lottery. But whatever device you choose to end your speech, *how* you present your conclusion should be given special consideration. As soon as your brief review or summary is delivered, it's time to move away from your notes or manuscript. If you must, memorize your final

Chapter 14 Speaking Before a Group 417

remarks. Once again, to elicit maximum audience attention, stop and pause for a few moments—and look carefully around the room. Then shift your talking rate into "slow" and deliver your final story, joke, quotation, or illustration, which should be designed in such a way that when you're done it is very clear you have reached the end. You need not tell your audience that you have finished—they should understand it fully. Save everyone from cute gestures and trite endings like a Porky Pig, "That's all, Folks!" Instead, slowly and deliberately pick up your materials and walk casually back to your chair or offstage. However, be prepared to acknowledge applause! If it comes, smile broadly, nod, lean, thank the audience, and leave.

In our next and final section (notice that transition) we look at a set of issues that both summarize and group together much of what we have presented in this chapter. The main idea we will use is the concept of *immediacy,* which was developed at length in Chapter 3, on non-verbal communication.

Enhancing Immediacy

We started off this chapter by talking about public speaking as extended conversation. Along that line, we maintained that to the extent you can make a preplanned, well-organized speech resemble everyday conversation, the greater your chances will be for success—for establishing a personal, one-on-one relationship with each individual in that audience. We reasoned that the "Mr. Rogers" approach encourages the audience to feel unique, to feel a special tie to you as a speaker. When an interpersonal relationship seems to exist between you and individual listeners, you stand a better chance of informing, entertaining, and persuading your audience.

Immediacy, as we defined it, refers to physical or psychological closeness.[21] That is, people who engage in behaviors that show warmth, friendliness, and liking are exhibiting immediacy. Conversely, those who behave in ways that seem cold, distant, and aloof are doing the opposite. Research on immediacy in interpersonal relationships demonstrates that immediacy generally begets immediacy. That is, people tend to respond in kind. For instance, we know that it's hard to stay mad at someone who hugs us and smiles warmly. By the same token, we are unlikely to want to spend a lot of time with a person who ignores us or frowns and mutters whenever we're around.

We also learned in Chapter 3 that immediacy gener-ates *liking.* We are easily attracted to those who appreciate us, approve of us, and enjoy our company. In other words, we like people who like us. This principle has important implications for public speaking. If you, as a speaker, engage in behaviors that communicate immediacy, your audience is likely to mirror such behaviors back to you. And, since we know that immediacy connotes liking, both you and your audience will believe the feeling is mutual. They will care about you as a person because you care about them.

A major problem is how to establish immediacy with your audience. In the context of public speaking, it's not easy to engage in immediacy behaviors that transmit messages of closeness. During formal speech events, it's seldom either appropriate or even physically possible to touch members of the audience. Nevertheless, there are a number of techniques you can use that will reduce the psychological distance between you and members of your audience.

In the previous sections, a number of nonverbal behaviors were reviewed that contribute to perceptions of immediacy or liking. We mentioned direct eye contact, head-nodding, smiling, forward body-leaning, vocal variety, and relaxed body posture or position.[22] In addition, certain *verbal* behaviors can affect the amount of immediacy your audience will perceive. Anytime you transform the words *I* and *you* to *we* and *us,* you're engaging in verbal behaviors of approach.[23] People tend to feel closer to, and potentially have a greater sense of commitment to, someone who suggests that "*we* need to work together on this" than to someone who states that "*you* should work on this." The former implies a sense of connectedness and association, whereas the latter insinuates detachment or estrangement.

Another verbal strategy to increase perceptions of immediacy with your audience is to elicit their *feedback,* whether it's verbal or nonverbal.[24] People like to know that you're interested in them personally and in what they are thinking or how they are feeling. You might say, "I'd like to hear your opinion about this. What do you think?" Then wait for their feedback. When someones does interrupt in order to volunteer an opinion or ask a question, be sure to follow through with encouraging comments, such as, "Good idea. I wish I had said that!" or "That's exactly what I mean; you're right on target." Of course, when an individual's comment is a little off or misses the point entirely, you may have to be more creative. For example, you can try, "You know, you may be right; I really hadn't thought about it that way." Or, "No question about it, you have a point. But before we can tackle that issue, let me finish here and I'll get back to you."

Nonverbal Immediacy Behaviors (IMM)

Instructions Below are a series of descriptions of things some public speakers have been observed doing during some of their presentations. For each item, please indicate on a scale of 1–5 how likely you would be to engage in each of the following nonverbal behaviors while presenting your own speeches or talks before a large group. Use the following scale:

5 extremely likely   **2** unlikely
4 likely   **1** extremely unlikely
3 maybe/unsure

_____ **1.** I would sit behind a table or desk while speaking.

_____ **2.** I would use a lot of purposeful gestures while talking to the group.

_____ **3.** I would use a monotone/dull voice when talking to an audience.

_____ **4.** I would look directly at my audience while presenting.

_____ **5.** I would smile at the group while talking.

_____ **6.** My entire body would feel tense and rigid while giving my speech.

_____ **7.** I would approach or stand beside individual audience members.

_____ **8.** I would move around the room while speaking.

_____ **9.** I would avoid looking at individual audience members during my speech.

_____ **10.** I would look at my notes frequently during my presentation.

_____ **11.** I would stand behind a podium or desk while giving my speech.

_____ **12.** I would have a very relaxed body position while talking to the group.

_____ **13.** I would smile at individual members in the audience.

_____ **14.** I would use a variety of vocal expressions while talking.

_____ **15.** I would engage in a lot of nervous gestures or body movements, such as wrinkling my note cards or switching my weight from one foot to the next.

Calculating Your Score

1. Add your responses to items 1, 3, 6, 9, 10, 11, and 15 = _____.

2. Add your responses to items 2, 4, 5, 7, 8, 12, 13, and 14 = _____.

3. Complete the following formula:

IMM = 42 − total from step 1 = _____

Then, + total from step 2.

YOUR TOTAL SCORE = _____

Interpreting Your Score

Possible range of scores for IMM (nonverbal immediacy): 15–75. (If your own final IMM score does not fall within that range, you made a computational error.)

The average or midpoint for the IMM is around 45. If your own score falls above 50 (or above the median of 45), you are a public speaker who is high in nonverbal immediacy. Speakers who practice immediacy behaviors during their presentation are perceived as more credible, attractive, sharing similar attitudes with the audience, and overall, they are thought of as more approachable and likable. Audience members enjoy immediate speakers and are more likely to be attentive to what these speakers have to say. In addition, audience members are likely to find immediate speakers as highly motivating.

If your score falls below 40 (or below the median of 45), you might want to learn and practice the specific immediacy behaviors reflected in the items from step 2. Without engaging in immediacy behaviors (i.e., low in nonverbal immediacy), you can expect audience members to yawn and fade from your presentation; encourage you to finish early; and hope that you don't take up speaking, lecturing, or teaching as a career! Nonimmediate speakers bore their audience. And worse yet, nonimmediate speakers make their audience feel anxious and embarrassed for them. In order to turn those negative perceptions around, we recommend that you practice nonverbal immediacy skills and incorporate them into your overall presentational style.

References

This scale was originally designed to assess teachers' nonverbal immediacy in the classroom. For purposes of this chapter, however, we revised the scale to assess how you, as a public speaker, might use nonverbal immediacy while giving a presentation before a large group. The original scale can be found in:

Christophel, D. (1990). The relationships among teacher immediacy behaviors, student motivation, and learning. *Communication Education, 39,* 323–340.

Richmond, V. P., Gorham, J., & McCroskey, J. C. (1987). The relationship between selected immediacy behaviors and cognitive learning. In M. L. McLaughlin (Ed.), *Communication yearbook 10* (pp. 574–590). Beverly Hills, CA: Sage.

Finally, you can enhance your immediacy by recalling names, places, or occasions that are especially relevant to individuals in that particular audience.[25] If you are unacquainted with any of them, you may need to do your homework prior to your presentation and learn something about the town, the building, or the occasion. One good strategy is to arrive early and introduce yourself to several key people—with the intention of learning something about the event itself and, of course, to obtain names that you can refer to within the text of your speech later on.

Initiating and maintaining a relationship of immediacy with your audience pays off. Both speaker and audience become more cooperative and appreciative of the communication exchange taking place. When you like your audience and show that you like them by employing verbal and nonverbal immediacy behaviors, they will respond in kind. They will mirror many of your own immediacy behaviors by leaning forward, smiling broadly, and giving you eye contact. With a responsive, enthusiastic audience like that, you're bound to be a success!

Before we leave this chapter on delivery skills, we want to provide some wisdom that goes back to Aristotle and Quintillian. It is advice that has held true ever since: Too much emphasis on delivery without a simultaneous concern for content or thinking can be just as distressing as the inability to express oneself eloquently.

Another important admonition is this: There is no question that college courses and textbooks like this one can help you to speak well. Commanding the principles and skills of communication so as to gain that ability has long been recognized as a source of *personal power.* What you do with that power, however, is entirely up to you. Thoughtful people who have helped develop those skills, from the time of Aristotle to the present generation of scholars, have always urged their students to speak truthfully.

Chapter Review

- Delivering a message to an audience requires above all that we have something to say. But to be effective public speakers, we must also take into account *how* we say it. Delivering a speech is much like conversing one-on-one. Whether we are talking with a good friend or lecturing before a large group, some of the same basic principles of communication set forth in previous chapters continue to apply.
- Good speakers plan and rehearse so that they *appear* as spontaneous, relaxed, and natural as they would seem in any interpersonal interaction. Furthermore,

public speakers must be able to engage in effective collective role-taking so as to read and adapt to audience feedback.

■ Reading from a manuscript and delivering a memorized speech offer the advantages of communicating accurately and precisely. However, both modes can pose problems of spontaneity and flexibility. The impromptu mode is in some ways the most difficult. Most speakers are trained in the extemporaneous mode, in which they rehearse and then deliver their speech from brief notes or an outline.

■ Establishing credibility with the audience is essential to effectiveness as a speaker. A number of specific recommendations help in getting an audience to perceive a speaker as competent, trustworthy, composed, sociable, and extroverted.

■ Performing the actual speech requires advertising the event and providing an introduction that builds speaker credibility. It is necessary to pay careful attention to physical appearance, level of composure,

eye behavior, and opening lines. In the middle stage, where the plot may begin to "sag," there is a need to stimulate audience attention and comprehension by meeting audience needs, being somewhat redundant and repetitive, using transitions and signposts, varying vocalic rate, volume, and pitch, and using silence, eye contact, gestures, and posture in ways that attract, rather than distract, from presentation.

■ Preparing for the "famous final scene" requires the usual summary, but planning is needed so as to leave a memorable impression on the audience. Here, the use of a variety of nonverbal techniques can make a difference in creating that memory.

■ The immediacy principle provides a way to pull together many of the guidelines and suggestions presented in this chapter. Effective speakers should make every effort to close the physical and psychological distance that always characterizes speakers and their audiences. Both verbal and nonverbal behaviors can help narrow that communication gap.

Key Terms

Adapting (to audience)   Adjusting one's message to perceived needs and interests of an audience on the basis of collective role-taking and feedback that they provide.

Competence (of a speaker)   A dimension of speaker credibility, a judgment on the part of members of an audience as to how much valid knowledge the speaker commands about the issue under discussion.

Composure (as speaker)   As a dimension of speaker credibility, the degree to which a speaker is calm, cool, and collected before a large audience.

Extemporaneous delivery   Delivering a speech from a well-organized, well-rehearsed speech outline, but not a complete text.

Extroversion (of a speaker)   As a dimension of speaker credibility, a judgment of an audience as to the degree to which a speaker is "outgoing," that is, people-oriented, talkative, and gregarious.

Impromptu delivery   A mode of presenting a speech that is delivered on the spot, with little or no lead time or formal preparation beforehand.

Manuscript delivery   A mode of presenting a speech based on reading it word-for-word to the audience from a written script.

Memorized delivery   A mode of presenting a speech based on a procedure that requires writing out the speech beforehand and practicing it over and over again until the entire text is committed to rote memory.

Sociability (of a speaker)   As a dimension of speaker credibility, a judgment on the part of an audience as to how friendly and warm a speaker is. Perceptions of sociability are based on how congenial a person seems to be.

Trustworthiness (of a speaker)   As a dimension of speaker credibility, a judgment of an audience as to a speaker's level of honesty, goodness, and decency.

Notes

1. Germond, J. W., & Witcover, J. (1989). *Whose broad stripes and bright stars? The trivial pursuit of the presidency 1988* (pp. 365–367). New York: Warner Books.

2. Schieffer, B., & Gates, G. P. (1989). *The acting president* (p. 342). New York: Dutton. Much has been said and written about all presidential and vice-presidential campaigns. For the sake of recency, we have used the Bush-Dukakis election example. One should not assume that the analysis provided by these or other journalist authors cited in this illustration necessarily reflects the collective or individual opinion of the authors of this text.

3. Schieffer & Gates, op. cit., p. 367.

4. Schieffer & Gates, op. cit., p. 351.

5. Schieffer & Gates, op. cit., p. 367.

6. The initials ACLU refer to the American Civil Liberties Union, a controversial and very liberal organization that provides legal assistance to selected causes and individuals when they feel that important civil liberties are at stake.

7. Schieffer & Gates, op. cit., 1989, p. 403.

8. For these and other examples of practice articulation phrases, see:

Fulton, R. I., & Trueblood, T. C. (1893). *Practical elements of elocution* (pp. 53–54). Boston: Ginn.

9. Ibid., p. 384.

10. Fenno, F. H. (1912). *Fenno's science of speech* (p. 139). (Chicago: Emerson W. Fenno.

11. Extensive research has been done on the relationship between credibility, ethos, or prestige and attitude change or influence. From the early writings of Aristotle to the more current works of researchers in communication today, this relationship is so well established as to be a "truism" in the discipline. For an overview of this association, see: Andersen, K., & Clevenger, T., Jr. (1963). A summary of experimental research in ethos. *Speech Monographs, 30*, 59–78; McCroskey, J. C., Richmond, V. P., & Stewart, R. A. (1986). *One on one: The foundations of interpersonal communication* (pp. 73–83). Englewood Cliffs, NJ: Prentice-Hall; McCroskey, J. C. (1986). *An introduction to rhetorical communication* (5th ed.). Englewood Cliffs: Prentice-Hall; Reardon, K. K. *Persuasion: Theory and context* (pp. 114–121). Beverly Hills, CA: Sage.

12. McCroskey, Richmond, & Stewart, op. cit., pp. 73–83; McCroskey, op. cit.

13. McCroskey, Richmond, & Stewart, op. cit., pp. 73–74.

14. Burhans, D. T., Jr. (1973). The experimental study of interpersonal trust. *Western Journal of Speech Communication, 37*, 2–12; Rempel, J., Holmes, J., & Zanna, M. (1985). Trust in close relationships. *Journal of Personality and Social Psychology, 49*, 95–112.

15. Nelson, P. E., & Pearson, J. C. (1990). *Confidence in public speaking* (4th ed.) (p. 172). Dubuque, IA: W. C. Brown.

16. For these and other research-based approaches for securing both attention and retention, see: Woolfolk, A. E. (1987). *Educational psychology* (3rd ed.) (pp. 240–254). Englewood Cliffs, NJ: Prentice-Hall.

17. Glasgow, G. M. (1952). A semantic index of vocal pitch. *Speech Monographs, 19*, 64–68; Richmond, V. P., McCroskey, J. C., & Payne, S. K. (1987). *Nonverbal behavior in interpersonal relations* (p. 102). Englewood Cliffs, NJ: Prentice-Hall.

18. Richmond, McCroskey, & Payne, op. cit., p. 102.

19. Ibid., p. 77; Knapp, M. L. (1978). *Nonverbal communication in human interaction* (2nd ed.) (pp. 294–314). New York: Holt, Rinehart & Winston.

20. Scheflen, A. E. (1964). The significance of posture in communication systems. *Psychiatry, 27*, 316–331; Richmond, McCroskey, & Payne, op. cit., pp. 56–58.

21. Mehrabian, A. (1971). *Silence messages.* Belmont, CA: Wadsworth; Mehrabian, A. (1981). *Silent messages: Implicit communication of emotions and attitudes* (2nd ed.). Belmont, CA: Wadsworth.

22. Ibid., 1971, 1981; Andersen, J. F., Andersen, P. A., & Jensen, A. D. (1979). The measurement of nonverbal immediacy. *Journal of Applied Communication Research, 7*, 153–180; and Andersen, J. F. (1979). Teacher immediacy as a predictor of teaching effectiveness. In Daniel Nimmo (Ed.), *Communication yearbook 3* (pp. 543–559). New Brunswick, NJ: Transaction Books.

23. Mehrabian, A. (1967). Attitudes inferred from neutral verbal communications. *Journal of Consulting Psychology, 31*, 414–417; Mehrabian, A. (1967). Attitudes inferred from nonimmediacy of verbal communication. *Journal of Verbal Learning and Verbal Behavior, 6*, 294–295; Gorham, J. (1988). The relationship between verbal teacher immediacy behaviors and student learning. *Communication Education, 37*, 40–53; and Richmond, McCroskey, & Payne, op. cit., p. 187.

24. Richmond, McCroskey, & Payne, op. cit., p. 187.

25. Gorham, op. cit., pp. 40–53; Richmond, McCroskey, & Payne, op. cit., pp. 185–187.

Additional Readings

Anderson, K. E. (1978). *Persuasion: Theory and practice* (2nd ed.) Boston, MA: Allyn & Bacon.

This introductory text in persuasion includes a number of chapters covering issues pertinent to delivery and the presentation of messages. Particularly noteworthy are the chapters on totalitarian persuasion and ethics.

Bettinghaus, E. P. (1980). *Persuasive communication* (3rd ed.). New York: Holt, Rinehart, & Winston.

This solid text on persuasive speaking includes important materials on persuasion in the media, small groups, formal organizations, and various other public contexts. Particularly interesting is the coverage of nonverbal visual factors in the delivery of messages. Discussions include recommendations for improving delivery.

Fisher, H. (1981). *Improving voice and articulation* (3rd ed.). Boston, MA: Houghton Mifflin.

This is now the classic book in the field of voice and articulation. It clearly distinguishes between pronunciation and articulation in discussing the variety of speech and delivery problems that can be improved in the classroom.

Guidelines are described for improving problems such as running sound and words together.

Klopf, D. W., & Cambra, R. E. (1991). *Speaking skills for prospective teachers* (2nd ed.). Englewood, CO: Morton.

This text is intended for individuals entering the teaching profession and for those interested in improving their in-class communication skills. However, the chapters are written for anyone interested in improving their speaking skills. The chapter on verbal communication processes is particularly informative regarding both the effective use of language and immediacy behaviors that communicate.

McCroskey, J. C. (1986). *An introduction to rhetorical communication* (5th ed.). Englewood Cliffs, NJ: Prentice-Hall.

This is a well-documented survey of the fundamentals of public speaking specifically and of communication more generally. Each chapter nicely blends the historical-critical and empirical perspectives around a particular topic. The book gives special attention to oral presentation and the effects of delivery.

Chapter 15

Public Speaking: Polishing and Fine-Tuning

Contents

Four Strategies for Making Your Language More Interesting
Use Imagery Imaginatively
   The value of concrete images
   Evoking images with similes
   Using metaphors to create strong images
Strive for Simplicity
Employ Intense, Animated Language to Add
   Excitement
Maintain Rhythm for Emphasis

Orchestrating Audience Response
Developing and Using Sound Bites

Managing Applause
Developing Your Own Rhetorical Style
Dramatic Style
Animated Style
Humorous Style
Chapter Review
Key Terms
Notes
Additional Readings

Key Questions

- It is much better to explain major ideas in abstract terms, rather than try to spell them out in concrete and specific ways. This challenges your audience to think about what you are saying, rather than getting bogged down in specifics. Right? Wrong! Wrong! Wrong!

- If you use simple language in a speech, it is a clear indicator that you are "talking down" to your audience. They will not like it and will regard you as a lightweight. It is better to impress them with your grasp of complex language and ideas. Right? Wrong! Wrong! Wrong!

- There is just no way that a speaker can anticipate an audience's response to a speech. If they want to applaud or respond in some other way during the speech, they will do it. If they don't they won't. There is just no way to control such behavior. Right? Wrong! Wrong! Wrong!

- In presenting a speech, it is best just to be yourself even if your style is a bit boring. If you try to add drama, deliver the speech in an animated style, or use humor, you will not seem believable to people and the speech will fail. Right? Wrong! Wrong! Wrong!

When First Lady Barbara Bush was asked to speak to the graduating women in Wellesley College's class of 1990, no one had any idea of the furor and fury that would follow. Over 150 of those students signed a petition complaining that the first lady was unqualified to speak of self-made success and accomplishments beyond the traditional roles of wife and mother. After all, they chided, Barbara Bush was a college dropout and famous only for her husband's political successes. With all the media attention focused on the Wellesley controversy, people across the country formed and voiced their opinions. Most Americans thought the first lady should speak to the graduating seniors regardless of a "tribe of spoiled brats."[1] After all, she was the first lady of our nation and deserved our respect. Others countered by citing the fact that neither Harvard nor Yale had ever considered inviting "Mr." Margaret Thatcher to speak at their commencements. Despite all the controversy, and to Barbara Bush's credit, she agreed to speak at the ceremony.

Picture the drama of that event: Barbara Bush would be speaking to a group of young women—many of whom were openly and defiantly opposed to her presence at that very special occasion. Moreover, the first lady recognized clearly that a number of those in the audience would fail to perceive her as a credible source to speak on career opportunities and alternatives. How many of us, even if we were professional speakers, would "welcome" a similar speaking event? Anticipating a potentially hostile or critical group would make any of us stay home! Rather than succumb, as others might have, to the hysterics of the event, Barbara Bush steadfastly prevailed, determined to prove the Wellesley students wrong.

More than at any other time in her position as first lady, Barbara Bush needed a professional speech writer.

In fact, she employed the services of several writers, all of whom had to consider carefully both the audience and the occasion. In light of the much publicized criticism of her suitability as a role model, she wanted and needed "to convince a new generation of women that there is honor and a deep, sustaining pleasure in motherhood" and marriage.[2] Writing and presenting a speech that would do all that constituted a tall order! And yet, the first lady delivered. According to *Time* magazine, "Barbara, who was once so shy she cried over having to speak to the Houston Garden Club, delivered the speech of her life." *Newsweek* remarked, "A Job Wellesley Done." And NBC anchor Tom Brokaw exclaimed, "One of the best commencement speeches I've ever heard."[3]

While Barbara Bush is credited for both the content and tone of the initial speech, speech writer Ed McNally actually drafted the address from conversations with the first lady. Several others on staff contributed as well. In the box on pp. 426–427 is the final, polished version of that text.

An in-depth analysis of the speech text itself reveals some rather unique features that contributed to its success. Consider, for instance, the writer's turn of a phrase. The first draft might well have read: "You don't have to live your life the way everyone thinks you should." But the final version said: ". . . [Y]ou need not, probably cannot, live a paint-by-numbers life." She also employed humor and a certain sense of with-it-ness: After quoting the well-known movie character Ferris Bueller, Bush replied, "I am not going to tell George you clapped more for Ferris than you clapped for George." Recognizing that she was the students' second choice as a commencement speaker, she countered with: "Now I know your first choice today was Alice Walker—guess how I know? Known for 'The Color Purple.' Instead, you got me, known for the color of my hair!" And, as expected, the

One of the toughest challenges to a speaker in recent years developed around an invitation to Barbara Bush to make a presentation to the graduating class at Wellesley College in 1990. The student group who invited her was strongly criticized by another group who claimed that she was inappropriate and not qualified because she had no accomplishments of her own, and that she was famous only because of her husband. Despite the uproar in the media that reported on the controversy, her speech was a resounding success. Her presentation included a number of rhetorical devices, strategies for the use of language, and other ways of polishing and fine-tuning a speech that adapted it well to the situation.

loudest cheer and applause came when she delivered this kicker: "Somewhere out in this audience may even be someone who will one day follow in my footsteps, and preside over the White House as the President's spouse. I wish *him* well." Barbara Bush used these and other rhetorical techniques in order to disarm and charm her audience.

What lessons for polishing a speech can we draw from this example? Transforming words and phrases from the bland and routine to the unique and inspirational involve what we call *rhetorical devices*. Strategies for the use of language, humor, and style all contribute to the overall packaging of your speech. To the extent that you can polish or refine your text and presentation, your chances for success significantly improve. That is not to say, however, that packaging alone can motivate an audience, embrace disparate groups, or persuade individuals to change their minds completely. But polishing and packaging can help to disarm hostilities with laughter, confront controversy without alienation, and ensure that everyone listens actively and empathically to your message.

In this chapter we will focus on those strategies that can help you convert a speech from one that is basic and mechanically correct to one that communicates with force and intensity, with passion and inspiration, and with snap and panache. We will help you transform your speech from one that is merely "good" to one that can be "great!" With your outline prepared, your evidence at hand, and your delivery well rehearsed, you must consider taking this important, final step—polish your speech. Employing only a few of our suggestions can help you make it unique, rhetorically exciting, and truly worth listening to.

"No One Can Say What Your True Colors Will Be..."

From Associated Press

Following is the text of Barbara Bush's speech at the Wellesley College commencement:

President Keohane, Mrs. Gorbachev, trustees, faculty, parents, and I should say, Julie Porter, class president, and certainly, my new best friend, Christine Bicknell. And of course, the class of 1990.

I'm really thrilled to be here today, and very excited, as I know all of you must be, that Mrs. Gorbachev could join us.

These are exciting times. They're exciting in Washington. And I had really looked forward to coming to Wellesley. I thought it was going to be fun. I never dreamt it would be this much fun. So, thank you for that.

More than 10 years ago, when I was invited here to talk about our experiences in the People's Republic of China, I was struck by both the natural beauty of your campus and the spirit of this place. Wellesley, you see, is not just a place, but an idea—an experiment in excellence in which diversity is not just tolerated but is embraced. The essence of this spirit was captured in a moving speech about tolerance given last year by a student body president of one of your sister colleges.

She related the story by Robert Fulghum about a young pastor finding himself in charge of some very energetic children, who hits upon a game called "Giants, Wizards and Dwarfs." "You have to decide now," the pastor instructed the children, "which you are—a giant, a wizard or a dwarf?" At that, a small girl tugging at his pants leg asks: "But where do the mermaids stand?" And the pastor tells her there are no mermaids. And she says: "Oh yes there are. I am a mermaid."

Now, this little girl knew what she was, and she was not about to give up on either her identity or the game. She intended to take her place wherever mermaids fit into the scheme of things. Where do the mermaids stand—all of those who are different, those who do not fit the boxes and the pigeonholes? "Answer that question," wrote Fulghum, "and you can build a school, a nation, or a whole world."

As that very wise young woman said: "Diversity, like anything worth having, requires effort." Effort to learn about and respect difference, to be compassionate with one another, to cherish our own identity and to accept unconditionally the same in others.

You should all be very proud that this is the Wellesley spirit.

Now I know your first choice today was Alice Walker—guess how I know? Known for "The Color Purple." Instead, you got me, known for the color of my hair!

Alice Walker's book has a special resonance here. At Wellesley, each class is known by a special color. For four years, the class of '90 has worn the color purple.

Today, you meet on Severance Green to say goodbye to all of that, to begin a new and a very personal journey, to search for your own true colors. In the world that awaits you beyond the shores of Lake Waban, no one can say what your true colors will be. But this I do know: You have a first-class education from a first-class school, and so you need not, probably cannot, live a paint-by-numbers life.

Decisions are not irrevocable, choices do come back, and as you set off from Wellesley, I hope many of you will consider making three very special choices. The first is to believe in something larger than yourself, to get involved in some of the big ideas of our time.

I chose literacy because I honestly believed that if more people could read, write, and comprehend, we would be that much closer to solving so many of the problems that plague our nation and our society.

And early on, I made another choice, which I hope you will make as well. Whether you are talking about education, career or service, you are talking about life, and life really must have joy.

It's supposed to be fun. One of the reasons I made the most important decision of my life, to marry George Bush, is because he made me laugh. It's true, sometimes we laugh through our tears, but that shared laughter has been one of our strongest bonds. Find the joy in life because as Ferris Bueller said on his day off: "Life moves pretty fast, and if you don't stop and look around once in a while you are going to miss it."

I am not going to tell George you clapped more for Ferris than you clapped for George.

The third choice that must not be missed is to cherish your human connections, your relationships with family and friends. For several years you've had impressed upon you the importance to your career of dedication and hard work, and of course that's true. But as important as your obligations as a doctor, a lawyer, a business leader will be, you are a human being first, and those human connections with spouses, with children, with friends are the most important investment you will ever make.

At the end of your life, you will never regret not having passed one more test, winning one more verdict or not closing one more deal. You will regret time not spent with a husband, a child, a friend or a parent.

We are in a transitional period right now—fascinating and exhilarating times, learning to adjust to changes and the choices we—men and women—are facing. As an example, I remember what a friend said on hearing her husband complain to his buddies that he had to baby-sit. Quickly setting him straight, my friend told her husband that when it's your own kids, it's not called baby-sitting.

Now, maybe we should adjust faster and maybe we should adjust slower. But whatever the era, whatever the times, one thing will never change: Fathers and mothers, if you have children, they must come first. You must read to your children, and you must hug your children, and you must love your children. Your success as a family, our success as a society, depends not on what happens in the White House, but on what happens inside your house.

For over 50 years, it was said that the winner of Wellesley's annual hoop race would be the first to get married. Now they say the winner will be the first to become a CEO. Both of those stereotypes show too little tolerance for those who want to know where the mermaids stand.

So, I want to offer a new legend. The winner of the hoop race will be the first to realize her dream—not society's dreams—her own personal dream.

Who knows? Somewhere out in this audience may even be someone who will one day follow in my footsteps and preside over the White House as the President's spouse, and I wish him well.

Well, the controversy ends here, but our conversation is only beginning, and a worthwhile conversation it has been. So, as you leave Wellesley today, take with you deep thanks for the courtesy and the honor you have shared with Mrs. Gorbachev and with me.

Thank you. God bless you. And may your future be worthy of your dreams.

Five Strategies for Making Your Language More Interesting

Many of us have listened to a speech, only to recall later our impressions rather than the actual words that were used or the facts that were presented. Similarly, we may not be able to remember how or why an argument was initiated with a good friend, but we certainly know how we felt at the time. Those experiences stimulated our *feelings* even if they did not remain in our memory. In much the same way, we should try to create long-lasting and positive emotional responses to our presentations. Facts alone cannot do that. Logical arguments alone will not suffice. To achieve lasting impressions we must rely on the use of colorful and appropriate language, words, and phrases, to create mental and emotional pictures for our audience. In this section, we will target a variety of specific strategies for using language that will assist you in your efforts to communicate beyond the facts to create happenings, episodes, journeys, and trysts—language strategies that will summon impressions, feelings, convictions, and sentiments.

Using Imagery Imaginatively

The technique of evoking **imagery** requires the use of carefully chosen words and phrases that appeal to our senses of touch, taste, sound, sight, and smell. This must be done in such a way as to create concrete, realistic impressions about what we are saying. This can be done by linking your images to others that are familiar so that everyone can almost see, smell, taste, and touch what you feel. In other words, rather than speak in the abstract about your ideas, select your words carefully so as to arouse concrete pictures in the heads of those to whom you are speaking.

The value of concrete images   Vivid images are most easily aroused with the use of **concrete** language. For example, assume for a moment that you are interested in persuading your audience to forego more welfare subsidy programs and, instead, create new jobs for the unemployed. Very explicit language can be used. For example, Governor Thomas Kean of New Jersey used this concrete language: "We offer poor America not the junk food of more big government but the full meal of good private sector jobs."[4] By using concrete language he was able to create vivid sensory images for his audience to experience and perhaps to re-examine their policies. Ap-

plying that same principle may help *your* audience vicariously experience equally vivid sensory images.

Imagery aroused with concrete language helps your audience both to attend to and to perceive your message with greater enthusiasm and accuracy than if they hear abstract messages. For example, suppose you had outlined a persuasive speech on the negative effects of television. Consider how you could make the audience "see" your point. Here's how John Silber, president of Boston University, characterized the "dramatic" effects of television on children:

> Invaded by television, the home is no longer a sanctuary in which children are protected from exposure to the full sordid range of human experience. They are flooded with sex, with violence, the perverse and the sublime . . .—and the result is nothing less than the pollution of their sensibilities. Their minds . . . their souls—are trashed.[5]

Or, look how Senator Lloyd Bentsen, Democratic candidate for vice-president of the United States in 1988, used concrete language to present images of disorientation and delusion. Bentsen was trying to influence our thinking about the previous Republican administration:

> My friends, America has just passed through the ultimate epoch of illusion: An eight-year coma in which slogans were confused with solutions and rhetoric passed for reality.[6]

In addition to drawing sensory pictures through concrete language, two rhetorical devices that are common in literature are often used to create images in our presentations. These are the *simile* and the *metaphor*. **Similes** create images through the use of an "expressed" analogy, whereas **metaphors** develop a picture by "implied" analogy. But even though they are different, both similes and metaphors spell out for the audience common features posed by comparisons between two seemingly dissimilar things.

Evoking images with similes   The audience usually knows when a simile is being used simply because they are made explicit by prefacing the comparison with the words *like* or *as*. Most of us recognize the more mundane and banal similes in common use, such as "slept like a baby," "hungry as a bear," "sly as a fox," "light as a feather," "silly as a goose," "poor as a churchmouse," and "dumb as a board." These are to be avoided—they are so used and abused that they will detract from your presentations.

There is no excuse for using boring similes because it does not take profound imagination to create similes that are novel or unique. For example, Eugene Dorsey, president of the Gannett Foundation, employed a number of similes in his efforts to characterize (and criticize) the rampant consumerism and materialism of the 1980s: "VCR's and compact disc players became as necessary as a can opener to a gold miner. . . . Rolexes sprouted on wrists like crocuses announcing spring."[7] Or, charging Republicans with making America a debtor nation, for spending money we didn't have, Governor Ann Richards (then state treasurer of Texas) lamented, "It's kind of like that brother-in-law who drives a flashy new car but he's always borrowing money from you to make the payments."[8] One of the best-known sound bites of the Bush administration had its origin in a simile. Referring to the numerous and seemingly disparate ethnic, religious, social, business, and neighboring communities in America, President George Bush exclaimed: "a brilliant diversity spread like stars, like a thousand points of light in a broad and peaceful sky."[9]

Using metaphors to create strong images Many times similes can be converted into metaphors by omitting the comparative "like" or "as" and, instead, labeling the object or event with another, apparently dissimilar label. In this way, the metaphor implies and yet creates a much stronger image than does the simile. However, metaphors, like similes, are often overworked. Such expressions as "dog-tired," "late-bloomer," and "can't see the forest for the trees" are trite. Metaphors can be rich, imaginative, and powerful. For example, Reverend Jesse Jackson, who is well known for his use of imagery, used a strong metaphor to arouse images of the poor and unfortunate children of a low-socioeconomic area in Los Angeles called Watts: "Their grapes of hope," he said, "have become raisins of despair."[10] He might have been tempted to employ a simile, such as "Their hope has turned to despair, like the grape into a raisin." But note how Jackson's metaphor is infinitely more powerful than the comparable simile. In one's mind, hope *becomes* a plump round grape; despair *becomes* a dried, shriveled raisin.

Metaphors are widely used to create powerful images. In that same speech, Jackson, in his attempts to relate to working people everywhere, claimed that he understood work through this metaphor: "I was not born with a silver spoon in my mouth. I had a shovel programmed for my hand." Or consider the metaphor Eugene Dorsey (of the Gannett Foundation) used to describe the Wall Street crash of October 19, 1987: "The floors of the New York Stock Exchange became a scene from 'Nightmare on Elm

Street.'"[11] Or how about the "cancerous individualism" of the "Me Generation" that John Silber, president of Boston College, blames for overlooking and neglecting the welfare of society "on which every individual is dependent"?[12] All of these speakers relied heavily on the metaphor to communicate an attitude, an idea, a policy, or a dream expressively and definitively to their audiences.

Strive for Simplicity

Sometimes it's the simple words and ideas that have the most impact on an audience. When uncomplicated language follows from complex thought, the contrast is so great that audiences are likely to catch hold to the idea quickly. For example, consider Nancy Reagan's "Just Say NO!" or George Bush's "Read my lips: No new taxes!" Regardless of your political position, you cannot deny your easy recognition of both of these short, simple phrases. In other words, clear, modest, and uncomplicated language can communicate forceful, powerful thought. A very effective example of the principle of simplicity in action appeared in Ann Richards's speech at the Democratic National Convention in 1988. Five times she told her audience that the Republican administration was "wrong."[13] She preceded each of these claims with a story. These were about farmers going under, working mothers who have trouble keeping their families together, industries threatened by foreign markets and unfair trade laws, and polluted air and water. She followed each story with the phrase "Well, that's wrong!" Richards then did a turnabout by telling the crowd that there's nothing "wrong with you—nothing wrong with you that you can't fix in November!"

Another good example of simplicity can be seen in the convention address of Senator Bentsen, who complained that the "Reagan-Bush administration likes to talk about prosperity. But the farmers in Iowa don't hear them. The oil field workers in Texas and Oklahoma and Louisiana don't hear them. The factory workers in John Glenn's Ohio don't hear them. My fellow Democrats, it is easy enough to create an illusion of prosperity. All you have to do is write hot checks for $200 billion a year!"[14]

Ronald Reagan also used the principle of simplicity when he claimed that "Facts are stubborn things" at least five or six times in a speech at the Republican National Convention in 1988. He used this simple phrase to show the party how bad things were and how much better they became during his 8 years as President.[15] Each time, "Facts

An effective strategy in polishing a speech is to strive for simplicity. A simple phrase, used repeatedly to follow each of a set of related complex ideas, can focus audience attention dramatically. Ann Richards, now governor of Texas, spoke in criticism of Republican candidate George Bush at the Democratic National Convention in 1990. She followed each explanation of a reason why he would be a poor choice for the office with the phrase "Poor George!" Soon the audience began to anticipate the phrase and cheered each time it was used.

are stubborn things" was preceded and followed by one kind of "misery index" after another—all of which, he claimed, had occurred under Democratic-controlled administrations. That same year, George Bush gave us his "bottom line" in support of a strong national defense in very simple terms: "I hate war. I love peace. We have peace. And I am not going to let anyone take it away from me."[16]

In all of these examples, the strategy of using simple, clear, concise language helped the audience focus on the core issues that were fundamental to each speaker's argument. The juxtaposition of relatively uncomplicated, straightforward talk with some rather sophisticated, complex thoughts and ideas quickly communicated to the audience how they should feel about an issue, how they should evaluate a policy, or how they ought to vote or behave. Thus, simple words can replace or comple-

ment big, bulging words and ideas that can often confuse and lose an audience. Short, lean (even redundant) phrases and words offer the audience a reprieve from information overload, and at the same time, they reduce ambiguity and facilitate comprehension.

Employ Intense, Animated Language to Add Excitement

Many times we find that the difference between a dull (albeit mechanically correct) speech and an exciting-listening experience is in the speaker's use of intense, animated language. Moreover, we find that vivid speech contributes a great deal to attitude and behavior change.[17] To illustrate, let's assume for a minute that your sister Juanita invites you to see a movie with her. Here's her pitch:

A speech that has now become an American classic was delivered by Dr. Martin Luther King, Jr., in front of the Washington Monument on August 28, 1963. Using a measured style of delivery, simple language, and vivid imagery, he touched the emotions of all people, regardless of their race or background. Heard by thousands at the site, and by millions on television, this speech is believed by experts to have provided an important turning point in the civil rights movement in the United States.

I read in the paper that a new movie has just come out and it's playing in the neighborhood. Wanta go?

Now let's insert some intense, animated language and see how the persuasive appeal changes:

Steven Seagal delivers again, but this time his new film shows him piercing the villain's lungs with a simple poke of his finger—and he even reaches inside this guy's eye socket, pulls out the eye ball, and then lobs it on the table as he leaves. Some really incredible stunts! Let's go!

Even though the violence may not be all that appealing to you, the contrast between the two presentations is dramatic. If you want to be moved and if you want to move others, intense, animated language offers an effective way to do it.

Unfortunately, our daily speech habits are filled with words and phrases that say little and act only as grammatical connectors. For example, the words *is, are, have, there, was, had, here, very, so,* and *well* communicate almost nothing and yet we use these words in almost every sentence we speak. By substituting for each of these words others that "act" or "do something," boring speech translates into lively, active exchange. Similarly, moving from passive to active voice injects vigor and vitality into your speech. Adding descriptive adjectives communi-

cates a sense of energy and emotion that simple subjects and nouns standing alone are unable to do.

To illustrate these points, let's examine the text of a speech presented by Martin Luther King, Jr., who was one of America's greatest speakers and a leader of the civil rights movement in the early 1960s. He spoke to thousands in front of the Lincoln Memorial in Washington, D.C., and to millions on television and radio. One of his speeches, in particular, has become classic both in the study of speech and in the history of our country. It was entitled "I Have a Dream."

With an intensity and vividness of language that few have been able to duplicate, King moved people—he touched the emotions of people of all races, colors, and creeds. A century after the end of the Civil War and the emancipation of all Americans, his impassioned speech stirred the dream of equality and freedom from oppression for every citizen. Consider these passages:

. . . But one hundred years later, the Negro is still not free. One hundred years later, the life of the Negro is still sadly crippled by the manacles of segregation and the chains of discrimination. One hundred years later, the Negro lives on a lonely island of poverty in the midst of a vast ocean of material prosperity. One hundred years later, the Negro is still languished in the corners of American society and finds himself an exile in his own land. And so we've come here today to dramatize a shameful condition.

In a sense we've come to our nation's Capitol to cash a check. When the architects of our republic wrote the magnificent words of the Constitution and the Declaration of Independence, they were signing a promissory note to which every American was to fall heir. This note was a promise that all men—yes, black men as well as white men—would be guaranteed the unalienable rights of life, liberty, and the pursuit of happiness.

It is obvious today that America has defaulted on this promissory note insofar as her citizens of color are concerned. Instead of honoring this sacred obligation, America has given the Negro people a bad check—a check which has come back marked "insufficient funds."[18]

The language of this speech is truly vivid. According to King, the life of African Americans was still "crippled," not just "hurt." These citizens, he said, aren't simply poor, they "live on a lonely island of poverty in the midst of a vast ocean of material prosperity." They "languished" and became "exiled" in their own country. The writers of our Constitution became more than simply authors in this speech; King called them "architects." Americans are "heirs" to the promises of life, liberty, and the pursuit of happiness. Overall, this classic speech relies heavily on intense, animated language that evokes especially vivid imagery. It also makes use of concrete language, metaphors, and similes.

To illustrate further the use of intense, animated language, we can look at a speech by Governor Thomas Kean of New Jersey. He was denouncing the effects of pollution on our environment: "Today," he said, "our air is plagued by acid rain—our oceans and beaches are sullied by sewage and syringes—our very future is threatened by sunburn from above and poisoned water from below."[19] In this case, Kean substituted the intense words *plagued* for *filled, sullied* for *dirty, threatened* for *potentially harmed,* and *poisoned* for *polluted.* With each substitution, the message became more vivid, intense, and passionate. These word substitutions, then, empower us as speakers to inform and influence the audience. And, from the audience's point of view, intense, animated language makes the presentation more gripping and appealing.

Maintain Rhythm for Emphasis

Great speeches have a rhythm all their own. The recurrence of specific sounds, words, or phrases meet the audience's need for regularity, predictability, and familiarity. Rhythm enhances the pleasure and heightens the sense

of emotion toward us as speakers, and toward the message we are trying to get across. A favorite device often used by skilled orators is the repetitive use of key words and phrases. These often become memorable media events and household slogans. What follows is an example of this repetition or *restatement* taken from Reverend King's "Dream" speech delivered 30 years ago:

I say to you today, my friends, so even though we face the difficulties of today and tomorrow, I still have a dream. It is a dream deeply rooted in the American dream.

I have a dream that one day this nation will rise up and live out the true meaning of its creed, "We hold these truths to be self-evident, that all men are created equal."

I have a dream that one day on the red hills of Georgia the sons of former slaves and the sons of former slave-owners will be able to sit down together at the table of brotherhood.

I have a dream that one day even the state of Mississippi, a state sweltering with the heat of injustice, sweltering with the heat of oppression, will be transformed into an oasis of freedom and justice.

I have a dream that my four little children will one day live in a nation where they will not be judged by the color of their skin but by the content of their character. I have a dream today.

I have a dream that one day, down in Alabama, with its vicious racists, with its governor having his lips dripping with the words of interposition and nullification, one day right there in Alabama little black boys and black girls will be able to join hands with little white boys and white girls as sisters and brothers. I have a dream today.

I have a dream that one day every valley shall be exalted, every hill and mountain shall be made low, the rough places will be made plane and the crooked places will be made straight, and the glory of the Lord shall be revealed, and all flesh shall see it together.

This is our hope. This is the faith that I go back to the South with.[20]

Even though not many people today actually heard this speech directly, or even saw it delivered on television in 1963, all of us can associate the familiar words "I have a dream" with civil rights, equality, and freedom from racial injustice. Martin Luther King relied on repetition repeatedly. Recall the final words of that same speech, "Free at last! Free at last! Thank God Almighty, we are free at last!"

Let's take a minute to examine *why* repetition or restatement made this speech so memorable. Notice how the use of rhythm or restatement establishes a pattern of expectations for the audience. It takes only a single simple restatement for the audience to develop the expectancy that a second or third restatement—and perhaps more important points—will be made. When the expectancy is fulfilled, that is, when the second or subsequent restatement is there, the audience feels rewarded and gratified that their prediction was warranted.[21]

Moreover, we happen to know that repetition almost always ensures retention. Consider how long you have known your ABC's. When did you study *that?* It was a long time ago, but you *still* remember all 26 letters. Furthermore, you will never forget their order. Such long-term memory storage is not all that surprising when you consider how often you probably silently repeat the ABC's as you search through the card catalog, the dictionary, or the telephone book to find the letter *j, u,* or *f.* Similarly, we learn and remember special words and phrases that we hear frequently. Many of us still remember the humorous interaction that Senator Ted Kennedy initiated with his audience at the Democratic National Convention in 1988. Highly critical of candidate George Bush, Kennedy had this to say:

> The Vice President says he wasn't there—or can't recall—or never heard—as the Administration secretly plotted to sell arms to Iran. So when that monumental mistake was being made, I think it is fair to ask—*where was George?*
>
> The Vice President says he never saw—or can't remember—or didn't comprehend—the intelligence report on General Noriega's involvement in the cocaine cartel. So when that report was being prepared and discussed, I think it is fair to ask—*where was George?*
>
> The Vice President claims he cares about the elderly—but evidently he didn't know, or wasn't there, when the Administration tried repeatedly to slash Social Security and Medicare. So when those decisions were being made, I think it is fair to ask—*where was George?*
>
> And the Vice President, who now speaks fervently of civil rights, apparently wasn't around or didn't quite hear when the Administration was planning to weaken voting rights, give tax breaks to segregated schools, and veto the Civil Rights Restoration Act of 1988. So when all those assaults were being mounted, I think it is fair to ask—*where was George?*[22]

Kennedy continued his assault and finally concluded with yet another repetition: "On too many tough issues, George Bush's only defense is that he was a hear-nothing, see-nothing, do-nothing Vice-President."

What these passages illustrate is that restating simple phrases or even entire lines adds rhythm to a speech. In addition, *rephrasing* with similar, redundant words or word series can add "pulse" or cadence to an otherwise ordinary presentation. This idea can be illustrated by George Bush's rhythm in the following passage.

I want growth that stays, that broadens and that touches,

finally, all Americans, from the hollows of Kentucky to the sunlit streets of Denver, from the suburbs of Chicago to the broad avenues of New York, from the oil fields of Oklahoma to the farms of the Great Plains.[23]

Twice, Bush rephrased in order to add emphasis and strength to his point. First, he asks for growth "that stays, that broadens and that touches." Second, he provides a parallel "from"/"to" series reminiscent of the song "America the Beautiful"—"from the . . . to the . . ." over and over again. In short, Bush wants growth that includes *everyone.*

Generally, then, rephrasing and restating key phrases and words all help to build the rhythm of the speech. In these ways, rhythm excites, triggers suspense, and compels the audience to anticipate. Besides eliciting attention, rhythmic speech subtly stimulates the audience to focus, to learn, and to remember central ideas in your presentation.

Orchestrating Applause

While imagery, simplicity, intense or animated language, and rhythm all contribute to making good speeches better, consideration should be given to the strategy of manipulating audience reaction throughout the presentation. There will be moments during your speech when you will want your audience openly to show their concern, express their anger, or back your point. There are a number of strategies that you can use to invite and promote audience approval of points made in your speech. Good speakers *know* ahead of time which of their lines or phrases stand a good chance of being remembered, reprinted, or taped for later media use. This lets them anticipate when their audience is likely to interrupt with clapping. In fact, a really good orator will build features into the speech to make sure this happens. In this section, we encourage you to plan for audience applause and to plan for what the news industry calls "sound bites," whether or not your speech is to be reported by media.

Developing and Using Sound Bites

The expression **sound bite** is really a metaphor for a brief passage, such as a sentence or two, taken from a press release or presentation so as to be reprinted or taped for later news reports. Sound bites usually represent some major idea expressed by the speaker. Time or space usually prevents printing or showcasing the entire text of a speech or even an extended conversation. Reporters are likely to select carefully a brief passage that best captures an emotion or idea stressed by the speaker. Consider the famous sound bite from the motion picture *Sudden Impact:* Clint Eastwood as Dirty Harry points a loaded gun at the villain and challenges him to make the wrong move, "Go ahead—make my day!" You probably can recall a number of other sound bites that have become household expressions. See if you can remember the origins of each of the following common sound bites:[24]

> Ask not what your country can do for you, but what you can do for your country.
> If it looks like a duck, walks like a duck and quacks like a duck, it probably is a duck.
> Men and women can't be friends because the sex part always gets in the way.
> Ginger Rogers did everything that Fred Astaire did. She just did it backwards and in high heels.
> Voodoo Economics *or* Swiss Cheese Economics
> A kinder, gentler nation
> Read my lips: No new taxes.
> The L'-word [Liberal]
> The mother of all battles
> Just the facts, ma'am

Not all sound bites become widely recognized. In fact, most are disseminated and then quickly forgotten. Sometimes the wrong kind of sound bite is picked up by the media and disseminated to households across the country—much to the chagrin and embarrassment of the speaker. When Senator Dan Quayle debated Senator Lloyd Bentsen on television during their 1988 vice-presidential campaigns, Senator Quayle compared himself to former President John F. Kennedy (against the advice of his debate coaches). His opponent, Senator Bentsen, used the opportunity to tell Quayle in a rather cold way, "You are no John Kennedy." That scene appeared on television repeatedly, much to the embarrassment of the Republicans. The Democrats loved it. In the long run, however, the Democrats were caught with foot-in-mouth sound bites on more than one occasion.

The point is, sound bites can hurt or help speakers. Avoiding those that will hurt, and planning for those that will help, is an important step in polishing any speech. The goal is to ensure that the right kinds of phrases are attended to and repeated to others, and picked up by the media if they are present. In the previous section, we discussed five strategies for the more colorful use of language. It is at this stage of polishing that sound bites are created. When you systematically select just the right word or lines to use, you are creating potential sound bites for the audience, or reporters and editors, to extract for later dissemination.

In Chapter 1 we set forth the concept of *schemata,* which are configurations of meaning that people organize and store in memory. Because sound bites offer a concise way of characterizing an entire theme or idea, they are natural schemata. They are "preselected" organizing schemes that make it easy for an audience to remember a main point from your presentation.

To carry this idea into practice, you must be particularly careful to capture the points or issues that are central to the speech when preparing your sound bites. Once you isolate a crucial issue from the supporting material, consider clever ways you might use language to reiterate that point. You will be helping your audience construct memory schemata.

Another theoretical concept that can be of help here is *connotative meanings.* You want to help your audience organize their soundbite schemata in ways that will ensure they are remembered. Here, the five language strategies we discussed earlier become tools for helping your receivers construct connotative meanings for your point or issue. Experiment with metaphors; select animated words and phrases; try the rhythmic song of repetition. These and other language devices will help the audience identify those passages in your presentation that *you* decide are relevant, interesting, and newsworthy.

Once you have created a sound bite and embedded it in your speech, you will need to prepare your audience for the coming event. The best and easiest way to do that is to use the pregnant pause, give eye contact—*really* look at your audience—and then allow the sound bite to escape from your lips. And when you do, *change the volume of your voice!* If you were speaking loudly before, speak the soundbite softly, or vice versa. These nonverbal delivery cues provide a sharp contrast to all that was said prior to the sound bite.

When your dramatic use of the word, phrase, or sentence is complete, give the audience sufficient time to construct the schema before you proceed with the rest of your speech. Expect the audience to emote, exhale, or applause. Wait for them to do just that.

Managing Applause

Making use of sound bites is only one strategy to ensure audience reaction. You also need to "invite" or encourage your audience to respond by applauding during your presentation. Beginning speakers are often afraid of audience input; professional speakers welcome it. Why the difference? Perhaps beginners fear a negative audience reaction, whereas professionals expect the opposite.

In order to activate your audience, you need to keep in mind an important principle: Audiences like to be involved. Even though they know that the norms require them to be quiet, passive, and polite throughout the entire presentation, they would much rather *interact*. None of us like to be talked *at;* we much prefer being talked *with*. To the extent that you can simulate a sense of interaction *with* your audience, the more likely they will feel like a participant in your "extended conversation" with them.

Audience support and responsive applause does not just "happen." We have to plan for it. Even if the audience wants to applaud, members are seldom willing to "break in" to the middle of your speech. The norms defining who is supposed to do the communicating in the speech context are pretty clear, and every member of an audience knows his or her listener's role: "Listen attentively; don't interrupt." However, those social expectations can be overcome. Watch carefully when a comedian delivers a joke. She or he finishes the story—and waits. What is the comedian waiting for? Laughter and applause, of course. Often, the comedian will actually start laughing, to communicate to the audience that they should laugh now—hoping that the suggested effect will follow. Similarly, professional speakers pause to wait for anticipated audience reaction. Cue cards or monitors accompanying the script often tell the speaker to stop and allow the audience to "interrupt" with applause.

We showed in our chapter on nonverbal communication that pausing and giving eye contact are important turn-yielding cues in normal, everyday conversation. Correspondingly, the public speaking context requires the speaker to *signal* nonverbally to the audience that it is "their turn." A long and purposeful pause from the speaker alerts the audience that they are *expected* to react. Because we know that most people cannot tolerate silence during interactions, the audience is likely to feel obligated to respond on cue. And, because eye contact further obliges the listener to respond, we can predict that speakers who pause *and* look directly at the group will compel the audience to say or do *something*. That "something" is well defined in the norms of communication that regulate public speaking. The natural reaction is to applaud. This type of audience reaction, then, is not difficult to orchestrate.

Developing Your Own Rhetorical Style

All great speakers carve out their own unique style. Sometimes that communication style is enhanced with accents or regional dialects; other times style is intensified with a predictable look or smile. We can define **rhetorical style** as *the overall qualitative way in which a speaker communicates, using verbal language patterns and nonverbal cues.* Perhaps one of the more difficult assignments for new speakers is to identify or discover a personal style of communicating that works well for them. But once they have been able to isolate a personal style, they can begin to showcase that style to their own advantage.

But what are the alternatives? How can a new speaker select a style that will be appropriate and natural? Actually, there are a number of easily recognized types from which to choose. Among them are the attentive style, open style, friendly style, contentious style, relaxed style, and many others. However, in this section, we will examine only three common rhetorical styles that have proved to be useful in public speaking situations: the *dramatic, animated,* and *humorous* styles. With these we can illustrate the basic idea of rhetorical style.

Dramatic Style

We all know people who tell stories so dramatically that they literally command our attention. Dramatic speakers are generally humorous, but they need not be funny to be dramatic. They are performers and treat the public speaking event as if they are "on stage" and "center front." They know how to build tension when they tell a story; they often use colorful words or metaphors; they exaggerate for emphasis; and they vary their vocalics over a considerable range to hold attention and create effects. In short, they act *dramatic*. They typically "work" their audiences so well that people respond with sympathy, interest, or surprise.[25]

One of the more dramatic speakers in recent U.S. history is General Norman Schwarzkopf, who became known as "Stormin' Norman" during the Persian Gulf War early in 1991. Much has been written about General Schwarzkopf, but virtually all Americans who tuned into television reports on the war agreed that he was dramatic. Because he used an effective rhetorical style, he could make even the most boring military briefing seem exciting and stimulating. During one of those dramatic briefings, a reporter asked the general what he thought of Saddam Hussein's military leadership in Iraq: "Hah!" the general replied, in a voice booming with disdain. And then he used dramatic nonverbal gestures, ticking off his contempt one-by-one on the fingers of his left hand: "Saddam is neither a strategist, nor is he schooled in the operational art, nor is he a tactician, nor is he a general, nor is he a soldier.'' Then the general paused, shrugged his shoulders, and concluded with a derisive turnabout, ''Other than that, he is a great military man.'' And then he grinned. (And so did his entire audience.) Besides the use of nonverbal vocalics, rhythmic repetition, gestures, and pause time, General Schwarzkopf communicated dramatically by directly contradicting himself. First he tells us what Saddam *is not;* and then he says what he *is* (with double meaning). Altering the conclusion so that the facts cannot possibly support the conclusion is one of many dramatic devices that a speaker can use.

Both overstatement and understatement are two other ways the dramatic speaker highlights or adds emphasis. Exaggerating a story to make it seem more than it is, or delivering lines with dry wit, are common uses of over- and understatements. A good example of dramatic over- and understatement was used by Governor Ann Richards in her 1988 condemnation of the U.S. defense budget: ''But when we pay billions for planes that won't fly, billions for tanks that won't fire, and billions for systems that won't work, that old dog won't hunt.''[26] Notice her exaggeration of the qualities of defense equipment followed closely by the hometown euphemism ''that old dog won't hunt.'' Like General Schwarzkopf, Governor Richards was using a dramatic rhetorical style.

Stories often provide another avenue of drama to a public speaking event. Good storytellers like Mark Twain, Tip O'Neil, Harry Truman, Walter Cronkite, and Will Rogers, all used a dramatic style. You may know others who can ''drag out'' an episode, a joke, or an event. Clearly, some storytellers take too long and bore the listeners, but good ones use the time and the tale to build tension and anticipation. Notice how Barbara Bush used the tale of the mermaid—and quickly linked its finish with her own purpose. Similarly, you can dramatize a story in your efforts to sustain interest in your presentation. Beginning or ending your presentation with a story is a dramatic way to make your point. Consider the opening story of a student's speech advocating increased federal support for AIDS research:

> Listen carefully to my story about Phillip. It is a true story. It is a tragic story:
>
> Phillip is only 15 years old. Phillip will never be 16. Phillip is dying. Phillip will never drive a car; never go to college; never be a parent; never have a professional career. Only a year ago, Phillip thought he would have all those things. But a year ago, Philip was in a car accident and was hurt badly. He needed a blood transfusion. The new blood was infected with AIDS. So instead of getting better, Phillip is getting worse.
>
> Phillip is dying. Ask me if we need to find a cure for

AIDS. Ask my Mom. Ask my Dad. Better yet, ask my brother, Phillip.

Without question, this dramatic opening commands the audience to listen thoughtfully to the remainder of the presentation. Audiences will find it hard to develop resistant arguments when they discover the emotional attachment the speaker holds toward the issue. By dramatizing that commitment, the speaker stands a good chance of involving the audience.

Animated Style

Dramatic speakers are often animated as well, using a lot of energy when they communicate. Energy, enthusiasm, and excitement are the central characteristics of the animated rhetorical style. Animated speakers exaggerate their nonverbal behaviors by gesturing broadly, smiling frequently, pacing purposefully, nodding knowingly, and raising or lowering eyebrows. In brief, animated speakers *emote*—and they show every emotion they are feeling.[27] Audiences always seem to know *exactly* what animated speakers think and feel. All they have to do is watch their face, eyes, gestures, and body movement.

You probably can recall animated speakers who gesture wildly with their arms—sometimes knocking over water glasses on the podium or table. These are people who cannot seem to either think or talk without their hands and arms. They stand out clearly from more restrained speakers. For example, contrast the styles of well-known entertainers. Consider Jack Benny and John Candy. What about Felix and Oscar? Bob Newhart and Arsenio Hall? William F. Buckley and Jesse Jackson? Aside from their particular biases, to which type of speaker would you rather listen? For how long? Most of us would rather attend to speakers whom we find emotionally arousing and sufficiently enthused about what they have to say. After all, enthusiasm is contagious. The more aroused and excited the speaker appears, the more stimulated the audience becomes as well. Furthermore, the audience is more likely to ''stay tuned'' to an animated, lively, energetic speaker as opposed to a dull, lifeless, unimaginative one. By smiling, nodding your head, and gesturing expressively, you can direct your audience to listen and, at the same time, solicit their support or approval of your message.

Humorous Style

If you suspect your style of communicating is a humorous one, you will need to get plenty of feedback from others to validate your perception—and not from just your mother! Most of us already know if we can be funny. For instance, do people laugh "politely" when you tell a joke? When you volunteer to tell a funny story, do your friends quickly interrupt and change the subject? Perhaps they are trying to tell you something about your style. Or do people tell you that you have a good sense of humor? Do they ask you if you have heard any new jokes lately? That is an entirely different message about your style.

How can we decide if humor is for us? It is a difficult decision because most of us typically serve as the audience rather than as the entertainer in humorous situations. Research is not of much help. Much of the research on humor has centered on the sense of humor at the individual level—what we, as individual receivers, perceive or label as funny. In contrast, a new line of research, initiated by Steven and Melanie Booth-Butterfield, focuses on individuals' predisposition toward using humor themselves. Their HO Scale (Humor Orientation Scale) appears on page 438.[28] Take the time to complete the scale now to determine how regularly or effectively you think you use humor when you communicate with others.

It turns out that people whose scores are high on HO (above 60) are more likely to be spontaneous in their encoding of humorous things to say and do, whereas those who score below 60 are more likely to plan their humor.[29] Apparently, anybody can be humorous—even those with low HO scores can be funny, assuming they have the opportunity to prepare their humor ahead of time. This is comforting, because the implication for public speaking situations is that we *all* can inject at least some preplanned humor into our speeches.

Whatever our score on the HO scale, being humorous in front of a large group of people can be difficult if our strategy is not thoughtfully planned. First, most speakers don't *feel* particularly humorous when faced with a large audience to whom they are to deliver a 20 minute presentation. Second, most speakers feel sufficiently anxious or tense so that any attempts at humor are likely to be bungled. Finally, speakers know that humor is in the eye (or is it ear?) of the beholder. In other words, even though we may find our stories and tales sidesplitting, it is the response of the audience that counts.

The important point is that if you think your speaking style leans toward the humorous, you should try to capitalize on that quality by *planning* to be humorous. But even if you are low on the HO scale, you can still use humor if you profit from preplanning advice. In large part this means preparing funny stories ahead of time. Locate interesting quotes or experiences that others have

said or done. Joke-telling reference books are available.[30] A good source is Fuller's *2500 Anecdotes for all Occasions*. For memorable quotes, use Bartlett's *Familiar Quotations*. The *Reader's Digest* offers a number of anecdotes. Almost anything by Mark Twain will contain quotable stories. Television provides a useful source for humor. Particularly useful are talk show hosts, such as Joan Rivers, Johnny Carson, Arsenio Hall, and David Letterman; or comedy shows, like "Night at the Improv!" "The Roseanne Barr Show," "Married with Children," and others. Recall some of your own experiences or ordeals, and rework them into humorous narratives or anecdotes.

It is essential to *practice* telling your story or joke. Add animation and drama to your presentation. Practice in front of a mirror and again, in front of your friends. Vary your vocalics, including rate, volume, and pitch. You might even try adding a southern accent or drawl to regional one-liners: "I'm busier than a cat covered up!" or "I live so far up the holler, you have to pipe in sunshine!"

Borrowing expressions from well-known media sources work best when you repeat their lines using the same vocalics and animation as the original owner. Imagine saying, "Can we talk? Can we really talk?" (Joan Rivers) without also increasing your speech rate, clipping your words, and nodding your head rapidly. Don't be afraid to use gestures, give direct eye contact, lean forward, cross your arms, shrug—use your body to communicate a sense of the ridiculous as well.

You must also be ready and willing to take some risks. Don't be afraid to look (and feel) foolish. Exaggerate your expressions: Roll your eyes, raise those eyebrows, lower your eyeglasses onto your nose (a great prop!), walk slowly and deliberately across the stage, gaze thoughtfully upward, put your hands on your hips—or use whatever other exaggerated movement that helps to reinforce your tale. Nonverbal behaviors are key to effectively presenting a story humorously. Consider how Jack Benny made a fortune out of saying, "Well!" His nonverbal behaviors associated with that single, innocuous word caused people all over America to laugh night after night. If you have never seen Jack Benny, how about Bart Simpson's "Have a cow, man!" or "Cowabunga!"? And then there's the controversial comedian, Andrew Dice Clay: "Unbelievable!"

There are several cautions to keep in mind when using humor: First, we know that a humor threshold exists for every joke, story, and anecdote. Worn-out sayings are more likely to initiate groans, rather than laughter, from your audience. We also suspect that there's a "story threshold" to every presentation.[31]

Second, speakers can try to be *too* funny. Recent re-

Humor Orientation (HO) Scale

Instructions   The following statements apply to how various people use humor when relating to others. Indicate the degree to which each of these statements applies to you by noting whether you:

5 strongly agree   2 disagree
4 agree   1 strongly disagree
3 neutral/undecided

_____ 1. I regularly tell jokes and funny stories when I am with a group.

_____ 2. People usually laugh when I tell a joke or story.

_____ 3. I have no memory for jokes or funny stories.

_____ 4. I can be funny without having to rehearse a joke.

_____ 5. Being funny is a natural communication style with me.

_____ 6. I cannot tell a joke well.

_____ 7. People seldom ask me to tell stories.

_____ 8. My friends would say that I am a funny person.

_____ 9. People don't seem to pay close attention when I tell a joke.

_____ 10. Even funny jokes seem flat when I tell them.

_____ 11. I can easily remember jokes and stories.

_____ 12. People often ask me to tell jokes and stories.

_____ 13. My friends would not say that I am a funny person.

_____ 14. I don't tell jokes or stories even when asked to.

_____ 15. I tell stories and jokes very well.

_____ 16. Of all the people I know, I'm one of the funniest.

_____ 17. I use humor to communicate in a variety of situations.

Calculating Your Score

1. Add your responses to items 3, 6, 7, 9, 10, 13, and 14 = _____.

2. Add your responses to items 1, 2, 4, 5, 8, 11, 12, 15, 16, and 17 = _____.

3. Complete the following formula:
   HO = 42 − Total from step 1 = _____.

   Then, + Total from step 2.

   YOUR TOTAL HO SCORE = _____.

Interpreting Your Score

Possible range of scores: 17–85. (If your own final HO score does not fall within that range, you made a computational error.)

   The average or mean score for the HO is typically 59 or 60. If your score falls below 50 (or below the mean of 60), you are among those who are low in Humor Orientation (not frequently funny and not particularly adept at telling jokes). If your score falls above 70 (or above the mean of 60), you are classified as high in Humor Orientation. HI HO's (HI HO?) use humor a lot and consider themselves able to tell a joke quite well.

Reference

Booth-Butterfield, Steven, & Booth-Butterfield, Melanie (1991). Individual differences in the communication of humorous messages. *The Southern Communication Journal, 56,* 205–218.

search on humor in the classroom, for instance, reveals that award-winning teachers use humor frequently, but not as often as other teachers do.[32] Apparently, informative or persuasive speakers who use more humor than their audience wants to hear are likely to be dismissed as "jokers" or "lightweights." Thus, anything they have to say will not be taken all that seriously. We recommend, then, that public speakers who choose the humorous style should be careful to use only moderate amounts.

Third, your decision to use humor must depend, in part, on the topic and the occasion. Speeches on drunk driving, AIDS, senility, and drug abuse are not inherently funny. Even if you find something humorous to say about these or related topics, your audience may perceive you and your joke as inappropriate. Speeches presented at a funeral or some other solemn occasion call for a compassionate, sensitive demeanor. Attempts at humor during those events may seem to be useful for alleviating tension or helping to heal, but speakers who are normally humorous usually decide to table their clever wit on such occasions.

Despite these potential pitfalls, we know that humor affects people in a number of positive ways. Research on humor indicates that speakers can go a long way toward building affect with their audience. Simply stated, audiences like speakers who use humor more than speakers who do not. Audiences perceive humorous speakers as friendly; they feel "closer" to speakers who use humor. It turns out that humor is actually a component of *immediacy*.[33] In Chapter 3 we examined the construct of immediacy in a framework of nonverbal communication. We discovered that individuals who use eye contact, gesture frequently, lean forward, nod their heads affirmatively, and smile are generally perceived as physically and psychologically close. In many ways, humor is immediacy behavior because it serves to decrease distance and enhance closeness between people. This finding is good news for public speakers who employ humor effectively and judiciously.

Within limits, humorous speakers are perceived as more competent and intelligent than nonhumorous speakers.[34] Perhaps people admire speakers who can be witty under tense and conspicuous circumstances. What we don't know about humor is its effect on comprehension and retention of information.[35] That is, does humor help us understand what we just heard? Does humor help us remember the speaker's point? The research findings on this issue are mixed. Some studies suggest that humor helps; other research indicates that there is no relationship whatsoever. Fortunately, no study finds humor to retard comprehension and retention.[36] Even so, we suspect that too much humor or humor that is unrelated to the point may actually interfere with audience understanding and recall of the message. Assuming that you are "appropriate" in your use of humor, however, we can predict that humor will most likely help, rather than hurt, your speech.

Whatever rhetorical style you select and develop, you will find that it overlaps with others. That is just fine. After all, dramatic speakers are often both animated and humorous; animated speakers may also be dramatic and occasionally amusing; and humorous speakers may employ both animated and dramatic behaviors in their attempts to be funny.

Finally, whatever style or combination of styles you decide is appropriate for you, the overriding goal is to help the audience decipher how the literal meaning of your message should be interpreted or understood. If you develop and use a rhetorical style with which you feel both competent and comfortable, audiences not only will enjoy your presentations but also will understand very well what you have to say.

Chapter Review

■ Transforming a good speech to a great one requires the use of strategies for using language. These include drawing sensory pictures through concrete or familiar language, and making comparisons with similes and metaphors to create mental images important for audience understanding of abstract ideas. Other strategies that make a difference include the use of simple, clear, modest language to express complex thought; selecting intense, animated words and phrases to build a sense of energy and emotion; and restatement or rephrasing to create a sense of rhythm, predictability, and regularity.

■ All speakers want, and sometimes need, is for their audiences to applaud at key points in their speeches. There is no need to wait until the end of the speech to garner audience response. Instead, audience response can be orchestrated through the use of strategies for including sound bites in the speech so as to capture attention, emotion, or recall of particular points.

■ Effective speakers literally invite their audience to react during their presentation. This is not difficult because audiences want to interact—even though they know their role is to be quiet and polite. One goal in polishing a speech is to stimulate that interaction.

■ Great speakers have their own unique style. Developing your own rhetorical style is an important step toward enhancing your stage presence. There are many styles to choose from, but those that have the most potential to affect the public speaking audience positively include the dramatic or suspenseful storytelling style, the animated or energetic style, and the humorous or comic style.

Key Terms

Concrete (language in speech)   Words and phrases that represent specific objects and situations with which most people are familiar in their daily lives. The opposite is "abstract." For example, an apple, an orange, and a banana are concrete objects; fruit is an abstraction.

Imagery (in speech)   Creating concrete, realistic impressions about what we are saying with the use of carefully chosen words and phrases that appeal to our senses of touch, taste, sound, sight, and smell.

Metaphor   A descriptive phrase used to draw attention to a quality of some object or situation in which descriptive adjectives are assigned that would not normally be applied. Metaphors serve much the same purpose as similes, but they omit the comparative "like" or "as." For example, "He is a block-head," "She has a fiery temper," or a more extended version: "The 19th century became a door through which great ideas rushed and tumbled."

Rhetorical style   The overall qualitative manner of delivery—that is, mode of acting and speaking with the use of both verbal language and nonverbal cues or techniques—in which a speaker communicates to an audience.

Simile   A word or phrase that draws attention to qualities shared by dissimilar things by prefacing the comparison with the word *like* or *as*. Common examples are "dead as a doornail" or "worked like a horse."

Sound bite   A metaphor for a brief passage, sentence, or other expression taken from a press release or broadcast presentation that can then be reprinted or taped for later news reports. Sound bites usually represent a major idea expressed by the speaker.

Notes

1. Kelly, D. (1990). Letter to the Editor, *U.S. News and World Report*, June 11, p. 8.

2. Carlson, M. (1990). *Time*, June 11, p. 21.

3. Clift, E., with A. McDaniel & C. Bingham. (1990). *Newsweek*, June 11, p. 26.

4. Thomas H. Kean, governor of New Jersey, "Keynote Address," delivered at the Republican National Convention, New Orleans, LA, August 16, 1988. Taken from *Vital Speeches of the Day*, Oct. 15, 1988.

5. John Silber, "Education and National Survival," delivered at the Presidential Convocation, St. Paul's College, Lawrenceville, VA, Nov. 4, 1987. Taken from *Vital Speeches of the Day*, Jan. 15, 1988.

6. Lloyd Bentsen, U.S. senator from Texas and Democratic candidate for vice-president of the United States, "Acceptance Speech," delivered at the Democratic National Convention, Atlanta, GA, July 21, 1988. Taken from *Vital Speeches of the Day*, Aug. 15, 1988.

7. Eugene C. Dorsey, president of the Gannett Foundation, "Giving Yourself Away," speech presented to the National Rochester Society, Rochester, NY, Apr. 20, 1988. Taken from *Vital Speeches of the Day*, July 15, 1988.

8. Governor Ann Richards, then state treasurer of Texas, "Keynote Address," speech presented at the Democratic National Convention, Atlanta, GA, July 18, 1988. Taken from *Vital Speeches of the Day*, Aug. 15, 1988.

9. President George Bush, then vice-president of the United States and Republican nominee for president, "Acceptance Speech," delivered at the Republican National Convention, New Orleans, LA, Aug. 18, 1988. Taken from *Vital Speeches of the Day*, Oct. 15, 1988.

10. Jesse Jackson, candidate for Democratic presidential nomination, "Common Ground and Common Sense," delivered at the Democratic National Convention, Atlanta, GA, July 20, 1988. Taken from *Vital Speeches of the Day*, Aug. 15, 1988.

11. Eugene C. Dorsey, president of the Gannett Foundation, "Giving Yourself Away," delivered to the National Rochester Society, Rochester, NY, Apr. 20, 1988. Taken from *Vital Speeches of the Day*, July 15, 1988.

12. John Silber, president of Boston University, "The Cycle of Poverty," delivered at the Presidential Convocation, St. Paul's College, Lawrenceville, VA, Nov. 4, 1987. Taken from *Vital Speeches of the Day*, Jan. 15, 1988.

13. Governor Ann Richards, then state treasurer of Texas, "Keynote Address," delivered at the Democratic National Convention, Atlanta, GA, July 18, 1988. Taken from *Vital Speeches of the Day*, Aug. 15, 1988.

14. Lloyd Bentsen, U.S. senator from Texas and Democratic candidate for vice-president of the United States, "Acceptance Speech," delivered at the Democratic National Convention, Atlanta, GA, July 21, 1988. Taken from *Vital Speeches of the Day*, Aug. 15, 1988.

15. Ronald Reagan, then president of the United States, "We, The People," delivered at the Republican National Convention, New Orleans, LA, Aug. 15, 1988. Taken from *Vital Speeches of the Day*, Oct. 15, 1988.

16. President George Bush, then vice-president of the United States and Republican nominee for president, "Acceptance Speech," delivered at the Republican National Convention, New Orleans, LA, Aug. 18, 1988. Taken from *Vital Speeches of the Day*, Oct. 15, 1988.

17. A number of studies support this relationship. See, for instance: Bodaken, E. M., Plax, T. G., Piland, R. N., & Weiner, A. N. (1979). Role enactment as a socially relevant explanation of self-persuasion.

Human Communication Research, 5, 203–214; and Burgoon, M., Jones, S., & Stewart, D. (1975). Toward a message-centered theory of persuasion: Three empirical investigations of language intensity. *Human Communication Research, 1,* 249–256.

18. Martin Luther King, Jr., civil rights leader, "I Have a Dream," delivered to over 200,000 civil rights demonstrators, Washington, DC, Aug. 28, 1963.

19. Thomas H. Kean, governor of New Jersey, "Keynote Address," delivered at the Republican National Convention, New Orleans, LA, Apr. 16, 1988. Taken from *Vital Speeches of the Day,* Oct. 15, 1988.

20. Martin Luther King, Jr., civil rights leader, "I Have a Dream," delivered to over 200,000 civil rights demonstrators, Washington, DC, Aug. 28, 1963.

21. Thrall, W. F., Hibbard, A., & Holman E. H. (1960). *A handbook to literature* (pp. 416–417). New York: Odyssey Press.

22. Edward M. Kennedy, U.S. senator from Massachusetts, "Where Was George?" delivered at the Democratic National Convention, Atlanta, GA, July 19, 1988. Taken from *Vital Speeches of the Day,* Aug. 15, 1988.

23. President George Bush, then vice-president of the United States and Republican nominee for president, "Acceptance Speech," delivered at the Republican National Convention, New Orleans, LA, Aug. 18, 1988. Taken from *Vital Speeches of the Day,* October 15, 1988.

24. Although most of these well-known soundbites can be easily recalled, their origins are often hard to trace. Importantly, these particular soundbites are good examples of how such expressions can be important to how speeches are received.

25. Norton, R. (1983). *Communicator style: Theory, applications, and measures* (pp. 129–153). Beverly Hills, CA: Sage.

26. This example is taken from Texas Governor Ann Richards, "Keynote Address," delivered at the Democratic National Convention, Atlanta, GA, July 18, 1988. See *Vital Speeches of the Day,* August 15, 1988.

27. Ibid., pp. 67–68.

28. Booth-Butterfield, S., & Booth-Butterfield, M. (1991). Individual differences in the communication of humorous messages, *The Southern Communication Journal, 56,* 205–218.

29. Ibid.

30. For an excellent discussion of the effects of humorous representations, see Kaplan, R. M. and Pascoe, G. C. (1977), "Humorous lectures and humorous examples: some effects upon comprehension and retention," *Journal of Educational Psychology, 69,* 61–65.

31. Gorham, J., & Christophel, D. M., (1990). The relationship of teachers' use of humor in the classroom to immediacy and student learning. *Communication Education, 39,* 46–62.

32. Downs, V., Javidi, M., & Nussbaum, J. (1988). An analysis of teachers' verbal communication within the college classroom: Use of humor, self-disclosure, and narratives. *Communication Education, 37,* 127–141.

33. Gorham, J. (1988). The relationship between verbal teacher immediacy behaviors and student learning. *Communication Education, 37,* 40–53; Gorham, J., & Christophel, D. M. (1990). The relationship of teachers' use of humor in the classroom to immediacy and student learning. *Communication Education, 39,* 46–62.

34. Bryant, J., & Zillman, D. (1979). Teachers' humor in the college classroom. *Communication Education, 28,* 110–118; Gruner, C. R. (1966). A further experimental study of satire as persuasion. *Speech Monographs, 33,* 184–185.

35. A number of studies have examined this relationship. More recent research has focused on the *type* of humor used and its effect on message comprehension and retention, including irony, satire, sarcasm, self-deprecating humor, and others. See, for instance, Gorham, J., & Christophel, D. M. (1990). The relationship of teachers' use of humor in the classroom to immediacy and student learning. *Communication Education, 39,* 46–62; Weaver, J., Zillman, D., & Bryant, J. (1988). Effects of humorous distortions on children's learning from educational television: Further evidence. *Communication Education, 37,* 181–187; Kaplan, R., & Pascoe, G. (1977). Humorous lectures and humorous examples: Some effects upon comprehension and retention. *Journal of Educational Psychology, 69,* 61–65.

36. As researchers begin to examine the types of humor employed in a message, we might begin to find that certain kinds of humor may, in fact, interfere with the message. For instance, Weaver, Zillman and Bryant (1988) found that irony and humorous exaggerations contributed to children's misperceptions of educational television programs. Whether or not that relationship generalizes to adult audiences sitting face-to-face with live speakers has yet to be determined. These same researchers suggest that the potential for message distortion may occur with the use of "insider jokes."

Additional Readings

Booth-Butterfield, S., & Booth-Butterfield, M. (1991). Individual differences in the communication of humorous messages. *The Southern Communication Journal, 56,* 205–218.

This research report describes the development of scale that measures a person's propensity to be humorous. Results indicate that people differ in unique ways in their ability to make humorous presentations. The degree of humor in a speech is also shown to be related to detail, situation, and the amount of speaker planning prior to performance.

Lee, C. I., & Gura, T. (1987). *Oral interpretation* (7th ed.). Boston, MA: Houghton Mifflin.

This popular text offers a complete introduction to the study and practice of the oral interpretation of literature. Each chapter is written to blend theory with interpretative practice. Pertinent topics discussed include the use of voice, language, imagery and the handling of difficult material, as well as other issues important to presenting literature effectively. The text offers a number of suggestions that are particularly helpful for polishing the presentation of messages.

Norton, R. (1983). *Communicator style: Theory, applications, and measures.* Beverly Hills, CA: Sage.

This text provides an overview of the founding research on communicator style. It defines the various styles of communication and discusses how each influences presentations. That is, how a person exhibiting a particular style is perceived by others, and how they are likely to present their speech as a function of their particular style.

Ratliff, G. (1981). *Beginning readers theatre: A primer for classroom performance*. Annandale, VA: Speech Communication Association.

Similar to the available oral performance and oral interpretation texts this book covers a number of topics relevant to refining the content of presentations in general.

Moreover, it makes a number of substantive recommendations for using language and the voice that apply to all types of performance.

Vital Speeches of the Day. Mount Pleasant, SC: City News Publishing Co.

This bimonthly periodical publishes the original texts of contemporary speeches. Each text is unaltered and authentic and represents a speech that was delivered shortly prior to its publication. This provides students with the opportunity to examine firsthand how speakers of all types polish and refine their presentations.

Glossary

Accommodation style A strategy for handling conflict in which people "give in" to their opponents. Accommodators are the opposite of competitors. They tend to be passive, foregoing their personal goals and preferring to let their opponents reach their objectives.

Active response Getting an audience to engage in a form of behavior in response to a request or suggestion by a speaker. Examples are holding up hands, clapping on cue, saying yes or no in response to questions.

Adaptation Various ways in which both message senders and receivers independently modify how they think and behave toward each other during the transmitting and receiving processes.

Adaptation (to audience) Adjusting one's message to perceived needs and interests of an audience on the basis of collective role-taking and feedback that they provide.

Affinity-seeking Using various communication strategies in attempts to get people to like you.

Agent (of socialization) Persons such as teachers, friends, or parents, or even mass media, that deliberately or unwittingly present to us learning experiences or "lessons" that play a part in the development of our personality.

Anomie (personal) A feeling of anxiety or distress arising from confusion concerning the social expectations of others.

Arbitrary (selection) The sounds and/or letters used to form words that refer to particular meanings within a given language are not initially selected by clear rules but rather in random or even capricious ways. Once they are selected and established in use, however, the relationship between word and referent becomes fixed.

Artifacts Physical objects that we possess, such as jewelry, handbags, pens, and briefcases (or even homes, cars, and offices) that provide meanings to others about our personal and social attributes.

Assertiveness-training group A specialized discussion group in which participants are given instruction in ways in which they can stand up for their rights and be more demanding in ensuring that they are treated with dignity and respect.

Assignment-based cohesion A type of cohesion based on the fact that members of a group have been asked (or ordered) to serve by their boss, are voted into membership by a valued constituency, or must serve for some other valid obligation or duty.

Assimilation A feature of the embedding process by which a message is reshaped into new interpretations (distortions) by the psychological characteristics and culturally learned habits of the receiver.

Attitude A relatively enduring organization of affective beliefs about some broad object (such as a policy, social category of people, or situation) that increases the probability that an individual will respond to that object in a manner consistent with those beliefs.

Attribution process The selection and assignment of various personal qualities, conditions, dispositions, or external social pressures to another individual that we believe are the causes of or influences on some aspect of that person's behavior. (See **implicit personality**.) Verbal messages to other people about what kind of person we are.

Audio conferencing Connecting people by long-distance telephone lines (sometimes with the parties in special rooms where they can make use of good quality speakers) so that they can talk to each other to hold a conference or meeting.

Authority The basis of legitimacy for the exercise of power.

Avoidance style A strategy for handling conflicts in which a potential participant chooses not to be a part of the confrontation but chooses to stay away from situations where disagreements and disputes are likely to occur.

Behavior-alteration techniques Including meanings in a persuasive message that are designed to arouse feelings of reward and punishment. These techniques are based on principles of behavior modification in learning.

Belief A kind of "statement of truth" that an individual accepts about some object (thing, situation, or event). Some are "factual" in that they do not involve any kind of positive or negative judgment or imply any kind of emotional orientation on the part of the person holding the belief. Others are "affective" in having a positive or negative component of feeling or judgment regarding their object for the person holding the belief.

Body language The (unsupported) idea believed by some that bodily actions, gestures, and other nonverbal behavior reveal more of our "true" thoughts and feelings than does our verbal behavior.

Boomerang An undesired effect of a persuasive message (speech) that "backfires." That is, it creates an effect that is the opposite of that desired by the person originating the message.

Bureaucracy   A deliberately designed plan of the goals, norms, roles, ranks, and controls in an organization.

Charismatic authority   Unique personal attractiveness that makes an individual exercising leadership seem very special to those who are led and therefore willing to accept his or her exercise of power.

Chronemics   The study of the way in which people use time to transmit nonverbal messages.

Clever Hans effect   The mistaken belief that an animal can use language as do human beings because it makes complex responses or initiates behavior using combinations of signs and signals. Such combinations can be a result of the animal responding to subtle cues unintentionally provided by an experimenter, or they may simply represent chance occurrence among a large number of unpatterned behaviors.

Coercion   Compelling someone to do something, or restraining them from acting in some way, by threatening them with consequences that they find unacceptable.

Cognitive reorganization   A modification of the feelings, beliefs, attitudes, motivations, or other internal components of an individual's cognitive structure (as a result of persuasion in the present context).

Cognitive restructuring   A form of treatment for fears (which can be used to reduce communication apprehension). The process centers on a subject's personal interpretations of an anxiety-producing situation and seeks to change them through training.

Cohesion (group)   That set of factors in every kind of group, large or small, intimate or formal, which moves the participants to maintain their membership and to perform the activities expected or required of them.

Collaborative style   A strategy for handling conflicts in which people work jointly or willingly in cooperation with an opponent. The collaborative style is characteristic of persons who not only are seeking self-related goals in a conflict situation but who also have a sincere concern for their opponents.

Communication apprehension   A fear or anxiety experienced by a person when anticipating or during communication encounters.

Comparative perspective   The study of animals (including human beings) that is based on a strategy of looking for general laws of behavior common to many species.

Competence (of a speaker)   A dimension of speaker credibility, a judgment on the part of members of an audience as to how much valid knowledge the speaker commands about the issue under discussion.

Competitive style   A strategy for handling conflicts in which people narrowly view all conflicts as win-lose events. They believe that winning is their only goal and that having a concern for their opponent is both unnecessary and unimportant.

Compliance   Yielding publicly or observably to an influence attempt without actually accepting the change privately.

Composure (as speaker)   As a dimension of speaker credibility, the degree to which a speaker is calm, cool, and collected before a large audience.

Compounding pattern   A pattern of distortion whereby an original message passed by word of mouth through a grapevine grows larger and more complex, gaining additional details and interpretations that were never a part of the original.

Compromising style   A strategy from handling conflicts in which participants reach agreement by making mutual concessions.

Computer network   A number of computers linked together by wires or a radio system so that their users can transmit files of data or other information and messages from one to another. Some are local and serve a given organization. Others are large-scale and reach to many sites in a country.

Computer teleconferencing   Using a computer network for the purpose of enabling people at diverse sites to communicate in the manner of holding a meeting or conference. This permits them to type messages for each other that can be read on each of their screens.

Concept   A label (symbol) that stands for and signifies a set of objects, situations, or events that can logically be grouped together and thought about as making up a class or category because they share similar properties or attributes.

Concrete (language in speech)   Words and phrases that represent specific objects and situations with which most people are familiar in their daily lives. The opposite is "abstract." For example, an apple, an orange, and a banana are concrete objects; fruit is an abstraction.

Conflict   A dispute in which different values result in claims to rewards or resources that are in limited supply, and where the main objective of the participants is to either neutralize or eliminate the prospects of their opponents to win what is at stake.

Conflict style   The manner in which an individual is likely to behave when anticipating or engaging in a confrontation.

Connotative (meanings)   Personal or unshared meanings that an individual uniquely associates with a referent because of past experience.

Consciousness-raising group   One in which people engage in discussions that help them realize they face mutual problems, such as sex discrimination, and how these should be defined and dealt with.

Constructive resistance   Resistance to persuasion that contributes positively to a situation, especially when the behavior being solicited is against ethical norms.

Context   The combined physical setting, sociocultural situation, and social relationships in which communication takes place. Examples are a wedding in a church or a sales meeting among employees in an office.

Controls (communication)   Messages that provide sanctions—that is, meanings of rewards for complying with, and punishments for deviating from, the communication rules shared in the group.

Convention A rule adopted within a particular cultural group (or language community) that specifies what patterns of meaning are to be labeled with what particular word or nonverbal indicator.

Cost/benefit ratio The ratio between the efforts that have to be made in establishing or maintaining a relationship to the rewards that it brings. (See *utilitarianism*.)

Counterargument A persuasive message in a speech that presents information intended to discredit a particular conclusion or position.

Credibility (of a message) The degree to which a message is judged to be valuable or worthless, critical or trivial, true or false. This will depend on the perceived sincerity and honesty of the source as evaluated by the audience.

Credibility (of a source) Simply, the degree to which a receiver sees a source person (group or agency) as trustworthy and the messages transmitted by that source as usually truthful. In more technical terms, a perceived characteristic of a source based on a combination of beliefs about that source's competence, trustworthiness, extroversion, composure, and sociability.

Criteria (in listening) Standards by which we decide whether a source or sender is credible, whether what the person is saying is believable, and whether or not the message is important to us in any way.

Cushioning function The benefit derived from having friends or family members who provide emotional support when events beyond our control in an uncaring world make life difficult.

Decision-making group One in which the goal is to arrive at orderly judgments, usually through a process of formal communication and discussion.

Decoding The assignment of meaning to symbols perceived by a receiver in the communication process.

Definition of the situation W. I. Thomas's principle of behavior, stating that if people believe something to be real, they will act as though it were real.

Denotative (meanings) Meanings that by established convention are to be aroused and experienced by a particular symbol.

Dependency-based cohesion A type of cohesion characteristic of organizations with a complex division of labor. Members are bound to the organization and to each other because all members perform specialized tasks that are in some way linked to and dependent on the tasks performed by others.

Destructive resistance Disagreeable, negative, subversive, or even rebellious behavior in response to legitimate attempts at persuasion.

Disengagement Communication strategies people use when they are attempting to withdraw gracefully (or not so gracefully) from a close association with another.

Dissociation A strategy of transmitting messages to another person aimed at achieving a reduction in the use of the unit-implying pronoun "we," and reverting back to the individualistic "you" and "I."

Distancing A strategy of transmitting verbal and nonverbal messages to another person with the goal of increasing both physical and psychological distance between the two parties.

Distortion An outcome of communication in which meanings intended by the communicator become compounded with, or displaced by, unintended implications as the meanings of the message are constructed by a receiver.

Dyad Two persons in a relatively enduring social relationship.

E-mail A system for sending and receiving typed messages on a computer network. It consists of software that permits word processing and hardware which allows a message to be displayed on the screen of a sending person and to be sent to a receiver's computer (where it can be displayed on his or her screen and be stored in the memories of the computers at each end).

Embedding pattern A particular set of distortions—*leveling, sharpening,* and *assimilation*—that may occur in a message when it is transmitted orally from one person to the next in a kind of serial pattern.

Emblems A category of nonverbal gestures that have established conventions of meaning providing direct verbal translations.

Encoding The assignment of symbols to meanings that a communicator intends to transmit to a receiver.

Enculturation The process of acquiring understandings of a culture (or subculture), including not only language skills but also shared beliefs, emotional orientations, attitudes, values, and everything that makes a person an accepted human being who "fits in."

Engagement That communication process by which people try to move their relationships from an impersonal to a personal basis.

Exchange theory A formulation originally developed by George Homans to try to explain all forms of human social interaction. Applied to communication, it argues that we implicitly count up the history of rewards received from interacting with the other person, weigh that against the history of costs, and make an estimate of the worth of the relationship to us. If rewards outweigh the costs for both individuals, then the relationship is likely to survive and gain momentum. If not, the relationship is likely to terminate.

Experiential group One in which the principal goal of participation is to make people feel better.

Extemporaneous delivery Delivering a speech from a well-organized, well-rehearsed speech outline, but not a complete text.

Extroversion (of a speaker) As a dimension of speaker credibility, a judgment of an audience as to the degree to which a speaker is "outgoing"—that is, people-oriented, talkative, and gregarious.

Fax (or facsimile)   An electronic device for reading, transmitting, and reproducing documents, graphics, or photographs over long distance telephone lines.

Feedback   Verbal or nonverbal messages deliberately or unwittingly sent by a receiver back to a source or sender while a message is being transmitted. Feedback permits the sender to modify the formulation of a message so as to enable the receiver to understand it better.

Fidelity   The degree to which the encoded meanings in a sender's message match those decoded by a receiver.

Formal communication   Communication between parties who are allowed or required by the group's rules to transmit particular kinds of messages to specific receivers using officially designated rules and restrictions.

Format   A manner in which a lengthy message (like a speech, article, term paper, or book) is organized. Usually this is in terms of some number of major sections, each of which is divided into subsections.

Forum   A type of discussion group usually based on brief presentations by each member of a small group who are introduced by a chairperson. Their presentations are followed by a considerable amount of participation by members of the audience, again coordinated by the chairperson.

Framing   The use of nonverbal gestures or other actions while talking so as to emphasize, complement, and reinforce what we are saying.

Gateway   A computer that receives transmitted information from one network, reformats it if necessary, and feeds it into another network in a form that it can accept.

Grapevine   Complex social pathways in a network of intimate groups within an organization through which informal messages are transmitted by word-of-mouth.

Group   (Technically) Two or more people who repeatedly interact together, regulating their conduct within some set of rules for communication and social activity that they mutually recognize and follow.

Haptics   The study of touch as a means of nonverbal communication.

Human relations perspective   An approach to managing organizations in which the personal and social characteristics of workers as individual human beings are critical factors in the work process. Managers try to motivate, encourage, and foster worker performance by taking advantage of human factors to make work more tolerable, under the assumption that this will increase output.

Human resources perspective   An approach to managing organizations based on assumptions that bonds of loyalty can be created between worker and employer and that workers have insights into production processes which offer valuable clues as to how both quality and efficiency can be improved.

Human use perspective   An approach to management in which workers are not thought of in humanitarian terms but simply as one more thing that can be "used," along with machinery, and "exploited" like raw materials.

Identification   A desire to emulate a particular individual because a person feels that he or she is like that individual or would like to be like that individual.

Imagery (in speech)   Creating concrete, realistic impressions about what we are saying with the use of carefully chosen words and phrases that appeal to our senses of touch, taste, sound, sight, and smell.

Immediacy principle   The generalization that people tend to approach things and others they like or prefer and avoid those they don't like or don't prefer.

Implicit personality   A set of assumptions quickly formulated about the personal characteristics of an individual one has just met. These are beliefs about that person's qualities and motives that are projected on him or her on the basis of limited information obtained in an initial encounter.

Impression management   Knowingly transmitting verbal and nonverbal messages that are deliberately designed to bring one or more others to believe that you possess a particular set of characteristics.

Impromptu delivery   A mode of presenting a speech that is delivered on the spot, with little or no lead time or formal prior preparation.

Informal communication   Communication that takes place in the absence of deliberately designed rules, barriers, or constraints—communication that is spontaneous and unrestrained. When communicating informally, people feel relatively free to say what they feel and do not constantly worry that their meanings will be misunderstood or that they will arouse hostile responses.

Information   Physical events, such as agitations of air molecules that enable a receiver to hear the voice of a communicator or light waves that make written symbols visible. Such information makes it possible to transcend space or time in the communication process.

Instincts   Inherited tendencies to act in complex ways. Many animals have elaborate instincts concerning such behavior as migration, reproduction, and communication. Human beings do not have instincts. Their behavior patterns are established by learning in a social environment.

Internalization   Yielding to influence because it is personally rewarding or useful.

Interpersonal communication   Communication that takes place between two people in face-to-face settings, over time, who then come to know one another better as their relationship moves from impersonal to personal.

Intimate group   People who make up either a human family or a peer group. The key factor is that communication is extensive, self-disclosing, and uninhibited.

Kinesics   The study of body movements—including

gestures, posture, and facial expression—that are used for nonverbal communication.

Labeling theory An explanation of how people respond to others by reinterpreting the nature of an individual's characteristics and social worth after that person has been given a negative "label" by some official agency. For example, the term *mental patient* causes people to assign numerous negative characteristics to an individual who is so labeled, whether the person has those attributes or not.

Language A complex of shared words, nonverbal signs, and rules for their use and interpretation according to agreed-upon rules within a particular human group or society.

Learned helplessness A feeling of inadequacy and stress arising from an inability to communicate in a predictable way with a person who is completely inconsistent in his or her responses to messages.

Legal-rational authority A basis of legitimate authority in organizations in which leaders are selected because they possess technical-managerial skills that qualify them to exercise power within a limited sphere which is narrowly defined by "official" definitions and rulings.

Leveling A general shortening of a message, such as a rumor, story, or other verbal account as it travels by word-of-mouth from one person to the next, as through a grapevine.

Linear A process that moves like a straight line, from a beginning to an end through specific stages.

Listening An active form of behavior in which individuals attempt to maximize their attention to, and comprehension of, what is being communicated to them through the use of words, actions, and things by one or more people in their immediate environment.

Machiavellianism A strategy for ending a relationship in which a manipulative individual desiring that goal is able to convince an unwilling partner, who is unaware of the strategy, that termination was in the partner's best interest and was his or her idea.

Management (as communication strategy) The communication strategies people use to maintain valued interpersonal ties.

Manuscript delivery (in public speaking) A mode of presenting a speech based on reading it word-for-word to the audience from a written script.

Meaning Responses that individuals learn to make, either to objects, events, or situations in reality that they experience through their senses, or to socially shared symbols which are used to label those aspects of reality.

Meaning (deep) The basic ideas implied by a message. The essential meanings that can be understood well enough for practical purposes.

Meaning (surface) The entire set of meanings that are encoded into a communicator's message, whether they are essential to understanding its basic ideas or not.

Meaning triangle A diagram showing that meaning, symbol, and referent constitute a kind of system, with each element linked by a convention. One element is the referent—a situation, thing, or even make-believe idea to which we have assigned some meaning. A second element is meaning—the internal configuration or schema of memory traces subjectively aroused in us by apprehending the referent. Finally, the symbol is the word, gesture, object, or behavior that we use as a cue to arouse the meaning in another (or even in ourselves). Conventions are agreements among participants.

Medium Any device, simple or complex, that extends the distance over which people can communicate or which overcomes time. Media carry or store information into which symbols are encoded by senders and decoded by receivers.

Memorandum From the Latin *memoro,* meaning "to call to mind." A stylized written document, widely used in organizational communication for the purposes of transmitting significant messages to one or more receivers through formal channels.

Memorized delivery (in public speaking) A mode of presenting a speech based on a procedure that requires writing out the speech beforehand and practicing it over and over again until the entire text is committed to rote memory.

Message ordering Often referred to as the *primacy-recency* question. That is, is it more persuasive to put the arguments favoring a position early in a message, or does more change result when arguments are inserted at the end of the message?

Metaphor Descriptive phrase used to draw attention to a quality of some object or situation in which adjectives are assigned that would not normally be applied. Metaphors serve much the same purpose as similes, but they omit the comparative "like" or "as." For example, "He is a block-head," "She has a fiery temper," or a more extended version: "The nineteenth century became a door through which great ideas rushed and tumbled."

Negotiation A process of communicating proposed solutions to a conflict back and forth between opponents for the purpose of reaching a joint agreement and thus resolving the dispute.

Nonsocial constraints (on attitude-related action) Nonsocial factors that reduce the consistency between attitude and action. For example, the act may be inconvenient, involve potential financial loss, pose risks, or be difficult to perform. Also, the person may lack opportunity or competence.

Nonverbal communication The deliberate or unintentional use of objects, actions, sounds, time, and space so as to arouse meanings in others.

Nonverbal immediacy Physical and psychological closeness to others, a condition that can be established through the deliberate use of nonverbal signals and actions.

Normative confusion (anomie) A condition in which communication norms have not been effectively clarified, or in which consensus breaks down about what kinds of messages, topics, or issues are approved and disapproved. Such confusion can be a major cause of group disorganization.

Norms   In general these are shared convictions about what kinds of behavior are approved within a group or society. In the case of communication, they are rules understood and accepted by the parties that define both the content and style of messages that are appropriate or inappropriate in a particular situation.

Norms (for communication)   General rules that each participant in a group is expected to follow concerning what issues and topics and modes of transmission are acceptable for communication to various kinds of other members.

Oculesics   The study of eye contact and pupil dilation in nonverbal communication as people use their eyes to indicate their degree of interest, openness, and even arousal.

Order (in format)   The sequence in which major points in a speech are to be presented. This can be in terms of space (a sequence of places where the events took place), time (the chronological sequence in which events happened), cause (which events brought on others as consequences), or by topic (which does not require a particular logical sequence).

Organization   A human group that has been deliberately designed so as to achieve a desired objective. Usually it has a relatively large number of participants whose activities are coordinated by complex rules for communication.

Organization chart   A graphic representation of the chain of authority and command in an organization, which also provides a guide to the flow of formal messages. It is especially helpful in understanding the vertical flow of communication—up and down the organization.

Organizational cohesion   That which binds members of an organization to each other and to the group as a whole. Realistically, it is based on a combination of sentiment-based cohesion within small groups of work associates, reward-based cohesion in more temporary task-oriented groups, assignment-based cohesion among members of decision-making groups within the organization, and dependency-based cohesion that is a product of task interdependencies in the overall structure.

Organizational communication   The transmission of messages through both the formal and informal channels of a relatively large deliberately designed group, resulting in the construction of meanings that have influences on its members, both as individuals and on the group as a whole.

Organizational subculture   The total pattern of all the shared beliefs, sentiments, attitudes, values, rules, special languages, and everything else that is produced and shared by the members of an organization. These cultural elements set it off from other organizations and the society as a whole.

Panel   A more formal type of discussion group in which participants are often experts or representatives of some sort.

The panel is usually coordinated by a moderator, and the discussion usually takes place before a live audience.

Peer group   A small group of close and intimate friends, often of the same general socioeconomic characteristics, age, and gender.

Perception   The psychological process of seeing, hearing, or feeling something (with the senses) and identifying what it is within interpretations provided by one's language and culture.

Personal idea (persona)   An older term for set of beliefs, meanings, and understandings that an individual develops about another person as a result of communicating with her or him. (This is closely related to what social scientists now call "implicit personality.")

Person perception   The processes by which an individual comes to know and to think about specific other persons, their characteristics, qualities, and inner states.

Personality   The individual's more-or-less enduring organization of meanings, motivations, emotional patterns, orientations, skills, and other attributes that make that person different in psychological makeup from all others.

Persuasion   Basically, efforts to *change* people in some way by using strategies of communication. More formally: a communication process in which a source or sender encodes and transmits messages designed to influence a receiving person's constructions of meanings in ways that will lead to changes desired by the source in the receiver's beliefs, attitudes, or behavior.

Pheromones   Chemical secretions that are used by insects and other animals in their communication processes. They are released in the air or are deliberately used to mark trails, territory, or readiness for mating.

Phylogenetic continuum   The idea from evolutionary theory that animals can be arranged along a kind of scale in terms of the complexity of their bodily structures and behavior.

Predispositions   Tendencies to approve of some things and disapprove of others that are shaped by attitudes, values, opinions, preferences, and so on. These factors modify our perceptions and interpretations of things that take place around us, because they lead us to like some stimuli and dislike others.

Prejudice   A configuration of emotionally held beliefs that results in a person making judgments about another on a categorical basis (as opposed to an individual basis) before they even begin to communicate or interact.

Presentation of self   Deliberately formulating and transmitting verbal and nonverbal messages about one's self.

Primary group   Intimate groups that are earliest in the experience of the human individual and which play a critical part in the person's psychological and social development. Essentially these are the family and early peer groups. Peer groups in adult life are also considered primary groups.

Principle of covarying attribution   A general rule

concerning the attribution of internal or external causes to a person's pattern of behavior. If the behavior is disapproved by others, they will tend to attribute it to negative personal qualities (an internal cause). If the behavior is approved, they will attribute it to external factors beyond the person's control.

Principle of delayed gratification   A belief that accepting costs or guarding resources in the present will pay off in significant long-term rewards.

Proxemics   The study of the meanings communicated by the use of space and distance.

Psychodynamic strategy   A traditional approach to persuasion resting on the assumption that the route to achieving behavioral change lies in achieving cognitive reorganization (such as altering beliefs or attitudes). In nontechnical terms: Based on the idea that "mind" controls "action," it follows that if feelings and beliefs ("mind") can be changed by persuasive messages (cognitive reorganization), overt behavior will be correspondingly changed.

Psychological reactance (against persuasion)   Strong feelings of determined resistance that cause a person to react against an attempt at persuasion.

Quality control circles   Small discussion groups composed of individuals from a particular unit in an organization (usually devoted to manufacturing) whose members all face the same production task. They meet with their supervisor to find ways in which their particular assembly work can be done efficiently and at a higher level of quality.

Rank (as influence on communication)   Rules that define communication patterns based on authority, power, and privilege within a group. For example, who can issue orders, who must always listen to whom, who has a right to speak first or last, and whose messages are regarded as more-or-less important?

Rank ineffectiveness   A situation in which members of a group come to believe that those in positions of power and authority lack legitimacy.

Receiver eccentricities   Personal attributes and individual differences that help or hinder our capacity to receive and interpret messages accurately.

Redundancy (in language)   Including more words in a message than are actually needed to express deep meanings. A condition of excess, duplication, or abundance.

Regulating   Using nonverbal signs and signals as informal "rules of order" to regulate the flow of talk among people who are communicating verbally.

Reinforcement learning theory   An explanation of how individuals acquire particular patterns of response to particular stimuli. Essentially, it states that individuals try out a number of behaviors (sometimes selected randomly) as responses to stimuli. If the consequence is positive or rewarding, a "habit" is established. That is, the behavior becomes part of their repertoire, to be repeated again and again in similar circumstances. Should the consequence be punishing, however, the behavior is likely to be dropped and replaced with an alternative response.

Repetitive (versus redundant)   Repetition is presenting the same message more than once with the same wording. Redundant means presenting the same message more than once, but with different wording each time.

Resiliency factor   The propensity of human beings to be flexible in their learning histories, and not to be rigidly shaped by a few negative consequences of their actions.

Reward-based cohesion   A type of cohesion based on the personal satisfactions or rewards that flow to individuals because they participate in a group. This leads them to maintain membership and work toward the goals of the group.

Rhetorical style   The overall qualitative manner of delivery—that is, mode of acting and speaking with the use of both verbal language and nonverbal cues or techniques—in which a speaker communicates to an audience.

Role confusion   A situation in which shared understandings are inadequate, ineffective, or unclear about who should transmit what kinds of messages to whom. Such role confusion is a basis for group disorganization.

Roles   In general, roles are specific activities that are expected from each participant who performs a specialized part in a group. In interactive communication, they are rules that govern who can say what to whom in a particular relationship.

Roles (communication)   A cluster of rules in a group that define what kinds of messages a person in a particular position has a right to send or receive, and who must pay attention to them.

Role-taking   An assessment by a source person, who takes the point of view of a receiver, of the best choices of message symbols, nonverbal cues, and other message construction strategies that can get the desired meaning understood. More simply, mentally taking a receiver's role, so as to be better understood.

Round table   A common format for informal discussion groups in which no audience is usually present and the participants arrange themselves in a circular pattern.

Salient characteristic   A feature or an aspect of an individual that stands out in an initial encounter with another person and serves as a dominant attribute around which that person constructs a pattern of initial impressions.

Schema   A pattern or configuration of traces of meaning that have been put together in an organized way and recorded in a person's memory.

Scientific management   A way of managing organizations in which those in charge look systematically at the design of their group and its processes and try to design ways in which incentives, the flow of work, and the exercise of authority over workers can operate most effectively and profitably. Early versions were concerned with time and motion studies.

Scripted or stereotypic (conversations)   Conversations that are highly standardized and predictable, like lines rehearsed in a play. Conversations can be classified as scripted or stereotypic if they follow clear, even rigid, rules in certain well-defined communication contexts.

Selective perception   An individual's assignment of a personally unique pattern of denotative and connotative meanings to some person, activity, situation, or thing. Such personal stamps of meaning come about because each of us has different memories of meanings linked to signs, signals, and symbols, and even to human characteristics, stored up from our lifetime of experience.

Self (self-image or self-concept)   That pattern of beliefs, meanings, and understandings each individual develops concerning her or his own personal characteristics, capacities, limitations, and worth as a human being. In other words, our personal conceptions of *who* we are, *what* we are, and *where* we are in the social order.

Self-disclosure   Communicating messages to another that reveal the nature of one's past, private thoughts, personal views, or deep feelings.

Semantics   The study of relationships between words and their meanings, and of rules that can add meaning when human beings use language for verbal communication.

Seminar   One of the oldest forms of small discussion groups, now commonly used in advanced study in colleges and universities. In its classic format, each student takes a turn at addressing a central question that is the focus of the discussion, and the mentor draws the important lessons out of various comments.

Sender/receiver reciprocity   Successful adaptation to each other in a communication encounter by engaging in both role-taking and feedback simultaneously.

Sender/receiver similarity   A condition in which both the message sender and the receiver have had sufficiently similar learning experiences in their language community so as to have acquired parallel meanings for verbal and nonverbal signs and symbols.

Sensitivity-training group   One in which participants learn to understand the points of view of people unlike themselves.

Sentiment-based cohesion   A type of cohesion based on bonds of affection that exist between members of a group.

Sharpening   The counterpart of leveling in the embedding process. A verbal message shrinks as it is passed on by word-of-mouth, and with each retelling it becomes increasingly organized around its more central or "salient" details, becoming more and more concise until it is only a kind of summary, or *precis*, of the original message.

Sidedness   A feature of a persuasive message concerning the degree to which the arguments it presents explain one side only or include and refute opposing arguments as well.

Sign   An event or situation in the environment that animals (and human beings) learn to associate with and use to anticipate subsequent events. Examples would be that clouds are followed by rain, the sight of the dish (for dogs) is followed by the availability of food, or (for human beings) a red light indicates that one must stop.

Signal   Noises or patterned movements that animals can make to which animals like themselves can respond. Examples are cries or postures that typically imply such matters as danger, the presence of food, or readiness to mate. Human beings also use many kinds of signals (whistles, bells, waving flags, etc.)

Simile   A word or phrase that draws attention to qualities shared by dissimilar things by prefacing the comparison with the word "like" or "as." Common examples are "dead as a doornail" or "worked like a horse."

Skills training   A form of treatment for communication apprehension based on the assumption that limitations in a person's skills in communicating influence their apprehension levels. To reduce the apprehension, the person receives training in skills through systematic courses.

Small group   One in which the number of members can vary from two to perhaps a dozen, but optimal size with all members participating fully in communication is something like *five*.

Small-group conference   A small discussion group in which several participants are brought together, usually under private conditions, to share technical information or to discuss some problem in their area of expertise.

Small talk   Informal discussions that focus on topics of general interest and of little emotional or personal significance, such as the weather, sports, or other matters that do not require self-disclosure.

Sociability (of a speaker)   As a dimension of speaker credibility, a judgment on the part of an audience as to how friendly and warm a speaker is. Perceptions of sociability are based on how congenial a person seems to be.

Social categories   A number of people who share some common characteristic by which they can be classified. Examples are gender, age, education, occupation, race, and so on. Often, people in such categories are said to be characterized by certain regularities in their behavior.

Social controls   Various kinds of verbal or nonverbal messages transmitted by members of a group to other members for the purpose of ensuring conformity to social expectations.

Social efficacy   Being competent as a social person—that is, being able to form, manage, and maintain all kinds of social relationships in an effective manner.

Social expectations   The shared and commonly understood rules that govern all kinds of human social behavior (including communication) in group settings. These are the *norms, roles, ranks,* and *controls* by which group members pattern their interactions with each other.

Social institution   A broad configuration of closely related cultural elements and organized social activities that are essential to fulfilling a perceived basic need of the social order. Basic to all societies are the following institutions: family, government, economy, education, and religion.

Social learning theory Sometimes called "observational learning theory," this extension of earlier, more general reinforcement theories was originally developed to try to explain how individuals learn by observing and then adopting the behavior and reactions of people who portray or "model" some activity.

Socialization Long-term processes in which deliberate or indirect lessons about the ways of life of groups are internalized, enabling the person to become a unique human being, a functioning member of a society and a participant in its general culture.

Sound bite The expression *sound bite* is really a metaphor for a brief passage, sentence, or other expression taken from a press release or videotaped presentation which can then be reprinted or included in later televised reports. Sound bites usually represent a major idea expressed by the speaker.

Stage fright A special category of the more general condition of communication apprehension that specifically focuses on anxiety about a public performance or speech before a group or an audience.

Stereotypes Rigid and usually negative sets of beliefs about the personal and social qualities of all people who are members of a particular social category. For example, a person may believe that all older people are confused, cranky, inept, poor, and in bad health.

Susceptibility The degree to which a person is more-or-less easily influenced by others because of his or her personal characteristics.

Symbol A label that is used by participants within a language community to arouse standardized meanings for aspects of reality. The initial selection of a label for that to which it refers is initially made in an arbitrary manner. However, before the label can be a part of the vocabulary of a language, the connection between label and labeled must be maintained consistently by an established convention.

Symbols Words, numbers, and other marks, objects, or signs to which we have learned to associate patterned meanings that by established conventions are shared by other members of our language community.

Symposium A very formal type of discussion group. The participants are usually a small group of experts. They are individually introduced by a moderator, and each then makes a speech about the theme. During or even between the presentations, the participants seldom talk with each other and simply take their turn in delivering their analyses or views.

Syntax Rules for ordering words in a sentence or any expression in such a way that their meaning is clear.

Task-oriented group A group in which people participate in order to achieve some good that they have mutually set as an objective.

Technologies The application of physical, electric, or electronic principles so as to produce working devices that accomplish some purpose. In communication, the use of such principles to produce media that extend the ability of human beings to communicate swiftly over long distances.

Teleconferencing From the Greek word *tele,* meaning "at a distance." The use of media to link spatially dispersed people for the purpose of communicating in ways that to some degree approximate the conditions of a face-to-face conference or meeting.

Territoriality A common tendency characteristic of both animals and human beings in which they define some fixed or semifixed space to claim or stake out as their own.

Therapy group A specialized discussion group in which participants who share a common difficulty meet with a coordinator who usually has some special insight into the problem. The underlying assumption is that if such people get together and disclose their experiences, thoughts, and feelings to each other it will help them in coping and feeling better.

Trace Imprinted records of experience registered in the brain by electrochemical activities of its nerve cells.

Trait (personality) A relatively stable and predictable pattern of behavior that characterizes a person; a feature of the individual's personality that makes her or him different from others. Examples are "stingy," "honest," "smart," "happy-go-lucky," and so forth.

Transaction Any kind of exchange—that is, an activity that occurs between, and mutually influences, parties acting together in some way.

Trustworthiness (of a speaker) As a dimension of speaker credibility, a judgment of an audience as to a speaker's level of honesty, goodness, and decency.

Two-sided message A persuasive message (e.g., speech) that presents both sides of a controversial issue.

Utilitarianism An explanation of human behavior formulated by 18th-century British philosopher Jeremy Bentham, in which actions are decided on the basis of the ratio between pleasure and pain that can be derived. He maintained that we choose to engage in those behaviors that maximize pleasure and avoid those that result in pain.

Vertical transmission The flow of formal messages either up or down in an organization with clearly graded levels of power and authority.

Video conferencing The use of video cameras, long-distance cables, or satellite relays and television screens so as to enable people to see and talk to each other in a close approximation to having them face-to-face in the same room.

Vocalics The study of the way in which vocal tones indicate meanings to others, such as that we are happy, sad, confident, nervous, culturally refined, boorish, and so on.

Voice-mail network A telephone-based system in which a network of users share a sophisticated centralized answering machine so that they can leave and store messages for others and themselves.

Wage incentive system   A formula for paying workers in production settings in which wages are tied to personal output. That is, earnings for a worker in a production shop are determined by the number of units the individual produces in a given time period.

Withdrawal/avoidance   A strategy of indirect distancing and dissociation in which parties communicate less frequently, are "too busy" to get together, and avoid making any definite future plans. The couple sees less and less of each other without the strain of confrontation and their relationship simply "fades away."

Acknowledgments

Illustration Credits

Patrick Maloney: pps. viii, ix, x, xi, 2, 4, 32, 66, 98, 124, 126, 156, 188, 220, 248, 250, 282, 312, 336, 362, 364, 396, 422. **Susan Carolla Iannone:** pps. 13, 17, 21, 24, 26, 52, 57, 116, 320. **Page 39:** Edward O. Wilson, from *Sociobiology: The New Synthesis,* © 1975. Reprinted by permission of The Belknap Press of Harvard University Press.

Photo Credits

Chapter 1   9 The Granger Collection. **10** © Tim Brown, Tony Stone Worldwide. **11** © Bill Owens, Jeroboam, Inc. **15** © Tim Brown, Tony Stone Worldwide. **18** © Orion, FPG. **19** © Mike Mazzaschi, Stock Boston. **20** © C. T. Zimmerman, FPG. **22** © Charles Harbutt, Actuality, Inc. **23** © J. Moore, The Image Works.

Chapter 2   35, 37 The Granger Collection. **41** © Ken Gaghan, Jeroboam, Inc. **42** © Richard Ellis, Photo Researchers. **45** © The Gorilla Foundation. **50** © Charles Harbutt, Actuality, Inc.

Chapter 3   70 © Chris Craymer, Tony Stone Worldwide. **71** © Nancy Davis, The Picture Cube. **75** © Ken Graves, Jeroboam, Inc. **77** © Charles Gatewood, The Image Works; The Granger Collection. **79** © John T. Turner, FPG. **80** © Marcy Nighswander, Wide World; Bettmann/Reuters. **85** © Jeff Rotman, The Picture Cube. **87** © Hella Hammid, Photo Researchers. **91** © Cary Wolinsky, Stock Boston.

Chapter 4   101 © Charles Harbutt, Actuality, Inc. **103** © Bob Daemmrich, The Image Works. **104** © Janet Fries, Photo 20-20. **107** © Ken Graves, Jeroboam, Inc. **108** © Frank Siteman,

The Picture Cube. **110** © Dick Luria, FPG. **111** © Eugene Richards, The Picture Cube.

Chapter 5   131 © Dan Bosler, Tony Stone Worldwide. **132** © Joan Liftin, Actuality, Inc. **133** © Richard Hutchings, Photo Researchers. **136** © Frank Siteman, Stock Boston. **138** © Bob Daemmrich, The Image Works. **140** © Rose Skytta, Jeroboam, Inc. **146** © Susan McCartney, Photo Researchers. **148** © Richard Laird, FPG. **151** © Jean Boughton, Stock Boston.

Chapter 6   160 © Andrew Sacks, Tony Stone Worldwide. **163** © Lawrence Migdale, Stock Boston. **165** © Arthur Grace, Stock Boston. **168** © Michael J. Okonlewski, The Image Works. **169** © Telegraph Colour Library, FPG. **171** © Jim Pickerell, FPG. **174** © Alan Carey, The Image Works. **177** © Bob Daemmrich, The Image Works. **183** © Polly Brown, Actuality, Inc.

Chapter 7   191 © Sheryl McNee, FPG. **193** © The Granger Collection. **195** © Rick Friedman, The Picture Cube. **200** The Granger Collection. **204** © Charles Harbutt, Actuality, Inc. **205** UPI/Bettmann. **210** © Telegraph Colour Library, FPG. **214** © Art Stein, Photo Researchers. **215** © D. Beretty, Rapho/Photo Researchers.

Chapter 8   223 Reuters/Bettmann. **224** © Richard Hutchings, Photo Researchers. **230** © Mark Antman, The Image Works. **233** © Walter S. Silver, The Picture Cube. **235** © Mark Antman, The Image Works. **238** © Chuck Keeler, Tony Stone Worldwide. **242** © Christopher Brown, Stock Boston.

Chapter 9   255 © Jane Scherr, Jeroboam, Inc. **257** © Sarah Putnam, The Picture Cube. **258** © Jane Scherr, Jeroboam, Inc.

259 © G. Walts, The Image Works. **264** UPI/Bettmann. **267** © Mark Trousdale, Profiles West. **271** © Ron Chapple, FPG.

Chapter 10   287 © Gloria Karlson, The Picture Cube. **289** The Granger Collection. **291** © David Wells, The Image Works. **293** Reuters/Bettmann. **297** © Bruce Roberts, Rapho/Photo Researchers. **298** © David M. Grossman, Photo Researchers.

Chapter 11   316 © Richard Hutchings, Photo Researchers. **317** © The Telegraph Colour Library. **319** © Dion Ogust, The Image Works. **327** © Richard Hutchings, Photo Researchers. **329** © Mark Antman, The Image Works.

Chapter 12   339 © Bob Daemmrich, Stock Boston. **341** © Ted Streshinsky, Photo 20-20. **344** © Alan Carey, The Image Works. **345** © Peeter Vilms, Jeroboam, Inc. **348** © L. Migdale, Photo Researchers. **355** © Dion Ogust, The Image Works.

Chapter 13   368 © Bob Daemmrich, The Image Works. **369** © Jim Pickerell, FPG. **370** © Bob Daemmrich, The Image Works. **374** © Dion Ogust, The Image Works. **385** © Bob Kalman, The Image Works. **388** © Bob Daemmrich, The Image Works.

Chapter 14   401 © Jeffry W. Myers, FPG. **402** © Mark Antman, The Image Works. **403** © Kent Reno, Jeroboam, Inc. **407** © Frank Siteman, The Picture Cube. **408** © Robert Hollister Davis, UPI/Bettmann. **415** © Howard Dratch, The Image Works. **416** © Alan Carey, The Image Works.

Chapter 15   425, 430, 431 UPI/Bettmann.

Index

Abelson, Herbert I., 285
Accents, 82–83
Accommodating conflict style, 324–325
Accuracy in communication, 25–28
  See also Index of fidelity
  in grapevine, 211–213
  media as limiter of, 225
Active response, to informative speech, 383
Active vs. passive listening, 105–106, 118, 119
Adaptation, 106, 108, 109
Adapters, 82
Adapting to audience, 400–401
Addington, D. W., 95
Adler, R., 95
Adler, R. B., 63
Administrators, in organizations, 190
Adorno, T. W., 186
Advanced Research Projects Agency. *See* ARPA; ARPANET
Advertising, 81, 91
Affective beliefs, 294
  attitudes based on, 295
Affinity-seeking, 267–269
  strategies for (table), 268–269
Age
  personal space and, 84
  small-group ranking and, 179
Agee, P., 310, 394
Agendas, 180
Agents of socialization, 346
Aggression, 315, 323
Ailes, Roger, 398
Alaska, video network in, 244
Algozzine, R., 94
Alkema, F., 94
Allen, J., 394
Allen, M., 310, 360, 361, 394
Allen, V. L., 121
Allport, G. W., 186, 219, 360
Alper, T., 95
Altman, I., 95, 155
American Sign Language (Ameslan), ape studies with, 44–46
Anatol, K. W. E., 334
Andersen, J. F., 96, 421
Andersen, K., 421
Andersen, P., 95
Anderson, A., 246
Anderson, K. E., 421
Anderson, N. H., 310
Anderson, P. A., 88, 421
Anger. *See* Conflicts
Animal communication, 35–47
  "Clever Hans" story, 34–35
  comparative perspective on, 35

human communication vs., 10–11, 34–35, 36, 38–39, 40–41
  inherited behaviors, 35–36, 37–38, 39
  learned behaviors, 35, 36, 39–41
  territoriality, 86
  touch and, 87
Animated rhetorical style, 436
"Anna," case study of, 47–48
Anomie (personal), 349
Answering machines, 234
Anti-Semitism. *See* Prejudices
Antisocial behavior-alteration techniques, 306
Anxiety. *See* Communication apprehension; Fear
Apes, 41, 43–46
Appearance, importance of, 74–75
  in public speaking, 412, 413
Appelbaum, R. L., 334
Applause management, 433–435
Appointments, time meanings and, 89
Apprehension. *See* Communication apprehension; Fear; Shyness
Approach/avoidance, immediacy principle and, 91
Arbitrary selection, principle of, 53, 55
Areas of responsibility, in organizations, 190
Argumentativeness Scale (ARG), 322–323
Arguments. *See* Conflicts
Argyle, M., 94, 155
Aronson, E., 121, 187, 279
ARPA (Defense Department Advanced Research Projects Agency), 236–237
ARPANET, 237, 239
Artifacts, 75–76
"Artificial languages," ape studies with, 46
Asch, S. E., 279
Asch, Solomon, 254–256, 257, 258
Assertiveness-training groups, 168
Assignment-based cohesion
  in decision-making groups, 182
  in organizations, 215
Assimilation, 212
Associated Press, 226
Atkinson, R. C., 360
Atkinson, R. L., 360
Atonson, E., 280
Attitude(s)
  action based on, 296, 299
  behavior and, 296–299
  creating or modifying, 295–296
  defined, 296
  learning theory and, 346–349
  resistance to changing, 299, 302
  in small talk, 143–144
Attractiveness
  importance of, 74–75

prejudices about, 116
  small-group ranking and, 179
Attribution process, 265–266
  principle of covarying attribution, 276
  self-disclosure decisions and, 270
Audience, for speechmaking, 371–374
  applause management, 433–435
  feedback from, 400–401, 402
  preferred delivery mode of, 405
Audio conferencing, 241
Authoritarian leadership style, 176
Authoritarian ranking in families, 174–175
Authority
  in organizations, 194–195, 197, 200
  in peer groups, 175
  in rational society, 194
Automated behavior
  decoding as, 20
  encoding as, 18
Automobiles, as signals, 76
Avoidance. *See* Approach/avoidance; Withdrawal/avoidance
Avoidance conflict style, 324
Azjen, O., 309

Baddeley, A. D., 121
Badzinsk, D. M., 154
Bakker, Jim, 408
Bales, Robert F., 171, 186
Balfantz, G. L., 360
Ball-Rokeach, S., 360
Bandura, Albert, 121, 346, 360
Bargaining, negotiation guidelines, 329–332
Bargh, J. A., 30
Barker, D. A., 95, 96
Barker, L. L., 94, 95, 96, 121, 122
Barnes, H. E., 30
Barnlund, D. C., 154
Baron, Paul, 237
Bartlett, F. C., 30
Bateson, G., 154
BATs and BAMs (Behavior Alteration Techniques and Messages), 198–199
Bauchner, J., 95
Baxter, L. A., 155
Baxter, Leslie, 150
Bear, J., 94
Beattie, G., 30, 63
Beatty, L. R., 114
Beatty, M. J., 122, 360, 361
Beauty, importance of, 74–75
Beavin, J. H., 154
Becker, H., 30
Becker, H. S., 279
Beckwith, J., 186
Bee, H., 186

Bees, communication by, 38, 39
Behavior
   attitude and, 296–299
   attribution process, 265–266
   beliefs and, 294–296
   learning theory and, 346–349
   listening, 102, 105–107
   meanings as form of, 15
   nonsocial restraints on, 299
   norms, 130
   resistance to changing, 299, 302
   resistance types, 302–303
   roles, 130–131
Behavior-alteration techniques, in persua-
      sion, 306
Behnke, R. R., 114
Beighley, K. C., 394
Beinstein, J., 279
Beliefs
   actions based on, 294–295
   attitudes based on, 295
   communication apprehension and, 346–
      349, 356–358
   defined, 294
   learning theory and, 346–349
   resistance to changing, 299, 302
   shaping or altering, 294–295
Believability. See Credibility
Bell, Alexander Graham, 232, 236
Bell, D. 30
Bell, R. A., 269, 280
Benedict, R., 186
Benedict, Ruth, 164
Benne, K. D., 187
Benne, Kenneth, 176
Benny, Jack, 436, 437
Benson, T., 218
Bentham, Jeremy
   exchange theory and, 144
   immediacy principle and, 91
   utilitarianism theory, 137–138
Bentsen, L., 440
Bentsen, Lloyd, 428, 429, 434
Berger, C. R., 63, 143, 154, 279
Berger, T. G., 155
Berkowitz, L., 333
Berkowitz-Stafford, S., 310, 394
Berscheid, E., 94
Bettinghaus, E. P., 309, 310, 394, 421
Bettinghaus, I., 63
Bingham, C., 440
Birds, learned communication by, 40
Birdwhistell, R.L., 94
BITNET, 238
Blame, in dyad disengagement, 148–149
Blumstein, P., 186
Boards of directors. See Decision-making
      groups
Bochner, A. P., 280
Bodaken, E. M., 440
Body language, 69
Body-related messages, 74–75, 81–84
   in public speaking, 415
Book, C. L., 154

Boomerang effect, 390, 391
Booth-Butterfield, M., 441
Booth-Butterfield, S., 441
Booth-Butterfield, Steven and Melanie,
      437, 438
Borgatta, E. E., 310
Boster, F., 394
Boster, F. J., 310
Bostrom, R., 310, 394
Bostrom, R. N., 121, 122, 247
Bower, G., 30
Bowers, D. G., 334
Bowers, J. W., 154
Bradac, J. J., 280
Bradae, J. A., 63
Bradley, Tom, 407
Brainstorming discussion groups, 167
Brehm, J. W., 309, 394
Brehm, Jack, 299, 302
"Briefings," problems with, 209
Briffault, R., 63
Bright, M., 62
Brilhart, J. K., 186
Broadhurst, A. R., 31
Brock, T., 310
Bronowski, J., 30
Brooks, W. D., 121, 122
Brown, R., 280
BRS information service, 239
Brummel, B. J., 186
Bryant, J., 441
Buckley, William F., 436
Buller, D. B., 96, 279
Bulletin boards, electronic, 239
Burgess, P., 94
Burgoon, J. K., 94, 95, 96, 279
Burgoon, M., 246, 280, 360, 361, 441
Bureaucracy
   classical theory of, 193–197, 200–206
   defined, 193
   as organizational prerequisite, 193
   Weber's principles of, 194–195
Burhans, D. T., Jr., 421
Burke, R. J., 154
Burkhart, J. C., 94
Burns, C. S., 154
Burroughs, N. F., 310
Bush, Barbara, Wellesley speech by, 424–
      425, 426–427, 436
Bush, G., 440, 441
Bush, George, 398, 399, 429, 430, 433
Business communication
   See also Organizational communication;
      Small groups
   changes in, 222–223
   letters, 230–231
   memoranda, 231–232
   by telephone, 232, 233–234
Buss, A. H., 360
"Buzz" groups, 167
Byrne, D., 154

Cacioppo, J. T., 394
Calabrese, R. J., 279

Cambra, R. E., 421
Campaign speechmaking, 398–399, 428,
      429–430, 433, 434
Campbell, E. H., 310
Candy, John, 436
Cantrill, J. G., 310
Carey, A., 218
Carlson, M., 440
Carol, J. B., 30
Casson, H. N., 246
Cathcart, R. S., 187
Cats, territoriality in, 86. See also Pets
Cattell, R. B., 186
CCS (Communication Competence
      Scale), 8–9
Cecchi, L. F., 186
Cegala, D., 121
Cellular phones, 232
Censure, in formal decision-making
      groups, 181
Cermack, L. S., 30
Cetaceans, 41–43
Chair, role of, 180, 181
Changing old impressions, 275–277
Charisma, defined, 194
Charismatic authority
   in organizations, 194
   in small-groups, 177
Cheney, G., 218
Cherwit, R. A., 63
Children
   personal space and, 84
   touch and, 87
Chimpanzees, 41, 43–45
China, Tienanmen Square, 293–294
Christophel, D., nonverbal immediacy
      scale by, 419
Christophel, D. M., 441
Chronemics, 89–90
Citations, in speechmaking, 376, 406
Clark, M. S., 186
Classroom, communication apprehension
      in, 348, 349, 350–351
Clatterbuck, G. W., 31, 143, 154, 186,
      187, 218, 219, 247, 279
Clay, Andrew Dice, 437
Clever Hans effect, 34–35, 46
Clevenger, T., Jr., 395, 421
Clift, E., 440
Clothing
   nonverbal communication with,
      76–79
   for public speaking, 412
Clusters, in memory organization, 16
Coakley, C. G., 121, 122
Cody, M., 63
Cody, M. J., 309, 310, 394
Coercion, 290, 291
Cognitive functioning, 292
Cognitive organization
   attitudes as part of, 296
   behavior and, 296–299
   persuasion and, 290, 292–296
Cognitive processing, 292

Cognitive restructuring for communication apprehension, 356–358
Cohen, A. E., 310
Cohesion (group), 181
 bases of, 181–182
 defined, 181
 dependency-based, 214–215
 organizational, 204, 214–215
 in small groups, 181–182
 in urban-industrial society, 193–194
Collaborative conflict style, 324
Collective role-taking, in public speaking, 401
Collier, G., 94
Committees. See Decision-making groups
Communication apprehension, 338–359
 causes of, 342–349
 consequences of, 349, 351–353
 defined, 340
 extent of, 340, 342, 353
 learning theory and, 346–349
 as personality trait, 340–342, 345–349
 reducing, 355–358
 stage fright, 353–355
 temporary, 342
Communication Apprehension test, 350–351
Communication Competence Scale (CCS), 8–9
Communication process, 5–31
 See also Animal communication;
  Human communication
 context for, 7, 9
 definitions, 9–12
 impact of changes in, 225–227
 information society and, 7
 settings and media for, 6
 significance of, 6–9
Communicator, defined, 12
Comparative communication, 10–11
Comparative perspective, 35, 36–37
Competence of a speaker, 405–407
Competition
 conflict inevitability and, 316, 317
 conflict style and, 323
 norms involved in, 318
Competitive style, 323
Compliance, 304
 beliefs vs. action, 295–296
Composure, in public speaking, 409–410, 411, 412–413
Compounding pattern, 212–213
Compromising conflict style, 324
Compton, N. H., 95, 394
CompuServe, 239
Computer applications
 in business, 222–223, 237. See also Network communication
 conferencing, 242–243, 244
 credit card authorization, 237
 in journalism, 223
 in military, 222, 238
 in speech preparation, 376
 in universities and research organizations, 238, 244
 for wireless networks, 238

Computer network, 236. See also Network communication
Computer teleconferencing, 242–243
Concentration, controlling, 118–119
Concepts
 acquisition of, 50–51
 defined, 51, 52
 negative attributes of, 51–53
Concrete language, in speeches, 428
Conference calls, 243
Conferences, mediated, 167, 241–244
Conflicts, 313–333
 active listening and, 106
 causes of, 325–328
 consequences of, 318–321
 context of, 326–328
 coping styles, 321–325
 cultural conventions about, 316
 defined, 317–318
 inevitability of, 315
 in marriage, 321, 326
 nature of, 315–321
 negotiation of, 328–332
 in small groups, 172
 stress and, 319–320
 in workplace, 314–315, 317–318, 319, 320, 325, 326, 327–328, 330–332
Conflict style, 321–325
Confrontation, in disengagement, 151
Connors, S., 246
Connotative meanings
 barriers to listening, 116–117
 denotative meanings vs., 58–59
 electronic mail and, 240
 sound bites and, 434
Conrad, A., 121
Consciousness-raising groups, 162, 168–169
Conspicuousness, as apprehension cause, 343–344, 354
Constructive resistance, 303
Consumer relations, as organizational communication, 191
Contact-oriented people, 85
Context, 7, 9, 12, 125
 See also Physical context; Social relationships; Sociocultural context
 attitudes vs. behavior and, 298–299
 basic features of, 130–132
 communication apprehension and, 341, 342–345, 354
 conflict and, 326–328
 distortion through, 26–27
 initial encounters and, 258, 261, 265
 interpersonal, 133–138
 receiver responsibility and, 110
 relationships in, 22, 25, 130–131
 sender responsibility and, 109
 in simultaneous communication, 24–25
 small group as, 159–162
 social constraints, 266
Controls (communication)
 in formal decision-making groups, 181
 in intimate groups, 175
 in organizations, 195

 small-group disorganization and, 182–183
 in task-oriented groups, 179
Controls (social), 131
 in decision-making groups, 182
 in intimate groups, 175
 in organizations, 195
 in small-group development, 172
Conventions
 See also Cultural conventions
 defined, 55
 eye contact, 84
 listening behaviors, 106–107
 meaning triangle and, 56–57
 principle of, 55–56
 time, 89–90
Conversations, 139–144
Cooley, C. H., 94, 154, 186, 246
Cooley, Charles Horton
 on media's effects, 227
 on personal ideas, 134
 on primary groups, 159
Cooper, J., 309
Cooperation, conflict style and, 323, 324
Copely, F. B., 218
Coping statements, in cognitive restructuring, 357
Coping styles, in conflicts, 321–325
Cornford, F. M., 30, 186, 309
Coser, L., 334
Cost/benefit ratio
 exchange theory, 144
 in interpersonal relationships, 135–138, 144–145
 utilitarianism and, 137–138
Counterarguments, in speech strategy, 392
Couples
 See also Interpersonal communication;
  Marriage
 disengagement by, 132, 147–151
 labeling of, 146
Covarying attribution, principle of, 276
Craik, F. I. M., 30
Crail, T., 62
Cran, W., 63, 64
Credibility
 persuasion and, 306–307
 presentation of self and, 274
 in public speaking, 405–411
 of source, 110–111, 306–307, 377
Credit cards, network use with, 237
Criteria, in listening, 104
Crockett, W. H., 30, 279
Cro-Magnons, speech by, 7
Cronen, V., 30
Cronkite, Walter, 436
Cronkhite, G., 310
Croyle, R. T., 309
Cultural conventions
 See also Conventions; Multicultural society
 barriers to listening in, 113, 115, 117
 conflicting, 213–215
 conflict management and, 316
 eye contact and, 141

Cultural conventions *continued*
  intimate-group roles and, 174
  labeling theory and, 256–257
  learning of (enculturation), 164
  meaning triangle and, 56–57
  in organizations, 213–215
  proxemics and, 85
  time orientations and, 90
  vertical transmission problems and, 210
Cultural sensitivity, importance of, 7. *See also* Multicultural society
Culture
  defined, 56
  specialized, 213
Cushioning function, in interpersonal communication, 137
Cushman, D. P., 155, 309
Czitron, D. J., 246

Dahnke, G. L., 31, 154, 186, 187, 218, 219, 247
Daly, J. A., 269, 280, 360, 361
Daniels, T. D., 219
D'Antonio, W. V., 63, 333
Darnell, D., 394
Darnell, D. K., 31
Darwin, C., 95
Darwin, Charles, animal studies and, 36
DATEX, 239
Davis, F., 63
Davis, K., 63
Davis, L. M., 218
de Sola Pool, I., 246
Debate, audience strategy and, 371
Decision-making groups, 162, 169–171
  assignment-based cohesion in, 182
  communication codes in, 179–181
  conflicts as productive in, 318, 320
  tasks of, 169–170
Decision-making in organizations, human relations perspective, 204
Decoding, 10, 11, 20
  distortion in, 25–27
  in simultaneous transactions, 22, 23
Deep meaning, 28
Defense Department Advanced Research Projects Agency. *See* ARPA; ARPANET
Definition of the situation, 148
  in Machiavellian disengagement, 151
DeFleur, L. B., 333
DeFleur, M., 309
DeFleur, M. L., 63, 121, 155, 219, 280, 309, 310, 333, 360
Delayed gratification, principle of, 145
Delia, J. G., 30
Deming, W. Edwards, 205, 206
Democratic leadership style, 176–177
Demographic information, in audience analysis, 371, 372
Dennis, E. E., 310
Denotative vs. connotative meanings, 58–59
  electronic mail and, 240
Dependency-based cohesion, 214–215

Dervin, B., 30
Despert, J. L., 95
Destructive resistance, 303
Deviant behavior
  labeling theory and, 256–257
  "salient characteristic" and, 256
Dewey, John, persuasive speech and, 384
Diabase, W., 279
Dickson, W. J., 218
DiGaetani, J. L., 121
Digital Equipment Corporation, first interactive computer by, 236
Dillon, K., 310, 394
Disassociation
  defined, 149
  from interpersonal relationships, 149–150
Discussion groups
  See also Task-oriented groups
  formal communication in, 166
  reward-based cohesion in, 182
Disengagement, in interpersonal relationships, 132, 147–151
Displays, offensive, 86
Dissension. *See* Conflicts
Distance, nonverbal communication with, 84–86
Distancing messages, 149
Distortion, 12
  compounding pattern, 212–213
  embedding pattern, 211–212
  factors creating, 25–27
  in grapevine, 211–213
  nonverbal cues and, 26
  verbal symbols and, 26
Dittman, A. T., 94
Division of labor, 194, 214–215
Divorce. *See* Disengagement
Dogs, territoriality in, 86. *See also* Pets
Dolphins, 41, 42, 43
Donahue, W. A., 360, 361
Donohew, H. E., 30
Donohew, L., 30
Dorsey, Eugene, 429, 440
Downs, V., 441
Dramatic rhetorical style, 435–436
Dress codes, 78–79
Duck, S., 155, 187, 279, 360
Dukakis, Michael, 398, 399
Duncan, S. D., 94
Duncanson, W. T., 154
Durkheim, E., 187, 219, 360
Dyads, 133
  See also Interpersonal communication
  communication in groups vs., 160–161
  labeling, 146
Dyer, F. C., 62

Eastern Airlines, 214
Ebentsein, W., 154
Economic institutions, 192
  impact of media on, 226
Educational institutions, 192
Efron, D., 94
Eggen, P. D., 394
Ehninger, D., 394

Eicher, J. B., 95
Eicher, Joanne, 78
Ekman, P., 94, 95
Electric shock studies, 303
Electronic bulletin boards, 239
Electronic mail (e-mail), 239–241
  conferencing with, 242
  efficiency of, 222
  military uses of, 222
  norms, 240–241
Elocution, 399
Ellis, A., 30, 63
Embedded communication processes, 12
Embedding pattern, 211–212
Emblems, 72, 82
Emmert, P., 94
Emotional support, in interpersonal communication, 137
Encoding, 10, 11
  as automated behavior, 18
  defined, 14
  distortion in, 25, 27
  in linear communication model, 14–18
  memory and, 16
  role-taking and, 16, 18
  in simultaneous transactions, 22, 23
Encounter groups, 167, 168
Encroachment (space invasion), 85
Enculturation, 164
Engagement
  defined, 132
  in interpersonal communication, 132, 138–144
Entertainment, as speechmaking goal, 370
Esser, A. H., 95
Etzione, Amitai, 190
Evaluation
  as apprehension cause, 344, 353, 354
  by listening, 103–104
Evolution of speech, 7, 30
Exchange theory, 144
Exline, R. V., 94
Experiential groups, 162, 167–169
Extemporaneous delivery of speeches, 404–405
Extroversion, in public speaking, 410–411
Eye contact, 83–84
  in active listening, 106
  cultural conventions, 141
  hecklers and, 415
  in public speaking, 401, 409, 414, 435
  as regulating cue, 71
  as small talk skill, 141

Face-to-face vs. mediated communication, 23, 223–227
Facial expression, 81–82, 106. *See also* Body-related messages; Nonverbal communication
Facsimile (fax) communication, 223, 234–236
Fact finding, as small-group task, 170
Factual beliefs, 294
Failure, memories of, as apprehension cause, 344–345

Falcione, R. L., 218
Families
  See also Intimate groups
  communicating in, 163–165
  communication norms in, 173
  conflicts in, 319, 321, 326–327
  control messages in, 175
  rank in, 174–175
  roles in, 173–174
  as social institutions, 192
  tradition as basis for authority in, 194
Farris, S. R., 94
Fast, J., 94
Faules, D. F., 218
Faupel, M., 95
Fax. *See* Facsimile (fax) communication
Fayol, H., 218
Fayol, Henri, 197, 200
Fear
  See also Communication apprehension
  in conflict avoidance, 324
  persuasion based on, 306, 392
  systematic desensitization for, 355–356
Feedback, 20–21
  in first-impression management, 265
  in interpersonal communication, 134–135
  mediated communication and, 225
  memoranda and, 232
  in peer groups, 165
  in public speaking, 400–401, 402
  in sender/receiver reciprocity, 108, 109, 119
  in simultaneous transactions, 22, 23
  vertical transmission and, 207, 208
Feierabend, R. I., 310
Feldman, H., 334
Feldstein, S., 94
Fenno, F. H., 421
Feshbach, S., 310, 394
Fiber-optic networks, 238
Fidelity index. *See* Index of fidelity
Fiedler, F. E., 187
Fight-or-flight responses, 85–86
First impressions, 253–275
  See also Initial encounters
  changing, 275–277
  in interpersonal communication, 139
Fishbein, M., 309
Fisher, A. B., 186
Fisher, B. A., 31
Fisher, H., 421
Fisher, J. D., 95
Fisher, R., 334
Fitzpatrick, M. A., 154
Focus groups, 167
Footnotes, oral, 406
Formal communication
  apprehension in, 343, 353–355
  defined, 180
  as organization need, 193
  in organizations, 190, 191, 206–210
Formal decision-making groups. *See* Decision-making groups
Formal discussion groups. *See* Discussion groups

Format, for persuasive speech, 384
Forums, 167
Frame, nonverbal communication as, 70
Frank, R., 218
Fremouw, W. J., 361
Frenkel-Brunswick, E., 186
Friedland, M. H., 360
Friedman, P., 279
Friedrich, G., 360, 361
Friendship
  See also Interpersonal communication;
    Intimate groups; Peer groups
  auditioning for, 140
  role expectations, 174
Friesen, W. V., 94, 95
Frost, J. H., 334
Fulton, R. I., 421
Furnishings, as signals, 76

Galvin, K. M., 186
Gardner, Beatrice and Allan, Washoe and, 44–45
Gardner, C. R., 154
Gardner, R. A., 62
Gardner, R. R., 279
Gardner, T., 62
Gates, G. P., 420
Gateway computers
  electronic mail role, 239
  in large-scale networks, 238
Gender
  letter-writing errors, 231
  personal space and, 84
  small-group ranking and, 179
  susceptibility to persuasion and, 305
General Disclosiveness Scale, 272–274
Gerbing, D. W., 310
Germond, J. W., 420
Gerth, H. H., 218
Geshwind, N., 62
Gestures, 81–82. *See also* Nonverbal communication
Ghandi, Mahatma, 194
Ghengis Khan, 194
Gibb, C. A., 187
Gilbreth, F. B., 218
Gilbreth, Frank and Lillian, 197
Gilbreth, L. M., 218
Giles, H., 279
Gill, T., 62
Gill, W., 96
Gilmour, R., 94
Glasgow, G. M., 421
Glenn, John, 407
"Global village" concept, 227
Goals of communication, 14
  initial encounters, 262–263
  in public speaking, 369–371
Goffman, E., 279, 280
Goffman, I., 279
Goffman, Irving, 253, 254
Goldhaber, G. M., 218, 219
Goodall, H. L., Jr., 187, 217
Gorham, J., 55, 419, 421, 441
Gorillas, 41, 43, 45–46

Goss, B., 121, 361
Goss, W. B., 63
Gossip. *See* "Grapevine"
Gould, J. C., 62
Gouran, D. S., 186, 187
Government institutions, 192
Grammar, 59–60
"Grapevine"
  defined, 211
  distortion of messages in, 211–213
  in organizations, 191, 207, 210–211
Green, J., 30
Greenbaum, H. H., 218
Greenfield, D., 246
Greetings, 271, 274
Gregg, R. B., 63
Gronbeck, B. E., 394
Grossberg, L., 30
Groups
  See also Small groups
  basic features of, 160
  cohesion in. *See* Cohesion (group)
  fear of talking to. *See* Communication apprehension
  influence of size on, 160–161, 193
  normative conflicts in, 327–328
  persuasion in, 290–292
Group vs. dyadic communication, 160–161
Gruner, C. R., 441
Gua (chimpanzee), 44
Gumperz, E. J., 280
Gura, T., 441

Hale, J., 310, 394
Hale, J. L., 94
Hall, Arsenio, 436
Hall, E. T., 95
Hall, Edward T., 84
Hall's zones, 84
Halo effect, in persuasion, 377
Hamilton, C., 121
Hand movements, 82
Hanneman, G., 31
Hansford, B., 122
Haptics, 87. *See also* Touch
"Hard copy"
  letters as, 229
  memoranda as, 231
Harder, R. J., 394
Harlow, H. F., 95
Harlow, Harry F., 87
Harper, N., 30
Harrison, R., 95
Hartley, E. L., 187
Harvey, J. H., 280
Harvey, O. J., 394
Hawthorne management studies, 201–203, 204
  specialized cultures and, 213
Hayes, C. H., 62
Hayes, Keith and Catherine, 44
Hays, W. L., 279
Haythorne, W., 186
Hearing, in human communication, 39

Heath, R. W., 121
Hecklers, handling, 415
Heider, F., 280
Height, small-group ranking and, 179
Heller, J., 95
Hellweg, S. A., 218
Henderson, A. M., 218
Henderson, L. S., 114
Henderson, M., 155
Herman, L., 62
Herman, Louis, 43
Heslin, R., 95
Hibbard, A., 441
Hickson, M. L., 63
Hiemstra, G., 246
Hierarchy, in organizations, 190, 191, 194–195, 207
Higbee, K. L., 310, 394
Higgins, E. T., 30
Hikins, J. W., 63
Hilgard, E. R., 360
Hill, Anita, 80
Hill, S. D., 95
Hill, S. R., 31
Historical background, 7
Hitler, Adolf, 194
Hjelle, L., 279
Hobbes, T., 187
Hobbes, Thomas, 6
Hocker, J. L., 334
Hocking, J. E., 94, 95
Hoijer, H., 63
Holman, E. H., 441
Holmes, J., 421
HO (Humor Orientation) Scale, 437, 438
Homans, G. C., 155, 186
Homans, George, 144
Homeowners' association, 166
Homophily, 406
Hortalsu, N., 155
Hosman, L. A., 280
House, R. J., 218
Houston, J. B., 186
Hovland, C. I., 309, 310, 394
Hovland, Carl, 306
Howell, W. S., 121
Howells, W. W., 30
Hudson, H. E., 247
Human communication
    See also Communication process
    animal communication vs., 10–11, 34–35, 36, 38–39, 40–41
    defined, 11
    humans without language, 47–49
    on phylogenetic continuum, 36
Human relations perspective, 200–205
    defined, 203–204
Human relations theory, 202
Human resources perspectives, 205–206
    human relations theory vs., 206
Human use perspectives, 195–197, 200
Humor Orientation (HO) Scale, 437, 438
Humorous rhetorical style, 436–439
Hunter, J. E., 360, 361

Hunter, J. H., 310
Hussein, Saddam, 176
Hymes, D., 63, 280

Identification, yielding based on, 304
Ilgen, D. R., 218
Illustrators, 82, 414–415
Imagery, in speeches, 428–429, 431–432
Immediacy, nonverbal, 90–92, 417
    in persuasion, 306
    in public speaking, 417, 418–419
    as small talk skill, 141
Immediacy, verbal
    in public speaking, 417, 419, 439
    self-test, 54–55
Immediacy principle
    applying, 92
    defined, 91
Implicit personality, 134
    selective perception and, 263
    theory of, 257–258
Impression management, 254
Impromptu delivery of speeches, 404
Inconsistency, communication apprehension and, 349
Index of fidelity, 27
    See also Accuracy in communication
    barriers to listening and, 112–117
    conflict as problem of, 326
    connotative meanings and, 58
    deep vs. surface meaning and, 28
    grapevine and, 213
    letters and, 229
    mediated communication and, 225
    memoranda and, 232
    in organizational communication, 208
    sender/receiver similarity and, 111–112
    specialized cultures and, 213
Infante, D. A., 323
Infants, importance of touch to, 87
Influencing others. See Persuasion
Informal communication
    defined, 173
    in organizations, 190, 191, 200, 203, 207, 210–213
    rules of, 172–175
Informal discussion groups, 166
Information
    defined, 18–19, 223
    listening for, 102–104
    mediated transmission of, 223–224
    as speechmaking goal, 370. See also Informative speech
Information services, on-line, 239
Information society, 7, 236
Information stimuli, 19
Informative speech
    as goal, 370
    increasing effectiveness of, 382–384
    organizing, 377–382
Inherited communication abilities, in animals, 35–36, 37–38, 39, 40
Initial encounters
    See also First impressions

affinity-seeking in, 267–269
context and, 258, 261
deciding what to say, 269–275
importance of managing, 258
management strategies, 261–269
one person vs. several, 258, 260–261
problems in, 258–261
Innes, H. A., 246
Innis, Harold A., 227
Insect communication, 37–38, 39
Instincts, 39
Intention, 14
Interactive communication, 12, 21–25
    encoding and decoding in, 22, 23
    feedback in, 20–21, 22, 23
    influences on, 23–25
    in public speaking, 400–401, 402, 434–435
    role-taking in, 22, 23
Internal communication, in organizations, 191
Internalization, yielding based on, 304
International communication, 238–239
INTERNET, 238
Interpersonal communication, 127–152
    characteristics of, 133–135
    context, 133–138
    defined, 132
    disengagement, 132, 147–151
    engagement, 132, 138–144
    group communication vs., 160–161
    management, 132, 144–147
    reasons for, 135–138
Interpretation, grapevine and, 211
Intervals, meaning conventions and, 89
Interviewing, for speech preparation, 375
Intimate groups, 161–162
    communication goals in, 162–166
    communication rules in, 172–175
    sentiment-based cohesion in, 181–182
Intimate relationships
    See also Interpersonal communication
    establishment of, 145–146
    norms of, 147
    withdrawal from, 147–151
Irreversibility, 14, 109
    of electronic mail, 241
    in interpersonal communication, 135
Irrevocability. See Irreversibility
"Isabelle," case study of, 48
Iverson, M. A., 186

Jablin, F. M., 218, 219
Jackson, D. D., 154
Jackson, J., 394
Jackson, Jesse, 429, 436
Jackson, R., 394
Jackson, S., 440
Jacobs, S., 63
Jandt, F. E., 334
Janis, I., 394
Janis, I. L., 310
Janis, Irving, 306
Janis, L., 309
Janiszewski, M. E., 154
Janowitz, M., 187

Japan, human resources perspective in, 205–206

Jargon, perception of competence and, 406

Javidi, M., 441

Jensen, A. D., 421

Jensen, J. V., 395

Jewelry, as signals, 76

Job interviews, communication apprehension and, 353. See also Initial encounters

Jones, J. P., 309

Jones, Jim, 176

Jones, S., 441

Journalism
computer use in, 223
telegraph's impact on, 226

Judgment, as small group task, 170

Juries, 169, 170, 285. See also Decision-making groups

Kahn, D. D., 155

Kaminski, L. P., 95

Kaplan, R. M., 441

Karlins, Marvin, 285

Kaul, J., 218

Kavchak, D. P., 394

Kean, Thomas, 428, 432, 440, 441

Kearncy, P., 310, 360

Kelley, H. H., 155, 280, 309, 310

Kelley, Harold, 306

Kellogg, L. A., 62

Kellogg, W. N., 62

Kellogg, Winthrop and Louise, 44

Kelly, C., 121

Kelly, D., 440

Kelly, L., 361

Kelman, H. C., 310

Kelman, Herbert, 304

Kendon, A., 94

Kennedy, E. M., 441

Kennedy, Ted, 433

Khomeini, Ayatollah, 194

Kilmann, R., 334

Kilmann, Ralph, on conflict styles, 321, 323–325

Kinesics, 81–82

King, B. T., 334

King, M. L., Jr., 441

King, Martin Luther, Jr., 431–432

KISS rule, for public speaking, 382

Kissler, G., 394

Klein, H. J., 218

Klopf, D. W., 421

Knapp, M. L., 63, 94, 154, 155, 279, 280, 310, 421

Knapp, Mark, 140

Koehler, J. W., 334

Kohler, W., 62

Köhler, Wolfgang, chimpanzee studies by, 43–44

Koko (gorilla), 45–46

Kollock, P. 186

Komsky, S. H., 247

Koontz, H., 218

Koontz, Harold, 195

Kramer, E., 95

Kreitner, R., 218

Kreps, G. L., 219

Krippendorf, K., 31

Krivnos, P. D., 280

Kuwabara, A. Y., 360

Labeling theory, 256–257

Labels, 49
See also Language
concepts as, 51
for interpersonal relationships, 146
negative, 51–53
symbols as, 53
as territorial signs, 86

Labor/management relations
See also Workplace
barriers to listening, 115
conflicts in, 319, 328
conflict style and, 323
human use perspectives, 196–197, 200
negotiation guidelines, 329–332

La Gaipa, J. J., 155

Laing, R. D., 154

Laissez-faire leadership style, 177

Lambert, W. W., 310

Lana (chimp), 46

Language
acquisition of, 49–50, 163
children raised without, 47–49
cultural differences and, 56
defined, 62
meaning and, 15–16
natural signs in animals vs., 40–41
origins of words, 53, 55
rhetorical devices, 425, 428–433
structural features of, 59–60

Language culture, importance of, 48–49

LANs. See Local area networks

LaPiere, R. T., 309

Larson, C. U., 310

Leadership
conflict avoidance role, 328
in discussion groups, 176
in organizations, 194
Sargent and Miller Leadership Scale, 178–179
in small-group development, 172
styles of, 176–177

Learned communication, in animals, 35, 36, 39–41

Learned helplessness, 349

Learning
acquisition of concepts, 50–51
acquisition of meaning, 49–50
of communication apprehension, 346–348
inconsistency and, 349
reinforcement theory, 347–348
resiliency factor, 348–349
socialization vs., 346
social learning theory, 346–347

Lee, A. R., 154

Lee, C. I., 441

Leen, R., 95

Legal issues
bulletin board systems, 239
electronic mail, 241

Legal-rational authority, in organizations, 194

Legitimacy of ranks, disorganization and, 182–183

Leibowitz, K., 88

Letters, 227, 229–231

Leveling, 212

Levenson, D. J., 186

Levine, J. M., 187

Lewin, K., 187, 394

Lewis, P. H., 246

Lexis/Nexis, 239

Library, 375–376

Lie detection, 73

Lieberman, P., 30, 64

Liebowitz, K., 95

Likert, R., 334

Linear, defined, 12

Linear communication, 12–21
mediated communication as, 223, 224
persuasion as, 288

Linden, E., 62

Lindsey, G., 279

Lindzey, G., 121, 187, 280

Lippit, R., 187

Lippmann, W., 63, 154, 309

Lippmann, Walter, 53, 294–295

Littlejohn, S. W., 30

Listening, 39, 99–120
actions required for, 105–107
active vs. passive, 105–106, 118, 119
adaptation with, 106, 108
barriers to, 112–117
defined, 101–102
evaluation and screening by, 103–104
importance of, 7
information acquired by, 102–103
planning for, 117–120
purposes of, 102–105
Receiver Apprehension Test (RAT), 114–115
as recreation, 104–105
sender/receiver reciprocity, 108–111, 119
sender/receiver similarity, 111–112
social efficacy through, 105

Lloyd, K., 394

Local area networks (LANs), 237–238
defined, 237
electronic mail on, 239–241
military uses of, 222

Locke, J., 30

Locke, John, 7

Lowery, S., 309

Luchins, A. S., 310

Luchok, J. A., 394

Lying, eye contact and, 83

Maccoby, E. E., 187, 394

Machiavellianism, in disengagement, 150–151

MacNeil, R., 63, 64

"Magic bullet" view of persuasion, 288, 289, 290

Mail, 227, 229
  electronic, 222, 239–241
Malendro, L. A., 95, 96
Mammals, learned communication by,
  40, 41–47
Management
  See also Labor/management relations
  focus on societal needs vs., 192–193
  human relations perspectives, 200–205
  human resources perspectives, 205–206
  human use perspectives, 195–197, 200
  scientific, 197, 201, 202
  theories of, 195
  "universal principles" of, 197, 200
Management (communication strategy), 132
  first impressions and, 258
  initial encounter strategies, 261–269
  in interpersonal communication, 132,
  144–147
Managers, in organizations, 190, 191
Mandel, W., 310
Mann, R. D., 186
Manrai, L. A., 154
Manuscript delivery of speeches, 402–403
Manusov, V., 94, 95
Markoff, J., 256
Marriage. conflicts in, 321, 326
Marriage encounter, 168
Mason, M. K., 63
Mass media, 81, 192
Mayo, E., 218
Mazur, A., 95
McCroskey, J. C., 95, 96, 217, 218, 219,
  310, 360, 361, 393, 394, 421
  Communication Apprehension report
  by, 350–351
  nonverbal immediacy scale by, 419
  Touch Apprehension Measure and, 88
  on trait-like apprehension, 340
McCrum, R., 63, 64
McDaniel, A., 440
McEwen, W., 31
McGinnies, E., 334
McGrath, M. A., 154
McGuire, W. J., 310
McLaughlin, M. L., 310
McMillan, C. J., 219
McNally, Ed, 424
McPhee, R. D., 218, 309
Mead, G. H., 30, 121, 154
Mead, George Herbert, 108
Meaning, 12, 14–16
  acquisition of, 49–50
  cognitive reorganization and, 292–294
  concepts, 50–51
  conflict as problem of, 326
  deep vs. surface, 28
  defined, 16
  denotative vs. connotative, 58–59
  in grapevine, 211
  information vs., 19
  labels for, 49. *See also* Language
  in meaning triangle, 56–58
  in memory organization, 16

parallel. *See* Meaning, shared
receiver responsibility and, 118, 119
resistance to changing, 276–277
selective perception and, 263–264
sender responsibility and, 109, 110
shared, 49, 51, 111–112
stereotyped, 51–53
symbols as labels for, 53
vertical transmission problems, 208–210
Meaning triangle, 56–58
Media. *See* Mass media; Radio; Television
Mediated communication, 221–245
  computer networks, 236–241
  face-to-face communication vs., 23,
  223–227
  military uses of, 222
  simultaneous transaction model vs., 23
  teleconferencing, 167, 241–244
  telephones, 232–234
  traditional written media, 227, 229–232
Medicine, as social institution, 192
Medium, defined, 224
Mehrabian, A., 94, 121, 421
Mehrabian, Albert, 90, 91
Members, in formal decision-making
  groups, 180, 181
Memorandum/Memoranda, 231–232
Memorized delivery of speeches, 403–404
Memory
  in decoding process, 20
  organization of, 16, 17
Merton, R. K., 309
Message ordering, in persuasion, 306
Messages
  control, 175
  distancing, 149
  organizational communication, 191–
  192, 207–208
Metaphors, 428, 429
Metts, S. M., 154
Meyer, J. L., 121
Meyers, R. A., 310
Michela, J. L., 280
Milgram, S., 310
Milgram, Stanley, resistance studies, 303
Military, mediated communication in, 222
Miller, G. R., 63, 95, 121, 154, 155, 279,
  310, 311
Mills, C. W., 218
Mills, J., 121
MILNET, 238, 239
Mineo, P., 94
Minutes, 180–181
Mirabito, M. M., 246
Model, defined, 12–13
Modeling, in social learning theory, 346–347
Molloy, J. T., 95
Monarchy, basis for authority in, 194
Mongeau, P., 310, 394
Monkeys, touch studies, 87
Monroe, Alan, persuasive speech format
  of, 384–387
Monroe, A. H., 394
Montagu, A., 95

Moore, L., 394
Moreland, R. L., 187
Morgenstern, B. L., 246
Morris, C. W., 154
Mortenson, C. D., 154
Motions, 180
"Motivated Sequence," 384–387
Motivation in organizations, wages as,
  196–197
"Mr. Rogers method" of public speaking, 399
Multicultural society
  communication issues in, 56
  conflict inevitability in, 316
  meeting new people in, 253
  negative concepts in, 51–53
Murphy, Dan, 236
Mussolini, Benito, 194

Names, remembering, 141, 143
National Science Foundation, national
  network study, 239
Neanderthals, 7
Nebergall, R. E., 394
Negotiation, 328–332
Nelson, D., 154
Nelson, P. E., 121, 421
Nelson, Paul, 413
Nervousness, 339
Network communication, 236–241
  computer conferencing, 242–243
  electronic mail, 239–241
  large-scale networks, 238–239
  on-line information services, 239
  proliferation of, 222–223, 236
  security issues, 238–239
  types of, 236–237
  voice-mail, 234
  wireless networks, 238
Newcomb, T. M., 187, 394
Newhart, Bob, 436
Newspapers, impact of technology on,
  223, 226–227
Newspapers. *See* Journalism
Nguyen, M., 95
Nguyen, T., 95
Nichols, R. G., 121
Nicholson, H., 94
Niditch, P., 30
Nimmo, D., 96, 218, 421
Nofsinger, R. E., 280
Noise, as barrier to listening, 113
Nonsocial constraints on action, 299
Nonverbal communication, 12, 67–92
  on answering machines, 234
  artifacts as, 75–76
  body-related messages, 69, 74–75, 81–84
  in campaign speechmaking, 398
  in changing impressions, 277
  clothing as, 76–79
  as complement of verbal, 70–71
  as contradiction of verbal, 72–73
  defined, 69
  distancing messages, 149
  distortion by, 26

e-mail problems, 240–241
emblems, 72, 82
eye contact, 83–84
first impressions and, 254, 264
gestures, 81–82
humor in, 437
immediacy and, 90–92
in informative speech, 383, 384
interpreting, 73–74
interview example, 68
kinesics, 81–82
in listening, 106, 107
misreading problems, 70
oculesics, 83–84
proxemics, 84–86
psychological closeness, 91
in public speaking, 398, 399, 400, 412,
    413, 414–415, 434, 435, 436, 437
regulatory role of, 71–72
sexual, in workplace, 79–81
simultaneous transactions model and,
    81, 90
in small groups, 161
time and, 89–90
touch, 87–89
verbal communication vs., 69
in video conferencing, 243
vocalics, 82–83
Nonverbal immediacy, 90–92
in persuasion, 306
as small-talk skill, 141
Nonverbal Immediacy Behaviors (IMM)
    scale, 418–419
Normative confusion, 182
Norms
of competition, 318
conflicts between, 327–328
Norms (for communication), 131
communication apprehension and, 343
in conflict negotiation, 328, 330–332
conflicts based on, 327–328
electronic mail, 240–241
enforcing. See Controls (communica-
    tion); Controls (social)
fax transmission, 235
in formal decision-making groups,
    179–181
of intimate dyads, 147
of intimate groups, 173
letter writing, 230–231
in organizations, 194
in small-group development, 171, 172
in small-group disorganization, 182
in task-oriented groups, 176
telephone, 232–234
Norton, R., 441
Novel situations, as apprehension cause, 343
No-win situations, 349
Nussbaum, J., 441

Objectivity of source, 376–377
Observational learning theory, 346–347
Oculesics, 83–84
in speechmaking, 414

Offensive displays, 86
Ogden, C. K., 63
O'Hair, D., 63
O'Keefe, B. J., 30
O'Keefe, D. J., 310
O'Neill, Tip, 436
One-sidedness, in persuasion, 306
On-line information services, 239
Open confrontation, in disengagement, 151
Oral footnotes, in speechmaking, 406
Order (in speech format), 384
Ordman, L., 309
O'Reilly, C. A., III, 218
Organizational cohesion, 214–215
Organizational communication, 191–192,
    206–215
accuracy vs. distortion (informal), 211–213
accuracy vs. distortion (vertical trans-
    mission), 208–210
Behavior Alteration Techniques (BATs)
    and Messages (BAMs), 198–199
consequences of, 213–215
defined, 191
formal, 190, 191, 206–210
informal, 190, 191, 200, 203, 207, 210–213
management-oriented approaches to,
    195–197, 200–206
voice-mail networks, 234
Organizational cultures, 213–215
Organization chart, 197, 200, 201
Organizations, 189–216
bureaucracy in, 193–197, 200–206
cohesion in, 214–215
defined, 190–191
Hawthorne studies, 201–203, 204, 213
social institutions, 192–193
sociocultural context of, 192–193
specialized cultures in, 213
Organizing a speech, 377–392
Orientation, in small-group development,
    171–172
Oshinsky, J. S., 95
Oskamp, S., 310
Overreacting, danger of, 111
Overstatement, as dramatic technique, 436

Pace, R. W., 218
Pallen, C. B., 246
Panels, 166
Parallel communication, 12
Parker, C., 121
Parker, E. S., 246, 247
Parsons, T., 218
Pascoe, G. C., 441
Passive vs. active listening, 105–106, 118, 119
Patterson, F., 62
Patterson, Francine, Koko and, 45–46
Paulus, P. B., 187
Pausing, as speechmaking technique, 434,
    435, 436
Payne, Roger, on whales, 43
Payne, S. K., 88, 95, 96, 122, 360, 361, 421
Pearce, W. B., 30, 280
Pearson, J. C., 121, 154, 186, 394, 421

Pearson, Judy, 413
Peer groups, 161
    See also Friendship; Intimate groups
communicating in, 165–166
control messages in, 175
in organizations, 203
rank in, 175
Pennock, G. A., 218
Perception, 19–20
concepts as basis of, 51
of confidence, 405–407
defined, 263
person, 264. See also First impressions;
    Initial encounters
selective, 263–264
stereotypes and, 53
Perceptual defense, 209
Perceptual set, 209
Performance evaluation, as small group
    task, 170
Perlman, D., 187
Personal ideas (personae), 134
Personality
communication apprehension as part
    of, 340–342, 345–349, 354–355
conflict and, 326
defined, 164
implicit, 134, 257–258
susceptibility to persuasion and, 305
Personal possessions, as signals, 76
Personal problems
barriers to listening, 113, 117
interpersonal relationships and, 137
Personal Report of Communication Ap-
    prehension-24 (CA), 350–351
Personal space, 84–85
Person perception, 264
Persuasion, 283–308
attitudes vs. behaviors, 296–299
defined, 289
dynamics of, 289–299
examples, 285, 286–288, 290–292, 293–294
halo effect, 377
importance of, 286
in jury trials, 285
linear vs. transactional views of,
    288–289
organizing a speech for, 384–392
resistance and yielding, 299, 302–304
as speechmaking goal, 370–371
strategies, 304–307, 390–392
types of, 286
Petrullo, L., 279
Pets, communication by, 39–40
Petty, R. E., 394
Pfungst, O., 62
Pfungst, Oskar, 34
Pheromones, 37
Phillips, Gerald, 338, 358
Phillips, G. M., 361
Phillipson, H., 154
Phylogenetic continuum, 36
Physical characteristics, small-group rank-
    ing and, 179

463

Physical context
  barriers to listening in, 113
  of "grapevine," 211
  influence of, 22, 24, 26–27, 130
  initial encounters and, 258, 261, 265
  for interpersonal communication, 134–135
  nonverbal communication through, 75–76
Physical events, 18–19
Piaget, J., 186
Piecework, 197
Piland, R. N., 440
Pisani, P., 62
Plato, on belief and action, 294
Plax, T. G., 95, 121, 186, 309, 310, 360, 440
Poker, 73
Policy making, 170, 204–205
Politics, management of first impressions
  in, 263
Polygraph, 73
Poole, M. S., 186
Porpoises, 41, 43
Porter, L. W., 186, 187, 218, 219, 309
Positive attitude, 143–144, 150
Postal service, 227, 229
Postman, L., 219
Postures, 81-82. See also Body-related
  messages; Nonverbal communication
Prager, K. J., 155
Predispositions, first impressions and,
  263–264
Preiss, R. W., 394
Prejudices, as barriers to listening, 114–
  116, 117
Premack, D., 62, 64
Presentation of self, 251–278
  See also Self-disclosure
  for changing impressions, 277
  common difficulties, 258–260
  deciding what to say, 269–275
  defined, 254
  management strategies, 261–269
Primary groups, 159
  See also Intimate groups
  families as, 163
Primary-recency question, in persuasion, 306
Primates, 41, 43–46, 87
Principle of covarying attribution, 276
Principle of delayed gratification, 145
Principled negotiation, 329–332
Principle of salient characteristic, 256
Prior communication, influence of, 22,
  23–24
Privacy
  See also Security issues
  as advantage of letters, 230
  e-mail problems, 240, 241
  fax transmissions and, 235
  memoranda problems, 232
Private discussion groups, 162, 166
Problem reporting, vertical transmission
  of, 207
Problem solving, small groups for, 167
Prodigy, 239
Prosocial behavior-alteration techniques, 306

Proxemics, 84–86
Psychodynamic strategy, 292
  for persuasive speech, 384
Psychographic information, in audience
  analysis, 373
Psychological closeness, 91
  applications of, 92
Psychological distance, establishing, 149
Psychological reactance to persuasion,
  299, 302
Psychology, animal studies and, 36
Public discussion groups, 162, 166–167
Public relations, as organizational communication, 191
Public speaking, 397–420
  applause management, 433–435
  apprehension about, 353–355. See also
    Communication apprehension
  audience analysis for, 371–374
  campaign strategies, 398–399
  content preparation, 365–393
  delivery concerns, 398–420
  delivery modes, 402–405
  establishing credibility, 405–411
  as extended conversation, 399–402
  feedback in, 400–401, 402
  goal determination for, 369–371
  importance of, 7
  nonverbal communication in, 398, 399,
    400, 412, 413, 414–415, 434, 435,
    436, 437
  organizing an informative speech, 377–384
  organizing a persuasive speech, 384–392
  performance techniques, 411–417, 434, 435
  "planned" spontaneity in, 400
  polishing the speech, 424–425, 428–433
  research for, 374–377
  rhetorical devices, 425, 428–433
  rhetorical styles, 435–439
  role taking in, 401
  topic selection for, 367–369
  training in, 355–358
Punishment-based persuasion, 304, 306
Purpose statement, for informative
  speech, 380, 381
Putnam, L. L., 218, 219

Quality control circles, 167, 206
Quayle, Dan, 434

Racism. See Prejudices
Radio, panel discussions on, 166
Rancer, A. S., 323
Rank, 131
  artifacts as indicator of, 76
  clothing as indicator of, 76–78
  communication apprehension and, 343
  in organizations, 194–195
Rank (communication)
  in formal decision-making groups,
    180–181
  in intimate groups, 174–175
  in small-group development, 172
  in small-group disorganization, 182–183
  in task-oriented groups, 177, 179

Rank ineffectiveness, as disorganization
  cause, 182–183
Rankin, P. T., 121
RAT (Receiver Apprehension Test), 114–115
Rather, Dan, 398
Rational society, authority in, 194
Ratliff, G., 441
RATNET (Rural Alaska Television Net-
  work), 244
Ray, C., 310, 394
Reagan, Nancy, 429
Reagan, R., 440
Reagan, Ronald, 398, 410, 429–430
Reality
  meaning and, 49
  social construction of, 148
Reardon, K. K., 310, 394, 421
Rebellion, psychological reactance, 299, 302
Receiver
  See also Listening
  audience for speech, 371–374
  decoding by, 20
  defined, 10, 11, 12
  distortion by, 25–27
  feedback by, 20–21
  perception by, 19–20
  in persuasion, 288–289, 305
  responsibilities of, 110–111
  role-taking and, 18
  sender/receiver reciprocity, 108–111, 119
  sender/receiver similarity, 111–112
  strategies for, 117–120
Receiver Apprehension Test (RAT), 114–115
Receiver eccentricities, 117–118
Reciprocity, 108–111
Recreation, listening as, 104–105
Redding, W. C., 218
Redundancy, 60
  in informative speech, 382–383
  as speechmaking technique, 413
References, for speech preparation, 374–377
Referent, 55–58
Refutation, with two-sided messages,
  306, 391–392
Regulating, nonverbal communication
  used for, 71–72
Reinard, J. C., 393, 395
Reinforcement learning theory, 347–348
  classroom experiences and, 351–352
Reis, H. T., 186
Relationships. See Social relationships
Religious institutions, 192
Rempel, J., 421
Render, M. E., 186
Repetition
  in informative speech, 382
  as speechmaking technique, 413, 432–433
Rephrasing, as speechmaking technique,
  433
Research, in speech preparation, 374–377
Resiliency factor, in learning theory, 348–349
Resistance to persuasion, 299, 302–303
  destructive vs. constructive, 303
  psychological reactance, 299, 302

Resolutions, in formal decision-making groups, 181
Reward-based cohesion, 182, 215
Reward-based conflict, 317–318
Reward-based persuasion, 304, 306
Reward and punishment
  in reinforcement theory, 347–348
  in social learning theory, 347
Rhetorical devices, 425, 428–433
Rhetorical styles, 435–439
Rhythm, in speechmaking, 432–433
Riccillo, S. C., 94
Rice, R. E., 246, 247
Richards, A., 440, 441
Richards, Ann, 429, 430, 436
Richards, D. G., 62
Richards, I. K., 63
Richetto, G. M., 218
Richmond, V. P., 88, 95, 96, 217, 218,
  219, 310, 360, 361, 419, 421
Rimm, D. C., 186
Rivers, Joan, 437
Roach, M. E., 95
Roberts, H., 187
Roberts, Henry Martyn, 180
Roberts, K. H., 218, 219
Robert's Rules of Order, 180
Rodman, G., 63
Roethlisberger, J., 210
Rogers, E. M., 246
Rogers, Will, 436
Rokeach, M., 309, 310
Rokeach, S. B., 155, 280
Role confusion, 182, 328
Roles, defined, 131
Roles (communication)
  in interpersonal communication, 135
  in intimate groups, 173–174
  in small-group development, 172
  in small-group disorganization, 182
  in task-oriented groups, 176
Role-taking, 16, 18
  in first-impression management, 265–266
  mediated communication and, 225
  memoranda and, 232
  in peer groups, 165
  personal ideas in, 134
  in public speaking, 401
  in sender/receiver reciprocity, 108, 109
  in simultaneous transactions, 22, 23
  in small groups, 172
  vertical transmission problems, 208
Roll, S., 279
Rollins, B. C., 334
Roloff, M. E., 154, 311
Rosa, E., 95
Rosegrant, T., 121
Rosenfeld, L. B., 63, 95, 121, 154, 186,
  280, 310
Rosensweig, M. R., 186, 187, 218, 309
Roth, J., 186, 219
Rothschild, J., 218
Round table discussion groups, 166
Ruben, B. D., 218

Rules for communication. *See* Norms (for communication)
Rumbaugh, D. M., 62
Rumbaugh, Duane, chimp studies by, 46
Rumors, grapevine and, 211, 212
Russell, R., 218
Rutherford, J., 394
Rytting, M., 95

Saddam Hussein, 176
Safran, C., 155
Saine, T., 95, 96
Salient characteristic, 256, 258
  labeling theory and, 256–257
  selective perception and, 263, 264
Samovar, L. A., 121, 187
Samples, B. T., 121
Sanctions, 175, 195
Sanford, R. N., 186
Sarah (chimp), 46
Sarbin, T. R., 121
Sarcasm, 73
Sargent and Miller Leadership Scale, 178–179
Sater, V., 94
Savage, B., 121
Saylor, K., 218
Scent, in insect communication, 37
Scheflen, A. E., 421
Schegloff, E. A., 63, 280
Schema/Schemata, 16, 17, 18
  in decoding process, 20
  linking informative speech to, 383
  prejudicial, 115–116
  sound bites as, 434
Schere, S. E., 95
Scherer, K. R., 95
Schieffer, B., 420
Schneider, D. J., 187
School experiences, communication apprehension and, 348, 349, 350–351
Schulman, L. S., 154
Schwarzkopf, H. Norman, 436–437
Science, as social institution, 192
Scientific management, 197
  Hawthorne studies and, 201–203, 204
Scott, M. D., 361
Scott, Willard, 368–369, 410
Scott, W. R., 186
Screening messages, by listening, 103–104
Scripted conversations, in interpersonal engagement, 139
SD. *See* Systematic desensitization
Seboek, T. A., 62
Secretary, in formal decision-making group, 180–181
Security issues, in network communication and, 238–239. *See also* Privacy
Seibold, D. R., 309, 310
Selective action, 210
Selective listening, 103–104
Selective perception, first impressions and, 263–264, 270
Selective retention and recall, 210

Self
  defined, 133
  in interpersonal communication, 133–134, 136–137
  presentation of, 254
Self-disclosure
  See also Self-presentation
  in experiential groups, 162
  in initial encounters, 270–274
  in interpersonal communication, 145–146
  in intimate group communication, 173
Self-fulfilling prophecy, with communication apprehension, 357
Self-image
  See also Self
  development of, 136, 137
  negative feedback and, 138
Self-improvement, groups for. *See* Experiential groups
Self-presentation, 251–278. *See also* Self-disclosure
Self-tests and questionnaires
  Argumentativeness Scale (ARG), 322–323
  Audience Analysis Survey, 472–473
  Behavior Alteration Techniques (BATs) and Messages (BAMs), 198–199
  Communication Technology Avoidance Scale, 228–229
  General Disclosiveness Scale, 272–274
  Humor Orientation (HO) Scale, 437, 438
  Nonverbal Immediacy Behaviors (IMM), 418–419
  Personal Report of Communication Apprehension-24 (CA), 350–351
  Receiver Apprehension Test (RAT), 114–115
  Sargent and Miller Leadership Scale, 178–179
  Small-Talk Scale, 142–143
  Student Resistance Scale, 300–302
  Touch Apprehension Measure (TAM), 88
  Verbal Immediacy, 54–55
Seligman, M. E., 361
Semantics, 49–60
Seminars, 167
Sender. *See* Source
Sender/receiver reciprocity, 108–111, 119
Sender/receiver similarity, 111–112
Senses
  in human communication, 38–39
  learned meanings through, 15, 16
Sensitivity groups, 162
Sentiment-based cohesion
  in intimate groups, 181–182
  in organizations, 204, 215
Sereno, K. K., 154
Sergeant at arms, role of, 181
Sex. *See* Gender
Sexual communication
  immediacy principle and, 92
  listening and, 100, 113, 115
  in workplace, 79–81
Shanahan, W., 394, 310
Shannon, C. E., 31

Shapiro, E., 246
Shared meaning, 51
    as basis of communication, 49
    in grapevine, 211
    sender/receiver similarity and, 111–112
Sharp, S. M., 280
Sharpening, 212
Shaver, K. G., 280
Shaw, M. E., 186, 187
Sheats, P., 187
Sheats, Paul, 176
Sherif, C. W., 394
Sherif, M., 394
Shills, E. A., 187
Shimanoff, S. B., 31
Shockley-Zalabak, P., 219
Shock studies, 303
Short, J. F., Jr., 218
Shulman, L. S., 143, 279
Shyness, 337–359
    in communication apprehension, 339, 340
Sidedness, in persuasion, 306, 391–392
Siegman, A. W., 94
Sight, 38, 39
Sigman, S. J., 31
Signals
    animal communication with, 39–40
    artifacts as, 75–76
    in speechmaking, 435
Signposts, in informative speech, 383,
        384, 414
Signs
    in animal communication, 39, 40
    defined, 39
    in human communication, 40
    territorial, 86
Silber, John, 428, 429, 440
Similarity, sender/receiver, 111–112
Similes, 428–429
Simmel, G., 154
Simmel, Georg
    on conflict resolution, 314
    on stranger as confidant, 139
Simmons, H. W., 310
Simpson, Bart, 437
Simpson, G., 219, 360
Simuel, G., 154
Simultaneous transactions model, 21–25
    See also Interactive communication
    in conflict negotiation, 332
    context in, 131–132
    interpersonal communication in, 134
    nonverbal communication and, 81, 90
    persuasion in, 288–289
    in small groups, 160–161
Singh, J. V., 218
Situations, leadership and, 177
Size of groups
    bureaucracy and, 193
    influence of, 160–161
    initial encounters and, 258, 260–261
Skills, small talk, 141, 143–144
Skills training, for communication appre-
        hension, 358

Skinner, B. F., 360
Sladen, F. W., 62
Small, A., 154, 218
Small-group conferences, 167
    teleconferencing, 241–244
Small groups
    cohesion in, 181–182
    communicating in, 157–184
    development stages, 171–172
    disorganization in, 181, 182–183
    intimate, 161–162
    nature of, 160–162
    optimum size for, 161
    rules for communicating in, 171–181
    task-oriented, 159, 162, 166–171
    types of, 161–162
Small talk, 139–144
    See also Initial encounters
    defined, 139
    in self-presentation, 271, 274
    skills used in, 141, 143–144
Smell. See Scent
Smith, Adam, wage theory and, 196, 200
Smith, J. M., 95
Smith, K., 309
Smith, R. G., 395
Snyder, M., 95
Sociability, in public speaking, 410
Social categories
    in attribution process, 266
    in audience analysis, 371
Social constraints, in attribution process, 266
Social controls, 131
    in intimate groups, 175
    in small-group development, 172
Social efficacy
    defined, 105
    listening as requirement for, 105
Social expectations, persuasion through,
        290–292
Social institutions, 192–193
    defined, 192
Socialization, 163–164
    communication apprehension and, 345–346
    learning vs., 346
Social learning theory, 346–347
Social position. See Rank
Social pressures, attitudes vs. behavior
        and, 298–299
Social relationships
    communication apprehension and, 343
    conflict and, 319, 321, 326, 327–328
    influence of, 22, 25, 130–131
    in interpersonal communication, 135
    mediated communication and, 225
    rules governing, 130–131
    in small groups, 171–181
Social roles. See Roles; Social relation-
        ships
Social rules. See Norms
Social validation, of a speaker, 408
Societal needs, social institutions and,
        192–193
Society, language as foundation for, 7

Sociocultural context
    conflict and, 326–327
    influence of, 22, 24–25, 26–27, 130
    of organizations, 192–193
    of small groups, 162–171
    technological change and, 244
Sociocultural persuasion, 290–292
Socioeconomic status, proxemics and, 85
Sommer, R., 95
Sommer, Robert, 85
Soskin, W. F., 95
Sound, 38–40
"Sound bites," 398–399, 433–434
Source (sender), 10, 11
    accuracy role of, 25–27
    credibility of, 110–111, 306–307, 405
    defined, 12
    in linear communication model, 14
    listening behaviors and, 106, 107
    in persuasion, 288, 289
    responsibilities of, 109–110
    role-taking by, 18
    sender/receiver reciprocity, 108–111
    sender/receiver similarity, 111–112
Source of evidence, 376–377
Space
    nonverbal communication with. See
        Proxemics
    personal, 84
Space allocation, as small group task, 170
Spaulding, J. A., 360
Specialized organizational cultures, 213
    conflicts between, 213–215
Speculation, grapevine and, 211
Speech, vocalics, 82–83
Speechmaking. See Public speaking
Spiker, B. K., 219
Sports, spectator, as social institution, 192
Spread-spectrum radio transmission, 238
Stacks, D., 31
Stacks, D. W., 63
Stafford, L., 361
Stafford, S., 310, 394
Stage fright, 353–355. See also Communi-
        cation apprehension
Staring, 83
Steinberg, M., 154
Stephens, M., 246
Stereotypes, 53, 266, 267
Stereotypic conversations, 139
Stevens, L. A., 121
Stewart, D., 441
Stewart, R. A., 310, 360, 361, 421
Stiff, J. B., 310, 393
Stimuli, 19
Stogdill, R. M., 187
Stoll, C., 246
Storytelling, dramatic style in, 436
Stover, S., 247
"Stranger on the plane" phenomenon, 139
Strangers, fear of talking to. See Com-
        munication apprehension
Street, R. L., Jr., 279
Stress, conflict consequences and, 319–320

Strice, G. F., 186
Strodtbeck, F. L., 186
Student Resistance Scale, 300–302
Subjective responses, meanings as, 14, 15, 16
Success ethic, conflict inevitability and, 316
Sudnow, D. N., 63
SUNYSAT, 244
Surface meaning, 28
Susceptibility to persuasion, 305
Suspending judgment, as listening skill, 118, 119–120
Sussman, L., 218
Swingle, P., 334
Sybers, R., 95
Symbiosis, 73
Symbols, 11–12, 53–59
    arbitrary selection of, 53, 55
    conventions about, 55–56
    defined, 14, 53
    denotations vs. connotations, 58–59
    learned meanings for, 15–16
    in meaning triangle, 56–58
    in memory organization, 16
    referents of, 55
Symposia, 166–167
Syntax, 60
Sypher, H. E., 30
Systematic desensitization (SD), for communication apprehension, 355–356

Tagiuri, R., 279, 280
Tagiuri, Renato, 254
TAM (Touch Apprehension Measure), 88
Tardy, C. H., 280
Task-oriented groups, 159, 162
    cohesion in, 182
    communication goals in, 166–171
    communication rules in, 176–177, 179–181
    decision-making, 162, 169–171
    developmental stages, 171–172
    discussion groups, 162, 166–167
    experiential, 162, 167–169
Tattoos, 75, 77
Taylor, A., 121
Taylor, D. A., 155
Taylor, Frederick W., management style of, 197
Taylor, F. W., 218
Taylor, L. C., 95
Technologies
    answering machines, 234
    computer networks, 236–241
    defined, 245
    efficiency of, 222
    fax machines, 234–236
    sociocultural impact of, 225–227
    teleconferencing, 241–244
    telegraph, 226, 227
    telephone, 232–234
Teleconferencing, 167, 241–244
Telegraph, impact of, 226, 227
Telephone, 232–234
    answering machines, 234

audio conferencing, 241
    fax communication via, 234–236
    feedback limited with, 225
    norms, 232–234
    voice-mail networks, 234
Telephone research, for speech preparation, 375
Television, panel discussions on, 166
Tenure, as territorial sign, 86
Territoriality, 84, 85–86
Tests. See Self-tests
Thayer, S., 95
Therapy groups, 167–168. See also Experiential groups
Thinking. See Cognitive functioning
Thomas, Clarence, 80
Thomas, K., 334
Thomas, Kenneth, on conflict styles, 321, 323–325
Thomas, W. I., 148, 155, 295, 309
Thoreau, H. D., 246
Thoreau, Henry David, on newspapers, 226–227
Thorndike, L. L., 394
Thought, language as foundation for, 7
Thrall, W. F., 441
Thurman, B., 95
Tienanmen Square demonstrations, 293–294
Time, meanings associated with, 89–90
Time and motion studies, 197
Todd-Mancillas, W., 394
Tompkins, P. K., 218
Tonnies, F., 187
Topic choice, for speech making, 367–369
Touch, 38, 39, 87–89
Touch Apprehension Measure (TAM), 88
Towne, N., 63, 95
Traces, 16, 17
    in decoding process, 20
Tradition, as basis for authority, 194
Training groups, 167, 168
Traits
    defined, 340–341
    leadership, 177
    personality, 164
Transaction, defined, 22
Transactional communication. See Simultaneous transactions model
Transitions, in informative speech, 383–384, 414
Transmission, as physical event, 18–19
Treece, M., 246
Trenholm, S., 30, 186
Trinkhaus, E., 30
Trueblood, T. C., 421
Truman, Harry, 436
Trust, in interpersonal communication, 145–146
Trustworthiness of a speaker, 407–409, 411
Truth seeking, as small-group task, 170
Tuckman, B. W., 186
Tuckman, Bruce, 171
Turner, L. H., 394
Turner, R. H., 218

Twain, Mark, 367, 436, 437
Two-sided message, in persuasion, 306, 391–392
TYMNET, 239

Umiker-Sebeok, J., 63
Understatement, as dramatic technique, 436
Urban-industrial society, bureaucracy theory for, 193–195
Ury, W., 334
Utilitarianism, 137–138
    exchange theory and, 144

Validity of evidence, 376–377
Values, yielding based on, 304
Verbal communication, 33–60
    See also Language
    by cetaceans and primates, 41–47
    in changing impressions, 277
    nonverbal communication vs., 69, 71–72
    semantics, 49–60
    sexual, in workplace, 79–81
    without language, 35–49
Verbal immediacy
    in public speaking, 417, 419, 439
    self-test, 54–55
Verbal symbols, distortion through, 26
Verinis, J., 279
Vertical transmission, 207–208
    accuracy vs. distortion in, 208–210
    memoranda used for, 231
Vicki (chimpanzee), 44
Video conferencing, 167, 241, 242, 243–244
Vocabulary, vertical transmission and, 210
Vocabulary, 59
Vocalics, 81–82
    in speechmaking, 414
Voice, nonverbal uses of, 81–82. See also Nonverbal communication
Voice-mail networks, 234
Volkhart, E. H., 155
von Cranach, M., 95
von Glaserfeld, E., 62
von Osten, Wilhelm, 34

Wage incentive systems, 196–197
Wages, management communication with, 196–197
Wagner, J. P., 218
Waldhart, E. S., 121
Walster, E., 94
Walther, J. B., 94
Warner, H., 62
Washoe (chimpanzee), 44–45
Wartella, E., 30
Watson, K., 121, 122
Watson, O. M., 95
Watson, W. H., 95
Watzlawick, P., 154
Wealth of Nations (Smith), 196
Weary, G., 280
Weaver, C. H., 121, 122
Weaver, J., 441

Weaver, R. L., 186
Weaver, W. 30, 31
Weber, M., 218
Weber, Max, on bureaucracy, 193–195
Weider-Hatfield, D., 94
Weimann, J. M., 95
Weiner, A. N., 440
Weinman, J., 94
Weir, T., 154
Wellesley College, Barbara Bush speech
    at, 424–425, 426–427, 436
Wenberg, J., 154
Western Electric Company, Hawthorne
    studies, 201–203, 204
Westie, F. R., 309
Wexner, L. B., 394
Whales, 41–43
Wheeless, L. R., 114, 280
White, R. K., 187
Whork, B. J., 30
Widner, D., 246
Wiener, M., 94
Wiener, N., 31
Wiggers, M., 94, 95
Williams, F., 121, 246, 247
Williams, Madelyn, 78

Williams, M. C., 95
Wilmot, W. W., 154, 155, 279, 334
Winning
    as competitive style goal, 323
    conflict inevitability and, 316
    norms involved in, 318
Wireless networks, 238
Wishner, J., 279
Wishner, John, 257, 258
Witcover, J., 420
Withdrawal/avoidance
    in disengagement process, 150
    in high communication apprehension, 352
Wolff, K. H., 154
Wolvin, A. D., 122
Wolvin, A. W., 121
Wolz, J. P., 62
Woodall, W. G., 95, 279
Woolfolk, A. E., 394, 421
Word-of-mouth communication. See
    Grapevine
Words, arbitrary selection of, 53, 55. See
    also Symbols
Workplace
    See also Labor/management relations;
        Organizations

communication apprehension in, 352–353
communication skills training in, 358
conflicts in, 314–315, 317–318, 319,
    320, 325, 326, 327–328, 330–332
discussion groups in, 167
listening in, 100, 105, 111–112
sexual communication in, 79–81
shared meanings in, 203
Written communication, nonverbal cues
    absent in, 73–74
Written media, 227, 229–232
    letters, 227, 229–231
    memoranda, 231–232

"Yerkish" language, chimp studies with, 46
Yielding to persuasion, 303–304

Zakahi, W. R., 55
Zanna, M., 421
Zillman, D., 441
Zimbardo, P. G., 361
Znaniecki, F. F., 155, 309
Znaniecki, Florian, 295
Zones
    Hall's, 84
    personal-space, 84

j